KARL BARTH

*His Life from Letters and
Autobiographical Texts*

Eberhard Busch

Translated by
John Bowden

WILLIAM B. EERDMANS PUBLISHING COMPANY
GRAND RAPIDS, MICHIGAN

First published in German as *Karl Barths Lebenslauf, Nach seinem Briefen und autobiographischen Texten,*
Copyright © 1975 by Christian Kaiser Verlag, Munich

First English edition copyright © 1976 by
SCM Press Ltd, London, and Fortress Press, Philadelphia
Translated by John Bowden from the second revised German edition, 1976

First paperback edition published 1994 by
Wm. B. Eerdmans Publishing Co.
255 Jefferson Ave. S.E., Grand Rapids, Michigan 49503
All rights reserved

Printed in the United States of America

Library of Congress Cataloging-in-Publication Data

Busch, Eberhard, 1937–
[Karl Barths Lebenslauf. English]
Karl Barth: his life from letters and autobiographical texts /
Eberhard Busch; translated by John Bowden.
p.   cm.
Translation of: Karl Barths Lebenslauf.
Originally published: Philadelphia: Fortress Press, c1976.
Includes bibliographical references and indexes.
ISBN 0-8028-0708-9 (paper)
1. Barth, Karl, 1886-1968. 2. Theologians — Switzerland — Basel —
Biography. 3. Basel (Switzerland) — Biography. I. Title.
BX4827.B3B86313   1993
230'.044'092 — dc20
[B]   93-1217
                                                    CIP

Contents

8 Joyful Partisan of the Good God
The years from 1955 to 1962 in Bruderholzallee 26, Basle

9 'The Last Steps that We Can Still Take'
The years of retirement, 1962–1968

Preface to the English Edition

In January 1966, when Karl Barth was almost eighty, he began to write an autobiography. He completed a first chapter, about his family history, but then put the work on one side and never went back to it. This was typical of the man, in that he was far more interested in the present and the future than in the past (though he was more aware of the past than some of his critics have argued) and far more interested in other people than himself, but it has doubtless deprived us of what would have been a fascinating and illuminating story. Fortunately, however, in this magnificent book by Eberhard Busch, Barth's last assistant, we have the next best thing.

What Pastor Busch has done, in a way which appears more remarkable the more one studies it, has been to describe Karl Barth's life as far as possible in Barth's own words, by constructing a gigantic mosaic of them and with great self-restraint limiting his own contribution to a commentary which holds them together. At the appropriate points he has also summarized and given the flavour of the majority of Barth's theological writings. Some of the basic material comes from Barth's published works, but inspection of the notes at the back of the book will show the extent to which the narrative draws on unpublished letters in the Barth archives in Basle and on records of informal conversations with various groups as well. (The photographs are mostly published for the first time and also come from the Barth archives; many of them are snapshots taken by amateurs.)

As a result, this book is an extremely subjective study, with all the characteristics of an autobiography. For example, it always gives Barth's own view of events and of his own person (and in this respect the reader should note that while Barth was a man who knew and spoke his own mind, whenever he came to talk about himself or anything in which he had been involved, a touch of ironical and amused self-deprecation always used to creep in). Again, this makes it the best kind of book about Barth to have at present: although there has been so much discussion about him from an early stage in his career, the time has surely not yet come for anything like a definitive assessment of his person or of his contribution to modern theology. That will be the work of a later generation.

Meanwhile, it is important to have the facts straight, and here they are. This book is also a chronicle: it sets out to give as factual an account as possible of those personal details, dates and events which seem important for an understanding of Barth the man. Rather than being an interpretation and an assessment, it is a report. Or to put it another way, it is not so much a portrait as a map, to be used to trace a way through the exceptionally rich landscape of Karl Barth's life. It is rather more accurate than those which have been available hitherto, but as Pastor Busch himself is the first to concede, it is still on a very small scale and does have a number of uncharted areas on it.

Karl Barth probably had a more varied and eventful life than any other modern academic theologian, not least because he was so aware of the wider dimensions of the world around him. Rebelling against his father's views, during his university days he was a committed liberal (and extraordinarily active in the life of his student associations). In his first parish, even before writing the two versions of a commentary on the Epistle to the Romans which was to make his name, he was notorious as the 'red pastor', because of his support for local workers and trade unions. From being involved in 'dialectical theology' during the 1920s, he struck out on his own to develop a new and distinctive theological method which finally resulted in a work of more than nine thousand pages, twice as long as the *Summa* of Thomas Aquinas, with whom a Pope compared him. He saw the dangers of the Nazi rise to power at a very early stage, and was removed by the Nazis from his professorial chair in Bonn in 1935; back home in Switzerland, however, he made himself equally unpopular in his own country by his unwillingness to condemn communism, his outspoken and critical opposition to the use of atomic weapons and his independent line on many topical questions. And through all this he pursued a variety of other interests, from music to military history, and maintained a wide circle of friends and acquaintances. Coming into close contact with him like this, one runs through a whole gamut of emotions, but it is impossible not to admire him, even at his most infuriating, for the way in which he clearly tried to care for his family, his colleagues, his friends and his students, even if his personal relationships were sometimes strained to the utmost by the claims of responding to a gospel whose reality and primacy for him stand out from every page.

If Barth's life is a fascinating human story, it is also an extremely important background to understanding his theology. He was always conscious of the danger of generalizations, and not only his political remarks but also his theological statements, even in the *Church Dogmatics,* arose out of particular situations and were not formulations of universal timeless truths. The most important factors in his theological thinking were his attempt to be obedient to the message of the Bible and at the same time his awareness of the particular moment in history in which he was living. It is likely that both his supporters and his critics have so far failed to see this clearly enough. What is beyond question, however, is that if even the *Dogmatics* are to be understood, the reader must know what was happening in the outside world while Barth was sitting at work in his study.

There has also been a good deal of discussion about which of the various stages of Barth's life was most decisive or most important. What emerges from this biography, however, is that they cannot be played off, one against another; they all belong together and each period has an importance of its own, not least the years from 1935 to 1945, which are discussed in most biographies of Barth with striking brevity, and after them the years immediately following the Second World War.

Because this is so much Barth's book, one hesitates to intrude on it further. It is, however, worth pointing out that maps, a family tree, explanatory footnotes and a bibliography of Barth's major works and their translations has been added to the English edition. References in the notes are to both German and English texts, but the translations are all my own; in a book with more than two thousand quotations, this has proved necessary, if only to make the text readable.

Finally, some essential words of thanks. First to Pastor Busch, who has not only provided a great deal of help with background information to elucidate obscure passages and provide material for footnotes, but has also graciously allowed this Preface to take the place of the somewhat different Foreword to the German edition on which it is based. He himself would want there to be a reference to those who helped him: Frau Nelly Barth and the Barth family, Dr Eduard Thurneysen and Dr Hinrich Stoevesandt. And while many people at SCM Press have actively followed the progress of *Barth* over the winter, spring and sweltering summer of 1976, Margaret Lydamore has laboured in a way which Hercules at least would understand.

JOHN BOWDEN

To the English Reader

'He founded not so much a school as an era.' The words once used by Friedrich Schleiermacher of Frederick the Great of Prussia and then later by Karl Barth of Schleiermacher may also be applied to Karl Barth himself. Certainly, there are 'Barthians'. But they differ so much from one another, and extend so far into the extreme wings of theology, that they can hardly be said to form a clearly-defined 'school'. And in any case, Karl Barth's influence is by no means restricted to the stimulus which he has provided for these 'pupils'. Many theologians who would not count themselves in such a group have nevertheless been influenced by him in an unmistakable way, even if their connection with him cannot be defined very clearly. More than perhaps any other theologian in the twentieth century, Karl Barth has dominated the subject-matter of theology and posed the questions with which the theologians of the different churches have been, and are, occupied, although they may want to 'go beyond' him, go back behind him or even protest against his answers.

This is what makes an account of the life of Karl Barth so important and so interesting. In the last resort it will serve to clarify the context in which Christian theology is studied today. The concern of this book is to show that just as Karl Barth's work was an essential part of his life, so too his life is an essential part of his work. It is significant that so many people did not really understand him until they had come to know him personally. Thus the reader will discover that Barth's 'doctrines' are not merely theoretical pieces of armchair wisdom, but explanations and discoveries which he came upon during the course of a life-long struggle and quest.

It also makes an account of Karl Barth's life rather difficult. It is not easy to describe a great mountain when one is immediately below it, and for the moment a classical biography of a traditional kind is perhaps impossible, because we are still too near to Barth. For that reason Barth's life and work have been presented from his own perspective, in his own words, and the biographer has been content to remain inconspicuously in the background.

My hope is that a new circle of readers in Britain and America will find that this book brings them joy and that they are prompted to further thought by the witness given by Karl Barth in the church and to the wider world.

Uerkheim, Switzerland
Easter 1976

EBERHARD BUSCH

Preface to the New English Edition

When I wrote this book nearly twenty years ago in the short space of just a few months, I did not come totally unprepared. Perhaps I was destined from birth to spend some years of my life in the presence of Karl Barth. By some peculiar chance, his grandparents, Franz Albert Barth and Sara née Lotz, who appear on the first pages of this book, became in 1840 godparents to my great-grandmother. The families of his and my ancestors belonged to the circle – and party in opinion – of the Swabian Kingdom-of-God theologian, Tobias Beck, who was then active in Basle. Later, in 1925, when my father was set on studying under Karl Barth, his pietistic family went up in arms against this, roundly condemning the professor as a seducer of young theologians because of his alleged denial of the resurrection. My grandmother, a simple lady, wanted to know the real truth; she wrote to the accused on the matter and received from him such a satisfactory reply that she thereafter declared outright in the face of her clan, "My son *must* study under Barth!" This he did so thoroughly that he went on automatically to become a member of the Confessional Church and a delegate at the famous Barmen Synod in May 1934.

I suppose, then, I was somewhat biased when I moved to Basel late in 1959 to begin my studies in theology and to hear, among an interested and interesting throng of students from many countries in East and West, above all, Karl Barth. These were the sunset years of his academic activity. His vigorous attacks on the infant baptism tradition in his lectures made us well aware, however, of how agile the aging teacher's mind still was. After he retired from teaching responsibilities at the age of nearly 76, I began to come into closer and closer contact with him, gradually – and officially from early in 1966 – taking over 'secretarial' duties for him, which had until then been dealt with by his generous – and at the time seriously ill – colleague, Charlotte von Kirschbaum. In the following three years, I experienced him in very different states – once more with great vitality and enthusiasm for work, and paying close attention to ecclesiastical and political developments, but then also in weakness, illness and deep inconsolability. In the evenings, in a small circle of people, and after the obligatory Mozart record had been played, he would sit with a glass of wine and recount memories from his eventful life. As early as that, I started up a collection of documents on the subject.

This really paid off when, in 1973, I set to work on writing a biography of Barth. I can still remember well the difficulty I faced. Does it not, I asked myself, quite simply require greater – even purely temporal – distance, if one is to meaningfully portray such a rich life, with so many turns, and which at almost every point provoked so much contention, approval and debate? And don't I – and for that matter anyone who were to take up the task – lack just such a distance? Moreover, if I were to write from the particular viewpoint of one of the then dominant theological perspectives (which also determined the interpretation of Barth), would it not then so easily become an all too subjective product of the moment? And would it then be able to do any kind of justice to the great varieties in the eight decades of this life? Faced with such problems, I finally decided on the unusual 'collage' style of this biography. Only recently, I was astonished to come across a letter, dated October 20, 1967, from the former General Secretary of the World Council of Churches, W. A. Visser 't Hooft, who had clearly spoken with Barth about the plan of writing a biography and proposed the following concept: "As there is such an inexhaustible wealth of material available, this biography is more a matter of ordering the material and allowing it to speak for itself. A lot should be simply quoted from letters, notes taken in discussions, etc." I could take these words as an exact description of what I in fact attempted back then in the Barth biography, without ever knowing the letter.

It goes without saying that today, after so many years, I look back on my product, which has become to a certain extent independent of me, with somewhat mixed feelings. On the other hand, I think that if I were to take up the task of such a biography afresh, I would do a lot differently. On the other hand, I tell myself that today I would perhaps no longer have the strength – or probably the courage – to bring such a book into the world. Not that I regret what I did back then! But that's how it is and therein hang together these two competing thoughts: so infinitely much has shifted and changed since then, in the world of politics and society, in Church and theology, in the relationships of the denominations to each other and in ecumenism, and not last in the field of Barth studies. There is no permanence in any of these fields and there never was. Anyone who wants to express an opinion on Barth today, can neither overlook this nor wish it were otherwise. "The times change and we ourselves change within them." And not only what we used to know changes (and increases) – albeit with the danger that thereby earlier insights are submerged – but also the view-points change, from which others and we ourselves used to think and judge. Anything else would be abnormal.

Firstly, as far as Barth studies are concerned, they have boldly progressed through the years. A complete edition of his works, which also publishes his hitherto unprinted works, has been ap-pearing continually since 1971 and is provisionally close to com-pletion. A bibliography of the secondary literature on his works is about to appear which catalogues over 14,000 works, thus pointing away into sheer limitlessness. For a time, it seemed as if two polarized schools of interpretation were forming, one claiming Barth for socialism and the other linking him with liberalism. More progressive, however, was and is probably for the present a wealth of individual studies, which track down with a magnifying glass both historically and theologically what has been overlooked and forgotten. This includes one study in which his dreams are used to analyze his psyche by all the rules of the art (result – after con-sideration of all the distinctions and disadvantages of such a char-acter: he must have been a schizoid type!). My impression is that these studies have treated more his 'beginnings' in his early work and far less the themes and theses in his later work, namely in his comprehensive *Church Dogmatics*, which is, after all, his most major *oeuvre*. Have we become too short-sighted to grasp a work that has, and demands from its readers, such far sights? In the light of this at least, the provocative title of a piece by: P. Eicher and M. Weinrich, *The Misconstrued Testimony of Karl Barth* (1986), is easy to understand. There is obviously still a wealth that remains to be discovered.

In the last twenty years, there have been above all certain far-reaching changes of atmosphere. At the moment it is still unclear what it will mean for our understanding of Barth that the cirucmstances of German history in the first half of the century and those of the East-West conflict, to which he made critical reference, have since altered dramatically. In the field of theology at any rate, it can be seen that that 'distance,' and moreover not just temporal distance, but distance from his works, has meanwhile showed itself. Consequently it has become for many a piece of history, reduced to knowledge of at most a few catchwords; and these catchwords are often linked – it must be admitted – with distinct caricatures. We can put it rather crudely: while K. Barth appears to have been insisting on Christian identity, today one hears calls from all sides for ('dialogical') communication of the Christian with the 'environment,' i.e., with the so-called human sciences, with human religiosity and with 'other religions,' with emancipatory self-conceptions, etc. In this context, an image of his theology has formed which sees its thought process 'vertical from above' as authoritarian, imperialistic, patriarchal and incapable of dialogue. His 'Christocentric' approach is attacked as the origin of all these improper things, the evils of which many promise to overcome with a new, pneumatological approach.

Might this not be just that 'Theology of the Holy Spirit' which Barth thought he perceived in his last weeks, like Moses looking out over the Promised Land? It should at least give us food for thought that, as he looked out, he could certainly not consider the counterpoint to Fundamentalism and Neo-Liberalism, which he would already see forming back then and which seems to dominate the landscape today, as such a 'Promised Land.' One should also remember that the problem of 'communicating' was not so alien to him, that he was aware of the danger, though, of leaving in the process of such communication one's own position with respect to God, to then come before others as an extended arm of God. We should also keep in mind that as unsuspicious an observer of

Western theology as the liberation theologian G. Gutiérrez noted aptly in 1984 that, in contrast to the type of theologian who begins with humankind, it was just 'Barth, the theologian of the transcendence of God,' who was the one who saw correctly what humans are like 'down here.' 'The one – Barth – starts "above," with God and feels with those who live in the hell of this world; the other goes from "below," from men, and scarcely notices the situtaiton of exploitation inherent in the world.' This may remind us that those catchwords simply cannot be correct and that a life in other times in itself does not necessarily guarantee progress.

This reminder can keep us however from seeing clearly that we do in fact live in 'another time' and are called in it to be responsible. New questions have arisen, in the light of which the answers of yesterday cannot automatically be the answers of today. New horizons have opened up, in the light of which it cannot be forbidden to at least *ask* whether the insights of yesterday might not have contained the restrictions from which we can and should free ourselves. New challenges and new dangers have become visible, in the light of which what was previously insignificant must gain in importance and what formerly stood in the foreground can step back for a while. Why then should not the task of a 'Theology of the Holy Spirit' be on today's agenda? So long as it is the *Holy* Spirit with whom we are concerned and not just a human spirit or even an evil spirit (1 John 4:1-3)! The history of theology and the Church is a path on which we have to walk and on which we cannot just stop where we want. She who walks this path, the Church of Jesus Christ, is after all a wandering nation, which cannot live in solid houses, but only in tents.

If this is true, though, what can a retrospective on the path and work of Barth mean for us and benefit us on our own paths today? I would like here to refer to three things.

Firstly: At the funeral of Barth in December 1968, W. A. Visser 't Hooft said, 'There will be times, when many will rediscover his message, and with delight.' E. Jüngel then also – even somewhat boldly – expressed the suspicion, 'that the future of the theology of Karl Barth still lies far before us.' I take that in practical terms also as an invitiation to see the purpose of a memory of K. Barth and his work not in the conservation of past 'good old times,' but in working with his theology in our own day. The changed circumstances in which we live today could be an opportunity, then, to reread what he wrote, and probably differently to his contemporaries and representatives of the first generation after him. And in the realization of this opportunity, the astonishing 'modernity' of his insights would reveal themselves. For if we scratch at the patina of his at first apparently so antiquated concepts and materials, we encounter theological thought with a forward drive that carries us along. It encourages Christendom and equips it to look to a future in which it can probably no longer 'enjoy a recognized world-scale validity and guaranteed continuity,' but has to exist 'as a small, very lowly community of aliens, but for all that, as a brotherhood, freed from much pure ballast and thus made mobile' (*CD* IV/4, p. 185).

Rejection of the *corpus christianum,* of Christian world domination, was not meant as a feeble retreat. That becomes fully clear only when one realizes in what sense he himself, in in-depth engagement with the spirit of modernism, rediscovered the relevance of the Biblical message. He recognized the problem of modernism as lying in the existence of the ab-solute human, i.e. detached – namely from God and from fellow creatures (cf. *CD* III/2, p. 276ff.; IV/1, p. 464ff.). He recognised it in the existence of the lonely *I,* which as such either enters into aggressive competition with others or loses itself in others and so becomes part of a mass (cf. *CD* II/2, p. 341ff.). His diagnosis was that Christendom is powerless in the face of this modernism or in fact produces it, so long as it considers God also as such an ab-solute, i.e., as someone detached from humanity, through whom a person in his or her autonomy and detachedness, in his or her absolutism, is only affirmed and validated. Barth's discovery of the relevance of the Biblical message reads in contrast that God is 'completely different'; this he is as the *human* God, the God who essentially steps into relationship with his creatures and lives in relationship with them. His self-determination is his "freedom of coexistence" and as such calls humanity forward, and we for our part exercise this self-determination as "freedom in community" (*CD* III/4, p. 128). One could probably say that Barth with the message which we have summarized in this way was bringing "Enlightenment in the light of the Gospel" (E. Jüngel). And we could encourage ourselves today with the fact that this is not directed against the

Enlightenment at the root of the modern age, but against the fatal dangers which have so clearly grown out of this root. This approach may show the absolutely 'modern' in Barth's theology.

Secondly: Even having perceived the forward-looking aspect in Barth's work, one can of course not maintain that he is just to be taken as the prophet of the outlooks and practices which concern 'us' today. His work doubtless also contains burdensome and restrictive ideas, which are not necessarily compatible with what is dear and precious to us today (just as he stood often enough in his own time in contradiction of 'prevalent' opinions). One will however, in the light of such ideas, have to guard against making the rash judgment that they have therefore inherently been superseded and are of no relevance to us. A Church and a theology stagnates in her respective present if she with her belief in the resurrection does not also seriously heed the voices of her forefathers in thought and action, as if they were still speaking today (Hebrews 11.4). She has also, and most especially, to listen carefully to those voices which appear not to affirm, but to contradict her. There is not only a geographical, but also a historical ecumenism, from which the Church in her respective present cannot dispense herself. Indeed that which we today find restrictive in Barth's theology may have less to do with his being tied to his own time than with the fact that he assumes such a time-spanning ecumenism and allows it to speak in his *Church Dogmatics.*

It was in fact he himself who drew attention to this: "In the one 'community of saints,' it is not only the living who are right, but also the dead, it is also not only the living who speak and act, but with them those who have gone before, their words and works, their history, which does not end upon their departure, but rather, often enough begins its decisive stage not until long after they have gone, among their descendants, a stage which stands in inseparable relation to the respective present" (*CD* IV/I, p. 747). The practical meaning of this insight is, however, according to Barth, that the confrontation of our contemporary understanding with the voices of earlier ages inevitably means a 'crisis,' in which "the present can always maintain it is right against earlier ages," in which it however becomes an open question, "whether it is in fact right" (*Protestant Theology in the 19th Century,* 1946, p. 5). This is doubtless to be applied even to the great teacher of theology K. Barth. It is only right that we can and should try to say what he tried to say, but *differently*. But we need his voice in order to be clear whether 'we' are not saying something different, but are saying the *same* thing differently to him. This is all the more true in the light of our final point:

Thirdly: It is just the theology of K. Barth, as scarcely any other in the modern age, that stands for the unrelenting question posed to theology and Church, the question after its spiritual substance. Anyone who practices theology inevitably exposes himself to this question. It is for this reason that Barth's theology has been compared with some justification to that of Luther and Calvin. This question is not to be misunderstood, however, as if it were aiming at an ecclesiastical self-preservation, let alone a flight of theology and church away from the secular and religious world into a Christian ivory tower. In 1959, he called the Church to take note: "She is the human creature which is destined, in her very being, to be for the rest, for the human creation distinct from her. She exists ecstatically, eccentrically: even with the world, to which she belongs, not in respect of herself, but entirely in respect of it, her environment. She saves and sustains her own life by using and giving it up for the rest of human kind" (*CD* IV/3, p. 872). The one who thought like that was worlds away from a 'Christianity' as an end in itself. However, he repeatedly confronted Christendom with the question, whether the lampstand which she is not to put under a bushel in fact has a *light* burning on it and whether this light might not be purely one lit by herself (or other spirits), instead of a light lit by the *Gospel* (Matt. 5:14ff.).

Barth also gave a particular answer to this question, and with increasing pointedness. The answer is inherent in the question. It reads that Christendom only then has justification for its existence and something to say and mean to its environment, if it is the Gospel of God in Jesus Christ from which it has lit its message. In one of the last public statements, Barth said, "The last word I have to say is not a concept, but a name: Jesus Christ." That the Gospel of Jesus Christ might take people over and give them a bad deal, of that he was less afraid than that Christendom, out of a wrong concern about this, might weaken it and water it down. For bound up with the purity in which it is accepted was for him the absoluteness and unrestrictedness of the understanding that God himself says a pure 'yes' to humans and in them to his whole creation. That which was peculiar to Barth in this was surely that he understood this great 'Yes' from God both as God's 'good contradiction' (P. Fischer) to the fatal egoism in which the human person, fixed on self, otherwise says 'Yes' to self. But he gave no less emphasis to that it is just the 'Yes' from God which frees this person to then also say 'Yes': to God, to fellow creatures and to himself or herself. In the Gospel understood thus, Barth sees the spiritual substance of Christendom embraced. It would be more than short-sighted to suggest that we today in our tasks, but also in our danger of fundamentalism on the one hand and syncretism on the other, did not need Barth's questioning after this substance and his answer to it.

With all the above, I signal my reasons for believing that the voice of Karl Barth in his works still deserves to be heard by the Church and theology of our age. This new American edition of his biography comes with my hope that it may enable readers, not to follow Karl Barth, but to follow the One to whom he pointed his contemporaries and also us today.

Göttingen,
2nd April 1992

EBERHARD BUSCH

List of Illustrations

1

'Karli'

Childhood, 1886–1904

Basle – his family's city

Karl Barth was born in Basle on 10 May 1886. He came into the world on a Monday morning, about five o'clock, at Grellingerstrasse 42, and he was called Karl after his mother's oldest brother.

His parents' names were Johann Friedrich ('Fritz') Barth and Anna Katharina, née Sartorius. They had only been living in Basle for a month when Karl, their first son, was born, and it was exactly a week since Johann Friedrich had taken up a new post there. Before that he had been for seven years pastor in the parish of Reitnau, in the canton of Aargau.[1] He had lived there for five years as a bachelor before meeting Anna; by that time he had already had a patristic study published (on Tertullian's interpretation of Paul) for which he had been awarded a doctorate of theology in 1881. This was one of the reasons why, somewhat surprisingly, at the beginning of 1886 he was invited to be a lecturer at the College of Preachers in Basle. This college had been founded ten years earlier by W. Arnold, a pastor who was also its Director, for the training of 'scriptural' preachers, mostly for the free churches, in opposition to liberal theology.

So Fritz and Anna Barth came to Basle. However, neither of them were strangers to the city. Both had been born and had grown up there. Their fathers, Karl's two grandfathers, were pastors in Basle from the middle of the nineteenth century onwards.[2] The Barth family originally came from Mülligen in the Aargau. 'My great-grandfather moved there to Kleinbasel* at the beginning of the nineteenth century and was in the tobacco business.'[3] The oldest

*Kleinbasel ('Little Basle') is that part of the city which lies within the bend on the right bank of the Rhine (see map on p. 504). Throughout the book, forms of place names familiar to English-speaking readers have been preferred (thus 'Basle', not 'Basel'), but at times, as here, it has been impossible to be completely consistent.

son of this Samuel Barth and Veronica Elisabeth, née Otto, whose name was Franz Albert (1816–79), studied theology. 'He was one of J. T. Beck's first Basle students, but he also held de Wette in great respect. He became pastor in Bubendorf, in Basle Land, which in 1833 had been made a separate canton, and in 1840 he was married by Beck, his teacher, to Sara Lotz. In 1852 he became a teacher at the Girls' High School (his subjects were religion and music!); finally, in 1861, he became what was then called "deacon" (third pastor) at St Theodore's church in Basle.'[4] 'He had a keen eye for anything contrived, inauthentic or exaggerated, and was blunt in saying what he thought about it . . . . He was convinced that in the present state of the church, which he lamented bitterly, there was no future for enforced demolition or reconstruction; the only possible way forward lay in quietness and hope, and above all in humble observance of God's serious warnings.'[5] 'When the family were together in the house on the Rebgasse . . . in the evening (preferably over a glass of beer), there was not only a great deal of music-making, but often a lot of political talk, of which they were fond. There was much support for Bismarck!'[6]

'I also have a special connection with Kleinbasel through my grandmother (Sara) Barth, née Lotz.'[7] Sara (1817–88) was the fifth child of Peter Friedrich Lotz, a silk-dyer, a member of the Great Council* and a master of his guild, and Sara, née Heussler. She was thus descended from a family who were 'hardworking and skilled at their trade; they were extremely lively, indeed rather wild', prone to sudden outbursts of temper which became almost proverbial and made the family name a byword.[8] The young Sara herself also evidently had a lively disposition: 'she was very sensitive, and a woman of action, with the less desirable aspects of such characteristics as well'.[9] 'As a pious Christian and a woman of prayer, however, she knew how to cope with these difficulties and others which came her way. She and my father (her seventh and youngest child) must have had a particularly close relationship'; however, he always spoke of his father, too, with the greatest love and respect.[10]

Karl's father, who was born on 25 October 1856, was a somewhat shy and sickly boy, who had to be treated gently. From 1871–74 he

---

*The Great Council is the government of a canton. In effect, the cantons of which Switzerland is made up are states, which e.g. make their own constitutions, found universities, confer professional qualifications, and so on. They may, and do, establish state churches, though religious toleration is enforced by the central power, the Federal Council.

went to the grammar school in Basle, where he happened to sit next to Eduard Thurneysen (1856–1931), who became a friend for life. Thurneysen's son, who had the same name, later became a friend of Karl Barth.

Jacob Burckhardt, Emil Kautzsch and Friedrich Nietzsche were among Fritz Barth's teachers; he remembered all three of them well, and especially the last. 'Personally, I can only speak of Nietzsche with great respect, since he was my teacher at school, and did not have the slightest unsavoury influence on me.'[11] Fritz followed the example of three of his brothers in deciding to study theology; he began in Basle (where, among other courses, he attended the lectures of Nietzsche's friend Franz Overbeck), went on to Leipzig and finally completed his studies at Tübingen. He was attracted to Leipzig by music, and to Tübingen by theology. There he came into contact with Adolf Harnack, who was then a young assistant lecturer.* At the same time, as he himself said, the figure of old Tobias Beck made an unforgettable impression on him: 'I had ample opportunity, at the eleventh hour of his life and of my studies, to get to know this most distinguished man, whose first lectures my father had attended in his day. He made the most profound impression on me; he became not only a teacher but a spiritual father who brought me out of the barren wilderness of self-satisfied criticism into the green pastures of the word of God. It is thanks to him that I was able to be sure of my faith and happy in it, even as a theologian.'[12] Shortly after his father's death and immediately after his ordination in 1879, Fritz Barth became pastor of Reitnau. People there did not easily forget the earnestness of his preaching, his outspokenness for the truth and his personal humility.

Anna Sartorius, whom he married there, also came from Basle. 'She was the granddaughter of a professor of literature called Karl Friedrich Sartorius, who also came to Basle from Germany, early in the nineteenth century, to teach at the grammar school.'[13] His forbears lived in Franconia, and one of them was a Consistory Councillor in Bayreuth. This Karl was 'rather too jolly a fellow; according to his printed sermons his theology was extremely rationalistic'.[14] By 1832 he had been expelled from the university for

---

*German *Privatdozent*. There is no precise English equivalent, because the German university system differs from those of Britain or the USA. The *Privatdozent* is on the lowest step of the ladder of a university teaching career; he will have qualified by passing his *Habilitation* examination and his lecturing is approved by the university, but he is not paid for it.

drunkenness, whereupon he abandoned his wife Sophie, née Huber, who was twelve years younger, and their children, and left Basle, dying three years later in Bärenstein near Annaberg in Saxony. Hence 'the mysterious cloak of silence over his name which I already sensed as a child'.[15] Shortly after his death, his widow married the former tutor of their children, Dr Karl Roth. Her oldest son, Karl Achilles (1824–93), 'with black hair coming down almost to his shoulders, a style which he maintained even when it turned white, right down to the day of his death',[16] became a theologian. After a short period in Bretzwil he spent the rest of his life from 1851 onwards as pastor of St Elisabeth's in Basle, at first at the old church and then at the new. Here for a time he was 'a fashionable preacher following a strictly orthodox, Reformed line'.[17] 'In the 1840s he had studied in Berlin with Schelling in his late period and then in Heidelberg with R. Rothe. As a result he had come to some degree under the influence of Schleiermacher, but subsequently, like so many of his contemporaries, he went over to a somewhat primitive theological conservatism, tempered slightly by the gentle pietism of my good grandmother.'[18] 'At the same time a repressed remembrance of his idealist father impelled him strongly in the opposite direction . . . My mother heard him say with his own lips: "Anna, the teaching of the Bible and the church is an edifice which will completely collapse if anyone should take a single stone from it." '[19] In addition, his grandson also saw him as a supreme example of 'the self-assurance with which the church of the time had put itself on the side of the "authorities" appointed by God'.[20]

This grandfather took as his second wife Johanna Maria, née Burckhardt (1832–1915). 'Through my mother's mother, therefore, I have the honour of being descended from the old Basle family of the Burckhardts; indeed, I am not too distantly related to the famous Jacob of that name' (who was in fact a cousin of Karl's grandmother).[21] Their common grandfather, Johannes Rudolf Burckhardt, was for many years pastor at St Peter's church in Basle. 'He has an unforgettable place in the history of the church in Basle and the history of early Swiss Protestantism.' His twenty-first and youngest child, also called Johannes, made a deeper spiritual impression on Barth than any of his ancestors. He was 'emphatically a pietist', but he was not 'narrow-minded, gloomy or severe'; he was 'joyful, and a joy to be with'. He had lively exchanges with Albert Knapp, Ludwig Hofacker and Emil Krummacher, and also with the older Blumhardt and Isaak Dorner.[22] After working for a short time in Wuppertal and at St Jacob's church in Basle, in 1827 he became pastor in Bretzwil, Basle Land, until the revolt (3 August 1833) in which the Land defeated the city and seceded from it. Because he was a citizen of the city, it was then impossible for him to continue to work there. 'At that time my grandmother, as a small child, was smuggled back to Basle through France in a basket' (while 'my grandfather Barth . . . was standing guard in front of the town hall').[23] At the end of 1833, Johannes Burckhardt then went to the canton of Schaffhausen as a pastor; this was the native territory of his wife Amalie, née Peyer, who was a descendant of the Zürich reformer Heinrich Bullinger: 'So in some way his blood, too, runs in my veins.'[24] Karl Barth's grandmother was the third of the Burckhardts' children and grew up in Schaffhausen. She went to Basle in February 1854, to marry Karl Achilles Sartorius.

The seventh of her nine children was Anna Katharina (born on 15 April 1863). She went to the Girls' High School in Basle and then devoted herself to keeping house for her oldest brother Karl, who was still single and a pastor — first in Fleurier and then in Bennwil. This Karl was the closest friend of Karl Barth's father Fritz when they were students.[25] So it came about that Fritz made the acquaintance of Anna Sartorius at the parsonage in Bennwil, on a visit from Reitnau. They became engaged on 15 April 1884 and were married only four months later, on 28 August. Fritz's old school friend, Thurneysen, was best man at the wedding.[26] Fritz and Anna Barth had very different dispositions. Fritz was cautious and restrained, while Anna was outspoken and energetic: 'When my mother had made up her mind about something, it was usually done.'[27] However, 'my father's tranquil and earnest manner, still waters which ran deep, was an excellent counterbalance to her happy and vivacious character'.[28]

So when the couple moved from Reitnau to Basle in April 1886, they were coming back to familiar home ground. Like them, their son who arrived so soon afterwards felt close links with the city of his birth for the rest of his life. He had a complex character and was critical and reserved towards established Basle society, but nevertheless he too was a typical Basle citizen. In fact, he felt that to belong to Basle was something special. 'We breathe a distinctive kind of air here.'[29] 'There is a particular spiritual tradition here, which probably has something to do with the climate of the place.'[30]

Karl Barth once spoke of Basle theology, 'as it is done here and will probably continue to be done until the day of judgment', in terms which would also seem to apply to the disposition of the typical Basle citizen. 'He is utterly conservative and has always been so, while at the same time secretly taking pleasure in the radicalism and extravagance of others. However, although he may find the latter frightfully interesting, he will probably steer clear of adopting it.' 'He has been immunized against the right wing by a kind of innate, mildly humanistic scepticism', and 'he is protected against the left wing by an acquired *savoir faire* which comes from constant practice in observation. So he will settle somewhere between these extremes, perhaps in the tranquillity of a little free-thinking or perhaps in the tranquillity of a little pious enthusiasm, while in all circumstances presenting to the world the picture of a healthy combination of freedom and moderation. He is always inclined to see all discussions as being essentially a mere dispute over words, and he is a triumphant exponent of the method of always letting others have the first and the last word, thinking his own thoughts without openly compromising himself in action.'[31]

One of the most obvious aspects of the citizen of Basle is his characteristic laugh. He produces a sharp, biting, aggressive, mocking burst of laughter, not a happy, Mozart-like smile. 'Basle isn't Salzburg, Prague or Vienna – Basle is Basle.'[32] Karl Barth also inherited something of the Basle way of laughing, though often enough he directed his laughter against the typical citizens of Basle themselves: 'I am glad to be only three-eighths a genuine product of the real Basle.'[33] He was never very happy about the annual pre-Lent carnival, the public occasion for this laughter, 'Because I have a deep-seated antipathy to masquerades.'[34] Yet he also saw quite clearly that the rough humour of Basle concealed an acute and sober consciousness of death. 'People here in Basle have long pondered on the transitoriness of all earthly affairs, the evanescence of human life . . . It is no mere chance that the celebrated "Dance of Death" was performed in Basle in the Middle Ages. I once read the travel journal of a Frenchman who came to Basle two hundred years ago and found a book which, he said, was unlike anything that he had found anywhere else. This was the *Basilea Sepulta* (*Buried Basle*), which appeared eighty years before his visit and contained detailed descriptions of the tombs here in Basle. This is why Johann Peter Hebel wrote his immortal poem, *Das Gedicht vom Röteler Schloss*, about transitoriness.* This, too, is why they bang the drum so loudly in Basle at carnival time and why there is such a compulsion, almost an exaggerated compulsion, to be jolly, as if there were a need to forget such thoughts for a day or two. But they will keep coming back again. This is why we have such an incomparable cemetery in Basle, the Hörnli cemetery. Perhaps it is all connected with the fact that the Rhine flows past Basle and keeps flowing for ever past: past the cathedral and the Pfalz, the Fair and the Mustermesse, the university and the Volkshaus, the Museum of Fine Arts and all the other buildings which are important to us citizens of Basle.'[35]†

This is where Karl Barth was born. It was not an easy birth. And when he came into the world, one of his aunts said that he looked 'quite terrible'. He comforted himself later with the rule according to which 'the ugliest babies turn into the most handsome children and men'.[36] He was baptized in the cathedral in Basle on 20 June 1886 by his grandfather Sartorius (who at that particular time was finishing off a manifesto against cremation!). Karl's godparents were Karl Sartorius (1856–1906), his mother's brother, in whose house his parents had become engaged and who had just moved to Pratteln as pastor there; Hans Burckhardt (1840–1923), an older brother of Karl's grandmother Johanna Sartorius, and finally his other grandmother Sara Barth, 'whom sadly I was too young to know';[37] she died eighteen months later. The young Karl spent only three years in Basle. During this time he thrived under the upbringing of his parents and a nursemaid – though his father's diary for 27 April 1887 has the frightening entry: 'Baby Karl falls off his cushion.' And on 12 June 1888 there is the significant remark, 'Karli cries all night.' 'Karli' – this was the pet name by which his parents used to call him.

One of his recollections from this time was of 'how someone from the "College of Preachers" came into our dining room in Grellingerstrasse, so this term at any rate must have made some impression on me in my earliest years'.[38] He also remembered 'being pushed in the pram as a small child from Grellingerstrasse along Aeschenvorstadt

---

*The poem is in fact called *Vergänglichkeit* ('Transitoriness'), and describes a conversation between father and son whose thoughts have been turned in this direction by the sight of the ruins of the Röttler Schloss (Barth's orthography differs), which lie just over the border, in Germany.

*†See the map on p. 503. The Pfalz is a terrace in between the cathedral and the river with a fine view; the Mustermesse is an exhibition site and the scene of one of the greatest annual Swiss exhibitions; the Volkshaus is a public hall, restaurant and library.

to the parsonage of St Elisabeth's church'. This was where his grandfather Sartorius lived: 'He was sitting in his armchair, and he had long white hair . . . I sensed something of his patriarchal character and the solemnity of his vocation. At a later date I was quite incapable of making anything like the same impression on my own grandchildren . . . Through no fault of her own, my good grandmother was the cause of a trauma which disturbed me from time to time right up until my manhood. I must still have been very small and she was involved in some sanitary measures on my behalf which my mother evidently thought to be beyond her own capability. She gave me a sharp look, the intensity of which was heightened by a pair of spectacles which she did not wear at other times . . . depth psychology at work!'[39] Karl also remembered the stethoscope in the hand of his uncle Wilhelm Bernoulli: 'He watched over my health in my tenderest youth and sounded my back and my chest with it.'[40]

In his earliest years he learnt to sing some Basle-German children's songs from his mother, and these proved very significant for him. They had been written by 'a theologian called Abel Burckhardt. He was not a great man, but I, at any rate, held him in high respect. He lived about a hundred years ago and was a contemporary of the more famous Jacob Burckhardt who was second pastor at the cathedral here in Basle.' His children's songs 'were the textbook from which I received my first theological instruction at the beginning of the last decade of the nineteenth century, in a form which was appropriate for my immature years. What made an indelible impression on me was the homely self-assurance with which these unpretentious verses spoke of the events of Christmas, Palm Sunday, Good Friday, Easter, Ascension, Pentecost, as though they could have taken place that very morning in Basle or nearby, like any other exciting event. History? Doctrine? Dogma? Myth? No. It was all things actually taking place. You could see everything for yourself, listen to it and take it to heart by hearing one of these songs sung in the language you were hearing elsewhere and beginning to speak, and you could join in the song yourself. Holding your mother's hand you went to the stable in Bethlehem, along the streets of Jerusalem, into which the saviour was making his entry, hailed by children of your own age. You climbed the grim hill of Golgotha and walked in Joseph's garden at daybreak . . . Was it all rather naive. . . ? Indeed it was very naive, but perhaps the deepest wisdom, with its fullest force, lies in naivety, and this kind of wisdom, once gained, can carry a man over whole oceans of historicism and anti-historicism, mysticism and rationalism, orthodoxy, liberalism and existentialism. He certainly will not be spared trial and temptation, but in the end he will be brought back relatively unscathed to firm ground.'[41]

In the middle of April 1888, the Barths were able to move from their flat into a family house nearby, Grellingerstrasse 36. In this house, a week after Karli's second birthday, a second son, Peter (or 'Bäti'), was added to the family. Hardly had the family settled down in the new house, however, than the 'positives', a conservative theological group in Berne, approached Fritz Barth, just before Christmas of the same year, with the wish that he should succeed Adolf Schlatter in a professorial chair which they financed. Fritz Barth accepted the invitation, and so after just three years the Barths again left Basle and moved to Berne. At the end of April 1889 they moved into Länggassstrasse 75, where they rented an apartment on the first floor.

Early childhood in Berne

A few days later Karl's father took up his new post. On the one hand he was an assistant lecturer in the University of Berne, with permission to teach dogmatics; on the other he was teacher of religion at a Christian private school, the 'Lerberschule'. This was named after its founder, Theodorich von Lerber, whose acquaintance Fritz Barth had already made in Basle.

Among his colleagues at the university, Samuel Oettli, the Old Testament scholar, came closest to his own views. Karl Marti, who succeeded Oettli in 1895, was more inclined to liberalism, but since the time when they had been students together, he and Fritz Barth had maintained a close personal friendship. In Berne, Fritz also came into closer contact with Carl Hilty, a noble and religious man who taught jurisprudence. In March 1891 the Berne administration appointed Fritz Barth *extraordinarius* professor, and in June 1895 he became *Ordinarius* Professor in Early and Mediaeval Church History.* In addition to the teaching work which this involved, he also lectured regularly on New Testament questions. Indeed, his real

---

*Again, there is no exact English or American equivalent to the distinction between *extraordinarius* and *ordinarius* professor. The *ordinarius* professor is so to speak the 'full' professor, the *extraordinarius* in some respects is like the American associate professor.

interest seems to have lain here. His two principal works were in fact on specifically New Testament subjects: *Die Hauptprobleme des Lebens Jesu* (The Chief Problems of the Life of Jesus) and *Einleitung in das Neue Testament* (Introduction to the New Testament). In addition to this, he showed himself to be a man of many other interests. He had a lively concern for doctrinal questions, on which he gave a variety of lectures at home and abroad; he involved himself with the affairs of the church in Berne, in which he held a respected place (from spring 1895 as a member of the Synod); he was open to the problems of the time, especially women's rights and social issues, and helped to found a Christian Socialist society to devote serious attention to the latter. In due course the scope of his activities made his name fairly well known. His writings were distinguished by their diligence, their circumspection and their thoroughness. For all his firm principles, he was a free man, who could maintain friendly relations not only with Adolf Schlatter but also with Adolf Harnack; both men visited his house from time to time. And although theologically he was counted a conservative, indeed precisely for that reason, he argued resolutely that the scholarly task of theology should be taken serious-ly, sometimes scandalizing the group with his views. He seemed in some way to sense the coming crisis, and as far as he was able he sought to act as a mediator between supporters and critics of tradi-tion, in the confidence that the gospel would continue to prove itself even in a changed world. Thus he manifestly sought some kind of middle way which went beyond the confrontation of 'conservative' and 'liberal'. This is probably why he was now on the whole 'one of those who were overlooked and somewhat despised by the theologi-cal pillars and props of the church'.[42] It was also one of the reasons why he did not really feel at home in Berne. For the same reason, however, much as he may have wished it, he was never offered a post outside Berne. He was considered for posts in the conservative faculties of Halle and Greifswald, but in a strange way his denial of the virgin birth in particular 'twice cost him a professorship'.[43] By way of consolation, however, in 1903 the University of Halle awarded him an honorary doctorate in theology.

'Thus it came about that I spent the whole of my youth among the people of Berne.'[44] The world in which Karl grew up was quite different from that in which he spent his later life. 'I have dim memories from my childhood of having heard people talking about Bismarck in a way which indicated that he was still alive.'[45] Bismarck was the man who was later to seem to Karl Barth to be the typical representative of the whole of that era. He himself felt that the first years in Berne were a very happy time. 'My earliest clear memories of my youth are associated with what was then still very much a country area on the outskirts of the Langgass Quartier, on the edge of the Bremgartenwald.'[46] 'We lived . . . right on the very edge of the city, so that woods, fields and gardens play a great part in my earliest memories and made a great impression on me. Then there were the arcades, fountains and towers of the old city, and the lakes and valleys of the Bernese Oberland.'[47]

Karl Barth spent this time among a growing family of brothers and sisters of whom he was the head. He and Peter were followed by Heinrich, on 3 February 1890, Katharina on 1 January 1893 and three years later by Gertrud, again on New Year's Day. 'Peter was my first and for many years my most faithful friend . . . He was always lively, always thinking up exciting ideas; one could always depend on his many-sided capabilities and he kept making even our solemn father laugh with his remarks and his escapades.'[48] The third boy, Heinrich ('Hinz'), on the other hand, was a quiet, shy, solitary child; he took offence very easily, but could himself be quite devastating with his sharp humour. A severe case of poliomyelitis most probably contributed to these characteristics; he had the illness in January 1891, when he was eleven months old, and it left him with a marked limp. 'Käthi' turned out to be a delightful 'gifted, lively child'.[49] Karl regarded himself emphatically as an uncle to Gertrud ('Trudi'), who was ten years younger. Doubtless he himself was the leading spirit among his brothers and sisters, to their qualified delight. 'I was the oldest child . . . in my family and did not always use my position in the right way: the consequence was that my brothers, in particular, bore a grudge against me all through their lives for having been so bossy then and having made everything grist for my mill.'[50] He came to be called 'Ulchen', a name made up of (K)A(r)l(i)chen, and when Pius X was made Pope, for a while he regarded himself as a new pope and claimed to be '*St* Ul(i)chen'. A dialect verse of his runs:

> My dearest people, here's my rule,
> I will no longer go to school
> Since now as pope I have my stool . . .

His parents brought up the family strictly, in the manner of the time, but they were also kind and understanding. 'Looking back on my childhood, I have to acknowledge now, at any rate, that my parents . . . brought us up in a good Christian spirit.'[51] This was his father's idea of bringing up a family: 'With God's help, parents direct the upbringing of their children and come to the aid of their inexperience with advice and discipline. Their hearts stay young through the happy games of their children; they relive their own childhood and experience much to make them exclaim, "Yea, Lord, out of the mouths of babes and sucklings hast thou ordained praise!" Children come under the healthy sway of the commandment "Honour your father and your mother", but in their turn they also educate us. We are humbled by the perception of our own errors in them, by the observation that a propensity to sin is even in children's hearts and that our strength often threatens to fail in the battle against it. These are other ways in which children are a blessing to us.'[52]

Karl later thought that his mother brought the children up much too strictly. She followed the principle 'Be very, very kind', but at the same time she constantly laid down the law (or what she thought to be the law) with an expressive shaking of the head, sometimes in silence and sometimes with words.[53] This kind of upbringing led to all kinds of clashes, 'the reasons for which I cannot now remember . . . One thing, however, is certain, that compared with so many others we had a very good life and must be grateful for a mass of things which we received without being aware of them.'[54] Thus Karl held his father in great respect and was deeply attached to his mother.

As far as diet went, 'our good mother conscientiously and inexorably carried out the instructions of uncle Wilhelm Bernoulli and later Professor Stooss on bringing me up . . . though today it is no longer thought appropriate to give children quite so much milk to drink'.[55] 'I shall never forget how, as a small boy, I had to drink a small glass of cod-liver oil every morning for many years. It was terrible, but it evidently did me good.'[56] Furthermore, 'we were rightly taught that the essential foundation for true contentment was to have plenty of sunshine'.[57] Punishment played its part in their upbringing. 'In one of my father's letters written in 1890 (when I was four years old), I read the remark, "Karli had to be beaten again today".'[58] There was a wardrobe in the Länggassstrasse house 'into which I was once shut because of my wild shouting in the street'.[59]

Karl did not allow himself to be intimidated by this measure; he somewhat perplexed his parents by asserting from the depths of the wardrobe that there was a certain need which he had to see to rather urgently. As a rule, however, his parents tried to put things like squabbles among children right by good advice rather than by punishment. 'On some occasions when we were young my father used to raise his finger towards us and say, "Behold how good and joyful a thing it is, brethren, to dwell together in unity."'[60] On the other hand, Karl believed that his mother had made an original contribution to the language with her occasional exclamation, 'We need to take one of them and beat the others with it.' As Karl's father understood a child's need for some rough and tumble, sometimes after lunch he found time for wrestling and boxing with his growing boys.

Of course they still sang the hymns of Abel Burckhardt in Berne, and soon Karl's parents sent him to Sunday School. '"Ruh, Ruh, Ruh, Ruh, himmlische Ruh!" (Rest, rest, rest, rest, heavenly rest) – I remember how when I heard this as a child in Sunday School I used to think of some kind of African wild animal (probably a kangaroo. . . !).'[61] However, one day the following incident took place. 'I had a well-meaning but rather silly Sunday School mistress who thought it proper to give us children a precise description of hell and the eternal torments waiting there for the wicked. Of course this interested us and excited us quite a lot. But none of us there at the time learnt the fear of the Lord and the beginning of wisdom in this way.'[62] At least that was Karl's father's view at the time, since he immediately withdrew Karl from Sunday School and from then on held a children's service for the family every Sunday in his study.

Karl made his first acquaintance with the Roman Catholic Church as a very small boy, at the age of five: 'I was on holiday with my grandmother . . . and we were staying in a Roman Catholic clergy house. I have always remembered how fond the priest was of a drink. I also went with him to mass. Of course I didn't understand what was going on, nor could I understand the Latin words, apart from the constant repetition of the phrase *Dominus vobiscum*. I identified the word *Dominus*, but connected it with my game of dominoes.'[63] At an early age he also made his first tenuous contact with the themes of Christian Socialism, through the name of Friedrich Naumann. 'I still remember the sub-title of his newspaper *Die Hilfe* (Help), which I sometimes saw on my father's desk: "Help for

God, help for one's brother, help for the state, help for oneself".
These strong words made an impression on me, though I could
hardly understand them. I felt that something strong, great and new
was on the way.'[64]

'Along to school the children go . . .'

Karl's education took a new shape on 21 April 1892, when he went to
school for the first time. '"Along to school the children go, and
soldiers go to war; let each one strive . . ." I can still hear my father's
rendering of this rousing verse at bedtime on the eve of the day when
I was to go off to elementary school. From this very first day onwards
I was never any good at mathematics, and my writing was never
beautiful, but I soon became a bookworm.'[65] 'From the most junior
classes until I left I had my schooling in what was then called the
Lerberschule and later the Free Grammar School.'[66] This was the
school in the Nägeligasse in Berne at which Fritz Barth was a teacher
from 1889 to 1912; from 1896 he was also one of the directors. It had
been founded in 1859 by Theodorich von Lerber with the intention
of providing school instruction with a deliberate 'biblical and positive' emphasis, as opposed to the official school instruction, which
was beginning to be shaped on freethinking principles. In accordance with this intention, at the school not only did every day begin
with prayer and chorales, but 'religion' was virtually the chief subject. In the year in which Karl entered the school, religious instruction was cut from six hours a week to three, whereupon von Lerber
resigned in protest from the school board and refused to allow the
school to be called by his name. Some time later the vice-president of
the school also resigned in protest against Fritz Barth's 'critical
remarks about the Bible' and his 'concessions to the left'.[67] As the
'positives' had their strongest support among the rich aristocratic
families in Berne, the Free Grammar School was predominantly
attended by the sons of these families. Consequently the school came
to be mocked, with some degree of justice, as 'this school built for the
sons of a few gentry with pietistic inclinations'.[68] Karl was never top
of the form. He did not have the ambition, nor the inclination in
some subjects. 'I never came more than second in class, and this did
not happen very often. My fierce antipathy towards mathematics
and the natural sciences, on which great stress was laid in Berne

schools at that time, on occasion still pursues me, even now, into my dreams. Regrettably, as a result we were never as well grounded in ancient languages as is usually the practice in German schools. Only history, and above all essay-writing, commanded my whole-hearted attention; when it came to the latter, in every class I was able to emerge head and shoulders above the rest of the competition.'[69]

For Karl, meeting his various teachers proved to be a matter of coming under more or less deep, moving and beneficial influences. There was a master called Pfister, who taught him 'to write with pen and ink'. 'I could not have written so many books had he not taught me how to deal with these things.'[70] Another master, Rudolf Huber, 'attempted to guide me to the peaks of mathematics'. '"They just don't want to know," he used to say of his refractory pupils, including myself. He was particularly fond of reading Psalm 104 in morning prayers. We were supposed to say prayers four times a day, but sometimes he made them rather brief. "Lord bless us, Amen", was one of his shortest. But really, that says all that needs to be said.'[71] Karl never forgot the 'saying which a teacher of religion impressed upon us when telling us the story of Jeremiah: "Ebed-melech, the negro, had some sensitivity"'.[72] Nor did he forget the remark which the French teacher used to make 'when the uproar in the class became too wild: "Aimez-vous les uns les autres!"'[73]

Karl never liked going to school. 'I tolerated the offerings and the demands of the lower school and the upper school as an inevitable cross which I had to bear.'[74] The free time after the claims of school had been satisfied was all the more important to him: it was a marvellous opportunity for him to develop his powers and his imagination to the full. 'I have much more vivid memories of the things which I loved to do and in fact did outside school hours during those years than of school itself.'[75] He proved to have two remarkably different sides to his character. On the one hand he was gifted with a very fine sensibility, which expressed itself especially in a sensitive and perceptive musical ear. His 'first encounter with great music' made an indelible mark upon him. 'I must have been five or six years old at the time . . . My father was musical and was fond of improvising on the piano . . . One day he was playing something by Mozart. I can still picture the scene. He began a couple of bars from *The Magic flute* ("Tamino mine, what happiness"). They went right through me and into me, I don't know how, and I thought, "That's it!".'[76]

But there was also quite a different side of Karl's character,

militant and even belligerent. 'Until I was sixteen, I lived and
dreamed of military exploits. My brothers and I would play with
lead soldiers for hours on end and did so with great seriousness.'[77]
From time to time Karl also enjoyed joining in 'real' fist-fights and
battles. Again, he could satisfy his enthusiasm for fighting by reading historical works about past wars. 'I shall never forget the first
book I read on this subject, when I was about seven or eight years
old: Christian Niemeyer, *A Book of Heroes. A Memorial of the Great
Deeds in the Wars of Liberation*, Leipzig 1818. I still have the book on
my shelf.'[78] It contained a 'bloodthirsty account of the wars against
"Buonaparte", whom it could not condemn too severely . . . So when
I was asked to construct a sentence with the object in the accusative,
I staggered my teacher by the prompt answer from my tender lips:
"Napoleon founded the Confederation of the Rhine." To think that
people later criticized me for giving history short shrift in my theo-
logy!'[79] Further reading matter was a 'bound copy of a substantial
German illustrated magazine from the war years 1870–71 . . .
Bavarians swinging clubs and "Turkos" in retreat were very prominent in the pictures, and when I had learnt to read, the text provided
extensive instruction on the battles of Weissenburg, Wörth, Sedan,
the sieges of Paris and Strasbourg, and so on'.[80] The hero of this war,
Bismarck, was also embodied before Karl's eyes in the form of a
nutcracker used in the family, which bore the Chancellor's features.

'The first war of which I was personally aware – though at a safe
distance! – was that between Japan and the old China in 1895.
Wasn't there a Japanese general at that time called Yamagata?
Anyway, I remember that I became very involved in the actions of
this man, and of the Japanese, who at that time were still very little
known in Europe, and followed them with great interest and excitement. Like any boy, I delighted in the victory of the lesser power over
the greater. From that time on the word "Japan" has always stirred
me, though I was less approving of some later undertakings of the
Japanese government and the Japanese army.'[81] It was even more
exciting when a King Chulalongkorn came from Bangkok to Berne
in 1897: 'He was escorted through the city in triumph by Swiss
dragoons, an event which so excited me that I had to go to bed with a
fever. The country was still called Siam then.'[82]

So Karl's life developed along these lines. Only part of it, however, was spent in the Länggassstrasse. On being promoted in 1895,
his father was able to look for a better house in Berne. He found one

at the opposite end of the city, east of the bend in the river Aare which girdles the old city of Berne, on the Schosshalde, from which there are fine views, on one side towards old Berne and on the other towards the Alps. The Barths lived in this area, at first, from the end of April 1895 to the beginning of October 1896, at Hoheweg 13, and from 1896 onwards in a new house which they had built for themselves at Claraweg 8. Karl lived here on the Schosshalde from when he was nine until his university student days, 'while the Aare kept on flowing past and the Gurten,* the Stockhorn and the Jungfrau kept tranquil watch over the beautiful countryside and Berne, old and new'.[83]

Holidays

Although Karl was never unhappy, even in this new part of the town, 'at heart I simply never got on well with the Bernese way of doing things'.[84] In the course of time he even developed 'an antipathy to a temperament and an attitude which, as I could see, often restricted my father and made problems for him. In a very different context, I was able to understand better what had disturbed me at that time when I came to read about Calvin's experiences with the same nation.'[85] This antipathy increased when he noted that in Berne a mindless and stupid hatred of the 'Baslerbeppi' was to be found everywhere.[86] So for Karl, who at home was brought up to speak a pure Basle German, holidays were the high points of his younger days, not only because they freed him from the burdensome pressure of school but also because he was usually able to get away from Berne. The family went to the Belpberg, to Beatenberg, to Sigriswil or to some other place around Berne, or even to Basle. When he was thirteen years old he wrote a poem:

> For holidays I always crave,
> as then I cease to be a slave,
> and life becomes worth living . . .

He especially remembered 'our family holiday in Lauterbrunnen – I think it was in 1893: that's where I caught whooping cough and almost left this world altogether. A year or two earlier we had gone with a number of relations 'to Kandersteg. I can still picture very

---

*The Gurten is a magnificent belvedere with a panorama of Berne, just outside the city; the Stockhorn and the Jungfrau are, of course, mountains.

clearly the complicated journey up there in a long procession of
carriages, in the last of which we had brought with us a small cask of
wine from Basle. I can hear the vigorous taunts of uncle Fritz
Sartorius, smell the horses and the leather harness in the pouring
rain, and finally see before my eyes the little house of a Herr Ogi,
which was far too small. Then I remember how uncle Ernst Sartorius played tunes on the trumpet by the Oeschinensee, like:
"Heavens! How beautiful it was . . .".'[87] 'I also had some memorable holidays near the Gerzensee, under the Kutzen in the Belpberg
area,* in a country house which at that time belonged to a Herr von
Muralt. I spent the summer months of 1896 and 1897 there with my
parents and the rest of the family. I regularly went on walks to
Gerzensee, on errands for my mother, to a friendly old lady named
Fräulein von Wyss, and on Sundays to listen to the sermons of Pastor
Hopf. His strict attitude left a lasting impression on me; I always
associate it with the hymn "Make my soul ready", which I heard
there for the first time. The country house on the Belpberg was a real
jewel from the eighteenth century, inside and out, with paintings by
Hogarth on the walls which gave me much to think about.'[88]

Coming from Berne, young Karl found Basle in particular a real
paradise. His grandmother lived there, and 'our regular journeys to
Basle to see our beloved grandmother Sartorius always turned into a
party'.[89] 'Now widowed, she lived at Nonnenweg 60, where to the
end of her days she was faithfully cared for and nursed by her
youngest daughter Elisabeth (our deeply loved Aunt "Bethi"). Visits
there were a real pilgrimage, and we used to look forward to them
more and more. There were all kinds of marvels in the house, for
example a picture of Lavater† with the inscription, "See nothing in
this figure but love of the truth which searches carefully and bears
witness to what it has found." There was also a large picture of the
arrival of the Pilgrim Fathers on American soil, being greeted there
most respectfully by Indians. Then there was an old-fashioned
peep-show with marvellous views which at that time gave us much
more pleasure than any cinema has done later. Lastly, and above all,

---

*The terminology in this section is somewhat confusing. It helps to know that Gerzensee is
both a small lake and a village, and that Belpberg can refer to a single mountain, a group of
peaks and a small town. The Kutzen is the highest mountain in the area.

†Johann Kaspar Lavater (1741–1801), who appears several times in the narrative, was a Swiss
pastor, poet, patriot and founder of the science of physiognomy.

there was a complete collection of the portraits of all the chief pastors of Basle. Everything there smelt of the past, especially of the eighteenth century and the beginning of the nineteenth. And indeed the past came alive in the figure of grandmother herself, with her black bonnet which seemed as much a part of her as grandfather's velvet cap had been a part of him.'[90] In addition, she herself had a lively interest in anything historical. The hobbies of two of her grandchildren in particular can be seen as a legacy of this: her younger grandson Heinrich once spent a whole month in Berne making a comprehensive 'historical and geographical calendar', while Karl (right down to the time when he became a professor) made an enormous collection of portraits of 'important personalities' past and present to which he was always adding.

'All her life she was small and slender, but her physical appearance concealed a resolute and unswerving will, and when she really wanted to she was quite capable of getting her own way. She was somewhat strict, but this strictness was modified and to some degree eclipsed by her great kindness and friendliness.'[91] 'Her depth of character, coupled with her clear understanding and gentle humour, made an exceptionally pleasing impression on all who came in contact with her. For advice and opinions she drew on her rich experience and always delivered them *sub specie aeternitate*; in an often disconcerting way she would hit the mark without causing offence.'[92] Aunt Bethi must have been an equally impressive figure – at any rate she was for Karl. 'She often went to stay in Bad Boll, and especially as a result of meeting Pastor Blumhardt, she increasingly developed an eye for signs of the coming of the kingdom of God. Rather than making her narrow-minded, her devotion kindled in her a love which went out to embrace all men . . . No wonder that as a result she was welcome anywhere! Wherever she went, she was loved in no time at all.'[93]

Karl's godfather Hans Burckhardt also lived in Basle. He was a 'respected figure in the old Basle silk-spinning industry and had amassed a considerable fortune . . . He was also a well-informed patron of the arts and still went out riding every day in his eightieth year. His name came to have an almost magical, mythological ring in the family, and we younger ones were only allowed to enter his fine old house on the Leonhardsgraben, with its imposing furniture, in our very best clothes, and after pressing instructions that we should be on our best behaviour.'[94] Since Karl was Hans Burckhardt's godson, he received a number of valuable presents – once, to his great delight, 'Thorwaldsen's "Expedition of Alexander" in plaster of Paris . . . over five feet long and eighteen inches high'.[95] Uncle Wilhelm Bernoulli was another member of the family who lived in Basle, in the Schärtlingasse, 'where . . . all the curiosities of this crookedly arranged house were embodied for me in a large tin bath in which one could have splendid games with real water'.[96]

And on the outskirts of Basle, in Pratteln, lived Karl's other godfather, Karl Sartorius. Karl loved to go to his parsonage in the holidays. 'Glorious Pratteln! How lovely you are! How happy I was when I was there,' ran a poem which he once wrote, when Pratteln was still in fact a lovely village. He once had an experience there which he used later as a parable of his own work. 'Feeling his way up the stairs of a dark church tower he unexpectedly caught hold of a bell-rope instead of the handrail, and to his horror heard the great bell ringing out above him, and audible not only to him but to others around.'[97] His uncle's property included 'a picturesque old tower above Pratteln' (it was called Hagenbächli) 'surrounded by a vineyard on a hill'. 'I've eaten many sweet grapes in its shade. From there you could look right over the countryside as far as the Vosges.'[98] A host of other relatives lived in and around Basle, and as a child Karl went from Berne to join in no less than five family wedding celebrations in the restaurant which had been built by his great-great-grandfather Huber.[99] Of course, meeting more distant relations was not much in his line: 'Tea-time chat and fussing around everywhere with uncles, aunts and cousins,' he complained at the age of sixteen.[100] 'Even when I was small, these family gatherings, like the solemn parades at uncle H. Burckhardt's, were something of an abomination to me.'[101]

Fighter and poet

Since the Barths had moved to the Schosshalde, Karl had grown into something of a layabout. He joined in street fights between his fellow schoolboys and the pupils of the City Grammar School – and also in fights between the sons of the aristocratic families of Berne and boys from poor or immigrant families (there were always tensions between these two groups among the pupils of the Free Grammar School). While he was living on the Schosshalde, Karl was also for some time the leader of a gang which was engaged even then in a

1.   *Old Basle – view of the Spalentor, about 1860.*

2. *Franz Albert Barth (1816–1879), pupil of Tobias Beck, pastor in Bubendorf and at St Theodore's Church, Basle.*

3. *Sara Barth (1817–88), also Karl's god-mother, came from 'lower-class Basle' and though frail, was an energetic woman.*

4. *Karl Achilles Sartorius (1824–1893), a conservative, orthodox pastor of St Elisabeth's Church in Basle.*

5. *Johanna Sartorius (1832–1915), a cousin of the famous Jacob Burckhardt, much loved by her grandson Karl.*

6. *Anna Barth (1863–1938), shortly after the move from the parsonage at Reitnau to Basle (1886), with her first son, Karl.*

7. *Johann Friedrich Barth (1856–1912), teacher at the College of Preachers in Basle, in 1888 with his son Karl, who was then two years old.*

8. *The Barth family in 1897, in front of their new house in Berne, Claraweg 8: Katharina, Aunt Bethi Sartorius, Karl (who shows signs of the beating he has just had from his father), Grandmother Sartorius, Gertrud Fritz Barth, Heinrich, Anna Barth, Peter.*

9.   Karl at the time of his confirmation in 1902, with Peter (aged 14), Gertrud (6) and Heinrich (12). Katharina had died three years earlier.

10.   On the election of Pius X in 1903, Karl (nicknamed Ulichen by the family) expounds rather over-enthusiastically the doctrine that any Christian may be made Pope.

bitter feud with another gang led by Martin Werner, a neighbour's child, who was later to become Professor of Dogmatics in the University of Berne (the feud was to be carried on afterwards, in a different way). In the winter he was equally active, skating on the nearby Egelsee. There is a significant entry in his diary (for 21 January 1899): 'Today I did a good deal of bashing up and got bashed up by plenty of people myself. There really is some splendid poetry in this active and passive.' Or on 9 February 1899: 'When I got up I thumped Bäti and he cried bitterly.' On 26 April of the same year he noted: 'Nothing much happened today,' and on the following day, 'Remarkably enough, nothing much happened today, either.' And on another occasion (25 May 1899), 'Our teacher Kacher got cross and pulled out two of my hairs, which are now in my museum.' He and the other boys also behaved badly at school. Indeed, they were so wild that his teacher Rudolf Feldmann (grandfather of Markus Feldmann, who was later to become a Federal Councillor), 'at the peak of one of the uproars which were common during his classes, solemnly cursed the miscreants. One day, he said, in our old age, we would be punished for all that we had done to him.'[102] In the same way, in 1899, 'I had a lively clash with my teacher Huber, the sorry aftermath of which is recorded in my diary every day for the next week: "Very sore about the punishment." A week later it reads, "Still sore about the punishment, but not so much." '[103] Inevitably, now there were often special remarks in Karl's school reports about his behaviour: 'dreams often', or 'three hours detention for misbehaving', or – about his behaviour in religious instruction – 'needs to pay attention'.

In these circumstances, the violin lessons given to him by an elderly Herr Jahn, from the time he was ten, did not make much progress. There is, for example, an entry in Karl's diary for 28 April 1899 which reads, 'Grandfather was in a bad mood during my violin lesson (and I didn't get on very well), so instead of being called "abominable boy", the flattering title which he has bestowed on me so far, I've now become "old fool"!' No wonder that 'for all the keen encouragement of music in our house, my violin practice was hardly productive'.[104] As a result, critical as Karl was about all dilettantes, he later became more and more 'a real listener instead'.[105] Nevertheless, in the course of time Karl did acquire a reasonable degree of competence on his instrument. He played in the school orchestra, 'where we performed resounding Handel and cheerful Mozart'.[106] But Karl was much fonder of singing than of playing the violin; he had a steady baritone voice.

His aggressive instincts were to some degree channelled when he entered the Berne cadets in 1897. 'Over four years I was given quite a methodical military education in the cadet corps which Switzerland had at that time. Despite my feeble attempts at marksmanship I managed to reach the rank of corporal.'[107] He had yet to feel any of the problems of militarism; on the contrary, he was notable for his 'passionate involvement in the exercises and route marches of the Berne cadet corps'.[108] When he had to report to recruits' school at a later date, in 1905, he was exempted from military service for health reasons (above all because of short-sightedness).

Soon after the Barths moved to Claraweg 8, Karl also began to write poems in ever increasing quantities. 'They say that the ink-bottle is as much a danger to the Barth family as the wine-bottle is to others.'[109] Karl's poems were inspired by his voracious reading of books on the history of warfare, and his discovery of Friedrich Schiller lent them wings. This classic writer was, he remarked, '*the great man during my time at the Grammar School. I had no more moving experiences than *Maria Stuart*, *The Maid of Orleans* and *Wallenstein* . . . In some way, Schiller seemed to me to be a model guide.' As a result of him, Karl became 'an idealist . . . it was still permissible to be one then, and I was one with great pleasure'.[110] Karl devoured Schiller's works. Not only that, but he was also fond of performing scenes from them with his brothers and sisters and their friends, in the summer house in the garden of Claraweg 8 or elsewhere. For example, 'I once . . . played the First Huntsman in a performance of *Wallenstein's Camp*.'[111] On another occasion he planned a performance of two scenes from *Wallenstein's Death* while on holiday in Beatenberg, with his brothers and Hans von Rütte, son of the pastor there. He wrote to his mother asking her to send off immediately 'large supplies of beards, sashes and so on . . . We would be most grateful to you, and if you don't, we shall lapse into profound melancholy.' Incidentally, while gazing at the Alps, he said with a sigh, 'If only Schiller could have seen all these glories, how amazed he would have been . . .'[112] In view of all this, it looked as though 'in some circumstances, I might have turned into an actor'.[113]

This reading and play-acting now also spurred on Karl to try out his own 'bold attempts as a dramatic poet'.[114] So, 'excited by the iambics of Schiller's *William Tell* and Körner's *Zriny*, for years I was active as a suspiciously productive dramatist'.[115] He wrote his first play at the age of ten: *Prince Eugen*, in five acts. This was followed by a considerable number of other plays, especially tragedies, including one which was actually written in French. When he was eleven or twelve he gave vent unmistakably to his heartfelt antipathy to the aristocracy of Berne in his play *The Henzi Conspiracy*. It began with a conspiracy scene (*Hauri*: 'I'm thirsting for the blood of aristo- crats' . . . *Jost*: 'Down with the oligarchy!' *All*: 'Freedom! Equality!'). It sets the devotion of the people (in broad Berne German: people should not 'speak a word against the nobility') off against the arro- gance of the aristocrats of Berne, who make mock of the 'lowly plebeians' (Government regulation: 'Everything will be said in an elegant, nasal and arrogant tone'). The play ends with a monologue by Henzi, who has been condemned to death. He has a prophetic vision of the future. 'I see the lords coming down from the thrones which they have usurped . . . All have equal rights . . . What a glorious time!' Karl wrote not only dramas of this kind, in which 'freedom' regularly appears as a key idea, but also a great many poems and 'historical articles' (on 'The Massacre of Eger', the battle of 'Neuenegg', which the people of Berne lost in 1798, and so on).

Karl proved to be especially productive in 1899 (from then on, incidentally, he had to wear spectacles for the rest of his life). The year was also memorable for other reasons, above all because on the night of 31 May his sister Käthi 'was suddenly and quite unexpec- tedly snatched away from the family circle. She was only six years old.'[116] She died of diphtheria, which the doctor had diagnosed too late. During the next summer holidays in Beatenberg, Karl began all of a sudden to collect together his writings up to that point, under the promising title, 'Karl Barth's Collected Works, dedicated to his grandmother'. In August, Trudi, who was three years old, also fell ill with diphtheria, and at the beginning of September Karl had to spend a month in hospital with scarlet fever. He then had a period of convalescence, which he spent in Basle with his grandmother, with whom he stayed until the middle of November. He again occupied his time with all kinds of writing. During this period, he went one day with his aunt Bethi to a dog theatre. 'It took quite a long time to begin, and then in the solemn silence I shouted, shrieked and barked so loudly that everyone started looking at me. I enjoyed that very much!'[117]

He naturally produced a literary narrative of a boat trip which he and his father had on Lake Geneva in April 1900. His longest play was written in 1901 under the title *Leonardo of Montenuova, or Freedom and Love* (it was dug up again by Bonn students in 1931 and performed under the aegis of Helmut Gollwitzer).[118] The play was 'a tragedy . . . with many violent deaths'.[119] In addition to the familiar warlike tone, however, this work also had some striking declarations of love.

> Fair maiden, now I must declare my love.
> Since first I looked upon you, I am yours . . .
> My heart beats madly, yet I am at peace,
> through love, new, greater powers are mine.
> The burden of my cares no longer weighs
> upon my spirit, and my fears are gone.
> The joy of youth shines forth in glorious light,
> for me the world is bathed in roseate hue
> and you, my love, your fairest face alone
> appears to me where'er I turn my gaze . . .
> Within your arms eternal happiness
> is all I seek, and towards you wends my way.

There was a reason for this new tone. Karl had fallen in love. His sweetheart was called Anna Hirzel, daughter of a literary historian at the university. She was the girl friend with whom Karl 'used to go skating',[120] and with whom he used to drink 'hot sugared water on the Neubrücke at ten centimes a time', which he generously expended. He also used to go to dancing classes with her, but 'to my sorrow I never became a good dancer'. 'She was the one I had in mind as the chief heroine of the play.'[121] However, the two of them parted and did not meet again until they were seventy, in Ticino . . .

Meanwhile, Karl had been increasingly cultivating his social life with great enthusiasm, and this gave his poetry and writing new horizons and new possibilities of development. Most of his friends were from among the pupils of the Free Grammar School. His closest friends in his own class were Werner Häberli and Otto Lauterburg, top of the form, both of whom later became pastors, and Wilhelm Spoendlin, son of a Zürich manufacturer who later became a lawyer. His father owned a large country house, Schloss Greifensee, where Karl loved to spend both longer or shorter holidays up to the beginning of the 1920s. Also in his class were René von Graffenreid, later a brigadier general, and Ernst von May, who was to become an officer in the Salvation Army; Albert Schüpbach and Hans Zurlinden went on to become doctors (he saw the latter again in Bremen). One class below him was Martin Nil (later a pastor in Grindelwald), a good friend of his – and of his brother Peter, and one class above him Adolf L. Vischer, whom he later met in the University of Basle as a gerontologist. Above all, he had a series of older friends and companions whom he admired and from whom he was ready to learn a great deal: two classes above him were Karl Buxtorf (later a pastor in Basle) and Gerhard Rüfenacht, while Gottfried Bohnenblust (later Professor of Literature in Geneva), 'the embodiment of an enthusiasm as learned as it was wise', was three classes above.[122] Siegfried Aeschbacher, the brother of the man who prepared Karl for confirmation, was six years older (and went on to become a doctor); Karl wrote a long ode to him as a 'fatherly friend'. Albert Schädelin, who as a pastor in Berne and a pastoral theologian was to be a trusty and lifelong friend of Karl's, was seven years older. Karl remembered Schädelin from his schooldays especially because of 'the class lists which were read out on speech days in the Nägeligasse chapel in a monotonous sing-song by our teacher, Ulrich Kriemler. If I am not mistaken, the one for a class far, far above my own regularly began: "First, Albert Schädelin, second . . ." (In the meantime I have learnt from the most reliable sources that historically this reminiscence is not quite correct. Still, I will allow it to stand: one should not want to "demythologize" everything!). One or two classes nearer the depths in which I was to be found could sometimes be heard the name of a pupil who is now a Federal Councillor.'[123] This was Eduard von Steiger. Karl did not get on very well with him even then. Karl's brothers Peter and Heinrich also went to the same school.

In November 1900, Karl and some friends founded a school society which they called 'Studia', the aims of which were 'the cultivation of friendship and learning'. They translated Caesar and read Schiller and Lessing. Karl (whose nickname was 'Finch'*), shone in poetry-readings and lectures ('The Fortress of Hüningen', '3 August 1833', 'Ludwig XIV', and so on). In 1902 he joined an older society, 'Patria' (and was now called 'Quicksilver'). He was even more involved in 'society activities, which are all the more

---

*German *Fink*. As well as being the name of a bird, in Switzerland the word has other associations: it denotes a happy, chirping person, and also a troublemaker.

attractive because of the amount of time and energy which they take up'.[124] By statute this society was made up of 'young abstainers from the Free Grammar School'. Its aims were 'friendship, sociability and education'. It was proudly conscious of its opposition to another society (not abstainers), which was more popular with the sons of aristocrats. Karl again produced various offerings for 'Patria', and sometimes even appeared as president. He gave lectures: on the Jesuits, on Richelieu (full of high praise) or on visiting the theatre: in his lecture on the theatre (a term which, of course, also includes opera), he not only likened theatre-going to worship, but also praised Wagner's *Tannhäuser* as a piece of 'powerful preaching': 'Why shouldn't we see a divine spark in the genius of a Mozart or a Wagner? Indeed, the theatre can also give us some very apt sermons.' Karl also took part in plays and wrote some poems and sketches for the society, including a 'grand, spectacular romantic opera, *The Sixth-Former's Dream*', in which he put new texts to arias by Mozart. For decades the 'Colour Song' which he wrote was the society's song. On these or on other occasions he continued to take further steps into the world of culture, sometimes tentative and sometimes bold, joining with youthful earnestness in all kinds of long debates. 'These were the years in which Haeckel and Nietzsche – "Is there a God?" – were on everyone's lips. They even penetrated the Free Grammar School, where anyone who had the competence was already discussing Schopenhauer, and then returned to Kant; the mighty and somewhat forceful Hermann Kutter was already beginning to appear on our horizons.'[125]

Confirmation

All this took place during Karl's last years at the Grammar School. During this time he had already made up his mind about his future profession. His decision was helped on by his encounter with Robert Aeschbacher, pastor at the Nydegg church, 'a preacher who at that time deservedly had an enthusiastic audience in Berne'.[126] He was a 'pupil and later a close friend of my father',[127] and theologically had 'at least one foot on this side of the line from which further progress needed to be made'.[128] According to Fritz Barth he 'refused to evade problems of theological thought, but immersed himself thoroughly and conscientiously, even if this seemed to undermine much of the tradition ... But he never regarded the question of Christian

thought as a purely theoretical one; it concerned real life . . .
Through severe inner struggles he arrived at the assurance that all
man's salvation is to be found only in Jesus, and it was now his joy in
life to proclaim this good news. However, he proclaimed it like a
shepherd, going out after those who are lost . . . He applied the
demands of the gospel to social life with such decisiveness that many
anxious people who could not understand him called him a socialist.'
His confirmation classes 'were so in tune with the understanding of
young people and so attractive in their sympathy and freshness that
people came to them from all parts of the city. The classes had to be
divided into several sections in order to accommodate everyone.'[129]

Karl, too, joined these confirmation classes. In 1901–02 he was
prepared for confirmation by Aeschbacher, 'to my great delight'.[130]
'The classes stick in my mind as having been quite extraordinarily
fascinating, not to say exciting . . . The main emphasis in his lectures
– I use this word quite deliberately, since I at any rate cannot
remember any catechizing (in the sense of a series of questions and
answers) or any discussion – was on teaching. Aeschbacher spent a
lot of time on apologetic and polemic against the ideas of Haeckel
and the other materialists which were extremely topical at the time,
but he also brought out in a positive way the meaning of the life,
death and resurrection of Jesus . . . He also told us something about
ethics; for example (long before Kutter and Ragaz), we heard some
of the first comments on the social question.'[131] 'Even then, to give
one instance, I learnt that the five mediaeval proofs for the existence
of God and the late orthodox theory of the verbal inspiration of the
Bible were very doubtful enterprises. And there was something else,
much more important. I learnt that it might be a good and excellent
thing not only to know and affirm the great statements in the
Christian creed, but also to understand them from within.'[132] 'Following the usual pattern at the turn of the century, the classes had a
very marked apologetic slant, but they brought me so close to the
whole problem of religion that when they came to an end I was well
aware of the need to learn more about it.'[133] 'On the eve of the day of
my confirmation (23 March 1902) I made the bold resolve to become
a theologian: not with preaching and pastoral care and so on in
mind, but in the hope that through such a course of study I might
reach a proper understanding of the creed in place of the rather hazy
ideas that I had at that time.'[134]

During the time that followed Karl 'went along all through the year to Robert Aeschbacher's sermons in the Nydegg church, which was packed almost to the roof (I shall never forget a series on Romans 1.16 and another on Psalm 23.1)'. 'I was completely wrapped up in them.'[135] While Aeschbacher proved the immediate stimulus towards studying theology, in a more indirect way Karl was influenced even more strongly by his own father, although he was not aware of the fact. 'The man who without question laid the foundation for my later involvement in theology was my father Fritz Barth . . . By virtue of the quiet seriousness with which he studied Christianity, whether as scholar or teacher, he became and remained my model. Often enough he was a warning to me, but I shall never forget him.'[136]

By then the beginning of Karl's university study was almost upon him. In the summer of 1904 he climbed the Titlis and the Urirotstock on a school trip, and during the July holidays prepared for the coming examinations with Spoendlin on the Greifensee. There he also met the family of a German pastor called Vietor. He played the violin a good deal with the daughter and sang with the son: they sang 'Ein Mädchen oder Weibchen' and other arias from *The Magic Flute*, 'ce magnifique oeuvre immortel du grand Mozart . . . même en baignant au lac'.[137] They also embarked on a 'nocturnal voyage' together, Karl smoking a great pipe 'with which I used to pollute the night air at that time'.[138] His written school-leaving examinations were held at the beginning of September 1904 and his oral on 15–16 September; the next day he was awarded his certificate. Thus 'I passed my matriculation, but only with a second class, having stumbled over chemistry, physics and the like.'[139] Two days later Karl was able to give his 'mule'* speech, in which he bluntly declared how reluctantly he had gone to school ('In honour you'll be held, of course, but don't expect me and my horse') and also how difficult the teachers had found this particular class ('Truly, the sufferings of Job or of the divinely patient Odysseus will have been less than the total number of torments and disturbances that we thought up for the Free Grammar School and its teachers!'). 'A journey to Frankfurt and Cologne, intended as compensation for the indignities which they had undergone', introduced Karl and William Spoendlin 'for the first time in amazement to the broad expanses of imperial Germany'.[140]

*Young men who have left school but not yet begun their study at a university are known as 'mules', German *Mulus*.

2

Theological Student

At university and as an assistant pastor, 1904–1911

The first semesters in Berne

'Then I began to study in Berne, with my father's kind but earnest guidance and advice.'[1] Karl Barth continued to live in Claraweg with his parents and went in to the university from there. On 17 October 1904 he matriculated in the theological faculty. Through the doors which were thus opened, he entered a territory which was still largely new to him. Of course his first impressions of theology did not go very deep. Somehow he felt that his theological teachers in Berne neither spoke to his condition nor commanded his attention. However, he attended their lectures and classes regularly and attentively. And 'at any rate I wrote down their solid, but rather dry wisdom assiduously, though without taking in its general outline'.[2] At the end of each semester, the zealous student took the notes which he had made so carefully and exactly to a bookbinder, and then went on to decorate the cover with all kinds of doggerel, anecdotes, sayings and caricatures. Thus a volume from his second semester has on it a picture of a careworn man with the caption: 'Sad father after lazy Barthli's exam.' There were some very eccentric figures among his teachers. 'At that time I learnt the New Testament under the direction of an old Berne professor by the name of Rudolf Steck', who occupied his lectures 'with amiable but rather tediously exact analyses'. He was 'one of the last and most extreme representatives of the Tübingen school', who put forward the view 'that all the letters in circulation under the name of Paul were inauthentic and belonged to the second century'.[3] Barth heard lectures on the Old Testament from Karl Marti, 'a strict pupil of Wellhausen',[4] 'who was also a great scholar . . . but what he had to say was a hopelessly dry kind of wisdom'.[5] 'In systematic theology we had a brave man by the name of Hermann Lüdemann, from Schleswig-Holstein, who could no longer live there because he had declared himself to be against Bismarck.'[6] 'Like Steck, he was a direct pupil of F. C. Baur.'[7] He constructed a theological system 'with his always ill-tempered sharp-sightedness' and 'with bitter attacks on Ritschl and his followers'.[8] It was based 'on the one hand completely on Kant, and on the other on what one might call positivism . . . He called himself an empiriocriticist. And in the first paragraphs of his lectures he dictated to us the thesis: "By virtue of his religious consciousness the Christian knows . . . !" Thus the religious consciousness, as an empirical fact, was – he assured us – the keyhole through which we could peer into the transcendent.'[9]

Karl Barth listened to these teachers without much pleasure. 'They were incapable of interesting me more deeply and to any lasting effect.' Nevertheless, 'what I owe to those Berne masters, despite everything, is that they taught me to forget any fears I might have had. They gave me such a thorough foundation in the earlier form of the "historical-critical school" that the remarks of their later successors could no longer get under my skin or even touch my heart – they only got on my nerves.'[10] 'At that time, as a student of nineteen, I smoked much stronger tobacco than anything which could be found years later under the brand of demythologizing.'[11] And, 'in my Berne semester I was earnestly told, and I learnt, all that can be said against "the old orthodoxy" . . . and that all God's ways begin with Kant and, if possible, must also end there.'[12]

'I followed my father's lectures and classes with incomparably more interest, but for that very reason I also looked out for new ways.'[13] In the four successive semesters which he spent at the University of Berne, Barth heard his father lecturing on 'The Parables of Jesus', 'Introduction to the Study of Theology', Church History I–IV, 'The Life of Jesus' and 'The Life and Writings of Paul'. But even these lectures failed to hold him. 'Quite apart from any personal or spiritual ties, I respected my father highly as a sound scholar – his picture still stands before me as I write. But I could not adopt what was then called his (moderately) "positive" . . . theological attitude and tendency.'[14]

The name of the philosopher Immanuel Kant has just been mentioned. It was his work which began to stand out for Karl Barth, even in these early Berne days, and to show him a course which he at first pursued with delight. 'The first book which really moved me as a student was Kant's *Critique of Practical Reason*.'[15] A few years later

Barth could even depict this reading of Kant in the tones of a conversion story: 'Then came the time when I began to make a great discovery. This was the discovery that the gospel was simple, that the divine truth was not a complicated, difficult construction with hundreds of different propositions and opinions and hypotheses, but a simple, clear knowledge, accessible to any child. I still remember vividly how this insight came to me. It was while I was studying a book the gist of which was that there is nothing good in the world and outside it, apart from good will.* This good will is the truth, the divine element in my life. I held on to that. It wasn't much, but it was something, and something could be made of it . . . The haze of questions and opinions in my head began to disperse, and its place was taken by three or four great questions: What is God? What does Jesus mean for us? What is the purpose of our life? How will we achieve this purpose? . . . I made a rule for myself: the simpler the better. I did not lose my delight in learning; indeed I studied more zealously and with more pleasure than before, but what I now looked for in books and from my professors was the true knowledge of simplicity. My aim now was to become more profound, clearer, more definite in *this* knowledge.'[16]

In his first semesters, Karl Barth's life as a student had another side: he was active in an association which for the moment occupied him and held his attention much more than his attempts in the field of theology. Shortly after his matriculation he was accepted into the very association in which his father had once played a vigorous part. He was nicknamed 'Skinny', and at this time strove to be as keen a member as his father before him. 'During this period I spent a great deal of time, money and energy in the students' association "Zofingia". It was not in the least bit infected by the youth movement which was then just about coming into being. At a later time I found my lifelong friends in quite different ways, but I could not regret this episode in retrospect, because of my highly coloured reminiscences of it.'[17] Hardly had he been accepted into the association than he and his companions proudly began to walk and to 'prance' up and down the city 'in our caps'.[18] Moreover, although he had only just left Patria, the abstainers' society at school, in a short time he became a very active beer-drinker. In any case he had already been a keen smoker for some time – as presents for his

*The quotation in Barth's words here comes from Kant's *Fundamental Principles of the Metaphysic of Morals*.

matriculation he had asked his grandmother for a 'long tobacco pipe', 'a lot of good tobacco' and 'plenty of cigarettes'.[19] In the association Barth found that 'the dominant tone is to my mind far too much one of *Gemütlichkeit* brought on by beer',[20] but he was very happy to join in it himself. In his very first semester he zealously attended all kinds of regular and extraordinary meetings of Zofingia – in Berne and elsewhere. He earned some of the money he needed by giving private violin lessons ('Isn't that quite ridiculous?').[21]

Through his contacts in the Berne association and in other groups of Zofingia elsewhere, Karl Barth came to know an impressive array of academics or potential academics. Especially in the Basle section, he made the acquaintance of people with whom for other reasons he was to have very close connections at a later date. There was Alphons Koechlin, later to be president of the Basle Church Council and an important ecumenical figure (1885–1965). He 'first came within my horizon at the Laupen festival of 1905. As General Secretary he carried the banner, and I went on his right as a probationer member.* When on occasions I marched rather roughly into the mass of people who were lining the route he gave me the gentle warning, "Do be polite to people, won't you!" This made a deep impression on me, though in later life I haven't in fact always been particularly polite.'[22] Then there was Lukas Christ (1881–1958), who was later president of the Baselbiet convention and whose father was already a friend of Barth's father. Barth remembered him 'always standing there like a rock. Because of his coldness and precipitousness I was even rather afraid of him when I was young, until he took me into his confidence and never withdrew again. We went through good times and bad together, year after year.'[23] There was Oskar Farner (1884–1958), who later represented 'the best possibilities of specifically Swiss theology and churchmanship' in Zürich. He was 'resolute and straightforward, truly open to every side';[24] Barth 'already felt very sympathetic towards his liberal background, with which I was in so much agreement over the most important things'[25], and this feeling increased over the years to

---

*Laupen is an attractive old town near Berne, scene of an unexpected victory of Berne over the Hapsburgs on 21 June 1339. Celebration of this victory was the occasion for a gathering of members of Zofingia, past and present, from all over Switzerland, the climax of which was a procession through the streets. 'Probationer member' is a colourless rendering of the untranslatable German *Hörnli-Fuchs*. The *Fuchs* ('fox') is a student who has been accepted into a student association but has yet to achieve full membership; such students wore special caps with a kind of horn at the front *(Hörnli)*.

come. Finally, there was Eduard Thurneysen (1888–1974): when he and Karl Barth first made friends, Thurneysen was 'a member of the Basle Zofingia, which was fully in tune with those very lively times. He was a young theologian, a pupil of Paul Wernle and Bernhard Duhm.'[26]

In the winter of 1906 Karl Barth made his mark on the Berne association and provoked long debates by a lecture, given on 20 January 1906, on a question 'which has preoccupied me since the day I entered Zofingia and has become a matter very close to my heart'. The lecture was on 'Zofingia and the Social Question'. Barth asserted that 'among us, too, . . . the gulf between capital and work, between mammonism and pauperism, in short, between rich and poor . . . is continually growing larger'. Referring to Leonhard Ragaz, he saw the social question as 'one link in the chain of development, or better *the* problem of mankind, which Jesus once posed to the ancient world'. Consequently the young theological student asked that Zofingia should stop being a 'robust gathering round the colours, whose essential national (!) task consists in handing down "honourable ancient student customs" to posterity in as intact a form as possible'. It should become an association 'filled with a new spirit, with the spirit of social responsibility towards the lower strata of society and above all towards ourselves'. His most vigorous opponent in the discussion was his former fellow-pupil at school, Eduard von Steiger, who had now become a law student.

During the same winter he also wrote two seminar papers (one on the New Testament and one on church history), having already written a long article during the summer for a seminar on 'The Stigmata of Francis of Assisi' (which he explained as being 'neuropathic', albeit miraculous phenomena). Then, on 17 March 1906, the first item in his 'bibliography' appeared, a report on the Tenth Aarau Christian Student Conference, which included a lecture by Adolf Schlatter. This conference had been instituted by Fritz Barth. For many years, three days had been spent each spring in lectures and discussions. According to the statutes, this was 'to arouse interest in religious questions among students, to answer them with the mind of Jesus Christ and to further Christian life among students'.[27] A month later, Karl Barth gave his first theological lecture in Berne to the academic Protestant Theological Society on 'The Original Form of the Lord's Prayer' ('Today we have taken a look into the workshop of historical criticism which – rightly –

cannot call a halt even before the highest and the holiest!').

The following autumn, on 17 October 1906, he successfully concluded the first stage of his study (with a first class) by passing the preliminary examination. Once again, he had prepared for it at Schloss Greifensee. In this examination a Swiss theological student had to demonstrate his knowledge of philosophy, the history of religion, church history and biblical studies. Karl took particular care over Hebrew, 'a language I have found myself fighting with since I first made its acquaintance. My father was very strong in it, and often reproached me, unfortunately to no effect, for being either unwilling or unable to get on with it.'[28] 'After the preliminary examination, according to Swiss practice I was ready for study abroad. I wanted to go to Marburg, while my father was very anxious that I should go either to Halle or to Greifswald. The consequence was that I went to Berlin, which was supposed to be more neutral.'[29] His school-friend Wilhelm Spoendlin went there with him, as did Oskar Farner, a fellow-member of Zofingia. When they reached the German capital, it was at a time of excitement over the sensation caused by the confidence trick which forms the basis of Zuckmayer's play, *The Captain of Köpenick.* * During the winter of 1906–07, Karl Barth had his lodgings in Halleschen Strasse 18, on the third floor. Of course he used to take his 'lunch' at Aschinger's.[30]† Over the Christmas holiday, which was the first he had spent away from home, he went to Greifswald to stay with Professor Samuel Oettli, a friend and former Berne colleague of his father's.

Harnack's pupil

Karl Barth studied very intensively in Berlin. Not, of course, with Reinhold Seeberg, whom his father was especially keen that he should hear. (In 1924, on one of his journeys through Berlin, he went to see an artificially prepared whale. He found it 'quite monstrous, the living, or rather the stuffed repetition of Seeberg's *Dogmatics!*')[31] 'I . . . wisely avoided Seeberg, foolishly, alas, took no notice of Holl; and instead went enthusiastically to listen to Harnack (and equally keenly to hear Kaftan and Gunkel).'[32] He heard Kaftan lecture on

---

*Wilhelm Voigt, a cobbler, put on a captain's uniform, arrested the Mayor of Köpenick, and made off with a large amount of money from the town's funds.

†A large restaurant, renowned for the cheapness of its food.

special dogmatics and Gunkel on Old Testament theology: 'It was thanks to Gunkel that it first began to dawn on me that the Old Testament might be a real option.'[33] Above all, however, he sat under Harnack (1851–1930) to hear his 'great lectures on the history of dogma'.[34] Thus he heard from Harnack's very lips the argument that 'the dogma of the early period was a self-expression of the Greek spirit in the sphere of the gospel'.[35] Karl Barth was even the youngest regular member 'of his church-history seminar on Acts . . . and was invited once or twice to his house on the Fasanenstrasse'. There 'I once met a man who was later to become very famous', with whom Harnack 'discussed all kinds of Baltic affairs at the family table: this was Count Hermann Keyserling'.[36] Nor did he forget how 'I saw Heinrich Scholz in Berlin as senior member of Harnack's seminar, among us lesser spirits. There was a touch of brilliance about him even at that time.'[37] For this Harnack seminar Karl Barth wrote a remarkably long paper (158 pages) on 'Paul's Missionary Work according to the Account in the Acts of the Apostles'. His conclusion was that 'Acts is and remains a secondary source for Pauline doctrine' – his teacher wrote in the margin, 'I would say, a primary source'. According to Harnack's written comments, Barth had 'discussed some matters in too general terms', but otherwise had worked 'very thoroughly and very capably, with circumspection and thoughtfulness'.

Barth now came to have a high regard for Harnack; he thought more of him than of anyone else, 'even Gunkel'.[38] 'None of the many Swiss who were with me there was more enthusiastic about the personality and the teaching of this man. My admiration reached such a pitch that because of the work which I had to do for his seminar and with which I was occupied virtually night and day for months, I almost completely neglected to take proper notice of the Kaiser Friedrich Museum and the other Berlin sights'[39] or 'to make necessary use of the manifold stimuli offered by the great foreign capital for my general education'.[40] 'I said to myself, "This is the great moment: here you are with *the* theologian of the day, why should you be bothered with museums, theatres and concert halls?" So I saw little of Berlin – I did not even hear the great speech by the Kaiser from the balcony of the Schloss against the centre and against Social Democracy.'[41] 'Instead, I saw and heard Harnack, if I may say so, very thoroughly indeed.'[42] At a later date, of course, Barth regretted that he had neglected to see more of Berlin – and in

Sefenwil he regretted that he had not signed up with Adolph Wagner for lectures on economics. However, he did go, incidentally, to a series of lectures by Walter Simons on 'Christianity and the Social Question'. And despite everything, in passing, he did take in something of the capital in all the splendour of the time: in the cathedral he was not very impressed with Dryander, the chief court preacher, but once at Schinkel's *Neue Wache** saw Kaiser Wilhelm II riding past with the Danish king to the salutes of the cuirassiers of the guard, which seemed to him like a fairy-tale.

Karl Barth now began to diverge noticeably from his father's 'positive' line. 'The possibility of understanding the Bible in terms of the history of religion began to dawn on me, and alongside Kant, Schleiermacher took a clearer place in my thought than before.'[43] Having 'worked through Immanuel Kant's *Critique of Practical Reason* and *Critique of Pure Reason* (which I read then for the first time, but equally intensively)',[44] he moved on to Schleiermacher, and from the time of the Berlin semester onwards, Schleiermacher was for years the leading light in his thought. 'In Berlin . . . along with Wilhelm Herrmann's *Ethics,* I bought myself a copy of Schleiermacher's *Speeches on Religion to its Cultured Despisers,* in R. Otto's edition, which I still use. Eureka! I had evidently been looking for "The Immediate", and had now found it, not with Hermann Kutter, who wrote his first book under this title, but with Schleiermacher . . . I was inclined to believe him blindly all along the line. Still (and this was surely in order), I also loved Eichendorff and was particularly fond of Novalis. Perhaps I was something of a romantic then myself! . . . One thing is certain, however, that even before 1910, in my innermost being I was a stranger to the bourgeois world of Ritschl and his pupils.'[45]

Just as he turned to Schleiermacher, something else happened to Karl in this Berlin semester which his father had sought to prevent by forbidding him to study in Marburg. In Berlin Karl became a committed pupil and follower of Wilhelm Herrmann (1846–1922): 'I can remember the day when I . . . first read his *Ethics* as though it were yesterday. That was in Berlin. If I had the temperament of Klaus Harms, I could speak of Herrmann as he does of Schleiermacher, or say what Stilling says of Herder: "This book started me

---

*Karl Friedrich Schinkel (1781–1841) was the most significant German architect of his time, and designed many notable buildings in Berlin, of which the *Neue Wache* (New Guardhouse) was one.

off in perpetual motion." With more restraint, but no less gratefully, I would prefer to say: "I think that my own personal interest in theology began on that day." '[46] Thus the semester in Berlin had in no way distracted Barth from wanting to study in Marburg; indeed, it strengthened his resolve. However, before his wish could be fulfilled, his career first took rather a bizarre turn.

In April 1907 he again enrolled in the University of Berne, and was immediately involved in a heated electoral battle for the presidency of the Berne Zofingia (against his former classmate Albert Schüpbach, later Professor of Medicine in Berne), which he won. In the words of a commentator, this election was a great surprise: 'A heretic had become pope. The fellow-heretics were in ecstasies of delight, the orthodox were utterly downcast. But neither hopes nor fears were realized. The new prince of the church made hardly any attempt to break with the old hallowed traditions. Now he acted in a completely orthodox way, quite in accordance with the rules. And this was a good thing. Had he resorted to coercion and pressure, he would only have hindered a development which was progressing gently of its own accord. So the semester followed a peaceful and normal course.'[47] In fact, for a whole semester Karl Barth now 'put as much effort into being president as I had once devoted to being a member of Harnack's seminar in Halleschen Strasse'. He had to concede that 'theology is lying completely fallow'. For most of the time, 'I sit with an official face in the Stadtbachgarten restaurant (the headquarters of the association), under the trees or on the sofa, and rule.'[48] Martin Nil was at Barth's side as his 'bodyguard': 'a faithful comrade, always ready for any kind of roguery . . . A Berne face, with all kinds of crannies and hidden dreams.'[49] Barth's time was now spent in meetings; in drinking morning, noon and night; in going to all kinds of festivals, balls and formal drinking-bouts; or solemnly carrying a banner right across Berne or down the Bahnhofstrasse in Zürich. Last but not least, the association went on various outings and excursions, 'the men with their stiff collars and the ladies with their fantastic white hats, in all their pre-war splendour'.[50] 'In Berlin, I "worked", but in Berne I passed my days in student glory . . . It was probably a time in my life when I had to "live it up" – I did live it up, to the full.'[51] Karl Barth was so preoccupied with it all that when Günther Dehn, a candidate for the Berlin cathedral chapter (and later to be his friend), came to visit the Barths at home, he would talk of nothing else all through dinner and dominated the conversation. 'I have a vague memory that after that evening I was sternly reprimanded by my father.'[52]

This summer also took on a special glow because of Karl Barth's first great love – a Berne girl called Rösy Münger. He had discovered her a year earlier. 'I spent the happiest hours with her' and, of course, also 'wrote her a lyrical (!!!) poem as long as your arm'.[53] 'Meeting her was one of the profoundest and most mysterious events of my whole life.'[54] Soon, however, all kinds of grievous complications began to come between them. It was like the song, 'They just could not get together.' Their parents were not in favour of their friendship or an engagement. And in an argument over the question, Karl Barth was even presented with the inexorable view: 'The will of your parents is the will of God.' Above all because of pressure from his parents, Karl parted company with Rösy in May 1910. 'I have never been able to forget this girl – she died in 1925.'[55] She was 'always in my thoughts: she had her questions, but she was loving and kind'.[56]

At the end of the summer semester of 1907, Fritz Barth was tired of his son's wild goings-on, and he spoke to him sternly in an attempt to guide his life into a more moderate course. He also wanted Karl to forget his friendship with Rösy and to think of other things. 'He felt that it was time that, with my liberal tendencies, I should hear some sound "positive" theology . . . so he sent me off to Tübingen, to Adolf Schlatter. I was to hear lectures by him and by Theodor Häring, a Ritschlian theologian who was nevertheless also a friend of my father's.'[57] Before Karl obediently yielded to his father's command, he spent four weeks during August 1907 as assistant pastor in Meiringen, a large parish in the Bernese Oberland.[58] The first sermon that he gave there (on Psalm 121) contains an extensive description of the mountains round Meiringen ('When the tones of the organ resound through God's house and the streams rush down, as always, from above, and the high snows give their greeting with eternal purity, who would not feel that "The prospect gives the angels strength" . . . ?'). His grandmother from Basle 'insisted on being present at my first children's class in the old church at Meiringen, half hidden behind a pillar. So I can hardly assume that she felt that I was doing it right.'[59] Barth had had some preparation for being an assistant pastor, since in the previous semester he had at least passed through a seminar on homiletics and had written his first sermon for it (on Mark 8.34f.).

In October he went off to Tübingen, 'at the bidding of my father, who was now much more insistent, and not according to my own inclination'.[60] In Tübingen his lodgings were at Neckargasse 10. 'When I put my head out of the window I could see the Hölderlin tower, and the Neckar bridge on the left. I really worked there, because I had to write a qualifying dissertation. At that time it was part of the Berne examination.'[61] He chose the subject himself: 'The Descent of Christ to Hell in the First Three Centuries.'[62] He treated it in a markedly historical way, and not as dogmatics. In the end the dissertation became a work of 194 pages. In addition, he zealously memorized what he needed for the examination and prepared himself for dogmatics by producing a thick collection of extracts, which he entitled, *'Consensus repetitus Fidei Christianae vere Lutheranae,* or, A Little Garden of Dogmatic Delights arranged for Children and Those who Love Children after the manner of C. E. Luthardt'. 'I worked in the library and in my lodgings from morning to night. And to give myself the air of a real Tübingen student of the time, I bought a very large pipe which stood beside me on the floor. I smoked it vigorously and worked.'[63] In the late evening Barth occasionally drank a glass of beer and also took part in all kinds of activities as a guest of the King's Society, the student association there.[64]

'Only one thing never happened in Tübingen: I did not join the ranks of the "positives".'[65] Barth felt so out of place in the lecture rooms there that in his fury he called the theological faculty a 'low dive' and Tübingen a 'wretched hole'.[66] He listened to 'Häring with astonishment (on Romans) and only enjoyed F. Fleiner on Canon Law': he went to hear Schlatter very irregularly, and then only 'with considerable resentment'.[67] He sneered at Schlatter's 'talent for moving difficulties elegantly out of the way without really tackling them.'[68] 'I was quite dismayed at Schlatter. I was now slanted so much in the other direction, towards Jülicher, Heitmüller and so on. So I could not bear the way in which Schlatter dealt with the Gospel of Matthew. After only three weeks I wrote a letter home to my father and said (in the words of the book of Jonah), "Lord, is not this what I said when I was yet in my country . . . that things would not turn out well." The shot went low. Only much, much later did I find my way out of this liberal swamp of my own accord, by quite a different route.'[69] In fact Barth actually met during this Tübingen period (for the first time on 27 December 1907) the man who was eventually to be of help: this was Christoph Blumhardt, whom he had already visited often in Bad Boll, 'though my eyes were not yet fully open'.[70] However, for the moment his father's command had proved ineffective, so that many years later his son came to the conclusion that 'One of the best remedies against liberal theology and other kinds of bad theology is to take them in bucketsful. On the other hand, all attempts to withhold them by stratagem or force only causes people to fall for them even more strongly, with a kind of persecution complex.'[71]

Herrmann's pupil

Did Fritz Barth also draw this conclusion from his son's behaviour? At any rate, when he had to admit that Karl was not being guided along the right lines, even by his enforced move to Tübingen, he finally allowed him, in April 1908, to go to Marburg, 'my Zion'.[72] Karl found lodgings at Hirschberg 4. Before the beginning of the semester he had already been able to hear Wilhelm Herrmann lecturing at the Aarau Student Conference ('God's Revelation to Us') – and also Leonhard Ragaz, with his stirring theme that God was meeting men today in socialism. And now 'a variety of circumstances brought about the fulfilment of my desires. I was able to go to Marburg as I had so longed to, and I could hear the lectures that I really wanted, from Herrmann and, above all, from Heitmüller. Jülicher's manner I found less to my taste.'[73] In addition, Barth also heard Stephan and Rade: he went to seminars on catechetics and homiletics, and in addition took note of the neo-Kantian philosophers there: 'There has been . . . a philosophical fervour which is almost priestly. This was impressed upon us at Marburg . . . by the figures of Cohen and Natorp.'[74]

But 'Herrmann was *the* theological teacher of my student years'.[75] He stood alone. Only because of him were the following three semesters in Marburg 'far and away my happiest student memory'.[76] 'On the one hand Herrmann was a Kantian . . . and on the other a pupil of the younger Schleiermacher, not the older. The first four of the speeches were so important to Herrmann that he told us in his seminar that they were the most important pieces of writing to have appeared before the public since the closing of the canon of the New Testament. I did not accept that from him without question,' but it did not in the least prevent Barth from listening to him 'with great respect . . . Especially since I myself had worked through the whole of Kant before I made my pilgrimage to Marburg! That is really where I came from: first I studied Kant's *Critique of Practical Reason,* and then I went twice through the *Critique of Pure Reason* almost with a toothcomb. At that time we thought that it was the way one had to begin theology. And after Kant, I then hit upon Schleiermacher.'[77]

Barth heard Herrmann lecturing on Dogmatics I (Prolegomena to the Concept of 'Religion') and Ethics, and on 5–6 June he copied out all Herrmann's lecture course from the previous winter (Dogmatics II). 'I soaked Herrmann in through all my pores.'[78] 'He showed us that theology could have its own professional fervour, not merely as a parasite on the fourth faculty, but in its own right. There was steel in Herrmann's voice.'[79] 'Herrmann was not ashamed of the gospel. So even his physical appearance was wholly lacking in that trait of wordly wisdom and cunning which too often makes the "systematic" theologian recognizable even at a distance. This trait was also absent from his theology, which some people have therefore found naive. Like the Marburg students, who grumbled about "advanced confirmation instruction" which was given in his lectures . . . and this at a time when the start of Troeltsch, with his world-wide programmes and perspectives, was nearing its zenith.'[80] Indeed, Karl Barth even thought that, 'Although Herrmann was surrounded by so much Kant and Schleiermacher, the decisive thing for him was the christocentric impulse, and I learnt that from him.'[81]

Yet Herrmann's theology was also peculiarly critical, in this very way. 'It should certainly be distinguished from old liberalism, and also from all "orthodoxy" and all "positive" theology. We deeply despised both of these: on the right hand and on the left we felt ourselves to be free and superior, progressing up the narrow ridge – as it was at the time.'[82] So Barth never forgot: 'The air of freedom blew through his lecture room. It was certainly not by chance that for decades, every semester a small party from Switzerland made the pilgrimage to Marburg and felt especially at home there. Our rebellious minds, repudiating all authority, there found satisfaction.'[83] During this summer no less than fifteen Swiss theological students were staying in Marburg. They met now and then at the Matthäi, a restaurant there.[84] In the middle of June Barth went with some of them to a theological conference in Giessen and over Whitsun went to 'a great feast of trumpets' in Bethel.[85] He got on particularly well with one of the Swiss who were there, Gottlob Wieser (1888–1973), and they were to be faithful friends for the rest of Barth's life.

Barth himself was to have an active summer after this semester: in the middle of July he wrote his papers for the final theological examination and 'for the second time did holiday duty as assistant pastor, this time in Pruntrut, in the Bernese Jura'.[86] Meanwhile he also had to go on to study for the second, oral part of the examination, occasionally in the following manner: 'Sunbathing in a green alpine meadow, classical nakedness, straw hat, cigar in the mouth, book under a parasol, insect-bites, sunburn.'[87] Then he went 'reasonably well-armed into the second examination' (on systematic and practical theology).[88] He passed on 28 October with a second class. 'In the end it proved that in contrast to the tendencies of my grandfather and my father, I had made myself a committed disciple of the "modern" school, which was still dominant up to the time of the First World War, and was regarded as the only school worth belonging to. In it, according to the teaching of Schleiermacher and Ritschl, Christianity was interpreted on the one hand as a historical phenomenon to be subjected to critical examination, and on the other hand as a matter of inner experience, of a predominantly moral nature. So I was not badly equipped in the autumn of 1908 for taking up a post as editorial assistant on the *Christliche Welt* (Christian World), a leading journal of the school, which was published in Marburg under the editorship of Professor Martin Rade.'[89] Barth did not yet want to go into parish work, although the Reformed congregation in Schwabach, a suburb of Nuremberg, did invite him.

On Wednesday, 4 November, Karl Barth was ordained by his father in the cathedral in Berne (the text of his father's sermon was Matthew 10.26f.). After that he could not wait to get back to Marburg, and left the very next morning. He now found lodgings at Hainweg 1. Of course he went to more lectures and seminars: in Jülicher's seminar he was proud to be given a place next to the professor. For the most part, however, his time was now filled with work for the journal. 'Work in Rade's house was cheerful and easy, and extremely interesting for a young man like me at that time, curious and thirsting for knowledge, and at any rate quite precocious. My main work was to read the many manuscripts which came in, make a preliminary decision about them, present this in an appropriate fashion to Martin Rade, and finally prepare the material that he selected for the printer. Countless quantities of manu-

The student

11.   *Karl Barth with fellow members of Zofingia in 1905 (he is on the right, next to the beer jug; W. Häberli is on the left, A. Schüpbach third from the left and F. Zulauf is on the right, with the banner). In 1907 Karl Barth was president of the Berne section for a semester.*

12.   *The traditional outing of Zofingia in May 1906 on the Aare, against a background of old Berne: Karl Barth is standing in the middle, with his friend Otto Lauterburg to the right of him.*

His Teachers

13. Martin Rade, Professor of Systematic Theology at Marburg, whom Karl Barth helped in 1909 with the editing of the Christliche Welt *(above left).*

14. The Berlin church historian Adolf von Harnack, whose lectures Barth heard in 1906–07 with such enthusiasm that he forgot almost everything else (above right).

15. The systematic theologian Wilhelm Herrmann, from Marburg, who sought to combine Kant and Schleiermacher, influenced Barth most of all. Barth followed his work for years.

16. Swiss theological students at Marburg, summer 1908. Karl Barth (standing above, right) is next to his friends Gottlob Wieser and Fritz Zulauf.

scripts which I and then the master thought to be less significant disappeared into a kind of theological Wolf's Glen* for a more or less extended interval, or even permanently . . . In his own generous fashion Rade let me do what I liked within certain limits, and from my standpoint (which at that time was somewhere between Kant and the young Schleiermacher), I seemed to myself to be quite important – something like a second mate. How could it be otherwise when, as far as the *Christliche Welt* was concerned, even the writings of Troeltsch, Bousset, Wernle, Gunkel and so on were completely dependent on my censorship? In time I was even allowed to burst into print with a couple of small reviews – I regarded them as masterpieces – and my self-importance reached its highest point when in the summer of 1909, as the Rades were going on holiday, I was allowed to edit and to take the responsibility for two numbers all by myself.'[90] Barth never denied that he learnt a great deal from his connection with Rade, in his study or in the 'sunny summerhouse on the Roten Graben'.[91] He gained many insights and attempted to put them into practice in his own way. 'The effects of working with Rade ranged from an unwearying diligence and openness in surveying the church and the world to the fluttering black cravats which for many years afterwards reminded my contemporaries of where and with whom I had spent my apprentice years.'[92]

In addition to his editorial work, Karl Barth also had time for his own research. He attempted 'to provide himself with real theological foundations through intensive study of Kant and Schleiermacher',[93] helped Horst Stephan with proofs and 'valuable notes' for the production of his book on the modern period (1909), and in June wrote an article on 'The Cosmological Proof for the Existence of God' (which had, of course been done away with by Kant and Herrmann). Incidentally, a further 'tragedy to excite fear and compassion' (*Iphigenia in Aulis*) flowed from his pen for a performance in his former society, Patria. And on Sundays he occasionally preached in the villages around Marburg or went on walks or trips on the Lahn with friends. 'While I was still a student, I once left the beauties of Marburg for a walk in the country with a good friend (Wilhelm Loew). We wanted to visit a pastor for whom we had both already preached. When we came to the place, we found that the whole village was celebrating a large wedding. We hadn't known of this

*A remote, forsaken spot – though doubtless not so eerie as the Wolf's Glen in Weber's famous opera *Der Freischütz!*

beforehand, but since we were there, we were treated like the people from the highways and the hedgerows in the parable: we were forced to come in. We were very pleased to do so, and in this way we took part in a local peasant wedding, much finer than the kind which are described and pictured in the best books . . . Throughout the whole of the feast . . . – and it was by no means short – the bridal couple were instructed to eat out of one dish, using one spoon, one fork and one knife.'[94]

Thus even now Karl Barth was in active and friendly contact with all kinds of people of the same age. His brother Peter and Martin Nil had also come to Marburg to study. In addition, Karl had also come to know one of Heitmüller's doctoral students, two years older than himself, Rudolf Bultmann (born 1884). And 'above all, I found two friends who are still friends today and will continue to remain so: Eduard Thurneysen . . . and Wilhelm Loew.'[95] He in fact already knew Thurneysen from Zofingia. 'We met again . . . in Marburg. But of those who were at that time regarded as German masters, Ernst Troeltsch made more impression on him than Wilhelm Herrmann, whom I preferred. At any rate he accepted the best that the liberal theology of the time had to offer with eagerness and success.'[96] Barth regarded Loew (born 1887) as one of the 'most brilliant contemporaries whom I ever met. He had a markedly individual character, he was highly intelligent and showed considerable independence in his judgments. He was not only widely read but also thoroughly well educated in theology and all related subjects.'[97] In company with Karl Bornhausen, an assistant, the friends formed a private working group which met regularly, to read together and for protracted discussions. Loew, immediately elevated to the status of an 'honorary Swiss' (and remarkably enough nicknamed 'Steamship'), was the real leader of this circle. 'At that time the name of Troeltsch stood in the centre of our discussions; it denoted the point beyond which I felt that I had to refuse to follow the dominant theology of the time.'[98] Did Barth already suspect what he later remarked about Troeltsch, 'that with him the doctrine of faith was on the point of dissolution into endless and useless talk'?[99] At any rate, even at this stage he would have nothing to do with Troeltsch, though in the winter of 1908–09 he did copy out all Troeltsch's lectures on the philosophy of religion from the summer of 1908.

In other respects, however, Karl Barth felt himself to be a 'committed supporter' of modern theology – 'as the 1909 *Zeitschrift für*

Theologie und Kirche shows'![100] In an article published there under the title 'Moderne Theologie und Reichgottesarbeit' (Modern Theology and Working for the Kingdom of God), which was composed at the end of his time as a student, he described the content of the 'satchel' which he had now acquired as 'religious individualism and historical relativism'. At the same time, in the article he deliberately considered the transition from study to pastoral work – discussing the objection that this transition was particularly difficult for the 'pupils of "modern" theology'. He asserted, however, that the difficulty could be overcome, and above all issued a warning against being led to give up this 'satchel' as a result of pastoral work. 'Anyone who was a real pupil, and not just a schoolboy, when he filled up his lecture notebooks with Herrmann and Harnack, will not want to take the course of a "flight into pastoral work".'[101] Barth himself was later surprised at 'the astonishing views that I happily put forward as a twenty-three-year-old candidate for the ministry to the horror of less consistent friends of Herrmann'.[102] In fact his article was so provocative that two distinguished professors, Ernst Christian Achelis at Marburg, and Paul Drews at Halle, simultaneously felt called to make replies. However, Karl Barth was not in Marburg to put his rejoinder on paper. Meanwhile he had gone into 'pastoral work'!

'At the end of my student days I was second to none among my contemporaries in credulous approval of the "modern" theology of the time. With the views that I have indicated, in 1909 I went into the pastorate.'[103] In his old age, Barth still liked to think that it was 'the good will of Providence that to some degree I was immunized by the magic of the *Christliche Welt*, by which I had been bewitched, against the over-hasty and unauthentic solutions of, say, the Seeberg school, while still remaining capable of searching for a better way out of the straits in which the whole of theology was then confined. But at that time I didn't even know that they were straits. The questions which I had to put to my masters and thus to myself were posed simply to gain an understanding within a set of problems which I regarded as immovable. What I owe to my time in the *Christliche Welt* is the fact that after that year I embarked on my life, went into the church and continued my further theological thinking not as a half-baked product of Marburg but for the first time as the real thing. It was necessary for me to have spent some time soaking in the atmosphere and the spirit of that autumn of the age of Schleiermacher – especially, perhaps, in daily conversation with the admirable Martin Rade, his family and his friends. Had I not at one time given it all my youthful trust, I would never have been able to make the discovery that I made seven years later, that now it really could come to an end.'[104]

Assistant pastor in Geneva

Karl Barth said his farewell to Marburg on 18 August 1909. A month later, on 16 September, after several weeks holiday during which he also joined in the celebrations for his parents' silver wedding anniversary, he went to Geneva: here, for a brief two years, he was to take the position of a *pasteur suffragant* to the German-speaking congregation of the *église nationale** there.[105] First of all he lived on the fourth floor at Quai des Bergues 21 (on the bank of the Rhône, near the Isle de Rousseau), and then from May of the following year in the villa Les Marguerites, in Avenue des Petits Délices 9. His special responsibility was to look after the area near the Rue des Pâquis. On 26 September Barth was instituted to his new office and gave his first sermon, which he based on Philippians 3. 12–15. It set out the intentions with which he was entering his ministry. 'And on the day I began my ministry, five minutes before I was to go up into the pulpit, the post brought me the new, fourth edition of Herrmann's *Ethics*, which the author had sent me. I accepted this coincidence as a dedication of my whole future.'[106] In his sermon, Barth explained, among other things, how he wanted to understand his ministry: 'To be good friends, pathfinders, leaders in the sphere of the inner life . . . we cannot do more. The time has gone for ever when pastors wanted to be seen, and were seen, not only as messengers but also as governors. We pastors and theologians have neither to administer nor to distribute religion: our task is always only to arouse, to encourage and to shape.' Above all, however, in view of his future work he was concerned 'to ask God to make Christ ever richer and clearer in our midst. Then all of us together, congregation and pastors, will be able to be something like friends and brothers and sisters to each other.'

The chief pastor of the church was Adolf Keller (1872–1963), who

---

*The relationship between state and church differs from canton to canton in Switzerland. Usually the Reformed Church and the Roman Catholic Church are 'established', and have certain civil responsibilities; as in England, the other churches can be referred to as 'free churches'.

was thus Barth's real superior. Barth found that he had 'an uncommonly rich and many-sided personality; theologically, too, I got on with him very well'.107 Keller was already a widely-travelled man; as a student he had done research on Sinai and had worked as a pastor in Cairo; later he was to travel even further on ecumenical work. He left Geneva the next October, to become pastor at St Peter's in Zürich. Because of the vacancy Barth had to look after the German Reformed congregation in Geneva single-handed for six months.108 During this period his time was taken up almost entirely with pastoral work. It was a relief for him, and provided some respite, when a new chief pastor was inducted at the end of February 1910: he was an equally widely travelled man, Pastor Walter, who had already worked in England, Moscow and Marseilles.

At that time Karl Barth was already paying great attention to the preparation of sermons. He wrote each sermon out word for word; they were quite long, and one usually took up about sixteen pages. The circumstances in which he prepared a sermon in December 1909 seemed to him to be so remarkable that he described them in detail. 'A few days ago they built a switchback below my window, on the island in the Rhône. It's a terrible thing, with lots of electric lights and a Swiss flag on the top. A machine somehow starts things off and now children of all ages are swooping down it . . . To add to their enjoyment and mine an orchestrion renders the songs from *The Merry Widow* and other classic tunes at regular intervals: I note with surprise and delight that all this will go on until the third of January, and think edifying thoughts about the joys and sorrows of preparing sermons in a big city.'109

In his Geneva sermons, Barth for the most part gave a systematic interpretation of the Epistle of James (with some interruptions): this was the very book on which he had heard Robert Aeschbacher preach at the beginning of his studies. Now he himself was preaching on it, in the proud self-assurance that 'had James known men like Luther and Calvin, Kant and Schleiermacher, to whom I have often referred here . . . he would have interpreted his text just as I have done, or very nearly so.'110 Besides, Barth's sermons were delivered in the most distinguished setting conceivable, 'in Calvin's very auditorium'111 and even 'in his pulpit',112 'next to St Peter's cathedral'.113 Calvin had once delivered his lectures in the same room and John Knox had preached there. 'However, I'm afraid that Calvin would hardly have been very pleased at the sermons which I preached in his pulpit then.'[114] Barth's sermons were very academic (in his sermon for Reformation Day 1910 he ventured to analyse Melanchthon's *Loci Communes*!). They were also very liberal, to the especial chagrin of his uncle Ernst Sartorius, who was a member of the congregation. Later, Barth himself had to shake his head at his brashness at the time. 'There I was, one hundred per cent a Marburg product. I knew everything, and knew it better than anyone else. And I entered the ministry and stumbled up the steps of Calvin's pulpit with an inexperience and awkwardness and unshakeable confidence reminiscent of the behaviour of a young St Bernard. When I think back on it, I seem to have been like that famous horseman on Lake Constance, who found that he had ridden clean across it without knowing.'[115]

Typical of his sermons were remarks like, 'The greatest thing is what takes place in our hearts.' Or, 'To each man goes out the call to be true to himself, namely . . . to that model of the best that anyone can become.' He told the congregation: 'Try to become valuable!' Or, 'Dear friend, think seriously about yourself.' As he explained 'Before I can know God, I must know myself.' He introduced Goethe's Faust as 'without doubt a true Protestant'. The congregation learnt that 'Calvin's view of the authority of the Bible would be quite wrong for us.' Critical light was shed on the Ten Commandments: 'Sometimes they contain too much for our needs and sometimes too little.' And once for a whole sermon he argued that 'James wrote the section which we are looking at now in a weak moment.' He attacked the Christ 'presented by the Chalcedonian Definition to the ancient church': 'I will gladly concede that if Jesus were like this I would not be interested in him.' But, 'If Christ begins to live in *us* . . . that is the beginning of Christian faith.'[116] From time to time Barth sent sermons delivered in this style to his father. Although Fritz hardly found his son's preaching to his taste, at least he had the wisdom to keep quiet, and not make any criticisms.

Not very many people came to services at that time. 'I once visited a sick old man and in conversation asked him to which church he belonged. He answered me in tones of some resentment: "Pastor, I've always been an honest man. I've never been to church and I've never been in trouble with the police."' Barth had the impression that this honest man 'has countless male and female counterparts in Geneva, in the German Reformed Church – chiefly male'. 'In living memory,' he remarked, of the eight hundred men in Geneva on the electoral roll, 'hardly one has appeared in the church . . . And I have seldom seen even the women's seats all occupied. So far the place has never been overflowing, or even full.'[117] In Barth's view this lack of interest in the church was probably connected with the 'consciousness and sub-consciousness of the free citizen of Geneva, saturated with a pietist complex', which caused him great trouble.[118]

In addition to preaching, he had to take confirmation classes in the church room in the Rue Pépinière. Here he came up against the same lack of interest in the church. In Geneva preparation for confirmation was limited to six months. But in his view, it was meant 'to give young people some coherence and clarity in their inner life. They will need it when they soon begin to lead their own lives.' Barth felt that the religious knowledge among his pupils was no better than 'that to be found among negro children on the Gold Coast'. For example, he asked them to name Old Testament prophets and was given the answer, 'Abraham and Eve'.[119] This lamentable state of affairs moved Barth to institute 'post-confirmation classes' each Wednesday evening which were intended to deepen the Christian knowledge of those who had already been confirmed; parents were also invited. On these evenings he attempted, in alternate weeks, to introduce the boys to 'Protestant missions' and the girls to 'personalities of Christian religion' (which included people like Athanasius and Socrates!).

The duties of the young assistant pastor also included pastoral care as well as preaching and instruction. He was zealous in visiting at that time and spent a great deal of time in relief work with the poor. He deliberately made acquaintance with real poverty, with the strong feeling that he was quite incapable of coping with it.[120] And as a result he was obviously prompted on occasions to express ideas about society – derived from Kant's categorical imperative.[121] At that time, too, he once criticized 'Kutter and our Religious Socialists' in public because for all their 'views on society . . . in practice they are the greatest subjectivists conceivable', incapable of 'really standing beside the rank and file of the poor'.[122] Barth's duties also included editorial work on a 'parish magazine' which appeared once a month. He put into the magazine some informal poems by C. F. Meyer, Herder and the Baselbiet pietist Annoni. He also wrote a number of contributions for it himself: for example in March 1911 an article on the saying, 'Do right and fear no one', at Easter 1910 one with the title 'Did Jesus really live?', and on the

Confederation Day of Prayer in 1910 one on 'God in the Fatherland'.
He also included résumés of two lectures which he gave in November
1910 and April 1911, in which he commended the hymn writers
Tersteegen and Novalis (the 'proclaimer of redemptive self-denial!')
very warmly to his congregation.

Special reference should be made to one of these small articles. In his
'Easter meditation' Barth dealt with the question 'Did Jesus really live?',
which was much discussed at the time. His own view, however, was that no
answer to the question was adequate for faith. 'The ground of our faith is
quite independent of all proofs and counter-proofs, and always will be.' 'For
faith is not a matter of accepting external facts and assuming them to be
true.' Rather, it is 'direct, living contact with the Living One'. So it does not
live on a 'series of external facts which have been handed down . . . Rather,
the ground of faith is the personal, inner life of Jesus. By that I mean his
human character, which is described to us as utter obedience towards God,
as complete love of his brethren and therefore as complete self-denial,
which does not halt even in the face of death.' He argued that this portrayal
of Jesus' character would be true in itself, even if the disciples had invented
it (which Barth did not believe to be the case). 'When we learn from this
portrayal what *God* is and what we shall *become,* then we *believe,* then we *have*
the assurance and the firm foundation that we need to be free and happy
men.'

Once the position of chief pastor was filled again, Barth was
occasionally able to get away from Geneva. In June 1910 he was
involved in a performance in Berne of Bach's *St Matthew Passion,* of
which he was very fond at that time. He went there again to take part
in the conference of a 'social-political organization'. In July he paid
another flying visit, to Marburg. Ostensibly it was to hear Karl
Bornhausen's inaugural lecture, but he went chiefly to have personal
conversations with Herrmann, and also with Heitmüller, Jülicher
and Rade. Then in August he went to see his father, who was
seriously ill (during the semester, Peter Barth had taken his father's
place!). After that, Karl spent the holidays with his grandmother,
reading Cohen copiously.

Above all, however, relief from his burdens in Geneva now
allowed him to spend more time in academic theology. He enlarged
his library by occasional 'forays' into the 'estate of my grandfather
on my mother's side in Basle'; in this way he finally got hold of the
sermons of Friedrich Schleiermacher, 'together with his letters,
Christian Morality and other writings'.[123] The special associations of
the place where Barth preached and the fact that in autumn 1909

there were Calvin celebrations in the Geneva theatre did not affect his theological thinking very deeply at the time. On the whole, 'in Geneva I was still living completely and utterly in the religious atmosphere that I had brought with me from Marburg, and especially from the circle of the *Christliche Welt* and its friends.'[124] 'I never regretted having tried to foist all that historicism and individualism on the people in Geneva, but in any case, they weren't having any. In fact I was quite happy making the most of the meagre resources which I brought to my work.'[125] Nevertheless, 'it may have been the spirit of the place . . . which caused me to deepen the experience I had gained from reading Schleiermacher again and again by making considerable inroads into Calvin's *Institutes*. I did not experience any sudden conversion, and at first thought that I could very well combine idealist and romantic theology with the theology of the Reformation. It was while holding this view that I had published a long article on faith and history which would have better remained unpublished.'[126]

This 'article', which was presented to a pastoral conference in Neuchâtel as early as 5 October 1910, but was only printed in 1912, showed Barth once again to be a committed Marburg theologian, and at the same time indicated that he was concerned with 'the problem of "faith and history", which was discussed so much in the first decade of the century and posed most acutely in the theology of Wilhelm Herrmann.'[127]

This extremely learned lecture contains in a nutshell all the features of Barth's theology of the time: his unswerving polemic against the 'orthodox' understanding of faith as holding certain things to be true, a view for which he even attacked the Reformers, and his definition of it in terms of 'inner experience' which has its 'ground' (not its object) in the 'inner life of Jesus'; his constant references to Kant and Schleiermacher, and even to Goethe and Schiller, as authorities; and hence his freedom to claim Francis of Assisi and Bodelschwingh, Michelangelo and even Beethoven as 'sources of revelation' alongside Paul. It is clear where he differs from Troeltsch and he interprets Calvin like Osiander. He welcomes Luther's 'If you believe, you have' and Melanchthon's exclusive concentration on the 'benefits of Christ', along with the 'sayings of old Angelus Silesius' ('If Christ is born a thousand times in Bethlehem and not in you . . .'). How could it have been otherwise, since he understood faith as 'the origin of the reality of life, the actualization of the possibilities of consciousness given in the *a priori* functions'?[128]

The maxims which Barth collected together (perhaps as early as that?) under the title 'Ideas on the Philosophy of Religion' also point in a similar direction. Beyond question, in Geneva he remained committed to the insights which he had gained in Marburg. Now, however, deep inside, he began to realize that 'the longer I had to preach and to teach, the more the work of academic theology seemed to me to be somehow alien and mysterious.' This was one of the reasons why the plan he had already begun to work out, to study for a doctorate under Herrmann, never came to anything. 'Circumstances and personal reasons got in the way of my aim to study for a doctorate in theology at Marburg.'[129]

Two events in early 1911 had an extraordinary effect on Karl Barth. One was the appearance in Geneva, at the beginning of February, of John R. Mott, the much-discussed 'apostle of the students and student organizer'. Mott's lectures moved Barth deeply, although he had serious reservations about the way in which Mott acted rather like an American businessman. 'He has only one tune, like old Dessau, but it's a good one: evangelization, mankind for Jesus and Jesus for mankind . . . One can detect a strength and a concentration of religious experience, the superiority of which we should be glad to recognize; just as our principles of individual and social morality may seem to be somewhat colourless against the reality which encounters us in Mott.' 'He is a personality: the reason why we give speeches and write books.' 'That is what I felt when I listened to his lectures in Geneva.'[130]

The other event took place on 28 April in the streets of Geneva. Thousands of Genevans, at the prompting of the City Council, demonstrated against the prohibition of gambling by the Federal Council. That evening Barth heard the uproar 'going on without interruption for at least five hours', and thought, 'Never in my life have I heard such powerful, harmonious and persistent pipings, shouts and taunts.' What flabbergasted him even more than this 'back-street hubbub', however, was the 'mindless phraseology to which the heads of our state descended'.[131] He was especially shaken that he heard a 'well-known Swiss statesman, Henry Fazy, say, "We respect religion, but people shouldn't bother us with it."'[132] Barth resolutely took up the cudgels against these Genevans and supported the prohibition of gambling in the conviction that this was 'simply one point in the enemy line', which for him was marked out by alcoholism, mammonism and libertinism. The moral that he drew from the event was that, 'What "the church" now has to do above all is to make the force of the kingdom of God felt by firmly saying "no".'[133]

At this time Karl Barth also made a significant personal decision. He became engaged – to Nelly Hoffmann. She was a member of his first-year confirmation class. She had attended very conscientiously and had been confirmed by him at Ascension 1910 in the Madeleine church in Geneva. She was born on 26 August 1893, the youngest of five sisters, and grew up first in Rorschach and then in Zürich. She had lived in Geneva since 1905. Her father, the lawyer Robert Hoffmann, town clerk at St Gallen, had died in 1894. So Nelly had been brought up entirely by her mother, Anna Elisabeth, née Hugentobler (1854–1934), who had gone with her family to Geneva so that they could have a good education in languages and art. Nelly was able to learn the violin at the conservatory there, but gave up studying music after her engagement. She was not yet eighteen when she became engaged to Barth, on 16 May 1911, a week after he had asked for her hand. As he wrote at the time, he was delighted at his engagement, 'with all the added depth and enrichment and purpose which it brings to life, with all the joy and intimacy which it promises.'[134]

A fortnight later, on 31 May, he gave a lecture (in French) to the pastors of Geneva which was a critical discussion of 'La réapparition de la métaphysique dans la théologie'. In it, as a good pupil of Herrmann and with emphatic reference to Melanchthon, he rejected both ancient metaphysics and the new metaphysics now again under discussion as 'une entreprise infructueuse aussi bien que dangereuse pour la théologie'. The reality which it encompassed was not to be taken as divine reality and had nothing to do with 'cette élévation pratique de l'âme, qui est l'essence de la religion'. However, this lecture was almost Barth's farewell appearance in Geneva, since another important turning point in his life had come into view. On 2 April 1911 he had given a trial sermon (on Matthew 5.10–12) in a village in Aargau. And the same month he had been chosen to be pastor of the community there. He gave his farewell sermon in Geneva on 25 June 1911 – on the very text on which his father had preached at his ordination. In it he expressed the hope that 'indifference to each other and indifference towards the highest things will give way to a mutual and common search. A Christian community, which at present only exists in the mind and on paper, must become a reality . . .'

3

Comrade Pastor

The years in the parish of Safenwil, 1911–1921

The pastor . . .

A new period of Barth's life began unmistakably in 1911, 'when like my father before me, I came to the Aargau as a pastor, to Safenwil, an agricultural and industrial community'.[1] According to a survey made in 1910, the village then consisted of 247 houses containing 1625 inhabitants. Of these 1487 were Protestants, of whom no less than 318 were schoolchildren. The village lies in a wide valley and at that time was changing considerably: it was becoming increasingly industrialized, whereas the number of those engaged in agriculture was dropping. It had electricity by the end of 1913. The population was growing steadily. A new school had just been built. Barth was only the fourth pastor to come to the village, since it was only about forty years since Safenwil had become a separate parish and had acquired its own church – principally through the support of a family called Hüssy. The church had been built on a piece of rising ground south of the village. Two texts were inscribed on the right and left of the pulpit, set high in the middle of the wall facing the congregation: John 13.35 and 14.6. The parsonage was on lower ground and a path led uphill from it to the church. 'I went this way often with a sermon in my head, good or bad, or at the head of a funeral procession, or with my confirmation candidates on some outing into the Gyrhölzli, or even behind the dung-cart.'[2] The parsonage was old, built in the Aargau style, and rather damp; it had earlier served as a school and a post-office, and bore the name 'Zum Fellenberg'.

Karl Barth moved into this house on 3 July 1911. He was installed in the church on the following Sunday, 9 July, in the afternoon: his fiancée, his friend Spoendlin and his aunt Bethi were there. His father preached on II Corinthians 4.1f., which contained 'the fine straight line of the biblical theology of experience'.[3] Karl himself preached his inaugural sermon on John 14.24. In it he expressed his joy that 'now after long years of change and wandering I have once again found a homeland and a friendly home in your midst'. He also stated his conviction 'that I am not speaking to you of God because I am a pastor. I am a pastor because I *must* speak to you of God, if I am to remain true to myself, my better self.' The very next morning Barth walked over to see his colleague in nearby Uerkheim, Paul Schild. Thus began a friendship which only ended with Schild's death in 1966.

For the next ten years of his life Karl Barth was now to live and work here in Safenwil. To begin with, while he was still a bachelor, he was looked after by a housekeeper, Fräulein Hanna, and surrounded by a host of cats. From now on his life was governed by the fact that 'he was a country pastor and that he took this ministry seriously and devoted himself to it with all his customary enthusiasm and dedication'.[4] 'I had a very lively time in every respect in this Aargau village. It was there that I first began at least to become aware of the full scope of the task of a Reformed preacher, teacher and pastor.'[5] For various reasons, it even transpired 'that my occupation with theology was now for years reduced to the preparation of sermons and classes, though I did this with extreme care'.[6] However, this was the very period when, by concentrating and reducing his work in this particular way, Barth was led to make some important discoveries. 'It was during my time at Safenwil that I changed my mind decisively in a way which also affected the outward form of my future career.'[7] Barth even thought that his later theology had its roots in his ministry at that time. 'It grew out of my own situation, where I had to instruct, preach and do a little pastoral work.'[8]

Barth saw as his principal task the writing of a Sunday sermon, week by week. On the first Sunday after his installation he began with a long series of sermons on the Lord's Prayer. In all he wrote and delivered about five hundred sermons in Safenwil which, as in Geneva, he wrote out almost every time 'painstakingly and down to the last detail'.[9] More than once the Sunday sermon 'was forced out with terrible birth-pangs'.[10] On occasions he had to spend two whole days on it; 'had to begin again five times';[11] or only finished preparing it on the Sunday morning. 'He did not read out these sermons on Sunday, but delivered them to his congregation freely, in a most impressive way.' Of course 'his sermons demanded a great deal of intellectual effort from the congregation'.[12] While as a rule he only

allowed two hymns in his services, he made up for this by the
remarkable length of his sermons. On the other hand the church
committee* soon began to criticize the unusual brevity of his funeral
services: to begin with he contented himself with a prayer and an
obituary.[13] Furthermore, as early as August 1911 he twice transferred the service 'with gratifying success' to the neighbouring wood
(Gyrhölzli).[14]

From the beginning he found it 'not only a fine old custom but a
necessity that our sermon should always be based on a "text", that
is, a word of Jesus, or of his Old Testament predecessors, or of his
followers, the apostles'.[15] He often chose short biblical sayings as
texts, or preached on a theme, like 'Prayer'; 'Reformation'; 'Pride';
'Mission'; 'Springtime is for Children', 'The Life of William Booth',
and so on. He followed liberal fashion in addressing the congregation
as 'my friends', or 'dear people'. To begin with – as in Geneva – the
content of the sermons was 'modern theology in the style of the
Christliche Welt'.[16] His review of Karl Heim's book on the problem of
certainty, written in 1912, in which he lauded Schleiermacher as the
brilliant leader of a new reformation, shows where he now stood and
continued to stand for the time being. However, 'while in this
pastoral work I was still very much under the influence of Schleiermacher, I did not of course talk in the language of his *Speeches* or even
along their original lines – as Schleiermacher himself did.'[17]

During the sermons of Barth's first period at Safenwil the idea
which comes out most prominently is that of 'life' or 'experience',
terms which were used so much in Marburg. Another significant
feature was his marked concern for 'honesty': the young pastor
wanted to be quite open with his congregation. At that time, for
example, he would tell them about the trouble he had had with a
text: 'I have not got that far yet. Up till now I have been too
preoccupied with other things – even with good things . . . I find
what I should be talking about today somewhat alien to me. I think
that's a mistake. But that's how things are. I must be honest.'[18]
Another striking feature even in this first period is his determination.
He makes bold and critical comments, such as: 'Oh yes, the pastor

---

*In this chapter, the distinction between 'church committee' *(Kirchenpflege)* and 'church
council' *(Kirchenrat)* should be noted carefully. The church committee was a group in Safenwil
consisting of six lay people, who shared with the pastor the responsibility for looking after the
church; the church council was the supreme church authority in the canton of Aargau,
consisting of seven members chosen by the synod, some of whom were always laymen.

should speak the truth, but he should not say anything against the businessman or against the manufacturer or against the teacher or against the trade unions or against the sports club or above all against me! Dear friends, the truth is not against anyone. It is *for* everyone. Believe me, I love you all equally, just as God loves us all equally.' But, 'my calling is to speak and to speak clearly . . . If I wanted to be liked, I would keep quiet.'[19] One last thing is remarkable in Barth's sermons of that time: their close connection with happenings and events of public life in the world, in his country and in the locality. Later he thought that the connection had been too close. 'During my time as a pastor . . . I often succumbed to the danger of attempting to get alongside the congregation in the wrong way. Thus in 1912, when the sinking of the Titanic shook the whole world, I felt that I had to make this disaster my main theme the following Sunday, which led to a monstrous sermon on the same scale.'[20]

At the same time, however, it is also worth mentioning that even in the first sermons given at Safenwil, surprisingly enough one can occasionally find a few sentences or arguments which run counter to the theology which Barth discovered in his studies and which dominate his theology elsewhere. Sometimes they even point beyond it.

Thus he can say quite directly, 'The message of Good Friday has its force . . . quite regardless of what you or I may say about it.' Or, 'Jesus does not disappear when fine religious feelings disappear. He does not have to be born, live and die for us a second time.' Or, just as in dialectical theology, 'Through Jesus all standards are turned upside down,' so that the impious '*are* men of God precisely because they know that that is what they are not'. Or again, 'What kind of Christians would we be if we learnt to look for God again in the future as the one who stands *before* us?' Or, 'There is only one kind of work for the kingdom of God, the work that God does himself.' 'It is not we who come, but God and his kingdom . . . the movement is not upwards, from below, but downwards, from above.'[21] However, statements of this kind stand out in Barth's early sermons like erratic features in a landscape which otherwise has quite different characteristics.

Barth's sermons did not create much of a stir. Indeed, 'I always seemed to be beating my head against a brick wall.'[22] True, he found a group of faithful hearers who understood him and went along with him, but they remained a small group. Part of the reason was that the population in general tended not to go to church – 'I have always explained the fact that going to church is contrary to the nature of the people of the Aargau by recalling the (former) Berne régime in which the pastor "survives" with the governor as the hated aristocrat.'[23] Part of the reason for Barth's scant 'success' in preaching was probably that his sermons were too little in tune with the Aargau mentality, which was characterized 'on the one hand by rationalistic ideas of progress and on the other by a sentimental pietism'.[24] So it seemed to him as though 'I and the people of Safenwil were always . . . looking at each other through a pane of glass.'[25] So Barth had often to preach to virtually 'gaping empty pews'.[26] However, he did not let himself be deterred by church attendance, 'which was usually so sparse',[27] from taking each new sermon seriously. He also connected the lack of a response with his own inner disquiet, his sense of searching and being on the way during that year, since this found expression in his sermons. 'Later I was sorry for everything that my congregation had to put up with.'[28] On the First Sunday in Advent 1935, when Barth once again stood in his pulpit in Safenwil, he looked back on his former preaching there and observed: 'I can see now that I did not preach the gospel clearly enough to you during the time when I was your pastor. Since then I have often thought with some trepidation of those who were perhaps led astray or scandalized by what I said at that time, or of the dead who have passed on and did not hear, at any rate from me, what by human reckoning they ought to have heard.'[29] Even before that he had said on one occasion: 'I am tormented by the memory of how greatly . . . in the end I *failed* as pastor of Safenwil.'[30]

He took almost as much trouble over his confirmation classes as over his sermons. The classes were usually held in a small room in the parsonage. As in Geneva, he 'proudly made up the course himself instead of going through a textbook'. He would summarize the content of each lesson in a brief statement, add some biblical references and then 'dictate my paragraphs like an old professor', lesson by lesson, to his pupils, so that they could write them down in their books.[31] He did not intend that the brief statements should 'be learnt off by heart: they were pegs on which to hang things, so that they could be recalled later'.[32] During his twelve years as a pastor, Barth rethought his confirmation course no less than eight times.

His first course had two parts: 'The way to Jesus' and 'The way to God' (with subdivisions: 1. Obedience; 2. Love; 3. Self-denial). At the beginning of the first part he dictated the following two statements to his pupils: 'By nature man should be distinguished by his *reason*, that is, by the fact that he thinks, wills and feels according to certain laws which he bears within himself. He fulfils his destiny by *applying* his reason or *striving* for what is true, good and beautiful. And this destiny is man's destiny with *God*, for God is eternal truth, goodness and beauty. To *seek* God means to *find* God (Plato). And therefore: this divine destiny for man is expressed most clearly in the inner law of the *will*. Each man should act as he believes *everyone* should act. Such a will is a good will (I. Kant).'

Barth adopted the following principle for giving instruction: 'Instruction cannot merely be teaching and learning: we must discover each other personally and become good friends.' He expected of his pupils 'participation, confidence, openness, questioning'.

He was resolutely against making services compulsory for confirmation candidates. But he was very strict that they should come to their classes regularly. 'A boy got his father to ask me whether he might be allowed to miss the last three classes – because of a course on pruning fruit trees . . . ! I gently asked him in turn whether he would also like to spend Good Friday (the day of the confirmation) among the fruit trees?'[33] As early as winter 1911 Barth obtained permission from the church committee to extend his classes in the last quarter of the year to three a week. His reason was that it would help to make 'discussion of practical questions more thorough and more personal'.[34] Since in addition he insisted that the confirmation classes should be given during working hours (by Swiss custom candidates were already fifteen years old), there were soon unending disputes with a manufacturer called Hochuli, who on one occasion simply kept the candidates in the factory and on a second occasion declared that he would stop taking on confirmation candidates as workers. On yet another occasion he sent confirmation candidates to Zofingen to be instructed. Finally, the church council in Aarau, which Barth summoned to his aid, also intimated that 'part of the trouble lies in the personality of the pastor'.[35] For a long time Barth thought it important that he should have a private conversation with each candidate before confirmation.

Preparatory instruction prior to confirmation classes had only been introduced in the Aargau since the spring of 1912. Barth saw its purpose as being to make the pupils directly familiar with the Bible and especially with the people of the Bible. He evidently worked out written principles for this instruction only from 1917 on. He also told Bible stories to the twelve- to fourteen-year-olds in the so-called 'children's class' on Sundays after the sermon (for those who were even younger there was a Sunday school run by a 'Miss Wilhelm').

And as in Geneva, at the beginning of his time in Safenwil Barth again arranged weekly evening meetings for those who had been confirmed, boys and girls alternately. On the whole he found teaching young people in all these different ways something of a burden which he did not feel himself really capable of bearing. This task was 'always a dreadful worry for me'.[36] Often he stood 'awkwardly in front of bored faces', and usually he 'simply ran out of steam, even in the most well-known things'.[37] 'The kingdom of God simply will not accommodate itself to my teaching methods, whatever stratagems I try.'[38]

Disciplinary problems were the least of Barth's worries in his classes. Once 'a boy left the church in protest, slamming the door behind him', or 'two boys were fighting during my efforts with the story of Athaliah, so I boxed their ears and kicked them out of the church'.[39] But these were the exceptions. Usually Barth got on very well personally with the young. During his first years he liked to hold his confirmation classes out in the open during the summer, instead of in the usual room. Every now and then he also went on walks and excursions with them, and every winter 'to heighten our mutual pleasure' there was also a 'great snowball fight'.[40]

In addition to preaching and teaching Barth was also responsible for holding Bible classes for the congregation during the winter and for giving lectures on the Bible or on church history to the Blue Cross temperance society. The Safenwil schoolroom was packed 'on the best days of my Blue Cross agitation period, when I used to tell the story of David and Goliath'.[41] At that time the Blue Cross had a considerable membership in Safenwil (as in the area generally) – this was the time when 'almost half the pastors were abstainers'. Barth, too, was an active member of the Safenwil group and therefore an abstainer: for some years he was even its president. Years later he abandoned abstinence again, and then learnt to his amusement that 'in the Blue Cross, theologians who are no longer abstainers are called "back-to-the-bottlers"'.[42] For a while he also acted as conductor of the large Blue Cross choir, where he directed proudly and with aplomb the singing of all the 'Idas, Röslis, Emmas and company'.[43] On one occasion at least they were able to perform Mozart's *Ave Verum Corpus*. He went visiting less often and when he did, he tended to pay a large number of visits all together, and then stop for a while. Occasionally the church committee asked him to go visiting more often.[44] But he thought that he could not expect much from 'an increased frequency of these encounters'.[45] In addition to Safenwil, his pastoral responsibilities also extended to the scattered communities of Rothacker and Walterswil, which lay on the other side of the nearby canton boundary, in Solothurn. He was always anxious to work closely with his church committee, a group which in Safenwil consisted of six lay people who shared the responsibility for looking after the church with the pastor. According to Aargau custom Barth never functioned as its president, but from 1911–19 he acted as its secretary, and was principally responsible for recording the minutes of its meetings. It was his desire and aim that the meetings should have some 'real content', with 'conversations about the good God and his relationship to the people of Safenwil', while questions about 'new tiles on the parsonage and so on were kept in the background as far as possible'.[46] He was delighted when the church committee later began to have lectures on Calvin, Zwingli, etc., at their meetings. Sometimes he went on excursions and outings with them in a horse-drawn carriage. From time to time he also arranged lectures in the church, and after his marriage his wife Nelly provided musical interludes. Sometimes even Barth himself joined in.

As village pastor he was often involved in some strange sidelines. In 1911–12 he undertook to give domestic science courses on personal hygiene and book-keeping. By way of a private joke he used the names of his friends and theological teachers for the examples he gave – e.g. 'stock held by the baker Julius Kaftan', etc. For a number of years he was also one of the school governors, and even became chairman of the board. In this capacity he succeeded, among other things, in introducing sports for girls.

In all these spheres Barth worked as pastor of the Reformed Church of the district. However, some of the Reformed inhabitants of Safenwil did not go to the services in the local church; they had attached themselves to a pietistic community called 'Albrecht's Brethren', which had been formed under American influence; they held services of their own in the 'chapel'. From time to time a preacher came out to them from Zofingen. Here Barth encountered the problem of pietism in a specific form, and in the course of time the group became his direct opponents. There were only a few Catholics in Safenwil, and they had to go elsewhere for mass. There was a 'Roman Catholic' village in the area, Rothacker, and Barth had many contacts with the priest there during this period. He was called

Grolimund: 'He was not very progressive, but he was a pious man, and we had many conversations. We talked about the Council of Trent and about the controversy between Rome and the Reformation', and also 'about mysticism, socialism and celibacy'. Thus this Catholic colleague 'had at least one important function: for the first time he brought me into living contact with Roman Catholicism'.[47] Both pastors kept in touch with each other right until their old age.

At quite an early stage, Barth's theological interest was largely concentrated on, and thus reduced to, his parish work, and he became less and less inclined to pursue his own course of research along the lines of liberal theology. In his view, one sub-conscious reason for this may have been an event which took place right at the beginning of his time in Aargau: 'The death of my father, which took place in 1912, may have been a contributory factor.'[48] His father died suddenly, from blood-poisoning, on Sunday 25 February; he was only fifty-five years old. Shortly before, he had given lectures in Berlin and Berne and the previous autumn had ordained his second son to the pastorate. 'This last period, in particular, had been extremely peaceful for him, in the bosom of his family.'[49] Karl hastened to his father's death-bed immediately after his Sunday sermon. 'He said farewell to his loved ones peacefully. One of his last remarks which we could hear, spoken as though to students in a lecture room, was: "The main thing is not scholarship, nor learning, nor criticism, but to love the Lord Jesus. We need a living relationship with God, and we must ask the Lord for that." '[50] At his funeral three days later, his friend Karl Marti, who represented a very different theological trend, praised Fritz Barth as 'an outstanding teacher, an excellent scholar and an admirable colleague'. Karl himself gave a moving sermon in Safenwil the following Sunday on the occasion of his father's death. And it may well be said that only from this point on did he really begin to see and to understand what his father stood for, since during his student days he had had many reservations about his views. Three years later he had a psychoanalytical conversation with a cousin of C. G. Jung, in which 'a splendid father-complex was brought to light'.[51]

. . . and comrade

There was something else which even more markedly lessened Barth's interest in the way of doing theology which he had once welcomed so vigorously. 'My interest in theology as such continued to be nourished by eager reading of the *Christliche Welt, Zeitschrift für Theologie und Kirche*, the works of Troeltsch, etc., but in the industrial village of Safenwil it had to give place to other things. 'My position in the community led me to be involved in socialism, and especially in the trade union movement.'[52] 'Class warfare, which was going on in my parish, before my very eyes, introduced me almost for the first time to the real problems of real life. The result of this was that my main study was now directed towards factory legislation, insurance, trade union affairs and so on, and my energies were taken up in disputes sparked off by my support for the workers, not only in the neighbourhood but in the canton.' So specialist theological books now gave way to books on economics: 'I had to read Herkner and Sombart (which in fact he had already bought in Marburg in 1908), and also the Swiss *Trade Union Journal* and the *Textile Worker.*'[53]

According to statistics from the year 1920, at this time 587 of the 780 wage-earners in Safenwil were employed in industrial work.[54] A small number of workers had employment outside the village, but the majority worked in Safenwil itself in Hochuli's knitting mill or in the factories owned by the Hüssy family, which was highly respected in the church as well as in the civic community: they owned a weaving mill and dye works and a sawmill. Here the workers were paid extremely low wages, and as they were not organized into a trade union they could do hardly anything to protect themselves. For the young pastor of Safenwil, the obvious thing to do was to come to their aid with theoretical instruction and practical support, and to give them advice about organized action. Here, of course, he had in mind the example of his father, who as early as 1894 had publicly pointed out the 'great and severe' social 'emergency' and had issued a challenge to 'change what has to be changed'.[55]

Barth began to give lectures to the 'Workers' Association' in the old school at Safenwil as early as October 1911. At first his approach was far too academic: he even introduced them to Cohen. However, he soon learnt from experience. 'The people here simply do not understand academic discussions of socialism . . . All they think of is local conditions . . . and they judge everything that one says in these terms . . . *Occasionally* a well-aimed shot which shakes the people is of some use. On the whole, however, it is better to wait until something *specific* comes up . . . Then all at once more light dawns on them than from a hundred sermons on social affairs . . . But one mustn't loose off at random, which is what I have done here several times' – with marked lack of success.[56]

The first lectures dealt with 'Human Rights and Civic Duty', 'Religion and Society' and the slogan 'Earn, Work, Live' (given in April 1912 in Fahrwangen). A lecture on 'Jesus Christ and the Social Movement' which was given on 17 December 1911 was published immediately in the socialist daily *Free Aargau*.

In it, Barth drew a contrast between the church, which for 1800 years had failed to deal with social needs, and Jesus Christ as the partisan of the poor, for whom there had been 'only one God, in solidarity with society', and according to whom one 'has to be a comrade to be a man at all'. True socialism was the true Christianity for our time. However, true socialism was not what the socialists were doing but what Jesus was doing. This was also the socialists' ultimate aim (but only their aim). Barth did not say all this in order to win the workers over to the church. How could he? 'Jesus is not the church'; indeed, with its 'pie in the sky' attitude towards material needs, the church was opposed to Jesus Christ. Barth spoke as he did, rather, because he believed that the kingdom of God was close to the poor and that Jesus identified himself with them. In this sense, 'the real significance of the person of Jesus can be summed up in the two words "social movement"'. Therefore 'the spirit which counts before God is the social spirit'.

Here Barth spoke so provocatively that the manufacturer Walter Hüssy immediately reacted by making a sharp attack on him in which he sought to ridicule the pastor as an ignorant idealist. However, Barth's equally clear 'Answer to the open letter of Herr W. Hüssy of Aarburg' (of 9 February 1912) demonstrated how well up Barth already was in this material. Shortly afterwards, anonymous correspondents also joined in the discussion, and on 13 February the president of the Safenwil church committee, Gustav Hüssy, a cousin of Walter Hüssy, sent in his immediate resignation in protest against Barth's attitude. There was also criticism from Marburg, where the lecture had become known, of the 'superficiality' of Barth's theology!

However, this opposition did nothing to deter Barth from his active support for the cause of the workers. For 'I regard socialist demands as an important part of the application of the gospel, though I also believe that they cannot be realized without the gospel.'[57] Barth so wanted to play a special part in the answer to these demands that he supported the workers with political schooling and instruction. Here his aim was 'to explain the people's cause to them in accordance with our better understanding and to make them take it to heart, at the same time, of course, illuminating its deeper presuppositions and their further consequences'. From the beginning, a characteristic feature of Barth's involvement in industrial questions was his refusal either to force socialism on the church or to attempt to give it a religious hue. Another characteristic of his position was that on the one hand he attempted to 'lead the socialists out beyond themselves'[58] (in the direction of those 'deeper presuppositions and further consequences') and on the other he showed them what could be done in practice about a particular situation. In his ethical counselling he wanted to prevent them from being diverted from their problems into the welter of bourgeois associations (which were so prized in the Aargau). At the time, however, he did not want them to carry on their necessary fight for a better righteousness, say, in the name of nothing more than a new egoism. Barth also saw a clear connection between the problems of the workers and alcoholism. Thus under his leadership the Safenwil 'Blues' sometimes acted in conjunction with the 'Reds'. Barth also saw the connection between the social question and that of militarism. This is indicated by his 'Dissenting view on Military Aircraft' (14 March 1913). Here, he dissociated himself clearly from the naive pacifism of the socialists of that time. It was impossible to be a half-hearted pacifist, and anyone who felt that war might still be a necessary evil could not suddenly shrink from using even aeroplanes. 'War is war.' He also kept up with the German Social Democrat Party from a distance: 'I was well aware of August Bebel and old Liebknecht, and saw the prophetic cloud hovering over the German Social Democrats before it disappeared.'[59] It was no coincidence that as early as spring 1913 Barth was regarded as a possible Social Democrat candidate for the Great Council. However, when the president of the Safenwil Workers' Association pressed him to become a party member that June, he thought hard and then said no. This fitted in with everything that he said during the course of this year in a series of sermons on the book of Amos.

His wedding took place in the midst of these activities and preoccupations. Meanwhile Barth had seen little of his fiancée, but he had carried on a lively correspondence with her. In 1912 her mother had returned to Zürich from Geneva, and Nelly herself had spent June to October of the same year in England as governess in the family of an army officer. She and Karl were married on 27 March 1913 in the

Nydegg Church in Berne, at the wish of the Hoffmann family. Barth's friends Thurneysen and Spoendlin also took part in the celebrations, which were 'on a modest scale and with relatively few guests'.[60] The couple went on a short honeymoon to Lugano and Milan. Barth found that in some respects his marriage had suddenly changed his life. 'With its gentle pressure, marriage sets to work on so many of the bristly features which are man's by nature and helps to suppress them . . . Moreover one is stimulated and helped in all kinds of good things: a wife gives loving criticism of sermons and speeches and is a spur to academic work; she is an extension of one's own work, looking after the girls' post-confirmation evenings, the mission classes, and so on.'[61] On a later occasion Nelly even held a political meeting for women. Her husband recognized that she was a wife 'who helps me to see things and to bear them'.[62] Barth's life was changed further when a year later, on 13 April 1914, he became the father of a daughter, Franziska Nelly ('Fränzeli').

Soon after the wedding, he had to devote himself to the preparation of a lecture on 'Belief in the Personal God', which he then delivered to the Aargau Pastors' Association at Lenzburg on 19 May. In this lecture he once again proved himself to be not only a product of nineteenth-century theology but also a man with an intimate knowledge of it.

He sought to demonstrate two things: first, that the different conceptions of God as a personal being and as absolute being were to be understood as the expression of different kinds of 'religious experience', namely the experience of the infinite value of the soul and of the supra-personal 'kingdom of God' respectively. He also sought to demonstrate that these two conceptions probably could not be *thought of* together, but that precisely because of religious experience they had to be held together.

Barth evidently sought here to reconcile his Marburg insights (under the keywords 'personality' and 'soul') with his new socialist discoveries (under the keyword 'kingdom of God'). Of course the liberals took the lecture as grist to their mill. And Barth asked himself whether his next move should not be to produce a 'philosophy of religion'. But this never came about.

Thurneysen and other friends

A few days after this lecture, on 1 June, Barth walked over to

Leutwil, where Eduard Thurneysen was being installed as pastor. His revered teacher Paul Wernle was also there. For the previous two years Thurneysen had been working in the Glockenhof at Zürich as a YMCA secretary. 'We met again in Aargau . . . as young village pastors.'[63] They already knew each other from student days. Only now, however, did the two become close friends. 'At this time I had countless anxious conversations' with Thurneysen.[64] 'Our villages were separated by several high ridges and valleys.'[65] Now there was some regular and rapid 'walking to and fro along the Friesenweg between the two places'. 'The first to shake their heads weren't either Jülicher or Harnack, but at best the inhabitants of Holziken and Schöftland as they looked down the road and saw the two strange wanderers between two worlds.'[66]

At that time Barth was able to cover the considerable distance 'in two and a half hours each way'.[67] He went even faster 'on my trusty bicycle'.[68] Barth was one of the first pastors in the canton to own one. He liked to set off so early that sometimes he arrived in Leutwil 'in time for a breakfast drink, very hot and shiny. Then we began to talk and brood a lot; sometimes we would mock other people and laugh at them. We would smoke a variety of cigars. We called it "digging, boring, knocking, ringing" – and indeed there was something of that sort about it. Then the next Sunday we went on even more vehemently, far above the heads of the astonished people of the Aargau: "God is, God counts, God wants" – until Epprecht and Schild (neighbouring colleagues) willy-nilly became our first theological audience . . . The Hallwilersee called from afar and the cocks crew and the sun shone kindly on the whole scene and looked down on us.'[69] 'Thus the old parsonage in Leutwil, which has now vanished off the face of the earth, became the scene of innumerable conversations about how to carry on our ministry: especially about our sermons and about the church in general and its task in the world. We did not know what great changes were in store at that very time. We only knew that we had to look for decisive, compelling words, more substantial than those which we heard around us. And we knew that we could no longer do theology in the traditional style of the discipline. So even then in Leutwil we were saying "no" in a great many directions.'[70]

'We walked untiringly backwards and forwards to meet each other, but that was not enough. We had an irresistible need to be real brothers, to share our thoughts about everything that was going on, as we used to say at the time, in the church, the world and the kingdom of God. And because we had no telephones in our parsonages . . . we began a lively correspondence which was carried on almost week by week.'[71] The whole correspondence between the two friends amounts to about a thousand letters. 'Our language at that time was rich, not to say over-rich, in images of every kind; military metaphors, especially those taken from artillery, played a decisive role . . . You must understand that as we were at war with the world during those years such metaphors flowed almost automatically from our pens.'[72]

Barth did not think that he was the dominant partner in the correspondence between Leutwil and Safenwil. 'It would be wrong to suppose that I was the one who provided the stimulus or made the contribution and that Thurneysen was simply the one who had to be prodded, the one on the receiving end.'[73] 'All my personal impressions of him can be summed up in the word *openness* . . . Thurneysen has the rare gift of being able to learn from others and, moreover, to learn from a person just what is worth learning from him. He then brings it alive in his own way. However, he is hardly ready to settle for well-defined positions or trends. If you are looking for his views it is no use expecting them always to be once and for all in one particular place. For all his decisiveness, he is a volatile man, and is always apt to spring surprises over points of detail . . . He gets on with people in an astonishing way. He can put himself in their place, walk with them and help them by understanding them (though from a more lofty vantage point and in a transfiguring light). He shares their sorrow or their joy. The very evident criticism which he brings to bear on them is almost always a radical, immanent criticism which is constructive by being comforting, helpful and friendly . . . His study and indeed his view of the church and the world is like Noah's ark: all kinds of animals can enter and leave again, saved for the time being, under the sign of the rainbow which binds heaven and earth together.'[74] Barth treasured his friend as he was, and even thought that 'he devoted special pastoral care to me'.[75] And in his own way Thurneysen was indeed a stimulus to Barth, and gave him a great deal.

Thurneysen also helped and stimulated Barth by being able to introduce him to the large circle of interesting friends and acquaintances who had been attracted by his open nature. For example there were Rudolf Pestalozzi, businessman and owner of an ironware business, and his wife Gerty, née Eidenbenz. In their years of travel both of these had come into contact with the Christian Socialist movement – in different ways, but both in England. When he returned to Zürich, Pestalozzi had found an understanding friend at the YMCA there in the person of Thurneysen. 'Through him he came to Religious Socialist conferences. As a first lieutenant in the Swiss army and a businessman, he seemed rather out of place. But he joined in. He was interested, and it aroused his interest.' Through Thurneysen, Pestalozzi then became friendly with Karl Barth. From that time on 'Ruedi' played more and more of an indispensable role in Barth's life: he supported him in many ways, listened to him and talked with him, acted as host, gave financial help, accompanied him on journeys and even acted as photographer. He was by no means poor. But Barth found that the way in which he used and gave away his money 'strengthened faith in the best sense of the term'. 'Indeed, in the hands of people like Pestalozzi money all at once became something different.'[76] Barth had an equally faithful friend in Pestalozzi's wife, who had an impressive 'delight in helping' and 'an inexhaustible gift of receiving and passing on information about every kind of new life-style, from Lucci-Purtscher and Bircher-Benner to Tolstoy and Gandhi'.[77]

Another person with whom Barth came into closer contact through Thurneysen was the Basle theologian Paul Wernle, who belonged to the history of religions school (1875–1936). It is hard to exaggerate the 'degree to which Wernle, through his brilliance in books and articles, held the attention of all Switzerland and influenced it in one way or the other'. This man, 'as *the* representative of modern theology at that time . . . meant a great deal to me'.[78] Barth corresponded with him and visited him in Basle. Indeed soon he began to provoke him, and found him all the more interesting as an opponent. He regretted their failure to arrive at an understanding. 'How much we could have had from him if he had simply been prepared to be a little more understanding . . . There is only a thin wall between him and us; I can clearly hear him knocking on the other side, but I no longer believe that we shall be able to get through to each other.'[79]

Another person whom Barth also got to know through Thurneysen at that time was to prove a much more positive stimulus. This was Hermann Kutter, who was then fifty years old (1863–1931). He had obtained his doctorate in Berne in 1896 and in so doing had come into close contact with Fritz Barth. Since 1898 he had worked as pastor in the Neumünster congregation in Zürich. Thurneysen knew him from his work there, and as pastor of Leutwil he soon introduced Barth to Kutter and his work.[80] The two of them visited Kutter in his house in Zollikerstrasse, and they also went to his sermons and especially to his children's classes. Kutter paid return visits to the Aargau. There were many long conversations, which could last all day. Kutter completely dominated them by the 'molten lava of his eloquence', 'like an uncanny volcano'.[81] Barth was 'amazed at his astonishing intelligence and mental powers'. 'Breathing fire, he thunders away about trenches and grenade throwers.'[82] Barth acknowledged that he had been stimulated in a crucial way by Hermann Kutter.[83] 'From Kutter I simply learnt to speak the great word "God" seriously, responsibly and with a sense of its importance.'[84] 'When he preached, and indeed in private conversation, he could impress on one that this was a deadly serious matter, which could not be taken lightly.'[85] And it was this 'prophetic thinker and preacher . . . who at that time, with a force unrivalled by any of his contemporaries, represented the insight that the sphere of God's power really is greater than the sphere of the church and that from time to time it has pleased God, and still pleases him, to warn and to comfort his church through the figures and the events of secular world history. Kutter said this above all in his earlier books: *Sie Müssen* (You Must, 1903), *Gerechtigkeit* (Righteousness, 1905) and *Wir Pfarrer* (We Pastors, 1907), with particular reference to the Social Democracy of the pre-War period.'[86] However, at that time Barth could still find little in the heavy style ('blaring') in which he presented this insight.

Through Kutter, Barth in turn came in contact with a whole group whose searching and thinking was along similar lines. At that time, in fact, a series of other Swiss theologians had given a particularly surprising twist 'to the "struggle for the kingdom of God" by endorsing and affirming the eschatology and the hope of the Social Democrat workers' movement, setting it up against the church, theology and Christianity. They saw it as the realization for our time of the faith which Jesus had not found in Israel.'[87] One of the most prominent and influential figures among those who thought and acted in this way at the time was Leonhard Ragaz (1868–1945). He put forward and disseminated this view of the 'kingdom of God' from 1902 onwards as the pastor of Basle cathedral (Eduard Thurneysen came to occupy the same position in 1927), and from 1908 he held a theological chair in Zürich (though he resigned it in 1921, the very year in which Barth became a professor, in order to devote himself completely to social and peace work). It was through the influence of Kutter, and decisively through that of Ragaz, that the Religious Socialist movement developed in Switzerland in 1906. Its journal *Neue Wege* (New Ways) began to appear in the same year.

This movement saw itself as the consummation of the dominant trends in church and theology, and took a stand against both the 'positives' and the 'liberals' of the time. As such it found increasing approval and support in Switzerland. In Barth's view, 'although "Religious Socialism" was also prompted by the younger Christoph Blumhardt's message of hope, by virtue of its critical and polemical presentation it was already a characteristically Swiss movement.'[88] Albert Schädelin, Barth's Berne friend, was also a committed member of the movement: 'He was a fiery character, critical and always on the go, yet as long as I knew him he was always concerned to be constructive. He was part of the bedrock in my own life . . . Thinking of him always seemed to me like looking at a safe stronghold.'[89] He was 'probably one of the first to listen to Hermann Kutter at that time and urged the rest of us to hear him. Later, of course, he was also one of the first to want to stand on his own feet in the face of Kutter's blast.' 'But . . . there were also Hans Bader, Emanuel Tischhauser, Karl von Greyerz and so many others, each with his characteristic ideas and passions. While outwardly they seemed to form a unity and indeed did so, the effect of their coming together turned many conferences into lively encounters, which then gave rise to numerous conversations in small groups or wider circles. Any young Swiss pastor of the time who wasn't asleep, or didn't live somewhere on the other side of the moon, or hadn't been corrupted in some way, was a Religious Socialist in the narrower or the wider sense. We were vehemently anti-bourgeois (we were better at knowing what we were against than what we were for). This was the time when a sceptic (Heinrich Barth!) wrote a verse about me and my activity in my village in Aargau:

'And the kingdom of God can be found,
not only in power but in sound.'[90]

Apart from its publications, the chief activity of the movement was its conferences. At the time they were rated very highly. Barth also took part in them, read *Neue Wege* and talked with the various heads of the movement. Without doubt his contact with Religious Socialism helped to confirm, clarify and further his theological search and his socialist involvement. But once again he could not completely identify himself with Religious Socialism. 'Ragaz and his Religious Socialists interested Thurneysen, and they interested me too. But I kept my distance.'[91] For, as the two of them somehow felt with some uneasiness from the beginning, 'Leonhard Ragaz developed what Kutter meant to be a view of the current situation and an interpretation of the signs of the time, not a programme, into the theory that the church must regard socialism as a preliminary manifestation of the kingdom of God. In other words, he made it a true system of "Religious Socialism".'[92] It was against this systematic approach among the Religious Socialists that Barth and Thurneysen reacted.

Another place for meeting and discussion to which Barth and Thurneysen went every year was the Aarau Student Conference. Since about 1910, the lectures and debates held there had shown a marked shift towards the 'practical and social questions of the present'.[93] 'This was the hey-day of the Aarau Conference, with all the dogmatic theologians and prophets, regular and irregular, who were brought from far and near to speak there.'[94] There, Barth had listened to lectures by leading representatives of what was still modern theology, like Wilhelm Herrmann, Ernst Troeltsch, Johannes Weiss, Theodor Häring and Paul Wernle, the philosopher Rudolf Eucken and the educationalist Paul Häberlin – and also to Heinrich Lhotzky, Johannes Müller and Friedrich Wilhelm Foerster, to Adolf Schlatter and to his own father, Fritz Barth. Now, however, it was the Religious Socialists who increasingly came forward to the speaker's desk – including representatives of what was then the youngest generation: the German Emil Fuchs, Albert Schädelin from Berne, Lukas Christ and Ernst Stähelin from Basle or even Barth's cousin, Albert Barth, from Schaffhausen.

Barth treasured the three March days in Aarau as a good opportunity for friendly conversations. He already knew a large number of those present from his school days and his time as a student, and from Zofingia. He also met a considerable number of them at the Religious Socialist conferences. Other members of his family were also very active there. He made contact with younger students and discovered new acquaintances and friends. Emil Brunner went there from Zürich, and Gottfried Ludwig, who was later to be so faithful a friend, from Berne (he was later pastor in Biel). Above all, Barth became more closely acquainted with a group of people from Basle – again partly through Thurneysen, who came from there. These included the lawyer Max Gerwig, who as central president of Zofingia took up 'the struggle for social renewal' in 1914[95] and at one point was to be Barth's colleague at Basle University; also Fritz Hoch and Walter Steiger, who were theological students. In addition, there were figures who have already been mentioned: Alphons Koechlin, Thurneysen's classmate Gottlob Wieser, Lukas Christ from Basle, who was 'reliable in his own fashion',[96] and Ernst Stähelin, Kutter's son-in-law and later a church historian at Basle, of whose studies and researches Barth had great expectations.

There were all kinds of further opportunities for meeting and discussion. There were other conferences to make pilgrimages to. And visits were exchanged between parsonages. Those involved did not hesitate to make long journeys on foot. So Karl Barth was often on the road here and there, and in turn entertained many visitors. Above all, however, he loved 'Kränzli', informal meetings of like-minded pastors in small and sometimes intimate groups in various places. These consisted of discussions of biblical texts, of members' sermons and of 'the situation' generally. While Barth shrank from official pastors' meetings, he was very concerned to 'win sympathy with the pastors wherever we can' in this informal way.[97]

Of course all these many contacts were the richest possible stimulus for Karl Barth. Various public statements which he made at that time in addition to his normal pastoral duties show his interests in the period immediately before the First World War and the matters which were of concern to him. On 24 August 1913 he held an abstainers' conference in Safenwil, and invited Lukas Christ to speak at it. He wrote an article against a Dr J. Kreyenbuhl, who had argued that Jesus must have been a legendary figure because of his abnormal personal characteristics. Barth countered that the great 'geniuses' still seem to be abnormal to the mediocre, whereas they are in fact the ones who are normal! He commented on the Aargau synod of Autumn 1913 in the newspaper *Basler Nachrichten* with the biting words, 'Nothing, nothing, nothing'. Apart from his ministry, however, his chief concern was with socialism, 'so that by degrees I could come to some understanding of it'. This gradually made his name known outside his own district, so he increasingly had the opportunity of appearing 'here and there as visiting preacher',[98] and could be heard talking about socialism in all kinds of sports centres, schoolrooms and restaurants. For example, on 1 November he spoke at the 'Grütli Association' (moderately socialist) in Entfelden, arguing that Switzerland, having achieved national and political democracy, should go on to achieve *'social* democracy'.

In connection with his work in the Safenwil 'Workers' Association' during the winter of 1913–14 Barth produced for his own use an extensive dossier on the 'workers' question'. In the new year he spoke there on 'The Gospel and Socialism' and 'The New Factory Act'. In 1914, as president of the Aargau Committee (which in fact consisted only of himself and his wife) he was involved in action against casinos; this was yet one more aspect of his concern with social questions (he was also still active in this connection in 1920). In a sermon in June about the Berne Exhibition, which was published at the same time in *Neue Wege,* he declared that 'the evil' of capitalism was the consequence of a world without God. He contrasted this with the Christian hope of a new world, brought into being by the 'living God'. In July, in both a lecture in Safenwil and a contribution to the *Christliche Welt,* he embarked on a criticism of Friedrich Naumann; he objected that because of his compromises Naumann no longer looked longingly for something better, 'beyond war and capitalism'. 'We should expect more of God.'[99]

In his sermons – and during 1914 he preached two long series on Romans 1.16 and Matthew 6.33 – he was particularly preoccupied with the question of God in the manner of the sermon mentioned above.

'In every sermon I must always be particularly careful when I get to the word "God".' 'The little phrase "God is" amounts to a revolution.' 'For heaven's sake' we must not confuse God's concern with the church 'or with other good and necessary efforts'. It must always have complete priority: *'First* God's concern, *then* ours.' If there were people who were 'completely serious about God all along the line', social problems would be solved. 'Socialism is a very important and necessary application of the gospel.' Jesus is the man who was quite serious about God: 'He lived in God.' For that reason he is 'the beginning of a human life' which triumphs over distress.[100]

The outbreak of the First World War

On 1 August 1914, the First World War broke out. As a large number of people from Safenwil were called up to guard the frontier (but not, to his regret, their pastor), Barth helped farming families for weeks on end with haymaking. Still, on a number of occasions, armed with a rifle, he joined the 'home guard' and spent nights on duty. He immediately set up a reading room in the parsonage for the soldiers stationed in Safenwil. However, this was the least part of his reaction to the war, the outbreak of which shook him and disturbed him to the depths of his being. 'In 1914 the whole world was preoccupied with the outbreak of war. I felt obliged to let the war rage through all my sermons, until finally a woman came up to me and asked me for once to talk about something else.'[101] From then on the war did not appear so directly in his sermons, but Karl Barth certainly continued 'to think about it and agonize over it at a distance. I was particularly involved because of my connections with Germany, but they did not shape my views!'[102] Above all, another event on the day war broke out set him off on a highly critical train of thought which led him to change his views radically.

On that very day 'ninety-three German intellectuals issued a terrible manifesto, identifying themselves before all the world with the war policy of Kaiser Wilhelm II and Chancellor Bethmann-Hollweg. For me it was almost worse than the violation of Belgian neutrality. And to my dismay, among the signatories I discovered the names of almost all my German teachers (with the honourable exception of Martin Rade).'[103] 'It was like the twilight of the gods when I saw the reaction of Harnack, Herrmann, Rade, Eucken and company to the new situation', and discovered how religion and scholarship could be changed completely, 'into intellectual 42 cm cannons'.[104] As a result, Barth did not know what to make of 'the teaching of all my theological masters in Germany. To me they seemed to have been hopelessly compromised by what I regarded as their failure in the face of the ideology of war.'[105] Their 'ethical failure' indicated that 'their exegetical and dogmatic presuppositions could not be in order'.[106] Thus 'a whole world of exegesis, ethics, dogmatics and preaching, which I had hitherto held to be essentially trustworthy, was shaken to the foundations, and with it, all the other writings of the German theologians.'[107] Barth made his protest against this failure that same August in a private letter to

Martin Rade, who had been relatively restrained. In it he attacked Christian endorsement of the war and 'the "experience" of war as a religious argument', as he put it in a sharp 'question' to Wilhelm Herrmann in November.[108] Without obtaining Barth's consent, Rade had the letter to him published by Ragaz in *Neue Wege*. At the beginning of January 1915 Barth was able to express his hesitations personally to Rade in Berne – the French pastor and Religious Socialist Elie-Joël Gounelle was also present at the time. Now, however, Barth's criticism soon began to develop and extend to nineteenth-century theology generally, as far back as Schleiermacher: 'He was unmasked. In a decisive way all the theology expressed in the manifesto and everything that followed it (even in the *Christliche Welt*) proved to be founded and governed by him.'[109]

For Barth the outbreak of the World War was 'a double madness',[110] involving not only his theological teachers but also European socialism. 'From *Sie Müssen* we had more or less definitely expected that socialism would prove to be a kind of hammer of God, yet all along the national war fronts we saw it swinging into line.'[111] Surely it was not long since 'in the cathedral in Basle the socialists of all lands had solemnly assured each other and the world that they would be able to offer effective resistance to the outbreak of any new war.'[112] And what happened instead? 'The apostasy of the party',[113] and in particular the 'failure of German Social Democracy in the face of the ideology of war'.[114] 'Many of us were completely flabbergasted. Our bold criticism began to recoil on us. We observed that there was a new public and a readiness for further insights.'[115]

However, despite his criticism of Social Democracy, at this point Karl Barth declared his solidarity with the Social Democrats (this was typical of him!); unlike Thurneysen, he became a party member. He joined on 26 January 1915. From then on the Safenwil workers called him 'comrade pastor'. Because in the pulpit 'I set such emphasis Sunday by Sunday on the last things, I could no longer remain suspended in the clouds above the present evil world. I had to demonstrate that faith in the Greatest does not exclude work and suffering in the realm of the imperfect, but includes them.' Conversely, Barth took this step in the hope that as a result he would avoid becoming 'unfaithful to our "essential" orientation, as might well have happened to me two or three years earlier'.[116] Thus Barth ventured to show outward solidarity only when he thought 'that now I can offer even my Social Democrat friends something better than I could before, where I stood alongside them'.[117] Nevertheless, 'I was now liberal in such a way that in contrast to the liberals there I could become a Social Democrat; they called me "the red pastor of Safenwil". But that didn't bother me. Today, of course, there would be nothing remarkable about it. But at that time it was a "bad" thing to be a Social Democrat. People called you a Bolshevik' – even in Aargau, indeed especially there. 'With the exception of a few resolute figures, the Aargau Workers' Party was hardly a dangerous enclave of the red International.'[118]

At the beginning of February Barth again paid a brief visit to Berne to explain his reasons for joining the party to his mother, who was disturbed about it. At the same time his brother Peter, now a pastor in Laupen, joined the 'Helvetic Association'. Karl remonstrated that people should first seek the kingdom of God and should not found special (e.g. patriotic) associations to achieve the 'other things' ('Good heavens, patriotism is not a political principle').[119]

Barth gave his first lecture as a new party member on 14 February 1915 in Zofingen. It was on 'War, Socialism and Christianity'.

He made it clear that since war had broken out, both Christianity and socialism were in need of 'reformation' and that each required the other. 'A real Christian must become a socialist (if he is to be in earnest about the reformation of Christianity!). A real socialist must be a Christian if he is in earnest about the reformation of socialism.'

In a similar vein, during the spring and summer he spoke about 'Christ and Social Democracy' (in Seon), 'The Future of Social Democracy in Switzerland' and 'What does it mean to be a Socialist?' His answer to the last question was that a socialist is one who is a socialist at heart. He also said that there was no question of improving man *before* improving his living standards or *vice versa:* the two things had to happen together and simultaneously. And before Barth's radical 'comrade' Willi Münzenberg came to see him in Safenwil he was told: you mustn't preach against the church here!

Meeting with Christoph Blumhardt

Meanwhile Barth also continued to be strongly affected by the confusion into which theology, socialism and thus his own previous thinking had been thrown as a result of the war. 'The need for me to preach proved a very healthy corrective and stimulus in the development of my ideas . . . Above all, it has become increasingly clear to me that what we need is something beyond all morality and politics and ethics. These are constantly forced into compromises with "reality" and therefore have no saving power in themselves. This is true even of so-called Christian morality and so-called socialist politics.'[120] 'In the midst of this hopeless confusion, it was the message of the two Blumhardts with its orientation on Christian hope which above all began to make sense to me. I owe my acquaintance with it to my friend Eduard Thurneysen.'[121] True, Barth had visited Bad Boll a couple of times as a student; but Thurneysen had 'the great advantage over him in knowing the younger Blumhardt personally'. He had come to know him well in his schooldays, when the Blumhardts were visitors to the family home. Now Thurneysen introduced his friend at Safenwil not only to Blumhardt's ideas[122] but also to Bad Boll and to Christoph Blumhardt himself. Here Blumhardt prayed and had pastoral conversations with the various pilgrims who hastened there.

In April 1915 Barth went with Thurneysen to wartime Germany: first, of course, to Marburg, where on 9 April his brother Peter married Martin Rade's daughter Helene. As a result Karl Barth was brought even closer to this Marburg celebrity ('Uncle Rade'); for all his strong reservations he was compelled to respect more and more the way in which Rade 'has watchfully and openly and readily gone along with everyone and everything in his own particular way, suffering and struggling through with them'.[123] At the wedding Barth also met Rade's father-in-law Friedrich Naumann (whose son-in-law was in turn Karl Barth's good friend Wilhelm Loew). 'When I met him, I had the impression, in contrast to his books and articles, which were written with imperturbable assurance, of a man who was not so sure of his affairs, because his secret awareness was beyond anything that he could express. At any rate, this uncertainty was the best thing about him.' However, 'his writings now fell short of his best insights'. Barth had a passionate argument with him, over a glass of beer, because Naumann said, in these very words, 'All religion is right for us . . . whether it is called the Salvation Army or Islam, provided that it helps us to hold out through the war.'[124] There could be no further progress along the lines of a Christian theology which still took itself so lightly.

Barth himself stayed in Bad Boll from 10–15 April. Here 'I was in the strange position of bringing Blumhardt greetings from

Naumann, probably the last he received. Naumann understood Blumhardt best when he was in a hurry and anxious to get on; not so well when it was a matter of waiting and listening. The unique feature, indeed the prophetic feature (and I use the word deliberately), in Blumhardt's message and mission was in the way in which the hurrying and the waiting, the worldly and the divine, the present and the future, met, were united, kept supplementing one another, seeking and finding one another.'[125] Barth heard a meditation of Blumhardt's (on 'Peace be with you') and had long conversations with him at this time. The way in which Blumhardt combined an active and eager search for signs and 'breakthroughs' of the kingdom of God with a tranquil, patient 'waiting' on God, and the decisive action which he alone could perform, was evidently important for Barth. Even more important was the fundamental connection in Blumhardt's thought between knowledge of God and the Christian hope for the future; through this he learnt to understand God afresh as the radical renewer of the world who is at the same time himself completely and utterly new. For Barth this could be – and had to be – the starting point for further developments.

Soon after his return he began to read Zündel's book on the older Blumhardt. He found that he was extremely moved by what he had encountered in Bad Boll. 'The new element, the New Testament element, which appeared again in Boll can be summed up in the one word: hope.'[126] By virtue of this hope, almost in isolation from the church, Blumhardt had been able to become a Social Democrat deputy – in the Württemberg assembly in 1900 – but he acted with a great spiritual freedom which particularly impressed Barth at this moment of his life. 'He simply passes over dogmatic and liberal theologians, those interested in religious morality and us socialists. He is friendly, but quite uninvolved. He does not contradict anyone, and no one needs to feel rejected, but at the same time he does not agree with anyone's views . . . I think that he would also have all sorts of things to say about the conflicts and problems which now affect us. But he does not want to say it; it is not important enough, because other things are more important to him.'[127]

Soon after his return, Barth took up the theme of peace in an article. 'It is not the war that disturbs our peace. The war is not even the cause of our unrest. It has merely brought to light the fact that our lives are all based on unrest. And where there is unrest there can be no peace.' But 'God is peace'. And where there is no peace there is no God – 'we do without him'. After his meeting with Blumhardt, a longing began to stir in Barth 'to show himself and others the essentials'.[128] But how? 'It was a time when I battered like a bumble-bee against all the closed windows.'[129] At first those who listened to his sermons merely felt that 'they were *particularly* difficult after my visit to Germany'.[130] Surprisingly enough, the prospect presented to him by the Religious Socialists, who were pulling the movement apart in a great many directions, reinforced his inclination to continue in the same direction the search which he had begun since his discovery of Blumhardt. Kutter and Ragaz were increasingly at odds; and Barth was particularly interested in their argument, which had a fruitful effect on him. The argument, in brief, was this. Kutter put more emphasis on the prophetic knowledge of the 'living God', whereas Ragaz was more concerned with active discipleship along the lines of the Franciscan ideal of poverty. Accordingly, the two sought to exploit the upheaval caused by the First World War in very different directions: Kutter with a summons to tranquil reappraisal, Ragaz with appeals for pacifist action. It was also significant that Kutter never became a Social Democrat, while Ragaz became one as early as 1913. The surprising thing now, however, was that Karl Barth was prompted to look for a way to overcome their differences. 'Isn't it better to strive for the point where Kutter's "no" and Ragaz's "yes", Kutter's radical tranquillity and Ragaz's energetic tackling of problems . . . come together? I believe in the possibility of such a position, even if I cannot describe it at the moment.'[131] At a Religious Socialist meeting in Pratteln at the beginning of September 1915, at which Hans Bader had reported on the difference, Barth realized even more clearly that he was 'always forced to follow Kutter in matters of emphasis' but that he 'could not rule out Ragaz's position on any important issue': 'Ragaz's endeavour to put principles into practice is an indispensable, though secondary, element, in spite of its evident "danger".'[132]

Barth searched. And in this search he found himself right on the fringe of the church. He now found extremely questionable the 'religious workshop in which one is forged as a pastor'. Indeed he even occasionally complained, 'If only one could be something other than a pastor.'[133] He was particularly annoyed at the 'universal spoonful of tolerance which especially in our local church is proclaimed to be the supreme good'.[134] 'Even before the First World War, I ended an account . . . of a cantonal synod held in Aargau which appeared in the *Basler Nachrichten* with the stirring words, "O Aargau, state religion, may God have mercy on you!" A further article which I wrote shortly afterwards to assuage my wrath over the church's up-to-date participation in the Berne Exhibition of 1914 (a stand) was sent back to me "with thanks" by the same paper.'[135] Official pastors' meetings, the 'chapter,' in particular always filled 'me with the greatest unrest and anguish . . . When I want to shout something out in the room, I have neither the voice nor the words, and I hang there wriggling like a roofer on his rope.'[136] On one occasion, however, he did in fact 'shout out in the room': this was at an autumn synod of his district church on 11 November 1915. He put a formal motion to the synod that it should abandon its traditional opening service, in order to demonstrate publicly (this was all Barth was concerned about) 'that everything, above all everything that has to do with the state, is taken a hundred times more seriously than God'.[137]

This was a trenchant criticism of the church. Yet Barth did not make it at a remove from the church; it stemmed from a 'necessary involvement in the church's affairs in the world'.[138] The significant thing about this criticism was the perspective from which it was made, namely that 'God' had to be taken seriously again in quite a different way. For Barth, the question of according God a place of central importance was becoming more and more fundamental. And since he had met Blumhardt, it was very closely connected with the eschatological question of the Christian hope.

It was in this questioning attitude that shortly after the synod, on 15 November, Barth gave a lecture in Basle on 'Wartime and the Kingdom of God', in which he put strong stress on 'the absence of God from secular circles'. Paul Wernle 'summed it up, not unfairly, with the epithet "apocalyptic"'.[139] Nothing new, Barth argued, was to be expected from 'secular circles', among which Barth also included human attempts at reform and even the church: 'The world is the world. But God is God' – the *'but'* is there because new things are to be expected from God. A week later he began a study week in Safenwil on the characteristic theme of 'The Christian Hope'. He opened the series of talks, and as they continued he called in as speakers Thurneysen, his nearby colleagues Robert Epprecht and Paul Schild, and his schoolfriend Ernst von May. Von May, now in the Salvation Army, impressed Barth deeply: 'Confronted with this man I was really ashamed of my bit of inner activity, all my questions about orientation and my bickering. Here was this natural and simple life in the love of God, in which everything was so organic and not at all contrived.'[140]

Meanwhile Barth also continued his activities with the Social Democrats. In the winter of 1915–16 he again 'ran in Safenwil a course on ordinary practical questions (working hours, banking, women's work, etc.) every Tuesday, plundering the dossier on these things which I assembled at one time'. Now, however, he did it 'without enthusiasm, simply because it is necessary and because I cannot yet go on to the one thing necessary for them in the way that it should be done'.[141] In addition, he also gave individual lectures from time to time, in Safenwil or outside. In a lecture at Safenwil on 4 December, on 'Religion and Christianity', he said something more about his involvement in socialism. 'I regard the "political pastor" in any form as a mistake, even if he is a socialist. But as a man and a citizen . . . I take the side of the Social Democrats.' And on 7 December, in a lecture in Baden on 'Religion and Socialism', he spoke in more detail about the critical significance of the kingdom of God:

'I can never find it where money is thought to be more important than people, where possessions continue to be the standard for all values, where in anxiety and pettiness the fatherland is thought more important than humanity and where people believe more and more strongly in the present than in the future.' And in so far as socialism points beyond such a way of thinking, 'Despite all its imperfections – one can talk about them quite calmly and openly – it is to me one of the most encouraging signs that God's kingdom does not stand still and that God is at work.'

In January 1916 Barth spoke on 'Our Attitude to the Church', arguing that this attitude should be critical of the church's 'organization' and 'religion', and in March, in Rohr, on 'The Will of God and the War'. The same March he also spoke on 'The Trade Union Movement' in Berne to a women's conference. His mother, who was keenly interested in all questions to do with women, was also involved in it. A few weeks earlier there had been a stormy argument in his parish between him and the manufacturer Herr Hochuli. It arose from a party to which the manufacturer had invited the confirmation candidates and at which there had been a good deal of drinking. Barth was surprised and scandalized and said what he thought about the party: in the next confirmation class he told his pupils that 'they had now had a taste of hell',[142] and in his sermon of

16 January on Psalm 14.7 he identified the 'captives' with the people of Safenwil under the power of mammon, which was capable of anything.

At the same time, however, Barth was now much more deeply disturbed and preoccupied by an idea which kept taking shape more tangibly: 'We must begin all over again with a new *inner* orientation to the primitive basic truths of life: only this can deliver us from the chaos arising from the failure of conservative or revolutionary proposals and counter-proposals.' At the beginning of 1916 Barth remarked that Ragaz's whole line of questioning was still not radical enough for him. The problem of 'war or peace?', about which there was so much talk and writing, had to give way to the radical and deadly serious problem of faith: 'With God or – as so far – without him? We must resolutely "look for another".'[143] It was with this intention that on the very day, 16 January, on which he caused a furore in Safenwil with his sermon, he gave a lecture in the city church of Aarau on 'The Righteousness of God' in which he tersely declared: 'Above all, it will be a matter of our recognizing God once more as God . . . This is a task alongside which all cultural, social and patriotic duties are child's play.'[144]

Barth showed that he was taking this task seriously above all by thinking hard again about his preaching. The problems associated with preaching soon also proved to illuminate the wider problem of how God is known. (Barth saw a close connection between preaching and teaching in that he now understood teaching strictly as a 'special instance of the task of preaching, with the aim of giving some idea of the message of the Bible. Educational considerations have to be left in the background.')[145] For a long time he had felt preaching to be a 'limitless problem'.[146] He had already recognized the inevitability of the 'depressing ups and downs' from which he suffered in his own preaching: there was 'a necessity in our whole situation of which we cannot wish to rid ourselves'.[147] Thus he once complained: 'I preached today with the clear impression that this *cannot* get through . . . because it is still far from getting through to me myself. We still make mighty postulations.'[148] It was the same in pastoral work and teaching. 'My visiting and my instruction are a laughable piece of bungling; I feel like someone trying to blow into a trumpet; my cheeks are all puffed out, and yet curiously no sound emerges.'[149] Barth found that preaching – like the rest of his pastoral work – never got any easier; indeed, 'it gets more difficult for me all the time'. He spoke of his 'increasing realization that our preaching is impossible from the start'.[150] This was doubtless because he now began to become clearer and clearer that preaching had to be quite different. It had to be radically concerned with 'God'. The most significant evidence of his preaching at this time is his sermon on Ezekiel 13, given three weeks after the fateful 16 January 1916. He had it privately printed and distributed it to all the houses in the village. In it he spoke in prophetic tones of 'the great unrest which is inevitable when God speaks to us', saying that the 'pastor who satisfies the people' is a false prophet. His sermon in the middle of March to the Aarau Student Conference on 'The One Thing Need-ful' was significant in another way. It was absolutely necessary, he said there, that instead of doing all possible kinds of things, 'we should begin at the beginning and recognize that God is God'. In 1916 he also gave a series of sermons on 1 John, which were again strongly influenced by his concern over the problem of how it was possible to talk to God.

However, the recognition that sermons must be concerned with God in quite a different way did not mean that Barth felt that he had 'solved' the problem of preaching. The strange thing about his train of thought was that it made preaching even more of a problem for him. At this time he found his predicament to be a lesson in itself. 'As a pastor I wanted to speak to people in the extraordinary contradic-tion of their lives, but to speak the no less extraordinary message of the Bible, which was as much of a riddle as life. These two factors, life and the Bible, have risen before me like Scylla and Charybdis: if these are the source and the destination of Christian preaching, who should, who can, be a pastor and preach?' This 'familiar situation of the pastor on Saturday at his desk and on Sunday in his pulpit crystallized in my case into a marginal note to all theology . . . it is not as if I had found any way out of this critical situation. Certainly not. But this critical situation itself became to me the explanation of the character of all theology . . . Why, I had to ask myself, did those question marks and the exclamation marks, which are the very existence of the pastor, play really no role at all in the theology I knew . . . ? Was my question only my own; and did others know a way out which I had not found? I saw the steps they took, but I could not recognize a way out in any of them. Why then did the theologians I knew seek to represent the pastor's perplexity, if they touched upon it at all, as being tolerable and superable, instead of understanding it at all costs, instead of facing and perhaps discovering in it, in its very insuperableness and intolerableness, the real theme of theology? Would it not pay, I also asked myself, to satisfy oneself how much light might be shed upon theology from this viewpoint?'[151]

Thus the predicament in which Barth found himself when preaching was not primarily a technical and practical matter (*how* do I say it?), but a problem which concerned the basic content of preaching (*can* I, *may* I, speak of God at all?). And the discovery that he now made was this, that to recognize the basic *difficulty* in speaking of God is in itself relevant knowledge *of God*. He felt that this discovery was a profound *change* from his previous theologizing. The new element was not a more satisfying answer to the question of God; but now the question had become a serious one for him. Not, however, in the sense of questioning the existence of God: God's existence was basically no more questionable than it had been before. 'From the beginning my question was how to develop my thinking about what I should say as a pastor, starting from the presupposition that God is . . . My levity at the beginning of my ministry was *not* a matter of taking that positive presupposition too much for granted and simply having no ear for the whole business of apologetic. The trouble was that I took so long to notice that really serious temptation only becomes possible and real on the basis of that positive presupposition. What do sceptics know about "life and death" questions? They leave the question "Does God exist?" open. Surely the sceptics' question always leaves one essentially as one was before, unshaken? Don't things become dangerous only *if* and *because* God is? In that case does not the decisive question recoil on one, because then setting out *and* continuing, scepticism *and* the supposed courage of faith . . . in short the whole of human independence and self-assurance, are weighed in the balance and finally found wanting? (This is notoriously not the case with the sceptics' question.) That is the question which I failed to recognize as a student or as a young pastor. It is *the* question, which then came down on me like a ton of bricks round about 1915.'[152]

While Barth's thinking was determined more and more by these problems, he increasingly moved away from the group of Religious Socialists, which in turn threatened more and more to disintegrate as a result of other differences. On 23 May 1916 Hans Bader called a conference of Religious Socialists at Brugg with the intention of bringing about a general reconciliation. A remarkable thing now

happened. Barth, of all people, was elected president of the conference (Thurneysen, Pestalozzi and the Baselbiet pastor Sandreuter
were on the committee), evidently because he was not regarded as a
committed supporter of either Kutter or Ragaz. He was given the
task of calling the next conference, in the autumn. However, at the
end of October Barth informed Ragaz through Thurneysen that they
were thinking of giving up conferences altogether – his reason being
that it was not the time for organized activities, but (as he was fond of
saying at this period) for a period of tranquil growth. Kutter felt the
same way, 'sending us younger ones home to our villages with strong
and healthy scepticism about all conferences'.[153] Kutter also visited
Barth in Safenwil at the end of October.

Ill-feeling developed between Barth and Ragaz in July for another
reason. Barth had sent Ragaz a review of Blumhardt's *Hausandachten
(House Prayers)* for *Neue Wege* under the title 'Wait for the Kingdom of
God' (with the last words in italics!). In it he wrote some words which
were unmistakably directed against the Religious Socialists: 'Our
dialectic has reached a dead end, and if we want to be healthy and
strong we must begin all over again, not with our own actions, but
quietly "waiting" for God's action.'[154] Ragaz refused to publish the
review because he rejected its argument as being quietistic[155] (it
then appeared in September in *Der freie Schweizer Arbeiter*). Thereupon Barth and Thurneysen met Ragaz on 3 November at the house
of their friend Pastor Richard Preiswerk in Umiken for a thorough
discussion. Things were smoothed down, but from then on contact
between Barth and Ragaz virtually ceased. 'Ragaz and I roared past
one another like two express trains: he went out of the church, I went
in.'[156] Nevertheless, when they met Ragaz tried – in vain – to get
Barth to succeed him in his professorial chair, from which he wanted
to retire. And when Ragaz was saying goodbye on Brugg station, he
whispered to Thurneysen, with a glance at Barth, that he was afraid
that 'those whom the gods love die young . . .'

The first edition of Romans

While this controversy was still going on, Barth's thoughts had
moved increasingly clearly in a particular direction. 'Over and
above the group of problems associated with liberal theology and
Religious Socialism, I began to be increasingly preoccupied with the

Pastor Barth

17. Karl Barth during his time in Geneva, where he worked as assistant pastor to the German-speaking church from autumn 1909 to summer 1911.

18. Nelly Hoffmann in 1906. She was one of Barth's confirmation candidates in his first year and became engaged to him in 1911. They were married in 1913.

19. From 1911 to October 1921 Barth lived in this house as pastor of Safenwil; it proved to be a storm center in many ways.

20.   *Karl Barth on holiday in the mountains at Saas-Fee in summer 1919, immediately before his revolutionary Tambach lecture.*

21.   *Karl and Nelly Barth with Markus (aged 1) and Franziska (2) in 1916, just as he was beginning work on his commentary on Romans.*

22.   *Barth and his friend Thurneysen at the Bergli in 1920, soon after it was first opened.*

Religious Socialists

23. *Hermann Kutter, pastor of the Neumünster, Zürich.*

24. *Leonhard Ragaz. In contrast to Kutter he was the activist.*

25. *Christoph Blumhardt, the counsellor and 'prophet' of Bad Boll.*

26. *At the beginning of the First World War Kaiser Wilhelm II delivers a speech written by A. von Harnack from the balcony of the Schloss in Berlin. ('Political parties are a thing of the past, I recognize only Germans.') The outbreak of war made Barth doubt his teachers' theology.*

Romans

27. Teachers from the University of Berlin on their way to a remembrance service in 1919. Seeberg, the Rector, is walking behind the two proctors, and behind him are the theologians Kaftan, Graf Baudissin, von Harnack, Mahling, Deissmann, Holl, Strack, Runze, Gressmann, C. Schmidt, Richter, Eissfeldt and K. L. Schmidt.

28. The beginning of the first edition of Romans, written in 1916; it marked a break with the dominant trends in liberal and positive theology.

idea of the kingdom of God in the biblical, real, this-wordly sense of the term. This raised more and more problems over the way in which I should use the Bible in my sermons, which for all too long I had taken for granted.'[157] At the beginning of June Barth had a few days' holiday with Thurneysen in Leutwil. Shortly beforehand, Thurneysen had married Marguerite, née Meyer, from Basle. Like Nelly Barth, she had had a musical training, and the two women enjoyed playing together; Karl Barth occasionally felt 'moved by the Spirit . . . to join in making music with them in the wildest of ways'.[158] During these June days Barth agreed with Thurneysen that 'for further clarification of the situation it would be necessary to return to academic theology'.[159] Barth had the impression 'that the area from which I draw resources for inner concentration and upon which I would gladly rely in working and speaking must be widened and deepened – otherwise I am in danger of coming to a dead end'.[160] At first it was clearer *that* something had to happen than *what* should be done. 'It was Thurneysen who whispered the key phrase to me, half aloud, while we were alone together: "What we need for preaching, instruction and pastoral care is a 'wholly other' theological foundation."'[161] It was at an 'evening rendezvous in Leutwil that for the first time we said aloud that we could no longer share the fruit of Schleiermacher'.[162] 'But where else were we to begin? Kutter was impossible too, because I had become extremely suspicious of his "living God" as a result of his wartime book *Reden an die deutsche Nation* (Speeches to the German Nation).'[163] For a moment Barth himself evidently considered a new study of Kant.[164] On the other hand, 'in a meadow above the Hallwilersee'[165] Thurneysen had 'raised the strange question whether we should study – Hegel. Nothing came of that.'[166]

'In fact we found ourselves compelled to do something much more obvious. We tried to learn our theological ABC all over again, beginning by reading and interpreting the writing of the Old and New Testaments, more thoughtfully than before. And lo and behold, they began to speak to us – but not as we thought we must have heard them in the school of what was then "modern theology". They sounded very different on the morning after the day on which Thurneysen had whispered that phrase to me (he had meant it in quite general terms). I sat under an apple tree and began to apply myself to Romans with all the resources that were available to me at the time. I had already learnt in my confirmation instruction that this book was of crucial importance. I began to read it as though I had never read it before. I wrote down carefully what I discovered, point by point . . . I read and read and wrote and wrote.'[167]

Barth was thirty at this time. He saw his writing as 'copy-book exercises in explaining my change of position and perspective just to myself and some friends'.[168] 'In the first place I really wrote the book only for myself and for the private edification of Eduard Thurneysen and other fellow-sufferers.'[169] 'I did not intend it as a dissertation. I simply wrote it out.'[170] If Barth was not under the tree in the garden, he worked at a small and uncomfortable desk at which his great-great grandfather Burckhardt and probably also Lavater had once meditated. It had come to him, along with a pile of books – from the possessions of his treasured grandmother Sartorius. She had recently died in Basle, on 26 December 1915 – and Karl Barth had spoken some simple biblical sayings over her grave.

What he was now writing 'for myself' was, of course, significant enough. 'Only now did I begin to think of my dead father "with reverence and gratitude", as I indicated in the Foreword to the first edition of *Romans* . . . And I do not want to conceal the fact that for a moment – remember the warning at the end of Mozart's *Seraglio* that "Nothing is so hateful as vengeance" – the idea came into my head that now I could and would get my own back on those who had so put my father in the shade, although he knew just as much (but in a different way)!'[171] However, Karl did not do this, since the study and research which he had begun involved him in much more important matters.

It was the discovery of the Bible which held his attention. He had now 'gradually become aware of the Bible'.[172] And so he expected that the new basis for which he was searching would come from a new attempt to be 'more open towards the Bible and to allow it to tell me what it might have to do with Christianity more directly than before'.[173] He looked for this above all from Paul's Epistle to the Romans. He had chosen to 'snatch it from our opponents', as he explained to Ragaz in November 1916.[174] The impression he got from his Bible study was of something quite surprising and strange. 'During the work it was often as though I caught a breath from afar, from Asia Minor or Corinth, something primaeval, from the ancient East, indefinably sunny, wild, original, that somehow is hidden behind these sentences. Paul – what a man he must have been and what men also those for whom he could so sketch and hint at these pithy things in a few muddled fragments! . . . And then *behind* Paul: what realities those must have been that could excite the man in such a way! What a lot of far-fetched stuff we compile about his remarks, when perhaps ninety-nine per cent of their real content escapes us!'[175]

Of course, there were 'still hefty quotations from Goethe and Carl Spitteler and even from Schiller'. 'At that time I was still in the process of coming out of the eggshells of the theology of my teachers.'[176] New teachers were added to the old, especially Tobias Beck, who was so revered by his father and grandfather. 'Among the books I inherited from my father I found many by J. T. Beck and made very good use of them.'[177] Barth thought that as an interpreter of the Bible Beck 'towered above the rest of the company, even above Schlatter. We also found some of his systematic approach accessible and it served us as a model.'[178] However, as Barth saw later, this new teacher not only helped him in his approach to the Bible but also presented new difficulties. 'My interpretation was more strongly influenced than I had noticed by Bengel, Oetinger, Beck and even by Schelling (passed on through Kutter). Subsequently this did not prove adequate for what had to be said.'[179] 'So at that time (and indeed later) I read the text of the Bible with very many different kinds of spectacles and naively displayed the fact. But by using all those different kinds of spectacles, what I honestly wanted to express (and was convinced that I was expressing) was the word of Paul.'[180] By listening in to the Epistle to the Romans, Barth believed that despite everything 'the apostle Paul gave me special evidence about the truth and clarity of the Bible's testimony'.[181]

What did Barth learn from this study? That all the Christian groups, trends and 'movements' of his time could not carry on as they were doing! 'Everything had always already been settled without God. God was always thought to be good enough to put the crowning touch to what men began of their own accord. The fear of the Lord did not stand objectively at the beginning of our wisdom; we always attempted as it were to snatch at his assent in passing. Thus the greater the zeal for God, the greater would be the reluctance to submit to God's real demands, since failure at that point means that whatever ensues, it cannot be new action or aid on God's part. In the last resort it will prove to be a reform, or the old situation in a new guise. From God's standpoint that is more of a hindrance than a help, since it continues to delude people about the need for the coming of *his* kingdom. Our 'movements' then stand directly in the way of God's movement; our "causes" hinder his cause, the richness of our "life" hinders the tranquil growth of the divine life in the world . . . The collapse of *our* cause must demonstrate for once that *God's* cause is exclusively *his own*. That is where we stand today.'[182]

In a whole series of new phrases, Barth was saying two things in particular. First, that men can never make 'God's standpoint their own partisan standpoint' and therefore that no individual or group simply stands on God's side over against others. Rather, in solidarity, together, they all share the responsibility before God![183] This was criticism of any form of individualism, especially in its religious form!

All human distinctions, between the religious and the irreligious, the moral and the immoral, become relative. 'The difference between mountain and valley becomes meaningless when the sun at its zenith fills both with its light.' 'The transformation of all values!'[184] Secondly, he stressed that the kingdom of God is not 'a rebellion within the old aeon but the dawn of a new one'; it is not 'a development within previous possibilities but the new possibility of life'. Thus there is a clear distinction between this kingdom and all human attempts at reform. 'Your light is an artificial light in the night, not dawn and daybreak.' But there is also a clear distinction between this kingdom and man's religious and moral possibilities: 'They do not create anything new.'

God's kingdom, however, creates something completely new in the world: 'Real knowledge of God . . . with its ultimate certainties, knows that it is at the beginning of its work, not its end; it has never finished with the riddles and the difficulties of life . . . Knowledge of God is not an escape into the safe heights of pure ideas, but an entry into the need of the present world, sharing in its suffering, its activity and its hope. The revelation which has taken place in Christ is not the communication of a formula about the world, the possession of which enables one to be at rest, but the power of God which sets us in motion, the creation of a new cosmos. A divine shoot breaks through its ungodly casing . . . There is work and struggle at every point and for every hour.'[185] Of course, a little later Barth began to ask whether these distinctions between divine possibilities and human possibilities were clear enough, above all because of his 'constant opposition of the picture of humanity as a growing divine organism to an empty idealism'.[186]

These two central ideas of Barth's defined his position in a number of directions: on the one hand over against the Romantic movement and idealism, and on the other against pietism. This had seemed especially problematical to him, 'a quite evil religious mechanism', during the appearance of an evangelist called Vetter in Safenwil in the middle of November 1916. Secretly he now also turned away

from Schleiermacher – and from his Marburg teacher: 'The last
direct sign of life I received from Wilhelm Herrmann was an inscription, written in the year 1918. It bore the laconic words: "None the
less, with best wishes from W. Herrmann." '[187] Indeed Barth now
even dissociated himself clearly from Ragaz and Religious
Socialism, for all his acknowledgment of it and dependence on it.
'Pacifism and social democracy do not represent the kingdom of
God, but the old kingdom of man in new forms. The criticisms and
the protests . . . which they sling against the course of world history
are of this world; they are born of need, and are no use.'[188]

Gradually Barth filled a first 'notebook with comments'[189] with
his 'copybook exercises', then a second and third, and gradually they
turned into quite a thick book. In July 1916, in the middle of the First
World War, he began writing it out. By September he had already
reached Romans 3.[190] Then he had a breakdown in health through
overwork, and this made it necessary for him in October to ask the
church council for a holiday to recover. During the following winter
he made only slow progress, and in March 1917 he seemed to have
come to a complete standstill preparing for chapter 5. He did not
return to his exposition for six months, but then with the intention of
finishing the book and having it printed within a year. In order to
make speedier progress, in October 1917 he asked the church council
for four weeks' study leave. He spent it after Easter in the 'Krähen-
bühl' in Zürich, in the house of his brother-in-law Richard Kisling, a
keen patron of the fine arts.

Even before his six months' break Barth had given a memorable
lecture, on 6 February 1917, during a study week at Leutwil – other
speakers were Emil Brunner and Gottlob Wieser. It was his first
public account of the results of his new Bible studies. The title of the
lecture was 'The Strange New World within the Bible', and in it he
argued that in the Bible we find something quite unexpected: not
history, not morality, not religion but virtually a 'new world': 'not
the right human thoughts about God but the right divine thoughts
about men', so that the Bible takes us out of 'the old atmosphere of
man to the open portals of a new world, the world of God.'[191] During
these six months Barth also wrote other lectures. At the end of April
he spoke in Safenwil to members of the Schoolchildren's Bible Circle
on 'Everyday Strength' – and now for a while he turned with
remarkable perception to pietistic figures of past and present.
In May he visited the pietists' Baden conference and studied

Hofacker's sermons with particular care. At the end of July he appeared with Ernst Staehelin to speak at a camp of the Basle Young Christians' Alliance at Buus in the Baselbiet about 'The Future of Christianity and Socialism'. Finally, on 9 October he spoke to a small group of women teachers on the problem of religious instruction ('Religion and Life'); his clear criticism of 'religion' here (as a private affair, as mere inwardness, as a quietist, ineffective attitude) is striking. Religion, he argued, by-passes life – life in the world and even more life in the Bible.

During these months Barth and Thurneysen prepared a small collection of sermons for publication – six each. He was somewhat hesitant, since 'Abraham, Isaac and Jacob did not have anything printed'.[192] Still, he thought it appropriate for once 'to provide an objective picture of the present state of our affairs' in this way, and to expose them to public criticism.[193] Even while the book was at the printer, Barth again complained about the trouble which preaching caused him. It had now become even greater. 'Our sayings . . . all remind me of bridges which are still only half built, staring promisingly, sadly, threateningly, or however one will, into the air.'[194] The book was published at the end of the year in Berne by the firm of Bäschlin under the title *Suchet Gott, so werdet ihr leben* (Seek God and You Will Live). According to the Foreword, it was addressed to 'people who share our disquiet at God's great hiddenness in the present world and the church and share our joy at his even greater readiness to break through all our bonds'.

Barth's sermons in this book are notably different from those in his first Safenwil period. His tone and style were now like this: 'Is it not the case that sometimes we are heartily sick of our previous "God" . . . But fortunately we are all involved in a revolution. What we mean yet do not meet, seek and find; miss and lack, yet do not discover anywhere; is a *living* God . . . the opposite of our previous "God", a God who is really *God* . . . Not a fifth wheel on the waggon but the wheel which drives all the rest . . . Not a notion, not a view, but the power of life which overcomes the powers of death . . . Not an adornment to the world, but a lever which is applied to the world! Not a feeling with which one toys, but a fact which one takes seriously . . . Only now do we begin to perceive him, the living God. There can be no question of our knowing him, of our "having" him, as the saying goes.'[195]

During those same months Barth again had a long holiday with his family: the Thurneysens and the Pestalozzis went with them. They went in June to Risch on Lake Zug, immediately after a visit by

Martin Rade to Safenwil. Barth did not neglect his family during
these years. He delighted in his children. There had been indications
of this delight even before the arrival of his first child, when he kept
writing impatiently in his diary, 'Where is the baby?' At her baptism
he had read aloud a somewhat liberal creed of his own and afterwards, at the family party, had joined his wife in playing on the violin
and singing the song 'Thoughts are free'. By now, this first child
Fränzeli was three years old. Meanwhile a second child, Karl Markus, had arrived (on 6 October 1915) and a third was on the way.
Christoph Friedrich ('Stöffeli') was born on 29 September 1917.
Barth's choice of godparents for his children is an indication of his
more intimate relationships. His daughter's godparents were his
own sister, one of his wife's sisters and his uncle Ernst Sartorius, with
whom he had been close in Geneva. For Markus, his first son, Barth
asked his friend at Leutwil to be godfather, along with Helene
Barth-Rade and a Dr Karl Guggenheim, a lawyer whom he had
known since his schooldays and who, in 1915, was stationed in
Safenwil as a soldier. He was godfather to the Pestalozzi and Spoendlin children, and the fathers in turn were to be godparents at Christoph's baptism.

During the holidays at Risch he went to Berne for a few days to be
official delegate at the party conference of the Swiss Social Democrats. On this occasion the conference passed a resolution which
Barth thought to be 'as generous as it was meaningless' in refusing to
defend their country.[196] Barth had spoken on this question the previous winter at several meetings of 'his' Workers' Association, and
in addition gave some analyses of the progress of the war. Soon after
his summer holidays he began to be seriously 'involved in several
considerable battles' in his village.[197] They did not, however, per-
turb him too deeply. 'As pastor of Safenwil I grew a thick skin . . .
Not much has got under it: it all passed over me.'[198] The battles
were now over the organization of trade unions among the workers.
The factory owners were against them, Barth was for them: 'in the
background, sometimes openly, and sometimes even a bit from the
pulpit'.[199] Barth saw the formation of trade unions as one of his chief
political concerns. 'The aspect of socialism which interested me most
in Safenwil was the problem of the trade union movement. I studied
it for years and also helped to form three flourishing trade unions in
Safenwil (where there had been none before). They remained when I
left. That was my modest involvement in the workers' question and

my very limited interest in socialism. For the most part it was only
practical. Of course I was also involved in other things. But I was
only marginally interested in socialist principles and ideology.'[200]
There were clashes in Safenwil over the formation of trade unions,
especially at the end of August and the beginning of September 1917.
Barth was the speaker at a demonstration and had his 'funeral
oration' for a worker published. In it he presented the
worker's death as an exemplary sacrifice for the 'cause of humanity'.
At that time he also paid a personal visit to Hochuli, the owner of the
knitting mill, and spoke with him 'in his villa, like Moses with
Pharaoh, asking him to let the people go out into the wilderness'. But
the conversation ended with 'a flat rejection and a declaration of war
. . . in which I was told that I was the "worst enemy" he had had in
his whole life'.[201] Barth's attitude in the affair now produced great
tensions in the community, which became polarized. This fact had
already emerged in June when, according to Aargau custom, the
confirmation of Barth's election fell due: 189 voted 'yes', but 85 voted
'no' or returned blank ballot papers. Tension grew when in the
autumn the socialists gained 'a majority of three to two against
liberalism' in the local council thanks to the strategic advice of their
'comrade pastor'.[202] The church committee took their pastor to task,
but his view was that their wrath was probably directed not so much
against his bit of politics as against 'my general line as a pastor,
which is evidently new, alien and unattractive both to the
bourgeoisie and to the socialists'. Church attendance fell. Indeed
what amounted to a 'leave the church' movement began to develop
in protest against the pastor.[203] On the other hand, Barth began to
gain the workers' trust as a pastor too. 'They came to me at the
parsonage. But they also came to church. The socialists were the
keenest audience for my sermons – not because I preached socialism
but because they knew that I was the man who tried to help them.'[204]

The church committee wanted to ban Barth from any political
activity, but of course he refused to comply. Nevertheless, for a while
he stopped giving political lectures. At the end of 1917 he even
ceased to be directly involved with the Religious Socialists. In the
summer he had opposed a reorganization of the movement to make it
more efficient. His reason was that 'a general offensive is *now* impossible without a struggle'.[205] Nevertheless, a conference in Olten
resolved on this reorganization on 10 December, with the obvious
consequence that both Barth and Thurneysen resigned from the

committee. Barth wondered whether he should now 'clear the table' at the next Aarau conference in a lecture against the supporters of Ragaz, but did not in fact do so.

Meanwhile, he had made the acquaintance of two Basle students of theology who were interested in Religious Socialism. They were very different, but both were to follow him on what was now proving to be his independent course. One was Wilhelm Vischer (born 1895), a Marburg student, who was sensitive and aesthetic. He was also ready 'for us to move to new ground, first of all under the vigorous thrust of Religious Socialism, and then in a more radical form of this movement'.[206] The other was Fritz Lieb (1892–1970). Unlike Vischer, he was an almost wild, electrifying character. He was a cousin of Frau Thurneysen and was later to become the brother-in-law of Gottlob Wieser and Ernst Staehelin; at that time he was studying under Ragaz and living with Kutter. He particularly impressed Barth as a 'thinker of astounding breadth, freshness and versatility'. 'From beginnings in Oriental studies, especially Assyriology, he had become preoccupied with Karl Marx.'[207] Barth had got to know him 'by the Hallwilersee' in the following way: 'You were adorned with one of those panama hats which were so popular at the time. No sooner had you got off the train than you immediately began to talk enthusiastically about a resolution you had just made not to have anything more to do with Swiss infantry rifles but to transfer to the sanitary corps. This demonstration was very much in Ragaz's line, and in those days, whether we approved of it or not, we were at any rate astounded by it and thought it extremely significant and promising.'[208]

Above all, the year 1918 meant a great deal of hard work for Barth in his interpretation of Romans – not that he was without his doubts: 'Does the good God really want this piece of writing?'[209] At the beginning of June he had finished 'a first reading' of the interpretation, and after looking through the manuscript carefully, on 16 August he could write in his diary, 'Romans finished'. At the same time he was well aware that 'there is still an immense amount which I have not understood and which later readers will have to discover'.[210] It was not easy to find a publisher for his book. 'Three well-known Swiss publishers refused to have anything to do with it, which was quite understandable at the time . . . It was the Berne firm of G. A. Bäschlin which finally dared to make the venture with the book when my friend . . . Pestalozzi offered generous financial support. There was no question of printing more than 1000 copies.'[211] The book, which has 1919 as its date of publication, was already printed by December 1918.

The First World War came to an end while Barth was reading the proofs. And amidst the confusion in which it ended, a general strike broke out in Switzerland in November 1918. At this time Barth complained, 'If only we had turned to the Bible earlier, we would now have firm ground under our feet. Now people brood alternately over the newspaper and the New Testament and really see dreadfully little of the organic connection between the two worlds, about which one should now be able to give a clear and powerful witness.'[212] This autumn, as earlier in July, a kind of influenza was so rampant that services at Safenwil had to be abandoned for a number of Sundays. Even Barth had to retire to bed – in the midst of the general strike. Hardly had he recovered, than 'I awoke as president of an eleven-member emergency commission with a capital of six thousand francs, which had been raised by our manufacturers'. So Barth now had quite enough to do, leading the 'final stages of the battle against the retreating influenza'.[213]

Shortly after this there was a rumour in his village that Barth had 'praised' the general strike. Although he could demonstrate that he had only *'appraised'*, i.e. explained it (as a consequence of the political situation), four of the six members of his church committee resigned on 20 November as a result of the rumour. Barth refused to be discouraged by this. On the contrary, in February 1919, after a long interval he resumed his activity in his Workers' Association with a series of lectures in which he 'expounded' political events – 'as our workers say of such explanations'.[214] For example, he spoke about the general strike, about the meeting of the 'Second International' at the beginning of February in Berne, and about the conference of the Swiss Socialist Party which took place at the time and rejected the Second International. Then he spoke about the Russian revolution, which he saw as an attempt which had to be made but was not to be imitated. He was also well aware of the problems in this attempt: violent revolution (which meant the establishment of the new society 'on the old foundations'), the exclusiveness of the working class (in contrast to the abolition of classes) and minority rule ('the acknowledged shortcomings of democracy are not improved by its abolition'). On May Day he even marched with his workers behind the red flag to Zofingen.

This was the last straw for many of the people of Safenwil. Others joined the manufacturer Hochuli in leaving the church; as he did not want to be without religion, he founded his own 'worship association'. On 10 August two civic parties made a move to disenchant Barth with his position at Safenwil by refusing him an urgently-needed pay rise (he had begun with a salary of 230 francs a month and even now was earning little more, less than the other pastors in the canton). As his socialism was given as the reason for this step, Barth declared that 'ill-feeling against him had been growing for two years and matters had now come to a head. It was a lie that he glorified Bolshevism and Spartacism; he had done precisely the opposite. He had warned the workers against it . . . He did not put out socialist propaganda, nor had he done so.' However, 'he was not ashamed of taking the side of the workers'.[215] Moreover, he would not be dissuaded from being pastor at Safenwil by any financial moves. His salary was then increased, with 99 dissenting votes.

Barth also produced two written statements on political questions at this time. In a 'Word to the Citizens of Aargau' he made them responsible for the degree to which the socialists had adopted radical positions. Because the people of Aargau did not take moderate representatives of socialism seriously, 'as in Russia and Germany' they were leading them to 'deny their own origin and become a devastating firebrand'. And in an article entitled 'What Should Not Happen', he warned the Socialist Party against joining the Third International, which was dependent on Russia. The question whether or not to enter occupied the Swiss Social Democrats for two years and shook the party to its foundations. The final decision was not taken until 20 December 1920 (in Berne). It was against the Third International, but at a price: a minority split off from the Socialist Party and formed the Communist Party. 'I was also in the audience and present as an eyewitness when there was a sharp split at the Swiss Social Democrat Party conference of 1920 between the Second and the Third – Muscovite – Internationals. The supporters of the Third International, finding themselves in the minority, left the hall in protest singing "Peoples hear the signal for the last affray". And who was there as one of the most resolute and recalcitrant of them? – Fritz Lieb!' (quite unlike Karl Barth).[216]

During 1919 Barth also came into conflict with some of his more distant relations (at least with the conservative ones). He appeared at the wedding celebrations of his uncle Ernst Sartorius in Basle. 'I gave an after-dinner speech about and against family life in general and in particular. It was felt to be extremely tactless. I can still see the devastating looks which uncle Hans Burckhardt directed against me, and the way in which uncle Fritz (Sartorius) sat on an armchair in a corner and announced his utter disapproval with a long drawn out "ay-ay-ay-ay" and what seemed to me to be a particularly impressive shaking of his double chin.'[217] Barth got on very much better with his closer family relations. He kept in regular contact with his mother through all the years at Safenwil and shared his thoughts and his activities with her. Karl's mother's sister, his beloved aunt Bethi, was no longer alive. After the death of grandmother Sartorius she had worked with prisoners of war and died on service in Bulgaria in August 1917. At this time Karl also kept up a lively correspondence with his two brothers. After first working in Laupen, Peter served from 1918 until his death as pastor of Madiswil. Heinrich had obtained a doctorate in 1913 for work on Descartes and in 1918 became a teacher at the Girls' High School in Basle. In the same year his mother moved from Berne and came to live with him on the Rheinweg. She looked after her son, who was still a bachelor, and also played an active part as a committee member of the Women's Aid Group. Karl was also particularly fond of his brother-in-law, Karl Lindt, who was a pastor in Berne. In May 1919 Lindt had married Gertrud Barth, who was reading law at that time. Her brother in Safenwil performed the ceremony. Links in the family were further strengthened when Barth became godfather of Peter's son Ulrich and Gertrud's daughter Hanni.

Once Barth had finished his interpretation of Romans he went on to new researches and investigations into the Bible. So while the political controversies mentioned above were going on, he was at the same time continually occupied in reading texts from the Bible, reflecting on them and 'interpreting' them. In part the work was a direct preparation for preaching, and in part it found expression only in private writing. In the winter of 1918–19 he worked on Acts, which he learnt to treasure as an 'admirable book, full of character and universalism', and then on I Corinthians. He wrote a 'mini-commentary' on chapter 15 in February 1919: 'The chapter is the key to the entire letter with its remarkably profound disclosures on this and that, which have their source in ultimate wisdom. Some of them have struck us recently like shocks from an electric eel.'[218] He was particularly preoccupied with Ephesians, which he had read through cursorily(!) the previous year for hours on end with his confirmation candidates. Now, in the summer of 1919, he gave a series of sermons on the book which during the following winter he then reshaped as a short commentary. The next summer he looked at the epistle again during a Bible class. The provisional results of Barth's biblical studies can be seen in a lecture which he gave at a conference of the Student Christian Movement in Aarburg on 9 June 1919 on 'Christian Life'. Standing in for F. W. Foerster, he wrote it in one night. It also shows signs of an insight which had become significant for him that spring during a lecture by his brother Heinrich to the Aarau conference (on 'The Knowledge of God'). The 'wholly otherness of the kingdom of God' needed to be stressed even more strongly over against all human conditions and movements.[219]

'The kingdom of God is the kingdom of *God*. We cannot conceive of the transition from the analogies of the divine reality to human reality radically enough. The pattern of development is a failure . . . The new Jerusalem has not the least to do with the new Switzerland and the revolutionary state of the future; it comes to earth in God's great freedom, when the time has arrived.' Of course this hope does not sap 'courage and strength . . . for the things of today and of this world', it supplies them.

The lecture showed that Barth's thought was now becoming even more concentrated and even more thoroughgoing in its 'radicalism'. His friend Adolf Preiswerk put it to him in this way: '*You* undertake great things – *I* couldn't do it.'[220]

The Tambach lecture and its consequences

Building on the basic themes of this lecture, during the late summer Barth then worked out a further lecture which all at once was to make his name known in Germany. Equally suddenly it was also to show how much what had hitherto been thought and said in a parochial setting was now to point a new way forward for his time. The lecture came about in the following way. Two pastors from Hessen, Otto Herpel and Heinrich Schultheis, called a conference for Religious Socialists to be held on 22–25 September at Tannenberg, a sanatorium in Tambach, Thuringia, owned by a Wilhelm Scheffen. Here Swiss Religious Socialism was to be presented to any Germans who might be interested. Ragaz was first choice as speaker, but he had to say no, so (evidently at the suggestion of the young

Alfred de Quervain, who was a student in Marburg at the time) the pastor of Safenwil, who was almost unknown in Germany, was asked to give a lecture. Until then his *Romans* had in fact been read and reviewed almost exclusively in Switzerland (Emil Brunner was one of the first to welcome the book, as early as February 1919!). At the end of July, Barth first took a holiday to recover his strength: he went with Thurneysen and Pestalozzi into the Bernese Oberland and did some vigorous walking and climbing there and in the mountains around Saas-Fee. Then, at the beginning of September, he wrote an assessment of the work of Naumann and Blumhardt, who had recently died, rejecting the former and endorsing the latter. After that he devoted himself to working out his lecture 'in an uninterrupted series of day and night shifts'.[221] On the day before the conference, accompanied by his Religious Socialist friends Hans Bader and Rudolf Liechtenhan, one of his cousins who was then a pastor in Basle and later became Professor of New Testament there, he first went to Frankfurt, where they visited the zoo and saw an operetta, and then on to Thuringia. Further interested parties from Switzerland arrived by different routes, among them Thurneysen and Wieser.

A variety of people, about a hundred in all, came to the conference. What they had in common was the fact that 'they were deeply concerned at the revolution which had taken place in recent years and now as Christians were on the look-out for new ways in political and church life'.[222] These were people who 'saw no personal place for themselves in existing church trends and who felt that these trends held out little promise of solving the tasks which faced the church after the collapse of 1918 . . . Most of them were either people from the youth movement or outsiders of various kinds, with quite remarkable life stories.'[223] Barth spoke on the last day of the conference, after lectures by Liechtenhan on 'The Christian in the Church' and by Bader on 'The Christian in the State'. He continued the series with the theme 'The Christian in Society', and the radical pacifist and pietist Eberhard Arnold made a formal comment. Barth's lecture was 'a rather complicated kind of machine that runs backwards and forwards and shoots in all directions with no lack of both visible and hidden joints'.[224]

In characteristic fashion, Barth set out the theme right at the beginning: the Christian, the source of promise and unrest for human society, is not any Christian (not even a Religious Socialist Christian); the Christian is 'the

Christ'. It was striking that Barth then went on to make a clear and fundamental distinction between Christ or the kingdom of God on the one hand and human actions, whether conservative or revolutionary, on the other. 'The kingdom of God does not first begin with our movements of protest. It is the revolution which is *before* all revolutions, as it is *before* the whole prevailing order of things.' In contrast to both conservatives and revolutionaries it is radically new, in such a way that it says 'no' to both of them, though in this 'no' the one is qualified by a relative affirmation of the other. Thus on the one hand protest against the prevailing order of things is certainly part of the kingdom of God. But on the other hand Barth also reckoned with 'parables of the kingdom of God', 'analogies of the divine' on the earthly scene. And in any case he found himself compelled to dissociate himself from the danger which he now recognized as such, 'of secularizing Christ for the umpteenth time, e.g. today for the sake of democracy, or pacifism, or the youth movement, or something of the sort – as yesterday it would have been for the sake of liberal culture or our countries, Switzerland or Germany.'[225] In this way the lecture was so to speak a farewell to a theology which Barth himself had followed for some time, and especially to Religious Socialism. Even more, it led to his alienation from Ragaz, who felt that Barth had vitiated the influence of this movement in Germany by 'dialectical distortion'.[226] At the same time, however, the lecture also announced a new programme: one can say that it contains in germ ideas which Barth was then to develop in detail in subsequent years.

His words in Tambach had an extraordinarily powerful effect on his hearers. 'In comparison with him, all other remarks and discussions faded into insignificance.' True, one person, Carl Mennicke, went straight back to Berlin in a fury, and in subsequent years Barth's audience followed very different ways, even into the ranks of the 'German Christians'. But at the time 'everyone was aroused in one way or another'.[227] 'I only began to realize that I had thought and said things for which I had to be responsible towards a wider public when for the first time, in Tambach, I saw the completely different post-war situation in Germany . . . Here all at once I found a group and the prospect of further groups of people whose disquiet was related to my attempts like answers to questions – answers which, in the vigorous discussion with these German contemporaries that now got under way, themselves seemed in turn to become questions. The welcome from more than one of these people who hungered for realities flabbergasted me.'[228]

Thus as a result of his Tambach lecture Barth found access to a wider circle of people who were involved in a parallel movement concerned with criticism and renewal. He already knew Rudolf

Bultmann from his old Marburg days. Among new acquaintances were the Religious Socialist pastors Dedo Müller, Wolf Meyer and Hans Hartmann (who had opened the conference with a concert!), Otto Herpel, and the philosopher Hans Ehrenberg, who then went over to theology. He also struck up a friendship with Günther Dehn (1882–1970), pastor of Moabit, a suburb of Berlin. The time and place when Dehn made an unforgettable impression on Barth 'was at our meeting in the railway carriage which was taking us to Tambach'; '(probably as a result of hearing some of my bold remarks) he gave me a quizzical yet friendly look which made me both fear him and love him – what Luther's catechism says of our relationship with God himself.' And in Tambach 'he spoke about the altar which Abraham had built for the Lord with an aura of mystery and excitement which at the same time both attracted me and made me want to keep my distance'.[229] And 'here I met Friedrich Gogarten, the pastor of Stelzendorf (1887–1967), who had also come there with two friends, Oskar Ziegner and Otto Piper, from the Wandervogel youth association in Jena. In quite a different way, he had been preoccupied in his village with thoughts and problems which were very similar to mine.'[230]

The effect of the Tambach lecture was to open doors into Germany for Barth. This was clear from the return journey which he made the very next February. Accompanied by his wife and the Thurneysens, he first visited Hans Ehrenberg in Heidelberg, who introduced him to two friends, Richard Siebeck and Viktor von Weizsäcker, both of whom were doctors. From there he went on to Stuttgart for a conversation with Eugen Rosenstock-Huessy, who had become aware of Barth and wanted to get in touch with him; for a short period there was a vigorous correspondence between the two. In this way Barth had an equally brief encounter with the 'prophetic' Patmos group, to which Rosenstock-Huessy and the Ehrenberg brothers belonged, though this was soon broken off again; these were 'positive relationships, but they were left very vague'.[231] Finally he went to Bad Boll, where he paid a visit to Blumhardt's wife and his successor Eugen Jäckh, and then travelled on to Munich, where he was met at the railway station by the Lutheran pastor Georg Merz, 'who held a copy of *Romans* above his head so that I should recognize him'.[232]

A man of many interests, Georg Merz (1892–1959) moved in Munich's liveliest circles. Here Barth's *Romans* came as a revolutionary discovery. Barth made friends with him on the spot. 'Merz is very good, and knows *Romans* better than I do myself. He comes from Friedrich Rittelmeyer and has some residual characteristics left over from that association, but he was very open with me the whole time, untiring in his questions, and a most congenial man . . . He laughs and talks delightfully . . . and in addition directs Lempp's publishing house with considerable theological acumen.'[233] Merz introduced Barth to Friedrich Heiler, Artur Bonus and Alo Münch, and had Barth to speak to a small group at which Hilde, the daughter of Kurt Eisner, was also present. Albert Lempp, the owner of Christian Kaiser Verlag, commented at the end in his broad Swabian dialect, 'It's all fabulously new to me.'[234] Christian Kaiser Verlag now took over the publication rights for *Romans*. 'Since the capacity of the Swiss market seemed to be exhausted after the sale of 300 copies (at any rate)', the book was 'handed over to Christian Kaiser Verlag, under whose auspices the remaining 700 copies found German purchasers and readers in the twinkling of an eye'.[235] It was also reviewed. The same year Barth suffered a 'very honourable but decisive' repudiation 'not only from Adolf Jülicher, who was at that time the acknowledged doyen of New Testament scholarship', but also from the young New Testament scholar Karl Ludwig Schmidt. Both compared Barth with the 'heretic' Marcion. But Bultmann too dismissed the book in a review with 'unmistakable irritation as "enthusiastic revivalism"',[236] while Walther Köhler compared Barth with Schwenkfeld and Harnack compared him with Thomas Munzer.

Some of Barth's new-found German friends paid him a return visit the following summer and autumn in Safenwil: Eugen Rosenstock, Wolf Meyer, Hans Ehrenberg, Georg Merz, Richard Siebeck, Friedrich Gogarten and Otto Herpel. 'What we learn from all these visits is that the good God has a great variety of lodgers.'[237] They told Barth a great deal – from a variety of perspectives – about 'all kinds of personalities and sensations in the young Germany of the time, the flashes of inspiration all over the place and the new ways which, for whatever motives, were sought and found with all kinds of thoughtfulness and enthusiasm.' Richard Siebeck even gave him 'a book about kidney diseases, but before I could attempt to understand something of it . . . it was taken away by my doctor and I never saw it again'. Still, Barth felt that Siebeck was 'ill-at-ease over his concerns in very much the same way as I was in mine'.[238] The doctor Barth mentions was Erwin Lejeune, a brother of the man who edited the Blumhardt prayers. He lived at Kölliken, and shared Barth's interest in Religious Socialism during the Safenwil years; the two of them even spent some time together studying Kant.

1920 was also the year in which Barth subjected the view which he had presented in *Romans* to new criticism and rethought it, after varied and intensive study. He read a wealth of theology and other literature, he studied the Epistle to the Colossians, worked on the Psalms (and compiled a 'prayer book' from them) and spent a good deal of time studying Calvin. A series of sermons on II Corinthians which he gave at the same time took him further into Paul himself.

In these sermons there is a strong emphasis on the crisis which God brings upon man from above: 'If there were no God . . . there would be no need for us to sigh . . . Because God is the cause of our sighing, we must sigh.' Furthermore, in these sermons Barth showed a growing sensitivity to distinctions in comparison with the universalist view of *Romans*. Thus he stresses that God's action is a free choice which can have two incalculable aspects. ('Light can delight *and* blind, wind can refresh *and* chill.') Or he now discovers the significance of the individual in the kingdom of God. ('God's relationship to us men is not a legalistic one, in which the principle holds that all citizens are equal before the law . . . It is a free relationship. It does not have an abstract concern with everyone but only with the individual.') Or he stresses that not all times are the same. ('The Bible does not support the view that God is God in the same way at all times.') Or he often points to the qualitative difference between the biblical period and the present. ('If anything must stop today, it is the arrogance which attempts to say what prophets, apostles and Reformers were allowed to say without producing proof of the spirit and of power.')[239]

As a consequence of his extended study, Barth's thought now moved 'independently of old Württemberg theology and other kinds of speculative theology. Only now did my opposition to Schleiermacher become clear and quite open; Emil Brunner was later to give a detailed account of why Schleiermacher's theology could not in fact be used. The first evidence of this change was a lecture on "Biblical Questions, Insights and Vistas", given at the Aarau Student Conference.'[240] A new feature in the lecture, which was based on an Easter sermon, was the extraordinary pointedness with which Barth here declared God to be 'the wholly other'; revelation to be the encounter with a crucified man; knowledge of God to be recognition at the 'boundaries of mortality', 'the wisdom of death'; the divine Yes to be hidden dialectically in the form of a No; Christian existence to be not 'owning, feasting and sharing' but 'relentless searching, asking and knocking'. The lecture, given in the Great Council Room in Aarau on 17 April, led to 'a clash with Adolf von Harnack which was almost of historic significance'.[241] Harnack, too, was present and had earlier spoken to the same audience on the question 'What assured knowledge can historians provide for the interpretation of world events?' Harnack was shocked by Barth's remarks. 'I can remember very clearly the dismay which he expressed in the discussion after my lecture: the state of affairs was now worse than it had ever been since Kierkegaard (I can still hear the Baltic sound of the name on his lips). And I can also remember his great courtesy towards an unknown country vicar who was so much younger than he.'[242]

How alienated pupil and teacher had in fact become was evident when a few days later Barth had an hour's 'interview' with Harnack and Eberhard Vischer, father of Wilhelm Vischer, in Basle. 'The two gentlemen thought that I would do better to keep my view of God to myself and not make it an "export article"(!). Finally I was branded a Calvinist and intellectualist. Harnack's parting shot was the prophecy that according to all the experiences of church history I would found a sect and receive inspiration.' Barth was disappointed. 'It is evident that the idol is tottering. Harnack gave the impression of being really a broken man; he knew astonishingly little outside his lofty wit.' A few days later, 'I went to see the wife of Professor Overbeck, and that was fine. She is a spiteful, lively, clever old lady . . . and portrayed her husband for me in a way that tallies to the hairsbreadth with our view of him.'[243] She showed me 'a great German Bible, opened it at I Corinthians 15 and said something to the effect that this was what her husband had enjoyed reading'.[244]

Franz Overbeck (1837-1905), Nietzsche's friend, 'whom one only had to mention in Basle at that time to make everyone's hair stand on end',[245] was one of those thinkers who now began especially to come alive for Barth and to help him further. In particular, 'the posthumous publications'[246] of this 'strange alien'[247] gave him a good deal to think about, and in the early part of 1920 prompted him to write a work of his own under the memorable title *Unerledigte Anfragen an die heutige Theologie* (Unresolved Questions for Modern Theology). In it he put forward the view that Overbeck, with his radical criticism of Christianity, had seen very accurately 'the *negative* side of the point which has now to be dealt with *positively*'.[248] Now he also studied

Nietzsche himself, though he gained the impression that 'Overbeck had more insight'.[249] He also read Ibsen and Dostoevsky; the latter in particular helped to clarify his mind and made a profound impression on him. Thurneysen was a 'guide'[250] in his reading and then went on to give a profound interpretation of Dostoevsky at the next Aarau Conference (1921). It should not be forgotten that in his renewed search Barth also found the painter Matthias Grünewald illuminating, above all 'John the Baptist in Grünewald's painting of the crucifixion, with his hand pointing in an almost impossible way. It is this hand which is in evidence in the Bible.'[251] For the rest of his life, Barth worked with a copy of this painting hanging above his desk.

Another figure whom Barth discovered at that time was Søren Kierkegaard: 'The first book by this man which I bought – it was in 1909 – was *The Moment*. I assume that I also read it then. But it cannot have made a very profound impression on me. He only entered my thinking seriously, and more extensively, in 1919, at the criticial turning-point between the first and second editions of my *Romans*; after that he could be seen in a more important role in my other literary works ... What we found particularly attractive, delightful and instructive was his inexorable criticism, which went on snipping and snipping. We saw him using it to attack all speculation which wiped out the infinite qualitative difference between God and man. Thus in that second phase of our revolution he was one of the cocks whose voice seemed to proclaim to us from near and far the dawn of a really new day.'[252]

One other person influenced Barth and helped him a good deal at that time; his 'philosopher brother Heinrich'.[253] Heinrich qualified as a teacher in the faculty of philosophy in Basle in 1920 with a work on the soul in the philosophy of Plato. On 23 November he gave his inaugural lecture on 'The Problem of Origins in the Philosophy of Plato', in which he was particularly concerned with Socrates' 'wisdom of death'. His brother from Safenwil was among the audience. 'With the help of my youngest brother',[254] Karl was now 'faced once more with the wisdom of Plato'.[255] At the same time Heinrich also showed him 'the possibility of a new understanding of Kant in the light of Plato'.[256] At that time Heinrich Barth had a fruitful influence on Karl's thinking with the concept of 'the wisdom of death' and, like Emil Brunner, stimulated him to a combination of a theological approach and Plato's philosophy of origins.

The second edition of Romans

All these intensive and extensive studies in 1920 finally made Barth recognize that he had to say 'the same things' that he had said in *Romans*, but in yet 'another' way. At the end of October, Gogarten visited him in Safenwil; at the Wartburg conference of the *Christliche Welt* his lecture on 'Crisis and Culture' had had a similar effect to Barth's at Tambach. Barth now learnt to treasure him as 'a dreadnought on our side and against our opponents';[257] 'Oho, a first-class cruiser of the best Dutch kind, doubtless the man . . . who will give the call to battle in Germany.'[258] Immediately after Gogarten left, '*Romans* suddenly began to slough its skin'.[259] As a new edition of *Romans* had become due, Barth resolved to rewrite his interpretation from scratch. He felt oppressed by the 'need to subject the book to a revision in which hardly one stone of the original edifice is left on another'.[260] 'At the time when this second book was being written, our eldest, who was then a girl of six, told anyone who was prepared to listen that "Daddy is writing another *Romans*, much better". What the angels may have said on this occasion is another question.'[261]

Barth worked with exceptional energy on the second version of his *Romans*. He wrote the 521-page book in a mere eleven months, sending the pages straight off to the publisher as he finished them. During this period 'my parishioners often had to put up with a pastor who lived in his study'.[262] In the midst of this strenuous work, at the end of January 1921, 'an enormous stone fell into the pool'; he was invited to become a professor in Göttingen, and this now goaded him on to even greater speed.[263] In thinking about Paul he felt like 'an old potter whom I once watched at work in a kiln: all you could see were his shoes sticking out',[264] or like a 'canoe trip on the Niagara Falls',[265] or like 'an act on the high trapeze'.[266] In August 1921 he said to Thurneysen, 'I shall never forget this hot summer. I amble like a drunken man back and forth between desk, dinner table and bed, travelling every kilometre with my eye already on the next one.'[267]

Thurneysen was very involved in the manuscript as it took shape. 'Some of his additions penetrated deeper than my original comment, others were explanatory and added greater precision of expression. I have adopted these additions for the most part without alteration, and they remain a silent testimony to his self-effacement. So close has been our co-operation that not even the specialist will be able to see where the one leaves off and the other begins.'[268] However, since early in 1920 Thurneysen had no longer been living and working in the Aargau, but in the industrial town of Brugg in St Gallen. This physical separation obviously did not lessen their intimacy; indeed they continued to become closer over their work on the second edition of *Romans*. A story about them went the round of their friends: 'We were said once to have spent a whole afternoon sitting opposite each other and smoking. After an hour *I* said, "Perhaps", and after another hour of silence Thurneysen said, "Or perhaps not!!!" That was said to be our conversation and the essence of our system . . .'[269]

Barth now had some help of another kind, from Fritz Lieb. Lieb made it possible for his older friend to put in some concentrated work at his desk by coming to Safenwil in May and June 1921 and taking over the church. Barth was again astonished at his 'boundless intelligence and honesty', and sought to direct his political extremism along rather different lines (especially after a visit by the wild Basle communist Handschin to Safenwil).[270] Barth vividly remembered a scene from this time. It was the day of the baptism of his fourth child, Robert Matthias, who was born on 17 April. 'Fritz Lieb was preaching for me that Sunday and taking Sunday School. I was to perform the baptism immediately after Sunday School in the midst of a host of relations who had hastened over for the occasion. But it was not as simple as that. Lieb was delighting the young people of Safenwil with the story of the building of the tower of Babel, and I can still hear the way in which the talk, with all its exciting details and its application to the present, flooded out into the open air through the church window like an irresistible deluge, until the storming of heaven had finally been described and displayed in all its futility and the baptism could at last take place.'[271] Barth's new friends Siebeck and Merz were Matthias' godparents.

While Barth felt that the first edition of his *Romans* had been written in a 'still very nebulous and speculative form', the second edition, which came into being page by page between autumn 1920 and summer 1921, presented the reader with 'sharply contoured antitheses'.[272] Between the first and the second editions Barth thought that he had moved 'from Osiander to Luther'.[273] True, 'even now there will be all kinds of oversights and dislocations, but I think that I am a *bit* nearer to the truth of the matter than before. At any rate, the pantheistic tinge has now been removed. I confess that while I've been lopping off all the luxuriant growths (correcting the

first edition) I've been feeling rather like Abraham having to sacrifice Isaac.'[274]

So now the second edition represented much more clearly than the
first the bold attempt to introduce a theology 'which may be better
than that of the nineteenth century and the beginning of the twentieth in that it is concerned quite simply with *God* in his independent
sovereignty over against man, and especially the religious man, and
seeks to approach God as we believe that we can see him in the
Bible'.[275] This attempt contained a radical criticism of the liberal
and 'positive' theology of the previous century, arguing that it had
ceased to acknowledge God as God.

'Almost all along the line, at any rate in all its representative figures and
trends, it had become *religionist* and thus *anthropocentric*; in this sense it had
become *humanist*. For this theology, to think of God meant to think in a
scarcely veiled fashion about man, more exactly about the religious, the
Christian religious man. To speak of God meant to speak in an exalted tone,
but once again and more than ever about this man – his revelations and
wonders, his faith and his works. There is no question about it: here *man* was
made great at the cost of *God*.' Over against this, Barth now recognized
'that things . . . could not go on like this'. He made the discovery 'that the
theme of the Bible – contrary to the critical and the orthodox exegesis which
we inherited – certainly could not be man's religion and religious morality,
nor his own secret divinity. The Godness of God – that was the bedrock we
came up against . . . , God's independence and particular character not
only over against the natural world but against the spiritual world also;
God's absolutely unique existence, power and initiative, above all in his
relationship to men.'[276]

For this reason Barth asserted, shouted, declared, spelt out in a constant
variety of new dialectical 'meanderings'[277] that God – is God. To make that
clear, he said it above all with an abundance of *negative* definitions (this is
where the second edition of *Romans* differed from the first): he stressed that
God could not be conceived of, that he was beyond this world, wholly other,
remote, alien, hidden, that he questioned and indeed negated man and
especially his faith, the church and all conceptions of the deity. 'God! We
don't know what we are saying. The believer knows our ignorance.' The
new world touches the old 'as a tangent touches a circle, that is, without
touching it. And, precisely because it does *not* touch it, it touches it as its
frontier, as the *new* world.' God's revelation is at the same time the 'most
complete veiling of his incomprehensibility'.[278] Accordingly the true
character of faith, doctrine, worship, the church, is always merely that of a
'vacuum', a 'crater formed by an explosion', a 'standing place in the air'. So
according to Barth God is not an opiate for men, but their limit: he does not
restore their equilibrium, but upsets them, confronts them with 'crisis'.
This most certainly means that 'we should not console ourselves, say, with

the fact that we are certainly upset'. The 'Pharisaism' of the tax-collector, who perhaps even boasts of his 'uncertainty and brokenness', and seeks to reach God at least through them, also falls victim to criticism. For God is *'beyond* both this world *and* the Beyond'.[279] And because God is even beyond the 'Beyond', he is not simply distant from the world – which is a view that Barth was often thought (wrongly) to put forward. Certainly he is far from those who seek him and think that they have him in their grasp. But he is not far from those who are far from him, who do not 'know' him, 'experience' him, 'have' him – though of course the fact that they do not have him is not the basis for any claim.

There were without doubt some very critical insights here, but Barth was concerned that his book should not be understood as a rebellion of the younger generation against the old or be confused with a general pessimism about culture (he felt only antipathy to Spengler's *Decline of the West*).

Barth later recalled a certain contradiction between his arguments and counter-arguments at that time. 'Looking back, first of all I *had* to speak in those gruesome terms about the transcendence of God, about the tangent and the "line of death" and so on, and had to foist all this teaching on Paul. But I didn't just foist it on him. It's there in Romans. But I was the one who first drew out these threads.'[280] 'At that time I ventured to say the following things in my interpretation of Romans 8.24ff. "Hope that is visible is not hope. Direct talk of God is not talk of God. Christianity that is not eschatology, utterly and without remainder, has absolutely nothing to do with Christ – Redemption is invisible, inaccessible, impossible, and comes to man as hope . . ." Well roared, lion! . . . I still think that I was ten times more right than those against whom my remarks were directed at the time and who at that time utterly repudiated them . . . My remarks at the time were rash (in the sense of being open to suspicion), but not because of their content. It was because they were not matched by others equally sharp and direct to compensate for their total claim. If we claim to have too perfect understanding of the gospel, we at once lose our understanding.'[281]

His manuscript was already complete on his desk by 26 September 1921. And it was *Romans* in this second edition (which appeared in 1922) 'which was to prove the most decisive contribution towards the author's fame for decades afterwards'.[282] 'All unaware, I had been allowed to take a step which many people had been waiting for and to do things for which many people were prepared.'[283] The astonishing response reminded Barth of the time when he had seized the bell-rope by mistake in the church tower at Pratteln. 'He did it unwittingly, and he has no intention of doing it again. The effect of it is to make him continue his climb as carefully as possible.'[284] As a piece of self-criticism, Barth put in his own printed copy of the book 'a dedication of the kind that one puts in a book when one is giving it to someone else . . . : "Karl Barth, to his dear Karl Barth, 1922"'', after which he put a quotation from Luther: 'If you feel or imagine that you are right and suppose that your book, teaching or writing is a great achievement . . . then, my dear man, feel your ears. If you are doing so properly, you will find that you have a splendid pair of big, long, shaggy asses' ears . . .'[285]

In the months gone by, the family had largely lost their father to his desk, as the parish had lost their pastor. But despite the claims on his time, he watched his children (now four) growing up, with care and delight. He still had time, for example, to comb his son Christoph's hair every morning, 'more for my own pleasure than for his gain and satisfaction'.[286] And he even found time to entertain the children by making up a kind of 'Happy Families', based on Safenwil. The 'families', each consisting of four cards, might be: officials (Herr Ammann the Mayor, the Town Clerk, Herr Hüssy the Great Councillor, Herr Dambach the Bee-inspector), famous musicians (Herr Schuermann the teacher, Hans Jent the teacher, Frau Barth the pastor's wife, Fräulein Wilhelm the hairdresser), important people (the nurse, the grave-digger, the school caretaker, the pastor), regulations (You must not: quarrel, gossip, take offence, engage in politics), or excuses (I'm not going to church because: it's snowing, it's raining, it's hot, I overslept).

The parish, too, may often have lost its pastor to his desk during the work on *Romans*, but at least it still had him there – and his 'dialectical', critical phase as expressed in the second edition of *Romans* was certainly also noticeable in his preaching and his classes. He was well aware of 'the gross burden and deprivation which my teaching imposes on the majority of my poor congregation'.[287] And he was also aware 'that people are not really "happy" at what I say . . .'[288] But he could not do otherwise.

And he believed that today 'we must go through these narrow gates with our congregations'.[289] Without doubt he himself suffered under the same burden. And he would sigh, 'I often . . . long for the flesh-pots of Egypt, where one had "something" to offer to the people",[290] or, 'I would much rather be Hosea than to interrupt the shouts of the harvest festival like Amos, which is evidently what is happening.'[291]

The way in which he arranged and presented his confirmation classes also shows how profoundly Barth's thought had changed since his arrival at Safenwil. One idea which now appeared often in his books was that of the 'two worlds': 'Just as the waters divide on the heights of the Alps, so in the mystery of God, which is our own mystery, two worlds come into being. Both are in God's hands. But he is hidden in *one* and known face to face in *the other*. *Here and now* shadows and darkness prevail. *There one day* we shall find light and glory. An *old* world is passing away, and a *new* one is coming into being.' Accordingly Barth contrasted creation and redemption, the righteousness of man and the righteousness of God, hell and heaven, death and life, time and eternity, judgment and grace, Adam and Christ. So he would say something like this: 'What we see here and now is incomprehensible, for we see good *and* evil, joy *and* sorrow, glory *and* dismay. God is indeed Lord of this world. "Let everything that has breath praise the Lord." But that must *become* true. This world is waiting to become a *wholly other* world.' Or, 'A long ladder reaches down from the most noble, through honest citizens and the thoughtless masses, to the prisoners in Lenzburg.* And God? His righteousness is an eternal righteousness equally far from and equally near to all, whether they are on the highest steps or the lowest. Man becomes righteous before God when a *wholly other* world dawns' (1921). In one lecture Karl Barth also described Safenwil past and present as part of the old world: 'School, restaurant, factory, church and cemetery, and lastly all the houses, each tells in its way how men would like to live. But even in our beautiful homeland, under all the roofs, on all the streets, and in every heart, the great and bitter battle for heaven and hell rages on' (1918). And we men? 'We men are wanderers between two worlds; we have become homeless in this world and are not yet at home in the other. But as such wanderers we are God's children in Christ. The mystery of our life is *God's* mystery. Moved by *him* we must sigh, be ashamed, be frightened and die. Moved by *him* we may rejoice, be brave, hope and live. *He* is the origin. So we keep going' (1921). And anyone who sees that he is such a wanderer becomes dissatisfied: 'He can no longer be content, but has many questions to ask. That's right. This is the way faith begins. Those who are always content should never be envied' (1919).

The completion of the second edition of *Romans* coincided with 'my farewell to the parish of Safenwil'.[292] Possible invitations to other churches – to St Theodore's in Basle or 'as early preacher† at St

---

*Lenzburg is a small town in the Aargau with an intact castle which is used as a prison for serious offenders.

†So-called because it seems that the practice of holding services there at an unusually early hour is of very long standing.

Martin's'[293] – came to nothing. And although he was considered for
the Nydegg church, in the event the people of Berne did not want
him. Now, however, he was invited to become a professor at
Göttingen: 'I owe my invitation to a chair at Göttingen (which I
received as early as the beginning of 1921) and hence my elevation to
"proper academic theology" not to the famous second edition of
Romans, but to the first, which afterwards faded into oblivion. (The
chair for Reformed Theology was a new one, founded with the help
of American Presbyterians.) One might well ask how this book made
the groups and individuals who at that time counted for anything in
the German Reformed Church think that I was suited to the task.
Given its content and style, no one will be surprised to hear that at
first I found it a novel experience to be addressed in so compelling a
way in my capacity as a Reformed theologian. First of all I had to
accustom myself to the function that I was supposed to have. In fact
the second edition of *Romans* which I had produced in the meanwhile
made it easier for me: one will hardly find the first edition distinguished by a particular Calvinistic content. What moved a man like
Professor Karl Müller in Erlangen (who was foremost in recommending me) or the retired pastor Adam Heilmann in Göttingen
(who was most energetic in getting things going) to invite me there
was surely the form of the book. It suggested that I was passionately
concerned with holy scripture.'[294] That a chair of Reformed Theology was allowed in Göttingen at all was the result of decades of
tough negotiation between the Reformed Church of North West
Germany and the Prussian Ministry of Cultural Affairs.*

At any rate, Barth was utterly surprised by the 'enquiry of old
Pastor Heilmann and later the Prussian Minister of Cultural Affairs
whether I would be willing to take up the honorary professorship to
be instituted in Göttingen. I said yes after the briefest period of
reflection, because I felt immediately that as things were my place
was with the young theologians of Germany and not elsewhere. I was
blindly confident that my concern must somehow be for my lustily
growing horde of children over there.'[295] Having prepared himself
by reading the biographies of Ludendorff and Scheidemann, Barth
went to Göttingen at the end of February. He looked round his new
place of work and spoke there on 27 February: he did not give a

---

*As will be evident from events described in the next two chapters, appointments to professor-
ial chairs were made by the Ministry of Cultural Affairs and professors were regarded as civil
servants.

lecture, but a sermon (on Proverbs 16.2), 'which is what I wanted to be judged by most in respect of my lecturing'.[296] In this sermon he said: 'The really important thing is not what we say, but what may be said to us.' And again, 'The *question* about God cannot disappear, come to an end, or be settled . . . We can never be finished with him and must always begin again afresh with him.' On his way back he went to see Martin Rade in Marburg, Otto Herpel in Lissberg, Karl Müller in Erlangen and Merz and his friends in Munich.

Hardly had Barth returned to his village than he had a momentary temptation. 'An excited contemporary came to me and asked me to stay in the area and stand for election to the Aargau Great Council and then to end my days – who knows? – as a member of the administration in this canton.'[297] But the temptation was now no longer so great for the 'comrade pastor' and he said no. A further appearance of Gogarten in Switzerland, for a lecture to the Aarau Student Conference in 1921, only strengthened Barth in his resolve really to follow the path of theological scholarship which had unexpectedly opened up for him in this way. Of course he was also anxious about the future: 'I'm about to tread on some extremely slippery ice.' 'I just can't imagine myself in the situation and cannot think that I will be anything but a great failure.'[298] In July Barth paid another brief visit to Göttingen with Pestalozzi, to make preparations for the move there.

It so happened that on his departure from Aargau the cantonal church council asked him to make a 'general report' (which was due periodically) on the life of the church there over the last eight years. He took the opportunity 'of saying goodbye to the church in Aargau'. 'I'm writing in quite a rage, just like old times.'[299] In his report Barth flayed the modern church's zeal for methods, movements and money and its indifference over the 'content of preaching that goes with them'. He demanded that: 'The church should be aware of its failure towards socialism. Then it should re-examine itself and its task, in order perhaps to be able to tackle a new question which is appearing in a different form . . . more open, more prepared for God.'[300] However, in the meanwhile Barth had developed rather a more positive relationship towards the church in his district, so that he was prepared to take part in a commission to work out a new church order from summer 1920 onwards. He opposed any 'decorative' confessional formulae.

On 20 June, he made the personal acquaintance of the young poet

Hermann Hesse at a baptism which he had to perform in the home of his brother-in-law Richard Kisling in Zürich. 'Again I was astounded at the pietistic narrowness of these artists. Evidently they are mostly preoccupied with the problems of their private existence.'[301] He had already made the acquaintance of two other artists in this brother-in-law's house, and saw more of them later: these were the sculptor Hermann Hubacher and the painter Cuno Amiet (who belonged to the Dresden 'Brücke'* group). At the beginning of October, immediately after completing *Romans*, Barth went with Thurneysen and Pestalozzi on a very satisfying walk over the Susten Pass. Then he hastily paid a great many visits in the village. It was time to say goodbye.

The choice of Barth's successor again put Safenwil in a state of agitation and excitement. Vigorous newspaper articles appeared attacking Barth. The liberals looked for a candidate of their own. Barth himself would have liked his brother-in-law Lindt as his successor. In the event, however, a compromise candidate was chosen, Pastor Hans Brändli from Zürich. And now 'with dwindling exceptions . . . the people of Safenwil displayed only one desire, to have a peaceful time again'.[302] Barth had mixed feelings about his departure. On the one hand he thought that 'over these ten years I have been an extremely unprofitable servant'.[303] On the other, 'the recollection of Matthew 10.14 was very close to my heart . . . and without religious arrogance'.[304] He gave his farewell sermon on 9 October. 'The text of my last sermon was: "All flesh is grass and all its beauty is like the flower of the field. The grass withers, the flower fades (that is true!), but the word of our God will stand for ever (and that is even more true)." '[305]

With this, one chapter of his life came to an end and another began. 'It may well be,' thought Barth, 'that we shall soon look back on all the trouble and turmoil and wearisome labour of this time as one looks back upon a happy boyhood. What is to come may be the heat of the summer.'[306] On 13 October the Barths set off for Göttingen. All their life they remembered Safenwil with particular affection. When Barth's successor visited him in Göttingen, 'I asked him to give me news about every home in the parish.'[307] And still later he kept finding occasion 'to visit the place again and again'.[308]

*A group of expressionist painters dating from about 1905, including Ludwig Kirchner, Erich Heckel, Emil Nolde and Max Pechstein.

4

Between the Times

Professor of theology in Göttingen and Münster, 1921–1930

Initiation into teaching

So Karl Barth 'left the beautiful Aargau and joined "the Swiss on
foreign service"'; he came 'to the distant city of Albrecht Ritschl
where, with an assurance which today seems to me quite incomprehensible, I immediately opened the books on which I had unexpectedly and suddenly been called to give academic lectures'.[1] He
found a home for himself and his family for the next four years at
Nikolausberger Weg 66. This was 'an imposing house in the "better" quarter of Göttingen'.[2] Barth was able to buy it from the
systematic theologian Arthur Titius, who had just been appointed to
Schleiermacher's chair in Berlin. His neighbours were the opinion-
ated liberal-socialist philosopher Leonard Nelson, a Professor Old-
enberg (whose wife was a daughter of Fritz Barth's friend Samuel
Oettli) and a lawyer called Lütgebrune, a presbyter of the Reformed
Church with strong German nationalist feelings.

For Barth, the move from Safenwil to Göttingen was a decisive
event. Although in essentials he wanted to say 'the same things as
were said in Safenwil',[3] much had now changed. 'The "movement"
stopped. Work began.' 'Now it was no longer a question of attacking
all kinds of errors and abuses. All at once we were in the front rank.
We had to take on responsibilities which we had not known about
while we were simply in opposition. Suddenly we had been given an
opportunity to say what we really thought in theology, and to show
the church our real intention and ability . . . And yet we were far
from being ready. It was not just a matter of building on and
reinforcing positions which we had already taken up. We had only
just begun on a course which each one had to follow laboriously in
his own sphere. First of all the details had to be ascertained, clarified
and above all tested. On close examination, many things were not

what they had seemed to be at first sight.'[4]

Barth rarely preached in Göttingen. True, he did give a sermon there in the middle of November on 'The Name of the Lord' (Proverbs 18.10). 'By nature theology is a flight from all human names ... to the revealed name of the Lord. Its "academic character" consists in knowing about *him*.'[5] This sounded like a basic reflection on his new task. By and large, however, preaching now had to take a back seat. For the most part he was much more involved in the academic sphere, 'at a decent distance from the holy of holies. The situation is perhaps rather like that of the people who according to Psalm 1 "meditate" on the law day and night.'[6] 'Now I was happily resolved to get down to theological research and teaching – in grim earnest, in my own way and in my own style. Ragaz and Kutter thoroughly disapproved. Of course I had only a little of the equipment I needed.'[7] With great respect for the demands of an academic teaching post Barth therefore sought with tempestuous zeal to 'acquire the necessary foundations for it ... through some hard work'.[8] 'The rather vague terms of my teaching responsibility meant that at least in some respects I was gradually able to catch up by assimilating at least the most essential material which, with no inkling of this future, I had neglected earlier.'[9] 'So before venturing on dogmatics, I announced some purely historical lectures – essentially for my own instruction.'[10]

The desk at which Barth worked from now on (until he retired) was the one 'at which my father had lived and worked so much more competently'.[11] 'Now I was studying night and day, going to and fro with books old and new until I had at least some skill in mounting the academic donkey (I could hardly call it a horse) and riding it to the university.'[12] Barth devoted himself to the preparation of his lectures with unprecedented zeal – 'almost always on night shift'.[13] 'More than once, the lecture which I gave at seven o'clock in the morning had only been finished between three and five.'[14] He always had to work 'rather faster than my natural tempo ... And our "complicating" points of view, which turn everything upside down, do not simplify matters: there is an everlasting battle between these "viewpoints" and the material, which keeps wanting to snap back into its old familiar commonplace form.'[15] The young professor often sighed over the 'mountains of material which I haven't mastered!'[16] Or he lamented how 'I have to find my way through the fog like a poor mule, still hampered above all by a lack of academic agility, an inadequate knowledge of Latin and the most appalling memory!'[17] 'The inside of my head is like a cage full of hyaenas *before* being fed.'[18] 'I feel like one of those men at the fair who hit a knob on a box with a hammer in order to send a ring or some such thing high in the air, but it keeps coming down again.'[19] 'So "teaching" = groaning; there's nothing "splendid" about it.'[20] In a short time Barth did in fact work his way into academic theology and indeed soon became very productive in it, but this was probably because even at that time he learnt to keep closely to the principle that 'if one moves too quickly – and this often happens for very good reasons – before doing what really has to be done first (as though this could wait), one always has to pay the price'.[21]

Hardly had he become accustomed to his new situation than at the end of January 1922 he was surprised by the 'sensational news' that 'I have been made a doctor of theology by the (Protestant) faculty at Münster' – 'because of his many and varied contributions to the revision of religious and theological questioning'.[22] This title, of which 'I was later deprived in 1938 by *force majeure* . . . thus gave me academic respectability after the event'.[23] But the honour was 'a comfort and an encouragement'[24] for Barth. He was also very satisfied with the reaction of his daughter Fränzeli; she asked, 'Would I now be able to make children well?'[25]

In his first semester Barth's main lecture was only for two hours a week. The subject – an exposition of the Heidelberg Catechism – showed that Barth was now in earnest about discovering the character of Reformed theology.

He understood the Catechism as the product of a point in time at which 'the disquiet of the Reformers turned into the church's complacency'. He therefore argued that the text had two aspects. 'I kept having to *approve* and *disapprove* of almost everything. I would consider the historical context and the meaning in each case and then decide on its usefulness for teaching one way or the other.' Thus the very first question is 'definitely not good', as a question about 'your only comfort', but 'fortunately the answer blows it up straight away'.[26]

As the subjects of his subsequent lectures on historical and systematic theology indicate, he deliberately continued his efforts to understand the Reformed 'heritage' over the next four semesters. His special responsibility (which, in the somewhat obscure directive from the Prussian minister Carl Heinrich Becker, dated 16 August 1921, was to teach 'Introduction to the Reformed confession,

Reformed doctrine and Reformed church life') also involved him with this particular tradition.[27] 'I can now admit that at that time I didn't even have a copy of the Reformed confessions, and I certainly hadn't read them – not to mention all the other terrible gaps in my knowledge.' 'Fortunately it turned out that my theology had become more Reformed, more Calvinistic than I had known, so I could pursue my special confessional task with delight and with a good conscience.'[28] But first of all he had to get on with it. 'In fact it was only at Göttingen that I again familiarized myself with the mysteries of specifically Reformed theology, burning the midnight oil in my struggle over it.'[29] By undertaking this work, Barth became more and more a committed Reformed theologian, and 'slowly but surely became intent on pure *Reformed* doctrine'.[30]

It was only now that the second, 'more Calvinistic', version of his *Romans* appeared – with a Foreword which uttered a 'bold battle cry full of Homeric taunts'.[31] In line with his discovery of 'the Bible' through his work on Romans, Barth could not resist arranging a series of exegetical lectures in his first semester as well as those on historical and systematic theology: they were on the Epistle to the Ephesians. 'Nowadays I tear my hair in amazement that I could dare to announce that I would lecture on Ephesians for only one hour a week. Of course I hardly got as far as the second chapter.'[32] Barth's exegesis was done in a very characteristic way. He saw his chief task as that of 'attempting a *theological* exegesis': not in fundamental opposition to interpretation interested predominantly in historical questions, but as a 'necessary corrective'. And so he now interpreted the Bible in full awareness of 'the double scandal . . . that some of the problems of the other exegetes hardly seem to interest me at all, while my questions and concerns do not seem to trouble them very much either'.[33]

Barth's academic activity at the time was far from being exhausted by lecturing. True, he did not yet feel confident enough to give regular seminars in Göttingen. But he was well aware that the students, in turmoil after the catastrophe of the World War, had a pressing need 'to put questions and to register objections'.[34] Barth made an attempt to satisfy this need as early as autumn 1921 by arranging an hour a week for questions in addition to each series of lectures, so that problems could be discussed in the light of what he had said. In addition he regularly invited his students to 'open evenings' in his house. Here too there was opportunity for lengthy discussions, though Barth always thought it sensible that they should be linked with certain texts – for example sermons by Blumhardt and Kutter, or Thurneysen's book on Dostoevsky (which had just appeared), or passages from modern writers like Shaw and Thomas Mann or even political autobiographies (von Tirpitz, Liebknecht, Scheidemann, etc.).[35] Not content with this, he provided yet another opportunity for discussion; every Saturday afternoon he went out on walks with a small group of interested students on which he either 'walked and taught' or 'taught and walked'.[36] On these occasions he used to have to answer question after question without stopping: 'Herr Professor, what do you think about . . . ? How do you know that . . . ? What do you mean when . . . ?'[37] 'And at the end of each semester there was an exuberant party with sketches and parodies which the students used to write themselves (this tradition was kept up in Münster and in Bonn). There had to be a take-off of the master, and Barth himself used to sit at the piano singing the unforgettable "Song of the Swiss Exiles" to his own accompaniment.'[38]

Barth gave his various academic lectures 'to an audience which to begin with was not very large, but very excited'.[39] Since he was a mere honorary professor, there was no compulsion on the students to go to his lectures; moreover, members of the Reformed Church were a dwindling and even despised minority in 'Hanover'. Nevertheless, he soon drew quite a crowd from the total number of about 180 theologians.[40] 'The students are now particularly interested in a professor who is still so to speak himself a student. They soon noticed that I had to prepare each lecture as I went along and so could give them completely fresh bread.'[41] In his first semester he had an audience of fifteen for the main lecture, and fifty to sixty for his lecture on Ephesians. In the next semester the audience at the main lecture had already risen to forty-two and in addition there were 'always trespassers, strange ministers and scholars and even renegades from the competing lectures by Stange'.[42] Among his audience at Göttingen were H. Landau-Remy, Heinrich Graffmann, Hans Erich Hess and Elisabeth Haas (later Frau Schlier); Hanns Lilje, Joachim Beckmann and William Niesel, later to become church leaders; together with the Bavarians Oskar Grether, Walther von Loewenich, Karl Nold, Wolfgang Trillhaas and Herrmann Zeltner, who were particularly popular; and Walter Nigg and Artur Mettler from Switzerland. The audience presented a motley picture.

Amerikalied. *(mit kritischem Apparat)*

3. Willst du dein Dienstbüchlein zerreissen,
Das dir das Kreiskommando gab,
Willst nicht mehr Schweizerbürger heissen,
~~So reis ins Land~~ Amerika. .....

Willst reisen

2. Ich sehe schon den Dampfer rauchen,
Der mir den Freund vom Busen reisst.
Die Zähre kann ich nicht gebrauchen,
Die mir in Fremdes Auge gleisst.......

1. ~~Es pfeift~~, die Ankerketten stöhnen,
Am Sprachrohr steht der Kapitän.
Bei ~~solchen schauervollen~~ Tönen
~~Wird~~ schwer, ~~nach~~ Amerika ~~zu gehn~~....

H es recht H   *H Hör ich*
H diesen unbekannten
H einen Freund nach Amerika gehen
zu sehn

4. Dich locken Kaliforniens Felder,
Wo man das Gold im Bande wäscht,
Was nützen dir die vielen Gelder,
Wenn du das teure Hochland nicht mehr häst ....

5. Leb wohl, ich wünsch dir gute Reise,
Vergiss das teure Hochland nicht.
Wo sich der Fremde Edelweisse
Und Alpenrosenkränze fflicht.......

schöne   *F seine*

6. Grab dir dein Grab im Wüstensande,
Verdirb am Sakramentostrom!
Ich bleib im lieben Schweizerlande,
Bei meinen Vätern will ich ruhn.......

7. Schon schwebt das Schiff auf salz'gen Wogen,
Das zieht ihn fort nach fernem Strand.
Ach Gott, er ist dahingezogen,
Das Nastuch schwenkt er noch in seiner Hand......

Den ehemaligen Bonner in Erlangen et Zürchen unvergesslichen Gedenkens
überreicht
von
Karl Barth

29. *The 'America Song', which Barth was fond of singing to his own accompaniment at end-of-term student celebrations. He dedicated this copy of the text to 'former Bonn students now in Erlangen', 1931.*

It included 'many war veterans, a company commander, a battery commander(!) and a lieutenant from the Austrian Imperial Guard (who does some paving for a few hours every day – in the middle of the street! – in order to earn some money)'.[43] Later semesters saw the appearance of 'deaconesses, old women, chemists, law students and other hearers'. 'One man even came with a rifle. However, he was not a *Stahlhelm** man, but a forester, straight from his work.'[44]

'I saw the young students of the time and listened to them in the lecture room and elsewhere. They are among my brightest memories. In those years they called themselves the "youth movement" – and they were young, and moved. Because I heartily approved of that, I quickly came to like them for their great openness and their agility on all sides. They in turn became my partners, often exciting and always stimulating, giving me immense help with their remarks, protests and objections in my theological research and teaching, which were now blossoming out.'[45] 'What I had missed in Safenwil I now had an abundance of in Göttingen: talking and arguing not only with books, but with people.'[46] 'I was more grateful than they could know for the gratitude which so many Göttingen students lavished on me.'[47]

A prominent group among them were the 'Schlüchtern Youth', 'a Christian youth movement which has its prophets and heroes in a settlement in Schlüchtern, near Frankfurt'. Barth also came into contact with them. In December 1921 he even visited Schlüchtern itself and its current leaders, Eberhard Arnold, Georg Flemmig, and Tillich's friend Hermann Schafft: 'another of those Germans, full of insights and moods, all tongue'.[48] And of course he came into close contact with the small group of Reformed students, 'most of whom unfortunately just have no clue. However, they have now suddenly become aware that to be a member of the Reformed Church might be more valuable than people in Germany are accustomed to suppose.' At Christmas Barth once delighted them by giving them 'biscuits, cigars and a copy of *Romans*', 'one each for the flesh, the soul and the spirit'.[49] 'In the midst of all these young men and women' Barth felt like 'a beekeeper at work among his hives, smoking vigorously so as not to be stung, or like a good father, looking after his children, teaching them, admonishing them, comforting them on all sides, and

---

*The *Stahlhelm* ('Steel Helmet') was a para-military organization with strongly nationalist ideas, founded in 1918.

often in a position to protect one against the other.'[50]

Teaching students, Barth was just one professor among others. He took note of his colleagues with some detachment and with his characteristic degree of curiosity and astonishment. 'One can observe the average academic and scholarly fervour (which seldom appear without a touch of Fichtean pride, though it too is surely respectable in its own way) on any street in a German university town.'[51] At any rate he had great respect for his colleagues in the Göttingen theological faculty. 'In the common room I felt small and despicable among these giants of scholarship' – or like a 'wandering gipsy . . . with only a couple of leaky kettles to call his own who to compensate occasionally burns a house down'.[52] There he might meet, say, 'Carl Stange, an apologist for modernism and positivism' – a 'fabulous diplomat' and a 'skilled advocate of Christianity';[53] 'Alfred Bertholet (also from Basle), whose subjects were the history of religions and the Old Testament; the critical New Testament scholar Walter Bauer; His Majesty the Privy Councillor Professor Dr Mirbt (church history, canon law and amusements of that kind); Johannes Meyer the pastoral theologian with his smooth blonde beard'; the New Testament scholar Alfred Rahlfs; and, from 1922, the liberal systematic theologian Georg Wobbermin. Their approaches were 'far too different' for Barth to want to make their closer acquaintance,[54] though he met them on various occasions, on committees and elsewhere. For example, on 25 March 1922 he was with them at the grave of 'blessed Ritschl . . . the centenary of whose birth we celebrated, standing there in top hats to dedicate a wreath to him, the founder of the fame of our Göttingen theological faculty'.[55] Indeed 'the faculty even tormented me a bit: they wanted to keep me under . . . On the black notice board where announcements of lectures were pinned they put mine next to the lessons of the teacher who showed students how to play the harmonium . . . that was the place of Reformed theology at the time. A gymnastics teacher was another member of our party . . . But I survived.'[56] And it was Stange who gave Barth to understand that in Hanover 'the Reformed church means no more than the millenarian sects!!'[57]

By and large, however, in essentials the paths of Barth and his colleagues simply did not cross. There were two exceptions. He found two scholars on the faculty, both church historians, of immediate interest. One of them was Erik Peterson, a young assistant lecturer, a sardonic individualist with all kinds of eccentricities who was convinced of the 'transitoriness of earthly things'.[58] Barth later heard him lecture on Thomas Aquinas in the winter of 1923–24 and learnt a lot, so Peterson seemed to him to have 'not a little grace'.[59] Barth was perhaps even more interested in Emanuel Hirsch, but in a different way, as an opponent who had to be taken with the utmost seriousness. Hirsch had come to Göttingen at the same time: a 'learned and acute man',[60] a 'skilled dialectician and acrobat', with 'a profound knowledge of Luther and Fichte, an effete figure of a scholar of the kind to be found in books, German nationalist to his very fragile bones, but a notable phenomenon'.[61] Barth often met him for arguments and disputes – in their studies or on walks together. As early as February 1922 there was an exchange of written memoranda between the two in which they expressed their theological differences in eleven theses and antitheses. Here Barth contrasted his view of the Bible as evidence of the concrete revelation of God with the view of the Bible as a general religious document.[62] But their relationship continued to be 'intimate and stimulating'. 'Lively battles' alternated with 'the discovery that we had other things in common . . . It was difficult to swallow his eccentricities, his Berlin ways and academic airs, his Wingolfisms* and all the other ingredients, whatever their names, but *my* varied ingredients were no less difficult for him.'[63]

Companions

While Karl Barth was looking for his own particular course to follow among the Göttingen professors and students, he had a number of more or less close companions and continued to find more. He met the most flamboyant of them at the beginning of 1922. Fritz Lieb made his appearance – in the middle of a strike – 'in a red necktie, fiery red'.[64] Then in the middle of February Friedrich Gogarten came to Göttingen and 'strode sedately up and down our stage for three whole days'.[65] It emerged that 'we were at one in some forthright negative views',[66] but essentially in nothing else. That began to hamper the development of their friendship. Gogarten was con-

---

*Wingolf was a student association founded in 1830 as an alternative to existing organizations, differing from them in rejecting duelling and other undesirable features of student life. It was not, however, teetotal. To begin with it was Christian and pietistic, but later became just another association, and at this time had a marked German nationalistic tone.

fronted with Hirsch and Rudolf Ehrenberg, a professor of physiology, who belonged to the Patmos group . . . 'He wickedly posed riddle after riddle to Hirsch and was therefore excluded from "Christendom".' He even 'said something about the Copernican world system which was the presupposition of modern civilization, prided himself excessively on the fact that he had exchanged nine letters with the philosopher Grisebach in which "a basic clarity" was achieved, and described himself as having a mission to the *literary* public, to the men of *culture* (of whom he himself was one; one only had to see his study in Stelzendorf). However, in his lecture on "Revelation and Time" (which in itself was a good effort), strangely in contrast to me he gave the students the impression of being a dogmatic theologian; largely because, just as in Aarau and without being able to speak any more clearly, he broke in at the decisive point with the Lord Jesus as with a club.'[67]

At that time 'he also came to my lectures and listened a couple of times to what I had to say about the Heidelberg Catechism and the Epistle to the Ephesians. Even now, I can still hear him telling me, before he went off back to his Stelzendorf: "Do you know, Karl Barth, I don't think that things will turn out as you expect. Before we can talk about the Heidelberg Catechism and the Epistle to the Ephesians, we must first know what history is." I asked him, "But how will you discover what history is?" He replied, "First I must tackle Troeltsch, Dilthey, Yorck von Wartenburg and some other great figures from the beginning of the 1920s (he himself had started from Fichte . . . but he broke loose later). Well, first of all we must find a concept of history and only on the basis of that will we be able to read texts like the Heidelberg Catechism and the Epistle to the Ephesians" . . . Even then, that is in the winter of 1921–22, I noticed . . . that we did not think in the same way. For me it was quite the other way round: first of all I wanted to study the Heidelberg Catechism and the Epistle to the Ephesians. Only then did I want to try to understand what "history" is. But these were two very different approaches.'[68] Again, this fundamental difference in understanding between the two did not prevent them from following each other's progress with friendly interest in subsequent years.

Another person with whom Barth came into close contact at the same time was Rudolf Bultmann. In fact he had known Bultmann for a long time, since 1921, when Bultmann was *Ordinarius* Professor of New Testament in Marburg. 'Of course Bultmann was also

involved in the break with liberalism . . . I thought I understood him
and perhaps he thought that he understood me. Certainly we sometimes said the same kind of thing.'[69] At the end of February 1922
Barth went for a first visit to Marburg, where first of all some
students were waiting for him 'in a den with plenty of copies of
Romans thoroughly marked in pencil'. He also looked up Rudolf Otto
('looking just like an Indian rajah') and the philosopher Paul
Natorp, to whom he gave a copy of *Romans*. On this visit he took part
in a rather strange 'cult', though of course 'completely without
contact with the numinous. Bultmann led the magic. The theme was
"night". The night of sorrow and death, the mystic and the common
night, everything that is associated with night, darkness, sleep, rest,
"silence", twilight, bed, and so on, was discussed and talked to death
in word, song and prayer.' Following this, Barth had 'a good evening
at the Rades' with Hermelink, Stephan and Bultmann, the night's
orator and mystagogue . . . Bultmann was much better than I feared
he would be from his cultic attempt.'[70]

In the same year, 1922, a largely favourable review by Bultmann
of the second edition of *Romans* appeared. However, 'for Bultmann,
"faith" and "faith" again was at the centre of his interest in my book
and his approval of it. He thought that what I had said about "faith"
would easily fit into a sequence with what Schleiermacher, Otto and
Troeltsch had discussed under the title of "religion". Then he even
dared to put Paul's own Romans in this very same series!'[71] The way
in which Bultmann took Barth's side here made Barth ask whether
they really had the same views. This question hung over their
meetings during the subsequent period. When Barth was writing the
Preface to the third edition of *Romans* in July 1922 he raised it in
connection with a specific point. Bultmann had argued against him
that in Paul there were other spirits in addition to the spirit of Christ.
Barth retorted that everything there was the expression of these
'other spirits'; the task of the exegete was simply to ask how far these
other spirits could nevertheless serve the spirit of Christ.

A few days after Barth's visit to Marburg he gave a lecture to the
Göttingen liberals on 'Church Life in Switzerland', in which he
ironically depicted his country as a 'dreamland' of all liberals.[72] At
the beginning of March Pastor Thurneysen of Brugg, who continued
to be his faithful friend during these years, put in an appearance.
'One can . . . say that to ground theology in the church and especially in the work of the pastor and to make it relevant is a charac-

teristic of the whole theological renewal movement . . . It should be known, however, on the one hand that Eduard Thurneysen saw the need for a church theology of this kind before anyone else; at any rate, he stimulated me to work in this direction. On the other hand, it should be noted that of all those who have made a reputation and a name within this new theology, there is hardly anyone who embodies it as a movement from the church for the church as characteristically as does Eduard Thurneysen.'[73] 'In Göttingen, too, I needed correspondence and an exchange of ideas with him more than my daily bread. This was just because I knew how my stories amused him and because I could confide to him as to no one else my constant cares and concerns, which seemed to increase rather than decrease . . . but also because it was always my deepest need to hear his judgment on what I had done. And though I had my star to follow, as he had his, I had to keep taking my bearings from him because I had to understand him and be understood by him in order to understand myself properly. Which one of us went ahead? And which one followed? We were as one, in a union which could never become boring because almost always we approached both things and people quite differently and saw them differently.'[74] They also continued to visit each other in their homes during the vacations, and Barth was specially grateful 'for all the happy hours I was able to spend with him in that neat parsonage in Brugg'.[75] However, because of the great distance between their homes, their contact now had to be limited for the most part to letters, and there was a lively correspondence between Brugg and Göttingen.

Hardly had Thurneysen returned home after his first appearance in Göttingen than another theologian arrived to whom Barth felt a theological affinity – though with rather more reserve, and for only a limited period. This was Paul Tillich (1886–1965). He was an army chaplain during the First World War and became an assistant lecturer in Berlin in 1919, where he was involved in a group concerned with Religious Socialist questions which included Carl Mennicke, Karl Ludwig Schmidt and Günther Dehn. At the end of March he visited Barth in Göttingen and got to know him through two long conversations. In one of them, two students 'assailed the stranger with incidental questions . . . while I filled my pipe or else had no answer for the moment'. 'The most remarkable things about him are his "antipathy to orthodoxy" and his mythology of history, in which the need for the supernatural, which he otherwise takes pains to suppress, comes pouring out.' In the other conversation, 'Hirsch took pleasure in setting us against each other, denouncing Tillich to me as un-Christian and me to Tillich as unscholarly. Of course we did not agree with this type-casting, although there is something in it. We could only make peace on our somewhat narrow common front against Hirsch, and otherwise on the basis that we should think and expect the best of each other.'[76]

'Dialectical theology'

After his second semester in the summer of 1922 Barth ventured to announce that his main lecture would be given four times a week. First of all he devoted himself to a series on Calvin, who was an unprecedented discovery for him; 'a waterfall, a primitive forest, a demonic power, something straight down from the Himalayas, absolutely Chinese, strange, mythological; I just don't have the organs, the suction cups, even to assimilate this phenomenon, let alone to describe it properly.'[77] Barth was so preoccupied with Calvin and his theology that he had to abandon a second series of lectures which he had announced, on the Epistle to the Hebrews, although he had done some preparation for it. He was glad that after all his work in August he could have a long holiday in Switzerland, chiefly in Klosters. From there he also went to Davos to see the 'wise man of Jena', Gogarten's philosopher friend Grisebach; although at that point he got on 'much better' with him than with Gogarten himself,[78] they never really hit it off. On another occasion during these holidays he paid a visit to the old poet (and Nobel prize-winner) Carl Spitteler, whom he respected greatly.

On his return to Germany, he again had his hands completely full. It was a 'sour' time. 'Not only did I have to keep on learning and learning, but as the representative of a new theological trend, I also had to show my credentials or save my skin in every possible circle by giving lectures and holding public discussions.'[79] In the course of time these lectures took Barth all over Germany, and introduced him to a great many scholars, pastors and lay-people; he was also able to discover the prevalent opinions and feelings in the churches. 'How huge and varied Germany is! And there am I like a commercial traveller with my little briefcase, going to and fro from express to local train, in waiting rooms and on platforms, with a pipe which rarely goes out.'[80]

During the break in the summer semester of 1922 Barth had the opportunity of articulating his theology and taking it out of the lecture hall to groups of pastors and theologians by giving three long lectures. (A fourth lecture on 'Revelation and Faith' was planned, but was never given.) For Barth himself these lectures were 'more a matter of fixing the questions which concerned me than of providing answers'.[81] The subject of the first, which was given on 25 July to a pastors' meeting in Schulpforta, Saxony, was on 'The Need and Promise of Christian Preaching'. 'The friendly invitation extended to me by the General Superintendent, Dr Jacobi, contained the request . . . that I should give you an "introduction to an understanding of my theology".'

Barth accomplished his task by first describing how he himself had come to see the critical situation of preaching as 'an explanation of the character of all theology'. Thus for him theology could only be the theology of the cross, which not only gives an answer to men's questions but at the same time poses a question itself – 'and does so in a way that leads even the most frightened . . . to the edge of a worse abyss than he had dreamed of'. And so Barth concluded: 'There is more hope when we sigh *Veni Creator spiritus!*, than when we exult as though the spirit were already ours. You have been introduced to "my theology" once you have heard this sigh.'[82]

The second lecture, on 'The Problem of Ethics Today', was given in September at pastors' conferences in Wiesbaden and Lüneburg.

Barth's starting point was 'that the present problem of ethics is disquieting, perplexing, aggressive. It makes its uncanny and disturbing entrance into the bright circle of our lives like a strange stone visitor.'* Here too everything was subordinated to the dialectical principle: 'Because *God* says yes to us, we must be as radical in saying *no*.' But at the same time he attacked Lutheran quietism: 'Ethics cannot exist without millenarianism, however small the dose.'[83]

The audiences were varied: in one place 'a gathering chiefly made up of over-burdened modern city pastors', elsewhere 'old-fashioned people', 'petrified toothless Ritschlians', and so on. In Wiesbaden Barth met the New Testament scholars Martin Dibelius and Karl Ludwig Schmidt, 'who were obviously on our side'.[84]

Without doubt the high point in this series of lectures was the third, on 'The Word of God as the Task of Theology', which was

---

*The reference is to *Don Giovanni*, by Barth's beloved Mozart; at the end of the opera the statue of the Commendatore (whom Don Giovanni had killed in a duel) responds to Don Giovanni's flippant invitation and comes to supper with him (with disastrous consequences).

given at Elgersburg on 3 October. The audience was made up of 'unsuspecting and self-assured "Friends of the *Christliche Welt*". The only way in which I thought I could get through to them was to give them a lively introduction to "the fear of the Lord".'[85] 'A sea of dreamy autumn Thuringian woods, green, red, yellow, and one of many farm villages in it with white gables and timber frames, and in the middle of that an old castle, and now indescribably, the parade of liberals . . . No, I can't describe it. I will just say that there was no lack of old men in a second childhood with open collars and short trousers.'[86]

The lecture which Barth gave here is probably the most pregnant expression of what was then called 'dialectical theology'. His theme was: 'As theologians we ought to talk of God. But we are human, and so we cannot talk of God. We ought therefore to recognize both our obligation and our inability, and in so doing give God the glory.' He ended with the characteristic question: 'Can theology, should theology, pass beyond the prolegomena to christology? It might be that the prolegomena says everything.' For nothing, even 'dialectical talk of God', expresses the 'word of God'; it can only be a reference to it. Certainly, 'anyone who says "Jesus Christ" may not say "it could be"; he has to say "it is". But which of us is in a position to say "Jesus Christ"?' 'No way leads to this event; there is no faculty in man for apprehending it; for the way and the faculty are themselves new.'[87]

For this lecture from the pulpit at Elgersburg Barth was flanked by plaster angels, 'one of which at any rate had a shield with the inscription "Repent" on it, which he pointed at me!' Barth's remarks again created a sensation and were regarded as the rebellion of a new generation against the old liberals, no matter how much Martin Rade tried to pour oil on troubled waters when chairing the discussion. Barth found allies here in Gogarten and Bultmann. 'Of course Gogarten also spoke, with heavy, obscure, but good words. He gave free rein to all his magic arts, so that Krüger (the church historian from Giessen), who spoke after him, declared that he was still quite "stupefied" by what the "young man" had just said.'[88] On the way home Barth could not resist going to see Luther's room in Eisenach.*

Barth repeated the last two of these three long lectures, which together represented a concise summary of his viewpoint, in a number of other places. His first journey to the Reformed churches of

---

*Commemorating Luther's stay in Eisenach from 1498–1501: these were his last, very happy schooldays, before he went to university in Erfurt.

North West Germany in the middle of October gave him much to think about. Unexpectedly he found understanding friends there, 'excellent people, with whom I got on very well indeed.' First of all he had to appear at Emden at a solemn 'convention in a dark-panelled "council chamber".' The Reformed preachers came 'from all sides . . . wearing black coats, through the endless avenues of trees, past windmills and dykes'. He then spoke in Nordhorn, near Bentheim: 'The world there has stood completely still, *no trace* of liberals! . . . Instead there were resolute old gentlemen who really have dogma in their bones.'[89] Only two weeks later, still in October, Barth went to Bochum, where he had to speak against yet another different background. 'Countless factory chimneys and fantastic machines, the air full of coal dust, the kingdom of Stinnes and Thyssen. Naumann would have composed some appropriate "devotions" here: "Jesus by the blast furnace" and so on.'[90] Finally, at the beginning of December Barth took a number of themes for discussion which had developed to a 'quarterly conference' of the 'positives' at Bremen. Here he was impressed in yet another way by the Hanseatic scene. On first meeting he found the Bremen doctor Karl Stoevesandt to be a friend 'who was as resolute in his Christian faith as he was well grounded in medicine'.[91]

Shortly after his return, Barth was visited in Göttingen by Johannes Müller, who was collecting drop-outs from the church at Schloss Elmau (a 'cross between a convalescent home and a dance school'): because of the aim of the house, they were ironically called 'personal hedonists'. However, his visit only confirmed Barth in his 'aversion for this spirit and for heavenly prophets'.[92] At this period Barth also parted company from the Patmos group, which was dominated by the Ehrenberg cousins, Eugen Rosenstock and Franz Rosenzweig among others; he had first come across it in Tambach and 'about 1919–20 it wanted to overwhelm me and choke me with its gnosticism'.[93] Barth came across Rosenstock once again in summer 1924, quite by chance; both were climbing the same mountain in Beatenberg, in Switzerland.

On the other hand, during the course of 1922 Barth discovered two other remarkable groups. The first was the small Renitenz Church in Hessen, which had come into being in rebellion against the Prussian Union, and in which the remarkable characteristics of the 'berserk figure' Vilmar survived in a 'very characteristic and noteworthy way'.[94] Barth was introduced to this form of Lutheranism in Melsungen by his friend Rudolf Schlunck (who died in 1927). Barth had known Schlunck since Tambach: 'His apostolate in the Renitenz church gave him a remarkable combination of narrowness and openness; he had a stab at inspiration, associated with a concept of the *church* at which I increasingly pricked up my ears.'[95] At the same time Barth made the closer acquaintance of the Kohlbrüggians, based on the Dutch Reformed church in Elberfeld. They too were a separate church which had been formed in protest against the Prussian Union. Their theology came from the 'Reformed hyper-Lutheran'[96] Hermann Kohlbrügge; with its remarkable Reformation structure, this theology was now a delightful discovery for Barth. The group was embodied for him in a particularly imposing way by the powerful bearded figure of the Duisburg pastor Fritz Horn, a typical 'outsider'; Barth was not very happy with his worldliness, 'which was deliberately put on for show', but was clearly delighted with him as 'a true Israelite'.[97]

In the winter semester of 1922–23 Barth dealt with Zwingli and the Epistle of James in his lectures. 'I presented James as a tough and good outflanking attack on Paulinism . . . Several times I had the opportunity I wanted to fire off a Religious Socialist broadside.'[98] On the other hand he was disappointed with Zwingli, although he approached him 'full of good will and trust', and with the intention of taking seriously his 'announcement that humanism *also* intends to have its share in the good God of the Reformation'.[99] Things were to turn out differently. While he was assiduously 'tramping again and again through these books, then still in the Schuler-Schulthess edition', all at once he underwent a 'negative conversion'. This stemmed from a 'night with Zwingli' at the beginning of January. What he now saw in this man from Zürich was 'simply the familiar modern Protestant theology, the very image of it, with a few eggshells from the early church thrown in'. Disenchanted, he broke off the lectures with a description of the battle of Kappel in which Zwingli lost his life.

During this thorough preoccupation with Zwingli, in January 1923 Barth also came up against the thorny old confessional controversy over the eucharist. 'Study of the *earlier* writings of Luther, where one can see it *come into being*, had convinced me that Luther's doctrine of the eucharist was incomparably better than that of Zwingli. His only mistake was that he persisted with it . . . It was a real piece of good fortune that Calvin came afterwards and got the two carriages moving again after they had become stuck in the ruts of an undialectical relationship; unfortunately, however, he was too late for all of them.'[100] On the basis of these views, in July 1923 Barth wrote an extended study of 'Origin and Purpose in Luther's Doctrine of the Eucharist'. In it he sought to follow Luther for quite a long way, in the end only to confront him with Calvin's qualification, 'Yes, but'.

The lectures on Calvin and, at the latest, those on Zwingli showed that once Barth had turned to the Reformed heritage, the heritage of *the Reformers as a whole* had begun to open up to him. In Safenwil he had still not really found a way into the Reformers. 'Of course I also studied Luther and Calvin to some extent. But because I did so through the lenses of spectacles to which I had become accustomed over my years of study, that was not the time and place when I first sought and . . . found access to them.'[101] In Göttingen things changed almost at a stroke. Barth now felt that his previous theological view was really a pre-Reformation position, 'somehow in a corner along with nominalism, Augustinianism, mysticism, Wycliffe, etc. It was not itself the Reformation, but nevertheless the Reformation later sprang out of it.'[102] 'Only now were my eyes properly open to the Reformers and their message of the justification and the sanctification of the sinner, of faith, of repentance and works, of the nature and the limits of the church, and so on. I had a great many new things to learn from them.' At that time 'I "swung into line with the Reformation", as they used to say', not uncritically, but certainly with special attention.[103]

In short, his theological work 'led us, as it had to, to the Reformers' understanding of the Bible and of God'. But 'what we had learnt on the detour from Blumhardt via Kutter was not forgotten'[104] – as is shown by Barth's argument at the end of 1922 with Paul Althaus, who was at that time Professor of Systematic Theology at Rostock, on the 'Foundation of Christian Social Ethics'. Barth showed that in the meanwhile he had not forgotten his concern for Religious Socialism; now, however, he could acknowledge it only on the basis of the 'justification of the sinner'. His discoveries in Safenwil and his new appreciation of the Reformers were combined during this period to form a characteristic theology in which the earlier insights were given a different emphasis by having a new foundation, while at the same time Reformation theology was put in a distinctive light. Because of its characteristic concentration on 'the Word of

God', this theology has aptly been called a 'theology of the Word'; the term 'dialectical theology' is less apt, but it does describe its characteristic thought-forms. 'Some observer or other used the term "dialectical theology" of us as early as 1922.'[105] 'In contrast to the historical and psychological account which the "religious man" tended to give of himself at the beginning of the century', the characteristic feature of this theology was 'its question about the superior, new element which limits and determines any human self-understanding. In the Bible this is called God, God's word, God's revelation, God's kingdom and God's act. The adjective "dialectical" describes a way of thinking arising from man's conversation with the sovereign God who encounters him.'[106] This theology had a certain 'affinity to existentialism, which was unknown to me at that time', and also to 'phenomenology'.[107] At the same time, however, it was deliberately opposed to the other theology dominant at that time. 'Were we right or wrong? We were certainly right: read the doctrine books of Troeltsch and Stephan! Or read *Dogmatics* like those of Lüdemann or even Seeberg, which were so thorough in their own way. They were dead ends, if anything was! What was unquestionably due at that time was not some shift within the traditional way of posing questions (that had been attempted by Wobbermin, Schaeder or Otto), but this particular change of direction. The ship was threatening to run aground: it was time to bring the rudder round 180 degrees.'[108]

This 'theology of the Word' was also felt to be a new theological trend and a new school. As such it attracted many lively minds from that lively time – even including Martin Buber. From 1923 on he was teaching in Frankfurt and had some contacts with Thurneysen rather than with Barth: 'He understands . . . our concern and looks on it very sympathetically.'[109] On the other hand this theology provoked the opposition of the representatives of almost all existing theology. Barth had a whole series of kindred spirits at his side in formulating it. And in January 1923 it was given what amounted to its own mouthpiece in the form of a new journal (which first appeared at every quarter and then every two months). In September 1921 *Christliche Welt* very nearly became the organ of the new theology, since Rade had wanted to hand over the editorship first to Barth and then to Merz. But the plan fell through and the philosopher Knittermeyer took over. In Switzerland, in August 1922, Barth, Thurneysen and Gogarten had resolved to produce a new journal. 'There is a picture in which Thurneysen, Gogarten and I are sitting opposite one another on the day when we . . . founded this journal. At that time I still had quite a large moustache, which suited me very well. Next to me was Gogarten, who also had a moustache – that was a legacy from the nineteenth century! I'm looking at him in a remarkably sharp and mistrustful way, while Thurneysen is sitting peacefully – clearly in between the two of us. There was much to be said for involving Gogarten in this journal. I did not want to say no. But I did not say yes from the bottom of my heart. I always smelt something about Gogarten which I did not quite like.'[110]

The journal was founded in a memorable place, the 'Bergli'. This was a small, simple summer-house up above Oberrieden (which at that time was still quite a quiet place), on the left bank of Lake Zürich, with an open view on to the Glärnisch. Barth's friends the Pestalozzis had had it built there, and it was occupied for the first time in the summer of 1920. Since then it had become a favourite place for Barth (and Thurneysen) to stay in; right down to the 1950s he always paid at least one long visit there each year. He was always attracted 'by the lovely tranquil atmosphere – what Richard Rothe used to like', and increasingly he felt the place to be 'a second home'.[111] He used to get his strength back here. But he would also work hard, preparing and writing out some of his lecture series, individual lectures and articles. Anyone who wanted to see him during the summer vacation had to make the journey there, but visitors were always given a warm welcome by the Pestalozzis, whose hospitality was inexhaustible. This, then, was the place where the decision to launch the new journal was also made.

Barth found Gogarten's suggestion that the journal should be called *The Word* intolerably presumptuous. 'Better to call it *The Ship of Fools* than this idolatrous encumbrance.'[112] It was then baptized *Zwischen den Zeiten* (Between the Times), after an article by Gogarten. Its first number contained contributions from its three editors. 'When we founded *Zwischen den Zeiten* . . . we thought we were passionately agreed in what we wanted. We rejected the positive-liberal or liberal-positive theology of neo-Protestantism from the beginning of the century, and we rejected the man-God we thought we had recognized as its sanctuary. What we wanted was a theology of the Word of God. The Bible had gradually convinced us young pastors that something of this kind was absolutely necessary and we found a model among the Reformers.'[113]

The majority of Barth's lectures and articles from the 1920s now appeared in the issues of *Zwischen den Zeiten*. At the same time, however, these issues demonstrated that there was already a large group (for the most part made up of younger theologians) which, like Barth, was working somehow for a change in theological thought. There was a close theological affinity between Barth himself and a large number of the contributors. In the first years, not counting the editors, the names of writers included Bultmann and his pupil Heinrich Schlier; Erik Peterson and Günther Dehn; Fritz Horn, Wilhelm Loew, pastor of Remscheid; Joachim Beckmann, vice-principal of the seminary at Göttingen; and the writer Otto Bruder, Blumhardt's son-in-law, who was working at Christian Kaiser Verlag. A large number of Swiss friends also made contributions to the journal: Albert Schädelin and Gottried Ludwig, Fritz Lieb, Alfred de Quervain, Emil Brunner, Heinrich Barth and Lukas Christ, who had already proved of great service in the second edition of *Romans* 'by smoothing out the roughness of my style in many passages – a very necessary piece of work'.[114]

Georg Merz supervised *Zwischen den Zeiten*. 'He was equipped for such a task by nature and grace equally. Once the group had been formed he constantly redeployed it and led it out to battle. The work was often laborious and always demanding, but he would encourage and soothe where necessary, supplementing it most happily with his own resources.'[115] Now that Merz was in control of publication, Barth naturally had more frequent occasion to come in contact with him. For example, at the beginning of 1923, Merz delighted Barth in Göttingen with droll reports from a 'Pandora's box full of news from places far and wide'. Barth also loved Merz's distinctive form of Lutheranism, which was 'so marvellously diluted' by 'an anecdotal view of the world which constantly bewitched me'.[116] 'Merz was a consummate talker, a virtuoso conversationalist, a romantic letter-writer and a genius as a go-between. He enlivened our varied company and held it together; wherever he went and stood and talked, he added a touch of spice as well as bringing enlightenment. For Karl Barth, too, his appearance was a festival. Barth kept his Bavarian students back at the beginning of the vacation and invited them along. Then Barth sat smoking, laughing and simply listening in his armchair, while Merz stood in the middle of the room and lectured.'[117]

The publisher of *Zwischen den Zeiten* was the firm which accepted Barth's *Romans* in 1920, Christian Kaiser Verlag in Munich. Merz was its director. Albert Lempp (1884–1943), who owned it, took quite a risk to begin with in concentrating from that point on publishing 'dialectical theology' – and deliberately forgoing the sponsorship of other publications which would probably have been more lucrative. Following the underlying concerns of dialectical theology, part of Christian Kaiser Verlag's publishing programme soon also included writings from the time of the Reformation and beyond. This was the firm which over the next few years published the 'Munich' edition of Luther edited by Georg Merz and Hans Heinrich Borcherdt, and the *Opera Selecta* of Calvin edited by Karl Barth's brother Peter and Wilhelm Niesel. So 'right down to the first years of the Third Reich, Christian Kaiser Verlag published Karl Barth, and continued to publish "dialectical theology" until it was shut down in 1943. It produced almost all Karl Barth's first books.'[118] Staking virtually everything on this one card paid off: 'Our publisher could not but be content with the course of events from his particular standpoint.'[119]

In the month when *Zwischen den Zeiten* was first published, thus beginning to give 'dialectical theology' outward form as a distinctive theological movement, Barth felt constrained to enter into a debate in *Christliche Welt* with Adolf von Harnack. This was implicitly an argument with liberal theology, which was still setting the tone.

Each wrote two letters discussing the problem of theology as an academic discipline. When Harnack accused his former pupil of being a 'despiser of academic theology', the latter replied that he had no objection to academic theology, but that in its modern form it had 'departed from its subject (which had last been clearly stated by the Reformation)'. When the Berlin teacher spoke of a possible 'ascent of God' through culture, historical knowledge, morality, and so on, his young Göttingen colleague tersely countered with Jesus' saying: 'No one can come to me unless he is drawn by the Father who sent me . . .' And when Barth put forward the thesis that 'the task of theology and the task of preaching are one', the head of the liberals retorted with the objection that the 'professorial chair should not be turned into a pulpit'. Although Harnack thought that Barth's 'answers to my questions only show the depth of the abyss which separates us', his last word in the debate was one of reconciliation,[120] for which Barth thanked him in a private letter a year later with 'real respect'.[121]

While Barth was preoccupied with the new journal and with this 'feud', there was a tense political situation in Germany. It was all the more striking that he was notably less involved in direct political activity, which had been so much to the fore in Safenwil. True, when he had been invited to Göttingen he had been asked not to enter into any new political associations, but at this time he had no inclination to do so either. The chief reason for this was that he was so exceptionally involved in theology. 'At first I had so much to do in laying foundations for my academic work that I was rather restrained in this strange land.'[122] 'But inevitably I had to start looking up from my books and journals and listen to what was going on. I saw a Germany looking in vain for a cure for defeat in the First World War and its consequences – the word "Versailles", spoken with a North-German accent, often resounded like a whiplash in my ears.'[123] 'The political incompetence of the Germans' seemed to him to be 'boundless'.[124] 'The period of galloping inflation over the winter of 1922–23 saw to it that the stranger from a neutral country now became familiar with every aspect of post-war Germany.' A further factor was the French invasion of the Ruhr at the beginning of 1923, over which feelings ran particularly high in Göttingen; it even made Barth's blood 'boil with indignation'.[125] Of course Barth could not but reject the nationalism which was now flaring up in Germany, and he was dismayed above all at the chauvinistic reactions of his colleagues: 'The German professors are real masters at finding ingenious moral and Christian grounds for brutality.'[126] And of course he could not agree with the political conservatism which he found among these 'Machiavellian professors of the university there, who still all swear on the black, white and red,* and by the Kaiser or Bismarck, and so on. Indeed, there was nothing left for me but to take up my position on the left wing again.' Thus Barth maintained his firm political views. But to begin with he was 'not very active politically. I had to work in my study. I had better things to do than to get entangled in German politics.'[127] So 'I simply had no time at this point for involving myself in political activity'.[128]

However, Barth's political restraint was certainly also connected with the fact that he was a foreigner in Germany, and to begin with really felt that he was one. That was why he liked to spend all his holidays in Switzerland. 'Switzerland was never far away during all the years I spent in Germany. I always returned there for holi-

---

*The old imperialist colours, which in the German republic had been replaced by a new flag of black, red and gold. In the years leading up to the Third Reich the black, white and red flag became a rallying point for the nationalists.

days.'[129] 'But it was also the case that after a holiday in Switzerland I was always glad to get back to Germany and the German people.'[130] Gradually he really did begin to find his feet there, so that in January 1923 (during the Ruhr conflict) he could say, 'I'm slowly beginning to feel a German.'[131] This was inevitable in view of his intensive involvement in the theological task which had fallen to him, and his direct encounters with German students and others. So even if he refrained from adopting any public political stances, at any rate he tried as far as possible to help those who were in difficulties because of the political situation. At the end of September he made a successful appeal in the Swiss Sunday paper the *Appenzeller Sonntagsblatt* in connection with the 'bitter distress of countless' of his Swiss countrymen as a result of devalution: 'Help me to bring at least some relief to the many people who are threatened and oppressed.'

After another short visit to Switzerland in April, in summer 1923 he lectured on the Reformed confessional writings. He took a delight in studying the many texts and in addition wrote an interpretation of I Corinthians. This gave rise to 'the book on I Corinthians 15, which was published in 1924'.[132]

Barth saw ch.15 as the centre of this letter (Bultmann questioned this in a review), so here he developed in a nutshell his view of biblical eschatology: he wanted to understand the 'last things' not as an end to history but as an 'end-history' with which any period is faced. 'Last *things* as such are not *last* things, however great and significant they may be. He only speaks of *last* things who would speak of the *end* of all things . . . of a reality so radically superior to all things that the existence of all things would be wholly and utterly *grounded* in it and in it alone; i.e. he would speak of their end which in truth would be none other than their beginning.'[133]

In June Barth also wrote a brief critical 'reply to an article by F. W. Foerster'. In it he said to this well-known (pacifist) ethical writer and educationalist that Christian ethics could not be a matter of adding Christian labels to a preconceived ethical programme; from the beginning it had to stem from a Christian basis, namely from the forgiveness of sins.

After holidays in Switzerland (at the Bergli and in Grandvillard), in the middle of September Barth again found himself in Emden, a year after his first appearance there. He was speaking on 'The Nature and Purpose of Reformed Doctrine', evidently a product of his summer lecturing at the university. He delivered it to the 'General Assembly of the German Reformed Church, which was still very traditional. For once, I wanted to make their beloved Calvin rather strange and terrifying.'[134] In the lecture he said: 'The question of right doctrine introduces us to the vacuum at the *heart* of our (modern) church and inside Christianity.' He went on: 'A church does not live on truths, however deep and living these truths might be, but from *the* truth, which a man cannot take up *selectively*, choosing between this or that doctrine, theory or conviction. He *must* grasp this truth, because it has *itself first* grasped him.' 'The Reformed Confession lays emphasis not so much upon the idea that man is justified by *faith* and not by *works*, as upon the consideration that it is *God* and not *man* who brings about this justification.' But this gives rise to the question: 'Is modern Protestantism of the left or the right . . . with its fundamental concession to the rights and dignities of man, anything more than a Catholicism tempered by negligible heresies?'[135] This visit saw the beginning of Barth's acquaintance with leading figures in the Reformed Church like Wilhelm Goeters, Wilhelm Kolfhaus, Hermann Albert and Hermann Klugkist Hesse, and with its Moderator, August Lang. On the return journey he also visited his pupil Paul Leo on the island of Norderney.

If the Emden lecture showed Barth's new application to the question of 'doctrine', the lecture on 'Church and Revelation' which he gave in Lübeck on 30 November showed his new preoccupation with the problem of the 'church'. The decisive argument here ran: 'The true Christian church is the community of those who have been *pardoned in judgment*. Its foundation, which must constantly be recognized anew, is not human religious experience but the divine word of revelation directed *to* man. This foundation of the true Christian church is in principle the *end* of Christian subjectivism and the *presupposition* of a real Christian prophecy.' Barth liked the 'Hanseatic splendour' of the city as much as he disliked the 'alliance of the old middle class with the church': 'at any rate, the pastors are still just as Thomas Mann portrays them.'[136] In December he repeated the lecture to Göttingen pastors. And at the end of February 1924 he set out for 'the great port of Leipzig' to give the Lübeck lecture yet again. (Shortly beforehand the Imperial Chancellor Michaelis, on a visit to Göttingen, had impressed him as being an 'absolutely honest man, doubtless a bit twisted by Christianity; wise, but not really significant').[137] At Leipzig, '"hundreds, not to mention more", as it said in a letter, were eagerly' awaiting him. There were students and pastors; among them, 'Karl Fischer came hurrying in from the country with head held high at the head of a band of resolute followers, and the valiant Aé,' and others. 'The pastors wanted chiefly to learn from me what they were to do with their Lutheranism in view of the manifestly different Calvinistic doctrine which I was commending to them. I told them to test everything and keep the best.' On this occasion, Bishop Ludwig Ihmels, who received Barth for a private conversation, 'impressed me in his own way'.[138]

During the winter of 1923–24, as well as giving an interpretation of I John, Barth was preoccupied in his Göttingen lectures with an old friend, whom he now saw in a new, critical light: Friedrich Schleiermacher. Of course, he too was a member of the Reformed church.

'As far as I know, no one either before me or after me has attempted to interpret Schleiermacher in the light of his sermons. This was what I first attempted to do in my lectures, moving on from there to his *Speeches*, to the *Soliloquies*, to the *Dialogue on Christmas*, to his *Hermeneutics* and finally, as far as time allowed, to *The Christian Faith*.'[139] Barth's general impression was that Schleiermacher 'does intelligently, instructively and generously what the useless folk of more recent times do stupidly, unskilfully, inconsistently and fearfully'. 'Of course one often wants to cry out in a rage that his theology is one enormous cheat. To see that things do not work like this makes the situation quite clear, but the question "What then?" is all the more alarming.' Indeed, Barth raised the radical question, 'whether the case of Schleiermacher is not a box on the ear which in part resounds back to the sixteenth century?'[140] Barth had the lecture on the *Dialogue on Christmas* printed separately at the beginning of 1925.

Another consequence of this series of lectures was Barth's review of a book by Emil Brunner which appeared in 1924. This Swiss theologian (1889–1966), who had Friedrich Zündel as a godparent and who had been assistant pastor under Kutter, had been led along very similar lines to Barth in his thinking, but had a quite characteristic emphasis of his own as a result of a lengthy stay in England. As pastor of Obstalden, in 1921 he had sided with 'dialectical theology' in his *Erlebnis, Erkenntnis und Glaube* (Experience, Knowledge and Faith), a book which contributed to his appointment in 1924 to the chair of Systematic and Practical Theology in Zürich. 'It then came about that in the course of the change of position which we made together, my friend Emil Brunner, in his book *Die Mystik und das Wort* (Mysticism and the Word, 1924), gave vivid expression to our aversion from Schleiermacher, which was inevitable in that connection. I had to review the book in *Zwischen den Zeiten*, and found myself in something of a predicament over it. Although there was much in it which I also held against Schleiermacher, I was not very happy with the way in which Brunner presented his case. First, because I did not regard the term "mysticism" as an adequate designation for Schleiermacher's intentions. Secondly (and here there are already some first indications of my later conflict with Brunner), because I saw him using F. Ebner's anti-idealistic logology . . . just as much as the proclamation of the "Word" (of God) in his fight against Schleiermacher and his victory over him. Finally, and above all: because although I too was clearly "against" Schleiermacher in my way, I was neither so certain nor so completely finished with him as Brunner undoubtedly was.'[141]

At an earlier date, in November 1923, Karl Barth had already become involved in a regular controversy with Paul Tillich – though he did not find it easy 'to spread out before the eyes of certain smug people who are not involved in our joint concerns my differences with a man like Tillich who, even across various considerable chasms, is so close to me'. The discussion between the two was ostensibly over the problem of the concept of 'paradox'. In essentials, however, it was concerned with the status of the person of Jesus Christ in theology. 'For "us", Christ is *the* salvation history', whereas for Tillich Christ was only the symbol of a revelation present and knowable always and everywhere – and thus a revelation which was 'given' and not, as Barth wanted to see it, 'a very special *event*, revealed only by God and only to be known in so far as we can be known by it'.[142]

Barth's dissociation from both Brunner and Tillich demonstrated how much his thought had taken him along his own ways and how little he was concerned simply to form a new school under the title 'dialectical theology' which would present a closed front to the outside world. Thus even at this period he began to differentiate his theological standpoint from that of the other dialectical theologians. To make his own special concern known he had published in February 1924 a first volume of lectures with the well-considered title *Das Wort Gottes und die Theologie* (ET *The Word of God and The Word of Man*), dedicated to his mother. Only with Thurneysen did he continue to feel wholly at one over what he wanted and the two were so much of a mind that in the same year they were able to produce a second joint volume of sermons, *Komm, Schöpfer Geist!* (ET *Come, Holy Spirit*). As in the first volume, there was no indication of which of the two had preached which sermon. Questions addressed to other theologians of this group increased. However, a journey with twelve students to Marburg at the beginning of February 1924 strengthened the impression that Barth was essentially in accord with Bultmann. The immediate purpose of the journey was to hear a lecture by Bultmann in which 'the *former* Marburg theology . . . came off really badly and the good cause really well'. On another day Barth 'gave further information along with Bultmann in the theological seminar (the two of us sitting at the head of the table smoking our pipes in solitary splendour like two rabbis). Marburg has now really become once again one of those places on the map of central Europe on which one's eye can rest with satisfaction.'[143] By contrast, relationships with Gogarten had already reached such a pitch that when the two met in Göttingen in July 1924 an open quarrel was threatening.

Barth's first Dogmatics

It was evident that Barth was now in fact steering an independent course within the circle of dialectical theologians from the way in which since early 1924 he had been working out a series of lectures on dogmatic theology. 'I shall never forget the vacation of early 1924. I sat in my study in Göttingen, confronted with the task of giving my first lectures on dogmatics. No one can have been more plagued than I was with the questions "Can I do it?" and "How shall I do it?". Alienated increasingly from the good society of contemporary theology and, as I saw more and more clearly, from almost the whole of modern theology, by the biblical and historical studies which I had hitherto undertaken, I found myself so to speak without a teacher, all alone in the vast field. I knew that the Bible had to be the master in Protestant dogmatics. And it was clear to me, as to other scholars of the time that in particular we had to take up the Reformers again. But, "How can I, if no one instructs me?" . . . It was then that Heppe's *Dogmatics* fell into my hands, along with the parallel Lutheran work by H. Schmid. It was out-of-date, dusty, unattractive, almost like a logarithm table, dreary to read, rigid and incredible on almost every page that I opened: in form and content very much like so many of the other writers on "the old orthodoxy" on which I had heard lectures for years. Fortunately I did not dismiss it too lightly. I read, I studied, I pondered and found myself rewarded by the

discovery that here at any rate I was in an atmosphere in which the
way through the Reformers to holy scripture was more meaningful
and more natural than in the atmosphere which was all too familiar
to me from the theological literature dominated by Schleiermacher
and Ritschl. I found a dogmatics which had both form and substance, which was oriented on the central themes of the witnesses to
the revelation given in the Bible, and which could also explore their
individual details with an astonishing wealth of insights . . . I found
myself visibly in the sphere of the *church* and, moreover, in the sphere
of an *academic discipline* which was quite respectable in its own way
. . . Nevertheless, it was also clear that a return to this orthodoxy (to
stick to it and to do the same sort of thing) was impossible. For even
in that early period the "bane of Israel" which hitherto I had met in
its neo-Protestant form, was already in evidence and was making
itself felt.'[144] Barth's openness to earlier Protestant orthodoxy (he
was by no means uncritical, but ready to learn) was something
which the others involved in 'dialectical theology' could not share,
and they could only shake their heads at this remarkable change of
direction made by him. His serious consideration of this particular
heritage marked the point at which their ways had to diverge even
more obviously.

While preparing for his first *Dogmatics*, Barth not only began to
listen to 'orthodoxy', but also developed a positive interest in the
Fathers of the early church and even to some extent in Catholic
scholasticism. Indeed, he scented still unknown theological possibilities in the realm of Catholic thought – so much so that he
resolved 'not to stand too firmly on the "ground" of Protestantism'.[145] Of course the *Dogmatics* which he then outlined proved to be
neither 'orthodox' nor scholastic. The really new feature about it
proved to be the 'stubborn persistence' with which he 'kept returning from every angle to the situation of the pastor in the pulpit'.

The first paragraphs set the tone for the whole work. The opening sentence
read: 'The problem of dogmatics is scholarly reflection on the Word of God,
spoken by God in revelation, and handed down in holy scripture by
prophets and apostles. This is what is and should be stated and heard in
Christian preaching today. By prolegomena to dogmatics we understand
an attempt at an agreement in principle about the object of this reflection,
the need for it and the way in which it should be carried on.' Above this
explanation Barth put a prayer by Thomas Aquinas: 'Merciful God, I pray
thee to grant me, if it please thee, ardour to desire thee, diligence to seek

thee, wisdom to know thee and skill to speak to the glory of thy name. Amen.'

Thus from the beginning he approached his task with the view that 'Dogmatics is reflection on the Word of God as revelation, holy scripture *and Christian preaching* . . . Its primary object, therefore, is neither biblical theology nor church doctrine, nor faith, nor religious awareness, but Christian preaching as it is actually given. This can be *recognized as* the "Word of God" by reference to scripture and revelation and is defined critically *by* the "Word of God" (which is the aim of the exercise). Thus the concept of dogmatics is the exposition of the *principles* of Christian preaching (= dogmas) based on revelation and scripture.'[146] Only from this perspective and in this sense did Barth then find the freedom for his reconsideration of the old 'orthodox' doctrines: the doctrine of the Trinity (understood as 'the problem of the inalienable subjectivity of God in his revelation'),[147] the doctrines of the properties of God (to be maintained against mysticism), of predestination (ordained before creation), of creation (i.e. creation from nothing), of the covenant (which precedes the fall), of the person and work of Christ, and so on. 'Don't think that this is old junk.'[148] 'What happens is that after much racking of my brains and astonishment I have finally to acknowledge that orthodoxy is right on almost all points and to hear myself saying things in lectures which I would never have dreamt could be so either as a student or as a pastor at Safenwil.'[149] Barth was somewhat uncertain about accepting 'natural theology', which he saw the orthodox reckoning with. On the other hand the 'immanence of God in the world' seemed to him to be a great truth, 'if only one holds fast to the *creatio ex nihilo* through everything'.[150] This was a step beyond *Romans*.

One curious feature of this first series of lectures on dogmatics was that Barth was able only to announce them 'in connection with someone wholly other, as "Instruction in the Christian Religion", so Lutheran was the façade of the Göttingen theological faculty at that time. Laughing fit to burst, I carried on this charade for three semesters.'[151] At Stange's urging, 'the theological faculty passed a resolution against me that I had to announce my dogmatics as *Reformed* dogmatics'.[152] However, Barth could not accept this: he did not want to surrender the 'ecumenical character' of his teaching.[153] At last he was able to begin under the compromise title, with an audience of sixty: 'I suffered considerably from Stange's parallel lectures.'[154] He gave the Prolegomena in summer 1924 (and also lectured on Philippians); Dogmatics I in winter 1924–25; Dogmatics II (the doctrine of reconciliation) in summer 1925 (and also lectured on the Sermon on the Mount); and Dogmatics III (eschatology) in winter 1925–26. However, he had already left Göttingen before starting on this last section. Barth was very well aware of the strangeness and the loneliness of his attempt at dogmatics. He saw it as an experiment, and sighed: 'O this centuries-old swamp in which we're stuck! It is so terribly difficult to keep on *thinking* the opposite, let alone to say it, to formulate it and to put it in context.'[155] So he was glad to be able to talk at length with Thurneysen during the summer vacation of 1924 in Pany (Graubünden) about the course he had adopted.

Over the following period he again gave a number of lectures in an attempt to present his theological views for discussion by a wider audience. At the end of October he delivered an interpretation of Philippians 3, based on his summer lectures, to a pastors' conference at Tennstedt, Thuringia. And at the end of November he went to Königsberg to lecture. (The day before he left, Hindenburg had 'made quite an impression' on him at the dedication of a monument in Göttingen!)[156] While staying in Berlin en route he heard a lecture by Seeberg and visited Lietzmann. In Königsberg itself he was so busy 'that I had almost no time to think of Kant'.[157] His lecture on 'The Word of God and the Word of Man in Christian Preaching' took up a chapter from the prolegomena of his dogmatics lectures of summer 1924. In it he argued that the task of preaching could only be to create 'attention, respect and understanding for God's own Word'.[158] The response to his views was along lines which had gradually become familiar: 'Yes (to overcoming subjectivism, immanentism, anthropocentrism – hurrah, hurrah! We've always said that) – But! (And yet . . . somehow there *must* be . . . our Luther taught us . . . precious heritage . . .)'[159] On this occasion Barth also got to know Hans Joachim Iwand (1899–1960), who had recently been given his doctorate – 'I was fond of him from our very first meeting in Königsberg . . . An incomparable fire burnt in him!'[160] On another day the same lecture 'was staged once more' in Danzig, 'in the sacristy of an old church'. General Superintendent Kalweit (with whom Barth was staying) 'spoke to his pastors in unconditional agreement'. The city itself seemed to him to be 'a real fairy-tale', and he gazed in awe and wonder at Hans Memling's 'Last Judgment'.[161]

Before Barth worked out further material for 1925, he heard a lecture in Göttingen by Hermann Graf Keyserling, who sought – in vain – to win him over to his 'school of wisdom'. On another occasion he met – with astonishment – the 'phenomenological' philosopher

The 1920s

30.   *For decades the Bergli, a country retreat owned by Barth's friends the Pestalozzis, became his home for the summer holidays, where he worked, rested and entertained his friends.*

31.   *The university in Göttingen. It was here that Barth worked hard from 1921 to 1925 in an attempt to make himself familiar with the demands of academic theology.*

32. *At the Bergli in summer 1922, the time of the founding of* Zwischen den Zeiten: *Marguerite Thurneysen, Gogarten, Lukas Christ, Thurneysen, Peter and Karl Barth, Richard Siebeck, Gerty Pestalozzi.*

33. *In 1924 Georg Merz introduced Charlotte von Kirschbaum to Barth; she soon became a loyal assistant and joined his household in 1929.*

34. *Barth's friends in Weggis, 1925: Gottlob Wieser and his wife, Lukas Christ and his wife, Walter Steiger, Marie Straub and Friedrich Gogarten.*

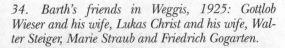

35. In summer 1929 Barth had a sabbatical semester which he spent at the Bergli studying Augustine and Luther, helped by Charlotte von Kirshbaum.

36. Barth and his mother in Münster, 1928; at that time she was sixty-five and was keeping house for him.

37. Barth's Munich friends Albert Lempp, who owned Christian Kaiser Verlag, for many years his publisher, and Pastor Georg Merz (below left).

38. On his first visit to Holland (May-June 1926), Barth was very impressed with the Calvinism he found there. One of the first people to draw attention to his theology was T. L. Haitjema (below right).

39.   *During the time he was at Münster, between 1926 and 1930, Barth gave a series of important lectures. On 9–10 June 1927 he spoke at an SCM conference on the Baltic island of Rügen.*

40.   *The Protestant Faculty of Theology at Münster, 1926: (sitting) Otto Schmitz, Johannes Herrmann, Georg Grützmacher, Georg Wehrung; (standing) Wilhelm Stählin, Karl Barth, Johannes Hänel.*

Moritz Geiger. And at the beginning of February he heard a lecture by Bultmann, who had made the journey with 'thirty to forty of his pupils'. The lecture revived Barth's suspicions about the theology of his Marburg friend. It was probably on this occasion that the following scene took place: 'One of the most unforgettable incidents of my life is a visit which Bultmann once paid me in Göttingen.' 'We sat down one Saturday in a small village outside Göttingen to have coffee and buns – which was a favourite pastime then.' Bultmann 'read aloud for hours from lectures by Martin Heidegger which he had heard and written down in Marburg. The purpose of the exercise was that we should attempt to understand the gospel witnessed to by the New Testament, like all matters of the spirit, by means of this "existentialist" approach.'[162] At any rate, Bultmann's visit went like this: 'In public we kept as close together as possible', but there was a series of private conversations 'in which our differences were also discussed . . . He reproached me for having no "clean" concepts . . . and I him for thinking in terms which were too anthropological, too Lutheran, too reminiscent of Kierkegaard (+ Gogarten) . . . But these are all points of difference about which one can have a profitable discussion.'[163]

At the end of April Barth again made a brief appearance in Switzerland, to give a lecture on 'The Scriptural Principle of the Reformed Church' in Basle, Zürich and Berne based on part of his summer 1923 series of lectures on dogmatics. In them Barth accepted the principle that the Bible, an earthly, human book, is a witness to revelation and thus itself the Word of God. So it is not merely a source of Christian knowledge, but its critical norm. In the middle of May there followed a respectful, but critical, discussion of his former teacher (who had died in 1922), 'The Principles of Dogmatics according to Wilhelm Herrmann'; a lecture which was first given in Hanover. His chief opponent here was Bernhard Dörries (who wrote a whole book against him in 1927) 'in the name of Lutheranism'. He then delivered the lecture 'to the died-in-the-wool liberals in Halberstadt', taking a large group of his pupils along with him. 'I have never before smelled so strongly that *this* history is *finished*; theological liberalism is *moribund*.'[164]

One can see how far Barth had moved away from the liberals, and at the same time from Herrmann and thus from his own beginnings, from the fact that he could now say: 'The church should always present revelation to men as "doctrine" (what else? Surely not in lyric poems . . . or as random emotional outbursts?). And it should always be presented with the claim that this doctrine is to be "accepted as true" (how else? Surely not as a fairy tale?). Would to God that our doctrine were so worthy of belief that it could compel such acceptance as truth.'[165]

About a fortnight later, on 6 June, he made an impression at the General Assembly of the German Reformed Alliance in Meiderich, a suburb of Duisburg, with a new lecture – on the 'Possibility and Desirability of a General Reformed Confession of Faith'. There he found 'the Reformed world on the lower Rhine really something to see' at close quarters, though he caused disquiet there by a remark associating pietism with rationalism. In the lecture, Barth gave as a condition for a Christian confession: 'God must will it, and his will must be recognizable from the fact that it has something *definite* to say in terms of dogmatics *and* ethics . . . Has the church something to say to the world, e.g. with reference to Fascism and so on?'[166]

During this period Barth was also concerned about his own future. For some time he had wanted to move on from Göttingen. The honorary professorship was badly paid, and the dispute with the faculty there over the announcement of his lectures on dogmatics had shown his lack of rights. Since then, 'my relationship with the faculty has been worse than ever'. So he thought that it would be best 'if I could find some way out of this mouse-trap'.[167] The possibilities of invitations to Bonn or Giessen (in December 1923) fell through, and the possibility of an invitation to Berne (in July 1924) did not attract him. In June 1925, Thurneysen surprised his friend by inviting him to succeed Kutter in early 1926 as pastor of the Neumünster church in Zürich. But Barth found this offer less attractive when at the end of February Kutter wrote a letter (to Thurneysen) in which he said that he could only regard Barth as a 'general rejection' of his own theology.[168] 'So Thurneysen was as unsuccessful in summoning me from Göttingen and my first exciting preoccupation with dogmatics back to Switzerland and into the pulpit ("the real arena of the kingdom of God"),[169] as I was unsuccessful in having him as my successor in Göttingen. Doubtless both these things had to turn out as they did.'[170] While Barth was still considering the enquiry from Zürich, another possibility suddenly emerged. 'At the end of the summer semester of 1925, just after I had finished my first three-semester course on dogmatics, I heard the news that . . . the Protestant faculty of theology in Münster had successfully proposed me as Professor of Dogmatics and New Tes-

tament Exegesis. Since the restriction of my formal status in
Göttingen had occasionally bothered me . . . there was no reason for
me not to accept confidently this confident invitation.' More precisely, this was an invitation to be '*ordinarius* professor in a post normally
occupied by an *extraordinarius* professor'.[171]

In August, Barth first had a holiday with his family on the island
of Baltrum in the North Sea. The party also included his old friend
Wilhelm Loew with his wife and children, to one of whom Barth was
godfather, and the family of his new friend Karl Stoevesandt. The
plan that the Bultmanns should also spend the holiday with them
was thwarted by the advice of Frau Bultmann that 'we should keep a
kilometre of water between us'.[172] Shortly beforehand Barth's family
had increased in size yet again. Another son, Hans Jakob, was born
on 6 April 1925; the Göttingen Superintendent Carl Mirow, Albert
Lempp and the wife of Barth's former Safenwil neighbour Pastor
Paul Schild were chosen as his godparents. In the holidays Barth
had time for his family; otherwise, because of the many demands on
his time, he only saw them 'swarming around and living as though
under glass'.[173]

Still, even at other times he would join in their interests and
activities. Occasionally he went cycling with his wife Nelly around
Göttingen, or (as in the summer of 1923) went with her to orchestral
rehearsals for the Handel Festivals in which she was involved.
Occasionally, too, he went with his children – he once called them
'K.B.'s collected works' – to the cinema or to the circus (which he
liked even better). Here 'balancing acts of the most remarkable kind
. . . interested the father more than the children'. On another occasion he went with his children to the zoo. 'Looking at the restless
hyaenas on land, the equally restless sea lions in the water and two
ibexes butting each other in the presence of a tapir gave us a good
deal to think about. We are probably somewhere near this whole
world (including the smell of game which surrounds these creatures), and who knows whether one day, after a transmigration of
souls, we shall not have to do penance for all kinds of things in a cage
like that before we can be put to a better use.'[174] Karl Barth was
enchanted by the 'bold phraseology' in a letter from his oldest son,
who greeted his parents courteously as 'one who is your true and
abiding son Markus'.[175] And he was quite amazed when his son
'Stöffeli . . . discovered for himself the doctrine of predestination in
its undiluted Calvinist form and presented it to me as his own

invention'.[176] As a small boy, the same son also surprised his father by asking, 'Do you know who Mr Essential is?' 'No, who is he?' 'God.'[177] Barth did not think that he could bring up his children as strictly as the older generation did in his childhood.[178] 'I brought them up on a very long lead – or rather, I hardly brought them up, but let them grow and get on with things. They always showed a great deal of confidence in me . . . and when they got older, I understood their own particular ways and kept in with them as well as I could. There were never tensions or scenes between us, but plenty of friendly exchanges which always taught me a lot. Each of them was an individual in his or her own way. And if criticism was due from my side, I certainly never kept it back. But everything tended to happen increasingly on the basis of a free and open friendship.'[179]

In September 1925 Barth stayed at the Bergli again. This time he got to know Charlotte ('Lollo') von Kirschbaum more closely. She was a Red Cross sister from Munich with a lively interest in theology. She came from Georg Merz's circles and it was he who had brought her along to Switzerland. The days there ended with Barth's first aeroplane flight – from Zürich to Munich. He enjoyed 'being able to look down on the earth from such a distance'. In October he gave a lecture to the Göttingen Autumn Conference on the mutual relationship of 'Church and Theology' and again during a 'Theological Week' in Elberfeld. Its main topic was the problem of the authority that theology should recognize. He felt compelled here to wage a 'running battle' with Erik Peterson, with whom so far he had gone along so expectantly.[180]

Münster

Then, on 25 October, he found himself in Münster, 'nest of priests and rebaptizers'. He lived a bachelor existence in lodgings run by a Frau von Flottwell in Warendorferstrasse 23. There, under a 'gigantic oil painting' of the 'emperor with the sideburns', Wilhelm I, he began work straight away.[181] He had to live alone to begin with because the sale of the Göttingen house and the purchase of a new one in Münster was a rather long-drawn-out affair. So he was by himself while he got to know the new surroundings to which he had suddenly been transplanted. 'The predominant characteristic of this area is its flatness. Outside the city the countryside is intersected by roads which from where one stands sometimes form one straight line as far as the horizon . . . The building materials here are red bricks (you see millions and millions of them) . . . and the dominant form of worship is Catholicism, which is evident in the persons of numerous monks, nuns and clergy of all kinds.'[182]

During the next months Barth saw his family only on visits: the longest one was at the end of the year, when what he liked best of all was playing Mozart with his wife and a great-granddaughter of Hegel's on Christmas eve. At the beginning of January 1926 he went from there to Danzig – Bultmann joined him in Berlin – for a theological refresher course for pastors and teachers of religion. To this group he gave an interpretation of Philippians 3 (based on the relevant part of his Göttingen lecture), while Bultmann 'spoke in tongues of fire on Pauline and Johannine eschatology'.[183] During this trip the two of them also went to visit 'the uncanny castle of the old knights of the order in Marienburg'.[184] Barth was again given a warm welcome by General Superintendent Kalweit, 'a wise, far-sighted man, *very much* up with things philosophically and theologically'.[185] When he returned to Münster he had to go on living there alone. And he was still by himself when Thurneysen came for a first visit – Charlotte von Kirschbaum also came shortly afterwards. He could not bring his family to Münster until 4 March; for the next four years they lived in Himmelreichallee 43 – in a house which was 'a real orgy of red brick'.[186] Barth thought that the name of the street was as symbolic as that in which his 'special friend' Althaus now lived. 'He also moved (to Erlangen) and now lives in Hindenburg-strasse.'[187] Barth also thought it symbolic in another way that his new home was mid-way between a zoo and a cemetery.

Meanwhile he had already survived his first semester in Münster. A high-point of this winter was his last long meeting with Adolf von Harnack, soon to be seventy-five years old. Harnack was staying in Münster for a lecture on 'The Significance of the Reformation for the History of Religion'. When Barth's old teacher came to see him, to his surprise his former pupil was interested in a commentary on the Gospel of John by Cocceius. The two then had a long conversation – about the task of a Protestant dogmatics. 'I was very impressed by the fact that he told me that had he to write a *Dogmatics* it would have to be called *The Life of the Children of God* (that seems to me to be a very significant expression of his particular Christian standpoint!).' Harnack also made enquiries – 'no polemic now' – about Barth's own work. 'If I wanted to sum up his positive significance for me, I would have to say that he gave me a vivid idea of the time of Goethe. He impressed on me indelibly that one must not forget the humanities – particularly if one does not want to seek the root and the essence of Christianity and theology in them (and here his way and mine parted).'[188] 'Harnack manifestly spoke for neo-Protestantism, for which the real object of faith was not God in his revelation but the man who believes in the divine. A theology which is governed in its thinking and speaking by holy scripture and the church will not be able to accord man such honour or think him so significant. But that does not mean that the concerns which led neo-Protestantism on its own particular course should be forgotten altogether. It has a legitimate place within the framework of the doctrine of the Holy Spirit'[189] – and at a later point in his *Dogmatics* Barth used the title suggested by Harnack as the heading for a section.

In his first semester in Münster Barth lectured – for one hour a week – on the last part of his 'Göttingen' dogmatics, i.e. on eschatology.

He began by asserting that: 'because it speaks of the boundary, of the end, Christian eschatology is fundamentally conscious of saying things which only God can say directly as they are'. Thus 'its object is not *the future* but *the one who is to come*'. Furthermore, 'Christian eschatology is not interested in the last things for their own sake. Conversely, here man is confronted with the mystery of the future *for the sake of revelation* . . . because the revelation which constitutes the Word of God is in itself eschatological.' It does not serve curiosity, but the Word of God. Finally, 'Christian eschatology is no idle knowledge'; it has 'the character of a claim to faith and obedience which directs itself specifically to man'.

This time Barth's main lecture (four hours a week!) was exegetical. In it he gave an interpretation of the Gospel of John, not without asking Bultmann for help with it.[190] It was significant for the method by which he interpreted the text that he 'drew his wisdom chiefly from the Greek concordance'.[191]

As early as in the introduction he observed: 'We only hear – still more, we only understand – the gospel when we *do not fail* to notice from the start the very real way in which it not only confronts us but comes to meet us . . . It is called canonical scripture . . . a word which from the beginning addresses us in the name of God and thus claims to be saying something fundamentally new to us. It is a word which has opened a conversation with us even before we have been able to hear it.' However, he went on to argue that this does not exclude either attention to the historical problems inevitably surrounding any book of the Bible because it is a word of man, or the need for the reader to be ready to listen as though he were still an ignorant pupil.

One new development in this semester was that for the first time Barth also had a regular seminar – on Calvin's *Institutes*. 'The best thing about this was probably that I made clear to myself and the students with much stammering and gesturing what understanding Calvin might possibly mean.'[192] On the basis of what he worked out there (and his 1922 series of lectures), Barth then wrote a lecture on Calvin which he gave in Münster in January 1926. He may also have resorted to earlier material when he gave a lecture early that year to Westphalian pastors on Calvin's doctrine of the sacraments.

Once again, then, he had a great deal to do in Münster. And he still did not find it easy to bear the burden which had been laid upon him. 'It is touching and encouraging that people are so keen and co-operative and that recently I have even gained the reputation of being a "scholar", but it does not alter the fact that often for many weeks on end I have had to cope with depressions of the foulest kind, have made plans to escape to a Swiss country parsonage, and so on. It is terrible *how* much we always find ourselves back at the beginning.'[193] Thus Barth from time to time felt a 'desire not only to "travel far, far away", but also simply to be able to "keep very, very quiet" about the Pope and Calvin and Schleiermacher'.[194] But that was just not possible. And so he had to go on and on under the burden of his tasks. He rarely preached at this time, and when he did so it was often from the pulpit of the Deaconesses' House in Münster. For the most part, however, he had to restrict his work and his speaking to the academic field.

He felt that the Westphalian students at his new university were 'rather a rough crowd'. Among his audience the 'tribal cohort whom I brought with me from Göttingen',[195] who made themselves felt vociferously, tended to dominate the scene all the more. But here too, from semester to semester, 'time and again good and even friendly groups kept forming'. Barth loved the German students: 'their openness, their delight in telling stories, their capacity to keep up with the professor and, once aroused, to spur him on to new heights'.[196] His colleagues in the relatively new Protestant theological faculty (it had only been in existence since 1914), with whom he now worked, 'all proved much more friendly than the Göttingen backbiters and poison-spreaders'.[197] And he found it pleasant that 'life in the faculty goes on, with what seems to be traditional friendliness and peacefulness'.[198] At that time his fellow-professors were Johannes Herrmann and Johannes Hänel for the Old Testament and for the New Testament Otto Schmitz, who had come to Münster in 1916 from the Basle College of Preachers: Schmitz was a man 'on whose good will one could always rely'.[199] The senior professor was the church historian Georg Grützmacher, 'who kept his pipe in his mouth even more constantly'[200] than Barth; the Reformed scholar Karl Bauer was also a church historian. Georg Wehrung was *Ordinarius* Professor for Systematic Theology, but he was oppressed by Barth's proximity and soon moved away. After Wehrung's departure from Münster Barth took his place, and Barth's place was taken by Wilhelm Herrmann's pupil Friedrich Wilhelm Schmidt, born in Berne. (Before Schmidt's appointment Barth had vainly proposed Wilhelm Loew for the chair, and then Werner Elert had turned down the invitation.) In the summer semester of 1926, Wilhelm Stählin, pastor of St Lorenz in Nuremberg (and later Bishop of Oldenburg), took up the chair of Practical Theology; he was a leader of the Berneuchen liturgical movement.*

Although Barth got on well socially with these professors, they provided less theological stimulus for him here in Münster than colleagues from the older and larger Catholic theological faculty. Here, of course, 'I came in contact with the Roman Catholic professors of theology. Occasionally I went to Roman Catholic services and there got to know the very solid Westphalian Catholicism.'[201] 'My encounter and acquaintance with this form of Catholicism became very important to me.'[202] Teachers on the Catholic faculty at that time included Franz Diekamp, a 'modern Thomist',[203] whose *Catholic Dogmatics* Barth often discussed later in his own *Church Dogmatics*, the moral theologian Joseph Mausbach, the New Testament scholar Max Meinertz, and Joseph Schmidlin, a specialist in mission. Barth got on particularly well with an assistant lecturer called Bernhard Rosenmöller, who was about the same age. Rosenmöller later worked in the philosophical faculty at Breslau. In a great many conversations with him Barth became convinced that in

---

*The Berneuchen group, which began in 1923, was concerned to find a form of church life which would speak to the young men who had fought in the First World War. The group believed that theology had to arise from a common life and to be grounded in sacramental worship.

the Roman Church, 'for all its fundamental errors, the substance has somehow been preserved better than in our own churches. As a result conversations can somehow become classic in a way which is quite different from what is possible and customary with us.'[204]

When Barth announced a series of lectures on 'The History of Protestant Theology since Schleiermacher' for his second semester in Münster, in the summer of 1926, he had the feeling that he was now 'really tackling something quite different from all my earlier tasks'.[205] The lectures proved that Barth was at any rate not so hostile to 'history' as critics of his *Romans* had argued – on the contrary, he occasionally wondered whether 'in a second life I might not turn completely to history, for which I have a secret passion'.[206] However, the choice of this subject also proved that Barth was obviously concerned to give an explicit account of himself in terms of the epoch from which he sought to make a critical departure in his theology. It was amazing how carefully and perceptively he turned to his encounter, with the declared aim of 'speaking of everything with all possible gentleness and sympathy: if the lecture is to succeed, it must take the form of a visit of the senior physician to a hospital . . . though this simile is probably too bold'.[207] At any rate, he was concerned to demonstrate in some way 'not only the suspicious nature of the whole enterprise, but also the good points of each particular individual or at least the forgiveness of sins which is promised to one and all'.[208]

Barth described the 'history' of the nineteenth century by portraying a series of typical theologians of this time. He had what were perhaps the two crucial lectures in the series, on Schleiermacher and on Ludwig Feuerbach, published separately in 1927 in *Zwischen den Zeiten*. He saw the theology of Schleiermacher as an attempt to make 'religion, revelation and the relations between God and man comprehensible as a predicate of *man*'. And he understood the anti-theology of Feuerbach as the undertaking of a 'sharp-sighted spy . . . reporting indiscriminately that the esoteric secret of the theology of the time was that theology had long since become anthropology'.[209] Barth regarded the Feuerbach article in particular as being also an indirect, critical enquiry to Gogarten, who he thought was indulging in all too 'Lutheran' talk of becoming *man* and of *man's* faith.

In the summer of 1926 Barth arranged another seminar, this time on the *Cur Deus Homo?* of Anselm of Canterbury. This first intensive encounter gave him a great deal to think about – ' "somehow" he is certainly right'.[210] In addition, Barth also gave an exposition of

Romans 12.1f., under the title 'Christian Life', in two Bible studies for the German SCM.

In the middle of this semester he, his wife and sixteen students went on an unusually memorable visit to Holland (from 28 May to 3 June). He spent 'seven extremely good and lively days' in this country, which he was visiting for the first time. Here he discovered a quite independent form of Reformed Christianity and a very distinctive type of man: 'something of that sea air which I so liked in Bremen and Danzig, and which could have such a healthy effect deeper into Germany (not to mention in Basle)'. The people had 'a very happy mixture of German and more western characteristics; one immediately felt at home among them'. They have been blessed with a 'treasure of a language, in which one says "beginsel" instead of "principle" – it's so much more pleasant!' Among the Christians, 'God be praised, Calvinism is predominant. Of course it's rather battered, but it is unmistakably Calvinism, with the problem of ethics instead of the "assurance of salvation". No knee-breeches, no spiritual games, no liturgical day-dreaming. It's all a bit dry and solemn, even among the young people, but still full of movement, like Rembrandt's "The Syndics" and "Night Watch". We sat in front of that in amazement for a long, long time.'

Barth found astonishing perception about his theological concerns here and 'an almost voracious urge to press on'. He was welcomed and taken round by Theodorus Lambertus Haitjema, 'the most important advocate of our "interests" in North Holland', who had just published a book about Barth's 'critical theology'. He first stayed in Groningen, where he repeated his Danzig lectures on Philippians 3; he also preached and was involved in a public disputation. The historian of religion who 'opposed' him was van der Leeuw; unfortunately Barth only saw him for a short time. He then went on to the 'really brilliant city of Amsterdam', which seemed to him to be 'just as watery as Venice'. He made the acquaintance of a small group of leading figures in the Dutch Reformed Church and came to respect them highly: Johan Eijkman, Nico Stufkens, Jan Pieter van Bruggen, Dirk Tromp and the much-respected preacher and scholar, Arnoldus Hendrik de Hartog (who was a weighty opponent). 'His teaching and his person were reminiscent of Kutter'; 'an imposing and dynamic man, a mystic. He does not listen for a moment when anyone else is speaking, but can give powerful testimony.' Finally there was Oepke Noordmans, who 'towered above the rest in originality and calibre'. At the end of this visit Barth gave a lecture on the relationship of 'Church and Culture' to a large audience at the Continental Congress for Home Missions, presided over by Reinhold Seeberg.[211] As he himself observed, 'after seven years . . . he wanted to take a rather different view' of the subject on which he had once spoken at Tambach. Barth wanted to consider church and culture in a characteristic way. He sought to see the basis of their relationship 'only in the decisive event of the speaking and hearing of the Word of God'. As a result of this, on the one hand he could say that 'The work of culture . . . *can* be like a parable . . . it can be a reflection from the light of the eternal Logos who became flesh.' And on the other, 'the hope of the church rests *on* God *for* man; it does not rest *on* men, not even on religious men – and not even on the belief that men *with God's help* will eventually build and complete that tower (of Babel).'[212]

At the beginning of the following winter semester Barth was still suffering from the effects of a bad riding accident in which he was involved at the Bergli at the end of August. The result of a medical examination was 'bruising of the right shoulder from the fall and contusion of the left upper thigh through a kick . . . I fell, somersaulted and finally came to a complete stop on the grass, unable to move a limb. Then, some paces away, I saw a telegraph pole on which the matter could have come to a very different end.'[213] In the autumn of 1926 Barth now set out on the task of giving a complete course of lectures on dogmatics for the second time. Since he had not felt that his first course (given at Göttingen) was ready for publication, this time he intended to have the lectures printed as they were delivered; so he announced the Prolegomena, Dogmatics I and Dogmatics II for the next three successive semesters. This new course was almost finished when he had another accident: in the dark he 'performed the trick of falling off one of the few hummocks in Münster which from a distance recall the possibility of hills'. As a result his leg was put in plaster and the lectures had to be postponed for a while.[214]

Some exegetical lectures ran parallel to the lectures on dogmatics, at least in the winter of 1926–27 and in summer 1927. First of all came a series on Philippians (in its final form), which was then printed that same year.

Describing his method of exegesis, Barth pointed out 'that although my purpose remains the same, I am not keeping to the procedure which I followed earlier with *Romans*, but am still seeking'. In fact, the sound of the Reformation was again clearly audible, as in this passage: 'From a man's point of view, in its decisive act, faith is the collapse of every effort of his own capacity and will and the recognition of the absolute necessity of that collapse. When a man sees the other aspect, that when he is lost he is justified . . . he sees himself from God's point of view.' But 'this righteousness does not become a psychological capacity; it remains in God's hand'.[215]

An interpretation of the Epistle to the Colossians followed in summer 1927; Barth was also able to make profitable use of a Catholic commentary, by Robert Grosche, in preparing it.[216] In the seminar at this time he first sat 'bowed over Schleiermacher's *The Christian Faith*, in order to communicate the mystery of wickedness in these really thought-worthy runes'.[217] Then (for two whole semesters) he went on to 'the interpretation of Galatians by means of the commentaries of Luther and Calvin'. Remarkably enough, quite independently of Barth, Bultmann had presented the same subject simultaneously to his seminar in Marburg. As he did later, Barth was already spending a great deal of time preparing for his seminar sessions: 'At any given moment I need to know just a little more than the brightest of the students.'[218]

'Doctrine of the Word of God'

For the most part, however, Barth's strength and effort during this period were devoted to his second progress through dogmatics. 'Rarely can anyone have begun to lecture on dogmatics for a whole course feeling so limp and so exhausted.'[219] He sat there 'day and night' trying to 'give the *Dogmatics* its new form', so intensively 'that at night I dream . . . of these mysterious three persons with their "hypostatic character" *ad intra* and *ad extra*, and of all the things that have to be weighed carefully and argued out on the safe Nicene line between monarchianism and subordinationism. So far I have been writing letters to Gogarten, to no effect, asking whether he knows anything about it all. Indeed I am probably the only professor of theology (with the exception of the Catholics, of course) who is racking his brains over it. But that's the way things must be now. Somehow I've set out on *this* voyage.'[220] What Barth was producing now was not, in fact, a mere repetition of the first course, but a complete new version which preserved the old structure. As with the second edition of *Romans*, 'here too hardly one stone remains on another'.[221] Barth himself was amazed at the pressure with which 'some demon or other is now forcing me write out everything twice'. But he thought that as a result 'everything is coming out much sharper'.[222]

These *Dogmatics* shared with *Romans* a 'protest against modern Protestantism (unfortunately all of it, apart from a few exceptions)'.[223] This 'protest' was given outward form by the frequent quotation of theologians who had 'not walked on the main road of more recent theology': 'the older and the younger Blumhardts, I. A. Dorner, Søren Kierkegaard, Hermann Friedrich Kohlbrügge, Hermann Kutter, Julius Müller, Franz Overbeck, A. F. C. Vilmar'.[224] In contrast to *Romans* and even more so to the 'Göttingen' *Dogmatics*, however, 'I had to take into account a great deal that I had boldly overlooked before, little self-made man that I was'.[225] This reference is to problems and dimensions of thought which were still to be found in earlier dogmatics and in ancient writers. Above all, however, 'I had to change my own learning a second time. I simply could not hold to the theoretical and practical *diastasis* between God and man on which I had insisted at the time of *Romans*, without sacrificing it . . . I had to understand Jesus Christ and bring him from the periphery of my thought into the centre. Because I cannot regard subjectivity as being the truth, after a brief encounter I have had to move away from Kierkegaard again.'[226]

However, in these *Dogmatics* Barth was only on the way towards moving beyond Kierkegaard and bringing Jesus Christ 'into the centre' of his thought. The decisive concept on which he took his bearings here was that of the 'Word of God' – later he would say 'Jesus Christ'. Thus he could say things like: 'The relationship between God and man, of which Christian discourse speaks in its pure form as the church's preaching, is *itself Word*. It does not become Word by being spoken of by man; it is Word from the beginning.' Although as in Göttingen Barth largely continued to relate dogmatics to preaching (indeed precisely because this was the case), he now wanted to understand it far more fundamentally as reflection 'on the Word of God proclaimed (in the sermon)'. The prolegomena in particular thus took shape as a critical counterpart to neo-Protestant dogmatics. Whereas neo-Protestant dogmatics usually discussed these general 'presuppositions' and conditions of Christian faith (philosophy of religion, psychology, etc) in the prolegomena, Barth now regarded the prolegomena strictly as 'an extract from the legomena of the *Dogmatics* itself which illustrates the whole work'. It was an introduction 'in the form of a preliminary leap into the subject-matter itself'[227] and thus a demonstration that the Christian faith does not have such general presuppositions and does not need them. Thus he composed the prolegomena virtually as an extended 'doctrine of the Word of God'.

Barth prepared this prolegomena for publication in the summer vacation of 1927; he spent August with his family at Nöschenrode in the Harz. This was his first book specifically on dogmatic theology, and Charlotte von Kirschbaum, who spent this holiday with the Barths, helped him with it. His intention was that the book should be the first volume of a *Christliche Dogmatik* (Christian Dogmatics) which was originally planned to extend over several volumes. In the preface, which was written in the Harz, Barth dealt with the suspicions of his own 'supporters' (he had Georg Merz particularly in mind) that 'the spring of the "message of the Reformers", which they had thought six years earlier could be the object of a quiet celebration, had been followed all too quickly by a dubious scholastic autumn'. He retorted: 'I was and I am an ordinary theologian who at best has a "doctrine of the Word of God" at his disposal and not the Word of God itself . . . Like any other theologian, therefore, I have had to give a bad impression and still must, seeming to "make a theology" out of the Word of God. I am not aware of ever having done anything but theology, whereas the Word of God will either have spoken for itself or not.'[228] At any rate, Barth felt that the time was ripe for presenting a comprehensive account of dogmatics; in any case, 'all kinds of serviceable preliminary work had been done'.[229] However, he was also aware of the novel character of his 'doctrine'. He therefore supposed that 'this dogmatics will probably have to go its solitary way, like my interpretation of Romans eight years ago in the field of modern biblical exegesis'.[230] Furthermore, he was also very clear about the tentative character of his dogmatics: 'It is not the ripe fruit of a life's work, but a beginner's attempt in this area': indeed he even thought that 'there are no real *Dogmatics* on the scene at present'.[231] He therefore deliberately called his work *Dogmatik im Entwurf* (An Outline of Dogmatics). And as he felt even more strongly this way in the future, the first volume of his *Christliche Dogmatik* was not followed by any more, and his further lectures on dogmatics at Münster remained unpublished.

In Nöschenrode, Barth once again saw Thurneysen for extended conversations: he also had a constructive conversation with the preacher Walter Kröker. It was here that he was posed a question which was to trouble him deeply for a number of months. Following the possibility of an invitation to Berlin, of which nothing came, he received an invitation to the University of Berne. This invitation made him wonder, unusually, for quite some time whether it would be possible to make the journey 'back from the high seas to the narrow channel' or whether he should 'continue to heap up my coal in Westphalia'.[232] What he should decide eventually became clear to him when all at once the Berne newspapers began a vigorous attack on him, over his alleged pacifism and his general lack of patriotism. At the end of October the Berne administration, while issuing the invitation to Barth, wanted to exercise its right to fill the next chairs to become vacant in Berne with liberals. Barth thereupon made his acceptance of the invitation dependent on the surrender of this 'right', and it fell through. He welcomed this outcome to the matter all the more since even in his youth he had not liked the character of Berne. 'The doors there would have had to open much wider if the invitation were to have been one which I could not refuse. This is what I wanted to provoke with my ultimatum to the Berne administration which was found so objectionable. Nothing happened, so in the end I had relative freedom to decide to stay longer in service abroad. A number of Swiss in earlier periods have felt happier here than in their homeland.'[233] The liberal Martin Werner was then chosen instead of Barth. This was the man who had put himself forward for the post with a crude pamphlet against Barth; Barth had told him sharply at Christmas 1925 that he could not recognize him as a conversation partner while he had 'ceased to share in the enquiry *with* me, and was simply teaching, agitating and fighting *against* me – there are certain limits'.

So Barth remained in his 'place' in Germany. Demands were made on him from so many sides that his decision to stay at work here must have seemed all the more to be justified. At the very time when he was occupied with his series of lectures on dogmatics he was preparing once again for some very active outside lecturing. His first task in early 1927 was a new approach to the old Reformation problem of 'faith and works' – in other words, to the way in which the question of ethics was illuminated and clarified by knowledge of the Word of God. He presented his reflections on the theme in two lectures, 'Justification and Sanctification' and 'The Keeping of the Commandments'; the former was more Lutheran in tone and the latter more Calvinistic.

Barth's starting point in the first lecture was that Christian preaching is a proclamation 'of the mighty acts of God' and not 'a proclamation of the acts and works of man'. Accordingly 'justification and sanctification' are together the 'achievement of grace' in man. It is not the case that one is an act of God and the other an action of man; rather *both* are 'an act of God in man'. 'So, *God* justifies and sanctifies.' Like a good Lutheran, Barth here explains justification as the *reconciliation* of the sinner and sanctification as the reconciliation of the *sinner!*[234] In the other lecture Barth stressed (over against idealism) that the Christian ethos does not consist in knowledge of a universal truth but in the fact that 'I am confronted with a claim which is really made and which really affects me'; this is a quite specific claim, 'and we have no control over its content'.[235] Barth added that first, man can hear God's commandment only with his promise, and secondly, we who are transgressors of the commandments can keep them only as justified sinners, i.e. only in faith!

Presumably it was the first of these lectures which Barth gave on a vacation course at the beginning of January 1927, and presumably he gave the same lecture again to his friends in Bremen at the end of the month. He gave the second on 9 March at the Aarau Student Conference, which he was visiting once again. As usual on any visit to Switzerland, he did not fail to see his mother in Basle, where he also met his brothers, his other relatives and his friends there. For some years after this stay in Basle he had a new, valued acquaintance in the person of Karl Hartenstein, the Director of the Basle Mission. He also stayed with the Thurneysens in Brugg – for the last time, as his friend was in the process of handing over the church to Hermann Kutter's son (of the same name) and moving into the parsonage in the Münsterplatz in Basle: 'Perhaps it is not always an enjoyable place in which to spend the noontide and evening of one's life, but at all events it is worthwhile and significant.'[236] Two years later, Thurneysen was also given a teaching post in pastoral theology at the University of Basle, as well as being pastor at the cathedral.

Between 29 March and 2 April Barth paid a second visit to Holland. On it he repeated his two lectures, first in Utrecht and then in Leiden. In Leiden he stayed with the church historian Albert Eekhof. 'I won over his wife completely by making the sound of a cock crowing and other farmyard noises to her three-year-old child.' As he noted, in Leiden he found himself in the stronghold of Dutch liberalism, but he found 'Calvinism' a 'basis for discussion' with the theologians there.[237] He gave his lecture on 'Justification and Sanc-

tification' again at a pastors' conference in Rudolstadt from 20–21
April; he found that he got on surprisingly well 'with the Gnesio-
Lutherans' whom he met there. Following that, he spent two days in
Dorndorf on the Saale, Gogarten's new parish. Gogarten was able to
travel into Jena from there and to be directly involved in academic
work as an assistant lecturer. The two sat down 'in a friendly way' for
long discussions, but found themselves 'shaking their heads' at each
other. Barth felt: 'There is nothing for it. We have to see how
questionable the tie between Barth and Gogarten truly is and yet
hide that fact from the world. On this occasion, Magdalene von
Tiling', a kindred spirit to Gogarten, also proved to be 'the model
woman and the model Lutheran'.[238] Barth then gave the same
lecture once again during a Baltic Conference of the SCM in Putbus
on the island of Rügen from 9–10 June. Here by the Baltic meetings
and discussions were less refreshing; indeed there was 'an unexpectedly lively clash with the Furche pietists, among whom I lived for
two days like a savage'.[239]

Encounter with Catholicism

A month later, on 11 July, Barth gave a new lecture to the university
group of the centre party in Münster on 'The Concept of the
Church'. The subject of the church was very much in the air at that
time. A book by Otto Dibelius, *Das Jahrhundert der Kirche* (The
Century of the Church), had appeared in 1926 and was widely read:
according to Barth, it was 'without exaggeration a worthless
book'.[240] His own interest in this subject had been aroused especially
by his encounter with Catholicism in Münster. He therefore felt the
time appropriate for giving an explicit account. This he did boldly
and vigorously in a clear, almost abrupt, clash with Catholic doctrine. 'For those who in the last resort are not one in Christ, taking
each other seriously cannot mean being good personal friends . . .
much as we all want to be that. It must mean taking upon ourselves
once again the whole burden of the opposition . . . on both sides' and
seeing the other man 'in his uncanny alienation from what for us is
the most central and unshakeable Christian truth. It means making
clear to ourselves that he too is shocked about us in precisely the
same way . . . To accept this enigma once again is to leave this place
a more thoughtful Catholic or Protestant, looking more longingly for

a peace in Christ which we do not yet know.'[241] Barth saw the
dividing line here above all in the Catholic attempt to claim control
over God's grace instead of allowing it the controlling power. He
connected this attempt on which the neighbour church had
embarked with its rejection of the insights of the Reformation and
regarded it as the one, fundamental error of Catholicism.

At the beginning of October, after the holidays in the Harz mountains, Barth paid 'a visit to the world of German students' associations at Burg Lauenstein in Thuringia'. This castle had been built
'most authentically by an invincible idealist in all the splendour of
the Middle Ages'. He had to speak there (on 8 October) 'in a real
"knight's hall"', on 'Theology and Modern Man'. In his lecture he
pointed out the dangerous risks run by modern man when faced with
the utterly superior, specific, binding and critical truth considered in
'theology'. He might either reject it directly (as in atheism) or
(worse) 'defuse' it (as in liberalism) or (even worse) seek to 'control'
it (as in Catholicism). At the end of the lecture Barth went walking
through the 'paradise' of upper Franconia with Charlotte von
Kirschbaum, with whom he had visited Bamberg in wonderment
early in the year. Still earlier, on 2 October, he had preached twice at
a 'Festival of Youth Associations' in Duisburg-Meiderich – 'in one of
those unbelievable congregations which are entirely made up of
theologians in disguise', and in which everyone keeps a keen eye
open to see 'that nothing is attributed to man and that grace alone is
celebrated'. For this very reason, Barth laid particular stress here on
sanctification. He was in this area again on 19 October for a lecture
during the second Theological Week of the Reformed Alliance in
Elberfeld – in 'one of those familiar Christian conference rooms with
a harmonium and all the trappings, weighed down to the gunwale
with pastors and well-briefed laity'. He had been asked to speak on
'The Word in Theology from Schleiermacher to Ritschl' – 'and of
course I was expected to kill off wicked old Schleiermacher'. 'However, I spent only a short time on him, so as to be able to devote more
time to a loving demonstration that revivalist theology and the
biblicists were of a piece with Schleiermacher and that the most
welcome events of the period were Feuerbach, Strauss and –
Kohlbrügge . . . Later, of course, there was a great cry of woe from all
those who had been attacked, but it was rendered impotent from the
beginning by the good Goeters, who had been called as an expert. He
could only concede that in historical terms, at any rate, everything

was "just as my distinguished colleague had said".'[242]

The following November and December Barth gave a series of five lectures in Düsseldorf on 'God's Revelation according to the Doctrine of the Christian Church' – an abbreviated and simplified account of his essential views in the Münster *Dogmatics*.

He could not, of course, accept the neo-Protestant interpretation of the revelation of God as 'man's self-revelation'. But it was interesting how he went on to deal at length with the argument that God only spoke of himself in revelation by virtue of the fact that man could not speak of him (thus also arguing implicitly with his own earlier position). Barth's new approach was: '*God* has come to me. That ends the delusion . . . that I have to speak of the way in which I have come to myself. God has *come* to me. That ends the delusion – and it *is* a delusion – that only God himself wills to speak of God's revelation. Since *God* has *come to me* . . . I can speak of his revelation and may do so, because I *must*.'

In early 1928 he wrote another critical lecture which was really a dialectical counterpart to the controversial lecture of the year before on 'The Concept of the Church'. Its title was 'Roman Catholicism: A Question to the Protestant Church'.

Here, too, Barth took an extremely critical view of Catholicism – but at the same time he found its completeness and consistency so imposing that he concluded that it could be resisted only by a 'Protestantism' which concentrated strictly on its own evangelical concern: this would be a Protestantism purified of the questionable elements which had found their way in from Catholicism. So for him the question posed 'to the Protestant church' was simply 'whether (and how far) it is a church – and whether it is the *Protestant* church'.[243] Using Karl Heim, 'one of our most authoritative theologians', as an example, he demonstrated 'how thin and endangered our line has become, and how banal the typically neo-Protestant form of argument is. I am convinced that it cannot be used against the Roman Catholic position. On the one hand it gives away too much of what we have to join the Roman Catholics in affirming, and on the other it tacitly takes over from them too much about which we should be arguing.'[244]

Barth gave the lecture in Bremen in the middle of March, and found promising conversation partners here in the philosopher Hinrich Knittermeyer and the pastor Karl Refer, who was interested in the Old Testament. He then gave it again in Osnabruck, now the home town of pastor Richard Karwehl, a brother-in-law of Georg Merz, with whom he had been friendly since 1922. Finally, he repeated it in the middle of April to the Lower Rhine Preachers' Conference in Düsseldorf. In Düsseldorf, especially, a short polemical remark about Bismarck 'unleashed a small storm of indignation, as though here I had attacked the holy of holies ("These are your gods, O Israel")'.[245]

Of course the controversy with Heim was not meant to be a rebuff to this former Münster theologian who was now at Tübingen, and Barth explicitly assured him of this in an open letter in June 1928. Moreover, their differences did not prevent them from being associated as editors of a series of theological studies which Christian Kaiser Verlag published from 1927 on, entitled *Forschungen zur Geschichte und Lehre des Protestantismus* (Research into the History and Doctrine of Protestantism). The third editor of the series was Paul Althaus, Professor of Dogmatics at Erlangen. A visit by him to Münster gave Barth a different impression from their published argument in 1922: he was an 'open and honest man with whom I had some good and enjoyable conversations, an opponent turned mediator. There must certainly be this kind of person.'[246] Although the differences between them became more acute, there continued to be 'cross-connections and fellow-feelings' between them, which were 'more subterranean, and not so easy to characterize on the level of "research and doctrine"'.[247] A respectable number of younger theologians sympathetic to Barth were among the authors of the first volume of this new series: for example 'my very competent pupil Otto Fricke', later pastor in Frankfurt;[248] or the Swabians Hermann Diem and Paul Schempp; or his doctoral students Wilhelm Niesel and Eduard Ellwein. From 1939 onwards, Ernst Wolf was the sole editor of the series.

From May to September 1928 Barth's wife and three youngest children lived in Switzerland. While they were away his mother looked after the household in Münster. For the previous ten years Anna Barth had been looking after her youngest son, Heinrich, but when he became engaged to Gertrud Helbing, daughter of the Basle publisher, her duties came to an end. In August she returned to Berne for the remaining ten years of her life.

During this summer semester Karl Barth made a critical study in his seminar of Albrecht Ritschl, whose theology seemed to him on closer consideration to be a 'tiresome and ostentatious positivism'. His over-riding concern was that 'his "self-confidence" should not be disturbed; in the end this was tantamount to giving an apology for himself and his bourgeois character, with the application of much real acuteness and knowledge'.[249] This time the seminar amounted

to sixty-three people, 'among whom I seem to rant like a Turk'.[250]
Barth had now gained the reputation of being a strict professor. He
required careful preparation for his seminars. And he was especially
feared in examinations, since in 'dogmatics' he expected precise
knowledge e.g. of the Reformation and even of early Protestant
orthodoxy. On the other hand, however, he himself felt that his
pupils kept him constantly on the run. He found students who had
come on from Bultmann in Marburg a particular trial. 'The great-
grandson of old Hase and lively Gretel Herrmann with the bobbed
hair were very much in evidence.'[251] Among the other students he
particularly liked Elisabeth Schulz and Anna Maria Rohwedder,
who went on to become teachers; later he used to stay with them on
visits to Hamburg. There was also Wilhelm Wedekind, 'the perfect
example of a restrained Hanoverian, respectful to the point of solemnity',[252] and Erwin Sutz from Zürich, one of a growing number of
foreigners. Other prominent figures among his audience at this time
were Edmund Schlink, Christine Bourbeck and Heinz Kloppenburg. Heinz Kloppenburg remembered that 'the decisive thing
about those years was that Karl Barth aroused a kind of theological
instinct in his students. People might go wrong, but quite apart from
any particular knowledge that he imparted, he kept putting the
pastor and the theologian on the scent.'[253]

Barth announced no New Testament lectures for the summer of
1928, but the next winter he gave a 'new edition' of his Göttingen
lectures on James. Much to his delight, these were the first lectures to
be attended by his thirteen-year-old son Markus, who sat 'a long
way behind the students on an empty bench'.[254] The rest of his
academic work this summer and winter involved him more closely in
a complex subject which he had first discussed in lectures during
1927: the problem of ethics. Now he lectured on ethics for two whole
semesters: 'a voyage beset with rocks'.[255] This voyage was all the
more exciting since various critics had lamented the lack of 'an'
ethics in Barth (his own brothers had complained of this most
recently, in 1928, in an animated conversation in Basle); Barth, on
the other hand, now began to fear that his colleagues Bultmann and
Gogarten were completely dissolving dogmatics into ethics (because
the term 'decision' had such a central place in their views).[256] So it
was significant not only that Barth was tackling ethics at all, but also
that he was doing so in detail and following the particular course on
which he had embarked.

In his ethics lectures Barth began with a detailed distinction between his own position and the broad tradition according to which dogmatics was concerned with God's action and ethics with man and his action. By contrast, in his view, in each of its disciplines theology is 'the description of the reality of the Word of God which addresses man'. Thus: 'Ethics, too, is concerned with reflection on the Word of God' – and, 'especially with reflection on the claim that this Word of God makes a claim on man'. However, the subject of ethics is not 'the Word of God which man claims, but the Word of God which makes its claim on man'. For Barth, this already decided the answer to the ethical question 'What is good?' 'Man acts well in so far as he acts as *one who has heard* the Word of God, and obedience is good. Thus goodness comes from hearing and so from the divine Word.' Consistently with his view, Barth required that the sequence and pattern of a Christian ethic should be specifically appropriate 'to the *Christian* understanding of the goodness of human action'. Accordingly, he himself arranged his ethics on a trinitarian basis, so that he dealt in succession with 'The Commandment of the Creator' (as the commandment of life); 'the Commandment of the Reconciler' (as that of the law); and 'The Commandment of the Redeemer' (as that of promise). The middle section was the most remarkable. Here God's command was given specific form by its orientation on sinful man, living in 'contradiction to God', and was therefore defined more exactly as the commandment of 'the divine contradiction which is experienced only by those whom God loves'. As he went on to describe each of the three forms of the divine command, Barth asked in each case: 1. How do we *know* the commandment? (In a man's calling, in authority, in conscience.) 2. What is the *content* of the commandment? (Following the ancient doctrine of the 'threefold use of the law': order, humility, gratitude.) 3. How do we *fulfil* the commandment? (In faith, love and hope.)[257]

Barth continued to pursue with some excitement the other great theme which had been important to him since his 1927 lectures, that of Catholicism, by reading St Thomas (*Summa Theologica*, Book 1) in his seminar during the winter of 1928–29. It was 'uncannily instructive' to him from all sides – 'uncannily, because the man has gone to work with such scrupulousness' that Barth found it extremely difficult to make any objections. 'He was aware of everything, just everything, apart from the fact that he did not know that man is a chess-player.'[258] Barth's interest in the problem of Catholicism, which was only intensified by Thomas Aquinas, led him to invite the Jesuit Erich Przywara (1889–1972) to a debate in his seminar. Przywara was living in Munich and had just made a name for himself through a book *Religionsphilosophie* (Philosophy of Religion). Before Przywara came to Münster, Barth had been able to welcome a whole series of acquaintances there as guest speakers, including Richard Siebeck, Paul Tillich and Hermann Kutter. In November, Albert Schweitzer also came. 'I told him in a friendly way that his views were a "fine specimen of righteousness by works" and that he was a man of the eighteenth century. After that, we talked and on the whole got on very well. There is no point in wanting to quarrel with him. He sees himself, like everything and everyone else, in relative terms, and it is certainly true that one should be compassionate. He gives us a great deal to think about.'[259]

However, for Barth the indisputable climax of this series of visits was that of Przywara at the beginning of February. After a lecture on the church he 'shone for another two hours in my seminar . . . and finally "overwhelmed" me for two whole evenings here. In this way he was an illustration of the way in which, according to his doctrine, the good God (at least within the Catholic church) overwhelms men with grace. The formula "God in and beyond man from God's side" is the motto of his existence, and at the same time represents the dissolution of all Protestant and modernistic follies and constraints in the peace of the *analogia entis*.'[260] Barth made the seminar session 'a kind of symbol': for the paper he 'put two seats behind the desk', and began by pointing out that 'after centuries, Protestant and Catholic theologians were again sitting "at one table" for a substantial, dynamic "conversation". They were not concerned with mere compromises but were seeking to understand their conflicting standpoints as clearly as possible.'[261] By his side, Barth had 'a little manikin with a big head' who 'was able to give an adroit and somehow relevant reply promptly, and in a kindly manner, to absolutely everything that was said to him. He was like a squirrel swinging from tree to tree, always with the Council of Trent or the Vatican Council behind him, knowing Augustine by heart and inside out . . . It was always the church, the church, the church, but it was the church moving in an extremely lively and varied way around the fixed pole of dogma, which was becoming more and more manifest. Przywara himself seemed to represent the visible unity of the church . . . but he was also formidably at home in the Bible. Paul was his favourite apostle. In the last resort, though, he was well aware of his own questionableness . . . He concluded his last contribution to the discussion in the seminar with the fine creed, "We men are all rogues." '[262] Przywara gave Barth a great deal to think about and to ask about in every respect.

A number of guest lectures which Barth gave under the title 'Fate and Idea in Theology' at the University Institute in Dortmund during February and March were obviously influenced by his reading of Aquinas and by his meeting with Przywara. In them he was principally concerned with the relationship of theology and philosophy. He showed how Christian theology had to make use of the two basic forms of human thought, 'realism' and 'idealism', but without being allowed to be caught up in that 'double aspect of reality: to be specific, seeking and finding God in fate or God in the idea'. Theology, he argued, is aware that this double aspect is transcended, 'not in a final synthesis that we have to achieve, but in the reality of God himself which is revealed to us'.[263] At this particular time an unmarried mother-to-be (who knew him only from his writings) approached him with a request for advice. Barth readily became godfather to her son when he was born in Dortmund that autumn; the son later became well known as the writer Peter Rühmkorf.

At the end of the winter semester, after giving these lectures, Barth left Münster behind him for a few months. He had been allowed a free semester in token of his rejection of the invitation to Berne. He spent it in Switzerland, where he again had his headquarters at the Bergli from the middle of April until the end of September. When he arrived there he was once again enchanted by the place: 'The buds are already bursting out all round the Bergli; there are flowers on all the tables; the twins are already gambolling stark naked through the meadows in the sunshine, we are already eating lunch in that memorable corner behind the house with its marvellous views, and all the indications are that things will get better and better – indeed almost better than our doctrine allows us to expect in this earthly life.'[264] Barth now occupied his time predominantly with theological studies, above all with intensive reading of Augustine and also of Luther. For once he was not pressed for time as he produced a new, more substantial version of a lecture on 'The Doctrine of the Sacraments' (which he had given a little while before in Emden). In it he argued that preaching ('the testimony of Christian *discourse*' to the Word of God) and the sacrament (the 'testimony of the *event*' to the same Word) had to go side by side. The special feature of this latter testimony was that 'it is something that is said to us and cannot be changed into something that we ourselves have said'.[265] Barth gave the new version at the beginning of June in the choir of the French

church in Berne, and at the beginning of July in Pratteln. On 8 July
he was involved in a discussion with the liberals in Zürich; Emil
Brunner and Oskar Pfister also took part in it. Some days later he
had a debate at the Bergli with theological students from Zürich
about the concept of 'revelation'.

During this summer Charlotte von Kirschbaum helped him with
his research and his work. He had now known her for a number of
years. She was born on 25 June 1899, the daughter of a Bavarian
general who had been killed in the First World War, and was a
trained Red Cross sister. Through Pestalozzi's support she had then
been able to go to a 'ladies' college' in Munich, where she had the
best possible training for secretarial work. She had also taken an
'advanced examination' for which she had had to produce a piece of
written work. Here Karl Barth acted as her ghost writer. During this
summer she now helped to expand his 'card index' by producing a
great many extracts. In October she returned to Münster with him
and from then on was to be of help to him for decades as his 'faithful
fellow-worker. She stayed by my side, and was indispensable in
every way.'[266] She soon familiarized herself with 'the theory and
practice of theology and the church through her daily contact with
them, and in so doing displayed not only a lively interest in this field
but also a remarkable gift of understanding and intelligence, and an
indefatigable capacity for work. Without her collaboration (and she
also filed my correspondence and even wrote some of my letters) I
could only have done a fragment of . . . my work.'[267] There was a
deep mutual trust and understanding between Barth and Charlotte
von Kirschbaum. Indeed, in her he had found a helper who had the
stamina to follow him on his long, distinctive course. Not only did
she keep with him, but in her own way she also influenced what he
did. She helped him as a partner and confidante in his questioning
and his progress onwards, in his meetings and in the controversies in
which he was involved; and also shared his moments of relaxation
and refreshment from work.

Her readiness to throw in her lot with Karl Barth in this way was,
of course, a risk for her: she put herself in an extremely unprotected
position. Many people, even good friends, and not least his mother,
took offence at the presence of 'Lollo' in Barth's life, and later even in
his home. There is no question that the intimacy of her relationship
with him made particularly heavy demands on the patience of his
wife Nelly. Now she had to retreat into the background. Neverthe-

less, she did not forsake her husband. She, too, attempted to follow his further career. In any event, it would have been impossible for Barth to carry on his strenuous work in the study and to entertain so many guests in his house had she not continued to fulfil her duties as wife and mother in the background. Barth and 'Lollo' were well aware of this. However, it was very difficult indeed for the three of them to live together. Barth himself did not hesitate to take the responsibility and the blame for the situation which had come about. But he thought that it could not be changed. It had to be accepted and tolerated by all three. The result was that they bore a burden which caused them unspeakably deep suffering. Tensions arose which shook them to the core. To avoid these, at least to some extent, was one of the reasons why in future Barth and Charlotte von Kirschbaum regularly moved to the Bergli during the summer vacation. It must be remembered that in addition to the many events of the following decades, Karl Barth, his wife and Charlotte von Kirschbaum *also* had to keep struggling to sustain and to tolerate their burden and the tensions it produced. Nor should it be forgotten that Barth's children, each in his own way, also faced the burden of this difficulty at home and suffered under it. Nevertheless, all through the years Barth had close friends who kept faith with him, and were well aware of this sore and vulnerable place in his life.

That summer, with 'Lollo' and the Pestalozzis, Barth also went on a tour of Italy (from 8 to 26 June). It was 'purely for pleasure, travelling for travelling's sake, a deliberate and complete break from the purposeful pattern of the rest of our lives . . . In Macerata (near Loreto) a fifth passenger suddenly joined us: no less than St Ambrose in five volumes, which I had noticed in the street market there, and which Ruedi's consummate business sense was able to acquire for me at twenty-five per cent discount. From then on Ambrose took his firm and often somewhat disruptive place in the back of the car, so that Lollo can be said to have entered Rome between at least two church fathers.' Barth was interested in Rome and most of all in the Vatican. 'St Peter's was the first thing that we saw in Rome, and we kept going back there afterwards with the feeling that this was the most lively place in this remarkable city . . . We climbed the famous cupola and gazed and thought very carefully about the vast outlay of mind and matter that can be seen from there. In the cathedral we followed very closely . . . the entry and exit of Pius XI for a blessing, in the midst of his cardinals, monsignors, chamberlains and guards, and surrounded by the people of Rome and visitors, clapping, waving handkerchiefs and shouting "Evviva". But that stone marvel was too contrived and too redolent of human success, and the old-fashioned Spanish march-past too much of a stage comedy, for us to feel that we had been warned about Christ, his prophets and apostles, and in some way of the last things.' As he kept coming in sight of the deep blue sea during the trip Barth was confirmed in his view that 'blue is *the* colour and in particular *the* theological colour. In comparison with it, Protestant black or papal violet are somehow aberrations or provisional stages.'[268]

It was really only after this journey that he began to take a broader view 'of the world or even of Europe'. 'Up to 1928 my first-hand knowledge was limited to Switzerland, the greater part of Germany and Holland. It was in 1929 that I first saw Italy.' After that he soon visited a number of other countries. 'I no longer know how I could ever have thought that I had so much to learn and so much to do in my study and its immediate surroundings that I felt no urge to go abroad. Perhaps this had to be. At all events, now I don't know how I could have become what I am if all those distant places, their past and present, and their people, had not spoken to me more or less clearly.'[269] It was once again thanks for the most part to Ruedi Pestalozzi – and his faithful Chrysler[270] – that Barth travelled more widely during these years.

As in earlier years and in the years to come, after visiting all kinds of Swiss and German friends he spent this summer at the Bergli. One particularly memorable occasion here at the end of May was a meeting with old Kutter, two years before his death. On both sides it provoked bitter regret for the way in which the two of them had moved apart in the meantime. Barth did not hesitate to tell Kutter 'quite openly what I thought of his talk of God, which said everything and nothing. But oh, oh, where was the answer? At least to the extent of three Sunday School lessons,* he kept assuring us that Jesus, Jeremiah and Paul had done precisely what he, Kutter, was doing and no more; that all my efforts at dogmatics and ethics and so on were all right as a game, but that they were really unimportant and undesirable because "today" the important thing was to be in accord with apostolic times by speaking "simply of *God*" . . . Neither steadfastness nor friendliness was any use – his floods simply over-

*Kutter took Sunday School lessons very seriously, and his own were notorious for their length.

whelmed us, as in his best days, though there were all kinds of good and spiritual things . . . On the whole though, to outward appearance it was simply a matter of the familiar application of Colossians 2.14f. to himself, a solitary triumph.'[271]

Then 'this fine summer' came to an end,[272] and Barth returned to Münster. Soon after his return he went to Berlin to discuss an invitation which he had just received from the University of Bonn and which he was very ready to accept. There he talked with his future colleagues Karl Ludwig Schmidt and Gustav Hölscher, and also had a meeting 'in a genuine Berlin Weinkeller' with his friend Dehn and with Gertrud Staewen, a social worker who in future was also to be very closely associated with Barth in his struggles (her sister was married to the lawyer Gustav Heinemann).[273] One result of the 'fine summer' (an indication of the research he had done during it, and at the same time a record of his argument with Przywara on the one hand and the rest of the 'dialectical theologians' on the other) was a long lecture on 'The Holy Spirit and Christian Life' which he gave on 9 October at another Theological Week in Elberfeld.

Starting from the thesis that 'The Holy Spirit is God the Lord in the whole of his revelation', Barth showed how the Spirit was involved in all the works of the 'Trinity', indeed even as 'Creator', 'Reconciler' and 'Redeemer'. By stressing the utter difference between God's Spirit and man's spirit, he rejected the identification of the so-called 'ordinances of creation' (an idea which was particularly popular at that time) with the Word of God. And by understanding the subjective realization of revelation as also being the act of God's Spirit and not as man's work, he saw the Spirit as 'the sole reality' of the image of God in man, fighting against 'man's hostility to grace' and creating divine sonship beyond the bounds of existence. The lecture was directed against the views of Augustine, with constant reference to Luther. Augustine is 'the classic representative of the Catholic view (which can also be found hidden away in Protestantism, or even openly dominating the field) that there is a continuity between God and man which is to be thought of as originating from man's side and which constantly threatens to make man his own creator and reconciler'. Because the connection between God and man which also exists from man's side is an 'event' in the Holy Spirit and only in him (that is, only as a gift of God), there is no connection apart from this 'event' – either before, as an innate property, or afterwards, as the product of some 'infusion'.[274]

Karl's brother Heinrich, who was now *Extraordinarius* Professor of Philosophy in Basle, also spoke in Elberfeld – on 'Ideas of the Spirit in German Idealism'. At this time Karl had 'great respect for the profundity and breadth of his field of view' and took 'great delight in the close link between the problems with which he was concerned and my own. I was, however, concerned about the degree of isolation in which he was treading his narrow path.'[275] Karl even thought that in Heinrich 'we have lost . . . a pastor'.[276] Yet from now on tensions arose in Karl's relationship with Heinrich; in a different way he also clashed with Peter and his 'baroque theology'. From that point on he occasionally complained that he could see 'the abysses of sibling complexes'[277] in his brothers.

The situation at the end of the 1920s

At the end of October Barth set about taking his last semester in Münster. He was now very much more established and at home in the German situation than he had been at Göttingen, especially since at the beginning of 1926 his status in the Prussian civil service had given him German citizenship as well as Swiss. 'I had become a person with dual nationality, so occasionally I was able to join in "Deutschland, Deutschland, über alles . . ."'[278] For the same reason, the new developments in the changing political scene did not escape his watchful eye. 'I followed the efforts of the few thoughtful people, the small groups of men of good will who took the "Weimar Republic" and its constitution seriously and wanted to build up a German social democracy, loyally seeking to secure for their country an appropriate territory among the still mistrustful neighbours by whom it was surrounded. I also saw and heard the so-called "German nationals" of the time – in my memory the most undesirable of all God's creatures whom I have ever met. They had learnt nothing and forgotten nothing, and torpedoed absolutely every attempt to achieve the best that was possible on that basis. With their inflammatory speeches they probably made the greatest contribution towards filling to the uttermost a cup of wrath which was then poured out on the German nation over the next two decades.'[279] 'In particular I found that with very few exceptions, the professors whom I came to know socially, in common rooms, sessions of the Senate and elsewhere, had what I can only describe as an attitude of sabotage towards the poor Weimar Republic. They did not even give it a fair chance . . . They poured scorn on the notion that the year 1919 might have been a liberation for Germany. With their philosophy of history, which they presented with the utmost assurance, they could hardly have done more in their sphere to prepare the way for Hitlerism. Should I . . . describe scenes which at that time I witnessed with amazement? For instance, there was the clash between the Münster Senate and the Berlin administration over three monstrous portraits of the Kaiser which the university did not want to part with. Or the time (in August 1929) when Flight Lieutenant Hermann Goering was received in the hallowed halls of the university and allowed to give us a fiery two-hour speech on the Langemarck Festival.'[280]* 'I was utterly wrong at the time in seeing no danger in the rise of National Socialism, which had already begun. From the very beginning its ideas and methods and its leading figures all seemed to me to be quite absurd.'[281]

Barth often thought later 'that I should have warned the Germans in quite another fashion against the disastrous courses on which they had inexorably embarked, even in the years between 1920 and 1930'.[282]

At this period, Barth also noted what was going on in Germany in the cultural sphere. In particular, 'in leisure time and on holiday I read what came my way of the *belles lettres* of that decade – even if the most obvious thing about them was that they were no longer "belles", but only an honest reflection of the situation that I have outlined. These were the books which were later outlawed by the barbarians as "seditious", as "asphalt literature", and some of them were burned.'[283]

Barth saw and described the attitude of the German Evangelical† Church, with which he had special links as a theologian, from much closer quarters and was much more involved in it. Towards the end of the decade the position became increasingly intricate. 'To my mind, things could never be right with it as it was. For two reasons. First, its leading organs and groups, at any rate, had an unmistakable bias towards the black-white-red reactionaries. And now that

*During the First World War an army company which had foolishly been made up completely of inexperienced students was wiped out in a bloody massacre. During the 1920s the German Nationalists portrayed this as the sacrificial offering of the cream of the nation's intelligence and celebrated the event in universities with great pomp.

†The German adjective *evangelisch* does not have the same overtones as the English 'evangelical'. Often it is synonymous with 'Protestant', but to use that translation all the time would fail to bring out the link between the *Evangelical* Church and the gospel *(evangelium)* which was stressed especially during the church struggle. *Evangelisch* has therefore usually been translated 'Evangelical', but with an initial capital.

for the first time it had found its own feet in independence from the state, it developed a remarkably pompous self-importance which did not seem to be matched by the content and profundity of its preaching. Here and there could already be found "bishops" of the kind who loved being bishops, and others who very much wanted to be bishops. And some of them, pooh-poohing the malice of the time and the storm-clouds in the heavens, saw the star of a whole "century of the church" rising on the horizon. I could not see either of these tendencies as being of any use to the cause of the church, and opposed them as well as I could.'[284] This opposition was given most spectacular expression in an article which Barth wrote at the end of 1929, entitled 'How long . . . ?' – Here, 'falling back into the style and spirit of those fine youthful days in Aargau', he attacked this 'pompous self-importance' with 'intense fury' as a Catiline 'conspiracy against the substance of the Protestant church': the complacent church was preaching to the winds 'with all its "Jesus Christ"; it was passing over man's real need, as it was passing over the Word of God'.[285]

Towards the end of the decade, a critical school which methodically took the field against certainties began to make itself felt, at least in theological circles, and proved a remarkable contrast to that complacent 'self-importance'. 'It was during 1928–29 in particular that the name of Grisebach occupied the centre of theological discussion. At any rate, for good or ill, anyone who wanted to join in as a theologian interested in systematic theology had to take on the "critical philosophy" which had been vehemently introduced into the theological sphere by him. The arguments which were produced were meant to "put him in question" completely. Vigorous conversations ranged to and fro and were given . . . literary form. All the more lively students listened in. The nucleus of a new theological school seemed to be developing . . . thinking back to those years one might see all that came upon us then and afterwards, say under the banner of "thoroughgoing eschatology" or "the demythologizing of the New Testament", as mere child's play, far exceeded by the radical character of "critical philosophy". At that time one could get the creeps and then get over them again, but after a while theological talk about this "critical philosophy" disappeared with remarkable speed.'[286]

In 1929 Barth had an argument with this group, in a review of a book on Luther by Hans-Michael Müller (the son of Johannes

Müller), a theologian who had escaped from Gogarten's school. He said of it: 'I would attempt to make clearer than Müller does that when I say "temptation" I do not mean the same thing as when I say "Jesus Christ".'[287] Man might not have control over God, but God could have control over him – and become flesh, thus creating a fact which the theologian may not question further with his critical principle; otherwise his theology would be without a subject.

Even in this first decade of his official theological activity, Barth could be seen to be doing theology in a fruitful way by the stimulus he provided for varied theological discussion and the many reactions and protests which he provoked. Indeed, for some time now a small library of works 'on Karl Barth' had been forming around his writings and it was growing larger and larger. It consisted of reviews and 'replies', with comment, praise and criticism; academic and popular articles, pamphlets and whole books, from writers representing the widest variety of trends and schools, age-groups and even confessions. In due course Barth could detect a response from distant foreign countries; there were reactions from 'far-away Iowa in North America', and it proved that 'even the Chinese are now no longer quite unaware of us'.[288] The first translations of his works – into English and Danish – were already appearing. At the beginning of the 1920s 'my teacher Harnack once said of me (crushingly enough!) that his colleague Barth seemed to be more of an object than a subject of academic theology'. Now at any rate he was an object as well, and it was true even in the 1920s that 'I could not complain that I had to exist like a rose blushing unseen; in fact there did seem to be something in the simile which I had once used of the man who has an unforeseen experience in a dark tower, seizing the rope of the great bell in his hand, producing the obvious result and drawing on himself the attention one might expect.'[289]

But Barth also became the *subject* of theological discipline and remained so. At this time he understood his theological concern to be primarily a search and a progress towards a tenable 'position'. In this respect he found it increasingly impossible to follow the dominant theological tendencies of the 1920s. 'In theology I saw the situation determined by three important factors. First, the dominance of the "liberal" trend which had been modern at the beginning of the century had been made problematical, but had yet to be shattered. Secondly, various different attempts were made to return to Luther, especially to the so-called "young Luther". This could, of course, easily lead on to a new Lutheran confessionalism. Finally, there were the beginnings of a new basis for theology in an "existentialist philosophy" which followed on from Kierkegaard. Anyone who could not decide for any of these three ways was advised to "winter his cattle", like the confederates after taking the Rütli oath.* In other words, it was better to get ready first and announce one's own proposal afterwards. That happened in my case. In everything that I produced during the 1920s I was still moving in the direction in which I really wanted to go.. These were no longer my student years, but they were nevertheless no more than years of apprenticeship.'[290]

Barth's search for the right course to follow meant that he was rather a solitary figure. His solitude became even greater when towards the end of his time in Münster it became unmistakably clear to him that the various leading representatives of 'dialectical theology' were increasingly moving apart. 'The so-called theology of crisis was obviously itself in a crisis, and the beams of *Zwischen den Zeiten* were beginning to creak.'[291] Over the years, the differences which could already be detected at the beginning of the decade had gradually taken on a more fundamental character. One reason for this was that since 1922 the theologians had continued in different directions; another was that they had not been clear enough among themselves about the extent of the differences which were there from the start. Anyway, these differences became so clear that in April 1927 Barth made the wise prophecy that 'perhaps once again there will be a great explosion within *Zwischen den Zeiten*'.[292] For the moment the tensions continued to be tolerable. And the comment made in 1928 by 'a young whipper-snapper that the leaders of dialectical theology were as divided among themselves as the generals in the Chinese revolution could be laughed at as a good joke and put on one side'.[293] The whipper-snapper was Hans-Michael Müller.

The tensions may have still been tolerable, but Barth at least felt them in full force. While Gogarten posed no problems for his

*The story of the Rütli oath, though little known outside Switzerland, enjoys the same popularity there as that of William Tell, whom it preceded by a few years. The traditional form of it is that in 1291, following a series of outrages and threats, Walther Fürst, baron of Attinghausen in Uri, Werner Stauffacher of Steinen and Arnold of Melchtal, all undaunted patriots, met in this secluded meadow to take a solemn oath that they would live and die in the common cause of resisting innovations and defending the inherited liberties of their valleys. In 1940, General Guisan (see p. 307 below) gave a famous speech at the Rütli, above the Lake of Lucerne, applying the legend to the policy of defending a central redoubt rather than the frontiers.

Swiss friends Christ and Wieser, for Barth he was the most questionable member of the group. 'After several years' issues of our journal,
no one with any knowledge could fail to see that Gogarten and I
understand the underlying programme of our theology in very different ways.' 'To see Gogarten preoccupied almost permanently
with questions on the boundary with philosophy or ethics and Barth
almost equally permanently preoccupied with the history of theology and dogmatics must even then have provided much food for
thought. Right from the start, the question "Why don't you do
anything about the necessary business of getting your presuppositions clear?" was neglected. There was equal silence over the
counter-question, "When *will* you get down to business?"[294] . . .
"When will you stop cheese-paring all over the place and get down to
the cheese?"[295] 'I always had the impression that Gogarten was
almost more interested in secularity as a background to the gospel
than in the gospel itself. He would never just sit down for once and
explain Christian faith itself to us, *without* these eternal side-glances
to the "world", whether it was the world of ordinances (as he used to
say), or the secularized world (as he would say later) – and he got
worse as time went on.'[296]

Barth's suspicions about Gogarten were only confirmed when he
had 'a vivid example' of the teaching being offered at Dorndorf,
which absolutely horrified him.[297] On 2 February 1930, Baroness
Magdalene von Tiling, from the Baltic, who was closely associated
with Gogarten, visited Münster. There was a discussion in Barth's
seminar 'in which this Frau von Tiling in a typical Gogartenish way
said to me: "Herr Professor, who are you really? You are a husband,
a son, a father, a professor" – and she mentioned various other
relationships which I had. To this I replied quite naively: "Yes, and
I'm myself! That is something, too." But she and Gogarten would
not have it. For them everything was determined by an "ordinance
of creation", according to which a person is a father, a mother, a
husband, an official, a Swiss, or whatever, and that is his or her
make-up. I objected, and said that I could not allow myself to be
dissolved into relationships in that way.'[298]

Barth had now also become increasingly suspicious of Bultmann.
He had 'evidently learnt from my *Romans* what difficult ambiguities
could in fact be found in the relationship between philosophy and
theology; quite soon afterwards, however, I wanted to *un*learn this as
thoroughly as possible'.[299] 'What I missed in him was very much like

what I missed in Gogarten. When is he really going to get to the point and say something substantial? When will he stop talking so much about the historical and systematic presuppositions of the message of the Bible, its context, and so on?'[300] It is striking that during all the years in Münster Barth avoided a direct conversation with Bultmann, though Bultmann urgently wanted one. Barth's first priority was to continue to 'work on his own account as positively as possible', and at the same time to 'leave time' for Bultmann and Gogarten to 'develop *their* contribution more clearly'.[301] Only at the end of January 1930 did Barth again pay a short visit to Marburg, with a lecture on 'Theological and Philosophical Ethics' (which he also gave to the University Association in Münster). This was a considerably revised extract from a chapter of his lectures on ethics in which he had developed the theme that 'philosophy is *not* the handmaid of theology. Theology, along with philosophy, can only seek to be the handmaid of the church and the handmaid of Christ.'[302] Barth also met Bultmann in Marburg. But 'I was not at all pleased with what I heard afterwards in the discussion, and still less with what Bultmann said in private conversations before it and after it.'[303] Once back home, Barth wrote a letter to Bultmann in which he expressed his fear that Bultmann's existentialist and ontological basis for the *possibility* of faith and revelation was an attempt to 'deliver theology once again into the hands of philosophy'.[304] This was not merely because of the link with existentialist philosophy but above all because Bultmann affirmed such a 'possibility' at all!

'It came about that within our journal and outside it I saw Emil Brunner, another member of our group, pursuing a theology that I increasingly came to view only as a return under new banners to the fleshpots of the land of Egypt, which I thought that he had left behind once and for all in our common exodus.'[305] In particular, Barth rejected Brunner's demand for a reconsideration of 'natural theology' (made in the interest of his 'eristics', a heightened form of apologetics). 'Ever since about 1916, when I began to make a marked recovery from the consequences of my academic study, my view of the task before our generation of theologians has always been that we must learn again to understand revelation as grace and grace as revelation. We must therefore move resolutely away from any kind of natural theology, "correct" or "incorrect", with a new resolve and a change of purpose. So when Brunner suddenly (say, after 1929) began openly to propagate "the other task of theology", the "point of contact" and so on, how could it be a mere late-night error on my part for me to say that I simply could not and would not agree with him?'[306]

At the same time Barth was also gradually becoming alienated from Georg Merz, who in 1930 was appointed professor at the theological seminary in Bethel. (To Barth's great joy, his old Swiss friend Wilhelm Vischer had been on the staff since 1928.) 'I also noted with astonishment that the far-flung readership of *Zwischen den Zeiten* and not least our director did not feel called upon to make any decision as a result of the split developing between the editors. Indeed, they did not even seem to notice that it was there. They were quite happy for my manifestos – which they were regarded as then – to speak in terms of the second and third articles of the creed (on Christ and the Holy Spirit), while insuring themselves with Gogarten, who spoke in terms of the first article (on the Creator).'[307]

Barth was self-critical enough to see that traces of the modes of thought which he now objected to among his friends were also to be found in his own earlier works. For example, there were traces of existentialist philosophy: 'I myself am unwittingly responsible for its introduction to theology with my 1921 commentary on Romans, though I was not aware of the fact at the time. I also paid my tribute to it in my well-known false start, the *Christliche Dogmatik im Entwurf* of 1927.'[308] Barth also thought that he had paid tribute to 'natural theology': 'How could I deny that I too have often in fact done "real natural theology", most recently, and still very obviously, in my 1927 article on "Church and Culture" and in some passages of my prolegomena, which appeared in the same year.' But towards the end of the decade Barth now regarded traces of this kind as 'eggshells, atavisms and regressions' which he purposefully sought to overcome and to erase.[309] By contrast, he found that his friends now sanctioned these very features as real ingredients of their theological approach.

Thus even by the very end of the 1920s there were deep-rooted differences and divisions among the representatives of 'dialectical theology'. At the same time, however, Barth also found new friends. And he continued to maintain valued old friendships – above all with Thurneysen, who was in fact of one mind with his friend over these questions and suspicions. 'It was a comfort, even if it was also a cause for disquiet, that I kept hearing just one man, Eduard Thurneysen, constantly confirming that he shared my concerns and that we two, at any rate, had once meant things differently' – that is, not in the way in which Gogarten, Bultmann and Brunner now meant them.[310] And in Germany, at least Wilhelm Loew agreed with Barth in his assessment of the situation. Barth gained the impression that 'our oldest German friend has also been the best'.[311]

One 'very remarkable friend' stood out among Barth's new-found acquaintances. This was the philosopher Heinrich Scholz, who had been given a chair in Münster in 1928. Barth had only made his closer acquaintance in the winter of 1929–30. Scholz was 'a former member of Harnack's seminar, and later Professor of Systematic Theology in Breslau – certainly not a conventional type . . . After that he became Professor of Philosophy in Kiel, working entirely, or almost entirely, with mathematical presuppositions.' 'He has an astonishing knowledge and love of the Greeks; of a Christianity with an Augustinian tinge, coming to a climax in the concept of *caritas*; and finally of the world of Goethe and everything connected with it. In addition he is an exquisite musician. What is remarkable and delightful about him is, of course, such a matter of personality that it is hard to describe and put into words.'[312] 'It was a small miracle that we became friends, when one thinks what different kinds of God's creature we were. He had moved away from theology into realms to which I could not follow him even one step, and I for my part had involved myself in a theology which, one might think, would only make him shake his head. Yes, and yet it all turned out so well: a relationship (as he would say) "of a magnitude comparable only with itself".'[313]

Barth came to the end of his last semester in Münster deeply concerned about the way things were developing in Germany in both politics and theology. The subject of the seminar had been 'The Reformation Doctrine of Justification'. In his lectures he had dealt (a second time) with 'Protestant Theology in the Nineteenth Century'. The lectures now had a different form. He no longer began with Schleiermacher, but prefaced the discussion of him with studies of Lessing, Kant, Herder, Novalis and Hegel. In this way Barth's presentation of Schleiermacher's theology was given a new emphasis. At heart, he was constantly preoccupied with the question whether 'dialectical theology as a whole' was not in process of 'adding up to a great restoration of everything that had been undertaken and carried out a century ago, in every theological camp'.[314] He was appointed Dean of the Faculty in the winter of 1929–30 and this brought him increased work. Not the least of his duties in this capacity was to settle the question of his own successor. He himself campaigned for Gogarten, somewhat unenthusiastically and eventually unsuccessfully, while the rest of the faculty pleaded for Emil Brunner, who said no. Otto Piper was in fact appointed to the vacant chair.

When Barth settled in Bonn on 19 March 1930 he had the feeling that the decade which now lay behind him was a period with a character of its own, which had now come to an end. 'I saw and lived through the 1920s as a period "between the times". It was like that obscure saying in Isaiah 21.12: "Watchman, what of the night? The watchman says: 'Morning comes, and also the night. If you will inquire, inquire: come back again.'"'[315]

5

Theological Existence Today

The years at Bonn, 1930–1935

The chair at Bonn

In early 1930, Otto Ritschl, son of Albrecht Ritschl (who had also worked there from 1846 to 1864), retired from the chair of systematic theology in Bonn. Karl Barth was invited to take his place. So now he moved to Bonn, where he found lodgings for his family in the south of the city, at Siebengebirgsstrasse 18, on the ground floor and first floors of a stately house. Pastor Landgrewe, a liberal, lived on the floor above. Barth's activity in Bonn marked the dawn of an unforgettable heyday for the Protestant theological faculty there. True, this 'most impressive period in almost 150 years of the history of the faculty lasted for only three or four short years', but during this time Bonn became a stronghold of Protestant theological learning. Its influence emanated in many directions, particularly as a result of the new approach to which Barth summoned Protestantism and for which he himself had laid the foundations. All of a sudden, 'unprecedented numbers of students' signed up for the Protestant faculty, and now too 'for the first time it encountered a lively response from the people of the Rhine which penetrated deeply into the Catholic sectors of the population'.[1]

On the whole, Barth got on considerably better with Protestant theologians who were his colleagues in Bonn than he had with his colleagues in Göttingen and Münster. The only exceptions were the Professor of Pastoral Theology, Emil Pfennigsdorf, and the Professor of Systematic Theology, Johann Wilhelm Schmidt-Japing, whom Barth had already come to know as a skilful 'opponent' in Bochum in 1922. However, 'he always begins with the great disadvantage of being ready in a terrifying way'.[2] He was 'the embodiment of the all-too-adaptable German intellectual of that period of transition'.[3] Barth had better relations with the others. First, there were the

41.   *From 1930 to 1934 Karl Barth worked at the University of Bonn. Here he began work on his* magnum opus, *the* Church Dogmatics, *and was also embroiled in the German church struggle.*

church historian Wilhelm Goeters, marvelled at for his great learning, and the *Ordinarius* for New Testament and Systematic Theology, Hans Emil Weber. 'His age and his attitude to life meant that Weber stood between the generations and what they represented. As a result, he felt threatened, disturbed and dissatisfied, but without being able to make a breakthrough on his own.'[4] There was also Karl Ludwig Schmidt, New Testament scholar and vigorous editor of the journal *Theologische Blätter* – 'an incomparable source of stories, jokes and intrigues of all kinds, but unquestionably wise';[5] 'over the years our relationship has swung from one pole to another', but 'we have kept meeting and joining forces at one corner or another'.[6] (Barth was equally pleased with Schmidt's original assistant Ernst Fuchs, who was an assistant lecturer from 1932 on.) He also had a special respect for Gustav Hölscher: 'an Old Testament scholar of a high critical calibre; in contrast to Schmidt extremely refined, with an attractive, clean-cut face. It took some time to arouse in him a love of theological questions, but it finally happened. He was determined not to allow any over-hasty nonsense in his own field.'[7] The vice-principal of the seminary, Friedrich Horst, also specialized in the Old Testament. Barth also met his former Göttingen colleague Peterson in Bonn: in 1930, however, Peterson was converted to Roman Catholicism. And once again, among his colleagues in other faculties, he met up with Richard Siebeck, who was Professor of Medicine.

In the following period two new colleagues joined Barth in the Protestant faculty. They were closely associated with him in quite a different way from those already mentioned, because they were personal friends and remained so. One was Fritz Lieb from Basle, who became a lecturer in Bonn in autumn 1930 and was appointed *extraordinarius* professor the following year. His interest in Russia continued to grow, and from 1929 on he joined Paul Schütz and later Berdyaev in editing the journal *Orient und Occident*. The other was Ernst Wolf (1902–71), who through Barth's good offices became *Ordinarius* Professor of Church History in 1931 at the early age of twenty-nine. He was 'the embodiment of what I would terribly much like to be . . . a real scholar who . . . possessed (*a*) the right view of creation in context; (*b*) a never-failing knowledge of all the literature on every conceivable subject between heaven and earth; (*c*) what seemed to me to be a quite amazing capacity for gathering all kinds of material in his writings, developing it and presenting it in a pointed way (when it was still all right to use that term).'[8] Their friendship began 'from that unforgettable morning in Bonn when I inquired somewhat dubiously whether he was a follower of Holl' and the two of them kept it up faithfully right to the end of Barth's life – 'although we certainly did not seem to be hewn from the same block'.[9] 'What a reliable and honest man he is!'[10] As a token of this friendship Wolf also asked his older friend to be godfather to his son Uvo.

At that time in Bonn Karl Barth was the main attraction and stimulus for theological students. He had larger audiences than ever before. 'All at once the small friendly ship at Göttingen had grown into an enormous export business, like the firm of Pestalozzi and Co.'[11] He began his first series of lectures in Bonn with an audience of 160,[12] and his open evenings soon became 'an almost uncanny exercise in mass production'.[13] The crowds caused special difficulties for his seminars, as he felt that these could only be carried on with a relatively small number of participants. He first adopted the expedient of holding each seminar twice and adding a further fifteen members to the thirty regulars. Then in addition to his seminar he also held discussion groups.* Furthermore, those taking part in his seminars had to have passed a preliminary examination. Here his sieve was so fine that for example in the autumn of 1931 two-thirds of the applicants were rejected. He also continued to be a strict examiner in theological finals, for which he now had to travel to Koblenz from time to time; he had no objection to 'surrounding the gates to the pastorate with a bit of fear and trembling'.[14]

Now there was also a sprinkling of Roman Catholics among his students, and in addition a growing number of foreigners. When an African appeared, Barth wondered whether he might 'perhaps be a herald of awakening Africa, which one day will put us into its pockets lock, stock and barrel'.[15] He was even further impressed by a Japanese, 'Kazumi Takizawa, who appeared in Bonn one day in the middle of a lecture on christology, looking for the right philosophy. He found a theology, sat on his bed with crossed legs and read the New Testament in Greek. After four weeks he took a competent part in discussion, and afterwards held his own Bible class. At the end of the semester he wrote an acute article against Bultmann – but

---

*There is no exact English equivalent to the German *Sozietät;* it is a discussion, in Barth's case usually of a text, lying mid-way in formality between the 'open evening' and the 'seminar'. It has been rendered 'discussion group' throughout.

for all that, he just did not want to be baptized!!'[16] Takizawa himself wrote: 'Since my fortunate encounter with Karl Barth in Bonn, the name of Jesus Christ has in a miraculous way become something from which I can no longer . . . detach myself.'[17] And the Bavarian Martin Eras, who became a Protestant under Barth's influence, recalls how 'he wanted to help us to become proper preachers'.[18] The theological students who flooded in from Germany delighted Barth by their extraordinary appetite for debates, which stimulated him immensely. At the same time, however, he saw evidence of the 'vices of German youth: they make a guillotine out of any principle they hardly understand, and chop off heads with it indiscriminately.'[19] Some of them came on from hearing Bultmann or Gogarten in order to hear Barth, so they were specially eager to have some clarification of the differences between these three, which were already in the air but not yet expressed publicly. From the students of the time a group of pupils emerged who kept particularly close to Barth. They included Georg Eichholz, Walter Fürst, Helmut Gollwitzer, Heinz Kloppenburg, Walter Kreck, Erica Küppers, Georg Lanzenstiel, Lili Simon, Karl Gerhard Steck and Hellmut Traub. At this time there was an uncommonly lively atmosphere among Barth's students. They were keen to study and discuss, boisterous in their approval and their questioning, so that even their teacher was worn out trying to cope with them. Some all-too-zealous 'Barthians' also began to put in an appearance. (In 1931 Dietrich Bonhoeffer remarked, half in jest: 'They have a sharp nose for pure-blooded people here. No negro passes for white!')[20]

Barth was forty-four when he began his academic activity in Bonn. And he was clear about the situation of a man of this age. 'By and large, at this stage a man has sorted out the main lines of his thought and actions. He has made himself known and, as far as possible, understood, to any of his contemporaries who are interested. For good or ill he has become a particular person to them. Did that mean that I was now "made"? No, remarkably enough, life was only just beginning. Now it was time for me to test and to prove, inwardly and outwardly, the position that I had adopted. Only now was it possible for me to justify my presuppositions and to develop their consequences. Only now did my arguments over other possibilities with other people become sharp and fundamental. And only now did I have to take on all kinds of practical responsibilities which began to prove oppressive.'[21] The tasks which Barth set himself caused him so much trouble that he often complained that 'I am getting more and more incapable of pulling things off'.[22] Or, 'Very often I have whole series of unproductive hours . . . Will there never come a time when one can bring out real wisdom and set it down on paper with fluency and elegance?'[23]

In the summer and winter of 1930–31 Barth first delivered his Münster lectures on ethics once again – to an audience which soon numbered 250. In addition he also gave his exposition first of James, and then of Philippians. He also gave a considerably revised section of his ethics lectures, on work, as a public lecture. The summer semester was interrupted in the middle of June by a visit which took him to Britain for the first time. He had been preparing for it for a long time by taking daily English lessons with the theologian John A. Mackay. He stayed for two days in London, where J. H. Oldham, the General Secretary of the International Missionary Council, had arranged all kinds of meetings with theologians and churchmen for him. 'My British friends . . . seemed more alienated than edified by the somewhat strict way in which I impressed on them the authority of the Bible, the majesty of God and the precedence of faith over morality – all in accordance with the state of my knowledge at that time. But I can also remember how, astounded by what I heard from them, I could not suppress a rather rude observation about the Pelagian character of the thinking which I encountered on this island' – in his tortured English he cried out; 'You are all Pelagians!'[24]

Barth then spent several days in Glasgow, St Andrews and Edinburgh. In St Andrews – 'a quaint miniature university in a glorious setting' – he was met by 'my very nice colleague Duncan' and the Old Testament scholar Norman Porteous, 'one of my former pupils'.[25] And in Glasgow, on 18 June, he was given his second honorary doctorate as 'the most-discussed theologian of Germany'.[26] 'The presentation of my doctorate was extremely solemn: I had to kneel down, as at a confirmation, and some incomprehensible Latin was murmured over me. The students were allowed to be their usual noisy selves during the proceedings.' Barth was also asked to buy a hood for the occasion: 'a kind of cowl in bright colours, the real token of honour . . . Afterwards I wore it to all the university occasions (in Bonn). I thought that I might as well be hung for a sheep as for a lamb and told the astonished medical professors and such like that I was the papal legate.'[27] He only got to know the theologian H. R. Mackintosh 'on Edinburgh station, where I was waiting for my train to London'. Mackintosh asked him 'with a very solemn face about my view of the reconciling death of Christ . . . my answer at that time must have been rather a paltry one. His personality made an unforgettable impression on me: the penetrating thoroughness . . . with which he struggled over the positions of nineteenth-century theology in the light of the Calvinistic traditions of Scotland which were still as alive as ever in him.'[28]

Pupil of Anselm of Canterbury

In July, Barth repeated in Frankfurt and Heidelberg his 1927 lecture on 'Theology and Modern Man'. In Heidelberg he bitterly offended the well-known women's leader Marianne Weber ('with some justification'). 'To make myself more comfortable, I took off my jacket and the starched cuffs which we still used to wear then, put them down in front of me and went on talking that way.'[29] During this summer semester Barth had originally planned also to revise the first volume of his 1927 *Christliche Dogmatik* for a second edition. It was clear to him that he must go on with publication of a *Dogmatics*. As he put it in an open letter to Karl Heim in April 1931, the only honest answer he could give to Heim's remark, 'We have enough textbooks', was a grim laugh.[30] All at once, however, he now felt strongly the inadequacy of his own first textbook on dogmatics – so much so that he began to delay the revision of the book. The 'blame' for this lay with Anselm, on whom he held a seminar during his first semester in Bonn. He had already come across this scholastic theologian in Münster. And 'in my prolegomena to the *Dogmatics* I made explicit reference to him, thus bringing down on myself in a flash accusations of Catholicism and Schleiermacherianism.' It so happened that 'in the summer of 1930 I held a seminar on Anselm's *Cur Deus Homo?* in Bonn. First of all the questions and objections of the students involved, and then most of all, a guest lecture (on 11 July) by my philosopher friend Heinrich Scholz of Münster on the proof for the existence of God in Anselm's *Proslogion*, aroused in me a compelling urge to deal with Anselm quite differently from hitherto.'[31]

Over the whole of the following year Barth paid a great deal of attention to following through Anselm's method of thought; then at the Bergli in the summer of 1931, he gave a final polish to the book which had emerged. This preoccupation made him recognize that he had to begin his *Dogmatics* again right from the beginning, that he had to free his thought in quite a different way 'from the last remnants of a philosophical or anthropological . . . justification and explanation of Christian doctrine'. 'The real evidence of this farewell is not my much-read little pamphlet *Nein!* (*No!*) attacking Brunner in 1934, but the book on Anselm of Canterbury's proof for the existence of God which appeared in 1931. I think that I wrote this with more loving care than any other of my books and that . . . it has been the least read of all my books.'[32]

This book is a detailed explanation of Anselm's formula *fides quaerens intellectum,* which now became the fundamental model for Barth's theological epistemology. Faith (*fides*) is defined here as the 'knowledge and affirmation of the word of Christ', or of the church's creed. And according to Barth's Anselm, in practice the task of understanding (*intellectus*) posed to theology consists of 'reflecting on what has been said and affirmed beforehand by the creed'. This understanding is achieved, however, in the form of a *search* (*quaerens intellectum*). 'On the presupposition that it is true that God exists . . . is one being in three persons, became man, and so on . . . ' the question asked is 'How far is that true?' That is the question, but it requires the whole of human understanding, in the knowledge that any theological statement is an inadequate, interim statement, capable of improvement, which needs to be accompanied by prayer and which is on the way to the final 'vision of God'![33] Before his book was published as a whole, Barth had a section from it included in the Festschrift for Ferdinand Kattenbusch.

Thus the link which Barth had established with Scholz in Münster was maintained, despite the physical distance which now separated them. Barth himself was amazed at 'the mysterious fact of our friendship; assured though it is, it is mysterious not only to others but even to ourselves'.[34] Indeed, according to Scholz the friendship really began at this point: 'At the beginning, during the years we were together in Münster . . . after a certain amount of close contact I came to believe that if one were to declare one's faith in Barth, one had to be prepared to be governed by him. But this was a mistake . . . He came to influence me in quite different ways, above all through the kind of subject-matter which he kept bringing up after the Münster years . . . When we got to know each other I was still regarded as a philosopher. And indeed I still was, in the sense that I was always at least on the way towards talking myself into his theology. This helped neither of us. In the end, separation brought about what proximity was unable to achieve.'[35] When he had the opportunity, Barth used to talk with other philosophers as he did with Scholz. 'My personal experience with philosophers is this: they have taken note of me and, somewhat unwillingly, have respected me, to the extent that I have given them a practical demonstration that as a theologian I feel no obligation to any of them.'[36]

During the course of the winter, at the beginning of December 1930, Scholz again came to his Bonn friend's seminar 'to present what were at that point very problematical views about the possibilities of Protestant theology as a discipline'.[37] The actual theme of the seminar was 'The Reformation Doctrine of Sanctification'. At this lecture Barth immediately attacked 'the suggestion he put to us at that time. He wanted us to wear scientific caps on our heads – and he had quite definite ideas about them: real scholarship looks like this or that. At that point it really was a matter of "Take it or leave it". So I had to say to him publicly, but in a friendly way: we can't gulp down any of these postulates, so there's nothing doing! But it was an interesting conversation between the two of us.'[38] In another conversation about the same problem Barth told Scholz that academic theology was based on the resurrection of Jesus Christ from the dead. 'He looked at me earnestly and said: "That goes against all the laws of physics, mathematics and chemistry, but now I understand what you mean."'[39]

Relationships with the other representatives of 'dialectical theology' continued to be disturbed. One indication of the state of affairs was that a conversation about their differences which these 'representatives' planned to have in Marburg at the end of October 1930 never took place. Gogarten and Brunner declined to come. Barth did not regret this in the least, since in his view the planned meeting could only have brought out the 'sadness of it all', 'the fact that we had discussed so much together and yet had agreed so little over fundamentals. It would have been difficult to discuss what had gone radically wrong between Gogarten and me after his discovery of the "doctrine of states" or between Brunner and me after his discovery of "eristics".'[40] After this, Barth did not feel very keen about the lecture which he had promised to give, on the same visit, to Bultmann's 'old Marburg pupils' on the theme of 'natural theology', which was such a burning issue at that time. To the great annoyance and chagrin of his Marburg friend he cancelled the lecture at short notice.[41] However, this was not a way of avoiding controversy, since he was putting forward *his* views about the subject, and about the theological methods of the other three theologians, in his book on Anselm. His argument that theology could only be a matter of subsequent reflections, made in the church on the basis of faith, also had another aim in view. It was to be understood as an indirect criticism of what he believed to be the character of 'natural theology' like that of Gogarten, Brunner and Bultmann, i.e. that by contrast it was seeking to establish presuppositions for faith by demonstrating its 'possibility'.

He did give another lecture, however, on 31 January 1931, on 'The Need of the Evangelical Church'.

In it he made a distinction between the essential, necessary and healthy need which arises from the fact that the Evangelical Church is a 'church under the cross', and the unnecessary and unhealthy need which arises when the church is 'in fact ashamed of the gospel' and 'does not recognize and accept the need that is part of its very being'. The former need must be affirmed, but a protest must be made against the latter. Barth's examples of the latter 'need' of the church were its assimilation of its message to contemporary modern categories like fate, authority, order and so on, and the 'hyphen linking Christianity and race'. 'What the German people needs today is the existence of an *Evangelical* Church, and not a *German* Evangelical Church.'[42]

Barth gave the lecture in the new hall of Berlin University. '1400 people had . . . poured into the hall in a crush which threatened their lives . . . It was often almost like a popular meeting, with interruptions for applause and protest. General Superintendent Dibelius, who was also at my lecture, replied to it eight days later in another lecture in the same place.'[43] In his retort to this lecture Barth assured Dibelius of his '*total* protest against the *whole* of the church which speaks the language of Dr Dibelius' – i.e. against the self-satisfied and self-assured 'Laodicenism' of the church.[44] From then on Barth 'often' found that the name of Otto Dibelius 'conveys something . . . of what I think I have to oppose more or less vigorously in accordance with the insight that has been given me'.[45] During this winter visit to Berlin he also took part in a discussion in Gunther Dehn's Neuwerk* circle. Nor did he neglect the museums; he especially liked 'the gate of the Babylonian temple of Astarte'.[46] Two weeks later he repeated his Berlin lecture in Bremen and Hamburg, and on

---

*The Neuwerk circle was one of the groups within the great revival of youth movements in Germany during the 1920s. Socialists, members of Bible groups, students and so on were particularly concerned to develop Christian forms of community and life-styles.

this occasion also visited his friends and pupils there. This time in Hamburg he also got to know Hans Asmussen, pastor of Altona.

During his lecture there Barth contracted an ear-infection which made him 'unfit for battle' for a few weeks.[47] Fritz Lieb gave his ethics lectures for the rest of the semester. Barth also had to discontinue his open evenings, which had attracted special attention during this semester because they were devoted to an analysis of the political programmes and ideologies of the German parties. Until he recovered, Barth kept himself occupied reading a great many books by Balzac – moved by the 'stupendous knowledge of the world and man which is unfolded there'.[48] He then had a period of convalescence with his mother in Berne. The long interruption to his work finally put an end to his bold plan to give lectures on the various disciplines within theology as well as those on dogmatics which he already had in mind.

Church Dogmatics

For his series of lectures on dogmatics Barth had originally wanted simply to repeat the Münster lectures; with a number of corrections, so that they could then be published as a somewhat revised second edition of the prolegomena volume which had appeared in 1927. Things turned out differently. 'When the first volume was before me in print, it showed me plainly how much I still had to learn about the subject and its history (I suppose the same thing happens to other people too: I could see this much more clearly than I ever could have done from a manuscript lying in a cupboard). The opposition which it encountered at least among colleagues was too general and too vehement, the intervening changes in the situation in theology, the church and the world generally gave me so much to think about . . . that I could not pay any attention to the gradually increasing chorus of enquiries, whether friendly or ironical, as to where my "second volume" had got to, nor even think of continuing on the level and in the strain of the initial volume of 1927. This first became clear to me when the four thousand copies of what had been published as the "first volume" began to run out and I was faced with a task of preparing a second edition. My experience with the new version of *Romans* years before was repeated: I could still say what I had said. I wanted to do so. But I could not do it in the same way. What option did I have but to begin again from the beginning, saying the same thing, but in a very different way?'[49]

It was predominantly as a result of his work on the Anselm book, which in the meantime had continued to make further progress, that Barth now recognized that he had to begin again afresh in dogmatics, and why he had to do so. 'Only a few commentators, for example Hans Urs von Balthasar, have noted that my interest in Anselm was never a side-issue for me. On the contrary, whether my historical interpretation of the saint was right or not, I took him very much to heart and absorbed him into my own line of thinking. Most commentators have completely failed to see that this Anselm book is a vital key, if not *the* key, to understanding the process of thought that has impressed me more and more in my *Kirchliche Dogmatik* (ET *Church Dogmatics*) as the only one proper for theology.'[50]

Barth now believed that he knew much more clearly than five years earlier what he wanted to do in the *Dogmatics* and what the centre of its content should in fact be. 'The positive factor in the new development was this: in these years I had to learn that Christian doctrine, if it is to merit its name, and if it is to build up the Christian church in the world as it needs to be built up, has to be exclusively and consistently the doctrine of Jesus Christ. Jesus Christ is the living Word of God spoken to us men. If I look back from this point on my earlier stages, I can now ask myself why I did not learn this and give expression to it much sooner. How slow man is, especially when the most important things are at stake! . . . My new task was to rethink everything that I had said before and to put it quite differently once again, as a theology of the grace of God in Jesus Christ . . . I have discovered that by concentrating on this point I can say everything far more clearly, unambiguously and simply, in accordance with the church's belief, and yet far more freely, openly and comprehensively than I could ever have said it before. In the past I had been at least partly hindered, not so much by the church tradition as by the eggshells of a philosophical system.'[51]

Concentrating on this point had its consequences. 'I cannot conceal the fact that in working at this task – I should like to describe it as a christological concentration – I have been led to a critical (in an exalted sense of the word) discussion of church tradition, the Reformers, and especially Calvin.'[52] Having in the 1920s swung in clearly behind the 'Reformation line', 'I soon saw that it was also necessary to continue it, to arrange the relationship between law and gospel, nature and grace, election and christology and even between philosophy and theology more exactly and thus differently from the patterns which I found in the sixteenth century. Since I could not become an orthodox "Calvinist", I had even less desire to support a Lutheran confessionalism.'[53]

Thus Barth did not want to write dogmatics in the tradition of any confession. He was, however, quite emphatic that he wanted to write a *'Church' Dogmatics*. And he saw this closer definition of his *Dogmatics* as a step forward from his 1927 attempt. 'In substituting the word "Church" for the word "Christian" in the title . . . substantively I am attempting to show from the start that dogmatics is not a "free" science. It is bound to the sphere of the church, the only place where it is possible and meaningful . . . That means, above all, that I think I now have a better understanding of some things (including my own intentions). To the very best of my ability I have excluded from this second version of the book everything in the first edition that might have seemed to give theology a basis, a support or even a justification in terms of existentialist philosophy.'[54] There were signs of this last point in the way in which for the first time Barth also wove into his revised *Dogmatics* critical remarks about Bultmann's approach and even prepared for a showdown with Gogarten. He did this by posing the question: 'How far is his anthropological basis for theology really different from the natural theology of Roman Catholicism and neo-Protestantism?' 'The text on pp.128f. (ET pp.125f.) comes from as early as summer 1931, and was immediately reported to Gogarten. I have never had a reply to it.'[55]

Church Dogmatics – that is what Barth now wanted to lecture and write about, and he was much more certain about it than in 1927. He did not want to lecture on systematic theology. 'There is a very problematical tradition behind the combination of this noun and this adjective . . . A "system" is a pattern of thought constructed on the basis of a number of concepts chosen in accordance with the criteria of a particular philosophy and developed in accordance with a method appropriate to it. But theology cannot be done within the confines and under the pressure of such a strait-jacket. The subject of theology is the history of the dealings of God with man and of man with God . . . which are expressed in the testimony of the Old and New Testaments and in which the message of the Christian church has its origin and content. Understood in this sense, the subject of theology is the "Word of God". Theology is research and teaching which knows that in the choice of its approaches, in its questions and answers, its concepts and its language, its aims and its limits, it is responsible to the living command of the Word of God – and to no other authority in heaven or on earth. To this extent theology is also free – because it is grounded in the sovereign freedom of the Word of God and the discipline which is governed by it. For that very reason it is not "systematic theology".'

But it is dogmatics! 'As "dogmatics", theology takes its bearings from the witness of the Old Testament and the New. It is concerned to demonstrate the truth of the message which has always been proclaimed by the Christian church and has to be proclaimed again today. It tests what has been recognized as this truth in accordance with public and individual testimony from past and present, namely dogmas. And today, as at any other time, it again seeks the truth from which the proclamation of the Christian church derives, which illuminates it and by which it is measured: it seeks *the* dogma.'[56] It is thus 'an essential function of the church', in that it controls and criticizes the life of the church by the truth of the Word of God. However, dogmatics can do no more than bear witness to this truth. Indeed 'it cannot want to prove the truth of the Word of God either directly or indirectly. It can only trust in the Word's demonstration of itself . . . This trust lends strength to its defence of itself against all other Christian and non-Christian thought-forms, ideologies, myths, world views and religions. As a result, dogmatics can and may be confidently presented to all men with openness, understanding and patience, in great hope for those who are still imprisoned by such views. And also because of this trust, dogmatics strives to be where possible the same basic and purely intellectual work as the other disciplines, in their midst but faithful to its own law.'[57]

When the first part-volume of the *Church Dogmatics* was published at the end of 1932 (dedicated to Rudolf Pestalozzi), readers could see that even in its external format it was different in several respects from the book of 1927. For example, 'I wanted to give more space to indicating the biblical and theological presuppositions of what I was saying and the way in which it was connected with the history of theology or took issue with other theologians. I have condensed all these things into the sub-sections in small print, and have arranged the dogmatic presentation so that non-theologians especially can read a consecutive text even if they have to skip its sub-sections.'[58] Nevertheless, these 'sub-sections' (at least the exegetical ones) were so important to Barth that he occasionally wondered whether he should not have them printed in large type and his own remarks in small type. Another difference from the *Dogmatics* of five years before was 'that I have thought it a good thing to make my exposition much more explicit . . . During the past five years I have found every problem very much richer, more fluid and more difficult. I have had to make more extensive soundings and to lay broader foundations.'[59] Whereas in the *Christliche Dogmatik* Barth could deal with the whole of the prolegomena in 463 pages, in the 514 pages (ET 489) of this first part-volume of the *Church Dogmatics* he could deal with only half of it (and in extent this eventually amounted to only the first third). The breadth of the account in this first part-volume itself indicated that the working-out of this *Dogmatics* would take Barth not just a number of years, but the rest of his life. Following the form he had adopted for his instruction in Safenwil, he divided the material in his *Dogmatics* into individual paragraphs, and began each with a proposition which he used to dictate to the students word for word.

Thus the prolegomena formed the content of the first part-volume of the *Church Dogmatics* – and then also the second. The numbering of them as I,1 and I,2 showed that the two volumes belonged together. Barth's plan was to go on in a further volume II to speak of God and then in three further volumes to speak of creation, reconciliation and redemption.

In essentials, the arrangement of the prolegomena was borrowed from his Münster lectures on dogmatics and even from those he gave in Göttingen. In each case Barth departed from the traditional view of the purpose of the prolegomena. This was not meant to deal with general ('preparatory', or 'introductory') presuppositions of faith and theology. Barth denied that faith had any such 'presuppositions'. For that reason, he saw the prolegomena as being a first step into the subject-matter itself, bringing about a first clarification of what revelation was and how it was to be spoken of. The prolegomena were concerned 'not with the things to be said beforehand, but with the things to be said first'. Or in other words: 'Thus in the prolegomena to dogmatics we are concerned with the Word of God as the criterion of dogmatics.' Thus the prolegomena in effect became a miniature dogmatics. Here (as already in Göttingen and in Münster), Barth began with a detailed answer to the central question: 'Who is God in his revelation?' He found the answer in the ancient church's doctrine of the Trinity. 'It is the doctrine of the Trinity which marks out the Christian doctrine of God as Christian.' But he related this doctrine to revelation more resolutely and more clearly than did the early church. In fact, he understood the doctrine as the interpretation of the statement, 'God reveals himself as the

Lord', and thus as an exposition of the truth that the God who reveals himself *can* reveal himself and that therefore in revelation we meet *none other than* the free God, God *himself*. For that reason it was also important for Barth to stress that in his revelation God is *'Father'*, *'Son'* and *'Spirit'* – not because man thinks so on the basis of his own impressions or his own judgment, but because God essentially is Father, Son and Spirit ('from the beginning,' 'beforehand and in himself'). In this sense Barth taught not only the 'economic' Trinity but also the 'immanent' Trinity as the nature of God.[60]

The content of the first volume of the *Church Dogmatics* was material which Barth presented in his lectures in the summer of 1931 and the winter of 1931–32. He lectured in the Auditorium Maximum in Konviktstrasse: in the summer at seven o'clock in the morning and in the winter at eight. A new feature of this series of lectures was that Barth opened each of them with a short devotion in which he read aloud the passage for the day from the Community of Brethren Bible readings* and led the students in a chorale. One of his main reasons for doing this was a very real fear that his group of students might become an all too knowledgeable, 'undialectical posterity'.[61] He shared this anxiety with them openly in his lectures: all at once they might become 'far too positive' in their enthusiasm over the rediscovery of the 'great concepts of God, Word, Spirit, revelation, faith, church, sacrament and so on', and think that 'we speak *of* them because we know how to speak *about* them with such relative freedom'.[62]

In summer 1931 Barth then dealt once again with Schleiermacher, 'whom he had already read and illuminated so often':[63] he studied *The Christian Faith* in his seminar and the *Brief Account of Theological Study* in his discussion group. Of course, in the meanwhile the students' interest had changed so much that – to his great astonishment – Barth did not make much progress with them here. First of all 'they simply did not want to taste this food, so I had to make great speeches about the historical significance of the man, if only to get them to read and think deliberately about the matter'.[64] One person, however, was delighted that Barth forced them 'to replace polemics with new attempts at interpretation: Georg Eichholz proved to be an interpretative artist of the first order'.[65] In July Dietrich Bonhoeffer took part in some sessions of the seminar. He

---

*The Herrnhut (Moravian) brethren publish annually a book of texts *(Losungen)* with Old and New Testament sayings for each day of the year, which then, as now, was widely used by individuals and in churches.

was only twenty-five but had already qualified as a lecturer; his friend Erwin Sutz also introduced him personally to Barth. Greatly impressed, Bonhoeffer reported that 'Barth is even better than his books'. 'He has an openness, a readiness to listen to any pertinent criticism and at the same time an intense concentration on the subject, whether a suggestion is made proudly or modestly, dogmatically or quite tentatively, which is certainly not primarily directed to the service of his own theology.'[66]

In the seminar Barth continued his custom of occasionally inviting distinguished speakers. At the end of June he had a session of this kind with the Orthodox theologian 'Georges Florovsky, whom Fritz Lieb had brought over from Paris'. 'I did not have an overwhelming impression that we really needed this Eastern theology' and the 'obscurantist effect of Russian thought-patterns'.[67] Later, Benedictines from Maria Laach also visited the seminar. During Barth's years in Bonn, friendly relationships were established with these monks, and he often visited them at Maria Laach (sometimes accompanied by his students). 'I once had to try to keep a straight face while listening to a reading there about the success of the Counter-Reformation in Bavaria.'[68] He also came in closer contact there with Damasus Winzen. Another Catholic whom he found stimulating was Robert Grosche of Cologne. Barth got on very well with him – within the limits of the principle which both affirmed, i.e., 'Genuine and profitable discussion is only possible where there is a confrontation involving real dogmatic intolerance. For it is only there that one confession has something to say to the other.'[69] During the winter, Erich Przywara reappeared at a session of Barth's seminar for a discussion of the 'problems of natural theology', over which there was so much dispute at that time, especially among the representatives of 'dialectical theology'. Przywara was in the process of having a book published on the *analogia entis*.* This title enabled Barth to pin-point the reason for his dissent from Roman Catholicism. 'I regard the *analogia entis* as *the* invention of Anti-Christ, and I believe that because of it one cannot become a Catholic. At the same time, I concede that all the other reasons one can have for not becoming a Catholic are short-sighted and frivolous.'[70] True, in repudiating the Catholic doctrine of the *analogia entis*

Analogia entis = analogy of being, i.e. any analogy which suggests that there is something in the being of man which has its analogue in the being of God. Such a view was anathema to Barth, for whom the analogy had to be an analogy of faith, itself given by God.

Barth did not want to 'reject the whole concept of analogy'. After his study of Anselm the concept as such no longer seemed to him to be unusable; indeed it now became almost a characteristic feature of his own epistemological method. He thought that there was probably an analogy, a point of correspondence, between God and man, by virtue of which man is 'capable' of knowing God. But – and this is where his passionate retort began – this 'point of correspondence' is not given to man by nature, by virtue of his situation, ontologically. It will, however, be given to him in faith *(analogia fidei)* since the only possibility of knowing God and his Word is to be found in the Word itself.[71]

In 1932 Georg Wobbermin made the criticism that Erik Peterson and Oskar Bauhofer had been converted to Roman Catholicism as a backlash from Barth's theology. Barth answered him on 18 June: on the contrary, he regarded Catholicism as 'an extraordinarily strong and profound conversational partner for Protestant theology. Indeed, in the last resort it was the only one which needed to be taken seriously.' Alongside it, idealism, anthroposophy, popular religion and atheism were 'child's play'. Of course he thought that Protestant theology as it was then was too weak to stand up to its opponent. 'I at least agree with these deserters that our army is for the moment essentially a defeated one.'[72] Three days later Barth wrote in another public letter to a Herr Hoffmann: 'The "general lack of interest in the Protestant church" can be explained from the fact that for about two hundred years the Protestant church has largely ceased to be interesting', because it had largely lost both its substance as a church and its form as a Protestant church. 'The Catholic church is generally "more interesting" because it has been able on the whole to preserve both its substance as a church and its (anti-Christian) form as the Catholic church.' He also remarked: 'The proclamation of the church is by nature political in so far as it has to ask the pagan *polis* to remedy its state of disorder and make justice a reality. This proclamation is good when it presents the specific commandment of God, and not good when it puts forward the abstract truth of a political ideology.'[73]

Before the storm

Over these months, political events also disturbed Barth to an increasing degree. This was the period during which the National

Socialists were making their presence felt increasingly clearly. For Barth, the German political situation was 'like sitting in a car which is driven by a man who is either incompetent or drunk'.[74] And he believed that now was the time to take up a specific position publicly. He did this on 1 May 1931 by becoming a member of the Social Democrat Party, in protest against the growing madness and the threat to democracy. He did not see this step as 'an acceptance of the ideas and world-view of socialism' but as 'a practical political decision', by which he identified himself with the party which he now found to be most aware of the 'requirements of a healthy politics'.[75] His wish for German politicians was that they should 'carry on their politics in the way which approximated most closely to the pragmatic approach of the Swiss communal councils and federal councils'.[76]

Even now Barth was being criticized here and there in a way that was to become increasingly familiar in future years. People said, 'that I am Swiss and not, as Hirsch so finely wrote, "a German from boot to bonnet",[77] and that he therefore could not feel like a German. Nevertheless, Barth thought that he could say with some degree of pride that 'in forming my opinions and defending them I paid very close attention to both German and . . . Prussian history – from Bismarck's life and speeches to the military actions of Frederick the Great and Moltke and the campaigns of the present century . . . I could give as good an account of details in this sphere as many of the German nationalists, whose assessment of the present situation I have been unable to follow, for all the information that I have assembled about their background.'[78] On the other hand, Barth could 'never forget for a moment that I am Swiss. I really did have dual nationality.'[79] And so on one occasion he said no less proudly: 'I am well aware of the Swiss element in me, but at the same time want to remain totally and unflinchingly in the centre of German theology and the German church. I can claim as my own the sentiments of the very secular poet Gottfried Keller:

> All hail to us, among the free
> Free words with passion let there be.

And if there is to be talk about my certificate of origin, I cannot think of a better way of showing my love of Germany and my identification with it than by remaining in the heart of Germany, even if I differ from so many Germans by being Swiss. How can that be a good reason for writing me off?'[80]

In October 1931, the very month in which the Reformed College
of Sarospatak in Hungary made Barth their 'Honorary Professor',
an incident developed which all at once seemed to intimate what was
in store for politics. German nationalist students in Halle organized
a wild protest against the appointment of Barth's friend Günther
Dehn – because of a (relatively) critical remark which he had made
in 1928 about the First World War. When 'the so-called German
students in Halle threatened to react to Dehn's appointment as
Professor of Practical Theology with an exodus to Jena or Leipzig, I
made a declaration of solidarity in *Theologische Blätter* with Dehn
personally and his views, and was joined in it by the editor, K. L.
Schmidt, and some other colleagues'. Bultmann, however, did not
want to add his signature. Over the following months no end to the
'Dehn affair' seemed to be in sight, and the theologians Hirsch and
Dörries supported the students, so Barth once again entered the fray
with the question 'Why not wage war all along the line? Why not
take on the whole of "dialectical theology" standing behind
Dehn?'[81] 'Let the fight be passionate, but scholarly.' An article in the
Zofinger Zentralblatt of December 1931 also shows how clearly Barth
saw the whole situation at this time and how seriously he regarded it.
In it, he characterized Fascism as a religion, 'with its deep-rooted,
dogmatic ideas about one thing, national reality, its appeal to foundations which are not foundations at all, and its emergence as sheer
power'. Moroever, it was a religion from which Christianity could
expect 'only opposition' and in the face of which Christians had an
even greater temptation, namely to conform to it.[82]

In the spring vacation of 1932 Barth travelled with Ruedi Pestalozzi from the Bergli to Berlin, where (before casting his vote for the
re-election of Hindenburg) he had to speak on 11 April to the
Brandenburg Mission Conference on 'Theology and Mission in
Modern Times'.

He understood missionary activity in the following way: 'By bringing about
a solidarity between the heathen within the church and the heathen outside
it . . . *in* the church and *with* all the world, the church can take seriously its
confession of the Lord who is the Lord.' The task of theology was not so
much to provide the missionary with 'weapons' as to ask him questions
about his relationship with the basis and the object of his activity. Here, too,
at every turn one could see Barth's tough struggles over the problem of
'natural theology', the *analogia entis* and the 'point of contact'. He thought
that the missionary message could 'only make contact at points which it has

first established itself, and not at points which were already there previously in their own right.'[83]

During this stay in Berlin Barth again met General Superintendent Dibelius, and also Siegfried Knak, Director of Mission, who
opened the discussion after the lecture by asking how Barth would
differentiate between Prussian and Swiss nationalist feelings. He
also met Bonhoeffer there. Bonhoeffer talked with him again during
a visit to the Bergli in the late summer of that year. After his return
to Bonn, Barth had a meeting with the Russian philosopher
Berdyaev.

In the summer of 1932 Barth continued lecturing on his prolegomena, and in his seminar he discussed Ritschl's *Instruction in the
Christian Religion.* In the following summer vacation he was able to
write the Preface to the first volume of the *Church Dogmatics* (at the
Bergli) and also the Preface to the English translation of the second
edition of *Romans*: 'The unselfish and laborious task of translating
this book into English has been undertaken by Sir Edwyn Hoskyns',
the English New Testament scholar. Thus Barth had an even greater
chance to influence the English-speaking world, though he warned
his new readers that they 'had in their hands the beginning of a
development' which in the meantime had continued inexorably.[84]
At about the same time, twenty-one of Barth's Passiontide and
Easter meditations appeared in a book of devotions published by
Furche Verlag. It is worth noting that at the very time when he was
turning to the *Church Dogmatics,* he also found the freedom to write
more 'popular books of edification'. In Bonn, as in Münster, he also
wrote meditations on the central Christian festivals for the large
daily newspapers.

In the winter of 1932–33 the seminar text was Book III of Calvin's
Institutes – 'first-class stuff for such exercises with young men'. They
learnt so much that Barth resolved to continue studying the text
during the next summer. In his discussion group he studied
Luther's Greater Catechism and on his open evening Emil Brunner's 'extremely loquacious' *Ethics.* In addition, during the winter
(and then again in the following summer) he arranged 'sermon
practices' with 110 interested students.

The distinctive feature of Barth's approach to preaching here was that 'I
dismissed as quite impossible the sermon on a theme which was regarded as
the only possible approach in modern seminars and examinations on
preaching, and treated the homily as virtually an essential article of faith.'[85]

Barth was in fact convinced that 'the whole trouble with modern Protestantism' was illustrated by the way in which 'its proclamation has become preaching on themes. Preaching on themes (the arrogant view that the preacher has something of his own to say to the congregation as well as, or in with, his interpretation of Scripture – *analogia entis*!) was and is quite simply the result of the neo-Protestant combination of biblical and natural theology in practical terms. Once the preacher wants his sermon to fulfil a second function over and above the service of the divine Word, and plans it that way, this second function wins the day and the preaching ceases to serve the Word.'[86]

In addition to his 'sermon classes' and other courses, Barth also had to deliver his main course of lectures on dogmatics. So he had more to do than ever – and the pressure was soon to increase.

Nevertheless, despite everything he always found time to join in playing Mozart string quartets – 'discreetly in the background as a viola player'.[87] At the same time he 'began to see e.g. Goethe in a new light, to read numerous novels (including many excellent examples of more recent English detective stories), to become a bad, but passionate horseman, and so on'. 'I cannot remember having lived so purposefully and so enjoyably in the earlier decades of my life – although these were very hard years.' Indeed, he believed that 'during these years I became *simultaneously* both very much more a man of the church *and* very much more worldly'.[88] And despite all the work there was still time, however limited, for him to be with his children as they grew up. Of course it was his wife who 'all her life devoted her energies faithfully and zealously' to the real work of bringing them up.[89] His oldest son, Markus, was already about to leave school, and with some astonishment, Karl Barth discovered that he tended to be involved with communist groups.[90] He had already shown his independence in 1930 by refusing to be confirmed. Christoph seemed to be more of a quiet and amiable child and Matthias was an imaginative boy 'living in some fairy-tale regions of his own';[91] Hans Jakob was passionately keen on his scientific collections, while his father thought that he might be a great racing driver or even a business man.[92] Matthias particularly impressed his father at that time with his fondness for preaching. He used to do it 'in a weird and wonderful way, from trees and other high points. This kind of impulse seems deep-rooted in the Barth family.'[93]

In the main series of lectures which Barth gave in the winter of 1932–33, he returned for the third time to the theology of the nineteenth century, on which he had already lectured twice in Münster.

'Their last form was a course that I gave in Bonn during the winter semester of 1932–33 and the summer semester of 1933, in which I examined first the "background" and then the "history" of Protestant theology from the time of Schleiermacher. (When the Hitler régime dawned, I happened to be occupied with Rousseau!) Both parts remain torsos. The "background" was meant to end in a study of Goethe, for which I had already done some preparatory work: I was particularly looking forward to it. I had planned to take the "history" as far as the time of Troeltsch. The limits of the academic semester prevented both parts from reaching their intended conclusions.'[94] The chief new addition to the old manuscript of the lectures was the description of the 'background', in which Barth developed the theory that 'it can be demonstrated that the famous criticism of dogma in the eighteenth century cannot be explained, as we have been taught, in terms of a breakthrough of truthfulness in the light of a changed picture of the world; it stems, very simply, from sentimental self-awareness, from a particular moral attitude of the time, rather than from any intellectual cause.'[95] It was also characteristic of Barth that he described pietism and the Enlightenment here as 'two forms of the *one* essence, outwardly more different than they really were'; both were united in their attempt to 'incorporate God in the realm of sovereign human self-awareness'.

In this third version of the lectures, as in the first, Protestant theology in the nineteenth century was described by means of typical theologians, with Schleiermacher at the centre: a figure who is the 'consummation of the eighteenth century and also transcends it' and is a 'church father of the nineteenth century'. He was seen as the representative of a theology in which 'man is left master of the field in so far as he alone has become the subject, while Christ is his predicate'. Barth added: 'The only consolation we can draw from this discovery is that this cannot be what Christian theology intends, and therefore could not be what Schleiermacher intended either. But this is really an article of faith.'[96] The theologians portrayed included not only the well-known figures, but such outsiders as Blumhardt and Kohlbrügge. Another new feature was that Barth *also* had some questions to the latter group.

Barth had a special purpose in pursuing this theme at this particular moment. He wanted to suggest to his students that 'the attitude and approach of the younger generations of Protestant theologians to the recent past of the church might be rather different from what they now often seem to regard, somewhat impetuously, as the norm – misunderstanding the guidance they have received from me. I would be very pleased if they were (to put it simply) to show a little more love towards those who have gone before us, however alienated they feel from them. A better exegesis and dogmatic theology must prove itself by the way in which its advocates acquire not only a sharper eye for the historical reality of their fellow-theologians of yesterday and the day before, but also a greater impartiality. We need openness towards particular figures with their individual characteristics and interest in them; an understanding of the circumstances in which they worked; much patience and a good sense of humour when we consider their obvious limitations and weaknesses; a little grace in expressing even the most profound criticism; and finally (even in the worst cases) a certain tranquil delight that they were as they were.'[97]

The mild way in which Barth spoke about the nineteenth century here, for all his criticism of it, led some people to ask whether he had not taken back his earlier criticism of this epoch. '"A new tone"? Certainly not, but perhaps played on the same harp: the tone of a string which belongs to this instrument, but can easily be missed. To speak in the context of an account of the past actions of certain people who are long since buried, and are out of the reach of further direct remarks which they could not benefit from anyway, is rather different from having to speak to certain living people in the thick of present activity in theology and the church. In the latter case one faces people who can still be shaken, from whom one can expect further developments, whose arguments and counter-arguments call for some sort of reply. In the former case the tone certainly has to be different.'[98] Barth had the section of the lectures on Gottfried Menken published in 1933 in the Festschrift for the seventieth birthday of Ernst Friedrich Karl Müller; the series as a whole had to wait until 1947 for publication.

'As though nothing had happened'

In the middle of the winter, while these lectures were going on, Barth's 'attitude and activities underwent a great change. This did not affect the content or the direction of my ideas so much as their application. And I owe this change to the "Führer".'[99] When first Papen and then Schleicher were made Chancellor, 'I raged in my study: I prophesied the end of everything and delivered gloomy predictions: "No good will come of this".'[100] Then, on 30 January 1933, 'the Führer' Adolf Hitler and his National Socialists forced their way to power in Berlin. Fritz Lieb made as if 'to throw the radio which was announcing Hitler's seizure of power out of the window. It belonged to our friend K. L. Schmidt.'[101] And even Barth, who on this particular day was in bed with 'flu, immediately knew 'where I stood and what I could not do. In the last resort, this was simply because I saw my dear German people beginning to worship a false God . . . Here I acted instinctively. I did not even have to think about rejecting all this.'[102] 'Rauschning was right when he defined the real esoteric content of National Socialism as pure, consistent nihilism which in the last resort was completely destructive and hostile to the spirit.' So it was clear to Barth that 'from the beginning the National Socialist policy on religion and the church could only be aimed at the eradication of Christian belief and its expression. But again, it could only move towards this goal . . . step by step, indirectly and in a variety of guises.'[103] Only now did Barth read Hitler's *Mein Kampf*; reading it merely confirmed him in his rejection of the new National Socialist régime.

However, it now transpired that the church was not equipped to deal with an 'opposition which had taken a hitherto unfamiliar shape'[104] and indeed that it was even incapable of recognizing the National Socialist state as such opposition. It transpired that 'over the centuries the Protestant church had in fact been "assimilated" as a result of all kinds of other less ostentatious and aggressive alien pressure to such a degree that it simply could not repudiate, promptly and confidently, the crude assumption that the church, its message and its life could be "assimilated" into the National Socialist State'.[105] To his grief and dismay Barth now saw even some of the friends who had joined him in the new developments after Tambach in 1919 and then in *Zwischen den Zeiten,* and even some of his former pupils and current students, either taking part in this 'assimilation' or at least accepting it without protest. For that very reason he now believed that 'where so many fell into line and no one protested seriously, I myself could not very well keep quiet, but had to undertake to issue the necessary warnings to the church about the danger it was in.'[106]

On the day after Hitler's seizure of power Barth had a discussion with Albert Lempp. He wondered whether it was not time to cease publication of *Zwischen den Zeiten.* The position was 'that I regarded Gogarten as one of those responsible for the ideology of National Socialism because of utterances like the speech on authority that he made during the 1920s. Then in 1933, I saw him appearing among the so-called Young Reformers* and for a while even among the "German Christians".'†[107] Barth therefore thought that he should dissociate himself publicly from Gogarten, if only to make things a little clearer. Once again it was agreed to keep *Zwischen den Zeiten* in existence, but as a compromise the names of the three editors no longer appeared. So in future Barth was responsible only for his own articles. He dissociated himself from the policy of the journal as a whole.

Otherwise he saw his 'first priority' in the period after the political revolution as being 'to urge the students for whom I was responsible to keep on working as normally as possible in the midst of the general uproar. I also felt it my duty to join in helping the Evangelical Church to carry on its work in the changed national situation, in other words to maintain the biblical gospel in the face of the new régime and the ideology which had now become predominant.'[108] To this end, in the very first days of the Third Reich Barth gave a lecture on 'The First Commandment as a Theological Axiom', the theme of which unmistakably defined what he believed to be the basic situation facing the church and theology. In it he detected a danger of having 'other gods' than God in every theological attempt to connect 'the concept of revelation with other authorities which for some reason are thought to be important' (like human 'existence', 'order', 'state', 'people' and so on) 'by means of the momentous little word "and"'. And he challenged Christians at last to say farewell 'to all and every kind of natural theology, and to dare to trust only in the God who has revealed himself in Jesus Christ'.[109] Barth delivered the lecture on his first trip to Denmark, in Copenhagen on 10 March 1933 and in Aarhus two days later. (This was only a few days after the burning of the Reichstag, on 27 February, which he believed 'to have been arranged by the National Socialists as a pretext for suppressing the press and the political opposition').[110]

Another effective means in the hands of the new authorities for suppressing opposition proved to be the 'Law for the Reorganization

---

*The 'Young Reformation Movement' was formed in May 1933 under a leadership including Walter Künneth and Hans Lilje; it sought to combine faithfulness to the Reformation with acknowledgment of the realities of the present situation and was thus thought by many members of the Confessing Church to have compromised itself from the start.

†The 'German Christians' were those among the Protestant churches under Hitler who were most keen to bring about a synthesis between Nazism and Christianity, identifying religious aims with national aims.

of the Civil Service', by means of which so many professors were subsequently dismissed or transferred. In March 1933 the Social Democrat Party informed those of its members who had been pressurized by the new state on the basis of the law that they should not 'sacrifice their academic status because of membership of the SDP': what was meant was that they should resign from formal membership and maintain 'private socialist convictions'. Barth corresponded with Paul Tillich on the matter. Tillich personally endorsed the recommendation, whereas Barth resolutely repudiated it and at this very point insisted on his *formal* membership of the party. 'Anyone who does not want me like this cannot have me at all.'[111] He communicated this view in similar terms to Bernhard Rust, the Prussian Minister of Cultural Affairs, at the same time asking whether in these circumstances he would be able to continue his teaching activity in the summer. Rust, who had once read Barth's *Romans*, allowed him to continue, but on condition that there was to be no 'formation of cells'. In June the SDP was completely prohibited and disbanded. When Barth was then asked 'directly by the Rector' how he saw his relationship to the SDP, 'I said: "I have arranged things with the Minister himself." So perhaps I was in fact the last member of the SDP in the Third Reich.'[112]

At all events, Barth could now continue his work unhindered during the summer semester of 1933. Strengthened by a stay at the Bergli in April, he took up a teaching load that was heavier than ever before: fourteen hours a week! As well as continuing the courses which he had begun in the winter, he gave his earlier lectures on John again (to some extent to replace Karl Ludwig Schmidt, who had just been suspended). The students were 'there in droves, and took things very seriously' – even 'Stahlhelmers and Nazis came in their uniforms'.[113] Barth impressed on them that for a theological student in the summer of 1933 'only quite serious theological work can have any real significance'.[114] In June he also arranged a working group on the 'Fourteen Düsseldorf Theses'. Barth played a decisive part in the composition of these theses (dated 4 June), which were a 'theological declaration on the form of the church'. They were one of the first words of warning to the church under the Third Reich and came from the Reformed Church. Their first thesis (identical with the first thesis of the Berne disputation of 1528!) ran: 'The holy Christian Church, whose sole head is Christ, is born of the Word of God, keeps to it and does not hearken to the voice of a stranger.'

Barth's first public comment on the new situation is to be seen in his writing *Theologische Existenz heute* (ET *Theological Existence Today*), composed virtually at a sitting on 24–25 June 1933. It was preceded by the first displays of Nazi power and a marked increase in membership of the so-called 'German Christian Movement', which was becoming more demonstrative. On 3–5 April it had demanded the assimilation of the church to the National Socialist state and had chosen the 'otherwise unknown and insignificant naval chaplain Ludwig Müller'[115] as its 'patron'. On 25 April he was given full powers in church affairs by Hitler. There had also been what Barth regarded as a highly suspicious and hasty attempt on the part of the heads of the church to establish a new church order, worked out by the triumvirate of Kapler, Marahrens and Hesse. The need for this was derived from the historical change of affairs 'in our beloved German Fatherland' and came to a climax in the demand for a central 'Reich Bishop'. According to Barth 'the idea of a bishop proposed in 1933 clearly aims to imitate a particular "state form", namely the "Führer principle"'.[116] The month before, Friedrich von Bodelschwingh had accepted an invitation to become Reich Bishop (on 29 May). Then suddenly, on 24 June, the magistrate August Jäger was appointed State Commissar for the Prussian Church. Bodelschwingh resigned his office the same day.

Against this background Barth wrote his battle-cry. He scrapped a first draft, in a sharp tone and couched in political terms, replacing it by a milder version. He thought that 'I could have said a great deal more, but I had to button my lips a bit, so that I could just say that'.[117] Nevertheless, the milder version was still strong enough to act as 'the first trumpet blast of the "Confessing Church"'.[118*]

Barth began by declaring that at this very moment it was important to do 'theology and only theology' – 'as though nothing had happened. This, too, is an attitude to adopt . . . and indirectly it is even a political attitude.' He described the teaching of the German Christians quite openly as 'heresy': the church 'does not have to serve men and so it does not have to serve the German people'. It has to proclaim the gospel 'even *in the* Third Reich, but not *under* it nor in *its* spirit'. Thus church membership is not determined 'by blood, nor by race either'. Barth caused particular offence by dissociating

---

*The 'Confessing Church' grew out of the 'Pastors' Emergency League' founded by Martin Niemöller in 1933, taking its name from the fact that it based its opposition to Hitler and the 'German Christians' on the confession of faith in Jesus Christ as the one Lord and source of belief. It set up its own church government ('Councils of Brethren') in all areas which had come under the official administration of German Christians.

himself equally sharply from the middle-of-the-road 'Young Reformation Movement'. This was supported by Heim, Künneth, Lilje and others, and stood on the one hand for the preservation of the independence of the church and on the other for a 'joyful yes to the new German state'. Barth objected that it did not stand in 'clear and radical opposition' to the German Christians.[119]

'I did not have anything new to say in that first issue of *Theological Existence Today* apart from what I had always endeavoured to say: that we could have no other gods than God, that holy scripture was enough to guide the church into all truth, that the grace of Jesus Christ was enough to forgive our sins and to order our life. The only thing was that now I suddenly had to say this in a different situation. It was no longer just an academic theory. Without any conscious intention or endeavour on my part, it took on the character of an appeal, a challenge, a battle-cry, a confession. It was not I who had changed: the room in which I had to speak had changed dramatically, and so had its resonance. As I repeated this doctrine consistently in this new room, at the same time it took on a new depth and became a practical matter, for decision and action.'[120]

On 1 July Barth also sent a copy of his work to Adolf Hitler with the declaration: 'This is a word to the German Evangelical pastors. I am recommending that they should reflect on their special position and their particular work in the light of the most recent events in church politics.'[121] The pamphlet had a tremendous effect. Christian Kaiser Verlag worked flat out to distribute it. A second edition had to be printed as early as 8 July. It was banned on 28 July 1934, but by then no less than 37,000 copies had been printed.

For the freedom of the gospel

Without doubt Barth's voice also became more influential now by virtue of the fact that he himself increasingly gained the ear of the Reformed member of the unfortunate triumvirate, Pastor Hermann Albert Hesse. Hesse (1877–1957), at that time Director of the Reformed Preaching Seminary in Elberfeld, emerged as the leading spokesman and representative of the German Reformed Church from the first days of the Hitler period. He listened more and more to Barth; he consulted him and used him 'so to speak as a theological corset'.[122] Finally he became one of the most resolute fighters in the 'Confessing Church'. He repeatedly summoned Barth, sometimes at surprisingly short notice, to Wuppertal to give him detailed advice. For example, this happened the day after the writing of *Theological*

Existence Today. Barth also met a group of pastors there. 'I have spoken, persuaded, shouted and cried until I was blue in the face. And I have formally begged a German Christian (Otto Weber, who was quite unstable, but had an important position) to abandon this heresy and return to the church.'[123] On 2 July Hesse summoned him again, this time to Berlin, where discussions were going on about the final form of the new constitution of the 'German Evangelical Church'. However, Barth was disappointed and travelled back early: he felt Hesse's attitude to be too yielding.

On 11 July the representatives of the churches adopted the new constitution, and three days later it became national law. On 20 July Hitler concluded his Concordat with the Roman Catholic Church. And on 23 July general elections took place in the Evangelical Church for which the German Christians (with massive support from Hitler) and a group called 'Gospel and Church', supported by the Young Reformation Movement, had set up competing lists of candidates. On the eve of the election Barth openly declared in an impromptu speech at a Bonn meeting, 'For the sake of the freedom of the gospel one cannot vote for these two lists.' 'The "Gospel and Church" group are saying in a secret, suppressed and restrained way what the German Christians are saying openly, loudly and without interruption.' Both were putting forward a message in which the freedom of the gospel and the gospel itself were being dissolved.[124] After the speech Hölscher embraced him in tears: this was a sign of the way in which liberal and dialectical theologians could become brothers in the battle conditions of the time.

At the meeting Barth himself supported a third list put together at short notice, 'For the Freedom of the Gospel,' along with Karl Ludwig Schmidt, Ernst Wolf, Hans Emil Weber, Gustav Hölscher and the lawyer Otto Bleibtreu. Despite the haste, in Bonn this list managed to collect ten per cent of the votes, and Barth was elected to the presbytery there. However, throughout Germany the election ended in a great victory for the German Christians. They gained three-quarters of the votes.

Thus it came about that 'in the summer of 1933 . . . because of the success of National Socialism and the suggestive power of its ideas, the teaching and organization of the German church ran the greatest danger of falling under the rule of the so-called "German Christians"'.[125] In fact the following months were dominated by this German-Christian victory. 'After some fuss, in most parts of the church administrative power fell into the hands of this party. For a while its spirit, its words and slogans, were dominant up and down the land.'[126] On 6 September the Prussian Synod passed the 'Church Law concerning the Legal Status of Ministers and Church Officials' which included the 'pernicious Aryan paragraph'.[127] According to this, non-Aryans or those married to non-Aryans could no longer be employed in the service of the church. On 27 September Ludwig Müller set himself up as 'Reich Bishop at the head of the Evangelical Church'.[128] The current love of abbreviations meant that he was known as Reibi. Barth, who was again staying at the Bergli over these weeks, felt that the situation was 'a public emergency' and that 'collaboration with this church régime' was 'acquiescence in the rise of heresy'. So 'I have refused to take the place offered me in the newly established theological chamber of the Reich church government and have resigned my membership of the theological examination department of the Rhine consistory.'[129] At this time Barth was deeply troubled over the failure of the church. 'All along the line Christians and theologians have shown themselves to be a much weaker, more glutinous and more ambivalent group than we ever dreamt that they might be even in the days of our greatest anger in the Aargau.'[130] He saw even long-standing friends either asleep, silent, or on the wrong side. And so he complained: 'Why must I be so isolated, even among those honest people with whom I would so like to agree and yet with whom I disagree to grievously?'[131]

However, this complaint did not prevent Barth from demonstrating publicly his break even with these 'honest' people – indeed precisely with them. In an editorial session in Munich on 30 September he told Merz that he was no longer in a position to collaborate in *Zwischen den Zeiten*. And on 18 October he composed a biting 'farewell' to this journal. His reasons included the following one: 'Some time during this summer I read . . . in *Deutsche Volkstum* Gogarten's acceptance of Stapel's theological dictum that for us the law of God is identical with the law of the German people. Once Gogarten had made this . . . confession it was a minor matter that a little while later he and his followers supported Ludwig Müller and Joachim Hossenfelder in church politics. In his remarks Gogarten had taken over the fundamental principle of the German Christians . . . on my part, as outright, angry repudiation of that principle seems equally consistent. When we appeared to be fighting together at the beginning of the 1920s, I always thought that it was against what can now be seen in concentrated form in the mentality and attitude of the German Christians. I cannot see anything in German Christianity but the last, fullest and worst monstrosity of Neo-Protestantism . . . I regard Stapel's maxim about the Law of God as being an utter betrayal of the gospel.'[132] So ended *Zwischen den Zeiten* – with an open break between Barth and others as well as Gogarten. Thurneysen joined Barth in this step, but Georg Merz could not understand it at all.

The gap left by the disappearance of *Zwischen den Zeiten* was filled by an 'occasional series of writings' which Barth and Thurneysen began to edit from October onwards and which were published by Christian Kaiser Verlag.[133] The great response to Barth's manifesto in June prompted him to call the series *Theologische Existenz heute*. With three exceptions, the first fourteen numbers, which appeared over the course of a year, came from Barth himself. The volumes which he wrote contained material (lectures, articles, sermons, theses, etc.) which documented and explained his opinions and attitudes towards the course of events in Germany. He used the forewords in particular to comment directly on the situation. In the late summer of 1934 issues of his contributions which had already been published were confiscated, and so he began to leave his topical forewords out of subsequent issues. These had obviously incurred the disapproval of the authorities in a particular way. However, he asked his audience to continue to read his contributions to this series as though they bore the sub-title 'between the lines'!* On 1 October 1936 he was finally prohibited from acting as editor of the series.

In another way, a journal which had been appearing from Christian Kaiser Verlag since April 1934, under the title *Evangelische Theologie*, set out to be a replacement for *Zwischen den Zeiten*, and its successor and heir. Thus to begin with it bore the sub-title 'A monthly journal continuing . . . *Zwischen den Zeiten*'. The editor was Ernst Wolf, helped by Wilhelm Niesel, Paul Schempp and Wolfgang Trillhaas. The contributors were mainly younger pupils and friends of Barth's, though he also wrote the occasional article himself.

Barely two weeks after the 'farewell' to *Zwischen den Zeiten* Barth was in Berlin for a lecture on 'Reformation as Decision'. 'I gave it on 30 October 1933 in the Academy of Singing.'[134] After a meeting of the Pastors' Emergency League Barth went there on the under-

---

*The German *Zwischen den Zeilen* differs from *Zwischen den Zeiten* by only one letter.

ground with Heinrich Vogel, deeply immersed in a conversation on Mozart, of all people. Although his lecture had not been advertised in any paper, the hall was full to overflowing.

Barth was to say something about the celebration of the Reformation. And he did so, but in the conviction that 'anyone who wants to celebrate Luther today must have a sword in his hand'.[135] He now saw the real characteristic of the Reformer as an existence in a 'decision' made for one of two alternatives which could be recognized clearly. The church was inextricably involved in this decision, standing on 'the one foundation, Jesus Christ', instead of, say, on that of 'Gospel *and* People'. Once again Barth condemned the 'dominant movement in the church today' as the 'last, most vital, most consummate form of the great neo-Protestant infidelity to the Reformation'. And he issued a summons to offer 'unrestrained and joyful' resistance: 'Smite their spears, for they are hollow!'[136] 'This one word, "Resistance!", aroused quite a tremendous response' at that time, 'so that I had to stop talking for several minutes.'[137]

A few days later, in a conversation with the American churchman and ecumenist Charles Macfarland, who had an audience with the Führer immediately afterwards, Barth emphasized that the Anglo-Saxon churches should now support the Confessing Church in one way and only in one way, by showing *theological* solidarity with its struggle against natural theology. But he also said that to put the church in the hands of Ludwig the Child, 'was rather like entrusting the defence of the Reich to the Captain of Köpenick'.[138] This remark, and other bold comments which Barth made later at the home of Pastor Gerhard Jacobi, were evidently reported by an informer, and later played a part in his dismissal. At Jacobi's home he discussed with a small group (in which he found himself in bitter opposition to Walter Künneth) the question whether it was still possible to remain in the church under German Christian domination. Barth pleaded that people should stay in, so long as they were not simply excluded. However, they should take the line that 'to collaborate now means to protest'. Above all, he warned against mere church-political tactics: 'We must be men who believe, first and last. That – and nothing else.' Still during this discussion Macfarland then reported that Hitler was willing to meet Jacobi. Thereupon the latter said, 'I will take Barth with me', but the meeting never took place.[139]

Back in Bonn, at a pastors' conference on 6 November, Barth

expounded seven 'answers' to the German-Christian 'Rengsdorf theses' (together with the arguments they rejected). At the same time he attacked 'the theology of the newly-founded Protestant bishopric of Cologne-Aachen' and the association of the Word of God with an 'autonomous world-view'.[140] On 11–12 November he went to Marburg with Lieb, Hölscher and Ernst Wolf for a thorough discussion of the situation in the church and in theology with Bultmann, who had had Heinrich Schlier and Hans von Soden with him. At the beginning of May there was a return visit to Bonn on similar lines. For a short period relations between Bultmann and Barth now became closer and more friendly; Barth was quite amazed not to see his Marburg friend 'appearing among the German Christians'.[141] Barth was also fascinated by the liberal Hans von Soden in a way which surprised Bultmann.[142] At the November meeting they even agreed on a common statement (against Reibi Müller), though this was overtaken by the overwhelming speed of events.

For on the following day (13 November) the German Christian teacher Dr Reinhold Krause, who was also a senior Nazi official, gave an extremist speech on 'The Popular Mission of Luther', to an audience of twenty thousand in the Berlin Sports Palace. In it, he played off the 'heroic Jesus' against the Old Testament and the 'Jewish element' in the New Testament and also poured scorn on 'dialectical theology from Paul to Karl Barth'.[143] This event immediately led to many splits and conflicts among the German Christians. Barth's view was that, 'Now we all have reason to be ashamed before God and the angels. There was so little knowledge among us that it needed the coarse paganism of Herr Krause to unleash the storm of a dismay which, had it been genuine, should have broken out at least the previous June.'[144] Hardly had Barth returned from Marburg to Bonn than he was summoned by Jacobi 'head over heels (to Berlin) for advice on the new situation which had been created by the notorious Sports Palace scandal'.[145] 'I found the group round Jacobi as agitated as an anthill, Bodelschwingh and Dibelius in its midst. Unfortunately things were not at all good.'[146] 'It would be an exaggeration to say that I found the group passionately concerned and preoccupied with the possibility of exploiting the situation created in church politics by the Sports Palace scandal and some outright suspensions of pastors. It had not been prompted to make the committed and fundamental reflection which was called for if it was to give good leadership to the church opposition at this particular time.'[147] Barth saw in this attitude the 'desperate danger that the conflict between neo-Protestantism and its origin in the Reformation, which has become evident in events in the church during this year, will once again lead nowhere, but regrettably be neutralized'.[148] There was a danger that now the place of the discredited German Christians would be taken by 'the church of brave people who say "shame!" to Hossenfelder only to wade deeper into the *analogia entis* and even further into the old mire.'[149] On the basis of these views he presented to 'the assembled leadership of the Pastors' Emergency League in Berlin' a memorandum which he had composed 'in a headlong rush'.[150] Of course, 'I never really had a chance, and there was even a regular opposition against me.' This also frustrated Barth's plan for a meeting with Hitler (and with Hindenburg).[151] To his regret, in Berlin Barth missed meeting Dietrich Bonhoeffer, for whose clear-sightedness he had such a high regard. Bonhoeffer had retreated to a pastorate in London for eighteen months. On 20 November Barth wrote to tell him that he should stop playing 'either Elijah under the juniper or Jonah under the gourd', and should come back 'on the next ship'.[152] Bonhoeffer followed his advice, though not on the next ship, and later the thought tormented Barth that he had in fact sent Bonhoeffer to his death.

On the other hand, on this occasion Barth did meet the Dahlem pastor Martin Niemöller (born in 1892). He had already met him at Wehrung's home in Münster in 1925 – and had the unfavourable impression, 'How Prussian!'[153] Even now, in Berlin, he could summon up 'very little confidence in him'.[154] It was only during the further course of the church struggle that he formed a very close personal friendship with Niemöller as well as finding him an ally in their cause. 'Niemöller was always "on the way". His career was more than a solitary progress. He has ignored almost everything in recent years that a German might consider important and urgent, whether rightly or wrongly (often unfortunately wrongly) . . . He can appear on the scene and be very strict, disciplined and determined, and then again – if he is on the attack or the defence, which often happens – he can adopt the kind of attitude which once drew on him the reproof of a chairman (it was Karl Koch): "Brother Niemöller, did that really have to be said like that?" In some circumstances he will gladly retract his remarks, but it can also happen that "Brother Niemöller" thinks that what has to be said cannot be said in any other way. Things are never boring while he is around, but they are often rather dangerous. And no one who comes into contact with him even superficially can fail to see that his concern is not with himself but with his cause. But it is not always easy to accept this vigorously aggressive, nervous, occasionally arrogant person as a supporter of the cause.' Over the next few years Niemöller was to embody 'the Evangelical Church in Germany with its distinctive approach and for all its limitations, as an opponent of National Socialism . . . There is an abundance of less well-known figures and less familiar names about which the same thing can be said. But Niemöller was the most outstanding of them all, and became to some extent a symbol.'[155] For Barth he was and remained 'a compass needle, which for all its mobility infallibly pointed forwards in the direction of the gospel'.[156]

Meanwhile, a busy semester was well under way. In it Barth gave the beginning of the second part of his prolegomena as lectures.

In fact, he began 'as though nothing had happened' with a compact outline of the doctrine of the 'incarnation of the Word', taking up the subtle problems of the christology of the ancient church and beginning with a section on 'God's Freedom for Man'. Indirectly, of course, all this was unmistakably topical. For example, Barth defined the incarnation (on which there was such strong stress in Lutheranism) as an act of God's freedom, and God's *freedom* as a freedom '*for* us', which was not totally and utterly arbitrary. He first spoke of reality and only then of the 'possibility' of revelation (which is therefore not already given by nature). He declared in a later section that 'revelation is not a predicate of history, but history is a predicate of revelation',[157] and finally stressed that the Old and New Testaments belong indissolubly together because they are related to the one revelation.

In addition to his lectures on dogmatics, during this winter he lectured (for a second time) on the Sermon on the Mount. In his seminar he dealt with 'The Doctrine of Justification' and in his discussion group with Bonaventura and Thomas Aquinas.

He had to preach again on 10 December. This particular sermon caused a stir by its clear recognition that 'Jesus Christ was a Jew'. It touched on the 'Jewish question – not because I wanted to touch on it, but because I had to touch on it in expounding the text (which on this occasion, too, was prescribed by the lectionary).'[158] Some of the congregation left the church in protest during the sermon. Writing to one woman from the congregation afterwards in a letter, Barth

confirmed that 'anyone who believes in Christ, who was himself a
Jew, and died for Gentiles and Jews, *simply cannot* be involved in the
contempt for Jews and ill-treatment of them which is now the order
of the day.'[159] Barth preached on other occasions during his Bonn
years, principally in the Schlosskirche in Bonn. There was only one
thing which put him off: 'Even during my youth I had an antipathy
to all ceremonial in worship. I was aware of always being clumsy
before the "altars" of the German churches where I had to preach.
In the old days in Bonn I once resolutely and independently put
myself behind the altar instead of in front, but I wasn't allowed to do
that a second time. There were also other reasons why my friend
Günther Dehn once said goodbye to me in the porch of the Poppels-
dorf church in Bonn with the stern rebuke 'Sermon, first-class;
liturgy, fifth-class'.[160]

Confessing Church

Only towards the end of 1933 did isolated opposition to the 'German
Christian' distortion of the church begin to give place to organized
resistance which was supported by whole congregations. 'In the
struggle against the Christianity *à la mode* of 1933, under Martin
Niemöller's direction first the so-called Pastors' Emergency League
came into being and then, on a broader basis, the Confessing
Church.' However, 'the struggle of the Confessing Church in Germany was not directed against National Socialism as such. It was
played out in the comparatively narrow sector of the question
whether the church would also continue to remain the church in the
future.' Barth felt that this sector was *too* narrow. Still, 'right up to
the year 1934 in Germany I myself thought that I should stick to this
line and not go beyond it, keeping quiet about my political opposition.'[161] Nevertheless, for Barth the theological dimension always
mattered most. And for all its limitations, the Confessing Church
offered real resistance. 'In the last resort, it is difficult to explain how
this happened. The senseless external pressure with which the German Christians sought to establish themselves everywhere, the
spiritual and intellectual inadequacy of virtually all their leading
people, surprise at the pagan background to the affair and perhaps
the beginnings of political disillusionment or even disappointment –
humanly speaking, all these things certainly played their part. But

there must have been some other factor at work when, at the beginning of 1934 . . . all of a sudden something appeared in the Evangelical Church which we might not have expected to find in Germany. Over a number of years we had good cause for our doubts, but all at once we noted an independent knowledge, strength and liveliness which was not subject to any worldly powers, but defied them when it had to.'[162]

One of the important events in the formation and consolidation of the 'Confessing Church' was a Reformed Synod held at the beginning of 1934. The Reformed Christians were in any case a particularly strong group within the Confessing Church. Remarkably enough, apart from Martin Albertz, who lived in Brandenburg, all its prominent spokesmen lived in Wuppertal: Hermann Hesse, Wilhelm Niesel and Alfred de Quervain in Elberfeld, and Paul Humburg, Karl Immer and Harmannus Obendiek in Barmen. The first three were all teachers in the theological seminary there, while the others were pastors in the Gemarke church, which played an extraordinarily significant part in the church struggle. Obendiek in particular 'represented "Wuppertal" for me in its most illuminating form'.[163] The focal point of the synod was the discussion of a 'Declaration on the Right Understanding of the Reformation Confessions in the German Evangelical Church Today', composed by Barth. 'I was asked to present the "Declaration" to a Free Synod of 167 Evangelical Reformed churches from throughout Germany, and allowed to explain it. Each church was represented at the synod, which met in Barmen on 4 January 1934, by a pastor and another elder. The synod adopted this Declaration without alteration, and the General Assembly of the Reformed Alliance for Germany, meeting at the same place, also adopted it on 5 January. At the same assembly it was resolved that membership of the Reformed Alliance was incompatible with membership of the German Christians.' An important clause in the 'Declaration' stated that the 'real problem' of the present was not 'how one could get rid of the German Christian nonsense, if that was God's will, but how it was possible to form a front against the error which had devastated the Evangelical Church for centuries'. It was this error which had been 'the error of the papist church and of the enthusiasts at the time of the Reformation', namely the view that 'alongside God's revelation . . . man also has a legitimate authority of his own over the message and the form of the church'.[164] Barth had already been saying this over and over again

42. *The family in early 1930: Grete Karwehl, Peter Barth, Markus, Charlotte von Kirsch-baum, Hans Jakob, Karl Barth, Franziska, Christoph, Matthias, Nelly Barth.*

43. *With English students, 1931–32: the group also includes his closest pupils, Helmut Gollwitzer (above, second from right) and Karl Gerhard Steck (second from left).*

44.   On 11 April 1932 Barth gave his lecture 'Theology and Mission' in Berlin, and he and
*Günther Dehn took the opportunity of voting for the re-election of Hindenburg. Barth had
joined the Social Democrat party a year before. Dehn was then the focal point of nationalist
agitation by students in Halle.*

45.   *Barth warned against any compromise
with the National Socialist state in his Theologische Existenz heute (June 1933).*

46.   *On the eve of the church elections, 22
July 1933, Barth spoke at a meeting in Bonn
in support of 'For the Freedom of the Gospel'.*

47. Reich Bishop Müller, Hitler's protégé, at a service for the dedication of Nazi banners in the Gustav Adolf church in Charlottenburg, a suburb of Berlin.

48. The original version of the Barmen Declaration composed by Barth in Frankfurt on 16 May 1934. It was accepted by representatives of the German Evangelical Church at Barmen on 31 May. The declaration, which rejected all authorities other than Jesus Christ, was the decisive confession of the Confessing Church.

49. Barth with his brother Peter, his son Markus and Ernst Wolf in Florence, on a happy trip to Italy in September 1934. In Rome Barth wrote his No!, attacking Emil Brunner, and arguing that 'natural theology' was the chief cause of the present confusion in the church.

50. With Pierre Maury and Willem A. Visser 't Hooft in August 1934 in La Châtaigneraie.

51. The end in Bonn: Barth's lectures are deleted for the winter semester of 1934–35.

in different ways for months. The novel feature here was that 'the resolution of the Barmen Synod gave this view a certain authority in the church'. So it was important to him to find that the Reformed Church would already allow him to speak in the name of the German Evangelical Church of the day. He also thought that his 'Declaration' had in fact 'said everything in terms which serious Lutherans would be able to accept without surrendering anything on their side'. It was, in fact, very important for Barth that the Reformed and the Lutheran Church should rediscover each other at this particular time, despite all their differences, so that they could bear united witness in the 'understanding of faith'. For 'the dispute in the church today is not about the question of the eucharist but about the first commandment. That is what we have to "confess". In the face of our need and the task which faces us, our fathers' problems must take a back seat; that is, they must be regarded as an academic dispute – still serious, but no longer divisive, no longer schismatic.'[165]

On the evening after the synod 'I had to give a lecture on "God's Will and our Wishes" in the Gemarke church in Barmen to a congregation of thousands (it was relayed into another hall where there were a further 1200 listeners). The psalms which they sang there sounded good and powerful. There is already something like a general rebellion against German Christianity. That was also the case on the following evening in Bochum and on the next in Lübeck: in the end, in both places the police had to bar the doors.'[166] In this lecture Barth again said an abrupt no to the question 'Is there a "natural revelation" in which God's will and our wishes might be one?'[167] 'This is put to us today much more sharply than it was to Luther and Calvin and so we cannot find a clear answer to it from them.' For Barth, all possibilities of resistance in the church struggle depended on this clear no. On the way back from Lübeck he heard a sermon by Hans Asmussen in Altona, which impressed him deeply: 'Every word carefully chosen and weighed.'[168] The Lutheran Asmussen (1898–1968) was 'probably one of the most striking church teachers' in the ranks of the Confessing Church and an 'original, spirited . . . theological writer'.[169] For a long time Barth and he were close comrades in the struggle – but 'unfortunately that was the only time when we were of one heart and one soul'.[170]

The days after New Year 1934 were 'nerve-racking days' for another reason. At that time there was a persistent rumour, publicly fostered by Reibi Müller, that Barth had been dismissed as a theological teacher. Evidently his dismissal had in fact been considered by the authorities, since he flatly refused 'to open every lecture with the so-called Hitler salute, when this was required of university professors and therefore also of me'.[171] At the very beginning of the winter semester Barth had told the Rector that he always began his lecture with a prayer and understood the whole thing as a kind of service; therefore the 'German salute' was out of place there. In any case, he said, it was only recommended and not required. In a written declaration, however, he further assured the Rector and the Minister of Cultural Affairs that he would not obey any order on this matter. So the rumour did not come out of thin air. Although at that time it proved to be a false alarm, Barth understood that his days in Germany were now numbered. Meanwhile, in Bonn Karl Ludwig Schmidt, Fritz Lieb and Ernst Fuchs had already been dismissed.

On the evening of 22 January Barth was again called to Berlin unexpectedly. The next day he was a highly undesirable guest at an assembly of church leaders and theologians which was to make preparations for Hitler's reception of seven representatives from each of the two church camps on 25 January. When Barth arrived at the meeting in St Michael's Hospice he was asked to agree to a memorandum introduced by the Tübingen theologian Karl Fezer. To his horror he could only regard it as heretical. 'I therefore said to Fezer on 23 January, "We have different beliefs, different spirits and a different God."'[172] 'That proved a bombshell. Wild tumult broke out. Fezer turned pale and was almost helpless, and some people (including Gogarten) shouted, "Can Barth be serious?" Others (like Rückert) wanted to leave the place and others again wanted to throw Karl (Barth) out. Yet others asked Barth to take back his remark and to show some Christian love. When calm had just about been restored, he began to speak again and said that of course he was in earnest. That was the situation between him and the German Christians. He had been saying it in his writings for nine months. Bishop Meiser moaned that this was the end of the Evangelical Church . . .'[173]

Nevertheless, Barth thought that he had to insist on his remark. 'That will have to be said emphatically and publicly as long as even the best representatives of the German Christians continue to drown the Word of God by the voice of a stranger. It is not a matter of persons, it is a matter of fact. The German Christian cause is false and rotten to the core. One can only be for it or against it. And as far as people go, if we are to get them to abandon this false and rotten cause we must be completely hard and completely cold about it. Anything else would not be love.'[174] Finally, in just under an hour, Barth himself sketched out a new memorandum for the reception by Hitler, but this was watered down and falsified by a declaration of loyalty to Hitler.

The reception (in which Barth did not take part) did not, of course, go well. 'The so-called leaders of the church' were once again utterly at a loss 'in a situation in which they should have been thinking simply of the church instead of trivialities (the classic example was the fact that the whole system of bishops has now come to nothing). As a result, many lesser people who had screwed up their courage a bit now became timid and subservient again.'[175] One of the very few people with whom Barth got on this time in Berlin was the assistant lecturer from Königsberg, Hans Joachim Iwand. He also had a long and critical conversation with Gerhard Kittel, the middle-of-the-road theologian from Tübingen, which led to a correspondence between them in June and July. Its subject was the understanding of revelation and the addition in German Christianity of a second source of revelation, and the confusion of the divine mystery of 'creation' with a human 'theory about race, blood, soil, people, state, etc.'

Barth spent the spring vacation with his mother in Berne and at the Bergli. A week after Easter he went with the Pestalozzis for his first long journey through France, during which he not only developed an enormous liking for French cooking, but also had to give a number of speeches. In Paris he had a reunion with Fritz Lieb, who had been expelled from Bonn: Lieb was having a 'lively time' there 'among the émigrés of all countries in the Café de la Paix'.[176] In a Dominican monastry in Paris he met 'the well-known spokesmen of the academic renewal movement in French Catholicism', Étienne Gilson, Gabriel Marcel and Jacques Maritain, and in a botanical garden in Boulogne-sur-Seine he had a discussion with the great scholars of the Sorbonne, Lucien Lévy-Bruhl and Léon Brunschvic. He spent an evening with the Student Christian Federation, and another at an ecumenical congress in which he was unexpectedly involved. But he was also interested in the bookstalls by the Seine and Napoleon's monuments. He went to a Strauss operetta and the Casino de Paris, where he marvelled at the apparently 'infinite number of possibilities open to a woman of moving her arms and even more her legs, wiggling, enticing, beckoning and frolicking in all directions.' And 'I thought again of the old question: "Why doesn't the church at least try to be as good at what it does as the children of this world with their singing, miming and dancing?"'[177] His guides to Paris were the pastors Pierre Maury and Willem A. Visser't Hooft – he had first met the latter in France in 1928.

While in Paris, Barth gave three seminars on Calvin from 10–12 April at the invitation of the Protestant Theological Faculty, and three lectures on the concepts of 'Revelation', 'Church' and 'Theology'. He spoke in French – on which Gerty Pestalozzi commented: 'Excellent! No one speaks French quite like that.'[178] As he was aware that 'much of most of what was said here had to be said for the first time', Barth gave a summary account of the leading ideas of his dogmatics. The third lecture contains his famous description of theology: 'Of all disciples theology is the fairest, the one that moves the head and heart most fully, the one that comes closest to human reality, the one that gives the clearest perspective on the truth which every disciple seeks. It is a landscape like those of Umbria and Tuscany with views which are distant and yet clear, a work of art which is as well planned and as bizarre as the cathedrals of Cologne or Milan . . . But of all disciplines theology is also the most difficult and the most dangerous, the one in which a man is most likely to end in despair, or – and this is almost worse – in arrogance. Theology can float off into thin air or turn to stone, and worst of all it can become a caricature of itself.'[179] On 15 April Barth preached on the 'Good Shepherd' in the Lutheran Church of Christ in the rue Blanche. What amounted to the second part of the sermon on John 10 followed three days later as an opening address to the Reformed Church Convention on the evening of 18 April, in the Bergkirche in Osnabrück. This division of the text of the sermon was meant to be a small indication that now the word of the Good Shepherd was directed 'to Germans and to Frenchmen, to Lutheran and to Reformed Christians, without distinction'. In the second speech Barth warned the assembly against any tactics or politics in which scripture and confession were 'only ornaments and not the foundation'. 'As though there were any other necessary truths which need urgently to be observed alongside the truth of the triune God!'[180]

Barmen

During the summer semester, Barth continued to lecture on dogmatics, and studied 'The Theology of the Formula of Concord' in his seminar and Augustine's *Enchiridion* in his discussion group. The seminar began with new excitements. On 30 April he was summoned for a long cross-examination (among other reasons, because of his remarks to Macfarland the previous October, which by some roundabout way had become known to the Ministry of Cultural Affairs). Following this, he was temporarily put under 'city arrest'. On 26 May his son Christoph had to make a rapid departure from Germany (because of a remark which the secret postal censorship had sniffed out): he went to Berne, where his brother Markus had just embarked on his first semester of theology – at the same time their sister was studying music and modern languages in Basle. However, Barth did not allow himself to be intimidated or to be deterred from resisting the interventions of the state in his own way.

To begin with, the church's resistance had on the whole been rather pathetic, but in the meantime it had been given a broader basis and more recognizable contours under the banner of the Confessing Church. At the end of May it was resolved to summon a synod from all over Germany to strengthen this 'Confessing Church'. To prepare the theological theses for the synod, on 16 May the Lutherans Thomas Breit and Hans Asmussen met Karl Barth, representing the Reformed Church, at the Basler Hof Hotel in Frankfurt. The theses then came into being in a remarkable way. Barth described it like this: 'The Lutheran Church slept and the Reformed Church kept awake.'[181] While the two Lutherans had a proper three-hour siesta, 'I revised the text of the six statements, fortified by strong coffee and one or two Brazilian cigars.'[182] 'The result was that by that evening there was a text. I don't want to boast, but it was really my text.'[183] The text was simply called a 'theological declaration', not a confession: 'the dear Lutherans would not have that'. However, 'in fact it was what people in the olden days used to call a confession, with all the business of accepting and rejecting: real anathemas have also been incorporated into the six articles.'[184]

The first Confessing Synod of the German Evangelical Church took place from 29–31 May 1934 in the Reformed church of

Barmen-Gemarke. It was directed by the Westphalian president Karl Koch, and 138 delegates from all over Germany took part in it. Representatives from the Rhineland included: from Barmen, pastors Immer, Humburg, Schulz and Viering; from Essen, pastors Graeber and Held and the lawyer Gustav Heinemann. 'At the synod itself, I was only in the audience. Indeed I was so much of a peripheral figure that they almost forgot to invite me there'.[185] The Synod appointed a twelve-member 'National Council of Brethren' to direct the churches, and passed one declaration on the legal situation and another on the practical work of the synod. But its undisputed climax was the acceptance of the 'Theological Declaration'. First of all, on 30 May, this was again discussed in a long committee session until far into the night. 'It was here that the first clause of the third thesis was given its present complicated form; Sasse and Althaus wanted to have the "sacrament" mentioned throughout, and I could not avoid insisting that the Holy Spirit should also be mentioned.'[186] The result was the statement: Christ acts in word and sacrament through the Holy Spirit! 'At the time I was sitting next to Wilhelm Niesel. When it was read, he nudged me and said, "What a delight for Calvin in heaven!" For in its present form (as a result of the Lutheran intervention) it has in fact become a typical Calvinistic text . . . Now I have always regarded Calvin as the ideal theologian of union . . . So I was delighted with what Niesel said.'[187] On 31 May, after Asmussen had explained the Declaration, it was accepted unanimously by the synod at 11.30 a.m. The delegates rose spontaneously and sang the verse 'All praise and thanks to God . . .' A few days later Barth read the 'Barmen Declaration' aloud solemnly in his lectures, and on 9 June he explained the meaning of the Declaration at a lecture in Bonn. Of course the unanimity which had been expressed in Barmen quickly proved to be only momentary and only partial. A markedly Lutheran and confessionalist opposition to Barmen, led by Werner Elert and Paul Althaus, took shape at the 'Ansbach Council' (11 June 1934); subsequently it turned into an increasingly pointed attack on the 'predominance of the influence of the theology of Karl Barth' in the Confessing Church (Künneth).

Nevertheless, the acceptance of the 'Barmen Declaration' remained a highly significant event. How did Barth understand it?

'At that time we were concerned with fixing certain Christian truths in connection with a definite and necessary *action*: it was necessary at that time for all the Evangelical churches and congregations in Germany to resist and attack the assimilation and alienation threatened by the German Christians. The church had to be strengthened by a reconsideration of its presuppositions and summoned to join battle boldly and confidently. With its back to the wall, so that it just *could not* fall, it had to "confess" by saying either yes or no. The making of this confession was the significant action which took place at Barmen.' 'What we wanted in Barmen was to *gather together* the scattered Christian spirits (Lutheran, Reformed, United, positive, liberal, pietistic). The aim was neither unification nor uniformity, but consolidation for united attacks and therefore for a united march. No differences in history or tradition were to be glossed over, but we were kept together by "the confession of the one Lord of the one holy, catholic and apostolic church", as the Declaration puts it.' Furthermore: 'This was the one and only centre around which we were gathered together at that time, as the clauses of the Barmen Declaration show: the one *Lord* of the church, *Jesus Christ*. This was the point at which we had learned from the confessions of the century of the Reformation, and needed to speak more explicitly and more precisely than they did. At that time we were asked too explicitly and too precisely not only *what* but *who* was the real ruler of the world and of the church. We were asked whom we would hear, whom we would trust and whom we would obey. It is a remarkable and indeed indisputable fact that the Synod of Barmen showed its unanimity and resolve on this very point, and it clearly stands out in the Declaration.'[188]

Thus the text of the Barmen Declaration was important for Barth 'because it is the first evidence of the preoccupation of the Evangelical Church with the problem of natural theology on the basis of the confessions . . . Barmen designated Jesus Christ, as he is witnessed to us in holy scripture, the one Word of God whom we have to trust and obey in life and in death. It rejected as false teaching the doctrine that there could be a different source of church proclamation from this one Word of God and (in the closing sentence of the Declaration) stated that to recognize the truth and to repudiate the error was "the indispensable theological foundation of the German Evangelical Church". This was a discovery, the significance of which went far above the heads of the poor German Christians and far beyond the immediate situation of the church in Germany. If it was taken seriously, it meant a purification of the church not only from the *new* natural theology which was specifically under discussion, but from *all* natural theology . . . There were protests – blunt words were said in Barmen by Hans Asmussen, who had to explain the Declaration there – "against the phenomenon which for more than two hundred years has slowly been preparing for the devastation of the church".'[189] There was only one thing which Barth later felt to be 'a failing': he had not made the Jewish question 'a decisive feature' of his draft of the text. 'Of course, in 1934 no text in which I had done that would have been acceptable even to the Confessing Church, given the atmosphere that there was then. But that does not excuse me for not having at least gone through the motions of fighting.'[190]

No!

In the summer vacation Barth drew a radical conclusion from the practical decision which had been made with the acceptance of the Barmen Declaration. In September/October he composed 'an outspoken piece of polemic'[191] with the brief, clear title *Nein! (No!)* directed against his former friend Emil Brunner.

In his work *Natur und Gnade (Nature and Grace),* Brunner had put forward the argument that 'the task of our theological generation is to find a way back to a legitimate natural theology'. Barth reacted to this with his 'angry' *No!* His view was that by arguing in this way Brunner was joining forces with 'the false movement of thought by which the church is threatened today, and at the decisive point'. Now he felt that he had to speak 'more sharply against Brunner than against Hirsch', 'because Brunner is closer to me, and I think that he is also closer to the Bible. So at present he seems to me much more dangerous than, say, Hirsch.' Barth's total rejection of Brunner's view that proclamation must seek a 'point of contact' in man and can presuppose its existence became celebrated and notorious. This, Barth argued, was enough to open the floodgates to natural theology. *No!* – for 'the Holy Spirit which proceeds from the Father and the Son, and is thus revealed and believed in as God, needs no other point of contact than that which he himself establishes.'[192]

Barth wrote part of the work, 'in the dawn light between 5 and 6 a.m.', in a memorable setting, 'at an open window on Monte Pincio in Rome', through which 'unmistakably St Peter' looked in from afar. This view gave him the critical insight that the 'Roman' danger of the *analogia entis* was a threat with Brunner.[193] During the summer 'holidays', which were otherwise filled with work, despite all the pressure of the period, he found time to make a trip to Italy with his brother Peter, his son Markus and Ernst Wolf. Even on the trip he had some incidental work on this particular writing to do. But on the whole he enjoyed life with an untroubled cheerfulness which did not desert him even now: he drank 'glorious wine'[194] in front of the Fountain of Trevi and 'let classical antiquity speak to me as it had never spoken before'.[195]

The breach with Emil Brunner demonstrated how Barth could lose even close friends at this decisive time. There were quite a number of them. He once complained that 'my life's work seems to lack a certain power of attraction; indeed, one characteristic of it seems to be a certain explosive or at any rate centrifugal effect'. However, at the same time he could 'also find new friends and sometimes very good ones'.[196] He did not find them among the German church leaders, from whom on the whole he was somewhat detached: he felt Bishop Wurm and Bishop Meiser in particular to be 'something of a brake on the whole church struggle' – 'not to mention Bishop Marahrens in Hanover!'[197] Karl Koch was still someone 'with whom I got on remarkably well' personally. 'I used to drink white wine or even a Steinhäger with him from time to time in an Italian restaurant not far from St Michael's Hospice.'[198] On the whole, however, it was chiefly the pastors who became good companions to Barth through the church struggle, because they were involved in it. Pride of place went to the pastors to whom he dedicated his book *Credo* 'in memory of all who stood, stand and will stand': Hans Asmussen, Hermann Hesse, Karl Immer (whom Barth called his counsellor), Martin Niemöller and Heinrich Vogel. Barth was particularly fond of Vogel, 'that special little Lutheran bird, who at that time was pastor in Dobbrikow in the Mark: not least because I can pull his leg',[199] but above all, of course, because he was so perceptive a fighter. 'Wizened and worked up, there he is all the time, waving his arms like a windmill and shouting "Confess, Confess". And in his own way, this is just what he does.'[200] Vogel had a son at this time and proudly called him 'Karl Martin Heinrich'. He asked the 'Karl' and 'Martin' who were celebrated by his son's name to be his godparents.

At the same time Barth also found treasured and faithful friends in two non-German pastors, the Frenchman Pierre Maury (1890–1956), pastor in French Ferney-Voltaire near Geneva, and Willem Adolf Visser't Hooft (born 1900), at that time General Secretary of the World Student Christian Federation. Barth had already got to know the two of them in April 1932, 'at my mother's home, where I was spending the holidays'.[201] There he had discovered that both of them were 'delightful people with whom one could converse well in French and German'.[202] Maury particularly attracted him. Barth saw his 'great charisma' as being 'that he was able to combine a very deep and objective theological thirst for knowledge with an undeniable sense of the human and the personal dimension. He was incessantly concerned to put these two gifts at the service of preaching the gospel in the community in both the broader and the narrower sense of the term. I have a very clear memory of all the conversations that I had with him, because he never attempted to conceal the difference between what he knew and what he didn't know – or even between what he absolutely insisted on knowing and what he did not want to know for various reasons! And I also think of him fondly because however often I saw him again subsequently, overburdened with work and full of cares, he never seemed indifferent or resigned. I always found him passionately interested, but positively and critically, in the questions which were our mutual concern. He certainly knew how to tell a story! And he knew how to listen and contradict. He could also keep quiet (at the right moment!) and declare himself satisfied (until the next time!).'[203]

Maury and Visser't Hooft visited Barth during this summer of 1934 for long conversations at the Bergli. And from then on Maury in particular often returned there. During these years the Bergli continued to be not only Barth's favourite holiday spot but also the meeting-place for many of his friends: an oasis in the middle of the rising storms and at the same time a secret armoury for the battles that had to be fought. Among the regular guests there were Ernst Wolf; the faithful Richard Karwehl from Osnabrück; Erica Küppers, an ex-teacher from Osnabrück ('confessing Erica* on the way, as I call her'[204]), who had begun to study theology under Barth along with some of her pupils; Gertrud Staewen, who was well informed and deeply involved; and Günther Dehn, whose laugh so delighted Barth: 'It was wise and yet hopeful, a combination which I found quite irresistible.'[205] There was also Herta List, a friend of Lollo's from Munich who always joined in 'with the remarkable melancholy which was her hallmark',[206] and of course Georg Merz. 'Like so many others, Merz had reverted so much to his origins (in this case Bavaria, Franconia and Lutheranism) that while I could remain personal friends with him, we hardly continued to hold the same views.'[207] Still, Barth continued to enjoy listening to his colourful stories – best of all while sitting on a stool belonging to one of the

---

*The allusion here is to the title of a journal, *Bekennende Gemeinde auf dem Wege* (Confessing Church on the Way), of which Erica Küppers was the editor. (In fact the journal – and the epithet – came into being after the period described here.)

children. At this time there was a remarkable mixture of anxiety and delight at the Bergli gatherings.

Many things were unforgettable: 'The long table in the narrow room, at which everybody ate; the beds in the open air and the little house itself, filled to bursting; all the people who stayed there, reading, listening to the most marvellous concerts on the gramophone, walking, and having intense conversations!'[208] In addition to the regular guests there were all kinds of further visitors: old and new acquaintances, friends, pupils and other interested people. During the day Barth was usually occupied most of the time with his work – and the articles, lectures and so on which flowed fresh from his pen were quickly communicated to those present. In the evening, however, they 'often joined in children's games. For instance, two people arranged to act the parts of characters from history or literature, went to look for possible costumes and had an appropriate conversation. The rest had to guess who they were.' Barth once played Novalis and another time Bodelschwingh. 'Or we wrote "poetry". That is, random rhyming words were chosen and everyone had to make these rhymes into a poem.'[209]

One of Barth's poems produced in this way, in which the last word of each line had been supplied, went like this:

> I do confess, this life is what I love,
> and yet I know 'twill fade away with time.
> The lasting joys are only found above
> (and now I have a word that will not rhyme).
> But surely it would be an error great
> to miss the echo of this distant song.
> And he is poor indeed who, in his state,
> Can miss both joy and love all his life long.

No doubt about it – life there was certainly 'loved'! 'Against the happy background of natural surroundings which radiated a deep peace there was this community of very different people who nevertheless felt at one in their search for truth and . . . were still aware what an important part conversation and the exchange of ideas play in developing knowledge.'[210]

In summer 1934 Barth also met his friends Maury and Visser't Hooft at another place: on the occasion of an international student conference in La Châtaigneraie. Here (on August 7) Barth spoke on 'The Christian as Witness'. He was enchanted by the background to his lectures: 'Lake Geneva, the Jura, the hills of the Savoy and the sun shining on the good and the bad alike . . . ' He was also battered with a storm of questions put to him by the participants: he felt 'like a man trying to swim against the stream in a raging torrent'.

Talking about the idea of 'witness', which was so important for him, he said that man became God's witness on the one hand 'in gratitude that God has already given us his own witness', and on the other 'in the hope that God will again give us his own witness'. He illustrated what he meant from a remark made by a Japanese, who 'revered Karl Barth for the inner life and Karl Marx for the outward life'. He observed: 'Everything will depend on whether he can leave *both* these Karls behind him and endeavour to move from human to divine wisdom.'[211]

In a variation on the theme developed in La Châtaigneraie Barth spoke on 11 September in French, in Vaumarcus, and on 12 September, in German, in Pratteln, explaining his understanding of the pastorate as 'Service of the Word of God' (which is achieved by God, who first of all performs the decisive service in us!).

Then, immediately after completing *No!*, he travelled back to Germany. On 14 October he took part in the famous Community Day* in Düsseldorf which was banned by the police when the crowd topped thirty thousand. After saying the Lord's Prayer together the people departed in a disciplined way for their various churches. 'That evening I had to climb into one pulpit after another. Afterwards I had a very bad night simply thinking of this unprepared production.' The same night Barth went on to Oeynhausen, where for two whole days he helped to prepare for a second Confessing Synod. Here he proposed that a representative of the theological faculties should be included in the National Council of Brethren and gave advice over a 'message' to be accepted there. His special contribution was the closing paragraph. There were strenuous negotiations. 'Time and again it was important to be on guard: here against anxiety, there against arrogance; here against paternalism; there against idle talk; here against political exaggeration, there against clerical over-emphasis. We had to avoid disaster and make sure that something really useful was said.' In all this he found Karl Koch a man 'who is very easy to work with, since recently he has unmistakably learnt a great deal'.[212]

Barth kept in the background for the actual proceedings of the

---

*The Community Day (*Gemeindetag*) was particularly popular during the time of the Confessing Church; congregations would meet in a central locality for a service, sermons, etc.

second Confessing Synod, which took place on 19–20 October in Niemöller's parish, Dahlem, a suburb of Berlin. When he felt that the representatives of Bavaria and Württemberg were trying to water down the confessional statements, he proposed a special motion attacking any 'weakening of the front'. To his surprise, in the end the synod went well and had a good outcome. 'The resolutions of the Synod of Dahlem clarified the status of the Confessing Church in connection with church law. But this clarification was dependent on the dogmatic clarification achieved at Barmen and stood or fell with it.'[213] At the Synod, the National Council of Brethren was expanded to twenty-two members, from whom the executive body, the 'Council of the German Evangelical Church' was elected. The members of the Council were Karl Koch, the Westphalian President, Thomas Breit, a senior councillor, Pastors Asmussen and Niemöller, the lawyer Eberhard Fiedler, and Karl Barth, as a professor of theology.

The end of the Confessing Church?

Barth went back to Bonn via Marburg. At the end of October he again stayed in Berlin, in order 'to set up the necessary guide-lines for implementation of the Dahlem resolutions' in the National Council of Brethren. On 1 November he came back to speak at the district synod in Cologne, and on 3 November went with the lawyer Wilhelm Flor to a meeting of the Confessing Church in the Beethovenhalle in Bonn (where he spoke on 'The Church Yesterday, Today and Tomorrow'). However, hardly had he begun his lectures and classes in Bonn when a stir arose in the Confessing Church which made it necessary for him to travel to Berlin again on 8 and 20 November. What had happened? 'Instead of continuing to work quietly on, the Council and the Council of Brethren became involved in endless deliberations over the vague possibility (supported by all kinds of rumours which had come to us through the back stairs of this ministry or that) that we might be recognized by the state. If that happened, we would be able to topple Reibi from his throne and rectify our illegal position. The great problem was: were we "tolerable" to the state in our present form? A group of extremely tough people (especially Bishops Meiser, Wurm and Marahrens), said "No" to this question.' They hoped that a more appropriate attitude to the state would lead to a closer contact with a wide spectrum of members and thus to the salvation of the 'people's church'. For this reason the group wanted either to get rid of the people round Barth (because of their theological, confessional and political views) 'or to banish them to an innocuous corner'. Marahrens even said: 'You, too, will hold the view that at present the greatest danger to the German Evangelical Church comes from Karl Barth.'[214] When even von Soden, the representative of Hessen, veered away on the new course, Barth said to him: 'Dear colleague, what do you think when you see Prussia against Hanover, Hessen, Württemberg and Bavaria? What does it remind you of? Wasn't it like that in 1866? And at that time wasn't the prince of Hessen blind?' But then even the Prussians fell: such 'admirable men' as Karl Koch, Karl Lücking and Joachim Beckmann assented to a line which Barth thought was in fact a matter of seeking to please the state instead of simply believing.[215]

The session which has been described as the end of *the* 'Confessing Church' took place on the night of 20–21 November. 'As a result of pressure from . . . the south German bishops and the pernicious Bodelschwingh', the National Council of Brethren 'was now disowned, despite the resolution of the Synod, and replaced by the Provisional Church Government . . . a demolition firm as far as the decisions made at Dahlem were concerned'.[216] What was decided 'without further synods, but in those nocturnal tumults in St Michael's Hospice, was this: Dahlem was invalidated, and while Barmen was "intact", and "unassailable", it was only a document.'[217] At that point, Barth thought, the Confessing Church had 'broken its back' and from then on could 'no longer go forward joyfully as it had done between Barmen and Dahlem'.[218] From then on 'its limitation was that while it had stumbled on the right insights (Barmen) and resolutions (Dahlem), increasingly and in the end irrevocably it allowed itself to be prevented from taking the relevant action.'[219] Barth saw that the leaders of the so-called intact churches were principally to blame for the revolution. 'At the same time it was the authoritarian and legalistic instincts and tendencies of an episcopal and consistorial ecclesiasticism, and politically the disposition of the German nationalists, that one saw turning into a brake on the Protestant resistance movement which was certainly the chief thing that prevented it from developing to its full potential.' Indeed the representatives of these churches and their attitude permanently 'left in the lurch those who were fighting earnestly and resolutely and constantly stabbed them in the back'.[220]

On 22 November Bishop Marahrens was made head of the Provisional Church Government – a man 'who in the National Socialist period publicly declared that the Nazi world-view was binding on every Evangelical Christian'.[221] Barth immediately left the National Council of Brethren. And he kept to his decision, even when many people (e.g. two hundred Confessing Church pastors from Brandenburg) asked him to have second thoughts. Hesse, Immer and Niemöller also joined him in leaving. Things now looked black for the Confessing Church. But also on 22 November Barth wrote to Niemöller: 'We have based our cause on God and not on success.' Two days afterwards, he said in a sermon in Bremen: 'The disciples of Jesus are men who are responsible to Jesus, and for that reason are responsible to no one else; they are wholly committed, and for that very reason are free men in their commitment.'[222] A further sermon (on the saying in Jeremiah, 'Cursed is the man who puts his trust in men, but blessed is the man who puts his trust in the Lord') followed on 28 November, on the eve of the main assembly of the Reformed Alliance which definitively and unanimously committed the Alliance to the line taken by the Confessing Church.

The end of teaching in Bonn

At this time Barth had made a further important decision, namely to refuse to give the oath of loyalty to the Führer on 7 November in the prescribed form which was required of him. This oath had been required of all officials when, after the death of Hindenburg on 2 August, Hitler had combined the offices of Chancellor and President and had taken them over himself (on 19 August). Barth had already heard the news at the Bergli. 'From the very first moment that I heard in Switzerland that this oath was being required, it was quite clear to me that when the request reached me I would be put in the *status confessionis* as specifically and as appropriately as could be.' Granted, 'I did not refuse to give the official oath, but I stipulated an addition to the effect that I could be loyal to the Führer only within my responsibilities as an Evangelical Christian.' 'After I had been invited to give the oath by the Rector of the university, Professor Hans Naumann, I immediately made representations to him and handed over my proposal for him to pass on to the Minister.'[223]

With that, 'my hour had come. I was suddenly suspended' (on 26 November). The reason given was that 'by his behaviour in office he has shown himself unworthy of the recognition, the respect and the trust which his calling requires'.[224] Barth never forgot how, on the day 'before my suspension, we sang together in the lecture room in Konviktstrasse the hymn:

> O may this bounteous God
> Through all our life be near us
> With ever joyful hearts
> And blessed peace to cheer us.
> And keep us in his grace
> And guide us when perplexed
> And free us from all ills
> In this world and the next.'[225]

The students found Barth's lecture room closed the next day, and Charlotte von Kirschbaum brought them the news of the forced suspension of the lectures. On 7 December the Rector presented the German-Christian Schmidt-Japing to the students as Barth's successor, whereupon one of them read a declaration which had been courageously written by three theological students, Martin Eras, Siegfried Hajek and Heinrich Quistorp, and was then signed by two hundred of them: 'We must reject the continuation of Professor Karl Barth's lectures and classes . . . by a substitute.'[226] The protest was no more effective than Barth's objection to the suspension at the Bonn court on 27 November. On 20 December the disciplinary chamber filed his dismissal with the administration in Cologne.

Barth had to appear before a tribunal, his head full of a rhyme which had come to him that very morning:

> Karl, we know, is hardly vile
> and yet he has to go on trial.

'I was accused, and an attorney charged me with having done what should not have been done in the Germany of that time. Three judges sat opposite me and looked at me with serious, mistrustful faces. And a bold young lawyer sat beside me and took great pains to demonstrate that it was not as bad as that. But everything took its inevitable course. I was found guilty and sentenced.'[227] Barth's lawyer was a cousin of Günther Dehn, Otto Bleibtreu (1904–59), the attorney and legal adviser of the Confessing Church of the Rhine, who had been dismissed from the judiciary because of his membership of the Social Democrat Party. The state attorney for the prosecution gave Barth the satisfaction of unwittingly demonstrating the aims of National Socialism: the oath, he said, 'in fact had unlimited content', and allowed no one to see for himself what was right before God. 'On the contrary, such an attempt was itself a serious crime. It went without saying that the Führer did not require anything that was against God's commandment.' Barth also defended himself. 'I flicked through a copy of Plato and read to the people the following passages from the *Apology* of Socrates: "Men of Athens, I respect and love you, but I shall obey the god rather than you. I believe that no greater good ever came to pass in the city than that of my service for the god ... And so, men of Athens, I am now making my defence not for my own sake, as one might imagine, but far more for yours, so that you may not by condemning me err in your treatment of the gift the god gave you."[228] By recognizing the state, the church affirms the limitation put on it for its own sake *qua* state, and the professor of theology appointed by the state is himself a state-appointed guardian of this limitation. It is his particular task to guard against the initiation of theories of the state like those currently in circulation and proclaimed by the state attorney. In the matter of the oath as in the question of the Hitler salute in lectures, I could only have done my duty on behalf of the state. They, the judges, should now declare in the interest of the state that there was no question of totalitarianism. If they did not do that, they should realize that they were making Hitler a god incarnate and offending most seriously against the first commandment.'[229]

At the hearing in Cologne, however, the question of the oath was only a peripheral matter, as meanwhile there had been some developments in the case. True, Barth's conduct had at first incurred criticism, even among some of his friends: Bultmann virtually asked him to 'withdraw' his condition for giving an oath.[230] But then, following the initiative of Friedrich Horst and Hans Emil Weber, the Provisional Church Government (on 7 December) and, in similar vein, the Reformed Alliance (on 14 December) had declared that for Christians, 'by its reference to God an oath excluded any action which would be contrary to God's command attested in holy scripture'.[231] So on 18 December Barth could report to the Rector in Bonn and the Minister of Cultural Affairs that 'the addition proposed by me as a condition of my taking the oath has become superfluous'.[232] The court in Cologne also recognized that now

Barth's attitude in the question of the oath was 'by itself no longer sufficient cause for a dismissal'.[233] However, it then went on to argue 'that the mere fact that the thought of this qualification had come to me proved that my attitude to the National Socialist state was incorrect, so I could not continue to be considered as a teacher of German youth'.[234] And on these grounds Barth was nevertheless punished by dismissal. On the evening of the same day twenty-five of his students in Bonn gave him a surprise by singing the hymn 'Now praise the Lord, my soul . . .'

This decision put an end to his academic activity in Germany. However, he continued to live in Bonn. On 4 February 1935 he asked the Church Government in Berlin to support an appeal against the Cologne judgment. He made his further involvement in the leadership of the Confessing Church dependent on the condition that the church 'explicitly makes my cause its own'. However, he discovered that 'when I approached the Provisional Church Government and the Council of Brethren of the time, who had brought this trial upon me, and asked for their formal support, I was left in the lurch by both these bodies and had to fight the whole battle by myself.'[235] When the National Council of Brethren did not accede to Barth's request, he stayed away from its session in Oeynhausen on 12 February, and on 24 February told Karl Koch that he did not think that he could continue in the Council of Brethren any longer, even as a guest. On 14 March he then lodged an appeal with the Supreme Prussian Court in Berlin on his own initiative – with arguments which had been worked out by Bleibtreu.

While it thus remained open for the moment whether he would resume his lectures again, he became more active in other fields. He preached on a number of occasions. On 1 December he reported on the problems of the Provisional Church Government to his former pupils and during this month gave an exposition of Luke 1 to them in four Bible classes. On 16 December he took part in a conference of the Young Reformed Christians of the Rhine, and on the 17th he gave a sermon to a large congregation in Barmen-Gemarke. On the 21st he sought to bring about peace between the East Friesian church administration and the Confessing Church there in a series of negotiations in Uelsen which lasted for hours. At the beginning of January 1935 he held a study group in practical theology with 'his' students in Kaiserswerth, at which he spoke on 'Sermons for the Congregation'. Then he stayed in Switzerland for several weeks: in

Grindelwald with his old comrade Martin Nil, in Berne with his mother, in Basle with the Thurneysens and in Zürich with the Pestalozzis. On 3 February he gave a sermon entitled 'Under the Word' at the Rhine-Westphalian Community Day in Barmen-Gemarke (on Jesus' stilling of the storm). And on 11 February he spoke in Mönchen-Gladbach on 'The Possibility of a United Confession', a theme which had become topical again as a result of the church struggle, but which was now being increasingly challenged by the growth of confessionalism within the Confessing Church. The day before, he had said his formal farewell to his Bonn pupils at a Bible study group for students at Bad Godesberg. He gave an interpretation of Psalm 119.67 and James 4.6 and ended with the words: 'We have been studying cheerfully and seriously. As far as I was concerned it could have continued in that way, and I had already resigned myself to having my grave here by the Rhine! I had plans for the future with other colleagues who are either no longer here or have been away for a long time – but there has been a frost on our spring night! And now the end has come. So listen to my last piece of advice: exegesis, exegesis and yet more exegesis! Keep to the Word, to the scripture that has been given us.'[236]

Barth's opportunities were constricted even further when on 1 March he was served with a total ban on speaking in public – at the station in Bonn.* Granted, this did not prevent him from giving a sermon on 26 March at the beginning of the Second Free Reformed Synod in St Nicolas' church at Siegen (on the commandment against making images, which had become particularly significant in view of the new ideology). However, this was his last personal public address in Germany. From then on his activity was largely limited to private conversations and discussions – above all with the various heads of the Confessing Church, and also with other contemporaries, including Josef Hromádka. He also wrote an article ('Answer to Erwin Reisner') in which he again dealt with the problems of natural theology and rejected even a negative 'point of contact' (in human despair and so on).

Although Barth's freedom was being restricted in this way, he now had the opportunity to speak elsewhere, and in a way which commanded a good deal of attention. This was in Holland, where from 8 February onwards he gave sixteen lectures at the University of

*Verbally, by the Gestapo.

Utrecht on 'The Main Problems of Dogmatics, on the basis of the Apostles' Creed'. He went there on Fridays week by week to give two sections of his lectures, and then came straight back. In the lectures he had a strong impression of speaking from the 'situation of a church militant' to an audience who still had time 'to do theology in a leisurely way'. However, he found 'that the situation of a church militant shows a close affinity to the great times in which church dogma arose'.

Barth called the book which arose out of these lectures *Credo*. In it, faith is understood as 'an act of the acknowledgment of the reality of God which comes to men', and to this extent as 'decision'. In other words, as 'the overcoming of the contradiction to this reality', it is also a 'confession', indeed a church confession. On several occasions he said: 'Christian faith stands and falls . . . by having God and only God as its subject.' But God is 'absolutely and exclusively God in his revelation'. Barth even thought that 'the great catastrophe of theology and the church' at that time springs from a misunderstanding of the 'three words "his only Son"'. If people would understand them, they would not want to recognize the 'Creator' in and for himself, and 'the knowledge of Jesus Christ' would also be the 'source of faith in creation' – in that case, however, people would not be dealing in human terms with 'an article of sight' but with 'an article of faith'.[237]

On his visit of 5–6 April Barth concluded his lectures with a question and answer session. Here he found the Haarlem pastor Kornelis Heiko Miskotte, whom he had known since 1928, a profound commentator.

In uncertainty over his future career he returned to Switzerland at the end of May. The question of a new post was becoming increasingly urgent. He had already spent a short time in Switzerland on 7 March, for the marriage of his daughter Franziska to a Basle businessman, Max Zellweger. Zellweger came from a family which was engaged in the silk trade, and was later to rise to the position of a Vice-Director in the Basle chemical industry. On this occasion Barth had already asked tentatively whether there was any chance that he might be given a chair at Basle. Visser't Hooft made an emphatic plea that he should be invited to a chair in Geneva. Despite all the hindrances, of course, he would much have preferred to remain in Germany – in a teaching post outside the university. At the end of April the Fourth Rhine Confessing Synod passed a resolution expressing its 'urgent concern that Professor D. D. Karl Barth should be able to continue . . . his work'.[238] But, as he discovered to his regret, he received no subsequent invitation 'in the form of a final and binding offer'.[239] Indeed he now began to detect unwillingness and opposition even in the ranks of the Confessing Church itself, partly because of his philosophy, partly because of his political attitude and partly for personal reasons. Bishop Meiser insisted that the Third General Confessing Synod, which took place in Augsburg at the beginning of July, could only be held if Barth were not invited nor present. So he took no part in it. And after what happened at the synod Barth for his part could not possibly rejoice in 'the new peace of Augsburg which has stemmed from it'.[240] He attacked the Confessing Church as it had been represented there with bitter words: 'It still has no heart for the millions who suffer unjustly. It still has nothing to say on the simplest questions of public honesty. When it speaks, it speaks only about its own affairs.'[241] Barth drew the conclusion that if the way of the Confessing Church 'really led from Barmen via Dahlem to Augsburg . . . then I have no alternative but to terminate my function here, which is really not a very attractive one . . .'[242]

From 21 May onwards Barth waited at the Bergli for clarification of his uncertain situation. He occupied his time preparing a lecture ('The Gospel in the Present') which he then gave during the time of the Augsburg Synod, first in Berne and then in Basle. In it he drew a radical conclusion from the church struggle. 'Christianity which wants the world to give it a reason and indeed a justification for its existence, has come to an end.' This meant that the church now had to become poor, and also that it was summoned to 'a completely new freedom in its confession and in its knowledge'.[243]

On 14 June a decision was at last reached on the case which was still pending in Berlin. The result was completely unexpected. The Cologne judgment was repealed and Barth was merely fined (a fifth of his annual salary) because of his refusal to give the Hitler salute and because of his remarks at Jacobi's in October 1933. However, satisfaction over the result was of short duration. On 22 June the Minister of Cultural Affairs dismissed Barth on the basis of the notorious paragraph 6 of the Law for the Reorganization of the Civil Service. Barth was immediately offered a chair in the University of Basle. 'It happened that I was dismissed in Germany on a Saturday and the very next Monday the Basle administration appointed me an *ordinarius* professor. So I was only out of work for the Sunday. I would like to call to your attention the fact that the two men who worked for my appointment here in Basle were both declared atheists. These were Councillors Hauser and Thalmann . . . *Dei providentia et hominum confusione Helvetia regitur** – as it happened?[244] Barth's appointment was made conditional on his acceptance of eligibility for Swiss national service, which he was glad to do in the circumstances. For the following period his former chair at Bonn was completely suspended – or rather made into a chair at the Technical High School in Berlin-Charlottenburg.[245]

So his years in Germany finally came to an end. The Protestant faculty of theology at Bonn, which had experienced such a meteoric rise in a short period and which had emerged as a tower of resistance in the church struggle, was now completely demolished. Barth's assistant Helmut Gollwitzer also had to go; he became a preacher in the Confessing Church and then Niemöller's successor in Dahlem. About the same time Ernst Wolf was transferred to Halle as a punishment and Friedrich Horst was similarly dismissed. Barth's departure was equally a loss for the Confessing Church, in two ways: they had lost a resolute fighter and a critic who had warned them against the lassitude in confessing which now threatened them. Of course Barth remained in close contact with the church even from a distance, but he no longer had any direct part in it. At the beginning of July the Council of Brethren of the Old Prussian Union wrote to its member churches: 'We are grateful to Professor Dr Karl Barth for the decisive service which he has shown to the Evangelical Church by reminding us once again, through his theological work, that the Word of God is the sole guide for the teaching and the order of the Church. The cause which he has represented . . . must never again be forsaken by those of us who are in the German Evangelical Church.'[246] Even Barth was reluctant to say goodbye to Bonn. 'I have spent the liveliest and richest years of my teaching life here.'[247] 'Things went so well that at first I was almost somewhat depressed when I returned home to Basle, where I was surrounded by narrower questions than I was there.'[248] Charlotte von Kirschbaum went with Barth and his family to Basle, 'leaving her fatherland and her friends' in order to go on supporting him.[249]

---

*'Switzerland is ruled by the providence of God and the confusion of man.'

6

A Swiss Voice

The years from 1935 to 1946 in St Albanring, Basle

Return to Switzerland

'Within three days of the announcement of my dismissal from Bonn, the cantonal council in Basle . . . invited me to a special chair in the university of my home town.'[1] Barth immediately accepted the invitation, not only because further work in Germany was now virtually impossible for him, but also because he thought that a Confessing Church which was ready for the sham peace of the Augsburg Synod 'could not at the same time have wanted my further services'.[2] On 8 July 1935 he and his family took up residence at St Albanring 186, not far from his birthplace (and not far from what is now Karl Barth Platz); exactly four hundred years after the arrival of Calvin in the St Albanvorstadt.[3] 'The famous Felix Weingartner' had lived in the house before Barth: 'when I moved into the house he gave me his voluminous life's work, a play about Christ!'[4] From one of the windows one could see 'not very far away the last out-runners of the Black Forest', and this reminded Barth of Germany.[5] As a consequence of this move Barth lived once again 'in the special air of Basle, which since 1899 I had only breathed on visits'.[6] From now on the rest of his work was done in the theological faculty, 'whose influence we had once been able to trace from Aargau with so much amazement'.[7]

Before Barth began work there, he had to fulfil a heavy programme of lecturing. However, he did refuse an invitation to be visiting lecturer to eight Japanese universities. Instead, at the end of July, he first gave four lectures on 'The Church and the Churches', at the invitation of Adolf Keller, in an 'ecumenical seminar' in Geneva, which were simultaneously translated into English and French, and then six seminars on the beginning of Calvin's Catechism. 'It was an extremely exhausting business, because I just had to be available to discuss things with every conceivable person from early in the morning until late at night.' In his lectures Barth showed a critical yet expectant interest in the ecumenical movement, which was slowly beginning to take shape, though 'All in all . . . for the moment this ecumenical business hasn't made much of an impression on me.'[8] He used the occasion to formulate his view of the ecumenical problem, developing the thesis: 'The question of the unity of the church must be identical with the question of Jesus Christ as the specific head and Lord of the church . . . Jesus Christ, as one mediator between God and man, is himself church unity, that unity in which there may indeed be a multiplicity of congregations, gifts and persons in the church, but which rules out a multiplicity of churches.' Thus the multiplicity of churches was not a sign of riches, but of need and of sin. It could not be overcome by mutual tolerance, and indeed the church could not be united at all; all that was possible was for the unity of the church which had already been accomplished in Jesus Christ to be *discovered* and *recognized* in obedience.[9]

At the end of August Barth travelled with the Pestalozzis and Lollo von Kirschbaum, at the invitation of his Prague colleague Josef Hromádka, to Mysliborice in Moravia. On this occasion he also visited Prague (he was especially moved by the Jewish cemetery) and went to Budapest and Venice on the way home. It was Hromádka who impressed Barth most on this trip and whom he thereafter regarded with respect: he thought him a 'pioneer' through and through. A special characteristic of Hromádka was 'an adaptability combined with an inner consistency which was a gift bestowed on him to help him at every stage through all his trials, great and small'.[10] Hromádka (1889–1969) was a Czech who had come to be a distinctive representative of 'dialectical theology' by very idiosyncratic ways and as result of deliberately following the old Hussite tradition. In Moravia Barth addressed a pastors' conference on 'The Theological Presuppositions of Church Order'.

In his lecture he pointed out that 'the present form of the church can no longer be accepted as a matter of course. Inevitably the form of the church will always be determined by definite historical, psychological, and above all theological presuppositions; however, reflection on it must be based on and supported by consideration of the mystery of grace and true obedience' towards God.[11] Barth was therefore obviously concerned to think through to their conclusions the insights he had gained from the German church struggle and to make Christians outside Germany share in them.

This was also his concern in St Gallen when on 24 September, for the first time since his return to Switzerland, he met a group of local pastors. There was quite literally a head-on collision. Barth declared (in a lecture on 'The Confession of the Reformation and Our Confession') that Christian confession was the obedient 'action of the church' by which it recognizes 'that Jesus Christ is . . . really the Lord'.[12] And he described the Swiss churches, measured by this standard, as 'confessionally weak'. But the lecture did not go down well. 'Our pernicious liberals . . . had expected that I would propose some kind of highly orthodox confession of faith and had armed themselves accordingly. My lecture made irrelevant the tirades which they had composed in support of freedom of conscience, biblical criticism, tolerance, etc., etc., but they could not resist directing them at me in person and required of me an acknowledgment that neo-Protestantism (*in toto*) was of the nature of the church.' Barth retorted with a 'small anathema against all anthropologisms', and 'on the streets and in the squares and at the café tables a cry of woe went up over my priestcraft, my popery and so on'.[13] And when in the discussion following his lecture he wanted to address the liberals 'casually and guilelessly as "friends", but not as "brothers"', the positives present were certainly not backwards in responding to such lovelessness with loud complaints; they also sang the hymn "Heart and heart unite together".'[14] The Goebbels press also made its own contribution to this outcry, using Barth's remarks as a pretext for blackening him as a notorious agitator among his fellow-countrymen. He himself was extremely disappointed as a result of this encounter with Swiss Protestantism. 'I came . . . fresh from the struggles and experiences of the German churches to ecclesiastical Switzerland and thought – evidently too naively – that at least I would be able to help to bring alive some of the different kind of questions which were asked here. But this proved to be impossible. I had the impression that here I was surrounded by considerable restraint – though people were certainly much more friendly – and could only swim against the stream.'[15] True, on 29 September Barth preached in the cathedral in Basle 'to an audience amounting to thousands' (on Matthew 6.24ff.: 'You *cannot* serve two masters'), and at first he was a 'foreign celebrity' in Switzerland.[16] But 'after a brief period of some notoriety', he had to pursue his solitary career as before.[17]

A few days later, on 7 October, at the urgent request of Karl

Immer, he risked returning to Germany to give a lecture in Barmen
on the subject of 'Gospel and Law'. This lecture was subsequently
regarded as his farewell to Christians in Germany, and for years
afterwards it was a subject of theological discussion.

He made a radical criticism of the German Christians and their doctrine of
'the law of the people' which went right to the heart of the differences
between them and the Confessing Church. In another way, indeed, he
provided an important corrective to Luther and certainly to Lutheranism,
posing specific questions to friends like Asmussen and Iwand. Barth's
approach was to reverse the traditional sequence of 'Law and Gospel'. He
believed 'that anyone who in all seriousness wants to speak of law first, and
only mention the gospel afterwards, on the basis of the law, cannot with the
best will in the world be speaking of God's law and therefore cannot be
speaking of his gospel either'. So it is 'not only hazardous and dangerous,
but also perverse, to want to read the law of God out of some event different
from *the* event in which the will of God is manifested to us in form and
content as grace'. Moreover, God's gracious action does not revolve around
itself; 'it is directed towards *our* action, towards a conformity between our
action and his.'[18] Consequently, the law *follows* the gospel.

Barth could not give the lecture himself; it had to be read for him
'by Pastor Immer in the church in Barmen, which was full to
overflowing and watched by the Gestapo. On the evening of the
same day, probably worried by the enormous crowds and the tumul-
tuous welcome from former pupils and supporters, the Gestapo
found it necessary to accompany us to the border in the slow overnight train.'[19] Barth was not to set foot on German soil again for ten
years – and what a decade that was!

At the end of October he took up his academic work in Basle,
teaching '"as though nothing had happened" – though some things
certainly did happen!' And the Rhine 'flowed past it all, with sadness or perhaps a touch of humour, down to Bonn, where Schmidt-
Japing and Stauffer were able to sprawl on our abandoned chairs'.[20]
Every day now he walked 'through the St Alban gate down the St
Albanvorstadt past the cathedral to the Stapfelberg, where in the
touchingly modest Auditorium "Maximum" of this university city I
continued to lecture on my dogmatics to all kinds of people' (first for
five hours a week and later for four).[21] Barth was to be occupied with
this task for most of the rest of his life, which from then on was spent
in Basle. In addition, in this first semester he held a seminar on 'The
Doctrine of Justification', and an open evening and discussion group

at his home. 'Ritschl' bored him so much as a subject for discussion that he changed it to 'Luther'.

Through his work Barth attempted 'to reconstruct the school which had been so sadly destroyed in Bonn, i.e. to make the students assembled here from many lands and of many tongues acquainted as extensively as possible with "Church Dogmatics", and above all to introduce just a little bit of Prussian tempo to the Swiss'.[22] These students now also included Barth's son Markus and from 1936 his son Christoph; there were also Walter Sigrist, later to become President of the Swiss Church Federation, the up-and-coming New Testament scholar Eduard Schweizer, the Scotsman Thomas F. Torrance and the Frenchman Georges Casalis. His audience in Basle also included all kinds of interested 'laymen'. Prominent among them were some society ladies, for example a Dr Burckhardt-Lüscher who, for twenty years, 'heard absolutely all my lectures and wrote them down with a ready pen'.[23] Barth suffered a little from the fact that 'my fellow-countrymen, the Swiss students, were rather harder ground to cultivate'[24] because of their restraint and the generally rather 'cooler and more confined atmosphere' than he was used to in Bonn.[25] Indeed he once complained that 'with very few exceptions they were hard to get moving and were preoccupied with rather primitive problems'.[26] 'In short, in outward splendour my teaching activity in Basle compared with that in Bonn rather as Herod's temple compared with that of Solomon.'[27] The student scene changed to some extent when they were soon joined by some quite noteworthy victims of persecution (on political or racial grounds) 'whose careers had been interrupted and who with a remarkable love of the subject had undertaken to study theology: one Ministerial Director, Emeritus Professor Dr Werner Richter (my former superior), one court lawyer, two advocates and Arnold Ehrhardt, a professor of law'.[28]

The frontier was still open, so that Barth could continue to have a number of German students and doctoral students, including Walter Kreck, Helmut Gollwitzer and Hans Heinrich Wolf. He found that most of 'the small group of German students who despite great difficulties found their way to Basle' later proved to be 'reliable and useful'.[29] The influx of German students to Basle was only stemmed at the beginning of 1939 by an official decree that semesters spent with Karl Barth were not counted as part of university studies.

Shortly after Barth's arrival, the theological faculty at Basle was threatened with dissolution. However, a proposal to this effect was rejected in the Great Council during the course of 1936 (the voting was 70 to 44). During his first three years in Basle Barth was only an *extraordinarius* professor. At first he had two seniors as colleagues in the faculty, the Schleiermacherian Johannes Wendland, whom he later succeeded, and Eberhard Vischer, Harnack's friend, 'a sturdy embodiment of the extraordinary academic spirit to be found at the end of the nineteenth century'. 'I shall never forget how openly and courteously he bade me welcome to Basle, although on earlier occasions I had given him cause for serious complaint.'[30] In 1938 he was succeeded by Oscar Cullmann from Strasbourg. The Old Testament professors on the faculty were Walter Eichrodt and Walter Baumgartner. Barth prized Baumgartner because of his zest for historical criticism, although they differed in their views and Barth found his colleague's teaching 'dry bread'.[31] Other members were the systematic theologian Adolf Köberle (until 1939), the church historian Ernst Staehelin and the New Testament scholar Karl Ludwig Schmidt, 'a colleague who was far superior to me in learning and debating power, but who always proved stimulating'; here 'once again he became my neighbour'.[32] To begin with, Eduard Thurneysen was the only one of his colleagues with whom Barth had 'a very close relationship'. Thurneysen 'represented the discipline of practical theology in our university and in particular taught the difficult art of preaching'.[33] Julius Schweizer taught catechetics and lectured with him. In 1936 Fritz Lieb also joined the teaching staff as *Extraordinarius* Professor in Systematic Theology. 'It is not saying too much to single him out as one of the most original members of the teaching staff of our university . . . His greatness consists in the single-mindedness which he displays on so many sides, the firmness with which he is so open and the mastery which (contrary to the poet's words) in his case does *not* show in his limitations.' He was competent to give instruction on Ancient Near Eastern and Russian cultural history, church history and especially the history of heresies, and every Saturday he also used to go into the country (with Barth's youngest son) to collect fossils; 'the fruit of these researches was presented in the developed form of a completely new hypothesis on the origin of the Jura for professional geologists to consider.'[34]

In 1936 the circle of theological teachers in Basle was also enlarged by two assistant lecturers, Alfred de Quervain, whose views on and arguments about ethics were 'always distinctive and had an original form and tone',[35] and Wilhelm Vischer. Barth came to have an affection for Vischer once again as a 'free, childlike troubadour of the good God', and also as 'an authentic heir and upholder of the old bourgeois traditions of the city of Basle and its families'. Barth felt that 'in his approach towards the Old Testament Vischer had a quite extraordinary gift which simply cannot be argued away by the objections which are made against him.'[36] In 1938, pressure from the 'liberals' led to the appointment of Fritz Buri as a counterbalance to Barth. Karl also came up against his brother Heinrich once more as a colleague in the faculty of philosophy, though relations between the two were steadily deteriorating. Throughout the Basle years relations between them were decidedly cool and sometimes almost 'unfriendly'. Karl felt that his brother's thought was now centred on a point which was 'just about diametrically opposed' to his own. Once again Heinrich regarded Karl as 'a man who would brook no opposition . . . but one has to show him once and for all that even he has his limitations'.[37]

Wilhelm Vischer, who had also been forced out of Germany, was at the same time pastor of Barth's local church (from early in 1936). He lived 'only a few houses away from us' and he now developed a lively relationship with the friend whom he had once visited in Safenwil. Barth particularly enjoyed going to hear Vischer's sermons in the old church of St Jacob. While Thurneysen attempted 'to say everything about any text' with great thoroughness, in his sermons Vischer wanted to interpret scripture 'much more narrowly than Thurneysen, that is, to present the quite special message which he heard and received from each particular text'. He had 'an innate gift for reinterpretation, and an astounding capacity for so to speak assimilating himself to a text, making himself its servant even down to its tone and mood, and thus allowing the biblical author to speak from his pulpit in modern words'.[38] Of course Barth also occasionally went to hear Thurneysen in the cathedral, and he also heard the other member of the trinity of prominent preachers in Basle at that time. This was Walter Lüthi, in whose sermons he found 'an exemplary form of good Swiss-Reformed theology'.[39] He saw 'application' as Lüthi's special strength, and 'often wished that one could combine Helmi Vischer and Lüthi in one person'.[40] Over the next period Barth's relations with Thurneysen became rather less intimate. Not only did Barth disagree with Thurneysen's tendency to generalize in his sermons, but he found that in spite of their continuing friendship,

Thurneysen's intellectual development since 1921 had somewhat alienated him from the problem of a church dogmatics and from the lessons Barth thought that he had learnt from the German church struggle.

Once he had settled in Switzerland, Barth also preached from time to time. This was mostly to stand in for Thurneysen or Vischer in the cathedral or in St Jacob's church, but for some time he also went back to Safenwil at least once a year. A further volume of sermons was published in 1935, and called *Die grosse Barmherzigkeit* (The Great Mercy), again produced in collaboration with Thurneysen. The sermons collected in this volume were an example and an indication of the conviction that Christian preaching is essentially preaching on a text, 'the interpretation of scripture': it may 'touch on' the 'questions of the day' but it should not discuss them thematically.[41] Barth believed that this was the way to approach the congregation, especially the modern congregation. 'In my opinion the best way to talk to unbelievers, intellectuals and modern youth is not to catechize their "capacity for revelation" out of them but to treat them quietly and simply, as though their objections to "Christianity" were not to be taken seriously (remembering that Christ died and rose for them also). They can then understand you, because they can see where you stand as a representative of Protestant theology, i.e. on the foundation of the doctrine of justification by faith alone. I have the impression that my sermons reach and "interest" my hearers most when I least rely on possible and already existing analogies to God's Word, when I least rely on being "able" to proclaim this Word, when I am least confident in my skill in reaching people by means of my rhetoric, and when instead I *allow* my language to be turned and *shaped* as much as possible by what the text seems to want to say to me.'[42] In accordance with Reformed tradition, for Barth the sermon was the chief element in the liturgy. 'For me a respectable sermon, a heartfelt prayer and energetic singing from the congregation would be quite enough if the weekly eucharist, which is of course part of all this, does not appear practicable.'[43] Barth occasionally had difficulty with prayers: 'For a while I tried the expedient of replacing what was given in the order for worship, not by extemporary prayers (I never risked that), but by loose collections of biblical texts from the Psalms. Only with advancing years did I begin to write these texts down word for word as I prepared my sermons, first for the end and later also for the beginning of the central action of the service.'[44]

At this time Barth's favourite hobby was riding. He had already been keen on it in Bonn, and now he went out with Wilhelm Vischer. He never forgot the many times 'we rode through the fields of Muttenz and Pratteln or dashed through the woods of the Hardt at an exhilarating gallop on the brown and the grey, thus representing at least half of the horsemen of the apocalypse!'[45] It once happened that on the following Sunday Vischer greeted him 'from the pulpit . . . : "Dear congregation . . . Up comrades, To horse, to horse . . ."'[46] Barth even ventured to insert in his *Dogmatics* the opinion (printed in small type) that 'a really good horseman cannot possibly be godless'.[47] He was also fond of riding with Walter Steiger, the pastor from Binningen, and once even went out with Emil Brunner.

Continuation of the church struggle

From the beginning of his time in Basle Barth continued to be very much preoccupied with the further course of events in Germany. He felt very close ties with the country. But because he saw that the 'lies and brutality, the stupidity and fear prevalent there were spreading far beyond the frontiers of Germany'; because he saw with terror the blindness of other nations towards the real menace of the Nazis, their systematic transgression of the first commandment, he had to oppose the country as it now was. There was nothing for it. 'For the sake of the preservation of the true church and the just state I had to persevere in my opposition to National Socialism even after I had returned to Switzerland. On that account I am labelled a sort of "public enemy number one" in Germany. The head of the Württemberg administration even described me in a public speech as "this good-for-nothing".'[48] Barth's opposition took many forms. He was chairman of the Basle Committee of Swiss Aid for (exiled) German scholars. He made many attempts to secure the awarding of the Nobel Peace Prize to Carl von Ossietzky. He looked out for grants for German students and new jobs for émigrés, put up non-Aryans at his home, and wrote letters to, for example, Bishop Bell of Chichester, Bishop Eidem of Uppsala and Marc Boegner in Paris, asking for the reception of Jews into other countries. He also made contact with others who were now unpopular in Germany: at the beginning of 1936 with Thomas Mann and the pianist Rudolf Serkin, and in November with the writer Ernst Wiechert. In September he corresponded with Martin Buber to see whether he could join in the argument about Gogarten's confusion between respect for God and respect for earthly authorities.[49] Gogarten's retort, a book entitled *Gericht oder Skepsis* (Judgment or Scepticism), in which he appealed for a liberation of 'German theology' from the 'sway' of Barth's theology, was published at the beginning of 1937.

Above all, however, from Basle Barth played a passionate and heartfelt part in further developments within the Confessing Church. He thought that 'now one could see much better from a distance than close to how dangerously the Confessing Church is swaying to and fro in the storm'.[50] He addressed a series of letters to the leaders of the Confessing Church, his friends and pupils, giving encouragement, advice and warnings – some were smuggled in by go-betweens, and some were written in code. And he received a constant flow of representatives of this group as visitors, either in Basle or at the Bergli: especially Immer and Hesse, Niemöller, Asmussen and Ernst Wolf. Wolf 'became increasingly close to me both as a theologian and a friend';[51] Erica Küppers, Käthe Seifert and Gertrud Staewen were also steadfast friends. He assured Robert Grosche that he took part in the German church struggle 'as though it were a part of us'.[52] He pleaded in vain for the release of Dr Weissler, a lawyer under arrest, and successfully, via Visser't Hooft, for that of his pupil Hellmut Traub. In December 1935, in the *Basler Nachrichten*, he criticized the 'unchurchly church government' which had just been set up by the Reich Minister of Church Affairs, Hanns Kerrl, so sharply that the German ambassador in Berne left in protest. In the middle of April 1936 he went to Driebergen in Holland to meet the lecturers from the seminaries in Wuppertal and Berlin, chiefly to discuss the problems that had arisen over his 'Gospel and Law' lecture. Here he found that Hans Asmussen was his chief opponent. He had hardly left Holland when the University of Utrecht awarded him an honorary doctorate of theology.

A striking feature of Barth's remarks on the church struggle after his return to Switzerland was a certain critical note, even against the Confessing Church, which became increasingly stronger. This made his position more and more lonely. He thought that 'one can and must reproach this Confessing Church for failing to recognize the real danger from the enemy early on and for not opposing the enemy from the start with the Word of God which judges human deceit and injustice, as was its duty as the church of Jesus Christ'.[53] In particular, he objected that the Confessing Church had not understood and in part did not even want to understand that the acknowledgment of the first commandment 'under National Socialism is not just a "religious" decision. It is not a decision of church policy either. It is in fact a political decision. It is a decision against a totalitarian state which as such cannot recognize any task, proclamation or order other than its own, nor acknowledge any other God than itself.'[54] So Barth accused the Confessing Church of having fought for itself, 'for the freedom and purity of its proclamation. On the other hand, it has kept silent, for example, over the treatment of the Jews, the astonishing treatment of political opponents, the suppression of the truth in the press of the new Germany and so much else against which the Old Testament prophets would certainly have spoken out.'[55]

Nevertheless, Barth also recognized the encouraging signs. 'When in Germany the press, the theatre, the trade unions, the universities, the army and so on were "assimilated", the Evangelical Church was one sector where the system came up against at least some fairly powerful resistance, and remained so. In the Jewish question, as elsewhere, the Evangelical Church may have been no more than a modest gleam, and often enough a barely flickering light . . . but right until the bitter end the darkness never overcame it.'[56] The reason why he thought that this light was 'barely flickering', especially in the second half of the 1930s, was because he saw that the Confessing Church was now taking flight in some respects. People were beginning 'to give way on all sides, to look everywhere for – shall we say it? – a more convenient substitute for what had been surrendered after Dahlem. And they began to find it: the "intact" even more in their local churches, the Lutherans again and even more in their confession, the Berneucheners even more in their mysteries. Now prisoners in their cells . . . discovered everywhere the wonder of solitary contemplation . . . The experience of the power of the eucharist among congregations led to a revival of the eucharistic disputes of the sixteenth century and people began to proclaim, with voices from the grave, that the full consolation of the gospel depended on the eucharist, that it was better not to share it with the Reformed . . . Not that these things were (or would be) evil or even insignificant.' But it was ominous 'that at that time they emerged as a result of a bad conscience, that they were *thrust forward* at a time when people had failed in simple obedience over the question of the body of Christ, and could be seen as a proper *quid pro quo*'.[57]

At the very time when the Confessing Church as a whole was involved in such a retreat, Barth by contrast became convinced that it was also necessary for Christians to offer direct, political resistance to the Nazi state. The grounds for this conviction were strictly theological, but they pointed increasingly clearly in that direction. However, it was only when he had returned to Switzerland that Barth stressed more and more strongly that the Christian resistance to National Socialism also had a political dimension. On the one hand he saw that his earlier hesitation to adopt a political standpoint was a failing: 'If I reproach myself over anything connected with my years in Germany it is that because I concentrated so much on my task in theology and in the church, and because as a Swiss I was somewhat reluctant to involve myself in German affairs, I omitted to give adequate warning about the trends which I could see in the church and the world around me, ominous though they were. I should have warned people explicitly as well as implicitly, publicly as well as privately.'[58] On the other hand, Barth also believed that in 1933 it had been important enough and hard enough for Christians first to fight 'in the well-defined and narrow sector of the question whether the church would continue to remain the church in the future'. 'If they are open to criticism, the charge cannot be that they began there, but only that they did not go on from there.'[59] Barth at any rate moved on further, in the direction of political as well as theological opposition to the National Socialist state. Barth's quarrel with this state may be said to have had two phases: in the first of them he was concerned to carry on the struggle *radically*; in the second, he was concerned to carry it on *consistently*.

Barth saw one of his tasks as being to interest Swiss church people in the German church struggle. He published a variety of articles with this in view, in particular the reports on the German church which he wrote every year from 1935 to 1939 in the *Zwingli Calendar*. He also gave a large number of lectures in which he informed his fellow churchmen about the concerns and the situation of the Confessing Church. In March 1936 he spoke in Schaffhausen (as the guest of the Swiss League of Nations Association) and in Basle; in September in Rifferswil and Chur; in November in Aarau, Zürich and Brugg; in December and in the following March in Basle again; and in the meantime in Neuchâtel, Lausanne and so on. In addition he was also asked for advice on press reporting of the church struggle from time to time by the director of the *Basler Nachrichten*, his cousin Karl Sartorius (the son of his godfather), and by their correspondent Herr Böschenstein. His 'good connection . . . with the Evangelical Press Service in Zürich (Dr Arthur Frey)' gave him even more influence: in this way he could bring 'all the most important developments to the public in the fastest way possible'.[60] In all the statements mentioned above Barth began from the thesis that, 'The trials and the suffering of the church in Germany affect every Swiss who is a conscientious member of his Evangelical Reformed Church just as much as if he were a German citizen.'[61] Thus he understood the German church struggle very much 'as a matter for Swiss Protestantism': 'Has it already woken from the sleep from which the German Confessing Church is beginning to awake, or is it going to continue to sleep on – for it, too, has undoubtedly been sunk in sleep for centuries?'[62]

Of course Barth found little assent to this thesis in Switzerland, and sometimes even direct opposition; moreover, this did not just come from 'the few not very important Swiss Nazis'.[63] 'To all appearances, at any rate, the church people of Switzerland are still in a remarkably carefree and undemanding realm in which everyone, from the Reformers, through the Oxford Group and the Religious Socialists, to our brave "positives" (who do not know how liberal they are), seems for the moment to have only one interest: not to let me impose on them, or (to get to the actual substance) not to let the German church struggle spill over into our own local churches which, God be praised, are so peaceful.'[64] 'The churches in Switzerland display astonishing solidarity. From my point of view they ought to have a better cause to be solid about.'[65] Barth's criticism of this whole attitude very soon involved him in all kinds of local controversies – as in autumn 1937 with the Zürich pastor Rudolf Grob and in March 1938 with Pastor Wolfer of the cathedral in Basle. He singled out the attitude of the Basle faculty to the German church struggle as being on the whole a 'chapter which I blush to remember'.[66] He thought it significant that instead of becoming involved in the problems over which there was such a hard struggle in the German church, the churches of Switzerland at this point began 'to hold the Oxford Group in particularly high regard'.[67] Emil Brunner was one of those who was caught up in it. A conversation on the matter with him, Gottlob Spörri and others, at Schloss Auenstein in January 1936, ended in a 'miserable' farewell.[68] At the time Barth put down his hesitations over the Oxford Group in an article ('Church or Group?'): 'One decisive point against it is that while it sets out to be a renewal of Christianity, it fails to respect its mystery, the freedom of grace and the sanctity of the name of God. Instead, all along the line, with all kinds of excuses and changes of terminology, it is turned into humanity and morality.' So 'if the church does not resist this movement, in the end it will be completely ruined by it.'[69]

Theological work 1936–1938

At the beginning of the summer semester of 1936, Barth caught up on his inaugural lecture, which was now due: it was on Samuel Werenfels, whom he understood 'as an excellent example of the kind of theologian Basle produces',[70] and therefore described him with critical affection. During this summer he studied the doctrine of the church in his seminar. The seminar came to a festive climax on 10 May when Barth celebrated his fiftieth birthday. Ruedi Pestalozzi gave him a subscription ticket for six Mozart concerts and he went to all of them in a week. Ernst Wolf, Hermann Diem, Karl Steinbauer and Albert Lempp presented him with a Festschrift published by Christian Kaiser Verlag, 'a collection of theological works in which once again my German friends have taken the most prominent part – with the kind of serious thought and research which has always been the pride of Germany, despite the time and energy taken up by their present troubles'.[71] Bultmann was also included among these 'friends', but Dietrich Bonhoeffer was missing because of an oversight. The book was also impressive evidence that Barth's influence now spread beyond German-speaking areas ·to Holland, England, Denmark, France and Japan – and 'that there have been more or less lively controversies in connection with my name even beyond the seas'.[72] The collection began with an article by Georg Eichholz on 'The Problem of the Theological Student', the first sentence of which ran: 'Scripture lies open before the theological student, scripture which remains open and is not shut.' With a special view to the situation in the German church, the book was to be called *Freiheit der Gebundenen* (The Freedom of the Fettered). The censors objected, and it could only be published 'by leaving out Asmussen's article and changing the offending title'; it was thus simply called

Theologische Aufsätze Karl Barth zum 50. Geburtstag 1936 (Theological Articles for Karl Barth's Fiftieth Birthday 1936).[73] The book also contained a bibliography of Barth's work which amounted to 202 items and showed that 'some of my books and other writings have now been translated into all kinds of foreign languages'. Barth also received all kinds of honours at the time, one of which was very curious: 'Enthusiastic friends have managed to give my name to a snow-capped mountain in New Zealand. One cannot ask for more. Yet amidst all this I have remembered that according to the gospel no one can add so much as a cubit to his stature.'[74]

At the same time the anniversary inevitably reminded Barth that he was gradually growing older: for some time he had 'seen the ranks of his own contemporaries growing thinner . . . and could already hear behind him the steps of younger ones. Now one knows that everything is at stake. Old age is coming nearer and with it what comes at the end of old age – if it does not come suddenly before then. For anyone who still has time and a goal to reach, this can only mean that everything and everyone become more sharply etched: the problems and needs of one's own position and career, as well as those of the world around, are felt more keenly. One is moved to a prudent haste, to a certain mild but dogged intensity in both work and talk. Now is the time when everything seems to be extremely serious, as indeed it is. One has to decide whether the gift of this short life also involves a responsibility and whether one has properly understood this responsibility, for all one's stupidity and perverseness. There is also the question whether despite one's own unfaithfulness, one has accepted this responsibility gratefully as a sign of the free grace of God.'[75]

Shortly beforehand, Barth had acquired his first grandchild, Sonja Zellweger. 'From time to time she was pushed very carefully through the city by her grandfather – to the astonishment of the neighbourhood. And people in Basle are easily astonished!'[76]

In the middle of June he went (with Hermann Hesse) to the jubilee celebrations of the Reformation in Geneva. With this commemoration in mind he had already lectured on Calvin at the beginning of the year in Zürich, Winterthur and Biel. It provoked some disapproval because 'I told my audience that I was sure they had come because of Calvin and not because of me': the lecture consisted almost entirely of quotations from Calvin.[77] At the Geneva festival Barth only preached a sermon; for the rest of the time he was in the audience of 'a congress which was concerned exclusively with the problem of predestination'. A lecture by Pierre Maury stood out from the discussions there, which were 'almost hopelessly bogged down in the old dilemmas': it was a 'reconsideration of the christo-logical significance and basis of the doctrine of election by grace in our time'.[78] 'The majority of those who took part in this Calvinistic congress were hardly capable of taking to heart what Pierre Maury was saying to them at that time. However, I remembered someone who read the text of the lecture with the keenest attention – that was me.'[79]

Barth read it with even greater interest because at the end of September and the beginning of October he was 'to make a trip to the Reformed Church in Hungary and Transylvania, to visit the theological colleges in Debrecen, Sarospatak, Klausenburg, Buda-pest and Papa, and to preach in Grosswardein'. At the same time he had to give lectures in Debrecen and Klausenburg on this very subject – each followed by a discussion.

In the lectures he criticized the classic doctrines of predestination and developed the thesis that: 'The word of God's election has nothing to add to the word of God's grace. But in a very remarkable and evidently indispens-able way it underlines it' – namely, by declaring that 'it means grace, grace to receive'. So 'election by grace, predestination, means grace in grace. Now grace in grace is the freedom and lordship of God in grace.' 'God's gracious election is the truth of revelation. To put it more specifically, it is the truth of scripture. Quite specifically, it is truth in Christ Jesus' and knowledge of it is 'a particular form of the knowledge of Jesus Christ'. From this standpoint Barth argued for a double predestination, but he under-stood *rejection* to have been accomplished on the cross – he therefore opposed any view which held that specific groups of people were elected or rejected.[80]

In addition, Barth gave a shorter lecture (in Sarospatak, Budapest and Papa) on the relationship between church and state ('People's Church, Free Church, Confessing Church'), a subject which had become particularly topical at that time. A striking feature of it was his derivation of the authority of the state 'from the reconciliation which has taken place in Jesus Christ'. In the light of this, he argued, the state has a significant function, no matter whether it uses it 'willingly, indifferently or unwillingly'. The church could have three forms corresponding to these three attitudes on the part of the state; each of them had its advantages and its dangers.

On the journey he noted the beauties of the broad Hungarian plains, the cities and, with special fascination, the gipsy chapels. But this time he was addressed, greeted and questioned by so many lecturers, students, pastors and even the Reformed bishops there that he once muttered to Lollo: 'My tongue aches just from talking.'[81] For these three weeks Professor Béla Vasady from Debrecen went with him everywhere as an interpreter. 'It was all very remarkable, very strange and yet very stimulating; not least the many banquets, which were extraordinarily rich for a Western palate. But all in all it was important to get to know the special characteristics of this country and its church.'[82] On the way back Barth could not resist visiting Mozart's Salzburg. However, he had to break his promise also to go to Fecetic in Yugoslavia and lecture on 'People's Church, etc.'; his 'chauffeur' Pestalozzi had to rush back to Zürich because of a currency crisis. On 30 January 1937 Barth was made an 'Honorary Professor' of theology by Klausenburg.

At the beginning of the winter semester of 1936–37, on 3 November, he had to give an academic lecture in the hall of Basle University on 'The Basic Forms of Theological Thought'. In his view, theological thought had to be biblical, critical and practical. It followed that 'theological thought, like medical thought, military thought or artistic thought, must be related to its subject matter: in this case Jesus Christ the Word of God as he is attested in the Bible'.[83] Over the same period he also repeated his lecture on 'People's Church' in Zürich and Neuchâtel. This winter he held a joint seminar with Adolf Köberle, on the Reformed and Lutheran interpretations of the Apostles' Creed. He also gave reasons for his critical attitude towards pietism at a conference of the Basle College of Preachers, where his father had once worked. And at the beginning of January he held a seminar in Lausanne on Calvin's Catechism.

At the beginning of March 1937 he set off on a new journey, to Scotland, where he was to give the Gifford Lectures at the University of Aberdeen. G. D. Henderson gave a 'running translation into English'. According to the will of their founder the lectures were meant to further the knowledge and dissemination of 'natural theology'. 'So in the summer of 1935, when the honour of the invitation to deliver these lectures was accorded me, I reminded the senate of the University of Aberdeen emphatically that "I am an avowed opponent of all natural theology".' In spite of this, the invitation was maintained, so Barth felt that he could only do justice to the task in the conviction that 'natural theology can only benefit by measuring itself against what from its point of view is the greatest of errors'.

Barth took as the basis for his remarks the text of the Scottish Confession of 1560. 'As I discovered on my arrival there, with some anxiety and some amusement, before 1937 it had been almost as unknown and inaccessible as the Helvetic Confession had previously been in Switzerland!' However, the lectures did not give any 'historical analysis' of the text. 'What did I do? I discovered for myself point by point the former sense of the confession, and then again point by point sought to discover how I could and must respond to the statements of the confession as one who was living and thinking today. Anyone who is interested in this can imagine what I understand and do not understand to be fidelity to the church's confession: it stands in contrast to an orthodoxy which has always been strange (not to say abhorrent) to me.'[84]

Barth's detailed remarks on the basis of this confession (which he liked very much because of its 'fresh Christocentrism') were in fact anything but natural theology. Again, it was astonishing how openly he could speak in the light of the revelation in Christ of a conjunction of 'the glory of God *and* the glory of man'. 'God alone is God. But God is not alone.' Since 'a real conjunction of God and man' takes place in Christ, man is 'affirmed and taken seriously in his existence; he is addressed as one standing over against God, God's partner, so that his independence is respected . . . God's love consists in the fact that although he does not need man, he does not wish to be without him.'[85]

The ten lectures which were given under the title *The Knowledge of God* were supplemented a year later (in the same place) by ten further lectures which followed on directly from the first series and were now given the title *The Service of God*. Here Barth spoke not only of the 'church service' but even of the 'political service of Christians', because Jesus Christ is also the Lord of the world.

In March 1937 Barth also visited Edinburgh, St Andrews and London. In London he met 'about thirty senior churchmen' and spoke to a group of German pastors and curates (on Romans 1.19f.). He also went to the theatre ('a dramatization of Edgar Wallace, with numerous dirty deeds') and a number of museums; in fact he liked the National Gallery best. On the whole, wherever he went he was delighted by the British people and their special qualities: 'They have an admirably sound view of the world situation at home and abroad, an assurance in always finding the middle way which is quite unhysterical . . . a most wholesome way of life, with well-banked-up fires which are splendid to sit around smoking and talking, porridge (ugh!) at the beginning of the day and whisky at the end . . . And . . . the kind of atmosphere in which you cannot be cross with anyone, just as you cannot make anyone really cross unless you virtually commit atrocities.' Barth could say this, although he heard the nicest people talking with 'incredible openness about . . . natural theology, pietism, "historical criticism" in the style of the 1890s, the "comprehensive church" (a favourite boast of the Anglicans), moral optimism and activism and so on'.[86] Because of this, when he was asked, 'What can we do for the Confessing Church in Germany?' he replied, 'What it needs is not expressions of sympathy or protest, but a solemn assent to Barmen I.'[87] On the way back he met Maury in Paris. The two of them celebrated French cooking as a 'devastating refutation of materialism': 'Veal, crab, mushrooms and so on appear there permeated with a spirit of which one has no inkling in any other country.'[88] Walking in the park between Versailles and the Trianon, both considered very seriously and at some length a plan for a new international theological journal to be called *Doctrina*. However, Barth then dropped the plan for fear of involving himself in new compromises.

In September, having expounded the Heidelberg Catechism to Swiss pastors in Davos, he interpreted the *Gallican Confession* to French pastors in the Ardèche. About two weeks later he found himself in Scotland again, to receive an honorary doctorate of laws at St Andrews. 'The celebrations in St Andrews were very interesting to me as new evidence for the unimpaired survival of the *corpus Christianum* in that fortunate land . . . In the evening I was able to shake the Duke of Kent by the hand. He didn't seem to be very clear about the significance of dialectical theology, since he only asked me whether this was the first time that I had been in St Andrews. I replied, "No, it's the *third* time."[89] On the other hand, unlike Thurneysen and Maury, Barth deliberately did not take part in the ecumenical conferences held that year in Oxford and in Edinburgh, though he had been involved in the preparation for them with a contribution on 'revelation' (which he had also given as a lecture in Geneva in April 1936). While he thought that on his travels during these years 'I have to some extent achieved my own "ecumenical movement"',[90] he was somewhat sceptical about the official ecumenical movement. 'Is it not the case that along with all the friendly and indeed useful contacts that one can make there, compromises and yet more compromises are the best that one can achieve in this international scene?' He found that the conferences confirmed his impressions and thought that, 'I am evidently not up to the particular logic and ethics and aesthetics of this business, and would prefer not to hear any more about it for a long time.'[91]

Despite all the many different tasks with which he had to cope, Barth was also, and principally, preoccupied with further work on his *Church Dogmatics*. In the summer of 1937 a new half-volume of the *Dogmatics*, the second half of the prolegomena (I, 2), was completed. The volume was 'terribly thick' (1011 pages, ET 905) – 'a real mockery of its title "half-volume"!'[92] 'In content it was only indirectly connected with the situation',[93] but it was connected, as was indicated by the quotation from Luther which was put at the beginning 'instead of a foreword': 'May Christ . . . sustain his little flock by his holy word . . . that it may be firm and steadfast against all the crafts and assaults of Satan and this wicked world, and may he hear its hearty groaning and anxious longing . . . May there be an end of this murderous pricking and biting of the heel, of horrible poisonous serpents.'

Following the doctrine of the Trinity put forward in the first volume, which essentially dealt with the 'subject' of revelation, the '*Lord*' who reveals *himself*, in this new volume Barth continued primarily to speak of the realization of revelation: first its objective realization, and then its subjective realization. 'The objective reality of revelation' is *Jesus Christ*, the 'incarnate Word', in whose reality God's freedom for man becomes an event. The reality of this freedom (and therefore not any capacity of man for becoming a bearer of revelation) also provides the basis for the *possibility* that God *can* become man. In contrast to Catholic Mariology (*and* natural theology!) Barth understood Mary as an example of the way in which man is involved in revelation, but does not 'co-operate' in it in any way: he is purely a recipient. Only in this sense did he also affirm the virgin birth (unlike his father at one time): it is not an explanation, but an indication of the mystery of revelation. This brief and compressed christology was then followed by a miniature pneumatology. For 'the subjective reality of revelation' is the *Holy Spirit*, in whose reality 'the freedom of man for God' takes place. Once again the possibility of such freedom was derived solely from the fact that it is really there – in the Holy Spirit, in the sphere of the church. Or is 'religion' an indication of a different possibility of such freedom, given 'by nature'? Barth answered this question in a section on 'God's Revelation as the Abolition of Religion': 'religion' is the enterprise of grasping after God (and is even attempted in Christianity, indeed, especially here) instead of receiving gifts from him, speaking instead of listening. 'Religion is *the*

concern of the godless man.'[94] It is not abolished by the constantly recur-
ring immanent criticism of religion (through mysticism or atheism), but
only through true religion: through Jesus Christ, who justifies the sinner. In
a further section ('The Life of the Children of God') there followed a broad
interpretation of the twofold love commandment – under the titles 'The
Love of God' and 'The Praise of God'.

The *attestation* of revelation is an inseparable part of it. Thus the two
following chapters dealt with the doctrine of scripture and of the church's
proclamation, each time determined by their christological and
pneumatological aspects. The first chapter discussed the problems of
'authority and freedom' – in the critical awareness that at the present time
'authority has all at once become a favourite secular word and "liberalism"
has all at once become a secular "taunt"'. Barth argued along the following
line: the church does not claim absolute authority for *itself* – nor does the
individual Christian claim absolute freedom for *himself*, but only for holy
scripture (here there was a critical discussion of the Catholic concept of
tradition and of the modernistic, tyrannical 'God in our own breast'). But
'under the Word' there is authority in the church (see creeds, 'church
fathers', confession) and there is also freedom (see the interpretation and
the application of scripture!). In the last chapter, on proclamation, there
was a fundamental discussion of the problem of 'dogmatics': dogmatics is at
the same time both critical *and* a servant of the church's proclamation. The
reason for this twofold aspect is that, while listening, it summons the
'teaching church' to hear the Word of God anew – and while teaching, it
summons the 'hearing church' to teach the Word of God anew. According
to Barth, dogmatics always involves ethics; indeed the relationship between
the two is that 'dogmatics must be ethics, and ethics can only be dogmatics'.
Finally, it cannot be any closed system, since the 'dogma' towards which it is
directed is an 'eschatological concept'.[95]

But had not the *Church Dogmatics* now itself become a closed,
'orthodox' system? In fact the charge 'has been made almost right
along the line, in every possible tone from friendly regret to blazing
outbursts of anger . . . that historically, formally and materially I am
now going the way of scholasticism. What am I to say? Shall I excuse
myself by pointing out that the connection between the Reformation
and the early church; trinitarian and christological dogma; the very
concepts of dogma and the biblical canon – all these are not in the
last resort malicious inventions of *mine*? . . . Or shall I merely be
astonished at a Philistinism which thinks that it should bewail
"speculation" where it fails to recognize its own ethicism, and fails to
see that not only the most important but also the finest and most
interesting problems in dogmatics begin at the point where the fable
of "unprofitable Scholasticism" or the slogan about the "Greek

thought of the Fathers" persuade us that we ought to stop? . . .
Should I bemoan the constantly increasing barbarism, tedium and
insignificance of modern Protestantism, which has gone and lost –
probably along with the Trinity and the virgin birth – an entire
third dimension (shall we say the dimension of . . . mystery); only to
be punished with every possible worthless substitute? Whatever the
right course may be, I can only ignore this objection . . . It is
precisely in relation to this disputed aspect that I am of particularly
good courage and sure of my cause.'[96]

In the summer semester of 1937 Barth had already begun on work
for the next volume of the *Dogmatics* (in addition to a seminar on the
eucharist, a discussion group on Wolleb's *Compendium theologiae christianae* and a lecture for non-theologians on the Heidelberg
Catechism). At that time 'I breathed again . . . in work on the *Church
Dogmatics* . . . Up to that point I had been fighting. I had had so to
speak to free myself from all kinds of conceptions and ideas,
theologies and heresies. Now, with polemic behind me, I could
simply go over to the doctrine of God and describe in positive terms
what and who God is.'[97] 'To say "yes" came to seem more important
than to say "no", though that is important too. Theologically, the
message of God's grace came to seem more urgent than the message
of God's law, wrath, accusation and judgment.'[98] The new volume
and its successor were together to develop *The Doctrine of God* (II, 1
and 2). In it, the reader was 'to learn what we mean by saying
"God"'.

Here Barth first of all dealt with the problem of the knowledge of God. His
principal statement ran: 'God is known only through God.'[99] From this he
concluded that there is no *possibility* of knowing God except on the presupposition that he is already *really* known (in the church) – and further, that to
know God is always pure *grace* – and furthermore, that this grace is matched
by only one particular form of the knowledge of God, namely *analogy*. Barth
continued to reject the Catholic *analogia entis*, according to which 'there is a
Being superior to God and creation in respect of which a comparison would
be possible between Creator and creature. Over against that I would say:
that is not the case . . . because between Creator and creature there is a
history and not a relationship as of two static substances . . . For that
reason I have gone on to speak of the *analogia fidei*.'[100] Barth stressed that
God is *known* in such apprehension through grace and in faith. He countered Feuerbach's argument by saying that God really is the *object* of the
knowledge of God, and natural theology by saying that this object is known
only in *revelation*. Furthermore, he spoke of a (Trinitarian) 'primary objec-

tivity of God', as a result of which God, unlike other 'objects', is the kind of object that we never possess in knowledge; rather, he always remains hidden, even in his revelation. Barth made a distinction between this and a 'secondary objectivity of God', manifest in his works and signs in the sphere of creation, by virtue of which man can know God, but only indirectly. He declared that 'natural theology', which in contradiction to revelation teaches an 'openness of man for grace', was the result of a 'bourgeois perversion of the gospel'. Besides, independence from revelation took not only the form of pride, but also that of humbleness and resignation, a refusal to accept gratefully where God has revealed himself in his grace.[101]

Barth also drew the material for his renewed differentiation over against 'natural theology' from his seminar on this subject which he held in the winter semester of 1937–38 (during this semester he also repeated his old lectures on Colossians and in his discussion group he continued to study Wolleb).

When *Church Dogmatics* I, 2 appeared at the beginning of 1938, the publisher was no longer Christian Kaiser Verlag. Barth had been forbidden to work with this firm by the Nazis in 1937. 'Stately' Munich was now replaced by the much more modest Zollikon, by Lake Zürich,[102] and Christian Kaiser Verlag by the Evangelische Buchhandlung there, which later became Evangelischer Verlag. For the rest of Barth's life this firm continued as the main publisher of his works, and its Editor and Managing Director, Dr Arthur Frey (1897–1955), became his close friend. The firm was essentially Frey's work. 'He brought it into being and achieved its considerable reputation with an astonishing understanding of the necessity for theological work, however difficult the external circumstances. He devoted himself whole-heartedly to it.'[103] To publish Barth's *Dogmatics* needed courage, especially at a time when the German-speaking market for books had been considerably reduced. 'I do not think that there are many publishers who could have brought such understanding and love to the business, and with them the farsightedness and the skill which were necessary for what could have seemed more than once to be a leap in the dark.'[104] 'Anyone who has known him on personal terms, who has been one of his friends, will never have forgotten the independence of his judgment and his decisions, which he has surrendered to no one. They will also have known his constant faithfulness towards his friends, in good days and in bad, whether they agreed with him or not.'[105]

In 1938 Barth acted as Dean of the Faculty of Theology in Basle. During the summer semester he not only continued to lecture on the

Dogmatics but also lectured on 1 Peter. In his discussion group he pressed on with Wolleb, and in a seminar on baptism for the first time 'came to completely negative conclusions over Calvin's arguments for infant baptism, at any rate'.[106] In addition, political questions were discussed at an open evening. In the winter, in his discussion group he studied 'Doctrine in the Church of England', and in the seminar the *Spiritual Exercises* of Ignatius. In the meantime, during the summer vacation, in September, he had given a lecture on 'Gospel and Education' in Muri, near Berne, for the Main Assembly of the Swiss Protestant School Association. In it he declared that the gospel was the message of Jesus Christ, 'the one and only "educated" man', and that it was therefore criticism of human attempts at education, a service and a hope.

Immediately after the lecture Barth again went into the Ardèche to give another course for pastors on the problem of preaching (for the last stage he travelled in a butcher's van 'along with his pigs'). He now came up against a 'terrifying individualism' among the pastors which he regarded as a serious hindrance, especially in the present situation. 'In the end I told them that what I would really like best would be to stay there, become a pastor in Vernoux or some other central point and then keep them all in order with episcopal authority.'[107] Nevertheless, Barth did find the pastors in sympathy with his views, and one of them was even inspired on the spur of the moment to ask Barth to be godfather to his son. At the beginning of October Barth led a course in the Baselbiet for teachers of religion on the Heidelberg Catechism. In November he gave a Reformation lecture in Oberwil and Uster, and in December a lecture in Basle on 'The Significance of Church Progress'.

'Political service'

In the very months during which Barth was concerned with all these various theological works and tasks, he was constantly and vigorously occupied to an increasing degree in following events in nearby Germany, as far as was possible and appropriate. In July 1937 he was able to gain a better and more detailed idea about what was going on behind the scenes in the Hitler régime from a long conversation with the former Senate President of Danzig, Hermann Rauschning, who had once been a leading National Socialist. On 8 October he composed an aide-mémoire for the Confessing Church in view of Himmler's 'Decree concerning substitute colleges': he advised that the prohibition which it contained should be strictly disregarded, as it directly threatened the life of the Confessing Church itself. He spoke about the Confessing Church at the end of 1937 in Lucerne and Olten, in January 1938 in Berne and Basle and then again in Arlesheim in the spring. When the 'Reich' annexed Austria in March 1938 he was again in Britain, to receive a further honorary doctorate of theology in Oxford and to deliver the second part of his Gifford lectures in Aberdeen. One of the lectures there dealt directly with 'the political service of God' which could also include 'active resistance to certain political authorities'.[108] He also gave lectures on the German church struggle in Oxford and Birmingham. In London he had 'a very good conversation with the Bishop of Chichester', George Bell, and he also visited the House of Commons, which was debating foreign policy: 'My impression here (in this "sacred play" between the English Government and the English Opposition) is that in human terms decisions are being taken about the political future of the world which one can regard with some degree of confidence.'[109] At this particular time Barth became so fond of the English people that he could say, 'If I were not Swiss, I would like best to be British.'[110]

At the beginning of July he went with Arthur Frey to Utrecht again, to meet leading members of the Confessing Church. He wanted to encourage them over their heavy task by reflecting with them on the questions of 'Gospel and Law' and 'Church and State'. A little earlier, on 20 and 27 June, he had given a lecture in Brugg and in Liestal which was a fundamental reconsideration of the whole issue. It then appeared (under the title *Rechtfertigung und Recht*, Justification and Justice) as volume 1 of a new series of writings which Barth edited, entitled *Theologische Studien*. This was his substitute for the series *Theologische Existenz heute*, in which he was no longer allowed to write.

The immediate reason for the lecture was to give the Swiss people 'clear information', so that they would not weaken before Germany over the annexing of Austria.[111] However, this information took the form of a return to basic principles.

In the lecture, he considered thematically the train of thought 'by which not only divine justification but also human justice becomes the object of Christian faith and Christian responsibility and thus also of the Christian confession'.[112] He thought that the Reformers had failed to see this clearly. In particular, he sought 'by exegesis to find a way to a better view of the problem of "church and state"'. His solution to this problem in fact differed from that of the Lutheran 'doctrine of the two kingdoms'; he had long fought against the latter as an 'error' and as the root of an ominous political quietism on the part of the church. By contrast, he now argued that: 'When the New Testament speaks of the state . . . we find ourselves in principle in the christological sphere. We are on a different level from when it speaks of the church, but the parallel . . . to the statements about the church in one and the same sphere, that of christology, is a real one.' Barth's approach to a positive evaluation of the state began from here. On this basis he asserted that democracy (i.e. the nature of a community which is built up 'on the responsible involvement of all citizens') was the form of the state which corresponded most closely to the gospel. He was even prepared to accept the legitimacy of Swiss national defence. Without wanting to speak of a confusion of state and church, he also derived the political task of the church from the same basis: it was not to be one of passive and subordinate obedience, but an active and responsible participation in the state. Of course, the church's decisive service to the state was, in Barth's view, its preaching: 'By proclaiming the divine justification, it performs the best service to the establishment and maintenance of human justice.'[113]

This lecture also formulated 'the theological presupposition' on which Barth himself at any rate sought to base his political statements and actions over subsequent years.[114] '1938–39 was a special time of sifting for the Confessing Church.'[115] Barth's integration of political and church resistance was largely misunderstood and then even rejected. Niemöller could no longer argue in its favour, since he was now in a concentration camp, and Asmussen underwent 'a kind of conversion' – in the sense 'that unfortunately, now the Confessing Church is even more passive towards state intervention than it ever was before'.[116] Barth became even more alienated from most of the leaders in the Confessing Church when during the following weeks he applied the view which he had put forward in *Rechtfertigung und Recht* in two specific ways. The occasion for the first was the demand made in the summer that German pastors should swear an oath of allegiance to Hitler. As early as May, in an 'opinion', Barth had already advised strictly against giving this oath. However, a 'fatal "Confessing" Synod' nevertheless recommended that the requirement should be fulfilled. Thereupon Barth retorted sharply: 'The good confession in which the Confessing Church in Germany has its human substance can be made only by disputing the error and the temptation which begins from the Confessing Synod itself.'[117] Barth also summarized his position on this question of the oath at a lecture in Zürich on 5 September.

On the same day his mother died in Berne after a long illness. He had visited her shortly beforehand and found her 'particularly alert, and indeed cheerful'. 'She talked to us about all kinds of things, old and new, as though she were already beyond us; she was perceptive and often very amusing . . . So I had a parting from her which will always be a happy memory.'[118] His friend Albert Schädelin gave the funeral oration.

In answering a letter of sympathy from Josef Hromádka, on 19 September, Barth gave a second application of *Rechtfertigung und Recht*. He told Czechoslovakia, threatened by Hitler's attack, 'that now every Czech soldier will stand and fall not only for the freedom of Europe, but also for the Christian church'.[119] 'In my letter to Hromádka – for the sake of the faith – I issued a summons to armed resistance against the armed threats and aggression which are now being made. It was not a call to a World War . . . but certainly to resistance.'[120] A loud chorus of protest began: apart from 'the whole of the German Press, which by command published the same article under a number of different headlines ("Professor of Theology is Warmonger", "Jews – Czechs – Karl Barth", "The True Face of Karl Barth")', 'anxious, troubled and above all dismayed comments rained down on me, even from those who were my friends and in sympathy with my cause'. The leaders of the Confessing Church dissociated themselves in a 'formal letter of censure'.[121] On 30 September, in the Munich agreement, England and France sanctioned Hitler's attack on half of Czechoslovakia. 'I spent a sleepless night after the Munich decision', and 'I wrote in my diary: "Catastrophe for European freedom in Munich". I saw myself unutterably alone in this view. At that time everyone understood "realism" to mean recognition of the facts created by Hitler. In all the churches, even here in Switzerland, thanksgiving services were held for the preservation of peace. Of course, six months later Hitler broke even that shameful treaty.'[122] In October all Barth's writings were banned in Germany. At the end of the month he gave a special explanation of his bold argument in an answer to his Swiss critics: 'If political order and freedom is threatened, then this threat also indirectly affects the church. And if a just state tries to defend order and freedom, then the church, too, is indirectly involved.' Granted, 'as a church it can struggle and suffer only in the spirit', but 'it would not be taking its own proclamation seriously if it remained indifferent here'. He added, 'We shall all have to pay for the fact . . . that governments, nations and churches allowed themselves to be deceived as they did before and after 30 September.'[123]

This stress on the political task of Christians did not alter the fact 'that the majesty of God, the eschatological character of the whole of the Christian message, the preaching of the pure gospel as the sole task of the Christian church were the thoughts which even now were the focal point of my theological teaching'. 'But the abstract, transcendent God who is not concerned with real men ("God is all, man is nothing!"), abstract eschatological waiting, without significance for the present, and the equally abstract church, only occupied with this transcendent God, and separated from state and society by an abyss – all that existed, not in *my* head, but only in the heads of my readers and especially those who have written reviews and even whole books about me.'[124] Barth's present attitude only confirmed this. Accordingly, he defended himself against the efforts of many of his followers 'who want to divide me into a theologian and a politician, and then want to be interested in me and to enjoy me only as a theologian (there are a number of people for whom the reverse is the case, who want to see me only as a politician), regarding the rest as a kind of embarrassment which they would like to put on one side, wishing that it was not there'.[125]

On 5 December Barth summed up his thoughts on the relationship of church and state in the present situation, which had been further clarified during 1938, in a lecture at Wipkingen (Zürich) entitled 'The Church and Today's Political Questions'. In it he remarked (a good three weeks after the 'crystal night', which was also the occasion for the meeting which he addressed*): 'Anyone who is in principle hostile to the Jews must also be seen as in principle an enemy of Jesus Christ. Antisemitism is a sin against the Holy Spirit.'[126] The lecture ended with Barth 'issuing a call to prayer against the Turks and describing this prayer as the most decisive thing the church could do in the political questions of the day'.[127] Barth said this at the first Wipkingen Conference (five of these conferences had been held by 1945). It was arranged by the 'Swiss Evangelical Society for Aid to the Confessing Church in

---

*Under the leadership of Goebbels, on this night an attack was launched on the Jewish community; 177 synagogues were burnt and 20,000 Jews arrested.

Germany' which had been formed in Zürich on 5 January 1938, chiefly on the initiative of the 'tireless pastor Paul Vogt' and with Barth's help.[128]

'The function of the society was originally more that of giving aid: entertaining tired colleagues or pastors' wives at Swiss holiday resorts' – including Walzenhausen, where Barth held a holiday course for members of the Confessing Church in August 1938 and August 1939. In addition there were also 'literary activities'; the circulation of leaflets and writings, some of them by Barth.[129] The society then became 'an enterprise more and more involved in the care of Jews and Jewish Christians who had been expelled or had escaped from Germany'.[130] 'Of the handful of Swiss people involved in this, who also had a serious commitment to Christianity,' Barth thought most of Dr Gertrud Kurz. She was an 'almost legendary figure', and 'with her indefatigable care and tireless appeals became almost a mother to German Jews, socialists, communists and internees'. There was also Paul Vogt, mentioned above, 'who over the years almost wore himself out in sacrificial service'.[131] 'In more than one respect he recalled Johann Kaspar Lavater.'[132] These were in the front line. On the whole they had to swim against the stream, but they symbolized 'the active participation of Swiss Christians in German suffering and in Jewish suffering caused by Germans'.[133] Vogt in particular was closely associated with Barth in this work, though 'the Creator certainly planned us and made us in rather different ways'.[134] Zwingli's hymn 'Lord, now stop the carriage'* made an unforgettable impression on Barth after he had 'often heard him (Vogt) . . . open meetings of the "Society for Aid to the Confessing Church" in Zürich with it'.[135]

Barth presented a simplified version of his Wipkingen lecture ('Church and Politics') during the first weeks of 1939 in a number of places in the Baselbiet (Oltingen, Gelterkinden, Kilchberg and Pratteln, and also in French at Môtier), 'because the north side of the Jura needs an especially good spiritual defence'.[136] People saw things here in black and white: 'We cannot be both Christians *and* National Socialists.' At the beginning of the year he was also able to make 'some last journeys to France, Holland and Denmark'.[137] In the first days of January he gave interpretations of parts of I Peter

---

*A famous Swiss Reformation hymn, 'Herr, nun selbst den Wagen halt', written by Zwingli before the disastrous first battle of Kappel, in 1529. The hymn depicts God taking over the reins of the carriage, which will otherwise go off the road.

and the *Gallican Confession* to pastors in Bièvres. In March he spoke in a series of Dutch cities (Utrecht, Leiden, Kampen, Groningen and Amsterdam) on 'The Sovereignty of the Word of God and the Decision of Faith'. In this lecture he asserted that the sovereignty of the Word did not exclude the decision of faith, but formed the basis for it and required it; however, this decision was only made rightly 'in responsibility before the Word of God . . . and in submission to his sovereignty'. Furthermore, 'as a proclamation of the sovereignty of the Word of God the decision of faith is . . . at the same time the proclamation of true humanity'.[138] Before he arrived, there had been a move to censor his lecture and he had been asked not to speak on political issues. He rejected censorship, giving the reason that, 'If those countries which are still free resort to such methods for fear of Germany, then we shall soon have a Hitlerite Europe, and I would not want to give even the slightest support to that.'[139] He also rejected the second request: 'Wherever there is theological talk, it is always implicitly or explicitly political talk also.'[140] While he was in Holland, Prime Minister Coljin, who was a Christian, took a particular interest in him. 'He had me watched by his police throughout the country and finally had me stopped in Amsterdam. Then he asked me very pleasantly to have a cup of coffee with him, though I didn't really want to.'[141] From Amsterdam Barth flew on to Denmark, where he repeated his interpretation of I Peter to a pastors' conference. As in Holland, he terrified his audience with the critical attitude which he had now adopted to infant baptism.

In the summer semester of 1939 he completed a further volume of his *Dogmatics* (II, 1). He dedicated it to the Universities of Aberdeen and Oxford. The second half of this volume was taken up with a chapter on 'The Reality of God'.

Here, rejecting a mere actualism, he considered the 'being' of God, though immediately afterwards he defined it as 'being in action' – namely 'in the act of his revelation',[142] rejecting any metaphysical speculation about God's being. In more precise terms, that meant that God's being was that he was 'the one who loves in freedom'. These dialectical statements had direct consequences for the doctrine of God's 'properties' or, as Barth preferred to say, God's 'perfections'. He sought to understand them strictly in terms of the revelation in Christ Jesus and at the same time thought that their 'fullness' was identical with God's 'nature'.[143] He understood them in terms of the 'divine love' and the 'divine freedom'. But in order to clarify the connection between these two forms of divine perfection, he saw each pair of complementary concepts as making up 'one' divine perfection: e.g. God's

Professor in Basle

52. *Barth as Dean (center) with his Basle colleagues. On the right of him are W. Baumgartner and W. Eichrodt; on the left, W. Vischer, E. Staehlin and K. L. Schmidt.*

53. *Barth was particularly fond of riding at this time – here he can be seen with Emil Brunner, a year after the angry No!*

54. *Discussing with his students during a session of the seminar at Basle, 1939.*

Involvement in the church struggle from Switzerland

55.   In April 1936 he met K. Immer, M. Albertz, H. Asmussen, H. Obendiek and W. Niesel for conversations at Driebergen (Holland).

56.   Conversation with Bonhoeffer's friend Franz Hildebrandt from Dahlem (and Charlotte von Kirschbaum) at the Bergli (September 1937).

57.   A lively discussion shortly before the outbreak of war in 1939: Charlotte von Kirschbaum, Barth, G. Staewen, E. and Asta Wolf, Ruth Pestalozzi, H. Gollwitzer; P. Maury is in the foreground on the left.

Lecture Tours

58. *Barth's first visit to the East, August 1935: Mysliborice in Moravia with the Pestalozzis, Charlotte von Kirschbaum and Gertrud Staewen.*

59. *On his first visit to Hungary, autumn 1936. Third from the left is Barth's pupil Dr. Török, and second from the right Bela Vasady, the interpreter.*

60. *Planting a commemorative tree in Klausenburg, Transylvania, autumn 1936; to the right of Barth are Bishop Vasahely and Professor Tavaszy.*

The Second World War

61.   Numerous refugees sought asylum in Switzerland.

62.   Barth lecturing in Gwatt on 6 July 1941.

63.   In April 1940 he became a soldier in the armed auxiliary.

64.   Climbing the Schilthorn with his sons Christoph and Markus, summer 1941. His son Matthias had met with a fatal accident a month before.

grace *and* holiness, mercy *and* righteousness, unity *and* omnipresence, and so on. For example, what is said towards the end of the book about God's patience leaves room for other statements and must not vitiate talk about his uniqueness (which amounts to the radical de-divinization of the world) or his omnipotence (though this does not mean that he can do 'everything', since he 'can' repent of some things and can hear prayers) or his eternity (which is not timelessness, since in it he has time for his creatures), or the indissoluble connection between his mercy and his righteousness. All this was said during these weeks and months of such hectic and melancholy political activity and stood out with comforting clarity against this background.

In summer 1939 Barth indicated his attitude to the political situation in a less indirect way by discussing the theological problem of the state in his seminar and texts on the German church struggle in his discussion group. From June on, his academic work had a new setting: at that time the university moved into new buildings on the Petersgraben and the theological seminar was transferred to the old university on the Rheinsprung. To inaugurate the new university Barth gave a festal sermon on I Corinthians 3.11 ('For no other foundation can anyone lay than that which is laid, which is Jesus Christ'). In the meantime he had also given a speech in Zürich and Basle on D. F. Strauss (taken from his earlier lectures on the nineteenth century). This was on the occasion of the centenary of the Strauss affair in Zürich.* He also made a translation of one of Dorothy L. Sayers' theological books: 'I have read her detective stories with quite special interest and amazement'. Barth did, however, find in her theology some of the 'Pelagianism which seems to be almost inevitable in England'.[144] The translation was eventually published in 1959.

Barth anxiously followed the course of further developments in Germany. This was the central topic of conversations which he had in November 1938 with Otto Klepper, in February 1939 again with Hermann Rauschning, in April with Heinrich Grüber, in May with Robert Grosche from Cologne and with Hromádka, and twice in September with Joseph Wirth, the old Chancellor. As early as April he had urged Visser't Hooft, as General Secretary of the Ecumenical Movement (which was in process of consolidation

---

*The controversial David Friedrich Strauss was invited to become professor of theology in Zürich in 1839. The devout Christians there were so scandalized that there was a revolt against the decision on 6 September which ended in bloodshed. Consequently the invitation was revoked.

then), to broadcast to Christians throughout Germany about the growing threat of war. The message he suggested was that 'Christians in every country should understand that the war was not against the people of Germany but against the dangerous usurpers in their midst. We ought to ask all Christians in Germany whether their conscience did not tell them to do everything in their power to prevent the war or a victory of the usurpers', either by refusing to take part in military service, by sabotage, or by other actions.[145] Visser't Hooft did not believe he had any authority to give such a message. But Barth's suggestion caused further agitation when he met Visser't Hooft and other friends (Ernst Wolf, Helmut Gollwitzer, Günther Dehn, Gertrud Staewen, Pierre Maury and Arthur Frey) at the Bergli over the end of July and the beginning of August. No one agreed with his request; his friends rejected it, 'perhaps simply because such a step was too unusual, too novel, too bold'.[146] Anxious conversations, punctuated by cursory reading of the Revelation of St John, 'hardly ceased during these days'.[147] Some of Barth's friends took him to the Zürich Exhibition. He regarded it (unlike the 1914 Exhibition) as a good thing, because 'immediately before the beginning of the great storm it has once again given us a delightful picture of the character of Switzerland and impressed it on our hearts'.[148] A portrait of Barth was even on show there – under the title 'famous Swiss abroad'!

In the shadow of the Second World War

When the Second World War broke out on 1 September, Barth was 'on a course for German theologians at Walzenhausen, where we were reading I Thessalonians and at the same time were very concerned about the practical question of how Christians in Germany should behave in the situation which obviously threatened. Should they remain this side of the frontier? Refuse military service? Shoot into the air? . . . Then early on the Friday morning the news suddenly broke, and after a good farewell, we parted.' Barth thought 'with sadness' of all the sorrow that this war would bring to 'many dear people in Germany' and to 'countless others in every land'.[149] But he also believed that now, at any rate, 'the beginning of the end of Hitlerism . . . has surely dawned. In that respect one could breathe a sigh of relief. And it is a good thing that the connection between National Socialism and Bolshevism, which so many people have so far denied, is now so obvious. In essentials everything has become much clearer. Now we know what the war is about. That is the great difference from 1914.'[150] 'It is a long time since there has been a war in which people on one side, at any rate, have known that it was all in a good cause and that any sacrifice was worth while. But there is also the other side. They must remain in ignorance and undergo sacrifices and sufferings for what is in all respects a lost cause. So we must certainly feel sorriest for the poor Germans.'[151]

The main thing about the following years was that Barth stayed at home in Switzerland. 'I travelled up and down my fatherland, giving lectures and attending conferences of all kinds, and learned to know it better than ever before. But Switzerland's frontiers were mine too.' 'I considered it my most immediate and important duty to play my part in seeing that theology should be carried on, thoroughly and "as if nothing had happened", in at least one place in an insane Europe – in our Swiss island, and especially in our border city of Basle from which one could simultaneously look over into triumphant Germany, which later suffered so much, and conquered France, which later rose again. And as never before, I was glad to be in a position to serve this cause, which was worthwhile, enduring and full of promise, no matter what happened.'[152] True, Barth sometimes complained because in so hectic a time, 'filled to the brim with world history', he 'could not be elsewhere joining in things which really mattered. But there is no escaping the fact that for the most part I must keep myself busy on the home front.'[153]

In the meantime Barth's audience in Basle had grown considerably smaller, partly because there were no foreigners and partly because a number of Swiss students were away on military service. Only one of his German students, Kurt Müller, was left, though he was a 'massive pillar'.[154] But Barth continued work imperturbably with the 'little flock' which remained. He lectured on his *Dogmatics* and studied classic texts with them. During the war years in the seminar he dealt with the *Confessio Helvetica posterior* (three semesters), the sacramental doctrine of the Council of Trent, Calvin's *Institutes*, Book III, Anselm's *Cur Deus Homo?*, Luther's Sermon on Good Works, Zwingli's *De vera et falsa religione*, the view of Catholicism in the Heidelberg Catechism and Calvin's *Institutes*, Book I, 1-9 (two semesters). The discussion group also studied church orders, the Formula of Concord (two semesters), works by Schleiermacher (four semesters), the problem of a Christian confession, Kant's philosophy of religion, Lavater's *Aussichten in die Ewigkeit* (Prospects of Eternity) and Luther's understanding of 'authority'.

Outside lectures now occasionally formed part of Barth's theological work. Thus in October 1939 he expounded Mark 13 to a pastors' conference in the Baselbiet, and in November he spoke in Berne on 'Christian Mystery and Human Life'. The 'Christian', he said, was the mystery: 'We cannot achieve it . . . it can only come to us. We cannot do anything about it, but it will do everything with us . . . It cannot be proved; it proves itself and is known as it does so.'[155] The lecture had already been given earlier in St Gallen, but not by Barth himself. He had been prevented from speaking by sudden abdominal pains, so at the last minute his lecture was read by Hermann Kutter Jr. In March 1940 Barth broadcast on 'The Reorientation of Theology in the Last Thirty Years', with special emphasis on dialectical theology. And in October 1940, in Travers in Neuchâtel, he began an exposition (in French) of the Apostles' Creed according to Calvin's Catechism which was presented at conferences spread over six or more years. It is significant that again and again he based his theological thinking on such texts, but they stimulated him to express his own thoughts. In this case a French-speaking audience which happily went along with him was even more of an encouragement.

This exposition was full of subtle points. 'Man's happiness is to allow God's beatitude to appear in human life, and God's beatitude consists in giving himself to man in the form of human happiness.' Or: 'Really to be man . . . we must believe in Jesus Christ.' Or, 'There is choice irony on God's part. He tells us: Since you have philosophy in you, well, have it and do your best . . . ! But on condition that your philosophy does not prevent you from being disciples.' Or: 'God is generous, free in his giving, the great liberal.' Or, 'Perhaps it is time for Christians to defend the French Revolution.' Or, 'We must beware of the idealistic spiritualism which makes us say, "God is too much of a spirit to have hands." No, he has hands, real hands at that (and not paws like ours . . .).'[156]

His pupil Jean-Louis Leuba later edited this spontaneous 'exposition' as a book, using notes on the lectures. During the war years Barth felt particularly close to theologians in French-speaking Switzerland, and especially in Geneva. His friends there included Jacques Courvoisier and Jacques de Senarclens; he also felt an affinity to the pastors of Neuchâtel, among whom Jean Jacques von Allmen was his contact, and to those in the Bernese Jura.

For all these other activities, his chief work was the continuation of his *Dogmatics*. And he was grateful 'that I can spend all my time studying and lecturing on these great things so peacefully'.[157] Everything that was said in the lecture room in Basle 'had a wartime background. Apart from the indirect effects, at the beginning and the end of the war one could hear its thunder in Baden and in Alsace, and the English and Americans roared unceremoniously over our neutral heads in the middle of it all and every now and then dropped something unpleasant. It is a good thing that the properties of God and predestination and all the rest could be put on paper and printed in the middle of all this.'[158] In autumn 1939, when the ravages of war had just begun, he had come to the doctrine of predestination within the framework of the doctrine of God. Again he dealt with it at some length: 'It all needs so much explanation if it is to be understood properly.' It proved 'necessary for me to clarify the exegetical background to my dogmatics even more fully than in the earlier parts'. It also proved necessary 'for me to depart even further from the territory of theological tradition than in the first part of this doctrine of God. I would have much preferred to keep to Calvin in the doctrine of predestination instead of departing so far from him. But that was not to be. The new direction became increasingly irresistible to me the more I allowed the Bible to speak to me about these things and considered what I thought I could hear.'[159]

The 'new direction' consisted in the fact that now – even more radically than in Hungary in 1936 – Barth took seriously the fact that 'the doctrine of election is definitely and clearly to be understood as *gospel*; it is not something neutral beyond Yes and No; it is not No, but Yes; nor is it Yes and No, but Yes in its substance, its origin and its scope. The doctrine of election is the *sum* of the gospel.' According to Barth it is neither an 'absolute decree' of God (Calvin) nor an inexpressible mystery behind revelation. As he formulated it, it is a 'particular decree' which discloses and fulfils itself in revelation. 'There is no will of God which differs from the will of Jesus Christ.' Accordingly, in Jesus Christ we have to do 'directly with the election of God himself'. But Jesus is not only 'the God who elects'; he is also 'the man who is elected' – he himself, and not some individual or group. However, he is elected to make the rejection of man 'his own concern'. 'In the election of Jesus Christ God has destined election, salvation and life for man, and rejection, damnation and death for himself.' So man's belief in God's predestination is a matter of 'not believing in his rejection'. 'However, in him, Jesus Christ, "the community" is chosen first, and not an individual.' And according to Barth, this community has the indivisible double aspect of Israel and the church: Israel chosen to represent the man who resists his election, the church to represent 'what should and may become in God's hands of the man whom he accepts and whose form he takes'. Barth did not mean this as a doctrine of universalism. He guarded against that by making 'the *open* multiplicity of those who are elect in Jesus Christ into a *closed* group' – whether the elect were a particular group of people or the totality of mankind. In view of this 'open multiplicity' the 'elect community' has no more urgent task than to proclaim the gospel of the grace of God.[160]

Barth moved on directly from the doctrine of predestination to the doctrine of *God's command* as the 'foundation of ethics', 'the sequence of themes is most appropriate'. Here he 'radically reshaped' his 1928 ethics lectures.[161]

The sequence was 'most appropriate', because in Barth's view the law follows the gospel and therefore ethics has the task of declaring 'the law as the form of the gospel'. Ethics 'has its basis in the knowledge of Jesus Christ because he is the God who sanctifies and the man who is sanctified in one'. And it 'belongs with the doctrine of God because the God who makes his claim on man in so doing . . . makes himself responsible for man'. In his ethics Barth therefore attached importance to two things: on the one hand to man's inability to hear the gospel of God's gracious election without being claimed by him, and on the other to the fact that the commandment which makes a claim on man is not an abstract law but the commandment of a gracious God. It is therefore not an 'ideal', but a commandment which has already been fulfilled. Ethics is an 'ethics of grace, or it is not a theological ethics at all'. And so the answer to the old question 'What are we to do?' is, 'We should do whatever corresponds to this grace.'[162]

During the progress of his theological work Barth found a new and extraordinarily stimulating companion in Hans Urs von Balthasar, a Jesuit and pupil of Przywara, who had come to Basle in 1940 as a Catholic student chaplain. Barth was soon also able to welcome him as a member of his seminar on the Council of Trent (in the summer of 1941), with the words 'The enemy is listening in'. He was criticized by von Balthasar in a number of ways, but 'there was no really impressive counter-attack. Perhaps he had been reading my *Dogmatics* too much (he dragged around II, 1 especially, in his briefcase, like a cat carrying a kitten).' And at any rate both of them were 'very much at one over W. A. Mozart and the need for national resistance'.[163]

Resistance!

This resistance kept Barth constantly occupied from the very beginning of the war. He took a resolute part in it, compelled 'by my concern for an orderly theology', and also guided by it.[164] 'Everything hangs together', he said of his various dogmatic and political theses at the time.[165] 'My sense of responsibility during these years of speaking about the matter was Christian – and there is none higher than that.' Barth did not join a party, as he had before, although he continued to support the line of the Social Democrat Party in Switzerland, which was extraordinarily alert in matters of resistance. However, it was not as a party member but simply as a Swiss citizen that he wanted to offer resistance. Again, 'I could only speak even as a Swiss citizen as my Christian faith allowed me to.'[166] Indeed, Barth was even convinced (as he once said to Hans Oprecht, a member of the party) 'that the enormous dynamism of the National Socialist heresy cannot be countered either by unbelief or by half-baked ideas of some kind or other. What is needed is something better and superior – and that certainly means Christian faith.'[167] But as a Christian he believed he had to be politically active.

Two considerations moved him in this direction. First, that *unconditional* resistance must be offered against Hitler – both ideological *and* military. He felt that what was at stake was nothing less than an attempt 'to halt the "revolution of nihilism"', which would deprive our life of all that makes it worth living'.[168] He therefore felt it wrong 'for the Christian churches, having spoken so thoughtlessly in nationalistic and militaristic terms during earlier wars, to want to keep equally thoughtless silence in a neutral and pacifist way in this particular war . . . They really should not object that the people of the democratic states are fighting against God; they should tell them that for God's sake we may be human and must defend ourselves against the onslaught of manifest inhumanity with the power of despair.'[169] 'And if no one else says this, the church must say it. The church must say what the guardians of our Swiss homeland can never say: it is necessary *in principle* for this defence to be made.'[170] Barth, who had long endured charges of 'pacifism', now had to hear accusations of 'militarism', even from some of his friends.

Another thought was also in his mind: that *Switzerland* was worth defending. 'More than ever over these years I have learnt to love and

to praise the cause of the free Confederation.'[171] 'What has been
entrusted to us in Switzerland is a particular way of ordering our
life . . . It is far from being perfect. But one can, may and should live
responsibly under this order. At any rate it aims at a free society in
which freedom serves the community . . . Such a state shines like a
light which, however small and (it must be conceded) however
wretched, must burn not only for itself but also for the future of all
nations.'[172] 'We had too much of our own to lose, and too much to
guard and preserve for a future Europe, to allow even a moment's
doubt that resistance had to be offered.' So 'in these years I became
more of a Swiss than I had ever been or expected to be'.[173]

Resistance along these lines now brought Barth into conflict with
what was then the official policy of his country. He felt this policy to
be a 'mixture of cunning short-sightedness and short-sighted cunning'.[174] Although he, too, recognized specific Swiss neutrality, he
did not feel that it meant that 'we should play no part in the events of
our time, but rather that we should take part in them in our own
particular way'.[175] 'From the beginning I have been able only to say
no to the interpretation of Swiss neutrality which the supreme
authority in the Confederation claims to be orthodox and compulsory. By that I mean the false and forced reinterpretation of our
military neutrality in terms of an "integral" neutrality, which our
Federal Council used in 1939 as a pretext for preventing not only
itself, but all Swiss citizens from demonstrating any Swiss interest in
the European conflict of the war years.' They wanted to 'tell us to
keep a blank face, while the others were fighting and shedding blood
for the "light of freedom" (where would we be now if they hadn't
done this?), and to act as though we saw no difference between Hans
and Heiri, Hitler and Churchill'. 'They left every door and every
gateway open for Goebbels' propaganda to come streaming in, but
wanted to stop us putting forward the real arguments against it . . .
And at that time, according to the very words of Federal President
Wetter, this standpoint was regarded as "the only possible Swiss
attitude" and accordingly protected by the police from any discussion. I regard this . . . standpoint . . . (along with certain scandalous
injustices in the treatment of foreign refugees and internees) as *the*
blot on the reputation of Switzerland at this time.'[176]

Part of Barth's resistance consisted in 'open letters' to other
churches and their leaders, exhorting them to the utmost steadfastness. Thus in December 1939 he composed a 'letter to France' (sent

by pastor Charles Westphal) which even 'caught the attention of Monsieur Daladier' and 'the Swiss censor as well as the French'. It earned him the taunt from Emanuel Hirsch that he was the 'deadly enemy of the German people' and 'from a Soviet commissar' that he was 'the enemy of the German-Russian alliance . . . and of atheism'.[177] His remark that 'Hitlerism' made it clear that 'Martin Luther was wrong about the relationship between law and gospel, between secular and spiritual order and power', and had brought about an 'ideological transformation and consolidation' of the natural paganism of the Germans, caused a considerable scandal.[178] Similar letters, urging clear and resolute resistance, were sent at the end of 1939 to the Bishop of Chichester and at the beginning of 1940 to Dutch Christians. At the same time Barth gave a lecture (in Tavannes, Berne, Herzogenbuchsee, Saanen and Delsburg) which also summoned the Swiss to steadfastness ('The Christian's Defence and Weapon'). In it he said that the Christians were on the way to a final battle which was 'much harder and more momentous' than earthly wars, but which spurred them on to fight 'transitory' human wars boldly and justly with human means. There were worse things than war, for instance the 'fanaticism' at present emanating from Germany. The war was necessary to do away with it. Because the censors objected, the lecture was not published until much later, and one sentence was deleted. While the German embassy in Berne was sending Hirsch's abusive pamphlet free to Swiss pastors, it sought to stop the circulation of Barth's new lecture. The Business Manager of Evangelischer Verlag, Hans Herren, caused some resentment by sending the lecture to the censor while it was being printed, without the knowledge of Barth or of Arthur Frey. So Barth had his next writings published by the Evangelische Buchhandlung in St Gallen.

In April 1940, '*Rechtfertigung und Recht* and Ephesians 6 became very topical for me. I reported for armed military service. I had been declared unfit when I was nineteen, but in my fifty-fourth year I was fit (so I had made some progress), and my bedroom now contained a helmet, a complete uniform, a rifle and bayonet, etc., so that I would be able to go out at any hour of the day or night to decide the issue.'[179] The result of this was that from now until the end of the war Barth had to be a more or less regular soldier for a couple of weeks every now and then – 'probably not a very good or dangerous fighter, but still a soldier, armed and drilled'.[180] In any case, at his urgent request, he was not just posted to office work (which is what his well-meaning superior officer had in mind!). He served for 104 days in all. All through May 'I practised my rifle shooting and many other military arts; I stood watch by the Rhine at darkest midnight and to protect the Basle reservoir slept on straw, if I slept at all. Once it happened that an unknown fellow-soldier, who heard only my sur-name, genially asked me how I avoided being confused with "Profes-sor Barth", and once I was almost put behind bars because while I was on guard at the arsenal I failed to recognize a corps commander and give him a proper salute. But this went down extremely well among my comrades from the less desirable and the less pious parts of Basle.'[181] 'I got on better than I could ever have imagined with the men of my country with whom I lived at close quarters day and night. And I was very, very happy to preach occasionally to these comrades of mine, ninety-five per cent of whom were non-church-goers . . . I learned once again how to write a sermon which is really aimed at a man.'[182] 'The very word "Jerusalem" caused difficulties for the soldiers.'[183] ' "Sentry Company V" – there are few memories that I would be so loath to part with.'[184]

'In the midst of the unrest of those days', while Barth was doing his first military service, his son Markus married Rose Marie Oswald, a banker's daughter who was studying theology; he had just finished his time as an assistant minister with Paul Vogt in Zürich and was about to become pastor of Bubendorf, 'where his great-grandfather Barth had had his first church about a century before'.[185] On the evening of 20 June, shortly before the cease-fire between Germany and France, Karl Barth's brother Peter died suddenly – 'perhaps he was really worn out by the excessive tensions and events of the time . . . before which he was in some respects defenceless'.[186] 'I had visited him four days earlier, without our having any idea of what was so imminent . . . He was preoccupied with events in France right up to the fever of his last hours: "We will not go back over the Loire!" Unfortunately that is just what "we" did do.'[187] The next Sunday Karl preached in the bereft pulpit at Madiswil on Psalm 46, 'the last biblical saying to comfort Peter'.[188] Karl, who thought that his contacts and relationships with his brother 'had been veiled in all kinds of mists, real and artificial', felt 'strongly the void which he left behind'. He respected his brother as an original Calvin scholar who pursued his studies 'soundly and thoroughly', but also with a certain sharp 'aggressiveness': a solitary man through and through, 'because what he saw as a unity of faith and thought, faith and action . . . in fact kept proving to be an idiosyncratic vision. 'So many things never came to anything.'[189]

'When our neighbour's apparently firm house collapsed like a pack of cards', Switzerland had a shock. Instead of its former four frontiers, the country 'now had only the one'.[190] 'We were living in a small room in which it was no longer possible to open the windows', in a 'country which had become a mousetrap'.[191] Consequently there was 'a great migration further into Switzerland by those living on the borders'.[192] In its wake, Frau Barth and her youngest son went to Beatenberg, where he was involved with the land army. There was 'hesitation and vacillation in the policy of a number of newspapers, as throughout the rest of Switzerland'.[193] 'There were "wise" people who thought . . . "We want to be clever, we want to fit into the new Europe".'[194] Or the heads of government, 'who thought that they should preach to us in obscure words that we too should now "put off the old man", confused us instead of ruling us.'[195] Even before General Guisan took a stand against defeatism on 25 July in his famous Rütli speech,* on 30 June (five days after the collapse of France) Barth was speaking at the district church festival in Signau, Berne, on 'The Church's Service to the Homeland', saying that this now also included military service and that any readiness for compromise should be fiercely challenged. Barth also sent his lecture to the General; here, as in his subsequent political remarks, he thought that 'the only line to follow is the one which the general indicated in his speech at the Rütli'.[196] He was kept informed of conditions in France by Maury, whom he met in Geneva in September, and by Georges Casalis, Thurneysen's son-in-law. In October he sent a letter to the defeated country: in the face of Hitler there could be no retreat 'along the inner line of religiosity', nor 'on any account could there be peace, or even a cease-fire'.[197]

At this time Barth was a 'member of a kind of secret organization for defence in case of an invasion' and for combating defeatism in Switzerland.[198] He even helped to found this so-called 'National Resistance Movement', along with Captain Hausamann, August Lindt, Hans Oprecht, Ernst von Schenck and others – on 7 September, in the station buffet in Olten. Membership was only by invitation and by subscribing to an oath. Among others, Wilhelm Vischer and Fritz Lieb joined it in Basle. The house in which 'the

*See p. 193

secret sessions of the Basle division of the National Resistance
Movement took place' was the former home of Barth's great-grandfather Lotz.[199] In this movement he collaborated positively with all
kinds of liberal and conservative figures. He came to prize the word
'liberal', 'so fine a word (outside theology)', at the very time when 'in
Germany it was becoming a jibe and a byword for all and any kind of
arbitrariness'.[200] Of course, he got on best in the movement with the
President of the Swiss Social Democrats, Dr Hans Oprecht. He
agreed with him that on the whole the movement was still 'much too
respectable, bourgeois, governmental': 'the movement could not or
would not offer the least resistance against the most important things
which have happened since 1940 (e.g. German trade treaty, tightening up of press censorship)'.[201] It was therefore hardly to be expected
that this 'club of harmless figures would seem very terrible to a
German occupation authority'.[202] On Barth's prompting, 'politicians' from the group made an appeal (curiously enough, written by
Barth himself) to the 'church', 'to make its own contribution
towards preparing the minds of our people for the crisis which now
threatens'.[203] However, the Reformed Church had already been
shown its involvement in the matter. It was warned in October by
the military censorship* (in a letter to Arthur Frey) that it 'was to be
involved in politics as little as possible'.[204]

Thus Barth already had 'one foot constantly in the political field',
'now telling the Christians that they must be Swiss citizens, and now
telling the Swiss that they must be Christians'.[205] He made this
latter appeal to the Swiss from November on in the context of an
interpretation of Romans addressed to a wider audience.

'This exposition came into being as the manuscript for a series of extra-
mural lectures given in Basle during the winter of 1940–41. One can hardly
detect in it the remarkable suspense which we experienced during those
years. I might just mention one unusual fact: I gave some of these lectures (I
think it was those on Romans 8) in the somewhat weather-beaten uniform
of a man of the "armed auxiliary". This *Shorter Commentary on Romans* is a
smaller and younger brother of the *Romans* of 1918 and 1921 . . . There is
always something new to learn from Romans. In this sense it is always
"waiting" (as I somewhat arrogantly put it in my 1918 preface) – particularly for me! . . . It will be seen at a glance that this is not an extract from the
older commentary . . . On both occasions my purpose has been . . . to let

---

*During the war the Swiss army staff performed the function of censorship; articles were
censored after they were printed and rules were laid down for the reporting of certain events.

Paul speak for himself. No interpreter can avoid the qualification "as I understand him". Nor can I. My hope has been . . . that Paul is strong enough to make himself heard even through the medium of interpretations which are still inadequate and which will continue to be inadequate.' In short, in this new interpretation Barth understood Romans as the presentation of a 'gospel' – a word which appears in all the sub-titles. Right at the beginning we hear that the gospel is power, omnipotence, 'the power which is above every other power, which is their limit, the point from which they are all governed'. However, it is power, omnipotence, the power of an 'omnipotent work of salvation' which is accomplished by one who as the judge is also 'the saviour'.[206]

But Christians were also to be summoned to be Swiss citizens. Barth took the oath which he had sworn in the Resistance Movement so seriously that the same November he wrote a lecture ('Our Church and Switzerland at the Present Time') in which he issued an urgent summons 'to do all that is in our power for the preservation of Switzerland'. He added that the future of Switzerland depended on 'whether we believe as Christians'.[207] He gave the lecture during the winter months in Pratteln, Liestal, Basle, Wattwil, St Gallen, Neuchâtel and at the end of April in Lausanne and Geneva, where it attracted considerable attention. In these last two places he discovered that at that time the recognition of the need for resistance was particularly weak in Romansch* Switzerland. As a result of the unrest which his lecture caused in West Switzerland, it came to the attention of Berlin. 'At that time there was even a diplomatic note' from the German side 'which is said to have been quite sharp, and because of that there was considerable anxiety in the Federal Parliament' in Berne.[208] This anxiety became even greater when in May Brigadier General Däniker brought the news from Berlin that people there were very offended by Barth's 'unrestrained attacks on Germany'. Before the censors prohibited the circulation of Barth's lecture, the resourceful Evangelische Buchhandlung in St Gallen had already published several thousand copies. When Councillor Eduard von Steiger, Barth's former fellow-pupil, reprimanded him in June for his intervention in politics, he could only reply: 'Even in the future I can only do what I feel necessary in the interest of reinforcing Swiss readiness for resistance in the context of my particular position and task.'[209] Von Steiger's view was that Barth,

---

*Romansch is a decayed form of Latin, somewhat more primitive than the North Italian dialects, spoken particularly round the Rhaetian Alps.

though 'garbed in clerical dress', was no more competent to argue with state politics than the authorities were to involve themselves in theological affairs. Barth protested both against the assumption that political decisions could be separated from theology and against the suspicion that his theology was only a disguise for what were really political arguments.

Shortly afterwards, on 6 July 1941, Barth took this intimation seriously by giving a lecture 'In the Name of God the Almighty' to an audience of more than two thousand members of the 'Young Church' in Gwatt, on Lake Thun (on the occasion of the 650th anniversary celebrations of Switzerland), and on 13 July to a considerable Romansch audience in Vaumarcus.

In the lecture, while he did not see Switzerland as a Christian country (rather, it was an 'unholy Switzerland'), he nevertheless understood it as a country with a Christian foundation. As 'a community of free peoples of free individuals allied by law', the Confederation was in fact, though undeservedly, 'like an Alpine twilight, a reflection of the gospel of Jesus Christ proclaimed to us and to all the West'. To preserve *this* Switzerland, its people were confronted with the uncompromising alternative 'either to surrender or to resist'. His choice in the face of the alternative was clear. But so that the resistance could be effective, Barth felt that he had to make some strong criticisms: 1. of the exploitation of the economically weak; 2. of the failure to have socialist representatives in the government; 3. of restrictions on the freedom of the press and freedom of speech; 4. of the curtailment of the right of sanctuary; and 5. of the lively trade between Switzerland and the Axis powers.[210]

The last part of the speech aroused exceptional attention and caused great offence. Barth also sent it to the General and to the Federal President. Printing was arranged so secretly that 16,000 copies of the lecture were already in circulation when it was banned on 18 July.

At almost the same time the censors banned a long 'Open Letter from Switzerland to Great Britain', which Barth had written at Easter at the invitation of the Revd Alec Vidler and Dr J. H. Oldham, in which he applied similar thoughts to England. The reasons for the prohibition of the Gwatt lecture, against which Barth immediately lodged an appeal, ran as follows: 'Just as in his earlier writings, Professor Barth uses his theological framework to support a position hostile to a foreign state, holding up a mirror to the Confederation in a way which is likely to disturb correct relations between Switzerland and this other state.'[211] In the middle of May Barth had already learnt that 'there had been talk at a recent conference of cantonal police directors about banning me from public speaking'.[212] In fact the censors prevented him from giving lectures which he had planned at the Teachers' Seminary in Muristalden (Berne) and the internment camp at Vouvry (Valais). He called the instructions which he had been given ('Speak theologically, but please not politically') 'an attack on the Reformed Confession', identical in content with the 'ominous error of German Lutheranism'.[213] The Theological Association of the canton of Berne and the members of the Fourth Wipkingen Conference backed Barth in his view. The man who 'at that time did everything he could to get the police to suppress my views and to make trouble by giving public speeches which could not be answered (he even refused me the right of personal reply)' was again Eduard von Steiger.[214] The head of the political department, Pilet-Golaz, joined von Steiger in taking personal action against the spread of Barth's political views. And voices were raised even in the National Council against his outspokenness. A Brigadier-General Schumacher suspected him of being an 'agent provocateur'. Malicious rumours about his supposed lack of patriotism were put in circulation. But again there were people among the censors and on the army staff who welcomed and supported his views and attitude and who were secretly able to circumvent actions taken against the publication of his works, with some degree of success.

From the beginning of July 1941, Barth had been living in a different house: he was only a couple of houses away from his former home and now immediately next door to his daughter's family. His new home was at St Albanring 178. The Barths moved house just after a great family tragedy. Karl's son Matthias, who had just begun the first semester of his theological studies, had been in a fall on the Fründenhorn on 22 June ('in the dawn of the very day on which the Germans marched into Russia') and had died the next day in Frütigen as a result of the climbing accident.[215] Matthias' death 'affected me more deeply than any yet', especially since Karl's son, 'although twenty, was still not fully fledged; he was still making very dreamy progress towards real life'. 'But we all felt that his life, during which he had always gone his own particular way, was so complete that we did not really dare to lament.'[216] He was buried in Bubendorf, and 'I myself gave the funeral address, on the first half of I Corinthians 13.12'.[217]

Barth was all the more grateful for some days of holiday at the end of July with his sons Markus and Christoph, in Mürren. In an article he gave a brief description of the way in which the 'relationship between the theological generations' had to be shaped, saying that the older generation should not be patriarchal and that the young should be ready to learn. In his own home, at any rate, he felt that 'the problem of the generation gap has played little part – or only a cheerful one', and he even thought that he could say that 'My grown-up sons are my best comrades – which is not a gift bestowed on every father.'[218] In particular, he found the two sons who were engaged in theology 'useful and stimulating companions'.[219] At the time Christoph was preparing to be assistant minister to Lukas Christ in Pratteln and to do his doctorate with Walter Baumgartner. In addition to his country pastorate, Markus was occupied with all kinds of theological research in such a way that theology, 'far from being a duty, is something of a passion with him'.[220] By contrast, Karl's youngest son, Hans Jakob, was now beginning very much to go his own way: he turned 'first to osteology (always from an aesthetic perspective), next to butterflies' and then, 'with the utmost dedication and effort, to painting'.[221] He left school early, in 1942, 'became a gardener and in addition soon acquired a certain skill as an artist'.[222] Later he became a free-lance landscape gardener.

During the holidays Barth climbed the Schilthorn again. During these years, as ever, he did not neglect the beauties around him. Indeed he thought that as he grew older he was 'much more susceptible to nature and to all kinds of human delights and pleasures which people tend to rush past in headlong eagerness in their earlier days – at any rate, I did'.[223] Because of the war he could no longer engage in his favourite pastime of riding, but he was fond of walking in the mountains. He went to the cinema quite often, above all to the films of the 'immortal Marlene Dietrich . . . (I don't know where she will have a mention in the *Dogmatics* – perhaps in eschatology, because she is such a borderline case?).'[224] He also cherished the custom of eating a slice of cheese in the Basler Kanne after going to the cinema. Every now and then he also went to the theatre or to a concert, or to the 'Cabaret Cornichon, which cannot be praised too highly' (because of its political attitude).[225] He usually had time for reading fiction only in bed at night, 'where I tend to devote a great deal of time to it'. In this way he in fact read a great deal, old and new. He once put down what he expected from a modern novelist in these terms: 'I expect him to show me man as he always is in the man of today, my contemporary – and vice-versa, to show me my contemporary in man as he always is. I expect the novel to give evidence on every page that its author not only knows this man properly and sees right through him, from the depths of his heart to his outward manners and mode of speaking, but also treats him honestly, i.e. loves him as he is and as he is not, without regret or contempt. Furthermore, it should tell me what its author finds special in this man – that and no more. In other words, it should have no plans for educating me, but should leave me to reflect (or not) on the basis of the portrait with which I am presented. Finally, its form should correspond to the portrait of the man whom it presents; its form should be necessary, strict and impressive to the extent that I do not forget the man I have been shown in his temporal and timeless aspects. I should be able to live with him, and indeed perhaps have to live with him, again and again.'[226] Finally, whatever Barth was doing, whether he was relaxing or at work, in jest or in earnest, he persistently smoked his pipe, filled with tobacco 'of the Maryland brand, which has already accompanied me on my twofold journey through the Epistle to the Romans'.[227] He once even said jokingly about over-zealous opponents of Darwin's theory of evolution: 'What a pity that none of these apologists thinks it worth mentioning that man is apparently the only being who laughs and smokes.'[228]

In the summer of 1941 he had a meeting at the Bergli with the founder of the Migros supermarkets, Gottlieb Duttweiler. Duttweiler impressed him very much: 'A kind of genius and artist of commercial life. Always beyond the merely conventional or obvious. Constantly having new ideas . . . Constantly dismayed at the folly not of the masses but of those who seem and are supposed to be leaders and experts. But somehow he also laughs good-naturedly about each and every one.'[229]

In November, at the fourth Wipkingen Conference, Barth almost came to break with the Swiss Society for Aid after Emil Brunner, followed by a majority of the gathering, had challenged an interpretation of the statement 'salvation *comes* from the Jews' put in the present tense. At the urgent request of Paul Vogt he maintained his association but only on condition that in future the Society gave up theological work and limited itself to charitable activity. This was essential, since he could not talk theology with anyone who had this understanding of the Jews. But when Emil Brunner all too eagerly accepted this limitation to charitable action, Barth immediately went on to stress the unity of theology and works of compassion and suggested that the next session of the Wipkingen Conference should discuss Romans 9–11.

A week afterwards, he called on the powerful chief of the foreign division of the Swiss police, Dr Rothmund, in Berne, to lodge an appeal on behalf of a number of immigrants. Immediately after his visit he also put his basic suspicions of the authorities in writing, in a letter to Rothmund: 'Dear Dr Rothmund – I wish that I could appeal over your head to your chief (von Steiger) – the church is not a department of the Confederation which as such must submit to and act in accordance with the plans and instructions of the Federal Council.'[230] When Barth was attempting to obtain some medicine for the revered Old Catholic scholar Ernst Gaugler through the English embassy in Berne at the beginning of January, he used the opportunity to make extensive enquiries about the attitude of England, from whose firmness he hoped for so much.

During this period he was even able to broadcast twice on the BBC. First, in December, he sent a message of 'about five hundred words in a foreign voice' to the Christians in Germany (which was immediately banned in Switzerland); it was a word of brotherly remembrance in all the suffering which the Germans and 'our brothers and sisters from Israel in Germany have to undergo' – looking towards the God who 'became and is our brother, to take all our sin and shame and death itself away from us and as our saviour to be the true Lord and victor over all kingdoms, powers and authorities on this dark earth'.[231] Barth was also able to send a message over the same transmitter in April 1942 to Christians in Norway: 'We think with concern of those who persecute you: they are to be lamented, you are not.' For 'what you must suffer' will bear fruit 'for the kingdom and for the church of Jesus Christ, for your fatherland and for the future of us all'.[232] 'Because of these two messages, on 18 August 1942 I was reprimanded by the Kuratel* of the University of Basle.'[233] Barth was given a closer idea of the German situation on 6 March 1941 by Dr Hans Bernd Gisevius and above all by Dietrich Bonhoeffer, who visited him on 4 March, 31 August and 19 September, when he travelled to Switzerland on a

---

*Kuratel – the supreme administrative authority for the University of Basle, without parallel in other Swiss universities.

secret mission for the counter-espionage department. 'At that time Bonhoeffer spoke to me of the plan to form a military government which would first of all halt the German troops . . . on the fronts that they then held and in the occupied territories, and would deal with the Allies on this basis. I remember very clearly Bonhoeffer's great amazement when I told him that I thought it impossible that the Allies would agree to this. The main topic of my conversation with Bonhoeffer at the time was . . . the question whether the planned new German government would be conservative and authoritarian, or have a democratic form.'[234] Barth was again able to get news direct from Germany when in the summer of 1942 he met the writer Ricarda Huch in Basle; she was on her way home after celebrating the golden jubilee of her doctorate in Zürich.

In March 1942, after the end of the winter semester and while the printing of *Church Dogmatics* II, 2 was almost complete (it had been finished during the winter), Barth was again due for another course of military service. He had to read some of the proofs of the book (898 pages, ET 806) at that time in Brunnen on the Vierwaldstattersee, on guard over a granary, and 'I was correcting them late at night in a federal guardroom. I might mention that one of my comrades asked me in the friendliest manner whether I had brought my carnival paper.* People in Basle will appreciate the significance of that remark.'[235] Barth dedicated the volume to the British and Foreign Bible Society in London, which in March 1940 had named him their 'Honorary Foreign Member'. At that time a number of unbound copies of *The Doctrine of Election* were smuggled into Germany under the title *Calvin Studies*.

God's good creation

In the following summer semester Barth began on a new theme in his *Dogmatics*, following on from the doctrine of God: this was the doctrine of creation (Vol. III). With it 'I have entered an area in which I feel decidedly less confident and assured. Were I not obliged to do so in the course of the general presentation of *Church Dogmatics*, I doubt whether I would have turned to this particular material

---

*A feature of the Basle carnival is a procession through the streets of various groups in fancy dress, each representing a particular topical theme. They carry with them long, narrow sheets (looking rather like galley-proofs), containing parodies and satirical verses.

quite so soon. I know of others to whom, in view of their greater gifts, interests and qualifications, I would gladly have entrusted the task of writing this part – had I more confidence in their presuppositions.' *Barth's* 'presupposition' here was that the knowledge of God's creation and the creatureliness of man 'is achieved only in receiving and responding to God's witness to himself, that is only in faith in Jesus Christ, in the knowledge of the unity of Creator and creature brought about in him'.[236]

'The only theological approach which I feel it possible to adopt has made it almost obligatory for me to begin the doctrine of the work of the Creator as such in the old-fashioned form of a thorough-going exposition of the contents of the first two chapters of the Bible.' It formed 'the kernel' of this doctrine of creation. It was striking that 'I have not tackled the obvious scientific questions raised in this context. I originally thought that this would be necessary, but later it became clear to me that there simply cannot be any scientific questions, objections, or even aids from natural science in respect of what holy scripture and the Christian church understand by God's work of creation. So in the central portion (of *The Doctrine of Creation*) a good deal will be said about "naive" Hebrew "saga", but nothing at all about the apologetics or polemics that might perhaps be expected. In fact I thought that the appropriate task for dogmatics here was exclusively to retell the "saga", and I then found the task more pleasant and rewarding than the dilettante torments to which I would otherwise have had to surrender myself. There is free scope for natural science beyond what theology describes as the work of the Creator. And theology can and must move freely where a science which really is science and not secretly a pagan *gnosis* and religious doctrine, has its appointed limit.'[237]

In accordance with this theological 'presupposition', which Barth wanted to use as a basis for his description of the work of creation, from the beginning he attached importance to the fact that 'The doctrine of creation, no less than the whole remaining content of Christian confession, is an article of *faith*.' It has no more to do with a further 'object' of 'natural' knowledge than the other aspects of Christian doctrine. According to Barth, this meant that while the creation is not the 'embodiment of the whole work of God', it is not a work of God which has been achieved or is to be understood in isolation; it belongs in the whole series of the one work of God. It is the 'accommodation for the history of the covenant of grace'. It 'makes possible the history of God's covenant with man, which has its beginning, its centre and its end in Jesus Christ. The history of this covenant is as much the goal of creation as creation itself is the beginning of this history.' Or, to put it another way: the creation is the 'external basis of the covenant' and the covenant is the 'internal basis of creation'. Barth's explanation of the 'image of God' in man was surprising: it consists (inalienably) in the fact that the Trinitarian 'self-encounter' of God the Father and the Son is 'reflected in God's relationship to man' and in turn in the human encounter of 'I and Thou', of man and woman. Barth termed this relationship of correspondence, with its particular differentiation, the *analogia relationis* – again in opposition to the *analogia entis*, and to make his concept of *analogia fidei* more precise. By understanding creation in terms of the covenant of grace and as having come about for that purpose, Barth was in a position to think of creation as God's 'act of good-pleasure' (and remember, this was at the height of the war). Referring to the old problem of theodicy, he explained it as a twofold act of good-pleasure: that the creation might really *be* within its bounds, and that it might '*be good*, seeing that it was justified by him'.[238]

'What I did in the last part of the volume on creation was a kind of vindication of Leibniz's honour which was probably not expected of me . . . Before I wrote the chapter . . . I had the sound of Mozart (the flute concertos, *The Magic Flute* or the horn and bassoon concertos) in my ears and that livened me up.'[239]

While this doctrine of creation was beginning to take shape, Barth continued to compose 'messages' to other countries, as he had done during the previous winter. He sent one 'by the underground' to Holland in July 1942; Hebelotte Kohlbrügge smuggled it over the border in a microfilm which she carried in her mouth: this was a 'message of deepest sympathy' for the present lot of Christians and others there. In it he encouraged the Dutch church to oppose the National Socialist state with 'prayer for the queen of the Netherlands' and 'in this way to express recognition of the just state, in so doing making a Christian confession of belief'.[240] In September and October he wrote twice to the United States, which meanwhile had become involved in the war. His first communication was a report for the political journal *Foreign Affairs*, in which he set out to describe the various situations in Germany, Holland, Norway, Denmark, France and Switzerland, saying that Europe now 'faced an end and a new beginning'.[241] Secondly, he answered in great detail seven questions which had been put to him personally in Basle and Geneva by the 'American churchman' Samuel Cavert. His main warning here was against any 'crusading ideology': the church must not, he argued, provide 'the necessary religious accompaniment' to the 'terrible sounds of war'. Nor should the war be understood as 'an instrument of divine vengeance' instead of as 'the last terrible instrument for restoring the public order which has been damaged and destroyed by common guilt'. It was only possible to have 'a good conscience' if the war against the Germans was 'in fact also being carried on for them'.[242] In November Barth again sent a letter giving warning and encouragement to the 'brothers and sisters' in Holland. He thought it very inappropriate that he always had 'to write such letters as a private citizen', and felt that 'from the start I am hindered by the fact that what I say will be accepted and treated only as my word'. Barth expected such messages to come from the Geneva office of the Ecumenical Movement. But at that time he 'often had cause to complain that while all kinds of useful observations were collected in Geneva and reports issued; all kinds of preparatory studies were made; all kinds of communications and correspondence were forwarded; all kinds of technical help were given . . . even in the most decisive moments of the history of these years nothing was to be *heard* from Geneva and thus from the Ecumenical Movement.'[243]

During these months Barth also continued to address the Swiss nation: at the end of July he gave a lecture in Basle on 'The Christian Community in Time of Trial', and in September he wrote a leaflet for the '1942 Day of Prayer'. In October he gave a lecture to teachers from the Ladies' College on 'The Christian in the State'. Of course he was also deeply moved by the stream of Jewish refugees which swelled again in the summer of 1942. He believed that 'today the Jewish question is virtually *the* question for statements of Christian belief'. He was all the more shattered that the government in Berne thought up and put into force 'a new law of sanctuary which was of little comfort and help to those who were being persecuted'. 'The Rhine will not wash away our guilt for having turned away ten thousand fugitives and having treated unworthily those whom we did accept.'[244] He saw three reasons *for* Swiss people to 'help fugitives. First, the Christian reason: the fugitives are our concern; not *although* they are Jews but *precisely because* they are Jews and as such are physical brethren of our saviour . . . Secondly, the national reason: the fugitives do us the honour of seeing our country as a last stronghold of justice and mercy . . . And lastly, the human one: we see in the fugitives what we have so far, by a miracle, been spared.'[245]

During this summer of 1942, without his seeking it, a remarkable friendship began which was to flourish for many years. It was with

Albert von Erlach, a doctor and health official, who often went to Germany for negotiations about exchanging prisoners. Barth came to know him as a 'non-partisan man of honour and a devoted friend'.[246] In July, for the first time he spent some days in von Erlach's 'aristocratic surroundings on his estate at Rosengarten by Gerzensee, a place which is frequented by Federal Councillors, foreign ambassadors, military attachés and even our General in person, and where very critical judgments are made on the whole world scene and on the Swiss situation.'[247] 'If there was anywhere that people, house and surroundings seemed to me to form an indissoluble whole, it was at the complex of Erlach-Rosengarten-Gerzensee.'[248] 'Fourteen Pekinese scuttle and bark right through the middle of it . . . in the background is a glorious terrace with old trees and in the background is the whole chain of the Alps, while in the house itself one can see quite marvellous things from the eighteenth century.' Here in August Barth met General Guisan personally, so that 'the chief of our army and its lowest ranks could take necessary counsel for the present and the future'.[249]

Of course, 'as far as politics were concerned, he was still banned from writing and speaking'.[250] In the autumn he discovered that for some time 'my telephone had been under police supervision'.[251] But because in the meantime the political scene had changed considerably, he thought that for the moment he could refrain from political remarks. The Swiss attitude hardened remarkably. And 'Tripoli fell on 22 January 1943, Stalingrad on the 31st. Then on 6 June 1944 the invasion of France began. The tide had turned in this Second World War, and I was happy to keep quiet about it until new questions arose.'[252]

So Barth could again concentrate more on his theological work. One new addition to his regular programme was the institution of a French-speaking 'colloquium', in addition to the pattern of 'lecture, seminar and discussion group'. In all his teaching he was constantly concerned to make his students aware 'that if correct knowledge is to remain correct, it must put out not only new leaves and blossoms, but also new roots'.[253] So at this time, too, his academic work extended further and further: 'Everything has its demands and its failure, its peaks and more level stretches, as happens if one has nothing else on one's plate.'[254] Barth now began to give more theological lectures. In October 1942 he spoke in Geneva on Romans 1 and 2, and at the beginning of the next year he spoke in St Gallen,

Basle and La Sagne on the problem of 'Community in the Church'. He felt that this problem was raised by the existence of various groups within the church and by the danger which might develop from insistence by each on the exclusive and absolute importance of its special concerns. His solution lay in the 'apostolic ministry' which was a critical counterbalance for these groups. On 7 May 1943 he gave a lecture to a meeting of theological students in Gwatt (Thun) which had great critical significance. In view of its repercussions it was comparable to the lecture on 'demythologizing' given by Bultmann two years earlier, which Barth noted with very mixed feelings.

In the lecture at Gwatt ('The Church's Teaching on Baptism') he explained the sacrament of baptism in the following way. It did not *bring about* the salvation of man ('causative'), but *attested* his salvation by the symbolic representation of his renewal in Christ ('cognitive'). As a consequence he argued for the rejection of infant baptism and put forward the demand that 'instead of being a passive object of baptism, the person baptized must again become a free partner of Jesus Christ, that is, freely deciding and freely confessing'. He was clear that the price for changing the practice of baptism in this way was to renounce 'the existence of the evangelical church in the Constantinian *corpus christianum*', i.e., 'the present form of the national church'. 'If the church were to break with infant baptism, it could no longer be a people's church in the sense of a state church or a church of the masses.'[255]

Barth regretted that the discussion in Gwatt ended with an 'episcopal charge by Koechlin. Now our students can go home quite contented. The *arbiter elegantiae ecclesiasticae** has told them that for the moment he is not completely convinced, and as he has said the last word, for the moment the matter is now settled.'[256]

In September Barth went 'to Leysin (near the Dents du Midi), where for five days I discussed all sorts of things with the tubercular students in the university sanatorium': lectures on 'The Christian and the State' (repeated soon afterwards in Safenwil) and 'La connaissance chrétienne', and a seminar on Luke 10. 'In the afternoons I went visiting their rooms.'[257] In October, Barth began a new seminar on Colossians with fifty to sixty pastors, which was again continued in several stages. He also continued the seminar on Romans in Geneva, though he had to abandon this because of the bad attendance. He then held the Neuchâtel seminar again in January 1944 in Lausanne 'with two hundred older and younger

---

*'The arbiter of church opinion.'

biblical scholars from that area'; among them he was particularly delighted with the New Testament scholar P.-H. Menoud.[258] In February he spoke at two places in the canton of Berne, in Biel and Kirchberg, on 'Jesus and the Nation'. There he presented 'Jesus' as the one who keeps company with people who have been deceived by false shepherds. The lecture later found a place, in concentrated form, in *Church Dogmatics* IV, 2. At the same time Barth gave an answer to the question 'Is Intellectualism a Danger?' for a student magazine. His answer was that talk of 'intellectualism' was a danger if it was an excuse for laziness in thought – and a danger if it was cultivated as an escape from action. His Basle seminar was on Zwingli and followed a particularly interesting course this winter. Barth attempted 'to take him out of the hands of the young people who seize him so assuredly and so roughly, and who have much less of a sense of humour in matters of natural theology than I myself have, and to make it clear to them that the man might not have had quite the views that our suspicious minds infer from his rather carefree terminology'.[259]

Barth's work was interrupted when on 15 March a terrible thing happened: 'The Rector of the University of Basle had to cut open the belly of the Dean of the Theological Faculty', in his capacity as a surgeon, to relieve the latter, Karl Barth, of a *hernia spigelii*. The patient was delighted later to be able to see 'at least some of my inner man through some transparencies which had been taken during the course of the operation (not because of my importance but because of the hernia)'.[260] Barth still felt the after-effects of this operation when he began the summer semester of 1944, in which he continued work on the great tenth chapter of his *Dogmatics*, 'The Creature' (anthropology), which he had already begun in December. Occasionally he felt this work to be a heavy burden for other reasons too: 'Why have I loaded myself with this *Dogmatics*, and thus required myself to know so much that could perhaps have been left unstudied, or at least could have been studied in rather less detail? But that is what has happened, and at least I cannot complain that I don't have enough to do every day and every week. What I in fact do is always only the least part of what I should really be doing.'[261] In addition there was a further 'burden': 'There is something exciting about the fact that for so many years now I have always had to make certain moves in theological thinking by myself and on my own responsibility. Only then do others come along and join me, and finally, when I have gone on to something quite different, even . . . the French, English and Japanese decide to approve of me a little. But that's my real problem.'[262] During Barth's convalescence, and as a consequence of the most recent volume of the *Dogmatics* to appear, relations with Leonhard Ragaz, which had been broken off for twenty-five years, were now revived in a new and friendly way. Barth was grateful and surprised to find Ragaz 'largely in agreement with me' in a review. In turn, Ragaz felt Barth's gratitude to be an 'act of discipleship which casts a glow of reconciliation on the remainder of my earthly days'.[263] He died a year later.

As the war drew to an end, Barth felt that his most important contribution was to persevere with writing his *Dogmatics*: 'That is *my* "aid"'.[264] But of course he also wanted to help war victims in other ways. So he himself worked away at looking for people ready to take in refugees, finding medicine for one, shoes for another, and so on. In June 1944 he organized a petition (on the basis of information given by the Zürich rabbi Dr Taube) to the (first!) Social Democrat to be elected Federal Councillor, Ernst Nobs. He pleaded that the government should take prompt and decisive action to help to save the Jews of Hungary. Shortly beforehand he had again withdrawn his agreement to a lecture trip in the USA (organized by Columbia University). One of the reasons he gave was that now, at the end of the war, his task was in Europe. Taking this task seriously, he became a member of a Swiss-Norwegian society and a 'Swiss Society for the Friends of Free German Culture'. He also took part in a 'Swiss-Soviet Union Society' and in Aid for Russian Internees. He became involved in the 'Soviet Union Society', because 'I have long been against the fear of Bolsheviks and communists which has . . . been rampant in Switzerland for years and an equally long-standing advocate of openness in this direction too.'[265] He felt this openness to be even more appropriate since Switzerland had profited from Russian resistance to Hitler.

'I am your friend'

'When a German defeat seemed certain', Barth felt that after his sharp warnings against an aggressive National Socialist Germany, by contrast he should 'challenge the general bitterness against Germany which was gradually gaining the upper hand'. So 'I attempted to circulate the slogan that we must now be both concerned and critical about the Germans.'[266] Barth adopted this approach for the first time on 23 July 1944 (six weeks after the invasion in Normandy and three days after the famous 20 July) in a lecture in Dürrenroth ('The Promise and Responsibility of the Christian Church Today').

He put in a good word both for the Jews and for the Germans in the same breath.[267] 'If any people today stand unambiguously before Jesus Christ, the one who has come to save sinners and not the righteous, then it is the Jewish people – and (in a remarkably similar way) alongside them the Germans.' So 'If the German war state lies in ruins, it cannot be our business to give a second judgment where God has already given his.'[268]

Barth felt the triumphant celebration of the 500th anniversary of the battle of St Jakob an der Birs, on 26 August, to be quite out of place. Since he was Dean of the Faculty of Theology this year he had to take part in it, 'joining in the festival procession in my academic gown', but he felt quite out of place. 'Over recent years we Swiss have been least like the heedless people of St Jakob.'[269] He was glad that a few days later he could escape the festivities and go to St Moritz and Davos, where he had to speak on 'The Nature of Catholic Theology' and on Galatians 4. He had similar misgivings when at this particular time Nikolaus von der Flüe was forced through in Rome as the Swiss 'national saint', with political support from the very Swiss statesmen who in recent years had been most vacillating (not to mention the fact that he objected in principle). He expressed his feelings in an article in November. At the beginning of 1945 he gave special consideration to the relationship between Switzerland and Germany, whose defeat was now a foregone conclusion, in a lecture on 'The Germans and Us', given in Couvet, Neuchâtel, Schönenwerd, Rohrbach,. Olten, Arlesheim, Aarau, Geneva, Le Locle, La Chaux-de-Fonds, Berne, Glarus and St Gallen.

In it he said that the Germans now needed friends, 'friends in spite of everything'. And in a paraphrase of Matthew 11.28 he went on to speak of *the* friend who now said to them: 'Come to me you unlovely creatures, you wicked Hitler youth and Hitler girls, you brutal SS soldiers, you evil Gestapo blackguards, you sorry compromisers and collaborationists, you sheep who now have run so patiently and so dumbly for so long behind your so-called leader! Come to me, you guilty ones and you connivers! Now you can and must see what your actions are really worth! Come to me! I know you well, but I do not ask who you are and what you have done. I can only see that you are finished, and for good or ill you must begin again. I will refresh you. Now I will begin again with you from scratch. These Swiss, puffed up with their democratic, social and Christian ideas which they have always cherished, may not be interested in you, but I am . . . I am for you! I *am* your friend!'[270] Barth thought that because the Swiss had hardly been affected directly by the German disaster, and indeed had often been all too weak against Hitler, they should be 'among the first to make that clear to ourselves'.[271] He said that because he was very afraid that 'our fatherland might be shamed a second time', as weakness towards a strong Germany gave way to harshness towards its defeated neighbours.[272]

There were some statements which Barth was to repeat frequently in the future. People, he said, should not talk 'only of a "friendship despite"'; 'every German must take responsibility for what had happened since 1933';[273] and 'the cure for the character of Germany must not only take account of the crass corruption of the Hitler period, but go back to the roots of the disease at the time of Bismarck and indeed of Frederick the Great'.[274] He said all this in the conviction that *this* end could only be followed by a *completely* new beginning. It was the end of a chapter which had lasted for very much longer than fifteen years. And the new beginning could not be for this long chapter to be reopened yet again. 'For me, the new German history, of which I should dearly love to be a part, begins with the opening of another chapter.'[275] Of course these thoughts provoked some opposition as early as the beginning of 1945: the Swiss felt Barth's attitude to be too friendly, and the German refugees felt it to be too radical. Dealing with opposition from the ranks of these refugees, in March and April he composed two open letters, one to Ernst Friedländer and one to Dr Hermann Heisler.

By contrast, he got on well over all these questions with the members of the 'Free Germany' Committee, with which he had been in close contact since December 1944. Indeed, 'St Albanring 178 was almost like a branch office' of this movement. 'Lollo von Kirschbaum was active presiding over the matter with Langhoff (the author of the novel *Moorsoldaten*) and the former Prussian Secretary of State, Abegg.' She sought to represent the Confessing Church there and got on extraordinarily well with the 'red and reddish people' who were active in this group.[276] Barth tended to keep in the background over this movement, 'in which . . . for the first time I became acquainted with notable communists and – less pleasantly – with communist methods'.[277] Agreeing to a request to make 'Free Germany' known to representatives of the Protestant exiles, on 10 February 1945 Barth invited a group including Karl Würzburger and Otto Salomon 'to a session at my home which I had to chair as a kind of honest broker'.[278] 'Unfortunately the Christian exiles did not cut a very good figure alongside the much greater simplicity of the goodwill of the others. The latter claimed to be atheists, but in fact reacted in a much more Christian way.'[279] 'I found these people utterly convinced of the lost cause of the German people'; without hesitation they 'acknowledged the responsibility of all Germans' and were concerned in a down-to-earth way 'with the practical tasks of union, reconstruction and restoration' in 'collaboration with all trends in Germany'. So Barth 'helped to establish contact between "Free Germany" and representatives of the Protestant exiles' until it was dissolved in December 1945.[280]

The source of Barth's thoughts and actions at this time became clear in an exposition of Matthew 28.16ff. given to 'a group of friends of the Basle Mission', at the beginning of April. 'Objectively, there is no other authority over and above that held by Jesus.'[281] A few days later he gave an answer to the question 'How can the Germans be cured?' which had been asked by the *Manchester Evening News*. Here all his wishes for the Allies' treatment of the Germans were neatly summed up: 'Show them how gentlemen behave when they are in power!' 'Give them practical instruction about the meaning of democracy, freedom, loyalty, humanity.'[282] It happened that on the very eve of Victory in Europe Day, 8 May, Barth was giving a lecture in Spiez (which was then repeated in Basle, Berne, Zürich and in an internment camp). In it he reflected on the 'spiritual basis for rebuilding in the post-war period'. What was needed, he said, was a new, responsible, human, shared, constructive and sober spirit – and this was the Holy Spirit. Although his authorship was kept secret, at the end of the war he himself had composed a message of thanksgiving, repentance and obligation from the Basle Church Council which was read the following Sunday from Basle pulpits.

And then, though only slowly to begin with, 'the door to the rest of the world opened again. For me this meant especially the door to Germany, where in the past I had lived so long, so happily and so much as a part of things, where I had left behind me so many good friends and also so many tough opponents.'[283] It 'tugged at my heart for the first time after so many years to be able to put a German address on a letter again':[284] his faithful Swabian friend Gotthilf Weber was the addressee. With Alphons Koechlin, Paul Vogt, Gertrud Kurz and Jacques Courvoisier he worked on a church

committee for aid to Germany, and with his colleague Ernst Staehelin on a secular committee.

At the same time he was now able to realize a plan which he had
made a long time before, for a published collection of 'all my more
important statements on the problems of the state, war, National
Socialism, Swiss resistance, etc., from 1938 on' – 'because I thought
it very important, especially with a view to future relations with
Germany, that I should make it clear what I said and what I did not
say.'[285] The title of the collection was *Eine Schweizer Stimme* (A Swiss
Voice). Of course the doors also opened in another way. Dr Eugen
Gerstenmaier made an appearance in Switzerland, and Barth commented in a furious article that the time might have come when 'the
old theological-ecclesiastical-political vinegar . . . slick, skilful and
pious, will be poured from the third bottle into the fourth instead of
being thrown away.'[286] In July he wrote in an open letter to the
'German theologians in prisoner-of-war camps' that Germany –
'poor as Job, poor as Lazarus, poor as the publican in the Temple' –
now had an advantage over other nations: 'there is nothing left for
her but to begin all over again'.[287] At the same time he assured
Martin Niemöller, who had now been released, of his heartfelt
sympathy – despite the notorious Naples interview,* which simply
showed Barth 'that he has now reached the end of the "journey from
the U-boat to the pulpit" '.[288] In the same month he had discussions
in Berne with Vogt, Frau Kurz, Visser't Hooft, Adolf Freudenberg
and Hans Bernd Gisevius over the 'ecumenical steps' which now
needed to be taken. Also in July he managed to go twice to Freiburg
im Breisgau, where he made pleasant contacts with the senior
French army chaplain, Marcel Sturm, and the lawyer Erik Wolf. He
even succeeded in bringing French and Germans round a table for a
conversation. His friendship with Erik Wolf, supported by mutual
respect, also dates from then. He regarded Wolf as 'the most
interesting of colleagues, skilled and learned in every direction, full of
melancholy humour and a good friend of Martin Heidegger too'.[289]

Throughout the summer of 1945 Barth held only his seminars,
while at his own request he was given a dispensation from his

---

*On 5 June 1945, Niemöller gave an angry interview in Naples (no doubt largely because
immediately after his release from a concentration camp he had been imprisoned by the
Allies), in which he shattered various 'mythological' views about him which were in circulation: he said e.g. that from the concentration camp he had volunteered for service in the army,
that his objections to Hitler were religious, not political, and so on.

dogmatics lectures. He wanted to use the time he thus gained to prepare his volume on creation for publication at last. However, his involvement in German affairs did not allow him to do this. The publication of the book was obviously delayed as a result, but also because he had some trouble in arranging the mass of material, which kept on growing, in the form which he had originally planned.

Barth had originally planned to present the doctrine of creation – like the doctrine of God – in two volumes: in the first, the doctrine of the Creator and the doctrine of the creature (anthropology), and in the second (to match II, 2) the doctrine of providence and the ethics of creation. In the autumn Barth then had merely the doctrine of the Creator published (i.e. without the anthropology, which was unsatisfactory in its existing form) in a volume which was (only) 488 pages long (ET 428). He managed this by leaving out a whole section on 'The Creator and his Revelation' (with sub-sections on 1. God and the gods; 2. Faith and world-views). In this section Barth had wanted to say that 'the revelation of God . . . is the criticism of all gods': 'It is the twilight of the gods in which they lose their divine authority . . . in which it again becomes clear that originally they were not gods but creatures.' He would also have wanted to say that 'accordingly' it was part of the nature of 'faith in the Creator' that there should be 'opposition to any closed picture of the world which required respect and authority for that very reason'.

In August he had a joyful reunion with Maury at the Bergli – and at the end of August and the beginning of September an equally joyful reunion with numerous German friends in their ruined land. For in an army jeep, 'I was able, under American auspices, to make a first and highly informative trip through Germany. I participated at Frankfurt in the reconstitution of the Council of Brethren of the Confessing Church, and later at Treysa in the organization of the official "Evangelical Church in Germany".'[290] 'It was not only a laborious but almost an adventurous journey.' Immediately after arriving in Frankfurt, Barth sat 'far into the night with my friend Niemöller'. At the session of the Council of Brethren there he was nominated as one of the twelve representatives of the Confessing Church at Treysa.[291] In Frankfurt he also visited old Frau Rade and Erich Foerster, got to know Gerstenmaier, whom he had previously treated so roughly – and 'I stood before the ruins of the Goethe-haus'.[292] In Treysa, Bishop Wurm, who was chairman of the meeting, made a deeper impression on him than at the time of the church struggle. 'I saw him there at the height of the fatal discussions about the future composition of the Provisional Church Government in honourable conflict with his own people from the district-church episcopal Lutheran German-national wing' – all in all in a way which compelled Barth's respect.[293] On the way back he visited Bultmann in Marburg and in Bonn saw the ruins of his former places of work. 'It is significant that at the conferences of theologians which I visited there was much talk of demons. "We looked Satan in the eye." Such statements were almost uttered with enthusiasm. I listened to them for a long time. Finally I couldn't keep quiet any more. "Are you about to slip back into a magical view of the world?" I asked my friends. "Why do you keep talking only about demons? Why don't you say outright that you were political fools? Please let your Swiss colleague admonish you to adopt a more *rational* way of thinking."'[294] When Helmut Thielicke once talked in the same way about looking demons in the eye, Barth answered: 'They don't seem to have made much impression on you!'[295]

Delighted as Barth was at his reunion with all the survivors, he was shattered by the degree of destruction and the loss of friends who had been killed in the war. Above all, however, he was worried by the appearance of the church which was presented to him in Treysa. 'The "German Christians" of 1933 had, of course, disappeared or gone underground or, in a few cases, been honestly converted. Nevertheless, to my astonishment I found in the official church roughly the same structure, grouping and dominant tendencies in which I had seen it hastening to its ruin in 1933. The progressive elements – those who had truly resisted between 1933 and 1945 and now wanted to translate into actuality the teachings of those years (Niemöller was one of the best among them) – were still on the scene and at work, but they were still a minority compared with the really dominant and determinative groups and authorities. I found the same old concern for preserving the formal, regulated character of the "district churches" – a concern which was not improved by an interest in all kinds of new and wonderful things, above all in a more pronounced confessionalism and clericalism and alongside this a preoccupation with liturgy which expressed itself in a great many fanciful ways. I found all this much more strongly in evidence than a concern for the question of renewing the Christian message from its sources and applying it to the new situation which had now emerged. The cause of the church always seemed to be the cause of some prominent person or circle, and not the cause of the parishes. At that time . . . I could discover little concern to look for the best way of simply proclaiming the gospel to the sorely tried people of Germany.'[296] So at least for the moment Barth could see all too little readiness for the new beginning which he had longingly hoped for at the end of the war. He attempted with renewed energy to resist the development which he saw in prospect. Why? 'Because I would like to rouse the German theologians from their intense involvement with sacrament, liturgy, confession, ministry, episcopacy and so on to face the real fact of the inward and outward needs of Germany and the real gospel which they should *say* to the people of Germany – in simple words, not mysterious ones.'[297]

Back in Switzerland again, Barth gave an account of his journey in an interview for *Weltwoche* ('And forgive us our debts'), and in a second interview a critical account of the Swiss attitude in the war ('Our malaise must become fruitful'). On 1 October he spoke in Neuchâtel and on 14 October at the sixth Wipkingen conference on 'The Evangelical Church after the collapse of the Third Reich'. Against the 'quite disloyal attempt' of Emil Brunner 'to wipe out aid work', it was resolved in Wipkingen that aid for the Confessing Church should be maintained.[298] In the lecture Barth also expressed his wish (which was communicated to Niemöller on 28 September) for the German church to acknowledge to an ecumenical body that in following Hitler the German people had taken 'a false course', that the present disaster was 'a consequence of this error' and that the church 'shared in the responsibility for the error'.[299] The so-called 'Stuttgart Declaration of Guilt' was in fact made four days later, but this sounded all too vague to Barth: 'In Stuttgart they were already far too much concerned with what they held against others',[300] he wrote to Asmussen, with whom he now had a final quarrel. They should not accuse others, they should not relapse into some kind of return to the *status quo* and above all else they should emerge from their slave mentality – these were the thoughts of a 'Word to the Germans' which he was able to present on a new visit to Germany 'at the invitation of the Württemberg Minister of the Interior in the Staatstheater in Stuttgart on 2 November 1945'. 'The Stuttgart speech (which I had already given once before at the University of Tübingen: there to an audience of two thousand, here to an audience of fifteen hundred) may at any rate be an interesting historical document. As far as I know these were the first occasions after the defeat of Germany on which a (civilian) foreigner . . . had spoken there in public and to a large audience.'[301] 'I think gratefully of the hospitality which I was able to enjoy at that time' in the home of Carlo Schmid in Tübingen.[302]

Then came the winter semester. Barth had begun lecturing on anthropology again, his seminar was on Calvin (*Institutes* I) and his discussion group was on Harnack's *What is Christianity?* During the semester 'one of the last of the Harnack group' died, Eberhard Vischer of Basle. 'I had to speak about him in the name of the university and the faculty. Years ago, when I undertook to write on *Romans* for the second time, neither Vischer nor I would ever have dreamed of that.'[303] During this winter, in December, Barth had the further task of giving the opening speech for a matinée of the Cabaret Cornichon in a Zürich cinema in support of the Society for Aid to Germany. He also gave a radio broadcast on New Year's Eve, looking back on 1945. With the dropping of atomic bombs on Japan at the end of the Second World War in mind, he spoke of his great concern for the future. 'For,' he thought, 'the end of the terrors of this war, which already seemed as great as they could be, thus merged into the prospect of the quite unforeseeable consequences of another. So the question of preventing any future war and establishing a solid and lasting peace this time became a matter of almost incontestable urgency.'[304] In January he held a seminar again in Neuchâtel (on baptism). In addition to all this he also had a great deal to do as a result of his rapidly growing correspondence. The number of visitors who came to see him also increased markedly. In January the Hungarian Laszlo Pap and the American Dr Cavert came. And in February Bishop Bell of Chichester, to whom, 'I said in the street, "You are the nicest man I ever met, but a little too nice."' Before Bell departed, 'by second class', Barth whispered into his ear: 'Not too much love for the Pope'.[305] Martin Niemöller came in February and in March: 'We enjoyed his visit more and learnt more from him than we expected.'[306] Barth had prepared for his visit to Switzerland by writing an article about him.

Barth lived through the whole of this first period immediately after the 'collapse of the Third Reich' convinced that the false 'prophets of a new Europe and a new world', now removed from the scene, had not had any really new aims. 'They found an all too appropriate consummation of the bad old days.' Allied to this was the conviction that '*after* them, Europe and even the world are at a turning point from which new ways and a new direction must be sought and found'. So despite all the disappointments and fears which had already emerged, he cherished the hope that in future 'it would be possible to attempt to live on rather *different* lines, not only from those on which we saw yesterday's assassins storm down, but also from those along which the rest of us jogged towards the point when one day we inevitably found ourselves in their hands'.[307]

7

Between East and West

The years from 1946 to 1955 in Pilgerstrasse 25, Basle

The two guest semesters in Bonn

For Barth, too, the task faced by the 'world' after the Second World War was that of reconstruction, and it needed to be tackled on all fronts. Barth wanted to play his part. Indeed he thought that in the volumes of the *Dogmatics* already written he had attempted 'to make a small contribution towards the fundamental basis of a future reconstruction of the German church and German culture'.[1] Early in 1946, however, the question arose whether he should not share in the reconstruction in another more direct way. 'The problem of German reconstruction seemed to me personally to be so vast, and made so complicated both by the world around and by the Germans themselves, that I saw myself faced with an alternative: either to return to Germany for good and devote what time and strength remain to me completely and exclusively to German problems and tasks; *or* to keep on with my real work – namely, the continuation and possibly the completion of my *Church Dogmatics* – confining my direct participation in German affairs, as well as in other foreign affairs that might possibly arise, to specific occasions. I felt that I ought to decide in favour of the second.'[2]

Nevertheless, Barth resolved at least to accept an invitation of rather shorter duration which represented a direct involvement in the reconstruction of Germany (because of it he declined to become Rector of Basle University for 1946). Even during his visit to Germany in August 1945, 'I was urgently asked by certain parties to further the work of reconstruction which was now needed in Germany by returning to Bonn.' Thereupon 'I said I would be prepared to come as a guest to Bonn for one or perhaps two summer semesters to support the work which had to be done there.'[3] The Basle Department of Education gave Barth paid leave for this and appointed Emil Brunner(!) his replacement in Basle for the summer of 1946. In the middle of April he had to move houses in Basle. He found his new home in a place 'with the attractive name Pilgerstrasse 25, not far from the Mission House'.[4] A few days after the move he set off with Charlotte von Kirschbaum for Bonn – unfortunately without the six Swiss students whom he would very much have liked to take. 'In the first days of May I went from Basle to Bonn on a Rhine freighter, under the sign of the Swiss cross.' 'We saw the changing landscape on the banks of the river in its old beauty and liveliness, in the full splendour of spring. But we also saw hundreds of destroyed bunkers. We saw sunken ships, broken bridges, bombed cities one after the other. We saw the symbolic figure of old Germany at the Deutsches Eck* shamefully knocked down and in pieces.'[5]

'While we were walking from the Rhine into the city (Bonn) beside our trolleys, loaded with cases and trunks, Günther Dehn came to meet us, laughing and the same as ever.' Barth found somewhere to stay in two small rooms on the first floor of Schlossstrasse 14: 'my study had to be both dining room and reception room – and my bedroom into the bargain.'[6] So now once again he found himself 'in the heart of Germany, the country which had concerned us so much from afar and over which we had so often shaken our heads. We were among these puzzling and stimulating and demanding people, a remarkable embassage from the hostile world outside and at the same time completely one of them, because inwardly we had felt so much for them.' 'First of all I devoted myself entirely to looking and listening, to observing and gathering impressions. There are so many overwhelming miseries which keep overlapping each other that at first one prefers to keep quiet and think, instead of jumping to obvious conclusions.'[7] One of the first people to whom he now 'listened' twice, for long periods (at the home of the Swiss Consul General, François Rodolphe von Weiss), was Konrad Adenauer, though Adenauer did not make a good impression on him. On one occasion 'Lollo spilt a whole glass of red wine on his trousers'.[8] Barth gave him an urgent warning – as he had already done to Gustav Heinemann in a letter in February – not to found a Christian Democrat Party. He thought that while the church should indeed have political commitments, these should not take the form of a Christian party. Indeed, he feared that as in pre-war days the

*The Deutsches Eck (German corner) is that part of Koblenz where the Moselle joins the Rhine.

German parties were acting 'like metaphysical sects of some kind'; for this reason parties should certainly not be formed *before* democratic practices had been established at the lowest levels.[9]

He had exceptionally friendly relations in Bonn with Dr Bleibtreu, the lawyer who had defended him in Cologne in 1934, 'who certainly "remains faithful", like his name'[10] – and now again with Bleibtreu's cousin Günther Dehn; also with Käthe Seifert, 'who sees everything that happens and immediately knows how to put it in the right context'.[11] It was only now that he really came to appreciate Wilhelm Goeters: 'He has described a whole world of its own: the Rhineland, the old Reformed Church, a whole host of regular and irregular characters of past times with all their inter-relationships, clear or confused, with their wisdom and wonder . . . How much I enjoyed listening to him when he began to expand on all his experience, as though it were today.'[12] Barth also had good relationships with the rest of his colleagues from the Protestant faculty of theology, Martin Noth and Hans Emil Weber, Heinrich Schlier and Hermann Schlingensiepen; the Dean, Ethelbert Stauffer, was a marked exception. They joined him on 10 May to celebrate his sixtieth birthday with utmost simplicity at the Bleibtreus (Ernst Wolf had also come over from Göttingen). The birthday meal consisted of a dish of potatoes and salad – 'and it was at least as meaningful and enjoyable as the finest cake at Pilgerstrasse could have been'.[13] He was also delighted to have a birthday letter from England signed by leading churchmen and theologians of all denominations. This was followed by a *Festschrift, Reformation Old and New*, edited by his theologian friend, Frederick Camfield, which appeared rather late. He also had a *Festschrift* from the French and the French-speaking Swiss, and birthday greetings from the Social Democrats, the trade unions, the Rhine church, and so on.

The summer semester did not begin until 17 May. In his lectures Barth wanted to present a 'Dogmatics in outline, following the Apostles' Creed'. 'A somewhat cautious but friendly welcome. After that, I read the text for the day as I used to . . . and then without any special opening remarks went on to talk about the nature and purpose of dogmatics.' The lectures 'were given at seven a.m. in the semi-ruins of the once stately Kurfürsten Schloss in Bonn, which had been taken over for the university. We began by singing a psalm or a hymn to cheer us up. About eight o'clock we became aware of the rebuilding in the quadrangle from the noise of the demolition crane

After the war

65. On board a Rhine freighter en route for Bonn, May 1946.

66. Barth lectured in the summer of 1946 in the ruins of the University of Bonn.

67. Swiss soldiers bringing aid to Bonn, 1946.

68. With his friend Martin Niemöller, who had just been released from a concentration camp (1946). They were to continue close allies in the future.

Visits to Germany

69.   *With friends at Herborn, March 1951: (standing) W. Niesel, W. Kreck, E. Wolf, H. Gollwitzer, O. Weber, and H. E. Hess; (sitting) G. Heinemann, K. Barth.*

70.   *Conference of the Society for Evangelical Theology in Wuppertal, March 1956: with J. Beckmann, H. J. Iwand and W. Schneemelcher.*

71.   *Lecture to the Goethe Institute in Hanover, January 1957: Bishop Lilje and Ernst Wolf are behind Barth and K. H. Miskotte is on the far left.*

which was breaking up the ruins. (Incidentally, my curiosity led me to discover, among the rubble, an undamaged bust of Schleiermacher, which was rescued and restored to a new place of honour.) The audience consisted partly of theologians, but most of them were students from the other faculties. Most people in today's Germany have gone through a great deal of suffering in one way or another, almost beyond imagining. I could see this in my Bonn students. With their grave faces, which had still to learn to smile again, they made a great impression on me. And *I* impressed *them*, as a foreigner, and as the centre of all sorts of gossip from old times. I shall never forget it all – and by a coincidence it happened to be my fiftieth semester. When it was over, my impression was that it was my best ever.'[14]

Those who knew Barth's *Dogmatics* would 'hardly find much that was new in these lectures'. However, they had quite a new and distinctive character, because on this occasion, 'for the first time in my life, I lectured without a script, and discussed the main propositions quite freely . . . The primitive conditions which I met with in Germany made it absolutely necessary for me to "talk" instead of to "read".'[15] He found that here it was 'quite impossible to be only an academic teacher (of course I never had been that, and so I fitted this situation quite well)'. 'To a great extent one also had to be a kind of missionary, Sunday School teacher, popular orator, philanthropist and so on.'[16] But Barth felt that in their particular form the lectures smacked 'of a document of our time, which has once more become a time "between the times" – and not only in Germany'. One of the key sentences in his remarks ran: 'There is only one Lord, and this Lord is the Lord of the world', Jesus Christ (who, he pointed out emphatically, was a *Jew*). 'Here we stand at the centre. And however high and mysterious and difficult the object of our search may seem to be, we may also say: here everything becomes quite simple . . . I may be a professor of systematic theology, but at this point I can only say to you, "Look, the alternatives are simple: it's either knowledge, or rank foolishness, so here I am in front of you, like a teacher in the lowest class of a Sunday School, who has something to say which a mere four-year-old can understand." "The world was lost, but Christ was born. Rejoice, O Christendom."' 'Several times during these weeks I was asked, "Aren't you aware that many people at these lectures are not Christians?" I always laughed and said, "It makes no difference to me." It would be quite dreadful if the faith of

Christians aimed at separating men and cutting them off from each other. It is in fact the strongest motive for bringing men together and uniting them.'[17]

Especially in the seminar (which was a discussion of the lectures) Barth found 'wild ideas rampant among undoubtedly gifted, receptive and alert young people'.[18] He therefore divided his seminar into small working groups which had to discuss the material among themselves first, before the seminar met as a whole. Other sessions studied the Barmen Declaration, and at the students' request there was also an evening at which a number of political questions were also discussed. The Bonn student of 1946 was 'a very different character from that of 1932 . . . But on the whole I cannot feel that he has changed for the worse.' True, he showed 'many signs that he spent his youth in rather a remarkable way'. 'But I never put to anyone the question whether "the German student of today might still secretly be a Nazi". I thought that everything would work out once the student found that he was being talked to, taken seriously and at the same time slightly encouraged, quite naturally and on a completely objective basis. This was my concern, and I found that I got on the right lines with him as quickly as with his predecessors (if not more so). I discovered a surprising degree of openness, willingness and preparedness, a rapidly developing understanding of the subject-matter and methods of theology, and lastly a gratitude which moved me deeply.' Barth also sought to give material help to the students and his other friends. He appealed to the Swiss to send a 'stout ship full of food and tobacco'.[19] 'From home – Berne – we were reprimanded for importunate demands for food.'[20] And how glad he was when in fact a convoy of aid did arrive in Bonn in the charge of 'a large group of officers, NCOs and soldiers in their familiar Swiss uniforms' – 'how splendid and peaceful they look in this place'. 'Then they all came along to the lecture and of course aroused a good deal of attention there.'[21]

Barth did not just teach. He also welcomed a large number of visitors to his Bonn home and dealt with an extensive correspondence. He skilfully established and cultivated numerous contacts with allied departments and individuals, above all with the Bonn University Officer, Ronald Gregor Smith, a Scottish pastor turned poet, 'a soul like an aspen leaf, full of good will, but much too refined for this world'.[22] 'In addition, I gave about twenty extra-mural lectures, usually before very large audiences . . . preached five times, spoke often on the radio and gave a series of interviews.'[23] The lectures, which were also given without notes, and were based on either slogans or brief statements, in fact only amounted to four different ones (apart from a lecture on 'Reformation or Restoration' in Siegburg which he improvised when he replaced Niemöller, who was suddenly prevented from speaking): they were on 'Romans 13', 'Christian Ethics', 'Christian Proclamation in Today's Europe' and 'The Christian Community and the Civil Community'. The second of the lectures indicated the outline of an ethics developed from a law understood in terms of the gospel which preceded it. The third gave a clear and far-sighted description of Europe's situation as now being 'between two millstones'. Europe was under serious threat from both West and East and under their influence; this situation was a chance for the church to proclaim 'a free and independent word'.[24] The lecture on 'Christian Community and Civil Community' aroused a great deal of attention: in it, however, Barth merely approached the subject along the lines of the fifth thesis of Barmen and felt that he had discussed it 'in terms of the Confessing Church in Germany'.

In the lecture he said that the church and the state were not to be understood as two realms set side by side. The relationship between them was like that of two concentric circles of different diameters. The state is 'outside the church, but not outside the range of Christ's dominion'. Because Christ is Lord over both, 'both have their origin and their centre in common'. In this way Barth ruled out any basis for the state in natural law or a doctrine of the 'autonomy of the world'. Here he spoke out against political indifference on the part of the church; against any political action by Christians which was not honourable solidarity with the world; against any Christian political decision which respected any other authority than that of its Lord. At the same time he stressed the 'capacity and need for politics to be a parable' analogous to the message of the kingdom of God proclaimed by the church. In speaking like this Barth did not believe that he had confused the two realms. Rather, he thought that Christians should 'enter the political arena anonymously', and not, say, as a Christian party.[25]

Three of these lectures and the series of lectures *Dogmatik im Grundriss* (ET *Dogmatics in Outline*) were soon published by Christian Kaiser Verlag in Munich. The last work, in particular, was then read a great deal and used especially by 'lay' people. Before the war, Christian Kaiser Verlag had for a long time been regarded as *the* publisher of Barth, but the Nazis had then banned it from distributing his books. Now it could publish some of his works again. On the whole, however, these did not amount to many since he was now really tied to the Evangelischer Verlag of Zollikon.

Barth's lecturing took him up and down West Germany: to Godesberg, Oberkassel, Frankfurt, Düsseldorf, Oberhausen, Cologne, Moers, Seelscheid, Berlin, Göttingen, Papenburg (Conference of the Society for Evangelical Theology), Barmen, Stuttgart, Munich and Schwenningen. Everywhere there were many people to greet and much to discuss. On his way through Münster he met Heinrich Scholz, and in Göttingen he met Friedrich Gogarten for the last time at his lecture on 'The Christian Community and the Civil Community'. 'He sat in the front row and made quite a Mephis-tophelian face at me. But he did not come up to greet me. And I thought it better that we shouldn't speak, because nothing could come of it.'[26] A high-point of his travels was a visit to Berlin, where Barth first 'had an unexpected meeting with Eduard Thurneysen on Charlottenburg station': Thurneysen was visiting his son-in-law who was with the French troops there, and also planned to give some lectures. 'I spent three almost indescribably full and busy days there with Germans, French, English, Americans and Russians. I talked to church people, Christians and communists . . . All the old historic Berlin is in ruins. The scenes are indescribable. Like a disturbed ant-hill it is teeming with all kinds of people, some of whom know what they want, some of whom aren't sure and some of whom just don't have a clue.'[27] 'I was received there in a very pleasant way by Lieutenant Tulpanov, the Soviet officer concerned with cultural affairs, and had a long conversation with the head of the Social Unity Party.'[28] 'I was taken into a room and there I found Pieck, Grotewohl and even Ulbricht with his little beard, a Herr Zimmer-mann and other great figures sitting at a long table. I sat opposite them in solitary state. Someone had somehow whispered that I was an important man and that they should have a word with me. It was a remarkable meeting just to look at – this long table . . . It reminded me so much of Leonardo da Vinci's "Last Supper".' 'I can still see the grimaces with which Ulbricht reacted to my all too Swiss advice.' 'I shall never forget two of the things that Pieck said to me on that occasion. First, he said, "Herr Professor, what we need in Germany is the ten commandments." I replied, "Yes, Herr President, especially the first!" The second remarkable thing that he said was: "In two years conditions here in the East will be so good that the whole of West Germany will eagerly come streaming in . . ." I replied, "We'll see . . ."'[29]

On his return to Bonn, Barth wrote 'Eleven Points of Criticism of the Allied Military Régimes',[30] which he had already presented verbally to Colonel Creighton, the officer responsible for questions of education and religion in the English zone. In it he complained that 'as a result of the mode of government and administration practised in Germany' by the Allies, the German people 'were still not being given any practical instruction in what they had never yet seen or known in their history: in a democratic way of thinking, pattern of life and politics (based on humanity, freedom, justice and so on)'. This criticism appeared in an English military newspaper and considerable notice was taken of it. However, Barth was careful to keep it from the Germans. He had other critical remarks to make to them. For he thought that instead of acknowledging their own guilt, they had already been far too quick 'to load it on to others' – under the leadership or with the collaboration of the church, which seemed to him 'despite Stuttgart (i.e. the 'Confession of Guilt' which was made there) still to be completely stubborn and unrepentant at the crucial point'.[31] He also bemoaned to the Germans the backward-looking attitude which came all too easily to the people and its churches and was connected with this unreadiness to repent. He regretted that politically there had been no attempt 'by the occupying powers to encourage the practice of democracy from below, first giving limited responsibility to very small groups, and *building up* gradually from there towards the large-scale features of a democratic state'.[32] He regretted that the question of the renewal of the church was made secondary to even more enthusiastic efforts in the game of 'opening up an "Eastern front"'.[33] And he regretted that the churches had prematurely 'resorted to the museum of the sixteenth century or the Middle Ages', instead of being concerned 'to rebuild the church from the ground upwards'.[34]

Barth returned to Switzerland at the end of August with rather troubled thoughts. During his holiday at the Bergli he was able to go to Zürich to hear Winston Churchill's famous Council of Europe lecture, which confirmed his general impression of allied policy: that the 'much-needed political wisdom being applied at present' was considerably less than 'the energy which had previously been expended in waging war'.[35] In October he spoke in Pratteln about his visit to Germany and in Safenwil about 'the church': his audience in Safenwil consisted of 120 of his former confirmation candidates who in the meantime had formed 'a society of their own with a committee, a crest and so on'.[36] During this period the BBC also transmitted a broadcast in which 'I said that it was time (not only in Germany) for the usual question from the church to the world to be reversed. For a change the world should discover what was really going on in the churches. Why was more justice not done to its great status and the claims which it raised?'[37] Then the winter semester began. Barth partly repeated his lectures on 'anthropology' and also took them further; in his seminar he worked on the Heidelberg Catechism and in his discussion group on Luther's *De libertate*. Since foreign students were at last allowed to come to Basle, the new university for once no longer looked like 'too large a garment for too small a child'.[38] Barth had also fought for permission to have six German students whom he had got to know in Bonn (they included the lawyer Helmut Simon).

Because the frontiers had been reopened, Barth's visitors increased considerably during the winter months. Now he could carry on a variety of conversations in which attitudes to the most recent past and the immediate future played an important part – he talked, for example, with Niemöller, Erik Wolf and Heinz Kloppenburg; with the Danes Sandbek and Regin Prenter; with Visser't Hooft; with the Polish bishop Jan Szeruda; with the Czech Josef B. Souček and the Hungarian Barnabas Nagy; with the American Elmer Homrighausen; and with the Swedes Ragnar Bring and Anders Nygren. He had a surprisingly friendly meeting with Nygren, who showed him 'quite a different Luther' from the one he knew in Germany.[39] 'I told the lively Scandinavians to teach us as quickly and as thoroughly as possible about this very different Luther which they claimed to have found in the Weimar edition.'[40] On one occasion Barth (who was only released from military service at the beginning of 1947) was able to shake General Guisan by the hand. The General was the centre of considerable controversy because of his critical account of the war period, but Barth told him, 'how grateful I was, as a simple citizen, for his report.'[41] On another occasion Reinhold Niebuhr invited himself. Barth received him in some trepidation, not knowing whether 'we would sniff at each other cautiously like two bull mastiffs, or rush barking at each other, or lie stretched out peacefully in the sun side by side':[42] at any rate, they had 'a good conversation'.[43]

During these winter months Barth often had to speak elsewhere. In Neuchâtel he began a seminar on the Lord's Prayer according to the Reformation catechisms (which was continued in 1948–49). In Tavannes, La Sagne and Morges he repeated his lecture on 'Proclamation in Today's Europe'. In a Basle church he spoke on 'Is the Bible the Word of God?' and in Zürich and Berne on the theme 'The German Student Today and Tomorrow'. One sentence led to a good deal of discussion and also to a public correspondence with the Heidelberg zoologist Erich von Holst: this was the remark that 'the type of conservative nationalistic scholar of the 1920s' (which was still represented by the majority of German professors) had 'prepared the way for Hitler and was still a danger today' because he was incapable of bringing up students to be 'free men'. It was significant that twice at the beginning of 1947 Barth was asked to co-operate in the ecumenical movement. To begin with, in the first days of January he had to give a lecture 'at an international conference of biblical scholars in Bossey'[44] on 'The Authority and Significance of the Bible'.

In it he said that since the 'subject' of the biblical witness 'is unique', the testimony, too, is 'itself the only one for the community at this time and the normative form of the Word of God for the world'. Thus 'the ecumenical unity' of the church 'is truth or illusion to the degree that the authority of the Bible, defined in this way, is valid or invalid for it'.[45]

Barth had to leave the conference suddenly in order to give a memorial address for his Basle predecessor, Johannes Wendland, who had just died. Then he had to prepare a 'paper' on the church (along with the Lutheran Gustav Aulén and the orthodox Georges Florovsky) for the Assembly of the World Council of Churches which was planned to take place in Amsterdam.

Under the title 'The Church – The Living Congegation of the Living Lord Jesus Christ', he put down in writing thoughts which in his view he was expressing for the first time with such precision and detail. They were on so-called 'congregationalist' lines. Starting from a strict understanding of the church as the 'event of its assembling', 'I have demolished the whole concept of church "authority" – in both its episcopal and its synodical form – and constructed everything (rather like the Pilgrim Fathers) on the congregation.'[46]

In the summer semester of 1947 Barth had Gustaf Wingren from Sweden as a replacement in Basle, while he himself went to Bonn. Once again he went by boat, but spent 'most of the time working in my cabin'. This time in Bonn he lived at Nuss-Allee 2, 'in the Geological Institute, an enormous building', lying 'in the middle of a park, so that from my place of work I looked straight out on to an enormous cedar of Lebanon'.[47] 'In some respects I found the situation different from the previous year. True, the academic presuppositions which most students brought with them had not changed essentially' – the results of an examination for the seminar were so bad that 'I had mercy' and accepted all the students. 'It was rather like my picture of the "restoration of all things"*.' 'But the size of my audience had doubled or trebled, partly as a result of special permission by the British military authorities. Again, the intellectual attitude of the students had hardened somewhat in the meantime and a certain rebelliousness was unmistakable, for all the attention which they paid to what I said. It cost me some effort to overcome it, but by the end of the semester I had succeeded. One witty little student from Württemberg called this effort the "stubbornness of a mule" which I had towards them.' 'My task in Bonn consisted first in giving four hours a week of university lecturing on "Christian Doctrine according to the Heidelberg Catechism", a one-hour public lecture on "The Christian Concept of Revelation" and a two-hour seminar on church and state.'[48] The lectures took place at seven o'clock in the morning ('by Swiss reckoning that summer it was five o'clock!'), 'in the Chemical Institute on the Poppelsdorfer Allee', where 'surrounded by glass and apparatus in all kinds of impressive shapes I plied my craft looking like a curious new edition of Dr Faustus'. 'To secure the use of this place for myself I had to stoop to one of the sorts of bribery which are the form here (I gave the caretaker a "Swiss food parcel", which is what everyone here dreams of).'[49]

The lectures on the Heidelberg Catechism were not meant to be a historical exegesis of the catechism but a dogmatic 'presentation of the gospel of Jesus Christ'. They were not about an idea or a rule of life, but about the gospel. As Barth remarked at the beginning, they were therefore solely meant to say, 'Give place, you spirits of sadness, for Christ the master of joy is entering in.' That was the message! For the gospel is not a 'dead possession that a man "has". One should beware of this capitalist understanding of Christianity . . . !' The gospel must always be sought afresh. 'No theology can do more than show man the way to the gospel, and only where that happens does its community live.' Barth followed the catechism in his

---

*Greek *apokatastasis panton,* the doctrine that all free moral creatures – angels, men and devils, will share in the grace of salvation (condemned as a heresy in the patristic period). Also known as universalism.

account, not to describe a 'Reformed orthodoxy' but to make clear that Christian thought is not only bound to scripture, but also – freely and gratefully – to the 'Fathers'. In this case, significantly, it was bound to the Reformed Fathers because their open recognition of the gospel was a guard against confessionalism, 'which I regard as the most questionable modern development here in German theology and in the church'.[50]

In his lecture on the understanding of revelation Barth saw the special characteristic of *Christian* revelation as being that it was an affirmative event, meeting man's needs, absolute and addressed to man. It disclosed an essentially hidden situation, inaccessible to man and outside his control. The disclosure was definitive in such a way that, 'coming from outside man', it fully claimed him.

As in the previous year, Barth again travelled up and down Germany giving lectures during this four-month stay. 'Again and again the broad German landscape, traversed by rapid car or (less pleasant) railway journeys; again and again rooms and churches full of people, discussions at which one must listen carefully to the points they raise in order to give a proper reply or make a statement; and always acquaintances appearing individually or in groups, with something to say, to ask, to complain about. Indeed, again and again the Germans with all their good and bad points, who continually interest me whatever they do and despite everything, and are masters at knowing how to pump things into one and out of one.' 'I gave lectures to very large audiences in Bonn, Godesberg, Cologne, Aachen, Velbert, Barmen, Neustadt, Dortmund, Münster, Darmstadt, Hamburg, Oldenburg, Berlin and Dresden – and finally in Frankfurt am Main, Munich, Stuttgart and Göppingen. And I preached four times in all – even wearing a ruff in Hamburg.'[51] Also in Hamburg he had to take part in a lengthy discussion on confessionalism and its relationship to politics, chaired by Hellmut Traub. In Oldenburg he spoke to the Society for Evangelical Theology, in Barmen to the Convention of Reformed Preachers, in Darmstadt to the Council of Brethren of the Confessing Church and in Frankfurt to the Reformed Synod. On one journey the car belonging to his friend the lawyer Paul Schulze zur Wiesche suddenly lost a wheel – 'fortunately the driver was very experienced . . . and was able to tame the twisting vehicle'.[52] In Neustadt Barth came to love the wine of the Pfalz and praised it highly. In Munich he also paid a visit to Bishop Meiser, and on the way there, in Nuremberg, saw Georg Merz, who seemed to be 'very well, cheerful and adjusted, at any rate personally'.[53] In Stuttgart he visited the government minister

Wilhelm Simpfendörfer, whose sons were studying with him. On his travels Barth used several lectures: the 'paper'on the church written for Amsterdam, his interpretation of the sixth thesis of Barmen ('The Message of the Free Grace of God'), and finally a lecture on 'Christ and We Christians', which set out to show the necessary 'basis' for all the efforts at reconstruction which he thought to be necessary. The second of these lectures stressed that God not only *exercises* 'free grace' but by his very nature *is* 'free grace', and that therefore the church not only *speaks* its message of grace but also lives by it.

Once again the climax of these lecture tours was his visit to Berlin at the beginning of August. There Barth not only lectured and spoke to German pastors and other Christians (and twice on the radio), but also talked with 'the great figures of the French occupation', with the 'British commandant', and the 'wise Asiatics Tulpanov and his adjutant Yermolayev'. He also talked to the Swiss ambassador, through whom he got to know Louise Schröder, the Mayor of Berlin.[54] On another occasion he spent 'a whole afternoon with a group of real flesh-and-blood German communists. Finally I said to them, "Let me tell you something from the Bible." And I recited to them the saying of Ecclesiastes: "Be not righteous overmuch, and do not make yourself overwise; why should you destroy yourself?" (adding that that could really also be said to the Western church!), followed by its continuation: "Be not wicked overmuch, neither be a fool, why should you die before your time?" (adding that that could now be said against, or rather for, you Easterners!).'[55] There followed a two-day visit to Dresden, where the Mayor, Martin Richter, showed Barth the 'exceptional devastation of the city'. He met lay representatives of the Confessing Church and, wherever he went, on the whole liked the Lutheranism that he saw. After his lecture (on 'The Church . . . ') to an audience of three and a half thousand, at a reception he sat 'next to a Soviet officer whose interest I caught by my after-dinner speech on Dostoyevsky and his attractive humanity. I said that the Red Army now had an important opportunity to show this humanity in Germany.' 'I still have a ticket stub from that evening: on one side it says "Confessing Church" – and on the other, simply and in large letters: "1 Schnapps". That happened only once!'[56]

On his journey into East Germany Barth already came up against the question of the attitude of the church in the East-West conflict which was just beginning; this question was to occupy him a great deal for a number of years. The other question which also claimed his attention in the following period, that of his attitude to Bultmann's programme of demythologizing the New Testament, also arose during this summer. Barth's opinion was sought by Bishop Wurm in his capacity as President of the Council of the Evangelical Church in Germany in connection with a question raised by Pastor Hans Bruns: how was Bultmann's description of the story of the 'empty tomb' as a 'legend' to be assessed (or condemned) and how was Bultmann to be disciplined and his influence limited? In a detailed answer Barth remarked that he regarded the term 'legend', if rightly understood, to be quite unobjectionable; his hesitations were over quite a different point. He objected less to demythologizing than to the "existentialist" pattern' which Bultmann used as a 'criterion for the interpretation of the New Testament'; and it was still very much open to question whether the questioner was not himself following this pattern. At any rate, Barth advised against any ecclesiastical disciplining of Bultmann; if he was to be opposed, then it could only be with a better theology.[57]

Teaching and research 1947–1948

After a few days' holiday (with Ernst Wolf) in the Engadine and at the Bergli, Barth continued to develop his 'anthropology' further in lectures in Basle. He returned to a discussion of Bultmann in an excursus. He objected to Bultmann's understanding of Easter (as the event of the origin of faith) by arguing that at Easter Jesus had appeared *to* his disciples and only *in this way* was their belief made possible. Here Barth raised a number of general questions about the whole programme of demythologizing: were there not also events which could be verified historically and were real happenings? Could the 'modern view of the world' impose its own conditions on our understanding of the content of the Bible? and so on.

This excursus was in a wider context in which Barth argued that man is man only in 'his allotted span of the past, present and future'. Similarly, it had been said earlier that man is man in that he accepts his responsibility before God; that he is man by 'being with others . . . I and Thou, man and woman'; and that he is man in his totality, soul and body distinct yet interconnected. 'I dropped a section which appeared in the first draft, on "Man and Humanity"', dealing with the individual, communities and society, because I was not sure enough of the theological approach to this question and therefore of the right way to treat it.' (However, in 1952 Barth arranged the separate publication of an exegetical excursus on Romans 5 which came from this section, under the title *Christus und Adam*: Christ and Adam). The other anthropological insights mentioned were introduced by and based on christological reflections: 'Jesus, Man for God' – 'Jesus, Man for Other Men' – 'Jesus, Whole Man' – 'Jesus, Lord of Time'. Barth argued even more emphatically than before that while anthropology was not christology, 'the man Jesus as the revealing word of God' was 'the source of our knowledge of human nature as created by God'. Barth thought that the non-theological disciplines might recognize individual 'phenomena of human nature', but not the 'real man' himself. This could be known only in Jesus Christ. The *'real'* man is not creaturely man in himself, nor is he the man who sins against his creaturely being; 'the real man is the sinner who shares in God's *grace*'.[58] Some readers of the book, e.g. Heinrich Vogel, took offence at the last section, in which Barth said that while in practice our death had the character of judgment, of itself it belonged to the good nature of man and that 'eternal life' therefore did not consist in either an alteration or a continuation of our present life, but in the revelation of our life as it had been.

This anthropology also contained arguments against Fichte, Nietzsche and Jaspers. By contrast, reference to the work of older theologians was 'rather sparse this time'. The reason for this was that 'the account here diverges even further from dogmatic tradition than say in II,2 . . . The only approach to the theological knowledge of man which I believe to be possible was not chosen by any of the older or more recent church fathers by whom I have taken my bearings . . . In contrast, to demonstrate the basis of my argument I also had to quote a great many biblical texts this time.' To his regret Barth felt that he could not find much help in contemporary exegetes, even from his friend Bultmann. On the whole, the time seemed to him 'not yet to have come when dogmatic theologians will be able to accept with a good conscience and with confidence the results of their Old and New Testament colleagues, and it will perhaps be clear on both sides that the dogmatic theologian also has responsibility for exegesis and the exegete has responsibilities towards dogmatic theology! Until so many exegetes have learnt their part in this common lesson better, or at any rate until they have practised it more thoroughly . . . the dogmatic theologian has no alternative other than to work out his own argument from scripture – running all the risks of the non-specialist.'[59]

Barth did not challenge the rights of historical-critical exegesis (in the biblical quotations in his *Dogmatics* he followed the modern Zürich translation with a frequency bordering on regularity).[60] But a characteristic feature of his exegesis was that he refused to involve himself in a discussion which was purely about the method of exegesis and was not involved in the exegesis of particular texts. He thought that 'hermeneutics cannot be an independent topic of conversation; its problems can only be tackled and answered in countless acts of interpretation – all of which are mutually corrective and supplementary, while at the same time being principally concerned with the content of the text'.[61] Another characteristic of Barth's exegesis was his rejection of the 'constraints of a method' in which the meaning of a biblical text can only be elucidated by the establishment of some historical precedent or influence. 'As though the "biblical" view were something which the Bible had in common with some hypothetical prototypes and then again with the apocrypha and pseudepigrapha . . . ! No, I am more sympathetic towards keeping to what the texts themselves say as they are, *as distinct from* what comes before them or after them. They say something *of their own* . . . What the texts themselves want to say has my "sympathy".'[62]

In the last part of the 'anthropology' which appeared in the winter of 1947–48, for the first time Barth could refer to books written by his sons: to a Göttingen New Testament dissertation by Markus Barth, *Der Augenzeuge. Eine Untersuchung über die Wahrnehmung des Menschensohnes durch die Apostel* (The Eyewitness. An Investigation of the Apostles' Perception of the Son of Man), and to Christoph's doctoral thesis under Walter Baumgartner, *Die Errettung vom Tode in den individuellen Klage- und Dankliedern des Alten Testaments* (Deliverance from Death in the Individual's Laments and Thanksgivings in the Old Testament). In 1947 Christoph had also prepared for publication his father's old Bonn lectures (from 1932–33), *Die Protestantische Theologie im 19. Jahrhundert* (ET *Protestant Theology in the Nineteenth Century*); then in the autumn he went out under the auspices of the Basle Mission to work in what was then called Indonesia. 'His last words, in October, as he got on the boat train to begin the journey to Borneo, were: "Everyone does what he can."'[63] Christoph became a theological teacher for native pastors in Bandjarmasin. Karl Barth now had a very close relationship with his sons and thought that the characteristics of each of them 'presumably reflects one side of my own nature and person'.[64] Karl often went to Bubendorf to hear Markus preach, and thought at that time, 'Of all the people I hear, Markus is the only one whose sermons I am glad to listen to.'[65] He was also fond of hearing Markus tell Bible stories to his five children – 'beautifully and faithfully'. As a grandfather, he hoped that 'in some way something of that seed will grow in all of them'.[66] He also followed the growth and development of his host of grandchildren with great interest, curious as to how their gifts might develop. 'Everything happens so quickly, and they all keep appearing in new editions.'[67] 'One of them wondered recently whether the many creases in my face had developed because I had spent so much of my life laughing.'[68]

In early 1948 Barth completed his doctrine of the 'creature'. It occupied III, 2 of his *Dogmatics*, a volume 800 pages long (ET 661), over which his student lodger Friedrich Herzog helped him by checking the final draft. He dedicated the volume to his friend Thurneysen on his sixtieth birthday – with the wish, 'May your old age be like your youth!' The winter semester was now drawing to an end. In his seminar he had given critical consideration to Calvin's concept of the church and he had taken 'a great deal of trouble', using Herrmann in his discussion group 'to show the youngest generation of theologians, to whom idealism is so completely alien, what we had thought forty years earlier to be the rock of salvation'.[69] In January he made the closer acquaintance of 'a promising young man from Berne', the writer Friedrich Dürrenmatt, 'an interesting, uncouth character, with both spiritual and worldly traits'. Dürrenmatt's attitude seemed to him 'like that of my 1921 *Romans*'. Barth had extensive discussions with Dürrenmatt, the producer Kurt Horwitz and the actress Maria Becker about the possibility of Christian drama: he took a positive view, at least over Dürrenmatt's play *The Blind Man*.[70] In addition, during the winter months Barth had to give a lecture on the situation of the German church as he had found it in 1947, which took him to various places (Safenwil, Neuhausen am Rhein, Zürich, Grabs, Weinfelden, Lugano, Thun and Basle).

He refused an invitation to a third summer in Bonn, not to mention the offer of the post of Rector of Bonn University. 'In retrospect' he thought his last stay 'too much of a failure. I did not present my case very well, and couldn't find the right words.'[71] But he was also too disappointed by the general developments in which he saw the German church to be involved. 'In view of the pernicious Lutheranism of the National Evangelical Lutheran Church of Germany (VELKD) . . . , the preoccupation with liturgy, the Bultmannian "demythologizing" on the one hand and the neo-pietism on the other, and lastly the new Evangelical-National course which Dibelius is evidently busy steering with his old powers', Barth believed that he could see the German churches, like German politics, on a great march back to antiquarianism.[72] So his impression was, 'that the doors there are closed to me, because I see only two choices. I must either take the general line, which in practice has finally been accepted even by the Confessing Church, though the words stick in my throat – or let loose an inarticulate cry which is probably foolish and incomprehensible because I don't know enough about the people and the circumstances there.'[73] All this influenced Barth's decision not to return to Germany again for a number of years.

So he remained in Basle and continued to lecture there. At this time there were some changes in the staff of the theological faculty. The Dutch ethics scholar Hendrik van Oyen took over the chair vacated by Köberle, since the majority of the faculty wanted a counter-balance to Barth. Barth himself supported – in vain – his pupil Georg Eichholz as a candidate for the chair. In 1951 the Kuratel appointed Fritz Buri *extraordinarius* professor for the same reason, to create a counter-balance. Wilhelm Vischer went on to Montpellier and Alfred de Quervain to Berne. For a short time 'old Bertholet lectured in Basle as a kind of honorary member of the faculty',[74] and Werner Bieder taught as an assistant lecturer.

From 1948 onwards the famous philosopher Karl Jaspers was one of Barth's colleagues in Berne. Barth had a great deal of respect for Jaspers, 'who has the gift of directing the attention of his colleagues, with all their disparate concerns, to the ultimate questions of human existence and keeping it there . . . Lecture room 2 – the biggest which we have here – is the scene of his public activity, while mine is in the more modest Room 1, immediately and literally at his feet. There are plenty of gifted young men going up and down the steps linking the two rooms, like angels up and down Jacob's ladder. I wonder whether a hundred and thirty or so years ago there was a similar connection between the places where Hegel and Schleiermacher lectured in Berlin, perhaps the other way round. The Basle students have made the comparison, not without some feeling of self-importance. The dispute over which faculty is now the "handmaid" has always been resolved by different people in different ways. But as this is more a dispute among idle onlookers than among professionals, we may consider ourselves both to be above it. We are agreed in our concern for knowledge of the mystery which both limits and governs the microcosm and the macrocosm. Each of us sees it from quite a different perspective and so from the first words each of us utters, our teaching cannot be the same. But we are also agreed that this mystery is intrinsically one and the same – and we are also agreed that it is worth devoting ourselves with all seriousness to bearing witness to it.'[75]

Since the frontiers had been opened again and were slowly reopening even for the Germans, the number of theological students at Basle increased considerably. As early as the winter of 1947–48, 'we had . . . become a truly ecumenical faculty virtually overnight. In addition to the Swiss, who were now in the minority, there were more than twenty Germans as well as Frenchmen, Dutchmen, Americans, Englishmen, Hungarians, Czechs, Norwegians, Danes, an Icelander and a Finn, all of whom wanted to learn something from me.'[76] In the summer of 1948 Barth's audience had grown so large that he had to move his lectures from Room 17, which he had used previously, to Room 1. In future, this was the place where he lectured on dogmatics: he was not particularly pleased with it, since he could 'hardly recognize the faces of the audience because they all have the windows behind them'.[77] During this summer semester his lectures dealt with the beginning of the doctrine of providence, his seminar was devoted to a discussion of the Reformers' interpretation of the Epistle to the Galatians and his discussion group dealt with Luther's Greater Catechism. Barth also gave a general lecture to students on the Creed.

Thus Barth's lectures continued to be the first public presentation of his *Church Dogmatics*. As they continued hour after hour, they were increasingly taking shape in writing. One might even say that these *Dogmatics* had their 'setting in life' in words spoken to pastors in the making. During his academic activity over all these years Barth took his seminars and the discussions which went with them quite as seriously as his lectures. 'The fact that I devote six of the ten hours a week that I usually teach to these exercises stems from the growing conviction that what can be communicated to the student in this form is probably the most immediately fruitful part of academic instruction. The student should be learning, by means of important texts, to *read*: at first to become aware, quietly and completely, of the content of these texts, to understand what he has read in its historical context, and finally to adopt a critical attitude towards it. For this he needs the stimulation, the guidance and the correction which is given him by a form of collaboration, in which on the one hand he is addressed and treated by the teacher as a regular fellow-researcher, and on the other he has to consider openly and carefully the attempts of his fellow-students . . . It is a matter of preparing the student for *teaching* by his active participation in *research*.'[78] To strengthen this active participation still further, in the winter of 1950–51 Barth introduced the custom of opening the sessions of his seminar 'with brief introductory reports on common work on the portions of the text under consideration at a particular time'.[79]

He was concerned in this way to supervise the progress of a sound younger generation of theological scholars. From soon after the end of the war he had again become the focal point for a considerable number of students working for doctorates or to qualify as lecturers: Felix Fluckiger, Eduard Buess, James Leitch, J. A. van Wyk, John Thompson, James M. Robinson, Friedrich Herzog, Eberhard Hübner, Guido Schmidt, Max Geiger and Heinrich Ott. But he never forgot that the future task of the theological student was usually work in the pastorate – indeed his instruction was primarily oriented in that direction. Furthermore, he also wanted this practical task to be the presupposition of those who aimed to be theological scholars and teachers. He thought that people would notice 'at every turn' if these would-be teachers had never made 'the "kerygma", to which there was so much appeal, their own responsibility, if they had never presented it in its canonical Old and New Testament form, with humility and patience, with delight and love, in preaching, instruction and pastoral work, serving a real community, instead of always just thinking *about* it and talking *about* it . . . That produces those academic theologians who are sometimes interesting but in the last resort always sterile because they have dissected the matter for so long and have lost their sense of proportion. All they can do is regard their standpoint as an absolute one and disport themselves arrogantly, proudly and vainly. They keep saying that what is important is unimportant and what is unimportant is important; they keep putting forward their own more or less arbitrary assertions in lectures and sermons – and are really in earnest only when there is yet another dispute in the faculty politics of which they are so fond.'[80]

'The Christian Community in the Midst of Political Change'

Although Barth did not go to Germany again for the summer semester of 1948, he did undertake another trip before the beginning of the semester: his second visit to Hungary. He prepared his material while staying on the Rigi, and then set off by air at the end of March. 'My colleague Charlotte von Kirschbaum and I were invited to make this journey by the Hungarian Reformed Church. My task was to give lectures to pastors, professors, church elders, students and other church and public groups in six towns . . . In Debrecen I preached on Good Friday in the "Great Church", which had just been restored after sustaining heavy bomb damage – on the "meek", who will "inherit the earth"! – and in Budapest I tried to answer questions (some of them uncannily specific questions!) in public for a whole morning. I met once again, or in some cases for the first time, most of the leading personalities in church and theological circles and I was able to have more or less thorough talks with them. President Tildy also received me in an open and friendly way. The Swiss Ambassador, Dr Feisst, reminded us of our own country in a most charming fashion. A Hungarian pastor (his name was Bodoky), whose mother was born in Basle, acted as my interpreter and kept faithfully by my side.'[81] The first of the lectures given there (in Sarospatak and Budapest) was entitled 'Modern Youth: Its Inheritance and its Responsibility'. 'In it I unleashed a storm of applause, quite unintentionally but very clear for all that, with a quotation from Kant: "Have the courage to use your own intelligence".' In the lecture Barth also said: 'The usual complaint of the old about the young might well be reversed today, and you might ask us what we really feel about not being able to bequeath you anything better; how we feel about having to send you on your journey from such unworthy beginnings.' The second lecture (which was given in Miskolc, Debrecen, Budapest, Papa and Sopron – and later also in Burgdorf and Vaumarcus in Switzerland) was about 'The Real Church'. In it the church was compared with the 'edifying spectacle that I cannot admire enough here in Hungary – how in a gipsy band every individual player has his ears and eyes glued on the leading fiddler, concentrating absolutely on the leader's improvisations, and hence playing inevitably and happily with all the others.' In the third lecture (given in Sarospatak and Budapest), 'The Christian Community in the midst of Political Change', Barth reflected the arguments of 'The Christian Community and the Civil Community', especially in connection with the fact that in the 'civil community' the 'political order' changes.

He pointed out that on each occasion such a change could be a dangerous temptation for the 'Christian community' *either* to set itself up in opposition to the new order in principle, by keeping to the old, *or* by identifying itself with the new in an equally partisan fashion. *Or* it could retreat into a false neutrality on an apolitical 'inner' line. On the other hand, 'the church best performs its service in the midst of political change when its attitude is so independent and . . . so sympathetic that it is able to summon the representatives of the old and new order alike . . . to humility, to the praise of God and to humanity, and can invite them all to trust in the great change (in the death and resurrection of Christ) and to hope in his revelation.'[82]

At precisely this point Barth thought that he was in agreement with his friends there, who were now under a communist régime. He found something which impressed him far more than the corresponding Christianity of West Germany: 'a church which is concerned to tread a cautious path between opposition to the new state and collaboration with it – which has clearly come to terms with the question of guilt – and which for the rest is concerned with evangelization and building up the community.'[83] 'And after I had listened carefully to everything, my comment was that I thought they were right.'[84] 'I might add that from a conversation which I had with some Czech friends (Hromádka, Souček, etc.) on the way home at Prague airport, I gathered that the problems are very similar there.' As early as May – after a visit from the pastor Janos Peter – Barth felt compelled to write to his friends in Hungary saying in an open letter that they now seemed 'to be going too far in the direction of compromise with the new order'.[85] He often repeated similar warnings over the subsequent period – in a conversation with Bishop Ravasz, and in letters to Bishop Bereczky and Janos Peter – though without making them known in the West. He did not want to add grist to the mill of anti-communism, which was busy enough as it was.

For this reason, however, he was soon overwhelmed by a real 'shower of rotten eggs and dead cats' from the Swiss press.[86] Emil Brunner, who 'in this matter doubtless had the Swiss temperament on his side',[87] publicly asked Barth why he did not 'issue a call to oppose communism and make a Christian confession' as he had done against National Socialism.[88] In his answer, made under the

title *Theologische Existenz 'heute'* (Theological Existence 'Today'),
Barth deliberately 'trained his sights on the unspiritual and cheap
appeal to principles';[89] the church of Christ never passed judgment
'on principle', but by individual cases, 'making a new evaluation of
each new event'.[90] One difference between the former period and the
present was that to 'deify' Bolshevism was hardly a serious temptation in the West, though this kind of possibility had been very much
the case during the time of the Nazi danger. But the church could not
simply 'repeat what any citizen could in any case read in his daily
paper'.[91] In essentials Barth's view was that, 'I am against all fear of
communism. A nation which has a good conscience, whose social
and democratic life is in order, need have no fear of it. Much less the
church, which is sure of the gospel of Jesus Christ.'[92] Barth also
discussed the question in July with students in a Belgian-German
camp at Schloss Rotberg.

Barth deliberately adopted a restrained tone in his answer to
Brunner, so as not to injure him again – as he had done in 1934 with
his abrupt *No!* And when he saw him at the beginning of October at a
meeting of the German-Swiss faculties, 'I was so nice to Emil Brunner, to the amazement of all . . . that people might have thought that
the millennium was . . . just round the corner, though the presence of
Martin Werner was enough to shatter this illusion.'[93] All the same,
in the following period there was no end to the 'popular excitement
. . . here in Switzerland' over the East-West conflict, which had been
expressed particularly after Barth's attitude towards 'Hungary' had
been made known. 'I finally had to make up my mind to demonstrate
once and for all my basic position in the matter, so I accepted an
invitation from the cathedral council in Berne and opened fire with
all guns, first on 6 February (1949) in the city church at Thun and
then . . . in the cathedral at Berne', on the subject that had been
assigned to him: 'The Church between East and West'.[94]

This lecture – which was also repeated in April in Geneva –
contained a fundamental account of Barth's view of the way in which
the church should behave in the present East-West conflict. And it
fuelled for months on end the polemical attacks from a large sector
of the Swiss press in the debate over 'Hungary' directed against
Barth and the 'Barthians' generally, and especially against Albert
Schädelin, Walter Lüthi (who had meanwhile moved to Berne) and
Alfred Fankhauser, the director of the seminary. The trial of Cardinal Mindszenty for high treason, which took place that same Feb-

ruary, heated up the polemic still further. Barth had in fact issued a warning right at the beginning of his lecture that 'those who are very passionately interested in the East-West question but little or not at all in the church' would take offence at his argument.

This argument was that the formation of an Eastern bloc and a Western bloc was based on a conflict of power and ideology and that the church had no occasion to take sides in it, either with the East and its 'totalitarian abominations' or with the West, as long as it gave the East grounds for just criticism. But today 'the way of the community of Jesus Christ in the present' has to be 'another, third way of its own', in great freedom.[95] It was doubtless characteristic of the hysteria of the time that the polemic against Barth which ensued overlooked this particular argument and limited itself rather to basing its charge that Barth was pro-Russian on the differentiation between National Socialism and Communism which was expressed more in a subordinate argument. His slogan 'Don't be afraid', which was now repeated again and again over the East-West question, provided the title for a collection of his sermons from the years 1934–1948, which were edited by Ernst Wolf in 1949.

The Assembly of the World Council of Churches in Amsterdam

During the months in which Barth was thus preoccupied with the East-West question – as a result of his journey to Hungary – another problem gave him a good deal more to think about and to do: this was the task of participating in the ecumenical encounter of the churches. His involvement in this arose from an invitation to take part in the First Assembly of the World Council of Churches in Amsterdam, and especially to give an opening speech on the main theme (which involved commenting on the four preparatory volumes). When this request was passed on to him in January 1948, he said no to begin with. At that time Hromádka urged him on: 'There are shoulders which can and must bear great burdens.'[96] 'Formerly I took no part, or only a small part, in the "ecumenical movement"; indeed, I had all kinds of criticisms to make of it, since I have always been suspicious of all movements as such. But in this case I must confess . . . my mind has changed.' It transpired 'that on closer acquaintance I could not but find this co-operation and co-responsibility both interesting and important'.[97] At the end of the summer semester of 1948 (at a time when he was also disturbed by the death of his brother-in-law Karl Lindt), Barth retired to the parsonage in Bubendorf to prepare for his address.

After a four-day preliminary conference of the four sub-commissions in Woudschoten, in which he took part, he gave his address in Amsterdam on the appointed theme: 'Man's Disorder and God's Design'.

'My lecture took the line that the theme should be stood on its head: that we should speak first of God's design and only then of man's disorder.'[98] Otherwise – Barth thought – there was a serious danger that Christianity might come to grief not only in its human descriptions and assessments of earthly needs, but finally also in its human plans and measures for fighting against these needs and overcoming them. So in his view it was necessary now to express again 'very definitely the Lutheran components of the gospel . . . over against this world-wide Christianity' and 'for good measure to quote Isaiah 8.10'. He criticized the preparatory studies above all for the view which could be found in all of them that 'as Christian men and as church people we ought to achieve what God alone can accomplish and what he will accomplish completely by himself. . . We shall not be the ones who change this wicked world into a good one. God has not abdicated his lordship over us . . . All that is required of us is that in the midst of the political and social disorder of the world we should be his witnesses. We shall have our hands full simply in being that.' He also criticized the preparatory studies in detail because they talked about 'Man's Disorder and God's Design' . . . 'and yet could say nothing in the four volumes about the return of Christ, God's providence and the Holy Spirit on the one hand . . . and property, capital, interest and so on on the other'.[99]

Otherwise Barth's official activity in Amsterdam amounted to giving an opening address at a special meeting of the Reformed Church and spending every afternoon as chairman of a committee on 'The Life and Work of Women in the Church'; though he did not succeed in convincing the 'Christian women' that 'besides writing Galatians 3.28 (which was about the one thing that they joyfully affirmed), Paul also said several other things on the relation between men and women which were important and right'. Finally he was involved in Section 1 ('The Universal Church in God's Design') which met in a gymnasium under the direction of Bishop Lilje. 'The discovery which I made as an actively involved member . . . of Section 1 was that theology as a whole must include some sort of "ecumenical theology", as well as "dogmatic theology" and "symbolic theology". "Ecumenical theology" is the art of encounter between the competent theologians of the various churches in the form of showing the disagreements within the agreement and the agreements within the disagreement and thus coming one step nearer, if not uniting . . . This was the art which I practised there especially in collaboration with Georges Florovsky, the Anglican Michael Ramsey (I was pleased by a remark of a third party on the relations between Ramsey and myself: "If things have gone so far, the millennium must be round the corner") and the Lutheran Anders Nygren.' 'I spoke my conference English come what might, even publicly at a press conference, and of course in all the section discussions.'

Barth also had numerous meetings on the fringe of the conference – for example with 'the Swedish archbishop Erling Eidem, who not only walked arm-in-arm with me half round Amsterdam but on the last day virtually put his arms round me and kissed me' – 'teasingly before the eyes of the zealous German Lutheran Edmund Schlink' – or with the 'colourfully garbed bishop of the Mar Thoma church in India, whose heart I was able to delight with the well-known better exegesis of John 20 (in favour of the apostle Thomas)'[100] – or with Georg Merz, who cheered Barth up with his remark: 'Ah, let me make my confession.'[101] He was one of thirty prominent figures invited to attend the coronation of Queen Juliana, along with Miskotte and Bishop Lilje. On this occasion he made the acquaintance of John Foster Dulles, in the 'inner court of the royal palace – I remember that Prince Bernhard was somewhere near': Dulles' look was 'cold and inattentive' and in other respects 'I did not like him at all'.[102] The food at court was 'just as a child would imagine it to be in a fairy tale'. A representative of Indonesia had also been invited there but was uncertain whether he should accept (because of the war with Holland). Barth was called in by the Indonesian delegation as an 'arbitrator'. 'I decided that a very good republican and a good Christian could well accept the invitation, but promised to accompany the little man into the presence of Their Royal Highnesses. I told him to bow no lower than I did.' 'In short, there was always something on from morning to evening, which I used to bring to an end with Pierre Maury over a small Bols in the hotel bar.'[103]

All in all, Barth regarded Amsterdam as 'a significant and pleasant affair. I was impressed and delighted: 1. By the phenomenon of the "young" churches. I spent one evening with a man from India (Devadutt) and another with a man from Ceylon (Niles), and realized that a general cessation of the "driving downpour" of the Word of God here in Europe would only mean that for a while it had moved somewhere else . . . 2. By the fact that although Christendom is deeply divided, unlike the UNO it has still achieved a remarkable unity. 3. By the relative independence of the negotiations and resolutions in comparison with what had been expected from this Amsterdam . . . 4. By the remarkable shift . . . of emphasis in favour of an approach from "above" downwards . . . in comparison with the preparatory studies and the Amsterdam negotiations. 5. By the result that the World Council has certainly not turned into a Western spiritual bloc.'[104]

Amsterdam involved some work afterwards. In October, Barth, Alphons Koechlin and Ernst Staehelin gave a report on 'Impressions of Amsterdam'. A correspondence developed with the Catholic Jean Daniélou, who had been offended by Barth's remarks about the failure of Rome to take part in the conference – and another correspondence with the American Reinhold Niebuhr, who accused Barth of quietism, though in such an inappropriate way that Barth thought 'that some day it may be necessary to air again the differences between American and our Continental ways of Christian thinking and speaking – differences that might be more important, and more fraught with danger, than the differences between the churches'.[105] Barth missed 'a third dimension' in the contrasts between good and evil, and so on in the thought of the 'Americans': the Word of God, the Holy Spirit, God's grace and judgment, etc. – 'all this not as principles but as designations of events'. The following March he attempted to demonstrate in a lecture in Wipkingen, Zürich, the significance of the ecumenical movement for the Swiss situation and especially for its future developments ('The Ecumenical Task in the Reformed Churches of Switzerland'). On this occasion a 'Swiss Church and Theological Working Party' was founded (with Gottlob Wieser as president, though it never really got off the ground). This took up the theological work of the 'Society for Aid for the Confessing Church', the welfare work of which was taken over completely by 'Swiss Evangelical Church Aid' (HEKS). Finally, in July Barth gave a report in Basle on the work of Section 1 ('The Scandal of the Disunited Church'). As a result of his involvement in 'Amsterdam' he now often had ecumenical visitors at home – this summer the Indian Sundar Rao, and Bishop Kulandra and S. Selvaretnam from Ceylon.

Barth had received all kinds of invitations to foreign travel at the Amsterdam Assembly. But he was still not interested in travelling to the USA and did not want to go to Germany again for the moment. One trip which attracted him more was to India and Ceylon, but this was abandoned through ill-health, as was a lecture tour of Sweden, Finland, Norway and Denmark which was planned for February and March 1949. He did, however, travel abroad to France, in September 1948, immediately after he had vainly attempted a reconciliation with Bultmann in Basle over the critical passage in *Church Dogmatics* III, 2. He addressed 'a conference of former members of the Student Christian Movement in Bièvres, near Paris, in the summer residence of the veterinary surgeon(!) of Louis XIV',[106] giving three lectures on 'The Reality of the New Man' (based on *Church Dogmatics* III, 2). This was 'in the course of one of those discussions which only come alive so splendidly in France'.[107] 'On this occasion I revisited Napoleon's tomb, Notre Dame and the Louvre, and saw for the first time the melancholy ruins of Port Royal aux Champs; finally I even reached the summit of the Eiffel Tower.'[108] In addition, 'I took a childish delight in looking at myself in the distorting mirrors in the Musée Grévin in Paris.'[109] And in Versailles 'we thought of Marie Antoinette and asked ourselves how all human greatness and guilt and misery could make sense and at the end of time appear as a unity, moving to its consummation.'[110]

Teaching and research 1949–1951

The summer months of 1948 had meant a great deal of work for Barth and he had had no holiday when the winter semester began, so he understandably felt tired. Yet he had to embark on new work immediately. To prepare for his lectures (on God's providence), he paid regular visits to the Basle zoo, 'to have a close look at all the animals again before I go on to speak of creation and providence'.[111] In his seminar and discussion group he dealt with the First Vatican Council and Schleiermacher – 'as winged monsters on the left and right of the *Church Dogmatics*'.[112] During his discussion of the Council he was constantly amazed and scandalized 'that the people in the Vatican in practice no longer know what to do with the abundance of spiritual power which was once promised to them. Their rule is really just as secular as that of any church council of a Swiss canton.'[113]

In Amsterdam Barth had made no bones about his disappointment over the failure of Rome to join in the ecumenical movement.

During the next months, however, he was surprised by a new and hopeful possibility of conversation with Catholicism which opened up so to speak at his very door, in Basle itself. In the winter of 1948–49 Hans Urs von Balthasar gave ten much-discussed lectures on 'Karl Barth and Catholicism', resulting later in his book *Karl Barth*, published in 1951, which attracted even more attention.[114] When possible, Barth went to the lectures – 'to learn more about myself'. Afterwards 'there were post-mortems with a very small group including Balthasar at the Charon'[115] (the Charon was a tavern near the Spalentor in Basle which Barth liked very much and which he often visited with his guests and students). 'The following conversation once took place there. Balthasar: "When I get to heaven, I shall go up to Mary, clap her on the shoulders and say, 'Well done, sister!'" Lollo: "And she will reply, 'Brother, you've got me wrong'."' On another occasion, when they had all been letting their hair down, 'Balthasar afterwards reflected quite placidly: "That's all right, at last we're quite alone and one can say what one thinks." On hell, he remarked (first, of course, in the Charon): "The dogma is that hell exists, not that people are in it."' At any rate, on these evenings Barth discovered to his amazement a Catholic theologian who 'envisaged a kind of reformation of the Catholic church and of Catholic theology from within. And now I was to be introduced like a new Trojan horse to bring it about (against Thomas and also against Augustine!).'[116]

During the winter the two of them went on one occasion to Einsiedeln (taking along Adrienne Kaegi-von Speyr, a friend of von Balthasar) where 'we listened to records of Mozart for almost twenty-four hours. We also had the opportunity of gazing in wonder at our remarkable friend celebrating mass in vestments in the Chapel of Grace.'[117] Stirred up by his revived and deepened friendship with von Balthasar, Barth's love of Mozart took on a new turn. Shortly after this expedition, 'I even let myself be carried away and devoted a special excursus to Mozart' – in the section in *Church Dogmatics* III, 3, on 'Nothingness'.[118] Barth now also bought himself a gramophone, which 'virtually became a centrepiece' at home,[119] and 'a large number of Mozart records, which can often be heard in my study. Following a tendency which I had even as a small boy, I have now concentrated completely on Mozart and have established that in relation to him Bach is merely John the Baptist and Beethoven Origen, if not the Shepherd of Hermas.'[120] Barth's objection to

Johann Sebastian Bach, otherwise so loved by theologians, was his all too deliberate, all too artificial 'desire to preach', while Mozart attracted him because he was free from such intentions and simply played.[121] So now there rang out 'over everything *The Magic Flute*, the symphonies, the concertos and the *Requiem* of that incomparable composer'.[122] 'Curiously, the ever-growing collection of records in my library is kept immediately below the Weimar edition of Luther.'[123] At this time Barth developed the 'splendid habit' of having one of these records resounding through the house 'almost every morning, as soon as I had had my shower upstairs'. This was 'a sign that a new day in the time allotted to me had begun'.[124]

After the end of the winter semester Barth went with Arthur Frey to Locarno to recover from his constant weariness, which had been heightened by a persistent attack of influenza and a minor operation. He thought that the reason for his miserable condition was that 'probably the "nothingness"' about which he was writing in his *Dogmatics* at the time 'was striving to keep itself dark'.[125] But he hoped that once again he would be allowed 'to rise on wings like an eagle or at least like a contented old sparrow'.[126] Over the following period his wife took her youngest son to spend several months with her sister in Portugal. And during this spring holiday Lollo von Kirschbaum stayed in Bièvres to give four lectures on a 'Protestant Doctrine of Woman' ('The Real Woman'), the significance of which she thought went beyond the Catholic view of Mary on the one hand and the existentialist interpretation of Simone de Beauvoir on the other. She had long been deeply concerned with this complex of themes. Some of her researches and insights had already found their way quietly into *Church Dogmatics* III, 2, and other parts appeared later in further lectures: in the spring of 1950 in Geneva on Simone de Beauvoir and at the beginning of 1951 in Basle on 'Woman's Service in the Proclamation of the Word'. Barth gave her 'ten rules for a speaker' to help her in her lectures. His advice was: 'Keep to the subject-matter you are dealing with and remember the audience you want to reach! Discourse is born on the way from one place to the other!' – and finally: 'Don't be afraid. Forget yourself and remember that all will certainly be well.' When the next volume of his *Dogmatics* appeared, he recalled in the Preface the 'twenty years' work' which his faithful colleague 'has quietly accomplished at my side. She has devoted no less of her life and strength to the growth of this than I have myself . . . I know what it really means to have a helper.'[127]

He completed *Church Dogmatics* III, 3 in the summer of 1949 (having begun it in the summer of the previous year). However, it only went to the publisher in the summer of 1950, since he recognized that because of its length he could not fit the ethics of creation into this volume, as he had planned.

'The three great themes of this volume – God's fatherly providence, his kingdom on the left hand and the ministry of angels – do not fall quite so readily under the one title "The Creator and his Creature" as the subdivisions of the earlier volumes. But the stricter formal systematization which attracted the admiration of some and the mistrust of others was not of vital concern to me. If I had and have any such concern, it is to hold fast at all costs and at every point to the christological thread, i.e. to what I have recently been accused of under the label and catchword "Christomonism". It is my one concern to cling to this in these spheres too. And my question to those who are dissatisfied is whether with a good conscience and cheerful heart Christian theology can do anything but finally and seriously remember "Christ alone" at each and every point.'[128]

This 'Christocentric perspective' had allowed Barth, the opponent of all 'natural theology', to write such a third volume on creation.

'In the doctrine of providence, which I would like to be seen as the real substance of this volume, I have found it possible to keep far more closely to the scheme of the older orthodox dogmatics *(conservatio, concursus, gubernatio)* than I anticipated. The radical correction which I have also undertaken will not be overlooked.' This correction consisted in the most consistent stress possible on the insight that faith in providence is (never an immediately accessible truth but) in the strict sense *faith* and indeed faith in *God* himself (and not a world-view or a philosophy of history), faith (not in some 'higher power' but) in the God of the *covenant* and the *gospel*. Therefore the action of divine providence was understood as 'God's faithfulness' in which 'he subordinates the creaturely event under his Lordship to the event of the covenant, grace and salvation and makes it serve these'. The next paragraphs were concerned with the problem of the relation of God's providence to *evil*, which Barth described as 'nothingness' – not as something which was not there (for it is in fact so real that it virtually overwhelms a man as soon as he thinks that he can resist it) but as 'really nothingness' (because it has been conquered in Jesus Christ). 'As far as possible I would like to avoid mentioning God and the devil in the same breath.'[129] This was Barth's chief concern. It was made clear in some excursuses which dealt at length with 'Leibniz's theodicy, Schleiermacher's doctrine of sin and finally with nothingness in the existentialists Heidegger and Sartre, always concluding that while they certainly had some inkling, in essence they knew nothing of nothingness.'[130] According to Barth, strictly speaking evil can be recognized as nothingness and nothingness as evil only in the one who has overcome it, Jesus Christ. Outside him it can only be misunderstood.

In the closing part of the book, which was written at the very time when the storm of the 'demythologizing controversy' was beginning to break, Barth turned with special delight to angelology. In it he declared the angels to be 'the pure witnesses to God'. In depicting modernist angelology, which he called 'angelology with a shrug of the shoulders', he had almost a carnival night in his class. 'And when I said that these theologians did not allow the angels an entry permit, let alone a permanent visa, the room was filled with shouts of laughter.'[131] When in this connection he was preparing material for the doctrine of heaven, he once went 'very cheerfully' into Lollo's room, saying: 'Heaven is really a very interesting place.'[132] On the other hand he mentioned 'the demons' in this context with obvious distaste and only 'very briefly and crossly'. 'I love angels, but have no taste for demons, not out of any desire for demythologizing but because they are not worth it.'[133] Here Barth dissociated himself from a trend in post-war theology (e.g. in Asmussen) in which demonology played an important role.

In the summer vacation of 1949 he considered for a time whether it might not be the time and place to give a critical lecture on 'Barmen or the Augsburg Confession'. In it he would have liked to have spoken to a German audience about the German church situation, which was causing him growing concern. He saw that the Lutherans there were attaching ever increasing importance to the Augsburg Confession. He had been becoming more and more suspicious of this confession during the summer semester in his seminar (parallel to this he was studying Wolleb's *Ethics* in his discussion group). It now seemed to him to be a 'deficient product . . . It really needs a wooden forehead and a brain to match to want to convince oneself and others that this is the rock on which today's church has to be built.'[134] But the lecture in which this was to be said was never given. Still, Barth confided these thoughts and hestitations to Ernst Wolf and Georg Merz during a holiday at the Bergli. He found that Wolf understood, but not Merz. 'I have never shaken my head so vigorously over him, and I have never liked him so much as during the days that we spent with him there. For me he is one of the most impressive examples of the way in which friendship between people means being attracted by them, attacking them with all one's power, not being surprised that in the last resort they cannot be changed, and nevertheless still allowing oneself to be involved with them.'[135]

In December Barth repeated his serious hesitations about the German Lutherans in a letter to the American Sylvester Michelfelder of the World Council of Churches, who was working in the central office (to his regret they were made public and caused some offence). He expressed his suspicions of their 'persistent confessional romanticism, their stubborn association with political reaction, their obscure ritual romanticizing, their feeble attitude at the time of the church struggle and more recently their sabotage of the unity of the Evangelical Church of Germany by splitting and forming the National Evangelical Lutheran Church of Germany'. The only people he excluded from these suspicions were some 'individuals like Iwand, Ernst Wolf and Heinrich Vogel'.[136]

However, during the summer holidays of 1949 he did write another lecture which was to be given on an unusual occasion. At the end of August Barth went to the 'Recontres Internationales de Genève', where he spent ten days in public discussions on the theme 'Pour un nouvel humanisme'. Along with the French Dominican A. J. Maydieu, he represented 'Christianity . . . among all kinds of intellectual children of this world'.[137] He himself contributed a lecture on 'The Actuality of the Christian Message' to this meeting. 'The philosophers and historians, orientalists and scientists, theologians and Marxists from all over Europe who were gathered there, not only before the same public but also really round the same table – each coming from his own particular place – spoke together openly and clearly, but also with commitment and at least sometimes with a degree of humour.' In the discussions Barth got on particularly well with Maydieu, who had already been a good and valued Catholic friend for a number of years. 'My Catholic neighbour and I were strikingly agreed that we should not put forward a "Christian humanism" to counter the ideas advanced by the other participants.'

'"Christian Humanism" is flawed steel . . . The central concern of the gospel is also with *man*. But what the gospel says *about* man, *for* man (even *against* man) and *to* man begins where the various humanisms cease . . . In the light of the gospel one can understand all these humanisms, affirm them to some extent and allow their validity . . . But in the end one must also counter all humanisms in the light of the gospel . . . ' 'At the same time they all smack a little of godlessness and idolatry. In Geneva, taking up the theme of the conference but also deliberately twisting its historical and abstract sense, I myself spoke of the "Humanism of *God*". By that I did not mean any humanity contrived and brought about by man, but God's delight in man as the source and the norm of all human rights and all human status.'[138]

'The result' of the conference can be summed up like this. In their search for a new humanism the old humanists felt that they were being squeezed between Christianity and Communism ("as between two plates in a denture", one of them actually said). However, they thought that they had been shown an escape, especially by the relativistic wisdom of the great Jaspers. So in the end we could go with a quiet mind by steamer to the Château de Coppet, where we thought about it all over a rich buffet presided over by the shades of Madame de Staël . . . An extra delight at these high jinks was the chance to see Pierre Maury regularly. The climax of our reunion was a visit to the Knie circus where the sea-lions . . . with their astonishing skill and their revolutionary anger, which broke out suddenly at times . . . again filled my cup of joy to overflowing.'[139]

After the Geneva congress Barth had a few days holiday by the Gerzensee, where once again he met General Guisan. He walked 'arm in arm' with him through the park – in mutual sympathy, 'since he too was now in high disfavour with the Federal Council' (because of his report on Swiss policy during the war).[140] Back again in Basle, Barth was visited by the Roman Catholic theologian Romano Guardini ('but I did not even begin to make contact with him, because he kept to aesthetics and world-views') and then by the American scholar Paul Minear ('there was complete agreement between the two of us over the most important things').[141] The following winter Barth began to lecture on the next volume of his dogmatics, specifically on ethics. In the discussion group he studied the Gallican Confession and the Belgic Confession, and in the seminar the doctrine of justification at the Council of Trent. Some of the most striking work done by his students this time came from Wolfhart Pannenberg. The same semester Barth also had 'to give a seminar on Calvin's *Institutes* I, 1–9, in Zürich, because Emil Brunner was in the Far East: presumably to win over the Japanese and the Indians to a "point of contact", while I sought to convince his students gently and without reference to him that Calvin at any rate had refrained from such arts.'[142] 'Beforehand and afterwards I regularly had a good meeting with Arthur Frey, and sometimes also with Adolf Keller . . . or Walter Gut.'[143] At one such meeting Barth came to know the Zürich psychiatrist Dr Hans Huber, who was 'fond of drink and literature'. He 'gave himself out to be an agnostic', but had a 'kind of wild interest' in theology, particularly in that of Barth, and now became very friendly with him over the next period.[144] At Huber's home in January 1950, Barth in turn got to know Emil Staiger, the professor of literature: 'I heard a good deal of bad Goethe theology, but tended to excuse him because he presented strict, pure and true doctrine in the case of Wolfgang Amadeus.'[145]

Barth's extra-mural lectures during this winter consisted for the most part in free elaborations of what he had already said in his dogmatics lectures. In the autumn he answered questions on *Church Dogmatics* III, 2 in the teachers' seminary at Muristalden and spoke in the Birsfelden Men's Association on 'Christianity has Failed'. In January he reported on the Geneva humanist congress in Zürich and Strasbourg. Strasbourg in particular 'gave me a quite brilliant reception; what with the authorities, the university, the military (!), the Catholic and Protestant churches, women in hats. I improvised speeches in French, gave two interviews on Radio Strasbourg, had a discussion with students (on political science and theology) and delivered a lecture with translations . . . all in twenty-four hours.'[146] In February Barth spoke in the Berne Zofingia, giving twelve theses on 'The Church as a Factor in Political Education'. And in March he had discussions with pastors from the Zofingen district and from Montbéliard, and with a group of 'Friends of Emil Brunner' in Zürich.

A talk given the previous December on Swiss radio on 'The Jewish Question and its Christian Answer', which was a simplified version of a passage from *Church Dogmatics* III, 3, aroused considerable attention. Barth argued that neither the special character of the Jews nor antisemitism could be evaded by means of a general concept of tolerance; moreover, what separated Jews and Christians in fact held them together, namely 'the Jew on the cross on Golgotha'. This 'caused some muttering among the Jews themselves and especially among the antisemites (who are in full splendour here in Switzerland, too)'.[147] In January and again in March 1950 it resulted in a 'religious conversation' with a group of young Jews in Basle ('Emuna'), 'to which of course all kinds of other Israelites came. I have never felt myself so much on Jordan's bank as in that closely-packed hotel room.' Barth felt that here he could 'only confirm' to his Jewish conversation partners 'that the messiah has already come, the law has already been fulfilled, morality is only an act of gratitude, and so on'.[148] The difficulty of conversation with Judaism on this point was again evident to Barth the following winter from a lecture by Martin Buber, in which 'half the Old Testament' – i.e. only 'Yahweh in the thunder-cloud of his wrath (or his hiddenness)' – 'was described very impressively'.[149]

In the spring holidays of 1950, Markus Barth took his father by car to Lake Thun for a theological conversation with two Old Catholic scholars, Arnold Gilg and Ernst Gaugler, of whom he thought a good deal. Barth had already come to know Arnold Gilg (1887–1967) when he was pastor at Safenwil and since then, 'over all the years of our acquaintance, looked to him with pleasure as a figure who was most reliable and promising in every respect in the face of the widespread confusion in theological research and teaching'. It was on this visit that 'I heard him give detailed information to an avid scholar on an intricate problem in Tertullian – liberally quoting names and page numbers of specialist journals which I had never read, and all off the cuff . . . as though anyone could do that!'[150] Shortly afterwards Barth spent a week, again with Markus, going 'through Burgundy to the Loire and along it . . . to the Atlantic ocean . . . We saw everything thoroughly: valleys, hills and plains, cathedrals and especially châteaux . . . and enjoyed the excellent food and drink which this country offers, eating crabs large and small, oysters and snails. Not the least of our pleasures was the free and open way in which the people live.'[151] Our topic of conversation during the journey was the explosive content of a new book which Markus was just writing. Originally he had rejected his father's criticism of infant baptism, but in the meantime he had come over to it and not only stopped having his children baptized but rejected the whole sacramental understanding of baptism (this was what his book was about). In the summer semester Barth's seminar studied Calvin's eschatology and his discussion group was on Mariology. Because he felt in great need of a rest, afterwards Barth went to the Bergli and spent 'the quietest and pleasantest holidays in living memory'. During them, in the morning he read aloud something from the 'ethics' which he was in process of writing, and in the evening passages from Gotthelf's works – between whiles he went walking or played table rugby and once went on an expedition to visit a cattle market. Nevertheless, even now many visitors found their way up there 'like a procession of ants': the Dutchmen Berkhof and Miskotte, the Hungarians Bereczky and Peter and 'the really delightful Professor Paul Lehmann from Princeton' to whom Barth gave a promise that he would visit the USA in 1952 (though he was unable to keep it).[152] Finally he went for several days with Arthur Frey to Gyrenbad in the Turbenthal – a favourite holiday place from then on.

1950 was also the year which Rome had pronounced a 'Holy Year'. It was obvious that this would arouse Barth's interest and attention. He had already prepared himself for it by his seminar in the winter of 1949–50. 'The Doctrine of Justification of the Council of Trent' seemed to him a 'bad, bad story', in the light of which one could only ask 'whether the *Una Sancta* will ever be able to take shape this side of the Second Coming'.[153] The question was to become considerably more pressing for Barth during the 'Holy Year.' Again with this festal year in mind his discussion group investigated Catholic Mariology in the summer and the encyclical *Mystici corporis* the following winter. In August a new papal encyclical, *Humani generis*, appeared. Barth studied it straight away and talked it over with von Balthasar, with much shaking of the head. He thought that this 'has almost, if not completely, extinguished the light of life for all my Catholic friends'.[154] Here he had in mind 'a whole chorus of German and especially French friends' who, like Balthasar, 'in different ways and with different emphases all seem to want to look in a new way towards the centre, the "author and perfecter of our faith" . . . who alone can make possible theology itself or any attempt at ecumenical understanding'.[155] Balthasar apart, for some time these friends had included the Belgian Dominican Jérôme Hâmer. Barth had been getting on better with Hâmer than when he was a doctoral student (doing work on Barth!); indeed he expected that Hâmer might be a new 'Alyosha'.[156] However, this expectation was later disappointed when Hâmer again seemed to Barth to be all too Thomistic and orthodox. A new addition to the circle was the wise French Jesuit Henri Bouillard, who wanted to do his doctorate on Barth, and not least the cheerful Gascon A. J. Maydieu, with whom Barth had had repeated meetings since Geneva. Maydieu refreshed him with his carefree answer to the question, 'Don't you think that Papal encyclicals should be taken more seriously in future, since this is expressly required in *Humani generis*?' 'Oh, that was only said in an encyclical and so it wasn't infallible.' On another occasion the two were talking again on the 'sorry theme' of papal infallibility. 'And when we had completely exhausted the subject, he said to me in a very friendly way, "Ne parlons plus du Pape, parlons de Jésus

Christ!" I replied, "In that case we are agreed." '157

Barth was also stirred by the announcement that on 1 November the Assumption of Mary would become a dogma by the pronouncement of Pius XII. It even made him want to join in the solemnities, 'to be there for once when somebody makes an infallible statement'. Moreover, 'I have always been particularly interested in Mariology because I have felt that it must be seen as the methodological principle of the whole of Roman Catholicism.' So Barth justified his wish to his Waldensian friend and former Bonn pupil Valdo Vinay.158 But in the end he could not take up the place in St Peter's which had been already reserved for him. It was obvious that he thought both the encyclical and the dogma to be questionable. 'The decisions made in 1950 have closed several doors, and in view of that we must keep our distance to begin with.'159 Still, 1951 saw the publication of 'the well-known book which Hans Urs von Balthasar has devoted to me, in which I find an incomparably more powerful understanding of the purpose of the concentration on Jesus Christ and the Christian understanding of reality thus implied in the *Church Dogmatics* than in most of the rest of the volumes in the small library which has now gathered itself around me'.160 However, as well as approving of Barth's christocentric approach, von Balthasar complained that there was a 'christological narrowness'. As a result Barth became somewhat restrained even towards him.

Before the winter semester of 1950–51 he began a new seminar course in Neuchâtel, on Calvin's *Institutes,* Book III, which continued despite lengthy interruptions. During this semester Schleiermacher was analysed again in the seminar (on the basis of his *The Christian Faith*): 'I built him up so much that in the end people even began to wonder whether he might not be right: a view which of course I shattered in the last session.'161 Barth had adopted a strict principle for discussion, which was continued in the summer: 'It is important that in the theological school of Basle, which is now oriented in such a different way, Schleiermacher should be studied not only with the same thoroughness and love as at any other place of education, but with even greater dedication.'162

Barth now sought more than ever to avoid all other duties than his usual teaching pattern. Once again (during 1951) he refused to become Rector of Basle. And he also excused himself from an invitation to Athens to celebrate the 1900th anniversary of the arrival of Paul in Europe. 'I think that they wanted to put me on the

Areopagus, to have me in the same place.'[163] If he did agree to something from then on, he preferred not to be a speaker but to join in discussions and to answer questions. He did this in December with ecumenists from Bossey and (in Schwamendingen) with pastors from Zürich. As the latter seemed to him to be rather 'buttoned up', he bade farewell to them with the song 'Do not tremble, do not fuss, the cottage won't fall down'.[164] In the spring he had a similar meeting with pastors from the Aargau.

In March he at last appeared again in Germany, not to lecture, but merely to join in conversations and to listen. Apart from a detour the previous autumn into Baden for a conversation with students, this was the first time that he had been there for four years. He took part in a theological conference of about seventy of his German friends in the Preachers' Seminary of Hessen at Schloss Herborn; this dealt with the topical questions of hermeneutics, 'Creation and Covenant', 'Law and Gospel' and the political situation. The speakers were Otto Weber, who was indirectly Barth's successor to the chair at Göttingen; Helmut Gollwitzer, who had just returned from captivity in Russia and was now teaching dogmatics in Barth's former post at Bonn; and Hans Joachim Iwand, about whom Barth said in Herborn that there was nothing finer than a Reformed Lutheran.[165] On his visit to Germany Barth was concerned to strengthen the church's opposition to the general 'reactionary tendencies'. He also attempted to warn them against a 'temptation' he saw to be very real for quite a number of them, pointing out the danger 'of doing theology by the criterion of an emotional reaction against the reactionaries in theology and the church'. However, he did concede that such an approach 'gives plenty of opportunity for letting off steam'.[166]

While Barth could snatch a little extra time for his work by giving up outside lectures, it was much more difficult to cope with the many individuals who wanted to talk to him at home in Basle with their problems, reports, questions and requests. He always wanted to be at the disposal of those who seriously sought his advice and his opinion as much as he could. And without doubt he himself needed continuing contact with a variety of people to stimulate and to develop his own thought.

One of the most impressive figures who came to him at this time was the Indonesian Takdir Alisjahbana, who asked him what he thought about the plan to found the new Indonesia on a 'liberal individualism' which proclaimed toleration. 'I warned the good man seriously against wanting to give his fellow-countrymen this medicine. Having tasted it, after two hundred years we had finally ended up with two world wars and Hitler, etc., and it was hardly an immunization against communism, which was obviously the thing he most feared. But I saw that I was preaching to deaf ears.'[167] Alisjahbana misunderstood Barth's answer and later accused him of being a spokesman for intolerance! Another time 'a delightful Armenian-American, Professor Haroutunian, appeared, bringing with him a pipe and four detective stories as presents. He then talked for a whole evening about his very remarkable views on the *filioque*, physical redemption and so on.'[168] Then the President of the United Church in Japan, Michio Kozaki, arrived: 'I discussed the main problems of the situation there with him.'[169]

Further work on the Church Dogmatics

On the whole, during these years Barth tried to concentrate with the greatest possible intensity on the continuation of his *Dogmatics*. He was convinced that this work was required of him more than any other, and it cost him a great deal of time and effort. During the course of a semester he had 'to produce at least eight manuscript pages of extremely complicated thought each day, in a state ready for the publisher'.[170] Four hours of lecturing on *Dogmatics* involved 'about thirty to forty hours preparation'.[171] And he thought that he was not a fluent writer. 'My life and work has always been much more burdensome than some people might now imagine.'[172] As he got older, he found that 'the lectures take much, much more out of me than they used to, so that I am now largely occupied with this central concern not only for the whole morning but also in the early evening and even on my free Wednesdays and Saturdays, tightening up and correcting the texts even up to the last quarter of an hour before the lecture'.[173] After that, the passages 'which I gave at the lecture in the afternoon' were 'put aside ready for the publisher'.[174]

Advancing age not only made work on the *Dogmatics* more laborious, but also drove Barth to more haste. 'Only the good Lord knows how long he will tolerate my efforts.'[175] At any rate, 'I now face the lower limit of the normal span of a man's life as envisaged in the Bible. I must get a move on. Inevitably there will be plenty of distractions and urgent requests and interruptions beyond my control. I think that I am doing justice to my academic duties with the ten hours teaching a week which I have been doing for years. Sleep and necessary recreation also need time. But where I see an engagement that I feel I can dispense with, especially if it is a formal one, I must take the time for myself.'[176] Barth regretted how often he now had to say no, how many things he had to put on one side or otherwise omit to do, because he did not have the necessary time over and above the 'oceanic production of the *Dogmatics*'. But this was the only way. The *Dogmatics* proved to be increasingly 'jealous of competition from any other undertakings'.[177]

Because he devoted himself so tenaciously to work on his *magnum opus*, a series of further weighty volumes (in terms both of their size and their content) came into being in relatively rapid succession. According to Charlotte von Kirschbaum, who had a closer view of the origin and growth of the *Dogmatics* than anyone else, in the case of each volume and each chapter it was 'always a breathtaking affair to see how such a chunk of rock evolved by almost imperceptible degrees through his constant concentration on innumerable and tireless efforts at chiselling and shaping'.[178] Seven volumes had already been finished, and an eighth was completed in the spring during which Barth went to Herborn. In view of the constantly increasing extent of the *Dogmatics* Barth occasionally asked himself whether he was building Solomon's temple or the tower of Babel. 'I am quite sure that the angels sometimes chuckle at my enterprise; but I would like to think that the chuckle is well-meaning.'[179] Occasionally he sighed deeply: 'Oh, what a good time I could be having! – contemporaries are now close to retirement or have already reached it. If only I had not been so arrogant as to dare to embark on this endless ridge walk twenty years ago! "What use is it?" often enough runs through my head; but then I find that each new vista which opens up on this journey proves so attractive and stimulating that I really would not have things otherwise, and I keep on taking one more step forward.'[180] In the meantime, the *Dogmatics* had proved so extensive that it made sense for Otto Weber to produce a concentrated survey of their contents in book form in 1950: so to speak an 'outline map of the territory of the *Church Dogmatics*, which has already grown so broad'.[181]

What Barth felt that he had learnt above all in preparing those eight volumes was 'that although I still enjoy a fight, gradually I have found more and more meaning in life and death affirmations'. 'Saying no is hardly a supreme art, nor is the overthrow of all kinds of false idols an ultimate task.'[182] In these remarks, one of the things Barth had in mind was the 'destruction' of theology prescribed by existentialism. Constructive, positive, edifying statements were more important and more central to him than destructive ones. So in his *Dogmatics,* controversies and direct polemic in fact faded more and more into the background. However, by 'positive and edifying thought' Barth did not mean the construction of a conservative and orthodox structure within which theology was to be carried on. He was indeed 'happy to be dubbed "orthodox"', as long as that meant being a theologian who was open and ready to learn from the Fathers. But he rejected any restriction to the doctrinal position of any teacher, school or confession. He could not and would not approve of the confessionalism which had become topical: '"Confessions" exist for us to go through them (not once but continually), not for us to return to them, take up our abode in them, and conduct our further thinking from their standpoint and in bondage to them. The church never did well to attach itself arbitrarily to one man – whether his name was Thomas . . . or Luther, or Calvin – and in his school to attach itself to one form of doctrine. And it was never at any time good for it to look back instead of forwards as a matter of principle.'[183] Barth did not want even his own *Dogmatics* to be understood as fixing a new doctrinal standpoint. 'I have never understood the whole *Church Dogmatics* as a house but as the introduction to a way which must be followed, as the description of the movement of something that can only be described in dynamic, not static, concepts. A house is a static object.'[184]

Barth did not expect that everyone should read all eight volumes. 'But anyone who does want to talk about me must certainly have read me. Moreover (if he is a serious person and not a journalist, and therefore not a theologian who thumbs through a book), he should have read me completely. Not everyone who thinks that he is able to know and say all sorts of things about me has fulfilled even this condition. So as before I can simply keep quiet about so much that I hear said of me.' But Barth hoped that his readers would not only read his work but also understand it – though they might not necessarily agree. 'We are not here to agree with one another and to pass compliments. If there are "Barthians", I myself am not among them. We are here to learn from one another, and to make the best of the literary works we present to one another. After that we go our way – not into a theological "school" but into the church – and we go it alone. Precisely because of that we must understand one another.'[185]

Barth dedicated the new volume of the *Dogmatics*, III, 4 (810 pages, ET 704), to the 'American Academy of Arts and Sciences in Boston' (which had a primarily scientific orientation). This was a sign of gratitude to them for making him their 'Foreign Honorary Member' on his sixty-fourth birthday. This time his pupil Heino Falcke helped in the preparations for publication. The publishers had the volume printed (like the rest of the *Dogmatics*) at the Graphische Anstalt Schüler in Biel, 'where an enthusiastic Herr Haag looked after things': 'He was so enthusiastic, that just as the setting for *Church Dogmatics* III, 4, was being completed, he even sang a bit of a chorale quite correctly to me over the telephone.'[186]

This new volume discussed 'the doctrine of creation . . . with a statement of the *ethical* questions and answers which arise in *this* field of Christian knowledge'.[187] Barth wrote this ethics on the basis of the following premises: 'The Word of God is truth and promise, but also *commandment*. It presents itself first as God's command to the creature, directed at the man who is his creature. It is also the word of God spoken in Jesus Christ within the sphere which is thus marked out: his commandment as his gracious offer.' This word of grace already claims man in his creatureliness. And 'in this combined view of the first and second articles of the creed, based on the previous volumes of the doctrine of creation', Barth wanted to write his ethics of creation, 'not in the light of an abstract law but in the light of the gospel'.[188]

For this reason he began by decisively rejecting the doctrine of 'ordinances of creation' – in so far as these are understood as being laws which are independent of the Word of God and capable of being known 'naturally'. Barth, too, recognized 'ordinances', but 'these are not things like laws, prescriptions, imperatives': they are 'spheres *in* which God commands and *in* which man is obedient or disobedient'. According to Barth, since the commandment of the Creator is *given to* the creature, these spheres are not a neutral realm, but are structures of humanity as it is manifest in Jesus Christ. Accordingly he divided his ethics into the four aspects of humanity which had been demonstrated in his anthropology: 'Freedom before God' (the holy day, confession, prayer), 'Freedom in Fellowship' (man and woman, parents and children, etc.), 'Freedom for Life' (the problem of suicide, the death penalty, war, exile – and work) and 'Freedom in Limitation' (profession, age, honour). Thus the central concept of these ethics is that of 'freedom': not understood in contrast to obedience, but as 'the freedom of the children of God' which is 'the freedom of obedience and therefore true freedom'. One striking feature of this ethics was that Barth began it with a discussion of the commandment to keep the sabbath holy. He made this commandment more emphatic and even thought that the 'commandment about the holy day explains all the others'. For it orders man to take delight in the fact that God in his grace 'has *taken* men's affairs into his *own* hands and thus *out* of the hands of men'. That means that the sabbath commandment bids a man *believe,* and *thus* to go to his 'work'.[189]

After the 'ethics' was published, in the autumn of 1951 Barth answered questions about the subject of the book put to him on Swiss radio by Ernst von Schenck.

The Doctrine of Reconciliation

Once the volume was completed, Barth, who was now sixty-five, faced the major hurdle in his *Dogmatics*, the doctrine of reconciliation. He reflected on the content and the arrangement of this doctrine during the holidays which he spent after the Herborn conference with Arthur Frey in Ticino, since he wanted to begin lecturing on it in the summer of 1951. He wondered for a while whether he would not do better to call the doctrine 'the doctrine of the covenant', but kept to the traditional title, although he interpreted it in the sense of the other. But how was he to arrange and divide up the whole work? In Locarno 'I dreamed of a plan. It seemed to go in the right direction. The plan now had to stretch from christology to ecclesiology together with the relevant ethics. I woke at 2 a.m. and then put it down on paper hastily the next morning.'[190] In his summer lectures, he began to sketch out a first section of the plan which he had 'seen'. 'I gave an introduction to the whole thing in the form of a paraphrase of "Immanuel", which was at the same time a prospectus of the whole' of the doctrine of reconciliation.[191]

The arrangement of the doctrine of reconciliation (which was then developed in three thick volumes amounting to almost 3000 pages) followed Calvin's doctrine of the *munus triplex*, the threefold office of Christ, as prophet, priest and king. Each of these three aspects was considered in turn, in terms first of christology, then of soteriology and finally of pneumatology. Furthermore, for a closer understanding of the three offices of Christ the first two were combined with the classic doctrine of the two states (humiliation and exaltation) and the two natures of Christ (true God and true man), whereas in the account of the prophetic office the *unity* of the two states and two natures was to be stressed. This gave the following artistic arrangement: 'The content of the doctrine of reconciliation is the knowledge of *Jesus Christ* who is 1. the true God, namely the God who humbles himself and thus brings reconciliation; 2. the true man who is exalted by God and thus reconciled to him, and 3. in the unity of the two is the guarantor and witness to our reconciliation. This threefold knowledge of Jesus Christ includes knowledge of man's *sin*: 1. his arrogance, 2. his sloth, 3. his lies – the knowledge of the event in which the reconciliation *takes place*: 1. his justification, 2. his sanctification, 3. his vocation – and the knowledge of the work of the Holy Spirit in 1. gathering together, 2. building up, and 3. sending the community, and of the being of Christians in Jesus Christ 1. in faith, 2. in love and 3. in hope.'[192]

Important decisions had been made in this arrangement. Barth no longer wanted to talk – as largely happened in the old tradition – of the person of Christ and of his 'natures' apart from what he had done for us: i.e. he no longer wanted to develop a christology independently of a soteriology. Nor, however, did he want – as largely happened in more recent theology – to talk of his work, of his 'significance' for us *(pro me)* independently of his person. Rather, he wanted to take the doctrine of his work wholly into that of his person and *vice versa*. Furthermore, he did not want to present an isolated doctrine of sin and certainly not one which was presupposed by the doctrine of reconciliation. It was to be directly incorporated into the doctrine of reconciliation and subordinated to it. Sin was thus strictly understood as a counter-movement against the action of God; as a contradiction not against an abstract, general law but against God's grace; as a contradiction which in truth cannot be known without grace, a contradiction which fundamentally comes too late and cannot do away with God's grace. Furthermore, Barth no longer wanted the decisive orientation of the knowledge of salvation to be merely on justification (as in Lutheranism) or on sanctification (as in pietism) or on vocation (as in the Anglo-Saxon churches); he wanted to do ecumenical theology by stressing these three perspectives equally in the light of the knowledge of Christ. Finally, he no longer wanted to put forward an independent doctrine of the Holy Spirit, but to regard it as an integral part of the doctrine of reconciliation itself. According to him it is to be understood strictly as the doctrine of the 'power of Jesus Christ' or as the power of the 'subjective realization of reconciliation' – which is not primarily achieved in the individual. It is realized first in the community and only after that, as a result, in the individual.

In *Church Dogmatics* IV, 1, which he now began, Barth was concerned merely with one aspect of the doctrine of reconciliation, the first: namely with the person and work of Jesus Christ in so far as he is 'true God'. For his account Barth again studied the christology of the early church – by means of Harnack's 'brilliantly' written *History of Dogma*; of course, 'somehow I tend not to believe a word of it; it *must* all have been different from what he would have us believe'.[193] According to Barth, the true Godhead of Jesus Christ is shown in the fact that – as true God! – he is 'obedient' to God (the

Father), that – as the eternal son of God – he becomes 'man's brother' and – as 'the Lord' – becomes 'servant' and humbles himself so that – as the judge – he becomes 'the one who is judged in our place'. In this way, precisely as true God he performs the priestly office. On the one hand, his view overcomes the static character of the concepts in which classical christology spoke of the 'natures' of Christ. 'Reconciliation is history' runs the very first sentence. On the other hand, this view also maintains – and Barth attached great importance to this – that the divinity of Christ is neither diminished nor obscured nor even transmuted by his humiliation; it is 'shown' precisely in it. Because God accomplished this priestly work especially on the cross, Barth understood Easter as the event of divine confirmation which establishes that 'Jesus Christ's action and passion were not apart from or against God but according to his holy and gracious will, and above all that his dying in our place was not futile but effective, not for our destruction but for our salvation'. Against any mere theology of the cross he said, 'There can be no going back behind Easter morning.' In the section on 'justification' Barth then sought to show that not only is man justified, but God also justifies himself, and that God's grace and righteousness are not opposites, because here God does right in his grace. In the ecclesiological section he showed that the church must be understood completely in the light of its 'head', Jesus Christ – as his 'body', he said, it is his 'earthly and historical form of existence'. The recognition that its head is at the same time the head of 'all mankind' (while it is itself only a part) means that the church is made relative. Consequently the statement 'outside the church there is no salvation' must be corrected to 'outside Christ there is no salvation'. According to Barth this amounts to a summons to the church not to keep to itself. One fact which gave rise to a good deal of discussion was that in deliberate antithesis to the 'doctrines of faith' in modern times, with their elevation of faith to be a principle of theology, Barth dealt with the faith of the Christian only at the end of the book and then did not devote much space to it. This discussion appeared under the title 'The Act of Faith' (in an attempt to overcome the false alternative of faith or works). This 'act' consists in a recognition, knowledge and confession which is directly related to the 'object of faith'.[194]

In working on the doctrine of reconciliation Barth was now preoccupied with the subject he believed to be at the heart of all theology, the knowledge of *Jesus Christ*. 'If one goes wrong here, one is wrong all along the line. If one is at least on the right track here, the whole thing cannot be completely wrong.'[195] Barth was thought to be 'christocentric', and indeed he was, in a quite definite sense. 'Of course I had to come a long way (or round a detour!) before I began to see better and better that the saying in John 1.14 is the centre and the theme of all theology and indeed is really the whole of theology in a nutshell . . . How does one really come to find the solution of all theological questions in Christ? . . . It happens when one resolutely and persistently seeks in Christ and is then able to make the discovery that *in fact* it is to be found in him: *in quo* sunt *omnes thesauri sapientiae et scientiae absconditi* (Colossians 2.3) . . . I have no christological principle and no christological method. Rather, in each individual theological question I seek to orientate myself afresh – to some extent from the very beginning – not on a christological dogma but on Jesus Christ himself *(vivit! regnat! triumphat!)*. On each occasion I then have to go about answering any particular question in a quite special way, or rather to allow myself to be led in a special way in the direction towards which I am looking. The methods must keep being renewed, changed, modified. I am very attracted to a remark by Hilary of Poitiers: *Non sermoni res sed rei sermo subjectus est.** There is a whole theological revolution in this saying, and if people had noticed it, many errors, much barrenness and much boredom in theology would have been impossible. The question of christological theology is first of all a question of *life* – the question of the confrontation of theology with the *res*, i.e. the one who is the *imago dei invisibilis, primogenitus omnis creaturae, caput corporis ecclesiae* (Colossians 1.15–20).'[196]

At the very time when he was occupied with the parts of volume IV, a plethora of interpretations and critical assessments of the theology of Barth's *Dogmatics* began to appear. In 1952, for instance, the Dutchman Marinus Pieter van Dijk and the French-speaking Swiss Maurice Neeser accused him of being 'essentially nothing but an existentialist', while in the same year 'Bultmann complained bitterly that I would not take existentialism seriously'.[197] Even the principal journal for theological reviews, *Theologische Literaturzeitung*, took note of Barth's position in its own way, having ignored his existence for thirty years.[198] And in 1953 the fundamentalist Cornelius van Til wrote a whole book to the effect that 'I was possibly the worst heretic of all time'.[199] Of the criticisms directed against him Barth took seriously only those concerned with his concentration on Jesus Christ. And there was certainly some criticism here. In 1951, in his book on Barth, von Balthasar made the charge that 'there was a christological narrowness in my work'. As Barth understood the charge, von Balthasar sought to avoid what he felt to be the narrowness by seeing holy 'repetitions' of Christ's history in addition to

*The word serves the content, not the content the word.

Christ himself. Against this Barth insisted that: 'The being and activity of Jesus Christ needs no repetitions. He is present and active in his own truth and power.' And he asked whether, if one saw things otherwise, 'Jesus Christ would not have ceased to become the subject and origin of Christian faith.'[200] 1951 also saw the first appearance of Bonhoeffer's *Widerstand und Ergebung* (ET *Letters and Papers from Prison*), which provoked a variety of contradictory interpretations. Because of the riddle they presented, Barth asked whether Bonhoeffer had really been done 'a good service' by their publication.[201] The phrase 'positivism of revelation' applied to Barth there[202] was subsequently used against him in a variety of ways. He could only observe, however, that he 'just did not know how to make sense' of this criticism: simply to put forward dogmas – 'take it or leave it' – 'Where do I do that in the *Church Dogmatics*?'[203] After Barth had been attacked harshly and fanatically for a long time by the Dutch Reformed Church (so that he wondered 'that I haven't died long since from so many refutations'),[204] in 1954 there appeared a book by a representative of this group, Gerrit Cornelis Berkouwer, called *The Triumph of Grace in the Theology of Karl Barth,* which gave him a great deal to think about because of its acute analysis and the questions it raised. The title itself indicated Berkouwer's criticism: that Barth spoke too 'triumphally', blunting the problem of evil with 'grace'. 'I'm a bit startled at the title, *The Triumph* . . . Of course I used to use the word and still do. But it makes the whole thing seem so finished, which it isn't for me. *The Freedom* . . . would have been better. And then instead of . . . *Grace* I would much have preferred . . . *Jesus Christ.* My intention, at any rate, has been that all my systematic theology should be as exact a development as possible of the significance of this "name" (in the biblical sense of the term) and to that extent should be the telling of a *story* which develops through individual events' – the story of a struggle, but a victorious one.[205]

Between the firing lines

While Barth was talking of 'reconciliation', the Swiss press was directing a real bombardment of criticism and polemic against him, more vigorously than before. How had this come about? After the Berne lecture of February 1949, he had continued to argue for a 'third way between East and West'. For this reason, in May 1950 he dismissed Ilya Ehrenburg, who had wanted to get him 'to sign the Stockholm (i.e. Moscow) peace appeal against the atomic bomb, empty-handed after a two-hour conversation'. 'I now react in a decidedly negative fashion to such obvious propaganda moves. He is then said to have denounced me as "bourgeois" . . . So one is always between two firing-lines.'[206] But Barth also refused to identify himself with the other side, and in any case, in the summer of 1950 he learnt from a sound source that he was under scrutiny from the American Secret Service and that 'in their card index I have a black mark against my name ("too many Eastern friends")'.[207] Barth was also concerned for this 'third way' when from the beginning he rejected German rearmament. He saw it as already being a serious heightening of the Cold War between East and West. He therefore followed with keen attention 'the dispute over the "remilitarization" of West Germany to fight against Stalin, which in Germany threw up waves of extreme irrationality as well as confessions of faith'. In October 1950 he stated his views on this dispute in an open letter to Wolf-Dieter Zimmermann in Berlin. Among other things, he said in it that: 'The Christian message today must be that we should not be afraid', and also, 'Anyone who does not want communism – and none of us do – should take socialism seriously.'[208]

As before, he rejected pacifism as a principle, but in the particular circumstances he was equally definitely against German remilitarization – and on this he agreed in principle with Martin Niemöller and Gustav Heinemann. Heinemann, who had recently had the courage to resign his ministerial post over this question, came to give a lecture in Basle at the beginning of December and on this occasion also visited Barth's home, where an extra session of the discussion group was held in his honour.[209] Barth described the character of his agreement with Niemöller in an article celebrating Niemöller's sixtieth birthday (1952): 'Not so long ago, a conversation between Martin Niemöller and myself went like this. Barth: "Martin, I'm surprised that you almost always get the point despite the *little* systematic theology that you've done!" Niemöller: "Karl, I'm surprised that you almost always get the point despite the *great deal* of systematic theology that you've done!" '[210]

Barth's plea for this 'third way' really meant a third way between the courses adopted by East and West. It meant a resolute plea for peace and against the Cold War. And at the same time it also included a decisive 'no' to anti-communism. 'Not that I have any inclination towards Eastern communism, in view of the face it has presented to the world. I decidedly prefer not to live within its sphere and do not wish anyone else to be forced to do so. But I do not see that either politics or Christianity require or even permit the conclusions which the West has drawn with increasing sharpness . . . I believe anti-communism as a matter of principle to be an even greater evil than communism itself . . . Have we forgotten . . . that only the "Hitler in us" can be an anti-communist on principle? . . . I think . . . that the Christian churches should have considered it their task to influence both public opinion and the leaders who are politically responsible by superior witness to the peace and hope of the kingdom of God. The churches have injured the cause of the gospel by the largely thoughtless manner in which they have identified the gospel . . . with the badly planned and ineptly guided cause of the West . . . By human reckoning, the cause of the gospel cannot be saved for a long time even by the best ecumenical and missionary efforts.'[211] Why this clear 'no' to anti-communism as well? 'Anti means *against*. God is not against, but *for* men. The communists are men, too. God is also for the communists. So a Christian cannot be against the communists but only *for* them. To be for the communists does not mean to be for communism. I am not for communism. But one can only say what has to be said *against* communism if one is *for* the communists.'[212] In this sense Barth was not a communist, but he was not an anti-communist either. And in this sense he summoned Christians to swim against the stream – and summoned them from both sides of the power blocs, 'in which men's pernicious propaganda prevents people on either side from seeing anything but the splinter in the other person's eye'.[213]

At this juncture, however, in September 1950 Federal Councillor Markus Feldmann attacked Barth vigorously in the Berne Great Council because of his views and accused him of endangering the basis of the state's existence by his ecclesiastical 'bid for power' and his friendly attitude towards communists. While still on holiday in Gyrenbad, Barth asked the politician 'why two men who were each in their own way trying to be Christians and Swiss citizens had to behave like this',[214] and suggested a meeting to see if they could reach some agreement. Feldmann accepted on condition that the questions to be discussed were fixed beforehand. Barth put seven short questions to him, but Feldmann took until February 1951 to reply, and then did not send a similar list of questions but an extensive refutation of Barth on the basis of his questions. In view of its content and style Barth could only regard this communication as 'a single indictment (– or perhaps one should say a "formal verdict"?)'.[215] He therefore refused to take part in the proposed conversation. To his great dismay, a little later Feldmann had the whole correspondence published (at the taxpayers' expense) 'without even asking me. The pamphlet was published by the Berne administration . . . and sent to newspapers throughout Switzerland.'[216]

After that there were storms of protest and dismay for months in almost all the Swiss newspapers and magazines, 'who thought that they had to show constant interest in my life by denouncing me in even the remotest little villages as a friend of the communists'. The *Schweizerische Politische Korrespondenz* even asked in all seriousness 'whether it was not time that the Herr Professor of Theology should at last be hauled before the courts'. 'I came off worst among the Social Democrats, and best in Spiez's *Volksfreund.*'[217] Albert Schädelin and Arthur Frey also defended their friend. About seventy Berne pastors sent him a declaration of solidarity, and 'a cake also arrived with an inscription in icing: *multorum corda non agricolae sed Barbae sunt!*'[218]* Barth himself resolved not to answer any of the accusations, but 'joyfully and in silence to exercise Christian patience: however, I cannot conceal the fact that this often turned into a decidedly un-Christian contempt for the human race'.[219] Barth indirectly explained his behaviour in the closing section of his 'ethics', which was written right at the beginning of the press campaign, in terms of the 'honour' which does not need to defend itself.[220]

At any rate, even now he was not ready to allow himself 'to be forced out of the narrow space . . . between East and West'. 'What we need now' are 'birds flying between East and West, and not partisan involvement'.[221] And precisely because he did not take sides with the Western cause, he thought that he could also warn Christians in the East not to make their 'affirmation of communism . . . part of the Christian message, an article of faith'. He first made the point verbally to Bishop Bereczky of Hungary (in Zürich) in the summer of 1951 and then put it explicitly in writing.[222] To his vexation, this warning, which was really only addressed to the Eastern Christians, was leaked to the Western press in early 1952

---

*'The hearts of the many are not for Feldmann ('field man'), but for Barth.'

from an unknown source. In a similar way, a conversation between Barth and a private group in Geneva in October 1951 about the 'influence of dollars' on the Swiss press was also made public and aroused new mistrust. Things only began to quieten down a little when at the end of 1951 Feldmann was elected to the Federal Council – not least because of his keen eye for 'friendliness towards the communists'. Barth remarked, 'That makes three votes against me in the Federal Assembly.'[223]

In January 1952 Barth was very pleased with the surprise news that 'His Majesty the King of England had the kindness to award me the Royal Medal for Service in the Cause of Freedom.'[224] 'Aha! Psalm 23.5! Now who is purged of all suspicion of communism by the most exalted figure of the Western world? But one should not praise the day before the evening comes.'[225] For 'by some strange application of a law of 1846',[226] the Basle executive council prohibited Barth from accepting the decoration: he only received it in 1962, when he retired. At that time, when working on *Church Dogmatics* IV, 1, 'I used the affair as a parable for the kingdom of heaven. It has come, but is still concealed by power and authorities.'[227] At the same time Barth also aroused considerable disapproval by objecting to the installation of a new stained-glass window in the cathedral in Basle. His view was strictly 'Calvinist': 'One can reasonably hold the opinion that the second commandment is meaningful and should be observed. "Do not make yourself any image" – at any rate in connection with Christian worship, even if it should be the most perceptive work of the most gifted artist.'[228] Whether because of this or not, when a vote was taken, the congregation decided against any decorated window.

Over the following months Barth continued to be constantly preoccupied with political questions which were always in some way connected with the East-West problem. On 10 May he had a discussion in Aarau about the church and politics with prominent lay people. On 25 May, on Swiss radio, he discussed the question 'What shall we do?', as 'small' helpless people who seem to have no influence on the present confrontation between the powers. His answer was: 'We should not worry so much!'[229] In the summer he was concerned about the dispute over German rearmament which had again stirred up the German church and now threatened to split it.

In a study called 'Political Decisions in the Unity of the Faith' he attempted to demonstrate the 'rules of the game' by which Christians made up their minds. He thought that the church could neither prescribe a political decision nor leave it open (as though it were merely a 'matter of discretion'); its task was to make the issues quite clear. On each occasion what was at stake was nothing less than obedience or disobedience towards God, and there was no third way between. With this argument Barth was implicitly challenging the mediating standpoint of his pupil Gollwitzer, who at that time had in fact described 'political decision' as a 'matter of discretion'.

In a letter to the editor of *Kirche und Mann* (Church and Man), Barth had earlier made *his* decision in the present situation quite plain: in rejecting rearmament he was 'one hundred per cent with Niemoller and Heinemann', even if they sometimes used 'ambivalent' arguments – 'I am also with Mochalski, and with anyone who honestly and resolutely opposes this development.'

In September Barth had a rare opportunity to gather information about the Vatican attitude to the questions of the day – in a conversation with Cardinal Tisserant at Colmar in Alsace. 'The meeting with the Cardinal was . . . interesting, although to this day I still do not know what the man wanted from me. I heard some remarkable things from him, e.g. that the Pope himself does not in fact want to choose between the Eastern and Western blocs, that he is not against communism as such but only against its *matérialisme athée*, that he is not *in favour of* German rearmament, that he does not consider the cases of Stepinac and Mindszenty as instances of *persécution de la foi.*'[230]

Demythologizing?

At least while he was working out his *Doctrine of Reconciliation*, writing it down and lecturing on it bit by bit, Barth was involved in another controversy besides the political one. 'It came about that we "old campaigners" from the 1920s and 1930s of our eventful century suddenly found that we had been overtaken and overwhelmed by a new theological movement. Its slogans were the "demythologizing" and "existentialist interpretation" of theological language. And the person who gave rise to it was no less than our former comrade Rudolf Bultmann.' 'What caused my restraint towards him' was 'not so much his "demythologizing" of the New Testament, to which the majority of his opponents objected, as his "existentialist interpretation" of its statements'.[231] 'As far as *demythologizing* was concerned, the enterprise left me cold . . . because I found it far too humourless. Moreover, following my experiences with modern man, who is after all the object of the exercise, I cannot regard it as being likely to be a successful instrument for "conversation" with this creature. To me at any rate, apologetics is an enterprise which is deeply suspicious and alien in all its forms, and therefore also in this reductionist approach. But I have certainly listened to the vigorous presentation of *existentializing*, which theological language is supposed to need.'[232] Barth watched this theological approach 'once again running into the dead end of a theological anthropology from which I thought it should have been recalled years ago. My critical starting point was once that "to talk of God" means more than "to talk of man in a rather elevated tone". Now I see that it has been discarded. There is no mistaking the fact that Bultmann and his pupils can sail nearer to the wind of the time than I, so I have to be content for my objections to be a source of amazement to many levels of the even younger generation.'[233]

Granted, Barth did not dispute that positive lessons could be learnt from philosophy – and even from existentialism. 'As Christians we must have the freedom to let the most varied ways of thinking run through our heads. For example, I can entertain elements of Marxism without becoming a Marxist . . . Today we are offered existentialism, and it too doubtless has important elements . . . I myself have a certain weakness for Hegel and am always fond of doing a bit of "Hegeling". As Christians we have the freedom to do this . . . I do it eclectically.'[234] Barth believed that the influence of philosophical thinking on theology could not and must not be excluded. But its use ought never to be a matter of principle; it should always be deliberately and recognizably eclectic.

Barth wrote the first volume of his *Doctrine of Reconciliation* 'with constant attention to the . . . rampaging Bultmann controversy'.[235] Indeed he regarded the whole volume as his answer to the teaching of his Marburg colleague.

'The present theological situation and also the particular themes of this book have made it necessary for me throughout to engage in an intensive though for the most part implicit conversation with Rudolf Bultmann. His name does not appear often, but his arguments have always been in my mind, even in places where, with his method and his results in view, I have deliberately ignored him.'[236] 'I think that one can only demythologize demythologizing by a better explanation of what Bultmann and his followers seem to have understood as no more than "myth" and shudder at with horror again and again.'[237]

The students, who were very involved in this question, followed the implicit controversy with Bultmann very attentively. Of about a hundred and sixty theological students in Basle, more than half now came from Germany. Above all in the seminars, 'these Germans were again a source of amazement to other nationalities and especially us Swiss because of their delight in mulling everything over and discussing it'. Barth thought that the Swiss were 'like the man at the pool of Bethesda; always arriving too late when it comes to answering a question'.[238] In the summer of 1951 Barth discussed Schleiermacher's *The Christian Faith* in his seminar; during the analysis of it Bultmann's burning questions were constantly in the background (the discussion group was devoted to Jacques Ellul's book on *The Theological Justification of Law*). So many American students were now coming to Barth's lectures that from this summer on he arranged a regular English language colloquium for them – in addition to the French one, which had already been in existence for a long time.

In July he had to take part in a preparatory conference for the World Council of Churches Assembly at Evanston. After that he had a holiday at the Bergli and then went with the Freys to the Golzern- alp ob Bristen, a lonely place in the hills where they still had to wash at a well in the open air. When he returned for the winter semester of 1951–52, he allowed himself to be persuaded by the students' great interest in the problems raised by Bultmann to tackle the arguments of the Marburg teacher directly. This time there was no discussion group, and the seminar was taken up with the question of 'Kerygma and Myth'. 'The room was . . . crammed full of people – more than ever before.'[239] 'The interest of the students made it inevitable that this time the questions raised by Bultmann and those prompted by him, and the arguments used on both sides, should dominate the discussion in a lively and sometimes heated fashion. It could not be our concern to resolve them in any way. But as a basis for a responsible reaction from each individual we had to make sure that in the end the nature of the problems became tolerably clear.'[240] When the Anglican bishop Stephen Neill spoke to the faculty about his church at the end of the semester, Barth thought that people had 'difficulty in restraining themselves from announcing their conversion to it'.[241] He wished he had a crozier like Neill's, so that he could summon certain theologians to business with 'an authoritative pastoral letter'.[242]

Barth had last seen Bultmann in person briefly in October 1950 at the home of his friend Baumgartner in Basle; as they parted Barth looked at the new Basle trams and said that they were surely a particularly important indication of the need for 'demythologizing'! On 18 March 1952 he was able to meet Bultmann again in the Charon and put his questions. Barth found his Marburg friend more open than ever before to his objections. 'He thought that he should think through the matter of the "objective subject" of faith again. That was indeed a gap.'[243]

Barth wrote out an 'extract' from the seminar work of the previous winter in a document which came into being during the summer vacation. It was not a polemical study of Bultmann but an 'attempt to understand him', as Barth indicated in the title.[244] Page after page was filled with nothing but unanswered questions. Barth sent a copy direct to Bultmann with a quotation from *The Marriage of Figaro:* 'O angel, forgive me.' Thereupon Bultmann sent back his long answer 'in a charming way' with the propitiatory continuation of the quotation: 'How could I be angry? My heart speaks for you.' In a further reply Barth said how puzzling it was that what Bultmann claimed to be *'the* appropriate interpretation' of the New Testament seemed to him to be a strait-jacket.[245] In his pamphlet on Bultmann, Barth added a postscript dissociating himself at the same time from his Basle colleague Buri: his impression of Buri's theology was that he 'has taken off the bathing trunks which Bultmann is still wearing'.[246]

In June, Barth gave another report on the question of demythologizing to the 'positive' pastors of Basle. And during this summer of 1952, at the same time as the Bultmann study, an exegetical passage on Romans 5 (part of the section omitted from *Church Dogmatics* III, 2) was published under the title *Christus und Adam* (Christ and Adam).

Barth understood this study as an indirect answer to the problem of the relationship of nature and grace which had been raised again by von Balthasar in his book on Barth. It was also an indirect reply to Bultmann, who later reviewed the study and completely rejected it. 'His title said all that needed to be said: "Adam and Christ according to Romans 5" (energetically turning the wheel back again).'[247]

There was also an echo of the Bultmann pamphlet in an invitation from Gerhard Ebeling to Barth to take part in a faculty conference about the problem of theological method in early 1953. Barth refused: 'It seems to me, not least on the basis of Bultmann's reply to my study, that it would be no use my entering this discussion once again.' He had had his say on the matter. He also believed 'that the question of the right hermeneutics cannot be decided in a discussion of exegetical *method*, but only in exegesis itself. And I think that I can see that discussion of the question of method *per se* now threatens to run out into nothingness.'[248]

Barth had finished the winter semester of 1951–52 quite exhausted, and weakened by the diabetes which had been diagnosed during the winter. But he soon recovered as the result of a strict diet ('How glad I would be to be rid of noodles!'[249]) and a holiday which he spent with his son-in-law Max Zellweger in Lugano. So he began the next semester with renewed strength. 'We took up Melanchthon's *Loci Communes* of 1521 in the summer, not only with the previous lively Bultmann seminar in mind, but also by a logical connection. It was almost as though once again we were dealing with a contemporary text. It is obvious that today Bultmann can appeal at least to a line which seems to begin in the Reformation theology inspired by Luther, and the members of the seminar were bright enough to be aware of this in the very first sessions.'[250] Among the students he was especially pleased this time with the Swede Gunnar Hillerdal. And how delighted he was when on his sixty-sixth birthday, at a boisterous seminar, the students read out 'a letter by Dr M. Luther which seemed to have come straight from heaven'.[251]

In the winter of 1952–53 Barth ventured on an unusual subject in his seminar – 'alone in the broad pastures!': the *Dogmatics* of the Hegelian Alois Emanuel Biedermann. 'What a laborious chase it was for me to arrange to get hold of the necessary copies, and rather shaming for the liberals.'[252] As they read this Zürich liberal together, Barth was amazed, for all his 'misgivings about his basic presupposition'. He 'attempted to commend him to the students as an object of modest respect and to make him understandable, especially to my many German students, as a typical product of the country'.[253] From now on he studied his own *Dogmatics* volumes in his discussion groups, as in the foreign language colloquia. Early in the year, stimulated as much as anything by the seminar, he set down his first-hand reminiscences of 'the world of free Protestantism' in a letter to Johannes Rathje. His complaint was that while it fostered friendships, there was nothing like 'the communion of saints' in it.[254] In May he again came into direct contact with the liberals, this time in Basle itself. This was 'on the occasion of the conference of so-called "Free Christendom" (at which Jaspers completely finished off those who had been shaken by Bultmann). I had a memorable evening in St Alban's parsonage with Buri and Werner: I gave them a friendly but firm invitation to return to the communion of saints which they had evidently left, but Buri told me that this was a "myth".'[255]

'Exaltation of man'

Early that same year, with the co-operation of his pupils Friedrich-Wilhelm Marquardt and Gerhard Bauer, Barth saw the first part of his *Doctrine of Reconciliation* (*Church Dogmatics* IV, 1) through the press. He had completed the volume the previous winter semester – so accurately that he finished delivering the material 'on the last day of lecturing just as the clock struck'.[256] He dedicated the 895-page book (ET 802) to his three sons. The oldest of them, Markus, had meanwhile gone off to the USA (at the beginning of February) to occupy a chair for New Testament in the Middle West, at a small, Presbyterian Seminary in Dubuque, Iowa, where Arthur Cochrane, a friend of Karl Barth's, also taught. Barth was present at Markus' last sermon in Bubendorf; he could not conceal the fact that 'I even cried a little in the church, because the ending and his farewell affected me so deeply.'[257] Christoph, Karl's second son, had home leave at this time. In July of the previous year his father had met him at the port of Amsterdam and been able to 'embrace him, deeply moved'. They then celebrated the reunion in style, 'not with a fatted calf, but by eating "wild duck"'.[258] Over the next few months, stimulated by Christoph's presence, Barth 'happily took up chess again . . . After battles lasting for hours I used to come off worst in a ratio of 4:1.'[259] At the beginning of May 1953 Christoph went back to Indonesia for a further five years, now to the college at Jakarta. And as Hans Jakob also went off to spend the summer painting in the neighbourhood of Munich, their father thought 'that with Jacob (Genesis 42.36) I could now say: "You have bereaved me of my children: Joseph is no more, and Simeon is no more, and now you would take Benjamin; all this has come upon me."'[260] But he comforted himself with the thought 'that the sun now constantly finds at least one of our family awake and at work in the service of the most beautiful of all sciences'.[261] Hans Jakob was now engaged to a nurse and masseuse, Renate Ninck, daughter of a Riehen psychologist who specialized in graphology; they were married in April 1954 by Gottlob Wieser. Their wedding came to an abrupt and shattering end when the bride's father suddenly collapsed and died in the middle of his speech. Thurneysen and Wieser spoke two days later at his funeral.

While Barth was working in increasing seclusion on his *Dogmatics* – 'Jerome in his cell', as one newspaper called him – his work was attracting increasing attention. At this point – among a whole series of visitors (including Visser't Hooft and Heinrich Held) – he also had 'an important visit from Geneva: Senarclens and Ryser, who brought me no more and no less than a handsome volume, containing the French translation of the first half of *Church Dogmatics* I, 1. The necessary thousand subscribers had been achieved, and still more were in prospect.'[262] From now on Barth's *Dogmatics* was to appear in French from the Geneva publishing house Labor et Fides. And it was the French-speaking Swiss pastor Fernand Ryser who from then on was to undertake the translation of the whole work. At the same time work on an English translation of *Church Dogmatics* was in full swing. I, 1 had been translated as early as 1936 by G. T. Thompson and was published by T. & T. Clark in Edinburgh and Scribners in New York. But then work stopped until in 1956 the translation was continued by a team of fifteen experts under the editorship of G. W. Bromiley and T. F. Torrance.[263] In 1959 the publishing house Shinkyo Shuppansha in Tokyo began to produce a Japanese version of the *Dogmatics*, translated by Yoshio Inoue, a professor of German. The original German edition of the *Dogmatics* circulated increasingly widely (finally there were over seven thousand subscribers), and in Germany in particular it was 'avidly bought and possibly also read . . . even without the blessing of the *Theologische Literaturzeitung* and other journals'.[264]

In the new semester, that of summer 1953, Barth began lecturing on the next volume of the *Dogmatics* (IV, 2), his tenth: 'Opening up the second line of the doctrine of reconciliation (from below upwards!) I first spent many hours talking about monasticism!'[265] 'What I am now seen to represent may provoke glad (or angry) surprise in some circles, as has occasionally happened before on the long journey of the *Church Dogmatics*. Those who still find its essence in the alternative 'either the ascent of man to God *or* the descent of God to man' (perhaps as a result of the confusion caused by my *Romans* of 1921), or who imagine (to their satisfaction or annoyance) that even in the first part of this fourth volume they can see little or nothing of the Holy Spirit's work of renewal, of the elevation of man, of his participation in the event of reconciliation, of sanctification and love, will now have to reckon with the fact that this aspect of the matter is treated with great urgency and at great length.'[266]

Having taken up the concerns of the Reformation in *Church Dogmatics* IV, 1, Barth thought that in IV, 2 he had done a bit more justice on the one hand to the concerns of Roman Catholic theology and 'what is there called sanctifying grace', and on the other 'to the pietists and "evangelical groups"'.[267] The reason why he could now take up these other concerns so openly was that he did not want to understand the relationship of Christ's exaltation to his humiliation, and that of sanctification to justification, as a mere matter of cause and effect. Nor did he want to see them as two different, successive acts. They were in each case two aspects of one and the same act, the one reality of the one Jesus Christ. 'Anyone who says "Jesus Christ" cannot just say "the humiliation of the Son of God"; when he has said that he has also said "the exaltation of the Son of Man".' To this extent, namely by stressing that the knowledge of Christ also has this other aspect, Barth dissociated himself from those 'who think inexorably in terms of Luther'. Again, he did not take up the concerns of the Roman Catholics or the pietists without considerable correction to the way in which these concerns were expressed by each of the partners in the conversation. The reason for this correction was that he wanted his presuppositions and reflections in developing the second aspect of the reality of Christ to be consistent with the first aspect. And this arose from his concern to take quite seriously that 'the man *Jesus*' is the one, entire foundation, power and guarantee for man's elevation and sanctification. Thus according to Barth men could only be 'sanctified' by participating in the sanctification which had already taken place, participating in *the* holy one, the *one* holy one. It was also remarkable in this new book that Barth – taking up the problem of the 'Life of Jesus' which was discussed at the turn of the century, and at a time when discussion of the historical Jesus was beginning again – here presented a detailed account of the *man* Jesus. However, in his account he did not go back behind the testimony of the gospels, but only followed it. He deliberately did not want to show any 'pre-Easter' Jesus, but only the 'royal man' seen in the light of Easter. In the section on sin he ventured the remarkable sentence: 'Sin is also stupidity and stupidity is also sin.' In the section on the church he described the community as a 'brotherly christocracy' in which the classic contrast between the spiritual church and the legal institution is not really a contrast; the setting up of an evangelical 'church law' was in fact part of its life. In the closing section on love it was possible to read the unusual remark that one could love God and Jesus directly – a point disputed by modern theology – and further that the neighbour who was to be loved was not just any fellow-man, but primarily the neighbour encountered in the community of Jesus Christ, since according to Barth love of one's neighbour is a testimony to the love of God which is essentially made 'by the neighbour' to me and by me to him.[268]

In contrast to former days, Barth had arrived at a more satisfactory relationship with pietists, 'although I could not simply adopt their view'. The reason for this was probably the change in his thinking which had taken place in the meantime, but in his view the pietists had also changed. 'If I am not mistaken, there is much more openness and thoughtfulness among them now than in the forms of doctrine and practice that I was aware of when I was younger – or thought I was aware of, for I am not ashamed to confess that I now understand them better than I did.'[269] This recalls in particular a friend whom Barth had known since 1937 and had come to value more and more: 'Richard Imberg, director of the Deaconess House of Siloah in Gümlingen: academically wild, but nevertheless a powerful theologian, whose warm humanity opened up to me a whole new side of the community movement.'[270] Imberg was, moreover, 'a preacher of universalism. I once said to him: "I don't believe in universalism, but I do believe in Jesus Christ, the reconciler of all."'[271]

While Barth was working his way tenaciously and steadily through the 'tunnel' of *Church Dogmatics* IV, 2, the summer semester of 1953 was taking its course. This time Helmut Gollwitzer had a stimulating effect on the discussion group and in the seminar the problems of 'those who think inexorably in terms of Luther' were now dealt with directly. The seminar was notable for the 'exceptionally large attendance (people on all the window seats and so on)' and 'much electricity in the air because of the theme, Luther 1520'.[272] Above all, it was because of 'the excitement that was in store for the numerous Germans who were taking part, since the prospect was that the result would not be further canonization but rather something like a degree of demythologizing of the great Dr Martinus'.[273] During his time at Göttingen Barth had already said in jest that *'anima Germanica naturaliter Lutherana'*,[274]* and now he often repeated the phrase in order to goad the 'German soul' into a critical treat-

*'The German soul is Lutheran by nature.'

ment of its tradition. The theme of Luther stimulated Barth into giving a contrasting seminar the next winter on 'Calvin's Doctrine of Justification'.

On his birthday that summer a flute trio, 'played by two students and our university proctor, who was a master of the viola . . . opened the day in such a festive manner that I asked the artists to repeat the performance (it was, of course, Mozart) the next day in the lecture room to an audience of 120 dogmatics students, with the result that even in this place there was an unusual splendour of light.'[275] The same month Barth travelled for a day to Männedorf to a 'conference of 160 (one hundred and sixty!) pastors' wives from all German-speaking Switzerland. I had to answer a great many written questions, including: "How can I be sure of my salvation?" and "Will we see our loved ones on the other side?" (Answer: Yes, but with others too!).'[276] The meeting went so well that Barth was happy to repeat it a year later. On another occasion he had a disputation with Hendrik van Oyen before the Basle pastors' association on the question of images in churches. He was against, and van Oyen for. On the way home Gottlob Wieser protested vigorously, 'You always want to be right', to which comment Barth retorted with a chuckle: 'But I always am right!'

Preparations for the World Council of Churches Assembly at Evanston

During the summer vacation – after some good days on holiday with the Thurneysens in St Luc – at the end of August Barth took part in the third preparatory conference of the advisory commission for the World Council of Churches Assembly at Evanston. He enjoyed this preparatory work more and more. A group of twenty-five experts had met for the first time from 20–30 July 1951, but Barth's memories of this gathering were not very happy. 'Yes, we sat there and talked for ten whole days. Americans (Niebuhr at their head!) with bright, healthy teeth, great determination and few problems . . . the British (the devastating Baillie from Edinburgh their most remarkable man), Germans (here the dear, profound Heinrich Vogel and the wise and quick-witted Schlink from Heidelberg deserve special mention), Hoekendijk . . . and Kraemer from Holland', Hromádka from Prague, Niles from Ceylon, the orthodox Florovsky and Roger Mehl from France, Wingren from Sweden

and the Baetas from the Gold Coast (both coal black, but I got on
with them very well), the intelligent Miss Daketa from Japan, who
very much wanted to learn German in order to learn some proper
theology (so in odd moments I introduced her to at least some of the
mysteries of the language), and Emil Brunner and myself from dear
old Switzerland.'[277] That time Barth was dissatisfied, even disappointed with the spirit in which the conference theme as a whole was
tackled. He argued in vain that the assembly should not be held in
the USA, but in New Delhi – and that the theme should not be 'The
Hope of the Church and the World' but, 'Jesus Christ, the Crucified
Lord, the Only Hope for the World.' When Niebuhr, reflecting on
the conference theme, had left eschatology 'on one side', Barth
'became angry and, having given up hope, wanted to go home'; but
the Japanese delegate was able to forestall him by arranging a
conversation between Barth and Niebuhr.[278] Nevertheless, he
returned to Basle 'with very mixed impressions', and doubtful
'whether I should continue. The Anglo-Saxons, the ecumenical
laughter, the eternal balancing of the various points . . . all this
finally tired me out.'[279] Barth regretted above all 'that we have to
tear our hair so much over Christian hope, of all things, instead of
rejoicing at it'.[280] At that time he summed up his understanding of
the special character of 'Christian hope' in an article for an American journal: 'The Christian's hope has its foundation in an event in
which all other human hopes end: in the death of Jesus Christ on the
cross of Golgotha.'[281]

It was possible to have a much more successful collaboration at
the second preparatory conference at the beginning of September
1952. This time the delegates assembled in the 'newly restored
Château de Bossey, near Céligny on Lake Geneva, in its beautiful
and peaceful surroundings . . . though at the same time as a group of
younger industrialists'. 'The commission had a number of non-
theologians (like the philosopher Donald MacKinnon) as well as the
inevitable theologians, and they played a vigorous part in it'; the aim
was 'to work out a unanimous report to present to the conference'. 'It
was by no means a straightforward task for twenty such different
people from such different origins and with such different
approaches.' However, in contrast to the previous year, people got
on very well at this meeting. 'Perhaps it was because now we had got
to know each other. And perhaps it was because in the meanwhile we
had all thought more about the matter, read our Bibles and therefore

Ecumenical activity

72.   *Work in Section I of the Assembly of the World Council of Churches at Amsterdam under the chairmanship of Bishop Lilje, 1948.*

73.   *Preparations in Bossey for the Evanston Assembly of the World Council of Churches, August 1953. On the left of Barth are Florovsky, Newbigin and Visser 't Hooft: behind him is Marie Claire Frommel (who later became his daughter-in-law), and on the left of her are H. Vogel, E. Schlink and D. T. Niles.*

74.   *Meeting with Cardinal Tisserant in Colmar, September 1952.*

75.   *With Geoffrey Fisher, Archbishop of Canterbury, in Lambeth Palace, July 1956.*

Time off

76.   Inspecting the Capitoline Venus in Rome, August 1954.

77.   Watching dog-racing with Dr Arthur Frey, Director of Evangelischer Verlag Zollikon, 1950.

78.   Near Bubendorf church, where his son Markus was pastor, with his grandchildren Anna and Peter Barth, 1946.

79.   In a break during preparations for Evanston in Bossey, with the son of Pastor Marcel Sturm, September 1952.

had automatically been brought closer to one another . . . And perhaps it was also because the needs of the day automatically brought us nearer to understanding. I would also suggest that it was because this time we had a chairman, in the person of the young Bishop Lesslie Newbigin from South India, who was able to bring us together and keep us together not only because of our common concern and the human links which joined us, but above all because of his spiritual discipline and his bearing and conduct from the beginning. The conference at Bossey was a small step on a long journey . . . But it happened that we not only spoke of the Christian hope but also grew together in it.'[282]

At the third preparatory conference people found that their respect for one another had developed even further. Barth himself noted with satisfaction: 'In these three gatherings in 1951, 1952 and 1953 we have come substantially closer together – even the Americans and I (Minear, Calhoun, Muelder and others are good people in their own way). Dodd, too, seemed to me to be a very good man and his theology was not bad (my hesitations are more on the ecclesiastical side). Best of all was the interplay with other continental theologians (which was not without its problems)'. (The theologians concerned were Schlink, Roger Mehl and Barth's friend Vogel, who would break out in ecstasy at any time and would perform his own musical compositions at the drop of a hat.) 'But if only the Anglo-Saxons would not make their phylacteries so broad and so long! I went to an Evening Prayer at which the Lord's Prayer was said twice and the Gloria five or six times. I said to them afterwards, "If I were the good God, I would reply to you in a voice of thunder, 'All right, that will do, I've heard you! . . .'"' The best diversion was provided by a small cat which once intruded into the service. It miaowed around here and there, finally sprang on the back of one of the most zealous worshippers and from there waved its tail to and fro like a banner. I expect that at Evanston a lion will perform a similar function.'[283]

At this conference, through concentrated team work, the 'report' of the commission on the main theme was given its third and final version. Barth was unanimously chosen to add a concluding word to this report which he produced in a day and which in fact won the assent of the whole commission.

It began by conceding that the great truth 'that Jesus Christ is the hope of the world . . . was worthy of much more appropriate thoughts' than were presented there. And it ended with some straight questions to the church: 'Is it an authentic witness to its Lord and head? Is it the pilgrim people, who have no abiding place here but look for a future one? . . . Is it the host of watchmen who, because they have already seen light in the East, know that a new day is now dawning . . . ? Is it the community which can already recognize the coming king in its hungry, thirsty, alien, naked, sick, imprisoned brethren . . . ?'

'The Gift of Freedom'

A month later, on 21 September, Barth again gave a lecture in Germany (the first for six years). This was in Bielefeld, to the Society for Protestant Theology. He made the journey there with two friends, 'the Swabian tin- and silver-smith' Harald Buchrucker and the Swabian pastor Hermann Diem, later to become an *ordinarius* professor in Tübingen. (With 'marked originality of character' Diem tried to build a bridge between Barth and Bultmann.)[284] On the journey, Barth became 'extraordinarily homesick for Germany in all its demonic and angelic confusion – so uniquely interesting and lovable'. The Bielefeld conference, chaired by Ernst Wolf, was one of Barth's most brilliant reunions with a vast multitude of his friends and pupils, old and new, from Germany and elsewhere. His one phobia was of the 'depressing sight of a host of non-Bultmannites who were most eager to throng around me!'[285] As far as he himself was concerned, he thought, 'It is definitely much better for my spiritual health to lead my usual life in the Swiss valley of humility.'[286] There were also about a hundred theologians from East Germany there, led by Walter Feurich and Johannes Hamel, who had just been released from prison. (It had been Barth who, early that year, had petitioned the East German Minister Wilhelm Zaisser for his friend's release.) Barth lectured to an audience of a thousand on 'The Gift of Freedom'.

In a tacit controversy with Bultmann, and in another way also with *the* 'freedom' which Western politicians had now inscribed on their banners, Barth argued that freedom was neither a natural right nor a possession which was bestowed by nature. It was God's gracious gift, grounded in God's own freedom. Freedom was not a formal power of control, a freedom of choice, but freedom in encounter, freedom *for* . . . Some remarks about the characteristics of a free theologian caused great merriment. For example, Barth said that he had the freedom 'always to begin his thinking at the beginning. This means taking the resurrection of Jesus Christ seriously as the guide for his reasoning . . . So much theology is undertaken and carried out in an earnest, pious, learned and ingenious way, but it lacks the light and serenity without which the theologian must be a sorry sight on this dark earth and a tedious teacher of his brethren, at best only to be compared with Beethoven and Brahms.'[287]

On the way back Barth visited Heinrich Scholz in Münster: 'We found him as cheerful in spirit as ever and also very alert, but physically he was very fragile.'[288] Barth then made a stop in the 'delightful Pfalz', to see Pastor Karl Handrich, in whose church he spent six hours answering the questions of a group of interested people; he was particularly pleased by the contributions of the assistant pastor Ferdinand Hahn, later to become a New Testament professor.

He returned to Basle extremely exhausted and resolved to cancel his plan to take part in the World Council Assembly in Evanston and to go on to give lectures at the universities of Columbia, Yale, Princeton, Berkeley and Toronto. 'The conference at Bielefeld impressed on me very strongly that I would be of more service to mankind – *if* I am at all – in producing these thick books than in anything that might be expected or required of me in America. I have also realized how quickly I get to the end of my physical resources on such occasions.'[289] So his part in the Second Assembly of the World Council of Churches was limited to the theological preparation of the main theme – about which he now lectured over the following months in Berne, to the pastors of Basle, to the Aargau synod, in the Zürich People's College and in St Gallen.

His pleasure in giving outside lectures now tended to diminish still further. 'I am not going to give any more outside lectures unless I feel very definitely called to do so by an occasion or a theme of my own, which is very seldom the case.'[290] So to an increasing extent he only accepted invitations involving 'answering questions' rather than lectures.[291] 'I have developed a technique of having prepared questions put to me by larger or smaller groups who want to hear my views. I then try to answer these questions in the course of the discussions.'[292] There was a session of this kind before the end of the year in Schwamendingen, attended by 'much of "better-class" Zürich and all kinds of people from east Switzerland'; it was solemnly opened with a Mozart quartet (and was repeated a year later).[293] A similar session was held in Reinach just after the beginning of 1954 with a group of pastors and then in March before an audience of three hundred in Stuttgart. The following day 'I heard a lecture about myself in Swabian-Gmünd' (by the musician Jürgen Uhde, whom he regarded very highly). 'The subject was "The Music of Mozart in the Theology of Karl Barth" (with musical illustrations, a splendid affair)!'[294] In the winter of 1953–54 Charlotte von Kirschbaum was also on her travels as a lecturer: she spoke on the biblical view of woman, in Hamburg and in Mülheim-on-the-Ruhr. In Basle itself, Barth was able to hear Rudolf Bultmann lecturing on 'Eschatology and History' (Bultmann was spending a guest semester in Zürich). Barth felt that the lecture 'said nothing new and was not very impressive about the old things'.[295] On another occasion he had a visit from the Danish theologian N. H. Søe, 'who like most Scandinavians is not very pleased with me: he thinks that I do not take the Fall, etc., seriously enough. Finally I summed up the conversation in the sentence: "We probably agree about Christ, but not about the devil."'[296] Regin Prenter and Gustav Wingren were prominent among the 'Scandinavians' who made similar accusations against Barth in their books. Wingren, starting from a 'God-devil pattern', argued that Barth left out all kinds of things in his approach. Barth's own view was that 'I can only be refuted by a comprehensive outline which corresponds to my own, and not by such . . . drollery.'[297]

In the summer semester the subject of Barth's seminar was a topical one: 'the prepared text for the main theme of the ecumenical conference in Evanston (August 1954): "Christ is the Hope of the World". We ended our consideration of it by composing a statement on the Jewish question to the leaders of the assembly. It did not achieve the desired result, but it had a certain *succès d'estime*.'[298] The majority of delegates to the Assembly rejected the statement, which required that Israel should be thoroughly integrated into the Christian hope. 'I did not think that the descendants of the old Amorites, Amalekites and so on would be the ones who destroyed the hope of Israel at this Christian conference.'[299] Barth may not now have been going to Evanston, but at least he had something of an ecumenical audience in this seminar: in addition to the Germans there were at that time more than thirty Americans, and representatives of many other nations – and 'fortunately also five Swiss'.[300] 'As he left, a Greek who was here for two semesters twice kissed my hand, either out of gratitude or because it is the custom there! And now there is a man from Uruguay who wants to study with me to gain strength for the fight against Voltaireanism. No, we have just about every-thing!'[301] Among the foreigners there, the cheerful South African Johannes Lombard stuck particularly close to Barth, persistently alternating between '"Sister Charlotti" [sic] and "little father" (that's me), always pursuing his rapid course either "in the seventh heaven" or "worried to death"'.[302] The fifteen doctoral students whom Barth had at that time also included Paul van Buren ('who later rushed so wildly out of my school'),[303] Shirley Guthrie, John Godsey, Charles Hall and others. The Germans included Rudolf Smend, Ekkehard Börsch, Holger Samson, Dietrich Braun, Jürgen Fangmeier, Trutz Rendtorff and Heinz Eduard Tödt. Barth com-plained: 'As a rule one only discovers who are the most involved students and what they are capable of towards the end of their stay in Basle. And one is rather sorry to see them depart, thinking that now things might really get going.'[304] In the discussion group the conver-sation kept coming back 'again and again to the question raised by some young know-alls . . . as to what the characteristic "thought-form" of the *Dogmatics* is. They feel that if they knew that, they could then decide whether or not to get on to the train which is apparently travelling inexorably from its specific starting point to its destina-tion.'[305]

On one occasion in the summer of 1954 Barth had a visit from a remarkable 'American specimen . . . from the Moody Bible Institute in Chicago . . . He came in, sat down and offered me a hundred dollars to write an article on the second coming of Christ. I was reminded of Judas Iscariot and politely, but firmly, declined. Then I pushed him out, but not without being told that the Bible said "Feed my lambs", while I seemed to be behaving as though it said "Feed my giraffes".'[306] Another time the English Old Testament scholar H. H. Rowley gave a personal description of his theory that Moses' monotheism was derived from his father-in-law Jethro. 'I said to him afterwards . . . "Now I'm going to tell my son-in-law what a glorious thing it is to have a wise father-in-law."'[307] Barth also had a visit 'from my quite remarkable colleague Bernd Gisevius', whose know-ledgeable accounts of the Hitler period always fascinated him. This time Gisevius again 'spoke very frankly after a good deal of Chian-ti'.[308] In August he again had a holiday in St Luc, with the Thur-neysens, the Freys and Hilda Heinemann. While he was there he 'climbed a mountain more than nine thousand feet high, called Bella Tola'.[309] After that he went on another trip to Italy with Lollo von

Kirschbaum, Ernst Wolf and the Pestalozzis: to Rome and Naples, but first to Florence. 'My great friend in this city is called Sandro Botticelli and he lives in the Uffizi. I paid him a lengthy visit.'[310] Barth was again astounded at the 'richness of line, combined with repose', and above all at the 'unfathomable knowledge, the questions and answers in the human *eyes*' of Botticelli's paintings.[311] On a further holiday by the Gerzensee Maury gave him a detailed report on Evanston.

Back in Basle, he met Hromádka, who visited him on the way home from the conference. For the most part their conversation was about the collaboration of Christians with a communist state. Barth urgently asked Hromádka not to depart from the 'narrow way' which 'the church in both West and East must seek and find in between the . . . ideologists on both sides'.[312] However, the request was to be understood on the proviso that 'Hromádka's little finger means more to me than the whole hands of some other contemporaries',[313] who were constantly attacking him.

After Barth had been to Gümlingen for a question and answer session arranged by his friend Imberg and a similar session with the 'positive' Basle pastors at Schauenberg, the winter semester began. In his seminar on 'Luther and the Enthusiasts' Barth again came up against the whole problem of politics and theology which had dogged him in the eventful post-war period. 'Each of the sessions produced some excitement. In the end Luther was as strange to us as he was at the beginning, if not stranger, and even K. G. Steck, who eventually rushed from Frankfurt to explain him (or to defend him), could not do much to alter that.'[314] 'My dear Germans' were somewhat perplexed, as at Barth's previous seminar, ' . . . that one can even put certain questions to their father Luther (whom each German theologian tends to make in his own image and then set up as a criterion)'.[315] During this semester Barth also regularly met twenty-five pastors from the Jura for discussions.

In the late autumn he took up an opportunity which offered itself for a direct political comment on German 'reconstruction' as it had developed over what was now a whole post-war decade. The opportunity was provided by an invitation from the Hessen administration to give a Remembrance Day address on 14 November in Wiesbaden. 'I considered everything that I said very carefully'[316] – and what he had to say was very pointed.

He spoke very clearly of the responsibility of even those who had been 'respectable' in the last war. Their chief victims had been the Jews, but they also included e.g. the *Rote Kapelle*.* Finally he asked for Remembrance Day to be celebrated with an active decision: 'As we must do our utmost to make sure that this never happens again.' Then he repeated what he had already said in two interviews in May and in the late summer (on the Geneva Conference and Adenauer's European Defence Union policy): Germany must be neutral and demilitarized, and remain so. He understood his stand '*against* remilitarization' to be a plea '*for* the demythologizing of the German character'.[317]

In saying this he was taking the line of Gustav Heinemann, Heinrich Grüber, Professor Ulrich Noack (who had visited him shortly beforehand in Basle) and Martin Niemöller, who had entertained Barth the evening before – and had handed over to him the golden cross,† 'which on this occasion I was allowed to wear for a moment for the first and definitely the last time'.[318] The speech stirred up a great deal of trouble. True, Barth dined afterwards with President Zinn of Hessen, but the Social Democrat administration dissociated itself from the speech immediately – and Barth regretted this more than 'the tumult of the Adenauer brigade'.[319]

Among the 'Adenauer brigade', Eugen Gerstenmaier attacked him very vigorously. Barth replied the next March with a brief article entitled 'Gerstenmaier with an Open Collar'. That same March he clashed over the same issue with Eberhard Müller and Hans von Campenhausen in Herrenalb, where he had been invited for a discussion with student chaplains from both East and West Germany. Von Campenhausen 'quivered with anger because Karl Barth gave his political views in such a way that those who differed were necessarily put in question'. Barth could only retort: 'Why don't you put forward your view with the same (Christian) commitment?'[320]

On the whole, Barth had the impression that in all the political views which he persistently put forward during the post-war years he was swimming against the stream, and that hardly anyone agreed with him. 'I evidently cannot change the fact that here, as in the rest of the "Christian West", we find ourselves in the exalted company of Dulles and Adenauer and thus mean to carry on the Cold War.'[321]

*The *Rote Kapelle* ('Red Chapel') was a group forming part of the Soviet espionage system in Germany.

†The golden cross is the sign of episcopal authority and is worn by bishops (or other equivalent heads) of district churches in Germany.

But this did not alter Barth's view of the Cold War. The many objections to his views which he had heard at first or second hand, at home and abroad, were 'a trial which has constantly dogged me over this decade and has also taken up my active attention . . . The older I become, the more I am confirmed in the view that – because things usually come to light in the right proportion of their own accord sooner or later – it is advisable, even if one has a good conscience, not to want to defend and justify oneself too zealously, if at all.'[322] More than anything else, Barth was confirmed in the view which he once reported to his Japanese colleague Kuwada (who visited him in the summer of 1955 with his oldest friend from Japan, Enkichi Kan): 'What we need to happen today in the interest of peace . . . is in the first place a spiritual Reformation and thus a conversion of Christians and of the Christian churches themselves – a conversion to the truth of their own message. And among other things that involves a good deal of better theology! And so we come to the contribution which I too have to make to peace among the nations.'[323]

In his vacations during these years Barth went to see the Pestalozzis in the Bergli less and less, although he had stayed there so often and so happily since 1920. There were personal reasons, as well as practical reasons, why he could no longer go there. He just did not want to. On both sides the interests which had once brought them together had now moved gradually, at first almost imperceptibly, in different directions. Indeed, as each became sorrowfully aware, in the course of recent years Barth's relationship with these friends to whom he owed so much had become much cooler. So for some time Barth had tended more and more to look for a new place in which to spend future vacations. For instance, in the spring of 1955 he settled in a holiday place rented by the Thurneysens, in a so-called Stöckli,* at Kapf in Emmental, with a glorious view over the meadows of the Bernese Oberland and over a 'sea of hills and valleys', with 'cows grazing and tinkling their bells'.[324] It was here that he prepared the last part of *Church Dogmatics* IV, 2, on 'Love', which was then delivered as lectures in the summer. During this semester he also continued a seminar on Schleiermacher's *Speeches*. During the following summer vacation he found time for all kinds of question and answer sessions (in Lorrach for Baden pastors, in Basle for Pfalz

---

*Stöckli is the Berne name for small cottages built alongside farmhouses to which parents retire in old age when the farm work has been taken over by their children.

pastors, and in Stuttgart for Swabian pastors). This time he also enjoyed his stay at another 'place of retreat which we have tended to visit since the Bergli shut its doors': this was his new 'Patmos', Gyrenbad,[325] a holiday resort 'still in the style of about 1890, but a wonderfully quiet place in the midst of the wooded hills of the Zürich Oberland. The visitors are simple, anonymous people, and it is a happy spot, with very good cooking – "and cheap", as old Grutzmacher used to boast after a stay in Switzerland. A bath in the waters every morning about 5.30 . . . an hour's massage every day and in the evening a cool drink at the tavern.'[326] 'Although in other respects I have my suspicions about the canton of Zürich, here it is just right.'[327] It was here that he wrote the Foreword to the next volume of his *Dogmatics* (928 pages long, ET 867). Help in editing the volume was given this time by Hinrich Stoevesandt, the son of his Bremen friend. In it he had to report among other things that 'from 1 October of this year I shall no longer be found in Basle at Pilgerstrasse 25, but at Bruderholzallee 26'.

This change of abode marked the end of a further period in Barth's life. The first post-war decade was now over. He was just about to move into the eighth decade of his life. His regular period of service as a professor had thus come to an end and negotiations were already taking place at the university about his successor. He himself did not want to take either a dramatic or a tragic view of the inevitable step into the next decade. 'The best thing is to keep busy with people and one's work, to be in the service of the good God himself in such a way that, like a pony, one is simply required to keep clearing one hurdle after another.'[328] 'A student recently asked me in well-chosen words, "What will it all be like when, if I may put it that way, you are no longer there?" He was quite right to remind me of this possibility. "Fast falls the eventide" is only too true of me.'[329] 'The shadows of our day are growing longer . . . But because they are cast by the light which shines before us, we cannot and must not look back on them, but must look *forward* to the great light before us.'[330]

8

Joyful Partisan of the Good God

The years from 1955 to 1962 in Bruderholzallee 26, Basle

1956 – year of celebrations

From October 1955 onwards, Barth no longer lived, as previously, in the centre of the city. The Barth household, which had now shrunk again, moved to 'the hill west of Basle, in much better air, with a great deal of green around us, in a substantially smaller and there-fore more modern and more comfortable house. No one will be able to turn us out, because I have bought it.'[1] The move there, to the so-called 'Bruderholz', was difficult 'in view of the extent and the complicated make-up of our household goods (hardly diminished by giving things away or selling them off – we needed thirty cubic metres of space in the removal van and seventy to eighty chests simply for books, all of which we had to nail down)'. Barth felt that the move was symbolic, 'reminding one of the transition from the old cosmos to the new (note the imagery of II Corinthians 5.1f.)'.[2] He now held his discussion group in the Bruderholz restaurant, a few doors away. It was a long way to the university and to the theological seminar. As a rule he travelled by tram. During the journey he occupied himself by composing advertising slogans, prompted by the posters he saw. 'Like Buchman in the Oxford Group, Knorr takes the lead in any soup', or, ' "Let's not wear hats", I've heard it said. You might as well not wear a head' (this was then in fact used by Arbon commercially) – though Barth himself had not worn a hat for years! Instead of this a beret served him as headgear.

The little room which from now on he used as a study was very small, like the rest of the new house. Here, too, Grünewald's Crucifixion hung over his desk and just below it a photograph of his father. To his left, as he sat at the desk, he had a view of the garden: 'small, but nice and quiet (our "Gertli", as my wife says in her incomparable St Gallen accent)'.[3] There was only room in the study for four chairs and a table, to entertain guests, and for the most important books, on shelves going up to the ceiling. These were the works of the Church Fathers, the Scholastics, the Reformers, the Orthodox and Schleiermacher; also Barth's own writings and his extensive literature on Mozart. The rest of his collection of books could be found in all the other rooms in the house, primarily in the adjoining study of Charlotte von Kirschbaum, and even in the garage. When Christoph later sent his father 'a piece of fabric decorated with symbols of the kind that only kings may wear in Indonesia', Karl Barth hung it in his study 'to protect and to cover my Pandora's box' – the Weimar edition of Luther![4]

The year 1956, which was now approaching, was especially significant because of his forthcoming seventieth birthday. But '1956 was . . . in fact even more significant for me as the bicentenary of the birth of Wolfgang Amadeus Mozart'.[5] 'For me, the most important commemoration of this year is that of the birth of the great little man in Salzburg in 1756.'[6] Barth enthusiastically celebrated the Mozart bicentenary, which fell in January, in his own way: by spending a good deal of money on buying new records ('Can one justify that in frugal Basle?')[7]; by writing a number of commemorative articles, one of which was a 'Letter of Thanks to Mozart' in heaven; and by going to a great many concerts. 'In one concert, in the Basle Musiksaal, at which Clara Haskil was playing the F major concerto, I even had a sudden vision of him standing there in front of the piano, so clear that I almost began to cry. That's quite a story, isn't it – such a story that even Balthasar with his mystical experiences listened respectfully when I told him. At any rate, now I know just what Mozart looked like in the last year of his life.'[8] Equally remarkable was Barth's confession in one of the commemorative articles, that 'if I ever get to heaven, I shall first ask after Mozart, and only then after Augustine and Thomas, Luther and Calvin and Schleiermacher'.[9]

However, for Barth the climax of the celebrations was that 'I was invited to give a commemorative speech about this man and his work at the festival arranged in Basle'. The speech was first delivered on 27 January in Thun, and then again on 29 January in the Grossen Musiksaal in the Basle Stadtcasino,* in between two Mozart wind serenades. It was broadcast live. Barth thought that his closer

---

*The Stadtcasino (City casino) is one of the largest public buildings in Basle, with a restaurant and large reception rooms as well as a concert hall.

attention to musicology would 'doubtless involve me in the same kind of conflict with the leading authorities' as 'I once experienced in my own field with Harnack, Troeltsch, etc.'[10] The lecture gave him the opportunity to think more closely about his attitude to Mozart.

The lecture was called 'Mozart's Freedom'. Barth saw this in the fact that 'he plays and does not cease to play', although he is well aware of human finitude and death. This play is characterized by a 'great and free matter-of-factness' and therefore by 'the absence of all demons': 'with him the subjective element never becomes a theme'.[11] 'I am not a man with particular artistic gifts or an artistic education, nor am I inclined to confuse or to identify salvation history with any part of the history of art. But the golden sounds and melodies of Mozart's music have always spoken to me – not as gospel, but as parables of the kingdom revealed in the gospel of God's free grace, and they continue to do so with the utmost freshness. Without it I could not think of what moves me personally in theology, in politics. There are probably few theologians' studies in which the pictures of Mozart and of Calvin can be seen side by side at the same level.'[12]

It was a happy coincidence that while Barth was preoccupied with Mozart in this way, his dogmatics lectures (from the beginning of the winter semester he had begun on the material for a new volume, IV, 3) were an extended and thoroughgoing discussion of the theological problem of the 'parables of the kingdom of heaven' in the human and earthly realm. He wanted to train Christians to have an eye for such parables and to reckon on their presence even outside the realm of the church. He gave the Mozart lecture again in June, in French, in Neuchâtel and Geneva. His remarks on Mozart soon made all kinds of remarkable contacts for him – for example, with the Heidelberg dermatologist Dr Greither and the Göttingen historian Hermann Heimpel, and even, after a long silence on both sides, with the Erlangen theologian Paul Althaus. He was also in touch again with his former fellow-pupil Albert Schüpbach, who asked him, 'Why do you bother so much with theology when you are capable of writing on other nice things as well?'[13] Curiously, Barth was very active in a Swiss Mozart committee, which included the writer and government minister Carl Burckhardt and the conductor Paul Sacher; he did not hesitate to make long journeys to its meetings. As a result he also had an impressive encounter in the autumn with the historian Jean R. von Salis at Schloss Brunegg. In March he discussed Mozart in Ludwigsburg with his friend the pianist and musicologist Jürgen Uhde, who attempted in vain to make him interested in Paul

Hindemith. But Barth had to concede 'that unfortunately I simply cannot make sense of any modern art (in all three of its forms). I am in no position to pass a negative judgment on it, which is why I don't think I have ever said a bad word against it. But it is a sad fact that I have no understanding of it, no eye or ear for it . . . Perhaps I shall discover in heaven what is so hidden from me now. But it is lamentable that this has not happened to me yet.'[14]

This last conversation took place during one of two interesting journeys which Barth made in March. The first took him to Wuppertal, to a conference of the Society for Evangelical Theology. 'The mockers call the affair in Elberfeld the "Barth Festival".' He happily repeated his Mozart lecture one evening – in a church full to bursting – and in a discussion gave his view on the political situation, which in West Germany was now strongly dominated by the question of relations with East Germany. 'My main argument is that "the problem of the church in East Germany is the church in West Germany".' With all seriousness Barth sought in this way to warn his friends against both the 'Scylla of a theology in the face of which politics becomes inessential', and the 'Charybdis of a policy in connection with which no one has any time for theology'.[15] On this occasion it also happened that 'I even had to oppose my dear friend Hans Iwand, who in important respects is far superior to me. He gave a lecture, in which he said with the great weight that only he can command, that I advocated a concentration of the whole of theology on christology! I was asked to give my opinion, so I said, "Sometimes I don't like the word christology very much. It's not a matter of christology, nor even of christocentricity and a christological orientation, but of *Christ himself*. Any preoccupation with christology – and I have been preoccupied a little with that – can only be a critical help towards coming to the point where we may have the experience of the disciples on the Mount of Transfiguration: "They saw no one, but Jesus alone." '[16] On the way home Barth visited his old friends Karwehl, Stoevesandt and Scholz. They were all getting on in years.

He made the second journey weakened by a persistent attack of influenza. It took him 'over the Gotthard, which was beautiful, and through the plains of Lombardy, which were not, to Venice', where at the invitation of the philosopher Umberto Campagnolo he took part in a conference of the Société de Culture Européenne – along with a group including Silone, Vercors, Stephen Spender and four Soviet intellectuals. 'It was quite pleasant to be included among the men of culture (I sat next to J. P. Sartre!), though my enquiry as to what culture might really be went unanswered. I improvised a little speech (in French) with references to faith, hope and love, and to those workers who are not *hommes de sciences, d'art, de littérature* and so on, like us, but are perhaps even more cultivated. Moreover on Good Friday and Easter Day (the affair took place on Holy Saturday) – I was praised by the head of the Soviet delegation as a "rrrevolutionary", although I was noticeably handicapped by the flu.' 'An Italian senator gave Lollo and me a personal tour of the Doge's palace.' 'We also went on a gondola ride and I fed the doves lavishly (with several hundred lira) so that they could be full for once. Then on Easter morning it was marvellous to hear a sermon at the Waldensian church (which could be deciphered from the biblical texts quoted), to go to the eucharist, and almost to be embraced by the delighted presbyters.'[17] Barth had a strange experience after that when he had a few days' rest with Lollo von Kirschbaum and Max Zellweger at the Signal de Chexbres near Vevey. On an excursion to France he was refused entry on the grounds that he was on some black list. He established that after the liberation of France they had forgotten to take his name off the list.

According to Basle law, at that time a professor was automatically retired at the end of his seventieth year. So for a long time it had been an open question whether Barth would still be able to teach the summer semester of 1956 as an *ordinarius* professor. For some months there was 'confusion over the question of my retirement and my successor – in which the thoughts of many hearts have become open', until finally 'the administration dryly communicated to me on a little bit of paper that although I had reached the legal age-limit, "exceptionally" my term of office "would be extended until further notice"', so no successor would be announced. 'It was Jaspers, of all people, who had spoken in the committee of my "secular" and "world-wide" reputation and had thus at least contributed to the event.'[18] Because he was feeling so weak after the attack of influenza and in order to spare himself for the impending festivities, Barth did not, however, lecture in the summer semester (in any case, for the past two years he had only lectured three hours per week). He only continued the seminar, the discussion group and the colloquia. In the seminar, having discussed two of Schleiermacher's shorter works in succession, this time he turned to the Roman Catholic doctrine of the church. This in turn stimulated him to study Matthias

Scheeben's *Mysterien des Christentums* (Mysteries of Christianity) in the seminar the next winter. In his view, Scheeben was 'certainly the greatest figure which the Roman Catholic church has recently produced in the German sphere'.[19]

In recent times there had been some changes in the Basle faculty of theology, and these continued. Karl Ludwig Schmidt had died at the beginning of January 1956 after a long illness; since the winter of 1953–54 his chair had been taken over by the Swedish Lutheran Bo Reicke. Mathias Rissi had become an assistant lecturer in 1954 and Eduard Buess and Martin Anton Schmidt (the son of Karl Ludwig) had joined the faculty earlier, in the same capacity, in 1951. The latter soon went to the United States, while in 1959 Buess became the successor to Eduard Thurneysen. In 1956 Max Geiger and Heinrich Ott also became assistant lecturers. In 1958 Ernst Jenni succeeded to Baumgartner's chair. On the whole Barth did not have any very intensive contact with his colleagues. 'Over the years I have had only occasional contact, if any, with most of my colleagues in the faculty – not to mention my own brother Heinrich', with whom relations had been chilly for years. 'Each went his own way, partly for practical and technical reasons, partly for deeper ones. This was far from being an ideal situation. Another reason is probably the very intensive demands made on some of us (not all) by our own work; and it may be said in part justification that each of us had something quite considerable under way.'[20] Among the professors from other faculties Barth knew the lawyer Max Gerwig .and the gerontologist Adolf Vischer from much earlier times. On the whole, his contact with them – apart from the historian Bonjour, and a few other exceptions – was little more than chance meetings in the common room. In a way he was very fond of the atmosphere there: 'Herr Kägi and Fräulein Bindschedler talk mild humanism. Herr Blin puts difficult theological questions to me which I have to answer in French, and Herr Wolfram von den Steinen laughs very mysteriously at everything. Nothing gets past the *universitas litterarum*.'[21] Barth always had a particularly high opinion of the biologist Adolf Portmann, whose academic attitude he thought to be a model for theologians as well.

Barth's seventieth birthday on 10 May brought home to him that he was now without doubt an old man. The same year was the centenary of his father's birth, and in the autumn this was commemorated at a small family celebration in Berne. Karl himself had long been a grey-haired grandfather. He had just acquired his tenth grandson – 'to match the volumes of my *Dogmatics* which have so far appeared'.[22] 'I feel like an old weathered fir tree, withered by sun, rain, wind and occasionally struck by lightning, bearing the inscriptions of all kinds of passers-by on its bark, but still standing in the same place.'[23] 'It is of course many years since I rode horseback through field and wood . . . Climbing uphill no longer tempts me (cf. Ecclesiastes 12.5a). And even the speed with which I work at my desk has become perceptibly slower.'[24] 'In my advanced old age – *all* my contemporaries as theological students have now retired – I should really be only an interested bystander', observing the actions of younger men. But, Barth thought, 'this move towards idleness (and possible decay) is not yet due. The admirable Dr Tschopp, to whom I submitted myself for a complete examination' (some while before), 'found both heart and kidneys in a satisfactory state. He even said of the former that it was like that of a young man.' So, 'in view of the troubles of so many other people I am thankful for undeserved blessings: I am not beset by any illness of which I am conscious; air, water, substantial nourishment and moderate exercise still help me to keep my vigour, and I am much better with my faithful pipe than I would be without it. The *Church Dogmatics* is the decisive factor in the preservation of my physical condition; it cries out to be completed and does not allow my head to hang or my hands to rest . . . How long things can remain so is another question.'[25]

Barth began his seventieth birthday, which fell on Ascension Day, by preaching a sermon (on Psalm 34.6), 'this time literally to the spirits in captivity', namely to the inmates of Basle prison.[26] 'Ernst Wolf put it succinctly: "Karl Barth has ended up in gaol." '[27] For two years now he had been preaching there regularly (and nowhere else). 'Martin Schwarz, who works there as a Reformed preacher and pastor, asked me to take his place there one day. From then on I have been there a few times each year and have always enjoyed being a guest in this household'[28] – twenty-eight times in all up to 1964. 'Some people have even toyed slyly with the thought of committing a crime in Basle in order to have an opportunity to hear him preach.'[29] Barth was attracted by this work – 'It is very evident there that people need firm contact with real life; at the same time the gospel becomes remarkably relevant and natural of its own accord.' 'Everything was somehow much more real than in an ordinary church, with the usual kind of Christians who are assembled there.'[30]

Barth usually preached on short texts – once simply on the words 'My grace is enough'. And he tried to preach the gospel as clearly as possible. Thus he said that the first Christian community had consisted of Jesus and the criminals who were crucified with him, and he strongly emphasized the little word 'all' in Romans 11.32. In one sermon he said, 'If anyone identified himself with prisoners, it was he', Jesus Christ; 'That is, the Lord who has mercy on you: this prisoner who is your liberator, the liberator of us all.' In another sermon he said that all men were accused, but that the court of Christ, the reconciler, was where we should have to appear. And in another sermon Barth stressed that 'the commandment of God runs: You may allow yourself to be loved by me', and in yet another, 'I am not sure whether Christmas is really in place in the cathedral or the Engelgasse chapel, where it is celebrated by the best people. But I am perfectly certain that it is in place here, in prison.'[31] The majority of sermons were followed by the eucharist. Moreover, 'in preparing and conducting the services, the prayers I used were just as important as the sermons themselves'.[32] Barth did not want merely to preach to his audience. In order to preach to them properly he also wanted to get to know them personally, and so he often went to visit them in their cells. For instance, he once reported that 'this morning I listened at length to three murderers, two confidence tricksters and one adulterer, added the odd remark here and there and gave each a fat cigar.' On another occasion he asked in amazement, 'Am I really something of an optimist or a walking embodiment of the heresy of the restoration of all things? I found it impossible to be despondent or disturbed over these men. Instead, I thought that I had seen something encouraging and cheering in each of them.'[33]

So 10 May 1956 also began with a service here. Following that, Heinrich Held, the President of the Evangelical Church of the Rhineland, gave Barth birthday greetings 'in an unmerited personal eulogy'.[34] Barth spent the afternoon with his family. They performed a short play for him in which Karl Barth, over a hundred years old, arrived at the gates of heaven, delivered his *Dogmatics* and eagerly asked to see Mozart. Some of his closest friends also took part in this family festival – all of them were now getting on in years or were already old. Others he would never see again, above all his beloved friends Pierre Maury and Arthur Frey, who had died shortly beforehand. 'Every Wednesday and every Saturday Arthur Frey would telephone me for a long conversation ("Arthur here"); and he was a good and utterly faithful friend to me (and to Lollo).'[35] This was also true of Maury. His death 'was a personal loss to us and a loss to the cause, of which we shall always be conscious. One feels drawn all the more to the friends that one still has.'[36] In succession to

Arthur Frey, Max Geiger became Editor and Managing Director of Evangelischer Verlag. Marcel Pfändler had already been proposed as Business Manager by Frey himself.

There had been another death in the family: 'my cousin the painter Paul Basilius Barth (1881–1955). Of course he lived in quite a different world. Towards the end we belatedly developed a remarkably good personal relationship.'[37] Karl Barth believed that his cousin had the gift 'of seeing much beauty with heart and eye. He avoided pretension, stiffness and obvious idiosyncratic whims, and showed insight, conviction and generosity.' 'There is a subterranean relationship between his efforts and my own; it is undefinable, but still very real.'[38] In 1954–55 Paul Basilius had painted two pictures of his theologian cousin, taking fourteen sittings over them. One had been commissioned by the Reformed Church in Frankfurt: 'they wanted to hang it in the presbytery room in a series which began with Calvin and John à Lasco'.[39] The other was bought by Barth's Basle friend Benedikt Vischer, who gave it to Basle University on Karl's seventieth birthday. The University hung it in the Regenzsaal 'alongside the portrait of a professor of gynaecology (also painted by P.B.B.!) and that of a professor of classical Greek'.[40]

Barth had insisted that his students should be allowed to come to the formal birthday celebrations on 11 May, at which the presentation of the portrait took place, and friends and representatives of various universities and churches evaluated his work. Pastor Vollenweider spoke in the name of the Basle church, Visser't Hooft in the name of the ecumenical movement, Constantin von Dietz in the name of the German church, and so on. Barth was also presented with a very large Festschrift, entitled *Antwort* (Answer), which had been edited by Ernst Wolf. 'Germans dominated it, but there were also many other contributors from all over the world, including an Indian Buddhist – a giant work.'[41] Seventy-eight writers contributed, and their work was evidence not only of the variety and number of Barth's friends in theology and in the church, but also of the wealth of stimulation which he had provided. One tit-bit in the volume was Thurneysen's release for publication of part of his correspondence with Barth between 1914 and 1921. Two years later, Barth in turn released the continuation of this correspondence between 1921 and 1925, and it was published under the title *Lebendige Vergangenheit* (Living Past) to celebrate Thurneysen's seventieth birthday. The Barth bibliography (up to the end of 1955), included as an appendix to *Antwort,* contained 406 publications and showed translations in twelve languages. In addition to *Antwort* there was also a series of further Festschriften from his Basle colleagues, from young Swiss theologians, from America, from Japan, from Lutheran theologians – and a volume of sermons by Rhineland pastors edited by Martin Rohkrämer. Barth was highly pleased with all these assessments, and with the flood of good wishes, but was bothered by the question 'What would Kierkegaard have said of such an occasion? How does it compare with the New Testament? What will it look like in the light of heaven?' 'The prophets of the Old Testament and the apostles of the New couldn't have seventieth birthdays like this.'[42]

So Barth did not want simply to accept uncritically the honour done to his 'person'. Especially when talking to his students, who also celebrated the event in a great many ways, he was concerned to direct their attention elsewhere. Certainly he was grateful for their friendly response. But he tried to warn them against understanding themselves as *his* pupils. 'Theology requires free men . . . And I would not like my life to result in the founding of a new school. I would like to tell anyone who is prepared to listen that I myself am not a "Barthian"; because after I have learnt something I want to remain free to go on learning.' Barth could also say that 'the criterion of a *good* "Barthian" – if there should be such a thing – is surely that Barth himself can and must learn something from him.'[43] At any rate, 'Emphasize my name as little as possible. There is only *one* interesting name, and bringing up all the rest only leads to false loyalties, and can only arouse tedious jealousy and stubbornness among other people. And do not accept anything from me without testing it. Measure everything by the Word of God, the sole truth, which is our judge and our best teacher! You will understand me correctly if you allow what I say to lead you to what *he* says. A good theologian does not live in a house of ideas, principles and methods. He walks right through all such buildings and always comes out into the fresh air again. He remains on the way. He has his eyes on the horizon, the high mountains and the infinite sea – and at the same time also has at heart the good and the bad, the fortunate and the unfortunate, Christians and pagans, his fellow-men from East and West, to whom he is allowed to make his modest testimony.'[44]

One of the lessons which Barth felt that he had definitely learnt during his long career was this: 'In all circumstances theology is a fine and joyful task . . . When I began it as a young man I was often troubled and saddened by it. Later I could see that if one understands theology properly, it takes one to a place which – for all the difficulties, all the laborious work that is required – is a happy one, where a man can *live* and long for the time when he will see "face to face" (I Corinthians 13.13): for himself *and* for others.'[45] Barth's birthday also made him take account of the course of his theological thought which now spanned roughly fifty years, and particularly of the change which had taken place since he had begun his *Romans*. He thought that there was not a 'new Barth', 'as many people have hastily assumed today'. 'But it is true that I have learnt some things on the way. At least I hope so. The way not to grow old, and to stay young with advancing years, is to continue to learn (in this case to study theology) and not to get tired of it. While once man apparently had no place in my theology, I think that over the years I have learned to speak of God the Creator and his relationship with man as his creature in a way which allows man a greater prominence. I think that now I can put things better by saying that man also has true freedom through the power of the free sovereign grace of God: freedom for obedience, the freedom of the children of God. I think that today I can understand and reverence more than before the wise patience of God, the outpouring and the renewing work of his Word and Spirit in man and in mankind. I do not think that I have forgotten and denied anything of what I learned and put forward earlier. But I think that in thinking and speaking about the great cause of God and man I have become more peaceful and happier than I could be when I was arguing fiercely against the attitudes current at that time.'[46]

This progress in thought had been struggled for and achieved over the years in an extensive collection of writings. Remarkably enough, Barth felt that this literary work had emerged only gradually. 'As far as I can recall there was no stage in my theological career when I had more than the very next step forward in mind and planned for it. On each occasion this step developed from the steps which I had already taken, and followed from my view of what was possible and necessary in each changing situation. I saw myself as the man who I had become so far. I used what I thought that I had learned and understood so far to cope with this or that situation, with some complex of biblical or historical or doctrinal questions, often with some subject presented to me from outside, often in fact by a topical

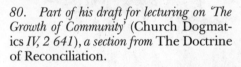

80. *Part of his draft for lecturing on 'The Growth of Community'* (Church Dogmatics *IV, 2 641*), *a section from* The Doctrine of Reconciliation.

81. *For thirty years he worked for the most part on the twelve thick volumes of his* Church Dogmatics. *Here he is correcting his draft (1959).*

82. *His study at Bruderholzallee 26, one of the few theologians' studies where, he pointed out, pictures of Calvin and Mozart could be seen on the same level.*

Friends

83. Hans Jakob Barth, Günther Dehn and Helmut Gollwitzer at Barth's seventieth birthday celebrations.

84. During the 1950s he found himself constantly in direct or indirect conversation with Rudolf Bultmann, his former colleague (pictured here in 1952).

85. Barth found himself in quite a different world as he made the acquaintance of his cousin Paul Basilius Barth, who painted two portraits of him (1954).

86. Emil Brunner and Karl Barth at their last meeting, at Bruderholzallee, 19 November 1960 ('the whale and the elephant').

subject, e.g. a political issue. It was always something new that got hold of me, rather than the other way round. I then tried to cope with this thing as well as I could. I found that difficult enough every time, so I could hardly think beyond the next day or the day after. I hardly ever had anything like a programme to follow at all costs. My thinking, writing and speaking developed from reacting to people, events and circumstances with which I was involved, with their questions and their riddles . . . I did not *want* to be, do or say this or that; I was, did and said it when the time had come. That is what working on the *Church Dogmatics* was like for twenty-five years: from one semester to another, from one week to the next. And it was the same with my other books, lectures, sermons and so on. They were like trees, large and small, which I saw shooting up, growing and spreading out before me; their life did not depend on me; I simply had to watch them with more and more attention. I prayed for my daily bread, got it and ate it, and let the next day look after itself.'[47]

In the middle of June 1956 Barth went with Hans Urs von Balthasar and Frau Adrienne Kaegi-von Speyr to Paris. There they were to take part in 'the doctoral examination of a Jesuit', Père Henri Bouillard, 'who had written 1200 pages about me. He was cross-examined about me for five hours (at the Sorbonne), and then we celebrated in a Chinese restaurant.'[48] This *viva-voce* examination 'was an extraordinary event, in that the "subject" of such a thesis should not really be still alive. That I was in fact very much alive and even there in person made the whole proceedings very tense, but also added a great deal of merriment.'[49] Bouillard was another of those Catholics in whom Barth discovered a surprising affinity to his own thought . . . 'In an astonishing way he too is very much *d'accord* with me. He is another one who wants to introduce me into Roman Catholic theology rather like a Trojan horse, but he also has his own critical little coda. Unlike Hans Urs von Balthasar, however, in this case it is not some holy little Thérèse or Elizabeth, but a transcendental *ontologie de la foi*, agreed criteria of a Kantian character. Still . . . there is much to suggest that I have another chance of becoming a kind of Catholic church father *in partibus infidelium*.'[50] Another 'valuable Catholic confederate, the bold Lucerne theologian Hans Küng', was also examined soon afterwards for his doctorate. 'At the Germanicum in Rome, and thus so to speak under the nose of His Holiness, he had written a work on "my" doctrine of justification.'[51] Barth had had a lively correspondence with him for some time. In

Hans Küng's book the reader would find 'razor-sharp arguments for the thesis that there is no essential difference between Reformation doctrine on the central point of justification as now interpreted and presented by me and the doctrine of the Roman church, properly understood. So far the book has not been repudiated by Catholic officialdom over there; on the contrary, it has been openly praised by several prominent figures. What is one to say to that? Has the millennium dawned, or is it just waiting round the next corner? How one would like to believe it!'[52] In January 1957 Barth wrote a foreword for this book (and was given an official *imprimatur* for the first time in his life!). In it, he said that if the teaching put forward by Küng was really Catholic, 'then, having twice gone to the Church of Santa Maria Maggiore in Trent to commune with the *genius loci*, I may very well have to hasten there a third time to make a contrite confession – "Fathers, I have sinned."'[53]

Two weeks after his journey to Paris Barth undertook another trip abroad. In autumn 1954, the Theological Faculty of the Reformed church in Budapest had bestowed on him an honorary doctorate in theology (his fifth); now in 1956 the University of Edinburgh gave him an honorary doctorate of laws (his second). He expressed his gratitude for these honours with dedications, to Budapest in *Church Dogmatics* IV, 2 and to Edinburgh in IV, 3. And he resolved to accept at least the second doctorate in person – in Scotland on 6 July. Accompanied by his son Markus, who had recently moved to the Federated Theological Faculty in Chicago as Professor of New Testament, he travelled to Britain. 'I was in London and Edinburgh, to receive a further Festschrift there (*Essays in Christology*) and to receive the title LLD in Edinburgh. In London I met the Archbishop of Canterbury (I looked in vain in Lambeth Palace among the many pictures of old gentlemen who had held this position for a portrait of Anselm), and in Edinburgh I was able to shake the Prince Consort by the hand.'[54] Prince Philip 'made some personal remark to me, but in the storm of applause I could not grasp it. There were speeches again in Lambeth Palace ("I have not read his books, but he is certainly a most outstanding man. However, I disagree completely with him"), not without a slight sense of humour.'[55] On this visit he also went to see Bishop George Bell again: 'An ecumenist without guile, who prepared a reception for me in his palace at Chichester the warmth of which I will never forget.'[56] Barth was seeing him for the last time.

By giving up his lectures for the summer he had a good deal of time and leisure for all kinds of other special activities. In the summer and autumn he again held a series of 'question and answer sessions': in Strasbourg and Geneva, with the 'positive' Basle pastors and in the Mission House there, and finally at the synod of the pastors from the Berne Jura in Tavannes (on *Church Dogmatics* IV, 2). He also went with his son-in-law and two sons to Mülligen in the Aargau, to see at first hand the place 'where the Barth family has lived since the eleventh century and presumably even longer. I, too, was completely at home there.' 'We were welcome and entertained there by the commune council and the rest of the people just as warmly as we had been in Britain by the Archbishop and the Duke.'[57] At about the same time, Barth had to re-examine his previous history in another way in a lecture which he had readily agreed to give.

'The Humanity of God'

In August, he again spent some days in Gyrenbad, during which he wrote this lecture virtually at one sitting; he then delivered it to an audience of Swiss pastors on 25 September 1956 in Aarau. It was in fact based on a talk on 'The Humanity of Jesus' which he had written earlier in the year for South German radio. The Aarau lecture – its characteristic title was 'The Humanity of God' – did not say anything that had not been said long before in the *Dogmatics*, but more than almost any other of Barth's works it publicized the way in which his thought had in fact changed profoundly since 'the beginnings of dialectical theology'. 'Remarkably enough it now came to people's attention for the first time, although they could have read it long before. For me it was a retrospective reflection, but for many people it was a discovery.'[58] In the very Great Council room 'in which I stood up against my teacher Adolf von Harnack' in the year 1920 and 'proclaimed my recognition of the "wholly other"'', Barth now presented a revision of his former theology.

'A *genuine* revision does not amount to a retreat after second thoughts; it is a new advance and attack in which what was said before has to be said again, but in a better way.' Barth certainly did not want to retract 'what forcibly burst upon us about forty years ago', in contrast to all the pious, liberal and 'positive' types of anthropocentric theology, namely the recognition that God is *God*. But he now wanted to develop this recognition in a direction which had earlier still been completely hidden from him: 'God is God in such a way that he also has the characteristic of humanity. In this form and in this form only was (and is) our view of the divinity of God to be contrasted with that earlier theology. There must be positive acceptance and not unconsidered rejection of the grain of truth which one cannot possibly deny in it, even if one sees all its weaknesses. God's very *deity*, rightly understood, includes his *humanity*. If Jesus Christ is the word of truth, the "mirror of the fatherly heart of God", then Nietzsche's remark that man is something to be overcome is a downright lie: in that case the truth of *God* is loving-kindness towards man – and nothing else.'[59] At the dinner which followed, the Aargau councillor Kurt Kim delighted Barth by alluding to a remark made by the former pastor of Safenwil, 'O Aargau, may God have mercy upon you'; he added, 'And God *has* had mercy on the Aargau!'

The thought here led in to another lecture on 'Evangelical Theology in the Nineteenth Century' which was given during the following winter in Hanover (on 8 January) in the course of a series of lectures ('Panorama of a Century') sponsored by the Goethe Institute.

In it Barth made clear that while he still had certain specific questions about this century – which he had once seen in such a critical light – he now could no longer simply say no to it. 'The nineteenth century is not finished, nor is its theology.' Why could Barth now think so openly and so positively even in this direction? It was most of all because he himself no longer understood 'theology' merely as a 'doctrine of God', but as 'theanthropology', that is, 'as "a doctrine of God and man"', of the communication and the community between God and man'.[60]

He gave the lecture in a large room, full to bursting, from which it was also relayed into two neighbouring rooms. Whereas in 1954 he had caused offence by his informal dress, this time he aroused attention by his formal tail-coat. Following the lecture there was a lively meeting with some friends and members of the Goethe Institute at the home of his former pupil Kurt Müller. There he had a cheerful meeting with Bishop Hanns Lilje, who acknowledged that he felt very much at home in this 'Diaspora'. 'At a late hour some adventurous dignitary put my beret on Lilje's head. It did not look at all bad on him.' When Barth accepted the invitation on this occasion to put his name in the Golden Book of the City of Hanover, a painting on the wall prompted him to show off his knowledge of history. He surprised the journalists present by seeming to know 'more about the victory won by the Hanoverians over the Prussians(!) in 1866 than they did themselves'.[61] On the way back from Hanover he met some of the Frankfurt philosophers by arrangement with Karl Gerhard Steck: they included Adorno, Horkheimer, Weinstock and Sturmfels. Here the remembrance of Heinrich Scholz, who had just died, proved to be a good bridge for the conversation between 'theology and philosophy', whereas mention of the late Heidegger simply brought conversation to a standstill.

In the winter semester of 1956–57 Barth was able to return with gusto to the continuation of his next volume, *Church Dogmatics* IV, 3. Having dealt in the first part of *The Doctrine of Reconciliation* with the humiliation of the Son of God and in the second with the exaltation of the Son of Man, in the third he was concerned to stress the *unity* of the 'God-man' Jesus Christ and his work of humiliation and exaltation. He only wanted to talk of this, however, by developing the statement that the reconciliation achieved in Jesus Christ, in his humiliation and exaltation, '*proclaims* itself by taking place'.[62]

Barth developed this succinct statement at length, distinguishing his approach both from the view that reconciliation is static and already complete and from the many doctrines according to which the disclosure of reconciliation to men is a matter of human artifice. 'The question of the significance and the scope of the "prophetic office" of Jesus Christ has led me in this third part of *The Doctrine of Reconciliation* to a theme which both in theory and in practice now appears widely prominent in the statements made in the church by all confessions, in a variety of contexts and under a variety of titles. But as far as I can see, this has so far lacked a theological basis which is firmly oriented on the gospel. One can find little or nothing in the theology of the Reformation and afterwards . . . about the decisive presuppositions on the basis of which we now think that we are free and compelled to pursue so zealously the problem of Christ (or the church) and the world . . . It cannot be my present purpose to enter properly into these discussions (say about mission, evangelization, the activity of the laity, church and culture, Christianity and socialism, and so on). My task is to discover the fundamental presuppositions, which are by no means obvious, and here everything ultimately compels me to the insight that the "confession before men" which has to be accepted and made all along the line does not just belong on the periphery but in the centre of the life of Christians in community – because it is grounded in the work of the living Jesus Christ. Indeed the problem of witness itself decides whether the Christian is a Christian or not, and whether the Christian community is a Christian community or not.'[63]

In his thoughts on this whole theme Barth began from basic considerations about the form of the risen Christ as the 'true witness'. 'If there is an axiom of Christian theology it is this: Jesus Christ is risen, yes, he is truly risen.'[64] From this point he went on to reflect on the concept of the 'witness' which for some time had been very dear to him. For Barth it had in fact become the embodiment of all Christian action (including proclamation). It had this significance in a twofold sense: that at best no Christian action can be a causal or instrumental realization, communication or representation of revelation, but only a human witness to it. However, as a witness man in fact 'co-operates' in reconciliation and takes part in its revelation *actively* (and not merely passively or receptively). Indeed Barth even thought that there might also be true words, manifestations of the one truth, alongside the one Word of God, outside the church as well as within, as a witness to the power of Jesus Christ to make even 'stones' testify to him. But because the church of Jesus Christ above all has to be understood as a community of witnesses, he stressed with the greatest firmness that it is not an end in itself: it 'is there for all the *world*, indeed for all men . . . It exists ecstatically, eccentrically . . . The centre around which it moves eccentrically is not simply the world as such, but the world for which God is.'[65] Barth saw the significance of the period between Easter and the return of Christ in relation to the task of extending the Christian witness. The volume therefore ended in statements about the Christian hope. One particular feature about them was the conceptual distinction between three forms of the one return of Christ: that of the resurrection, which had already taken place; that of the coming of the Holy Spirit which was taking place in the present; and that of the parousia, with its universal, total, definitive revelation, which would take place in the future. Another special feature was his dialectical approach to the question of 'universalism', which Barth's critics constantly saw as a danger in his work. One could certainly not count on it (as on any of God's grace); one had, however, to remain open to it (because grace is always greater than our heart).[66]

On the day that the Hungarian revolt broke out, 23 October 1956, Barth was beginning a section of his *Doctrine of Reconciliation* under the title 'Jesus is Victor'. In June he had been able to talk with Bishop Bereczky and in October with Professor Laszlo Pap (who had once been his pupil in Bonn) both about the Hungarian situation and about his concern over the danger that theology there would conform with the ruling régime. The subsequent winter months were now 'completely overshadowed by a preoccupation with world events and, even more oppressively, with the way in which we saw our Swiss society approach them. With only a few like-minded people on my side, I felt more isolated during these weeks than at any time since 1933 in Bonn and 1938–41 here in Basle. There was hateful witch-hunting of the few Workers' Party people, and senseless clamour for the termination of Swiss neutrality . . . Even among the Christians, everything seemed to be tottering.'[67] During these days 'a very dear colleague of mine preached a sermon in Basle cathedral on Matthew 8.28ff.: the expulsion of the demons from the possessed man into the swine. He did it very well and showed how one day the demons would be driven even out of the Kremlin. After the sermon I told him that he had forgotten only one thing: the swine into which the demons were driven. Often in such cases they are ourselves.'[68] The preacher to which Barth refers here was in fact Eduard Thurneysen.

Barth's view was that communism had 'pronounced its own verdict on itself' in Hungary and that 'it did not need ours'. Furthermore, before being interested in the splinters in other people's eyes, people should take the beams out of their own. He would now most of all have liked to write something to this effect, 'alongside which the *Theological Existence Today* of 1933 would have sounded like a gentle murmur'.[69] But he then asked himself 'whether today it might not be a matter of Amos 5.13 or I Samuel 3.11'.[70] So he did not write anything, but kept quiet. And 'because I kept quiet about it all (not just for the usual "two minutes silence") but all the time, unfortunately I now made myself unpopular in my homeland once again.'[71] And outside it as well! 'The question "Why is Karl Barth silent about Hungary?" has been raised against me even from America' – by Reinhold Niebuhr. 'But Karl Barth has remained silent and knows why.'[72] 'It was obvious that this was not a genuine question. It did not arise from the practical problems of a Christian who seeks an exchange of views and fellowship with another, but from the safe stronghold of a hard-boiled Western politician who wanted to lead his opponent on to thin ice, either to compel me to accept his primitive anti-communism or to unmask me as a crypto-communist, and in either case to discredit me as a theologian. What could I have said in reply?'[73] Still, precisely because he kept quiet, Barth was then in a position to help Hungarians in danger in their own land. 'I intervened on behalf of five people, received a courteous telegram from a minister in reply, and in fact achieved what I set out to do.'[74]

An indirect comment on the Hungarian crisis and especially on Western reactions to it was clearly contained in the statements to which he was led in his dogmatics during the summer semester of 1957.

Here he stressed remarkably strongly that Jesus is 'the victor' only as 'the victor of Gethsemane and Golgotha', the 'complete victor' only in his 'complete defeat', which with the 'growing greatness of the Word of God' in the course of history also means a deepening of darkness and of contradiction; thus the 'action' of Jesus the victor in the present always also consists in his 'passion' and his 'fellow-suffering' with the 'brethren'. He then showed that the lie, more than anything else, was the peculiarly Christian form of sin – and demonstrated this in a broad exposition of the book of Job. According to this the theology of Job's friends, while intrinsically correct, presented itself as a lie in the specific situation of Job's suffering. Here Barth was unmistakably incorporating his thoughts about the current discussion of atomic warfare, and about the problems of a 'Christian West' in general.

He also had some further duties in addition to his dogmatics lectures. He had already prepared two radio broadcasts during the spring vacation: one was on the problem of 'Immortality' (which in his view was a real problem for Christians); the other was on the question of 'The Individual in Modern Times' (threatened both by 'depersonalization' and by 'the retreat into the private sphere', but in either case called to freedom). He also gave a lecture in Neuchâtel on the problem of infant baptism in Calvin. On another occasion he heard a lecture in Basle by Gottlieb Söhngen from Munich on the *analogia fidei*, welcoming him with delight as the forerunner 'of a new Catholic theological learning'.[75] As in the winter, he also took a few days' break during the summer semester – this time to travel for a week (from 7 to 12 June) up and down Bavaria. He visited Frau Maria Lempp, was delighted to hear Karl Steinbauer preach, spent the night at the home of the mother of his dear friend Frau Liselotte Nold, and had a last exchange of reminiscences with Georg Merz, who had aged considerably. They had come to differ in their views more and more over the last decades, but they were still very close. After walking a little way arm in arm, they said their farewells. The climax of the trip was Barth's participation in a conference of the Bavarian Pastors' Brotherhood in Rummelsberg, at which Bishop Dietzfelbinger made a great impression on him. Here he himself had to answer questions at a public discussion. It was concerned with the problems of liturgy, to which he reacted with some pointed arguments and counter-arguments – goaded on by his partly 'anti-Calvinistic' (and at any rate decidedly Lutheran) opposition. His comment on the idea of a heavenly church is characteristic: 'Not an eternal church, which already bores people here on earth!' Or on the liturgy: 'The primary celebrant is Jesus Christ himself' and the secondary celebrant is the whole community, not the pastor. Or on the sacrament: 'There is only *one* sacrament – the one who has himself risen from the dead.' Or on preaching: 'It is not only proclamation, but also petition and adoration', and it is strictly 'an act of the community'.[76]

He was not very keen on German Lutheranism, as he had come to know it in the period immediately after the war. Now he had met it again in Bavaria, and it still interested him so much that he resolved once again to make a thorough study of the newer Lutheranism in his seminar during the winter of 1957–58. He attempted to understand it by taking up Werner Elert's *Dogmatics*. 'To be honest, for all our efforts, this really was not a success. We stood in horrified amazement at the phenomenon of a systematic theology characterized on the one hand by a sombre historical fatalism and on the other by an equally pig-headed confessionalism, in which we could only recognize the centre of the biblical message from a distance. I do not think that the seminar will be in a hurry to study any other product of this school, which is extremely barren, despite its deep sincerity.'[77]

The number of students who wanted to hear Barth now increased rather than decreased. On the whole, he found that their interest in Bultmann's questions was fading. 'I was particularly pleased to be able to note that the attention of the rising generation seems to be shifting from the question of method, which has been all too dominant in the field over the last decade, to the question of content.'[78] Now some of Ebeling's students used to travel over regularly from Zürich for Barth's seminar and discussion group – a practice that was to continue for years. Prominent among them that winter was Eberhard Jüngel, who 'played a lively part in the discussion'.[79] After his excursion into modern Lutheranism, Barth was glad to take refuge again in Calvin for the seminar in the following summer. He was also eagerly sought out by the Swiss communist Konrad Farner. 'One curiosity: my "pupils" in the English-speaking colloquium during the summer semester included no fewer than four American colleagues who, like others before them, were very keen to use their sabbatical leave for a stay in Basle.' And another curious thing: only *one student* took part in the French-speaking colloquium – 'and he was an Italian Waldensian'; there were, however, pastors from Alsace.[80]

The 'conversations' with all kinds of groups which now almost entirely took the place of Barth's former lectures had a similar form to his seminars and his colloquia. He asked for written questions which he then tried to answer in the course of subsequent discussion. It transpired that he had an astonishing aptitude and agility in developing his views and insights in connection with the objections and criticisms which were put to him directly in spontaneous discussion. During the winter of 1957–58 he talked in this way with missionaries at the Basle Mission House, with Basle pastors, with the sisters of the Evangelical Convent of Sonnenhof in the Baselbiet, with members of an ecumenical course at Bossey and with seminary students at Tübingen – and the following summer he also talked with the Lutheran Preachers' Seminary at Hildesheim. The 'conversations' in the Basle Mission House were repeated fairly regularly every year. Missionaries on home leave could discuss the problems which concerned them – and it was the same with the people at Bossey, who came to Basle every year on a day in January for discussion, led by one of the professors of theology, either Hans Heinrich Wolf or Nikos Nissiotis.

'We are concerned with life'

The year 1958 was marked out for Barth in a special way by his preoccupation with the question of atomic rearmament, which pressed on him from various sides. He had already spoken on this subject twice in 1957. On Good Friday he had endorsed the appeals against atomic weapons made by Albert Schweitzer and by the eighteen protesting German scientists with a succinct comment: 'People in both East and West should rise up against the madness which is in evidence here. We are concerned with life. We are concerned with people.'[81] Then in June, in a telegram to Radio Warsaw, he had called on the world powers to renounce atomic weapons – even unilaterally, if necessary.[82] In 1958 Barth discussed the problem above all in the context of the possible issue of atomic weapons to the Swiss or the German army. In April, the German church brotherhoods presented a petition to the Synod of the Evangelical Church in Germany at the heart of which were ten theses which designated even preparation for atomic warfare a sin. Its critical culmination was the tenth thesis, at which 'a real cry of dismay went up, and the weaker brethren at least sighed gently'.[83] Hans Asmussen spoke out particularly vehemently in opposition – with the counter-argument that not only dropping an atomic bomb, but even not dropping an atomic bomb, might be a sin. The polemical title of his article, 'Denial of the Three Articles of Faith', referred to the tenth thesis, which ran: 'No Christian can adopt a contrary position or even be neutral on this question. Either of these positions amounts to a denial of all three articles of the Christian faith.' When the rumour was spread in German newspapers that Professor Barth was not in theological agreement with the ten theses of the 'petition', he let it be made known 'that I agree with these theses (including No. 10) just as if I had written them myself'.[84] It was easy for him to say that, since he was in fact the anonymous author! However, over this question he kept in close contact with representatives of the brotherhoods. For this reason Ernst Wolf visited him on many occasions, together with Hannelore Hansch, Martin Rohkrämer and Helmut Simon. In the summer he had a conversation about it with Gustav Heinemann – 'with whom I quickly got on to "Du" terms before he became Federal Chancellor'. On 31 July he had a discussion on the same question at Feldberg with the Christian students association of Freiburg im Breisgau. Here, however, 'it unfortunately emerged that the dear and wise Erik Wolf (unlike his vigorous wife) is completely on the wrong track'.[85] Also this summer, Barth presented through the brotherhoods six theses which were concerned with this whole group of problems: 'Barmen Today. A Revival of the Repudiation made at Barmen 1934'. He wanted to give a lecture based on the theses at a conference of the brotherhood in Frankfurt at the beginning of October, but in the end he had to say no because he was so tired.

Barth was against atomic rearmament not only for Germany but 'for any state or nation. Atomic war cannot be a just war in any sense; it can only be universal annihilation.'[86] In view of the zeal of so many politicians to acquire these weapons nevertheless, he sometimes complained that he had the 'impression that we all live in a madhouse or in a kindergarten or, to put them together, in the children's section of a lunatic asylum: *kyrie eleison*.'[87] Thus Barth was also automatically against atomic weapons for Switzerland. However, in his protest he came up against widespread opposition: first of all in the Theological Commission of the Swiss Church Federation, to which he had belonged for some time (and for which in 1958 he prepared an opinion on Anglican-Presbyterian reunion). This Commission also had to concern itself with the question of atomic weapons. There were 'radio-active' sessions as a result of which two opposing views ultimately emerged within the Federation: 'One was inspired by Ernst Staehelin. This began from the fact that the creation was unfortunately still broken and was evidently to be broken even more (deep sighs). Therefore, it went on to argue, we had to support our atom-brandishing Federal Councillors and military authorities (*who* should have been on this troubled side but Eduard Schweizer, which is what happens to someone who has been flirting with Bultmann for years!). The other view was inspired by me', supported by the Berne Old Testament scholar J. J. Stamm.[88]

Barth also discussed the question with a divisional commander of the Swiss army, Alfred Ernst – who was reading the *Church Dogmatics*! He had come to know Ernst at the end of 1957 and had learnt to respect him 'both as a man and as a Christian (unlike others from that dark place Zürich!)'.[89] From that point on they wrote to each other and exchanged visits regularly: the theologian was interested in military questions and the commander in theology. Of course the two disagreed over the question of atomic weapons. Again, even Ernst did not succeed in making Barth change his mind. He maintained his view that – apart from any objections in principle – general acceptance of atomic weapons also meant an end to the political neutrality of Switzerland. He therefore joined Heinrich Buchbinder and Fritz Lieb in an initiative* against the introduction of nuclear weapons into Switzerland. Among the theologians, apart from Lieb, Gottlob Wieser was 'almost the only one who stood publicly beside me' in this whole complex of questions: he impressed Barth 'by the circumspection, the repose and the courage of his personal attitude'.[90] Barth was also at one on this question with Hanns Dieter Hüsch, whose cabaret he was fond of visiting and with whom he occasionally had personal meetings at this time. However, official policy took so little notice of these objections that in July the administration even prohibited the holding of an International Congress against Atomic Warfare in Basle. When such a congress did take place in London, Fritz Lieb was able to present to it a written greeting from Barth. Barth put forward the view that it was probably no longer possible to fight directly against atomic rearmament. The only course was the indirect one of overcoming ideological differences and the anxieties in the world-political situation which were caused by them.

The East-West conflict claimed his attention in yet another way in

---

*'Initiative' here is a technical term. A Swiss citizen has the right to make proposals on certain political matters to the administration of the canton or the Federation, and if he can gather enough support, a vote must be taken on these proposals, which are adopted if they secure a majority.

the summer of 1958. In July he put his new view of the position of the church between East and West in the form of seven theses in a 'postscript' to a work by Josef Hromádka.

In them he said that the church on both sides should not let itself be bound by anything, even by tradition, ideology or the interpretation of history – other than the task to preach the gospel. This task was to be undertaken in an utter openness of faith in which men could start from the view that 'Jesus Christ also died for "Marxists"', and he even died for "capitalists", "imperialists" and "Fascists".'[91]

These theses indicated implicitly, if not explicitly, that in Barth's view he and Hromádka were still at odds. For Barth this difference was one reason why – unlike so many of his friends – 'I could not really feel at home in the air of the ("Prague") All Christian Peace Movement, although I was very sympathetic towards it.'[92] The unresolved question continued to bother them both for years, without ever damaging their open friendship. To their mutual sorrow, however, they were never able to clear things up completely between themselves. Barth thought that he could get on better over this point with his two other Prague friends, Josef Souček and Jan Milic Lochman. At any rate, he could do nothing but repeat himself in new phrases: the gospel puts us in a place 'above the clouds of the conflicting and feuding ideologies, interests and powers in the present "Cold War"'. He was therefore 'most allergic to any identification of theology with social and political thought, and also to any drawing of parallels or analogies between them in which the superiority of the *analogans* (the gospel) to the *analogatum* (the political insights and views of the theologian concerned) did not remain clear, uninterchangeable and visible'. However, Barth did not see a standpoint above the conflict as an excuse for social and political indifference. Rather, it was the stimulus to a 'resolute attitude in which we can be of help with our Word, for the sake of God's will. We must show solidarity with *the man* by showing solidarity with men: of the left and the right, sufferers and fighters, the just and the unjust, Christians and atheists, while at the same time being sympathetically critical towards them.'[93]

In August Barth wrote a whole pamphlet in the form of an 'open letter to a pastor in the German Democratic Republic'. In it he gave all sorts of pastoral advice on the questions posed to him from East Germany about the existence of Christians there.

First of all, in a free paraphrase of 1 Peter 5.8f., he gave an explanation of what 'standing firm in the faith' might mean in East and West. The real 'lion' which had to be resisted (whether as an 'Eastern lion' or a 'Western lion') was not some external threat to Christians, but the temptation 'to howl with the wolves or to be afraid of being eaten by them, in short, to active godlessness'. Resistance did not consist in some kind of fight, but in simple readiness to 'believe earnestly and joyfully in God, to whom it is our task to bear witness'. In particular, it was not important to fight hard to defend the existence of the 'national' form of the church. Rather, the calling of Christians in the German Democratic Republic might be to 'live exemplary lives, showing the rest of us a Christian community already seeking and perhaps finding a new way for a church *for* the people (rather than *of* the people). Indeed, of the two Germanys, the Eastern zone might be God's favourite.'[94] Barth wrote this letter virtually at a sitting in the Thurneysens' holiday house at Kapf in Emmental. There he read it out to its first audience, which consisted of Lollo von Kirschbaum and Gertrud Staewen (who had joined in the family holiday, as they had done so often in the past), and Hellmut Traub, who used to have holidays quite close by.

The letter was on the whole gratefully received by the Christians to whom it was addressed, but this time newspaper reaction was overwhelmingly critical in both the East and the West, and especially in the Swiss press. Barth remarked with some disappointment: 'I don't expect ever to be *d'accord* with the Swiss again in this life.'[95] 'Sometimes at night I plan another pamphlet with the title *Letter to a Pastor in Seldwyla,* in which I would like to tell this people living on the other side of the moon that for once they have a counterpart.'[96] He also incurred displeasure in West German government circles with the views that he put forward in the letter. The Federal President Theodor Heuss intervened when Barth was to be awarded the 'Peace Prize of the German Book Trade' in autumn 1958, and it went to his Basle colleague Karl Jaspers instead.

'Not to become tired but to go on and on . . . '

The relative isolation in which he now found himself did, however, make him do something. Early in the next year he had the urge to pay another visit to some of the brotherhood people who had become close allies in the debate over atomic warfare and to have further conversations with them: there were Hannelore Hansch in Durlach, Helmut Simon in Karlsruhe and then all kinds of close friends in and around Stuttgart. In Stuttgart, Dore, the wife of his friend Gotthilf

Weber, cheered him up with a question in broad Swabian dialect, put with a sigh: 'Ah, Karl, will we never be able to be part of the crowd again?'[97] But he understood the sigh. In view of the amount of resistance and misunderstanding which had arisen because of his attitude to East Germany and to the question of atomic warfare, he again felt an 'odd man out', 'one of those lonely figures whose voice is not strong enough to come through the bawling of the majority of our pious and impious contemporaries in the West and in the East, and who often enough long to be able once again to be part of the common herd; and because they cannot do that either, they lose courage.' What was to be done in this situation? Barth's short, matter-of-fact answer was: 'Not to become tired, but to go on and on . . . !'[98]

Not to become tired but to go on! Immediately after finishing this open letter, he *had* already gone on and had turned to quite a different subject, which hitherto he had not tackled so directly: this was the question of the relationship between theology and philosophy. He found himself having to consider this question because he had been asked for a contribution to a Festschrift for his brother Heinrich, who would be seventy in 1960. And so – again at Kapf, during summer 1958 – he wrote an article in which he sought to understand and clarify his views on 'the contrast and the similarity between the philosopher and the theologian'.

He did this on the presupposition that in the first place *both* are confronted 'with the one unique, entire truth', and secondly, *neither* is in a position to talk 'down from heaven', since this truth is 'superior to both of them'. Barth thought that the real difference between the philosopher and the theologian was not in their subject matter but in the 'order' and 'sequence' of their concern for knowledge. As he strives for knowledge the theologian thinks from above (from God) downwards (to man) and only in this way from below upwards, whereas the philosopher adopts precisely the opposite approach. Barth thought that if the theologian is asked how he arrives at his special approach, 'he must answer directly and without qualification, without being ashamed of his naivety, that Jesus Christ is the one and entire truth through which he is shown how to think and speak, just as strictly as the philosopher is given his task.'[99]

Writing to the philosopher Wilhelm Weischedel, with whom he corresponded over this article in 1960, Barth said: 'Of course there is a "dispute" here. But perhaps it is something that can only be carried on in practice, and not discussed – with the philosopher thinking, speaking and writing as a philosopher and the theologian as a theologian. I let myself be talked into doing this just this one time.'[100]

Not to become tired, but to go on! In the summer, when he was writing the Festschrift article for his brother and the letter to East Germany, Barth felt a great weariness in another way. He was just physically exhausted, and could not shake off this tiredness. Now he noticed his age more than ever before. During the previous summer semester he had once complained, 'What a trial from week to week. Lollo thinks that she has never seen me otherwise than in this laborious onward movement . . . but subjectively I find the burden growing increasingly heavy. Every now and then Lollo orders me just to stop for an hour and get some fresh air.'[101] Now more than ever he needed vacations and real holidays, not filled with more work but purely for relaxation. And now he discovered how salutary it could be simply to do nothing in particular: ' . . . to read a bit and then stop again; to fill a pipe and smoke it, to enjoy the surroundings or perhaps even to stare into space; not to want to compose and write out any sentences; not to have to lament any lost hours because they have all been gained.'[102] During these years he regularly spent his spring holidays in Brione in Ticino, usually accompanied by his son-in-law Max Zellweger, whom he particularly liked. ('He is the original Basle citizen, through and through.') Barth usually met several friends there, including Helmut Gollwitzer, Ernst Wolf and Gustav Heinemann. He spent the summer holidays at his other customary resorts, and now, too, he often went to his children's holiday spots.

In the meantime, during his semester work, he deliberately took steps to keep himself alert. His habit of having a cold shower in the morning continued to be punctually and zealously maintained, as did his rule to sleep 'year in and year out with the window wide open'. In addition he did 'deep breathing in the evening and exercises in the morning – "dogmatics in movement"'. He also allowed himself now from time to time to 'enjoy a complete course of that royal jelly whose prominent consumers include Adenauer and Pius XII as well as myself', together with 'all kinds of extra vitamins'. 'In addition I have a very reliable doctor whose instructions I observe strictly, all the more since he is reasonable enough not to think of questioning a man's pipe.'[103] Thanks to all this – and thanks to what was evidently an especially strong constitution, Barth was still on the whole very fit for his age. If from time to time he became tired and exhausted, he was never really ill, though he was often troubled by a bad back. Rather, 'in comparison with others of my age I am remarkably and undeservedly healthy and can keep "jogging along", as Lollo says, not without emotion, at various theological exercises.'[104] So he tended to note and accept as a great gift the fact 'that the good God still has patience with me, still gives me breath and a few ideas for writing, and still brings me lots of nice students'.[105]

Despite his increasing need for rest, Barth did not yet want to think of going into retirement. And the claims on his time and his attention, which were increasing rather than diminishing, from all sides and through all kinds of commitments, would not allow him to think about it. One of the things he kept having to do in addition to his academic and literary writing was to deal with an extensive correspondence, in which he was asked about a great variety of matters. Another task was receiving all kinds of people who wanted to talk to him or to visit him. He was still constantly sought out by 'lots of dear and interesting people, but there are *so many* of them and they do take up time'. There were periods when 'hardly a day' went past 'when I did not have to cope with some lengthy visit'. Older and younger pupils and friends came, theologians known and unknown, and churchmen and laity from various European countries, with all kinds of reports and questions. 'Even Indians and Chinese appear on the scene.' And Japanese – 'the gratitude and generosity which the people of this distant country shower on me day by day and year by year quite puts me to shame.' In addition, not only serious scholars came 'from the land of America', but dozens of curious people ('May I take a picture?').[106] Barth usually dismissed the latter by recommending them to visit the giraffes and rhinoceroses in Basle Zoo. Among the visitors who appeared at the Bruderholz in the autumn of 1958 was 'remarkably enough, a man from the Indian Mar Thoma church. I could not refrain from expressing to him my high regard for their special apostle.' Then there was Paul Tillich, 'a charming man, though his theology is quite impossible (Oh dear, I have undertaken to hold a seminar on him for the whole winter!)'.[107] One of Barth's problems in getting on with Tillich was that he saw to his regret that Tillich (like Niebuhr) still thought of him 'as though I had been asleep since 1920'.[108]

The seminar on Tillich in the winter of 1958–59 was concerned above all with a 'diagnosis of Tillich's "method of correlation": not a good business, but I constantly try to interpret him for the best and to defend him against the students, who want to snap around him like hunting dogs'.[109] This semester Barth also began to be an outpatient at the Basle eye hospital: in future he had to go there at regular intervals for checks on his eyesight, which was in danger. In the seminar next summer he wanted once again to give an explicit account of his own theological epistemology to his students – in contrast to Tillich's approach which they had just studied. He therefore based the seminar on his book on *Anselm*, which had just appeared in a new edition after being revised by Hinrich Stoevesandt. There were also some individual engagements during this semester: he spoke once (in Berne) with members of the Preachers' Seminary at Wuppertal, then with pastors from Neuchâtel, and another time at his old student association Zofingia, to which he was invited back for the next winter.

He was also involved in the Calvin jubilee, which was celebrated in Geneva in the summer of 1959. For a long time Barth had thought Calvin an incomparable theological teacher, and he presented Calvin's thinking to his students as a model. Calvin also stimulated his own thought a great deal and gave rise to many questions. So in the summer of 1957 and again in summer 1958 he had arranged a Calvin seminar.

In the first seminar, 'It emerged again and again that if there are any grounds for infant baptism, they are not those which Calvin attempted to present.'[110] In the second there was a discussion of Calvin's eucharistic doctrine, in which it again proved that, 'It is inevitable that we shall have serious reservations even about these classic theologians: especially about Calvin's doctrine of God, his view of predestination which is based on it, and its consequences in all areas of his interpretation of Christian faith. But it is not difficult to bracket off this problematical complex. Then one can rejoice at seeing Calvin's clear view of the centre of the gospel.'[111]

Further seminars on Calvin were to follow in the winter of 1959–60 and the summer of 1960: this time on Calvin's epistemology *(Institutes* I, 1–9), which had preoccupied and disquieted Barth for a long time.

The celebrations led Barth to write two articles giving an account of his feelings about Calvin. In addition to an article on 'Calvin as Theologian', he also wrote a preface to an edition of the *Institutes*. In it he said:

'Unlike Luther, Calvin was not a genius, but a conscientious exegete, a strict and tenacious thinker and at the same time a theologian who was indefatigably concerned with the practice of Christian life, and life in the church . . . He is a good teacher, of a kind which has been rare in the church – who does not hand over to an understanding reader the results of his study, but asks him to take it up and to discover new results in his footsteps. Only a Christian and a theologian who has learned in Calvin's *Institutes* to pursue the truth with which he is concerned by using his own eyes and ears can be a "Calvinist".'

Barth often wished that the Germans had had the same attitude towards Luther. At any rate, he himself did not want to be a pupil of Calvin in any other sense. Nor did he want to be a teacher of *his* pupils in any other sense either.

At the time of the Calvin celebrations, on 6 June, the University of Geneva bestowed an honorary doctorate of theology on Barth. This gave him especial pleasure – because the honour was closely connected with the commemoration of Calvin and because it came just fifty years after the beginning of his own work as assistant pastor in Geneva. Finally, 'this is the first time that responsible Swiss authorities have said such a friendly word to me'. But the Calvin celebrations in which Barth was immediately involved pleased him less – about as little as the celebrations fifty years before. 'The whole thing seemed to me to be a well-meant but monstrous extravaganza (Calvin would have said 'une mommerie'). I constantly had to think of the question "How can you believe, who receive glory from one another?"'[112]*

About a month later, Barth came back to Geneva, this time to welcome his son Christoph who was arriving at the airport for home leave. He had last seen him in the summer of 1957. Shortly after his return to Indonesia Christoph had married Marie-Claire Frommel, a theologian in the service of the World Student Christian Federation there. She was the daughter of a Geneva professor of pharmacology and the granddaughter of Gaston Frommel, a professor of theology, of whose almost glowing pietism Barth had had an unforgettable experience at a student conference in St Croix in 1905.[113] He met his new daughter-in-law for the first time at Geneva airport – and her first child. This grandson was only two months old, but already 'charmed me by notable signs of intelligence, musicality

*John 5.44.

and piety'.[114] In view of the expansion of the family circle by this new daughter-in-law, Barth thought: 'I am now a rich man in every respect, with no less than three such distinguished daughters-in-law. Each of them gives me all sorts of things to think about, because none of them is an ordinary kind of person, one of those tedious stereotypes of whom the landscape elsewhere is so full.'[115]

During this winter semester, on 22 November 1959, Barth received another honorary doctorate of theology, in Strasbourg. 'This time I was able to give my paw twice to General de Gaulle – whose fat autobiography I have just started reading.' The General, who had just become President, 'seemed more congenial than one would imagine from the pictures in the paper and acted with a benevolent matter-of-factness . . . but for the moment it is probably all up with democracy in France.'[116] Barth was glad to use the occasion for conversations with friends and acquaintances there, with Georges Casalis and André Dumas, Roger Mehl and the Dominican Yves Congar. Subject-matter for conversations was provided by the burning problem of Algeria and the Council which had been announced by the new Pope John. 'At that time I asked . . . Père Congar, "What can the rest of us do for the Council?" He replied, "You should pray for the Council!" – That was a proper answer.' In fact, about then Barth did pray publicly and openly for the Pope in a service. There was great head-shaking afterwards. '"He prayed for the Pope." I replied, "Yes, but he certainly needs it."'[117]

In the winter of 1959–60 Barth received two other rare compliments: at Christmas a lead story appeared about him in *Der Spiegel*; he himself had suggested as a headline, 'A joyful partisan of the good God'.[118] And after the New Year he was even 'represented in person on the stage' on carnival night at the so-called 'Zofingerkonzärtli'; he was made the subject of a sketch. Among the jokes was a riddle: 'What is the difference between perpetual motion and Karl Barth?' 'None,' came the answer. 'Ah,' came the retort, 'but perpetual motion is im*poss*ible, while Karl Barth is im*plaus*ible.'* As Barth remarked, 'In Basle they really take care that no tree grows to heaven.' 'I then had myself photographed in the interval with the young man who was impersonating me. This is the way in which one

---

*The joke sounds even feebler in English that in German. The original word-play is on two words for impossible (High German *unmöglich* and Swiss *unmeeglig*), with the accent on the first syllable of the former and the second of the latter. The former means 'physically impossible', the latter 'impossible as a person'.

has to cope with such situations, at any rate here in Basle.'[119]

The category of 'answer'

With the lectures of winter 1958–59 Barth was able to finish another volume of the *Dogmatics*, IV, 3. It was so long (1107 pages, ET 963) that it had to be published in two parts – so this time the reader got 'two halves that were "bearable" (in the strict sense of the word)'.[120] Hinrich Stoevesandt again helped him with the proofs. So that he could prepare the ground for the next volume of the *Dogmatics*, Barth gave up his lectures on dogmatics the next summer.

At the beginning of the winter of 1959–60 he then got down to lecturing on the material for a volume IV, 4. '"You eternal cornucopia", Balthasar said to me – because my writing seemed to go on and on.' In preparing for this new volume, 'during the summer I read the New Testament again from A–Z and word for word (if only I knew what to do with Revelation!), and made a great many notes. Now it's breaking over me like a river, and inevitably over my future hearers and readers! . . . It is curious still to be so much a beginner at the age of seventy-three.'[121]

Even now, of course, Barth could not concentrate solely on this work. While he was feeling his way forward step by step into the new material he still accepted some outside invitations to write or speak. Thus in December 1959 he spoke to staff of the Basle hospitals on 'Christian Ethics'. And when he was staying at Brione again in the spring, it did not take him long to produce 'a remarkable article on "The Possibilities of Liberal Theology Today"', which had been commissioned by the *Journal of Swiss Freethinkers*. 'I advised them to look once again at Biedermann or Schleiermacher or Martin Buber or Ragaz. They should look for their salvation there, but I could not give them any guarantee that they would find it.'[122] On 10 May, his seventy-fourth birthday, Barth this time found himself 'on a lightning journey to Fulda – not as a pilgrim to the tomb of St Boniface . . . but for a meeting of German prison chaplains and counsellors, who had invited me there for a conversation about the theological problems of this particular sphere of work . . . This journey could not be more than a short diversion, undertaken in the middle of a semester, but in Würzburg we allowed ourselves to be held up quite seriously by Tilman Riemenschneider.'[123]

While answering a question in Fulda, Barth made some basic statements about the problems of punishment and imprisonment with which he was continually confronted at first hand as an occasional prison visitor and preacher. When asked whether some men had a predisposition towards crime (implanted by God), he replied that people were probably predisposed to crime through illness, but that even the healthy suffered from bad predispositions ('are these less dangerous?'). There was no divine predisposition towards evil, but only 'a divine predisposition towards salvation (election)' *for all* lost men. And when asked about the nature of punishment, he replied that it must be understood, administered and accepted as a pastoral measure, and not as expiation.

On 19 July Barth went over to Strasbourg for the day for another question and answer session, which took place within the framework of a World Student Christian Federation conference. The students showed an agitated and involved interest in the social questions of the modern world. Further speakers there were his ecumenical friends Visser't Hooft, Lesslie Newbigin and Daniel T. Niles.

At the end of the summer semester of 1960 – by now Barth had been in his Basle post for exactly twenty-five years – the University of Basle celebrated its five hundredth anniversary. While the Senate was arranging details of the celebration, 'I had a dispute with the majority, led by Jaspers'. They wanted to restrict invitations to Western universities – but *all* of them (including Madrid, Guatemala, Honduras, etc.), while excluding 'any representation whatsoever from the countries behind the Iron Curtain'.[124] Barth composed a petition to the Department of Education and wrote a newspaper article against this division into 'worthy and unworthy guests'. Though in the end there was some compromise in the matter, this did not make him alter his decision not to take part in the celebrations.

While they were going on he went back to Gyrenbad, where he continued to work on his *Dogmatics,* and Lollo von Kirschbaum prepared the lectures which she was soon to give in Germany.

However, Barth wrote at least three pieces in connection with this anniversary. For a Festschrift he wrote an article on his understanding of 'systematic theology', the discipline he represented. And in articles for the two large Basle daily newspapers he gave his ideas on the place of the 'Faculty of Theology' within the university.

In one of the articles he explained the practical task of this faculty: it consisted simply in 'seeing that future pastors have the necessary "brief-

case" for exercising their profession and the necessary instructions for using
it. They will need much more important things than this in their ministry.
But they will also need their briefcase and a clear head, and we can and
should offer them that, or a start towards it – they should go on studying
afterwards!'[125] In the other article he tackled the question whether there
was still a place for theology in the modern university. In his view, 'The
specific task of theology today, which I have attempted to get down to in my
life's work, is to show again all along the line what Christianity really is –
with all its consequences and all its dangers. And at least from my own
experience I can say that theology *will come into its own again* and be respected
to the degree that it does just that. But theology as mediation, evasion,
exaggeration, falls flat today more than ever before.'[126]

The new volume of *Dogmatics* which he was still writing steadily in
the meantime, 'was to contain (parallel to III, 4) a chapter on special
ethics, this time from the standpoint of the reconciliation of the world
with God effected in Jesus Christ . . . The intention now was to
present Christian ethics as the free and active answer of man to the
divine work and word of grace (IV, 1–3). The Christian life would
thus be depicted in its most intimate form in a progression beginning with recollection of the divine gift that demands this free
responsive action and makes it possible, and continuing with a
description of the response required of man.' Barth repeated the
statement which he had already made in III, 4: Christian ethics
cannot itself give commands, but only guidance on the right way to
put the question 'What shall I do?' so as to hear God's answer readily
and openly. If *Church Dogmatics* III, 4 was seen from the central
perspective of freedom, IV, 4 was now to be seen from that of
faithfulness (corresponding to the covenant of grace). However,
when Barth approached the central part of his ethics of reconciliation – 'the real heart of the chapter' in terms of content – for a while
he rejected the development he had originally planned to come
immediately after the individual features of the term 'faithfulness'.
Instead of this he decided to discuss the 'various practical aspects of
the Christian life' along the lines of the Lord's Prayer. He therefore
arranged the central part around the individual petitions of the
Lord's Prayer. But his plan was that before all this, at the beginning
of the ethics of reconciliation, there was to be an account of the
doctrine of baptism as the 'basis of Christian life': baptism was seen
'as the work of God himself in the form of baptism with the Holy
Spirit, and as a liturgical human work in the form of baptism with
water'. The book was to end with a treatment of the Lord's Supper

'as its conclusion and crown'. This was regarded as an account of the renewal and support of Christian life. Here Barth evidently wanted to understand the Lord's Supper as the obedient action of the community in response to the 'renewal and support' which was brought about by God himself and by God alone. Thus he wanted to understand the eucharist 'as the thanksgiving which responds to the presence of Jesus Christ in his self-sacrifice and looks forward to his future'.[127]

In this doctrine of baptism he decisively rejected infant baptism, as he had done in his 1943 work on the subject. But this time (convinced by his son Markus' study of baptism) he also rejected the sacramental understanding of baptism by water. He now wanted to term only the resurrection of Jesus Christ and the outpouring of the Holy Spirit a sacrament. And in so far as this 'sacrament' was the basis of the Christian life, he wanted to speak of 'baptism with the Holy Spirit'. Now according to Barth this is strictly to be distinguished from baptism with water, which is a purely human action; baptism with water can only be seen as an answer to and a petition for baptism with the spirit. Nevertheless, Barth stressed, baptism with water has its basis in Jesus' own baptism. And as the first official step in Christian life it is significant for all further steps.

In what followed Barth went on to develop his ethics by means of the Lord's Prayer because he thought that 'praying and working' (*ora et labora*) in fact belong very closely together. Indeed, saying 'Abba, Father', is virtually 'the basic act of the Christian'. Barth began by discussing 'zeal for God's honour' in accordance with the first petition. By that he understood above all the way in which Christians suffer because God is so known and yet so unknown to the world, the church and themselves (as demonstrated by unbelief, atheism in its various forms, and so on). It is striking that Barth – for all his criticism of 'natural theology' – could now even say that God is known to the 'world' – not subjectively but objectively! Here he took up more positively than ever insights from the beginning of Calvin's *Institutes,* which he had studied in the seminar in both the winter and the summer of 1960. In interpreting the second commandment Barth then went on to talk of the 'struggle for human righteousness'. This, in his view, is directed against the 'uncontrolled powers' – what he means are those powers which come into being when the possibilities of human life are emancipated from man and rule him, just as man is emancipated from God (he cited political absolutism, money, ideology, and also fashion, sport and trade!). Barth stressed emphatically that the kingdom of God can be neither realized nor even prepared for by man. It is 'a factor *sui generis*' not only over against the world, but even over against the Christian world.

At this point, however, Barth broke off work not only on this book but also on the *Church Dogmatics* altogether. At this stage three small extracts from the material he had prepared for *Church Dogmatics* IV, 4 were published as contributions to the Festschriften for his friends Kornelis Heiko Miskotte, Erik Wolf and Ernst Wolf. The contribution to the Festschrift for Ernst Wolf's sixtieth birthday was noted particularly for its bold combination of three concepts which had often been played off against each other in the history of theology: *'extra nos – pro nobis – in nobis'.*

When Barth saw the Bultmannites now stressing the *pro me* ('for me') and the pietists the *in me* ('in me') of God's saving action, he thought that he could now join in the conversation, hence the title. But he believed that he could do so only on condition that 'we' (pro *nobis* and in *nobis*) was substituted for 'I' (pro *me* and in *me*) and that above all the fundamental presupposition of the *extra nos* (outside us) was tenaciously maintained. What he said in his new section about the understanding of Christian existence as a 'free responsive action' was in fact also his special contribution to the conversation with pietism on the one hand and with the Bultmann school on the other. And since in this understanding of Christian existence he stressed both the fundamental reference to encounter with God's action *and* human life lived on man's own responsibility and by his decision, his thesis was both a critical alternative to talk about existence and decision in the two groups, and a positive acknowledgment of the questions which they posed.

'. . . to sigh and to hope'

It so happened that at this very time Barth had many promising contacts with at least one of these groups, the pietists. On 6 October 1959, even before he embarked on *Church Dogmatics* IV, 4, he had a whole-day conversation with a group of German and Swiss community people, which had been arranged by Pastor Max Fischer. It also included the Göttingen architect Otto Knobloch, whom Barth had long known and valued. The conversation was prompted by Barth's open acceptance of the 'concerns of the pietists' mentioned in *Dogmatics* IV, 2. To begin with, Barth recalled his early opposition to pietism and also the pietistic opposition to him. 'It is a good thing that we have all made some progress since then. We talk together in the certainty that we are agreed in essentials. It is now a question of clearing things up, not of fighting.' But of course what remained to be cleared up was quite considerable. The discussion centred predominantly on the question of establishing a clear boundary and division between believers and unbelievers. Barth could not understand the importance which the others attached to such a boundary and could not approve of it. They, for their part, could not accept the remarkable way in which Barth's theology made a relative matter of this boundary, and they therefore opposed his argument that 'We believers . . . must always become what we are . . . The others are already what they are to become.' This thesis marked the frontier beyond which mutual understanding was for the moment impossible.

The same frontier was evident in a conversation Barth had with Billy Graham, in August 1960. His son Markus brought them together in the Valais. However, this meeting was also a friendly one. 'He's a "jolly good fellow", with whom one can talk easily and openly; one has the impression that he is even capable of listening, which is not always the case with such trumpeters of the gospel.' Two weeks later Barth had the same good impression after a second meeting with Graham, this time at home in Basle. But, 'it was very different when we went to hear him let loose in the St Jacob stadium that same evening and witnessed his influence on the masses.'[128] 'I was quite horrified. He acted like a madman and what he presented was certainly not the gospel.'[129] 'It was the gospel at gun-point . . . He preached the law, not a message to make one happy. He wanted to terrify people. Threats – they always make an impression. People would much rather be terrified than be pleased. The more one heats up hell for them, the more they come running.' But even this success did not justify such preaching. It was illegitimate to make the gospel law or 'to "push" it like an article for sale . . . We must leave the good God freedom to do his own work.'[130]

By contrast, a meeting which took place before the beginning of the winter semester, on 12 October 1960, on the whole generally proved to be extremely positive. It was with German, Dutch and Swiss representatives of the Herrnhut* communities. The conversation which Barth had with them on the premises of the Basle community was as memorable for him as that with the representatives of pietism. It transpired that in recent years he had also discovered an affinity to Zinzendorf, the odd man out among the pietists of his time. As early as Christmas Eve 1952, he had written to Bultmann 'that I have increasingly become a Zinzendorfian, since I really

*Herrnhut is a village east of Dresden where a group of Moravians under Christian David formed a community on a site presented by Zinzendorf. From there the movement spread to other parts of Germany and Switzerland.

began to be concerned only with the central figure in the New Testament – or rather, to see all and everything only in the light and the perspective of this central figure'.[131] So Barth began by confessing to the Herrnhut representatives: 'If Zinzendorf was right about the main thing – not always in the right form – in taking as his centre Jesus Christ, all of him and him alone . . . if he was right in his view that the reconciliation of God with the world had already been completed, in his understanding of the relationship between gospel and law, in his view of the church as the community of the Lamb, the living Christ, then I may say in all modesty that I too am right. The whole of my theological thought revolves round this point, and this is where I am attacked. Zinzendorf and I stand and fall together.'[132]

About six months later, in the middle of May 1961, Barth had a similar conversation with the preachers of the Swiss Methodist Church in Reuti-Hasliberg. This also took place in a cordial and eirenic atmosphere, except that Barth could not say the sort of things about John Wesley that he had done about Zinzendorf. The conversation turned above all on the question of the 'experience of salvation' and the preaching of repentance. Barth's comment on 'experience' was: 'I do not deny the experience of salvation . . . But the experience of salvation is what happened on Golgotha. In contrast to that my own experience is only a vessel.' On preaching repentance he said: 'I always find it uncanny when we are given a picture of the church in one place and modern man in another; and we, the Christians, are the ones who are calling for repentance . . . This makes one side friends and the other enemies. And if the world thinks, "Here are people who think they have and know it," it reacts bitterly. As Christians we cannot be open enough. We can only say to the others, these people in the cinemas and in the sports stadium, "You are our brothers and sisters, come and take the great step of following Christ *with us* . . . " If we do not want to be "foremost" among sinners, we cannot say anything to the other sinners.'

So despite all the questions which remained, Barth now came to some sort of understanding with these representatives of the various communities. However, to his regret the dialogue with the other group which he still had in mind as he continued his work on the *Dogmatics*, the Bultmann school, went less well. Still, at this time at least one door opened a little wider, thanks to the Tübingen New Testament scholar Ernst Käsemann. In January 1960 Barth and Käsemann had first exchanged friendly letters. At that time Barth invited him over to discuss 'the problem of the relationship between exegetical and "systematic" theology, which evidently disturbs us both.'[133] Käsemann in fact came in the middle of May, and Barth disconcerted him at this first meeting with the 'simple' question: 'Tell me, what does "historical" mean? And "critical"? And what is the significance of the hyphen between the two words?' Anyway, further conversation showed that Käsemann was the representative of the Bultmann school with whom Barth seemed most likely to be able to reach an understanding.

It was this school (and no longer so much its master) which was now giving its colouring to theology, at least in the German-speaking world. The scene was largely dominated 'by the experiments of the former members of the house of Bultmann, now deeply torn by internal conflict, and by the delight of students in these experiments'.[134] Indeed, Barth thought that he 'would not be surprised if the business still had a considerable future in the many variant forms in which it is represented in the Bultmann school.' But he did not think that these 'experiments' would produce any results or take things further. 'I find it significant that present-day Old Testament scholars have on the whole adopted much better methods, especially in regard to the old (yet always new) theme of "faith and history", than the authoritative New Testament men, who to my amazement have armed themselves with swords and staves and have once again undertaken the quest of the "historical Jesus", a quest in which now, as before, I prefer not to participate.'[135] Barth no more approved of the attempt at this 'quest' of a 'pre-Easter' Jesus, to be considered apart from his resurrection, than of the attempt made among the representatives of this school (e.g. Ebeling) to compress theology into the framework of an 'isolated doctrine of faith' – and a faith for which it would be essential to dispense with 'the object of a personal encounter'.[136] He could only see such an attempt as a step backwards in theology. 'On the Bultmann line the nineteenth century has again become a paradise for many people, to be lost or regained. We can hardly do anything one way or the other; the history of the Spirit runs in spirals like this. I read somewhere recently that a "post-Barthian age" is now dawning and told my students that this might indeed be the case, but that they should be quite clear that it was now up to them to do things differently, and better, in a responsible way.'[137]

Barth believed that the predominance of the Bultmann school

should be seen 'in close connection with what I have felt with increasing misgivings to be the reactionary character of politics, the church and church politics in West Germany since the end of the war'.[138] 'Now the Bultmannites of all colours rule in theology and the indestructible Adenauer in politics.'[139] Still, in view of this situation Barth wanted to ask himself, 'without for the moment seeing an answer, "What went wrong?" In the end we have produced a theology which was certainly better than that of our predecessors and yet we are incapable of saying "Stop!" and "Go!" to the general reaction (and I include the attitude of the Bultmannites in that). The whole situation calls for a new song to be sung to the Lord. Will we be the ones who sing it? . . . Or will we all incur a great judgment – old and young, wise and foolish – which in some way may teach a lesson to those who come after us? That's certainly something to think about, and I do so often . . . But in the end I feel the best thing to do is to read a psalm, or a hymn by Paul Gerhardt (like 'You are a man, you know that well'), and then to sigh or to hope depending on which one it is.'[140]

Another contemporary with whom Barth now sought unsuccessfully to reach an understanding was his Zürich colleague Emil Brunner. A reunion arranged at the Bruderholz on 19 November 1960 by the American missionary to Japan, John Hesselink, who had just gained his doctorate in Basle, ended disappointingly. The hoped-for reconciliation of the two former friends somehow did not work out. It seemed to confirm one of the remarks that Barth had made earlier to a reporter from the BBC, in an interview about his relationship to Brunner: it was like the relationship between an elephant and a whale: 'Both are God's creatures, but they simply cannot meet' (earlier Barth had used the same comparison to describe his relationship to Bultmann).[141]

Although he was now almost seventy-five years old, Barth still had an amazing capacity for work. Material still flowed from his pen and in spite of his occasional physical tiredness, his spirit was unquenched. This could be seen from an article which he wrote in 1960 for a periodical published for German exiles. In it he saw a 'homeland' only as an 'unmerited gift', and roundly disputed that anyone had 'an absolute "right" to a homeland'. His remarks caused a storm of protest among the exiles, in which they were joined by the writer Agnes Miegel. He made further public comments during 1961. On one occasion he spoke in a radio series on the theme of

'Freedom'. Another time he gave his views in a broadcast series 'What does the Professor Think?' (he had already been in it in 1960). Then he wrote a newspaper article on 'Possibilities of Confessional Coexistence'; his view was that possibilities existed only when people were aware of the differences between the confessions as well as their common features and took them seriously. He also gave an answer to the question 'What is our Greatest National Task Today?' for a Zürich newspaper in connection with the Swiss national festival. His answer was that humanly speaking, Switzerland now had to be 'above disputes (especially those of the Cold War), and at the same time in solidarity with the real concerns of the rest of the world' (above all the Third World); if it did that, it could be 'confident of its own good cause and sure of its future'. Barth here expressed his long-considered thought that 'the awakening of Africa and Asia' would probably be *the* problem of the future. And he also expressed his conviction that 'any Swiss engineer, teacher, doctor or missionary involved out there (for the Third World) is doing the best thing that can possibly be done for our land and people today'.[142] He had already said the same thing at the end of 1960 when he had made a broadcast to his fellow-countrymen on New Year's Eve. He also had a few brief question and answer sessions about now: in the Basle Mission House; with Zürich pastors; with members of his church at the Bruderholz; with Catholic students from Paderborn and their professor, Albert Brandenburg; with the inmates of Basle prison and with the Basle pastors. He also gave a brief lecture on 'Church and Theology' in Zofingen, which he visited in September while on holiday in Gyrenbad. To his satisfaction his former president of the Safenwil church committee also spoke there.

Swan song

Barth celebrated his seventy-fifth birthday in May with a group of his closest friends. These were joined by Bishop Jacobi of Oldenburg and Joachim Beckmann from the Rhineland. On this occasion, 'I made my Dutch friend Miskotte fearfully angry by saying that I was waiting for an opponent – but for an opponent who met me on the same ground, at the same length, and got the better of me. For I was well aware of the transitoriness of my work.' 'I never thought that I had had the last word in the *Church Dogmatics*. It is very clear to me

Lectures and conversations

Especially when talking informally, 'he is all there. There is an openness, a readiness for objections . . . and along with this such concentration and impetuous insistence on the point, whether it is made arrogantly or modestly, dogmatically or completely uncertainly' (Dietrich Bonhoeffer).

87. Lecturing on the Dogmatics, *1961*.

88. With pastors from Bavaria at Lempp's house by the Starnberger See, 1957.

89. In a seminar discussion.

90. In conversation with Charlotte von Kirschbaum, Helmut Gollwitzer and Hermann Diem in Brione, March 1962. Gollwitzer was turned down as Barth's successor by the Basle administration the next day.

91.   The presentation of an honorary doctorate of theology in Strasbourg, 22 November 1959, with President de Gaulle in the centre.

92.   Public discussion before an audience of 2000 in Chicago, April 1962, with Fr. Cooke, E. J. Carnell, J. J. Petuchowski, Markus and Karl Barth, Jaroslav Pelikan, William Stringfellow, Hans Frei and Schubert Ogden.

93.   Trial shot with an American Civil War rifle by the St. James River, May 1962.

94.   With his friends Max Geiger and Dr Alfred Briellmann at Leuenberg, February 1968.

that the thing could have been done differently and better on every page.'[143] For the celebrations, 'a collection of my articles was edited by Karl Kupisch in Berlin under the remarkable title *Der Götze Wackelt* (The Idol Totters). When he told me that he wanted to give the book this title, I was first somewhat shocked . . . and told him that everyone would connect it with me! "So he is now seventy-five years old: *the* idol totters." But he told me that he did not mean it that way.'[144]

His birthday reminded Barth of his limitations in another way. Some time ago he had remarked, 'I hope that I will know the time when the students who still gather around me cheerfully and in large numbers will have had enough of me.'[145] They still came in large numbers – in Basle terms: there were more than eighty at the English-speaking colloquium alone, 'some of whom come to it by car from Heidelberg, Tübingen and Zürich. It continues to include some astonishingly bright and capable people . . . For the lectures I also have a Japanese (in addition to three negroes from the Cameroons and three Indonesians) who puts everything from A–Z on tape, and afterwards runs it through five times, thus learning German and theology at the same time.'[146] Barth still also taught some doctoral students, including Gyula Barczay, Keiji Ogawa, Karl Hammer, Hans Ruh and the Americans Marion Conditt, Daniel Fuller, James Wagner and Alexander McKelway. But he thought that he could now see and feel that the time had come for him to retire from his public teaching post. He thought that he could no longer fill it adequately, in view of the fact that 'I have become so fearfully laborious and anxious about all my writings'.[147] For some time he had had to write out every lecture twice before it was given.[148] And he could not lecture for more than two hours a week. Indeed, he had to concede 'that often I am simply tired of working'.[149]

So in accordance with his own wishes, the summer semester of 1961 was to be his last. In his seminar he was obviously preparing to handle the Lord's Supper in his own *Dogmatics*: having discussed the Catholic doctrine of the eucharist during the previous winter, he now considered the corresponding Lutheran doctrine. Indeed, he had it firmly in mind that after his retirement he would at least press on with the groundwork for his *Dogmatics* as far as possible. In the *Dogmatics* this summer he reached his great 'ethical' exposition of the second petition of the Lord's Prayer, 'Thy kingdom come', down to the point at which, in a long consideration of the two Blumhardts, he referred to the people through whom his understanding of the kingdom of God had begun to grow at the beginning of his long career. He concluded it with a verse from a hymn:

> Jesus is the conqueror who vanquishes our foe,
> Jesus is the Lord before whose feet the world lies low.
> Jesus comes with victor's might,
> And through the darkness leads to light.

In a brief postscript Barth said that he had now been active in teaching for forty years. And he compared these years to the wandering of Israel through the wilderness. What he now faced first was not a time of rest, but, like Israel after 'the conquest', a new struggle.

Meanwhile the discussion over his successor had long been under way. It dragged on for an unusually long time because 'political difficulties ("McCarthy difficulties") have arisen over the choice of my successor' – it was Gollwitzer from Berlin.[150] There was virtually a 'little Basle church struggle (indeed an all-Swiss struggle) over Gollwitzer, in which I did not take part, and in which the thoughts of many hearts were laid open.'[151] In this struggle it was asserted that Gollwitzer was politically intolerable for Switzerland, and the old hostility to Barth's theology and politics flared up again. It was impossible to settle the appointment before the end of the semester. So it fell 'to me after my retirement from academic teaching, to hold my seminar and classes, and to lecture once again in the winter semester of 1961–62, as my own substitute and the substitute for my still unknown successor.'[152] The dispute over the succession dragged on through the winter. 'It was an almost apocalyptic triumph of folly and malice of many kinds.'[153] It was clear enough 'that they do not want to give me any successor in whom I might take any pleasure'.[154] 'What fools the people of Basle and the Swiss generally are, that they let slip an opportunity, which will never occur again, to have such a spirit and head and heart' – namely Gollwitzer – 'in their midst. And what a shameful mess they've made of things.'[155] 'I hide my head and am ashamed of my ancestral city, of Switzerland and of the supposedly free world. The Last Judgment is probably not far away, as Luther would have said, but he did add that in the meantime another few trees could be planted.'[156] In the end, it turned out that Barth's successor was not to be Gollwitzer, but the young Swiss, Heinrich Ott.

Barth's farewell to teaching in fact proved to be 'a kind of ignominious dismissal'.[157] Following Barth's last lecture on 1 March 1962, the political economist Edgar Salin, in his capacity as pro-Rector, gave a speech in which he dealt critically with Barth's political attitude. However, the students reacted to this parting shot with vigorous demonstrations and cries of protest. Salin's reaction was a cruel end to Barth's last semester, in which he had discussed 'The Christian Life' according to Calvin in his seminar. In his lectures, instead of continuing with his *Dogmatics*, 'I wanted to seize the occasion for a swan song, and to give myself and my colleagues a brief account of what I had looked for, learnt and represented from among all the ways and detours I had so far followed in the field of evangelical theology during my five years as a student, twelve as a pastor and forty as a professor.' So 'I chose the form of an "introductory" discipline of the kind which has not appeared on the timetable of our Basle faculty for a long while. I could not complain about bad attendance. First of all we had to move into the larger lecture room 2, and finally into the hall.'[158]

Barth divided this 'Introduction to Evangelical Theology' into four parts each with four sections, about 'The Place of Theology', 'Theological Existence' (in wonder, concern and commitment), 'The Threat to Theology' (from solitude, doubt and temptation) and 'Theological Work' (study, prayer and service). In an introduction he explained that theology was a modest and free, critical and joyful discipline. A new feature in the first section was the distinction between the Word of God on the one hand and the word of the Bible and the church (as the mere *testimony* – primary and secondary – to the word of God) on the other. The distinction was evidently a correction to his earlier doctrine of the threefold form of the Word of God (in revelation, Bible and preaching).

Barth also understood his introduction as an account of his 'alternative to the *mixophilosophicotheologia* (a word coined by Abraham Calov in days long past) . . . which in its time seemed to make such an impression on so many people as being the newest of the new'. He therefore said once again that the theme of theology is not man, not faith, but *God*, and 'the God of the *gospel*'. Nor does it ever speak of God as an afterthought and in passing, as though, 'like the English crown, he were only a symbol'.

Although Barth was speaking emphatically, at the same time it was striking how open was the piece of theology which he now presented. For Barth this openness was rooted in the fundamental answer to the question, 'How does theology come to be theology, the human logic of the divine Logos?' His answer was: 'It cannot be that.

But the theologian can have the experience that God's spirit comes upon him and over him. Then he does not resist, nor does he seize it by force, but rejoices and makes his own contribution by way of response.' With the same open approach he could ask: 'Could not such a problematic theologian as Albert Schweitzer (still seen in a theological perspective) have chosen a better part, and along with him the first and best of those who have attempted here and there, without any theological reflection, to heal the wounded, to feed the hungry, to give drink to the thirsty and to prepare a home for fatherless children?' And equally openly at the *end* of his official career, he said of theological work: 'Anyone who sets out to do it can never proceed by building with complete confidence on questions which have already been settled, results which have already been achieved or conclusions which are already assured. He is directed every day, indeed every hour, to begin again *at the beginning*.' The crown and conclusion of this series of lectures was the last one of all, on love. Its final sentence was a recitation of the ancient Christian hymn of praise: *'Gloria Patri et Filio et Spiritui Sancto. Sicut erat in principio et (est) nunc et (erit) semper et in saecula saeculorum!'*[159]

9

'The Last Steps that We Can Still Take'

The years of retirement, 1962–1968

Travel to the USA

On 1 March 1962 Barth had delivered his farewell lecture and begun his retirement – if it could be called that.[1] Contemplating the prospect of this stage of his life he had once written that what 'an old man is and does can be thought unwise if he seems to have stopped considering that demands may still be made on him and is merely repeating automatically answers which he has given before. It is not as if an old man has no future, and therefore no authentic and full life of his own, but only the past. Nor is his only option to think back on the past, happily or unhappily, without doing anything, as though in the calm of a holiday evening . . . As if he were allowed to freeze and to solidify the river of responsibility at the very point where it should flow more torrentially than ever, in view of the approaching falls and the imminence of the coming Judge! . . . From the Christian standpoint one may simply add the supremely positive fact that an old man has an extraordinary chance of having to – or of being allowed to – live in terms of a verse which he has often sung with gusto:

> With force of arms we nothing can,
> full soon were we downridden;
> but for us fights the proper man
> whom God himself hath bidden.'[2]

So it was perhaps significant that Barth began his 'retirement' by undertaking a journey which took him further afield than any other yet. 'Directly after my farewell, at the beginning of my seventy-sixth year (younger colleagues now do this much earlier and more often), I spent seven weeks in America, where I had to give lectures at different places in the east, west and centre of the continent.'[3] Since the end of the 1920s Barth had had numerous invitations to go there and had always said no. He had happily given as his excuse that enough Americans came over to see him and to study with him: 'I think . . . that in this way I can be more genuinely useful to America than if I were to travel, like so many Europeans.'[4] Recently Barth had almost reconciled himself to the prospect that 'I shall only see America from my modest corner in one of the lower parts of heaven'.[5] But he actually saw the country during his lifetime. He was accompanied on the flight by Charlotte von Kirschbaum and his son Christoph, and in the USA his son Markus also joined the party. He was anxious about the tour, wondering 'how I will stand up to it all in my honourable old age', whether 'I will disappoint everyone or whether I will make a fool of myself on this occasion.' Barth's main purpose was 'to see and listen to' fellow theologians.[6] But he was also to speak there – and took with him the first five lectures of his *Einführung in die evangelische Theologie* (ET *Evangelical Theology*), which had been translated by his pupil Grover Foley.

He enjoyed the journey. Christoph even said that he was 'the most enthusiastic member of the party' . . . Barth himself hoped that he was not the most 'pleasure-seeking'! 'However, I cannot deny that during these weeks the life, the country and the people gave me extraordinary delight.'[7] What a wealth and variety of impressions! 'I can only sum them up in the word "fantastic", which plays an important role in a play by Tennessee Williams which I saw in New York. Yes, fantastic: the unending panorama of rivers, plains, hills and mountains between the two oceans, which I flew over by aeroplane or sped through by car: the deserts of Arizona, the Grand Canyon (which for good reasons I refrained from going down into), the Bay of San Francisco and the Golden Gate Bridge – Chicago and New York with their buildings towering to heaven and their streets filled with the constant, coruscating movement of countless cars, with their swarms of individuals from all countries, classes, races and walks of life – the organization and standardization of the whole of life (even of church life and of academic theology) which to some extent competes with divine providence – the pertinent and sometimes almost impertinent curiosity and descriptive power of the American reporter', whom Barth had to face in three large press conferences. 'I also found "fantastic" the thousands of people who streamed in to my lectures and public discussions, and the mass of publicity with which I suddenly found myself surrounded and which was completely new to me.'[8] *Time* magazine even had a lead story about Barth on the occasion of his visit to America.

First of all he stayed for about three weeks in Chicago, where he lived with his son's family. Here he had a great many conversations, with students, with businessmen, with Talmudic Jews, with actors, with Catholic theologians, with a small group of real live communists, with Mircea Eliade, the historian of religion and with the evangelist Billy Graham. He also delivered five lectures here, and on 27 April was given an honorary doctorate in theology. Here, too, under the chairmanship of Professor Jaroslav Pelikan, on two evenings he joined in a public discussion: 'an open "round-table" conference with a Jesuit, a Jewish Rabbi, a liberal Protestant, an orthodox Protestant and a layman', the lawyer William Stringfellow, whom he held in very high esteem. 'That evening we had between two and three thousand in the audience. Imagine that in the Grosser Musiksaal in Basle! The discussion was quite open, and the differences which inevitably emerged were neither disguised nor exaggerated, but tackled passionately and yet pertinently: "Everyone should talk together openly", as we say so often.'[9] Barth concluded by saying that if he were an American theologian he would try to write a theology of freedom – 'a theology of freedom from any inferiority complex over against "good old Europe" ', but at the same time of freedom 'from a superiority complex . . . over against Asia and Africa', and so of freedom 'for humanity'; a theology in which the Statue of Liberty in New York would be demythologized to become an expression of the coming freedom, which by contrast would be based on the freedom for which 'the Son' makes men free.

From Chicago Barth made a detour to the theological seminary at Dubuque, on the Mississippi. After the weeks in Chicago he also stayed in Princeton, to deliver his *Evangelical Theology* as the Warfield Lectures and to take part in a public discussion before an equally large audience: here he was warmly welcomed by Dr McCord and by his former Bonn 'English teacher', Dr Mackay. In Princeton he also heard a sermon by Martin Luther King. Unfortunately there was no time for any discussion; only for a photograph to be taken under the church tower. From there he went on to Washington, where he was received by the Swiss ambassador, August Lindt, and spent a whole evening in conversation with men from President Kennedy's staff. He celebrated his seventy-sixth birthday in Richmond – and the students there sang 'For he's a jolly good fellow'.

There followed a visit to Los Angeles and San Francisco, especially to the Theological School at San Anselmo, and finally a second visit to New York and to Union Theological Seminary.

'I had some experiences over there which other visitors to America might not think important or which for other reasons they might not have.' These included seeing the inside of American prisons. Because Barth had been a preacher in Basle prison he wanted to see American prisons, and in fact managed to do so. He found conditions in some of them so terrifying that at a press conference he compared them with Dante's *Inferno*. Because of his involvement in the racial question he was also interested in 'the notorious district of East Harlem, north of Manhattan', and was taken through it 'under the safe conduct' of Stringfellow, who was working there. His curiosity in these two directions was also satisfied 'by the wealth of information provided by two extraordinarily vigorous women', Mrs Anna M. Kross, champion of prison reform, and Dr Anna Hedgeman, 'the advocate of a new American negro movement concerned with civil rights'. The third thing he was anxious to do was to visit the battlefields of the American Civil War. He thought this was important 'because I felt that I could see that what was born there, amongst a great deal of grief and sorrow, was the reality and the myth of modern America'.[10] So he also went to the 'various scenes of the decisive battle of Gettysburg which was fought on 2 July 1863 . . . where a smart young officer showed me and explained to me all the things that I knew from books. Among the sights was a monument to Luther(!), standing in front of the Lutheran seminary in which General Lee had his headquarters at the time.'[11] On this visit, 'in a ruined Civil War fort by the St James River, I fired a hundred-year-old musket and to the honour of the Swiss army even hit the target – an event which could with good will be regarded as symbolic of my other capabilities and successes.'[12]

Conversations

Only after his return from the United States did Barth really feel that he now had to get used to the life of a retired professor. He said that at first he was very satisfied 'with the way in which I live, being able in my modest "retirement" simply to read a great deal in peace and quiet (an attractive combination of spiritual and secular books), though I am too often battered by the unending talk of existentialism from powerful jaws . . . But I can already see that this cannot be a permanent state.' Without the constant pressure of lecturing he planned to do more work on the *Church Dogmatics*. 'Now I must return to my primal state, when before I had any students I even wrote two commentaries on the Epistle to the Romans.'[13] However, Barth was far from sure whether he should really devote himself to continuing the *Dogmatics*. 'If only I had not fallen victim to a weariness bordering on *accidie* over the whole of the present theological situation! In the face of the thrust of our theological existentialists, the more I go on the more I can only feel disgust and abhorrence . . . Does it make any sense for me to write a thirteenth or fourteenth volume, if the twelve volumes I have written so far have not been able to prevent the outburst of this flood? Do we not need other new tongues to bring it to a halt? Do people only pay me attention out of respect, without really listening? . . . What if I have now had my day, and am simply being asked to look around a little, "in oriental tranquillity, despising all activists"? After all, that is the way in which others use the time they still have left?'[14]

However, for the moment he left the answer to this question open. At the end of July he went to Flims in Graubünden, where he had to talk to three hundred Protestant booksellers. Other speakers were Walter Lüthi and the Methodist bishop Ferdinand Sigg, whom he enjoyed hearing. Barth's contribution took the form of a 'question and answer session', which turned above all on the question of 'the possibilities for the church in a totalitarian state'. Barth replied: first, 'that all states in fact have something of the totalitarian state in them', and secondly, 'that there is only one possibility, for the church in the totalitarian world and the totalitarian state', namely to gather 'around Jesus'; 'the church is the circumference and he is the centre – that is its possibility.' Barth's reply to the rather personal question about the life of an ageing theologian was also significant. He reported that as he grew older, he found less pleasure in saying no, in 'demolishing and dismissing', and more in saying something positive. But he added the thought that this change was not just to be attributed to a growth in wisdom; 'the weakness of old age probably has quite a lot to do with it.' He was also preoccupied with this question in other respects, and wrote a little later: 'It is also my experience that one becomes wise and gentle in old age and in retrospect, but that the fire still glimmering under the ashes cannot simply be quenched. When one grows old, pencil strokes take the place of ink, pastel colours the place of oil, and the ocarina the place of the trumpet, with all the advantages and disadvantages.'[16]

During this summer Barth also had 'some pleasant times' with his 'son, daughter-in-law and two very original small boys from Indonesia'. In September he went off on holiday with his friend Ernst Wolf to the Walchensee, 'where I succeeded in breaking my right arm'.[16] He even had to spend a couple of days in a hospital in Bad Tölz. From there 'I was let out for a few hours, heavily bandaged, to take part in a small theological conference (held by Christian Kaiser Verlag) in the Josefstal'.[17] Barth enjoyed the conversations here with his colleagues, and especially with Gerhard von Rad, to whom he confessed his amazement that the Old Testament theology of the time had on the whole been so little attracted by existentialism. After his accident 'Lollo told me frankly that I was the worst invalid that she had ever met'.[18]

Having dropped all his teaching activity in Basle during the summer, in the winter Barth was eager to do some more work with theological students. 'Basle University was now utterly disgusted with me', so he resolved in future 'to hold a few strictly private colloquia in the neighbouring restaurant, the Bruderholz. However, the noticeboard will show a clear "will not lecture".'[19] Barth was able to keep up these colloquia for several more semesters, and always discussed sections from the *Church Dogmatics,* each about thirty pages long, in them. Thus the student in his 'discussion group' or in the English- or French-speaking colloquium was invited 'to join me in the questions, hesitations and objections which presented themselves to me, and to hear my replies to them'.[20] Barth was amazed that 'I still seem to have the ear of the youngest theologians'. In fact 'more students came than ever before', and proved to be 'my most effective refreshment'.[21] The English-speaking colloquium had 'fifty to sixty participants, and this time also included an eight-year-old-child, brought by his mother who had not been able to get hold of a baby-sitter. Next time, some baby or other will certainly appear in order to be informed about the basic concepts of ethics, and so on.'[22] Even larger numbers of people came to the German-speaking discussion group, again including a small contingent from Zürich. The students came from a variety of teachers. However, after a certain period of acclimatization, Barth again had the impression that 'a prophecy was fulfilled – not from the Bible but from

Rilke'. 'They laughed and slowly cheered up.'[23] In addition, Barth now regularly arranged a more intimate tutorial session for a small group of his pupils, especially his doctoral students. Here he watched the friendly interplay between the German Jürgen Fangmeier and the American Grover Foley; on occasions his old friends Eduard Thurneysen, Dietrich Ritschl and Martin Anton Schmidt also joined in. Some doctoral works were discussed in these sessions, and also all kinds of new theological literature – including books by Jürgen Moltmann, Wolfhart Pannenberg, Heinrich Vogel, Oscar Cullmann, Teilhard de Chardin, Eberhard Jüngel and Milan Machovec. Machovec, an atheist from Prague with a remarkable interest in theology, was once invited over by Barth for a discussion with the group.

In addition to the 'informal extra instruction'[24] which Barth now gave regularly, he also had a number of other commitments. Towards the end of 1962 there was an amazing period when for a few months he was again fresh and agile enough to be able to fulfil an almost uninterrupted series of engagements and undertakings. True, he was surprised that he 'had . . . a quite considerable need and capacity for sleep'.[25] The consequence of this was that 'I now give way to the habit which I utterly despised in my earlier decades of having an afternoon siesta; although I read somewhere that the bed is the brother of the coffin.'[26] Old age was making itself felt in other respects too: 'physically and also mentally, in the decline of a certain zest for life. I would so much like to have it and enjoy it, but it now fails me.'[27] For the moment, however, this did not prove a serious hindrance to Barth. He was still active and could express his views in a great many ways and a great many different directions. So he could even say: 'I still have no peace and quiet . . . because I get so many visits and letters – and I am asked by larger or smaller groups here and abroad to answer their questions.'[28] 'Indeed, it's rather like living in a beehive. I imagined that retirement would have been rather quieter.'[29]

At Christmas 1962 he wrote an article in a consumer magazine on 'God's Birth'. Above all, however, the beginning of his retirement was disturbed by a series of 'questions and answers' and interviews. 'I like these conversations very much. They really keep me alive.'[30] And as he remarked on another occasion, it was not just because of his declining strength that his public speaking now almost exclusively took the form of such conversations, rather than lectures. 'I believe that the time of long lectures, when someone spoke for an hour and the audience was condemned to sit and listen to whatever they were given, is . . . perhaps over – not just for me but for everyone. What we need in theology and in the church is – Oh, I don't want to use that wretched word again – "conversations". What I mean is simply that we should talk together and try to arrive at answers together, instead of someone trying to present something to other people as though the Holy Spirit had dictated it to him in person.'[31]

A meeting of this kind took place on 26 November 1962 in the Blue Cross hostel in Basle between Barth and agents of the Blue Cross in Switzerland. The subject was 'Evangelical Freedom'. 'I cheered them on by saying, "Good, you can and should go your way with the Blue Cross in evangelical freedom. That is a right and necessary thing. Don't be embarrassed about it. Do things as well as you can."'[32] In January 1963 he met ecumenical students from Bossey, Zürich students and members of the Reformed Bruderholz community for question and answer sessions. That same month he caused offence in his home country in an interview on his opinion of modern Switzerland: in it he suggested 'that we were in danger of being the "village idiots of Europe". Oh, this "sin of the tongue", which I keep committing again and again.'[33] The title of the interview was, 'We have no Sense of our own Relativity'. He called off a visit to Prague and East Berlin which he had planned for the beginning of March, on which he had wanted to have more conversations, because he could not face the effort involved. But in the middle of May he set off on the first of three visits to Paris which he was to make during the course of 1963. On each of the three occasions he made himself available for a television interview with Georges Casalis, a friend with whom he got on so well 'in things both great and small'.[34] On the first visit he also held a question and answer session at the Protestant faculty of theology, and on the second, at the end of October, he had a four-day colloquium with a hundred and twenty pastors in Bièvres (on his *Evangelical Theology*).

In June Barth spoke again at a question and answer session in Basle with an ecumenical group of students and also at the City Mission – the president was his son-in-law Max Zellweger. On 15 July, seventy-four members of the Church Brotherhood in Württemberg appeared for a cheerful whole-day conversation, in particular about the political service of the Christian. After the summer vacation, he gave interviews: in September to a Basle newspaper (about Rolf Hochhuth's play *The Representative*); in October to the BBC and North German radio; and in November to South German radio on the Barmen Declaration, the thirtieth anniversary of which was approaching. On 12 October he received a group of Göttingen students for a conversation about his views on understanding the Bible, human freedom, the nature of academic theology and eschatology. Then on 4 November he had a discussion with youth chaplains from the Rhineland on very similar questions. Almost the same questions were put to him again on 2 March 1964 at a whole-day conversation with the Repetents and students of the Tübingen Stift.* In the middle of November 1963 he also had a further question and answer session in the 'evangelical convent in Gelterkinden. The sisters kept wanting to be told what admirable vows they had taken and to be otherwise encouraged.'[35]

All these conversations took place in a splendidly eirenic and indeed often cheerful atmosphere, sometimes interrupted by loud laughter – except for that with the youth chaplains from the Rhineland. Here there was a vigorous argument over Bultmann and his followers, about whom the group was very much in two minds. One young man 'blurted out: "Herr Professor, you have made history, but now you have become history. We young ones are breaking out into new territory." I replied, "How nice, I'm pleased to hear that. Tell me something about this new territory." Unfortunately he couldn't. . . . There are a great many attractive young men in the church today, who tell us that almost everything must be changed. But they will only be able to indicate a credible new direction for the church when God speaks to them, they give him a hearing, and can go on to tell others what should replace the present scene.'[36]

In many of these conversations and interviews Barth expressed his surprise over the present state of Protestant theology. He felt that the current situation was a 'theological Vanity Fair'. 'Tillich and the Bultmannites rampage on the platform along with the problematical shades of Bonhoeffer. And poor Bishop Robinson in his *Honest to God*, which has sold 200,000 copies, has drawn off the froth from all this to put it on the market as the ultimate wisdom – and has been singled

---

*The Stift at Tübingen is perhaps the most famous hall of residence for theological students in Germany, dating back to the Reformation. The Repetents are the élite of the students, academics in the making who are preparing for their doctorates or to qualify as lecturers, and who help by teaching the younger students.

out for praise by Bultmann into the bargain.'[37] 'The theology of this bishop, which now also shed a rather lurid light back on to these German theologians',[38] seemed to Barth to be wretchedly 'flat-footed'.[39] He expressed similar criticisms at the beginning of 1964 in a preface to a new edition of his study of Bultmann. There he advised 'my colleagues, young and old, who are so keen to find a standpoint "beyond Barth and Bultmann", to stop doing it and instead to follow either the one or the other consistently along his way and to pursue it to the end. They will not find Rudolf Bultmann and me – or Tillich and me – or even Bonhoeffer (styled, of course, in the present fashion) and me as heraldic lions on the left and the right of the door which leads to the paradise of a new and better theology.'[40]

In a large number of these conversations Barth was asked one question which proved of considerable importance in current discussions within Protestant theology: 'How is the text of the Bible to be understood?', in other words, the hermeneutical question. Barth felt that one could run into a dead end here, not so much over the problem itself as over its promotion to a theme to be tackled in isolation. There seemed to be 'a return to the situation from which we thought we had escaped in 1920'. So he mocked the 'short-lived talk about hermeneutics',[41] and felt free to be 'deeply offended or even considerably amused at hearing the fortunes of the "language event" on the theological market, which I follow attentively (I am inclined to call its most vociferous promoters either the troop of Korah or the international union of garden gnomes)'.[42] In the conversation with the Rhineland pastors Barth gave his own view of the problem: 'It is not so much a matter of our encountering the witness of scripture as of our encountering the one to whom the testimony of scripture bears witness.' To encounter him it was necessary to pray, but also to work, and the work which needed to be done was to read the evidence with the aid of historical criticism – asking 'whether and how far' it bears witness to 'him'. But in no circumstances may 'the freedom of the Word of God . . . be limited through a sovereignty which we already impose on its testimony: it must be allowed its own sovereignty. The details of the problem are not simple. What has to happen will always keep becoming a new problem. Of course we all have some kind of ontology or world-view in our heads. And that is not prohibited . . . But when we read the Bible we are not to think that we are dealing with an ultimate authority which has to put itself at our disposal . . . What we have to do, rather, is quite simple: we must see that we keep the doors and windows open. We must not keep to a room which is "after the flesh", even if this "flesh" seems pious and rational flesh. No, we are in this room, but: "Open the window!", "Open the door!" so the wind can come in.'[43]

In these conversations and interviews Barth also expressed his hopeful and delighted surprise over modern Catholicism. 'A short while ago we were all thinking of Catholicism as a quite rigid structure, but now all at once it is on the move, and in a very interesting direction.'[44] Barth had a very high opinion of Pope John XXIII, who died in June 1963, as an exponent of this movement. 'It seems to me remarkable that this old Angelo Roncalli has in fact shown the papacy to be so rich. After a man like that one cannot continue to argue as insistently against this institution as one could in the past. He was a good man.'[45] 'One can go back three hundred, six hundred years and pass over all these other popes: none of them seems to have been a *pastor bonus*. But now we have seen one who has at least shown some quite definite characteristics of the good shepherd.'[46] Barth also followed the Second Vatican Council very attentively as an indicator of the new movement, gaining information about its lively course not only from written reports but also directly through Hans Küng, who was involved there as a *peritus*, and Oscar Cullmann, who was there as a Protestant observer. In the autumn of 1963 he was even invited by Cardinal Bea's secretariat to take part in person as an observer at the third session of the Council. But he had to refuse, as he did not think that his health was up to it. One little detail which he liked to mention as a pointer to the new movement was the inclusion of Joseph in the canon of the mass. 'I find this biblical figure, so moving and obedient and subservient, much more appropriate as a *protector (et exemplar) ecclesiae* than Mary, with whose function that of the church cannot be compared.'[47] In 1963 Barth expressed his amazement at the new Catholicism in a long interview for the journal *Réalité* headed 'The Churches are Coming Together', and in an article entitled 'Considerations on the Second Vatican Council'. In the latter he wrote that 'the signs of renewal within Catholicism must be much more interesting to us than the rather tedious question of the possibility of future "dialogue" with Rome'.[48]

Barth also undertook a good many other projects in 1963. In the middle of April he travelled with his son-in-law to Copenhagen. From there he had received 'the utterly unexpected news that he had been chosen to receive a prize previously awarded to such illustrious names as Winston Churchill, Albert Schweitzer, Igor Stravinsky and Niels Bohr because he, too, had made his contribution to the spread of European culture'.[49] 'How fortunate that Kierkegaard no longer lives there and cannot object that the real prophets were usually remembered with stones and not with such prizes.'[50] At the presentation of the Sonning Prize on 19 April, Niels Hanson Søe gave the *Laudatio* for Barth, while Barth in his speech of thanks sketched the history of his relationship to Kierkegaard. The gist of it was that 'I regard him as a teacher through whose school every theologian must pass at some time. Woe to anyone who has failed to do that. But he should not remain in it, and he will do better not to return to it.'[51] Soon afterwards, Barth wrote a further article on Kierkegaard to this effect, on the occasion of the 150th anniversary of his birth in May. He gave the greater part of the prize, which amounted to 110,000 Danish crowns – 'even Zacchaeus did not do more'[52] – to the Basle Mission and the City Mission, to Swiss Church Aid and to the relief fund of his family village of Mülligen: he used the rest to pay off the mortgage on his house.

In the same year Barth received a second significant award; a further honorary doctorate was bestowed on him on 6 November in Paris. The main purpose of his third visit to Paris this year was 'to receive (to the sounds of the Marseillaise) the *Dr ès Letterès h.c.* bestowed on me by the Sorbonne (I remembered the Reformers who in the sixteenth century were sent to the stake by the very same Sorbonne!).'[53] Here the *Laudatio* was written by the philosopher Paul Ricoeur.

A week after his spring visit to Copenhagen, Barth had to give a lecture on 'theology' to three hundred students, mostly from developing countries, who were in Basle as guests of the Mustermesse.

In it he accepted Marx's criticism of religion, but remarked that 'Christianity is not a religion'. He further declared that God was the one 'who in the man Jesus Christ gives the proof of his existence, beside whom there is no other'. He went on: 'There may be a religious West, but there is not a Christian West: there is only Western man confronted with Jesus Christ.' And he added: 'It could well be that one day true Christianity will be understood and lived better in Asia and in Africa than in our aged Europe.'[54]

In the middle of June a contribution by Barth appeared in the *Zürcher Woche* entitled 'For and against Atheism'. In it he was responding to an invitation to join in a discussion of the atheism of the Stuttgart professor Max Bense, but he explained straight away why he could not do that: 'A "Christianity" which needed to be defended by one professor when it was attacked by another would not be worthy of its name.' Furthermore, God in Jesus Christ has 'once and for all put an end to any talk of "atheism", whether in Max Bense's case or my own.' Besides, his 'opponent' should not be anxious about his rationality. Christian faith was not against thinking but for it. However, the thinking had to be of a certain kind: 'thinking means reflecting.' And finally: what was dangerous was neither the mild atheism of Bense nor the wild atheism of the East, but the *practical* atheism of Christians.

This summer Barth also wrote an article on characteristics of 'Reformed Theology in Switzerland' (which later appeared in a Festschrift in honour of his former critic Berkouwer). He disputed 'that, as I once heard a German colleague rudely say, the activity of Swiss theologians is confined to processing German tobacco for use at home.'[55] He claimed, rather, that in Switzerland theology took a specific form: it was characterized by a 'certain dry radicalism', 'a striking matter-of-factness', a 'marked tendency for mediation' and a love of ethics and pedagogy. Also this summer he wrote quite a different kind of article at the request of the Reformed church in Brandenburg: this was a 'theological opinion' on the 'Ten Articles on Freedom and Service' in which the East German churches had just formulated their understanding of their relationship with the state. He found that they lacked a thorough-going christological and eschatological focus and a clear connection between the concepts of 'freedom' and 'service' which would result in a 'freedom for service'.

Again in 1963 Barth had a large number of visitors: 'almost innumerable individuals who all claimed a considerable amount of time'. They came from many countries. Above all, of course, there were 'the Germans, for whom I was specially born'; once there was even 'a young Jesuit from Spain who is resolved to involve himself energetically in the reversal of the relationship between nature and grace, and also a very pleasant Salvation Army officer from France', to whom Barth defended his cherished lifelong habit of pipe-smoking, though he conceded, 'le péché ne commence que par la cigarette'. 'In short, I cannot in any way complain of loneliness.'[56] In the summer – after several days in Klosters, at Kapf and (for the last time) at the Bergli – Barth spent his holidays in Gyrenbad with his Dutch friend Kornelis Heiko Miskotte. Barth was very eager for conversations with him, because this man more than almost anyone else had followed the appearance of the volumes of the *Dogmatics* 'with such delighted understanding and such understanding delight'. He valued Miskotte as the 'seer and poet among my friends' and was impressed by 'the breadth and depth of his knowledge of all realms of literature, which is so much greater than my own'.[57] In December Barth then had a moving last meeting with Paul Tillich: 'I warned him that now might be the time to get himself straight. But he didn't seem to want to do that very much.'[58]

'Not completely finished'

During 1963 Barth's working pace had still been considerable, but from about the beginning of 1964 it began to decline noticeably. On Christmas Eve 1963 he gave a sermon in Basle prison on John 16.33 which attracted a good deal of attention and was broadcast direct by Swiss and South German radio. At Easter 1964 he preached there once again – on John 20.19-20. At the end of February he gave interviews to Hessen radio and North West German radio, and then in May to South West German radio and to the American journal *Christianity Today*. The same month also saw the publication of a short article on the four hundredth anniversary of the death of Calvin; it was not uncritical, but written in marked gratitude. At the beginning of April he even ventured a further journey to the Rhineland: he went to Mülheim, to take part in a conference on the question of postponing baptism for small children. He wanted to hear a lecture which his son Markus (who had recently moved from Chicago to a teaching post in Pittsburgh) was to give there. And he also wanted to support by his own participation those who were waking up to the problem of baptism and asking questions about it. About a year earlier, on the occasion of a visit by the Westphalian Church President Ernst Wilm to Basle, he had sought to enlist the support of church administrations for this concern. 'When he left me, I called down the street, "Don't let your spirit be quenched!", but I had the impression that he wasn't inclined to do anything about it.'[59]

About this time, however, Barth's health began to decline. In spring 1964 'an indisposition began which gradually developed into a regular illness'.[60] After his seventy-eighth birthday he told his friends: 'Despite some signs of the beginning of the collapse of this earthly tabernacle, I'm not completely finished. Not yet.' But he still complained: 'Quite frankly, I had imagined growing old would be rather easier. I also thought that "retirement" would be somehow more comfortable.'[61] In August he had to go into the Bethesdaspital in Basle for a prostate operation. 'I was looked after patiently and kindly by friendly and skilled deaconesses and other sisters.'[62] ' "The Lord will preserve you to do more work," an American professor of medicine said to me; he was travelling through here and was also interested in the functioning of my lower organs.'[63]

Hardly had he recovered from the operation than Barth had to return to Bethesda for another lengthy stay. 'Shortly before Christmas 1964 I had a slight stroke which for half a day robbed me of my speech – perhaps a sign, in view of the much too much that I have said in my lifetime. Then, possibly in unconscious protest against the undue disparagement of the third evangelist by prominent New Testament scholars, and certainly to the edification of the deaconess who was caring for me, the name Zechariah (Luke 1.22) clearly passed over my lips as a description of my state. Quite soon afterwards I was able to say more about the situation. Nothing like this has happened to me since – at any rate, not yet.'[64]

Soon after his return from hospital he was able to talk at length and answer questions again – for example, in an interview with the Dutchman George Puchinger on the history of his attitude to Roman Catholicism. Hardly had he fully recovered, however, than yet another stay in hospital proved necessary, this time in the Basle Bürgerspital, 'where I had marvellous experiences at the receiving end of modern medical science (for a full four months!)'[65] – from July to October 1965. 'I had the opportunity of a very existential experience of the skill and knowledge of the doctor and the apothecary who are so highly praised at least by Jesus Sirach 38 (a prophecy of the Basle chemical and pharmaceutical industry!): I also found that the care taken of me by a whole host of dear sisters was beyond all praise.'[66] He arranged regular evening prayers with these sisters, even allowing a Catholic present to say the 'Ave Maria'. For one of them he wrote some 'test questions for the choice of a husband'. 'The nicest thing that the nicest of the sisters who looked after me in the Bürgerspital said to me was that I was a "sisters' brother".'[67]. In hospital, Barth soon gained new strength and pleasure 'in reading what other theologians write and above all in singing this and that from the hymn book. And my pipe seldom goes out, even in hospital. In addition to the Bible, remarkably enough I have read a good deal of Goethe.'[68]

At the end of October Barth returned to the Bruderholz again, 'thankful to God and man that I am still alive and can read, carry on conversations, smoke, sing psalms and chorales, listen to Mozart, enjoy my fourteen grandchildren and exist from day to day in this positive kind of way'.[69] 'It has clearly been the good pleasure of God to give me for the moment . . . a further span of life.'[70] 'My physical weakness has still not completely disappeared – I call the region in which it makes itself felt Zürich-Niederdorf – and it is painful for me and a burden on those around me. However, for the moment it isn't dangerous. The activity in my head is evidently not hindered by it.'[71] However, for the future it proved that 'I often have to fight with a quite inexplicable sadness in which all the success that life has brought me is *no use at all*.'[72] 'But I used to say, and still tell myself constantly, that the good God and the angels probably wanted to know (and still want to know) whether I am in a position to do something about *living out* a few of the fine things that I have been *writing* over the past fifty years.' Moreover, 'Others have had to go through years and years of hardship, while I have been granted enough and more than enough days of good health.'[73] But at the same time Barth saw more clearly than ever that 'in the life of every man there are shadows . . . deep shadows, which will not go away. Perhaps it is God's will that they should not go away, so as to keep us where we are, as those who are beloved of God and can keep on loving and praising him.'[74]

After his second prostate operation Barth had to be looked after for the remainder of his life because he now had to wear a catheter. A nurse came in once or twice a day to see to his needs. Otherwise he was taken care of by his wife Nelly: she looked after me 'as well as a nursing sister, or even better'.[75] For some time Barth had been under a local doctor, 'Alfred Briellman, my Catholic doctor friend, who is forty years younger'. He came 'at frequent intervals to cheer me up . . . we always have new conversations about medicine, about people and about Christianity and the church'.[76]

While Barth was being restored 'to a relatively acceptable state of human dignity',[77] he suffered another blow. 'My faithful helper Charlotte von Kirschbaum, who had been at my side since 1930 and had been indispensable in every way, was incapacitated by a much more serious illness than my own (diagnosed definitely at the end of 1965) and was put out of action as far as the *Church Dogmatics* was concerned, having taken an immeasurable part in its origin and progress.'[78] For some time she had been showing increasing symptoms of a brain disease which by the beginning of January 1966 had progressed so far that she had to be moved to a residential nursing home. Barth looked forward week by week to the 'hour which I spend every Sunday with my dear Lollo von Kirschbaum at the Sonnenhalde in Riehen. . . . But because of her brain disease she is now only a shadow of what she once was.' When he used to go to visit her, Barth above all used to sing chorales to her. Once when she was saying goodbye to him, she said, ' "But we did have a good time, didn't we?" . . . She's a great lesson to me in all her frailty.'[79] After her departure, Barth took on one of his students, Eberhard Busch, on a regular basis, to deal with all his secretarial work and to help him in other ways. 'Lollo' only died after ten years of suffering (on 24 July 1975): 'it was a long, slow departure . . . she went further and further away'.

By December 1965, Barth was wanting to preach in Basle prison once more – but he no longer could. He never went again. So his Easter sermon of 29 March 1964, 'The disciples were happy when they saw the Lord' (John 20.19f.), was his last sermon there. It was also the last of about six hundred and seventy sermons which he had written in his life. Although he had written so many sermons and also had them published, remarkably enough, 'sermon meditations were a literary genre which I never attempted . . . I always find it difficult even to "meditate" on a sermon which I am to give myself, so I don't know whether I could be of any help to others.'[80] Barth now only listened to sermons. For years his favourite preacher had been Pastor Fritz Dürst, who worked on the Baselbiet side of the Bruderholz, in Binningen-Bottmingen. But Barth also went to the services of the Basle Bruderholz community and in addition now often visited the local Catholic church assigned to Brother Klaus, 'whose pastor apostrophized me publicly as the "Church Father of the Bruderholz"'. Indeed for a while Barth even attempted to bring about an ecumenical meeting between these two communities, 'which I visit alternately as a kind of "go-between" '.[81] When he was prevented more and more from going to church, he used to listen on the radio every Sunday morning, 'not just to one, but to two sermons, one Catholic and one Protestant'.[82]

One volume of Barth's prison sermons was published in 1959 under the title *Den Gefangenen Befreiung* (ET *Deliverance to the Captives*); a second appeared late in 1965. As with the first volume, the sermons were not only given in the prison, but also printed there.

The title of this second book of Barth's sermons, *Rufe mich an!* (ET *Call for God*), was also deliberately meant to be a reference to his understanding of the sermon as such and indeed of the whole act of worship. 'As the centre of the life of the community, worship has to be seen as a whole; moreover, all of it must represent a call to the gracious God.' So worship begins with a hymn sung by the congregation and with 'the expression of its gratitude, its penitence, its special prayer for God's presence and support in the specific act of its meeting for worship. This is expressed by the member of the congregation who is leading the worship. It culminates in the sermon, in which the call becomes an address and a proclamation in the interpretation and application of a word of scripture (a short text is better than a long one). From there the service moves towards the closing prayer. This briefly sums up the content of the sermon (now in a direct appeal to God), but also develops the act of worship so that it becomes the most comprehensive intercession possible . . . for all other men, for the rest of the church, and for the world. In the second hymn the congregation makes this closing prayer its own', and the service (as Barth understood it in his old age) ends with a blessing.[83]

On the basis of these thoughts, Karl Barth had now arrived at some specific views of the way in which services should be held and even about the disposition of the congregation. He thought that they should sit round in a semi-circle, and that 'the ideal solution to the problem of forming a central focus' was to erect 'a striking wooden table, which should be easy to put up, but clearly different from an "altar". It should be provided with a movable desk, since it would have to serve both as a pulpit *and* a table for the Lord's Supper *and* in place of a font . . . Pictorial and symbolic representations are out of place in the Protestant church. (The reality of the person and work of Jesus Christ can only be represented by the activity of the community in worship in the narrower sense of the term, and then above all in life: no pictures and no symbols.)'[84] He also thought 'that the organ should be replaced by four wind instruments to support the singing of the congregation – it seems to me out of place in the context of Christian worship, and belongs in the concert hall rather than the church'.[85] Barth also suggested that taking the collection 'should not be left to the end, as people were going out', and above all that the eucharist should be celebrated regularly. 'Why is the Lord's Supper not celebrated every Sunday in every church (at the very least in the presence of the whole congregation) – even if this is at the expense of the length of our sermons and our excessive organ music? It would be legitimate liberation for the preacher and his audience . . . ! And occasionally baptism could form the beginning of the whole service (also without an unnecessary flood of words). Would this not make us a comprehensive "church of the Word" – the Word which did not become speech, but flesh?'[86]

Barth's physical limitations, which had increased further as a result of his age and his illnesses, prevented him from preaching any more. But he did not want them to prevent him from doing at least some work of a different kind. Indeed, he thought: 'In my opinion, in view of the many ways in which our life is distorted inwardly and outwardly, that is the best, and perhaps in the end the only human answer to the question "What shall we do?" We should keep occupied and try to concentrate on what may be required of us at any one time – without making any claims ourselves. One cannot heal any real sorrows that way. But one can learn to bear them fruitfully and worthily.'[87] So while Barth was no longer active in the pulpit, he could at least be active at his desk. The desk at which he now sat was no longer the one which he had taken over from his father and at which he had written out by hand the whole of the *Church Dogmatics*. He now had a 'splendid new desk, given by the Presbyterians in Pittsburgh in exchange for the old one (which has become a museum piece there with an inscription)'.[88] At this fine new desk, in January 1966, Barth began with great zest to write an autobiography. He prefaced it with the words:

> What are we, and what do we have
> on this whole earth,
> which has not been given to us,
> Father, by you?

And he started off with a demonstration that man's life is not his own in another sense, by beginning with his ancestors. He took especial care to give a patient and loving account of his great-grandfather Karl Friedrich Sartorius, whom he found particularly interesting, since the family had kept completely quiet about him because of his serious weakness for alcohol. Hardly was this chapter finished, however, than Barth resolved to put his work into cold storage for the moment.

The first interruption to the biography was the celebration of his eightieth birthday on 10 May 1966. He, too, had now become a great-grandfather. And now that he had grown so old, on this anniversary he could contemplate an extensive range of 'descendants'. 'We really have . . . a close and splendid connection with them all,' he thought.[89] The times when he had danced round the lighted Christmas tree with Maxuli, his daughter's oldest son, and Peter, Markus' oldest son, were long, long past. In the meanwhile Markus' five children and Franziska's four had grown up, and had begun to go their own ways. There were even two great-grandchildren (children of the Zellwegers' second daughter) in whom he found delight. 'More and more, my own life is becoming that of a small child.'[90] Dieter, the Zellwegers' youngest son, received some theological instruction from his grandfather while he was at school and then decided to specialize in theology; he was the second of Karl's grandchildren to do so. Hans Jakob's two daughters, who were even younger, also came to their grandparents' home often. In 1965 Christoph and his wife and three children (they had a fourth in 1967) had left Indonesia for good and were now living close by. Karl Barth was particularly pleased to be able to increase his knowledge of the Old Testament from conversations with his son Christoph. However, in the autumn of 1967 Christoph left again with his family; this time for Mainz, where he had been appointed to an Old Testament chair. Shortly before his eightieth birthday, Karl Barth sketched out how he would like to keep on the right side of the rising generation in a 'Rule of life for older people in their relationship to the young'. This said, for example: 'You must make it clear that your younger relations have the right to go their way in accordance with their own principles, not yours.' And: 'In no circumstances should you give them up: rather, you should go along with them cheerfully, allowing them to be free, thinking the best of them and trusting in God, loving them and praying for them, whatever happens.'

Barth celebrated his eightieth birthday in wonder that 'I have lived to see this day, when so many of my former contemporaries and sparring partners have departed from us, some long ago, some more recently.' He was still alive; although 'more than once it looked as though I might have to join the ranks of the departed'.[91] Heinrich Barth and Paul Tillich had died the previous year. When he last visited him at the end of 1963, Tillich had told Barth about a visit to Palestine. Barth believed 'that he now knows better about the inscription which he discovered in Nazareth and of which he disapproved so much, saying *Hic verbum caro factum est.** One day we too will certainly know better, praising "the putting in context".'[92] In April 1966 Emil Brunner had also died. Shortly beforehand, Barth had sent him a message through his friend Peter Vogelsanger: 'If he is still alive and it is possible, tell him again, "Commended to *our* God", even by me. And tell him, *Yes,* that the time when I thought

---

*'Here the Word was made flesh.'

that I had to say "No" to him is now long past, since we all live only by virtue of the fact that a great and merciful God says his gracious Yes to all of us.'[93] These words were the last that Brunner heard in his life . . . Then Paul Althaus died in May and Friedrich Gogarten the next winter. Bultmann 'and I are now the last somewhat rotten pillars of an earlier generation'.[94] Bultmann wished Barth 'good courage' on his eightieth birthday; this was the last personal word exchanged between them.

As a curtain-raiser to the birthday celebrations there was a Mozart concert in St Martin's church under the direction of Max Geiger. At the official birthday celebrations on 9 May, a great many dignitaries were present in addition to Barth's closest theological friends, from Switzerland, East and West Germany, France, Norway (Professor Reidar Hauge), Holland, the USA and the USSR. There were such different people as the politician Gustav Heinemann; the diplomat and historian Hans Bernd Gisevius; the historian Edgar Bonjour; the physicians Fritz Koller, Gerhard Wolf-Heidegger and Paul Kielholz; the corps commander Alfred Ernst; Paul Vogt and Gertrud Kurz (who were involved in 'peace' work); and the von Stockhausens (a husband and wife who were painters, and whom Barth had got to know in Ticino). The Rector of Bonn hung round his neck 'a heavy golden chain which was worn by the same Federal President Heuss (when he was an honorary senator of the University of Bonn) who did not want to have me in Frankfurt that time'.[95]*

In view of Barth's ignominious departure to retirement the Rector of Basle now rehabilitated him. And Jürgen Fangmeier presented him with a voluminous Festschrift which he had edited with Max Geiger and Eberhard Busch, entitled *Parrhesia*. It contained thirty-two contributions, this time – with few exceptions – consisting of articles by 'young, younger and even the youngest' theological scholars. Barth replied to the bouquet of greetings with a speech of thanks in which he compared himself with an ass, namely the one who 'was allowed to bear the Lord Jesus into Jerusalem'. 'If I have made any contribution in my life, it is as a relation of this ass, who at that time went on his way with an important burden. The disciples said to its owner: "The Lord needs it". And so it seems to have pleased God to have needed me in our time, just as I was, and despite

*See p.434.

all the nasty things which have been said and can still be said against me. I have been used and I have been there. "The battle went on, the enemy was beaten and I sat on the baggage cart." *That's* how I have been there, and that has been my contribution. I have been there.'[96] Some days after the festivities '*three* important men appeared from East Germany to congratulate me: Gerald Götting, Hans Seigewasser and the publisher Günther Wirth of Union Verlag: they came in a tremendous car of Russian make (which was gaped at for three and a half hours in front of my house by the people of Bruderholz) and loaded with presents like the three wise men from the East (including Meissen crockery!).'[97]

Ad limina apostolorum

When the birthday celebrations were over, Karl Barth did not want to back to his autiobiography and become involved again with himself and his past. So he finally stopped work on it 'in order to turn once again to the theological present'.[98] He did not want to do this, however, 'in the form of a contribution to the discussion on the foolish "God is dead" movement, which has proved on both sides of the Atlantic to be the last and most glorious fruit of illustrious existentialist theology'. Much less did he want to be involved 'in the equally stupid "confessional movement", into which some people, who are neither called to nor capable of it (either mentally or spiritually), think they have to rush in order to contradict the rest'.[99] As early as the middle of March, Barth had briefly made known his views on the confessional movement. In his remarks he asked whether its confession also included statements against atomic warfare, against the involvement of the USA in Vietnam, against the new antisemitism and in favour of a German peace treaty with Eastern Europe, recognizing the 1945 boundaries. 'If your *correct* confession of Jesus Christ, crucified and risen for us according to the testimony of holy scripture, includes and expresses that, then it is a *right,* precious and valuable confession.' If it does not, then it is '*not right,* but a dead, cheap, fly-sieving, camel-swallowing and Pharisaic confession'.[100] In an interview on North German radio in May Barth repeated these thoughts – and added that he regarded this movement, 'like the whole Bultmann school, as a single regression into the long-obsolete questions of the nineteenth century'.

95. *Barth on his eightieth birthday in conversation with the Catholic theologian Hans Küng and the Reformed preacher Walter Lüthi. Hellmut Traub is on the left.*

96. *With Bishop Willebrands in front of the Colosseum in Rome, September 1966.*

97. *Draft of a letter of 13 March 1968 to 'His Holiness,' Pope Paul VI.*

98. *With the heads of the Swiss churches at Leuenberg, 28 February 1968: Bishop Kury, A. Lavanchy, Bishop Vonderach, H. U. von Balthasar, Bishops Hasler and Hänggi.*

Barth in old age

99.   He was very fond of playing chess: here with his grandson Lukas, who was very good at driving him into a corner.

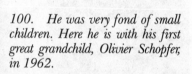

100.   He was very fond of small children. Here he is with his first great grandchild, Olivier Schopfer, in 1962.

101.   With his wife Nelly, his son-in-law Max Zellweger and his second great grandson, June 1968.

While Barth found this whole complex of questions insubstantial and inconsequential, he took an 'increasingly keen interest in the results of the Second Vatican Council' and post-conciliar Catholicism.[101] 'Having been long interested in the much more urgent and objectively much more important problem of Roman Catholicism, on my sick-bed I read not only Goethe, Jeremias Gotthelf, Gottfried Keller and other good authors, but also all the news and the texts (primarily German) that I could get from the Council.'[102] During the spring and summer of 1966, 'I then made a serious study of the sixteen Latin texts produced by the Council and of at least some specimens of the abundant literature devoted to the Council.'[103] Here Barth saw that at every step 'this thing which is called "Catholicism", and which is so remarkable to the rest of us . . . is now involved in a movement from new beginnings to new goals. The new movement must give us much more to think about than all the traditional elements which are still unmistakably part of Catholicism and which (perhaps for our edification) will have to stay a while longer.'[104] He happily counted himself among 'those who take delight in the serious and powerful movements which have arisen in the Catholic church before and after the Council, and which are evidently continuing, without optimism, but in Christian hope'.[105]

'Do not worry, I am not going to become a Roman Catholic!'[106] 'There is no sense in "conversions" from us to the Roman Catholic church or vice versa (*peccatur intra muros et extra*). They can only make sense where they have the necessary form of "conversion" – not to another church but to Jesus Christ, the Lord of the one, holy, Catholic and apostolic church. In essentials, on either side the important thing is for each one, in his place in his church, to allow himself to be called to faith in the one Lord and to his service.'[107] But Barth asked himself with increasing disquiet whether such a 'conversion' might not be made more decisively in 'new Catholicism' than on the Protestant side. 'What if one day Rome (without ceasing to be Rome) simply overtakes us in the question of the renewal of the church on the basis of the word and the spirit of the gospel, and puts us in the shade? What if we have to see the last becoming first and the first last, and the voice of the good shepherd finding a clearer echo there than with us?'[108] Barth certainly did not want to overestimate the renewal in the Roman Catholic church. Indeed, he believed that 'I can see all too clearly into the misery that prevails even there'.[109] In particular, what Barth hoped for as the renewal of the church in the sense of a conversion to Jesus Christ was not necessarily identical with the concerns of the 'progressive' wing in the Catholic camp. He also had his reservations about them; above all, he was worried that 'some Catholics are becoming all too Protestant' and that 'the errors which have been with us since the sixteenth century' might be repeated.[110] Hence his warning: 'Think of Pope Pius IX – young revolutionaries easily become old reactionaries!'[111] But for all his hesitations, Barth would not again give up his 'quiet brotherly hope', 'coupled with a readiness in the meantime to help to put our own house in order in matters great and small'.[112]

In the early part of the year Barth had already given some stimulus to the renewal of monasticism when – at the request of the Benedictine abbey of Montserrat – he had put forward some views on 'monastic life'. He said that such special communities of brothers or sisters were *especially* dependent on free grace and that their task and their significance was to be 'in exemplary fashion' the brothers and sisters of *all* Christians and *all* men. In June, Hans Küng came from Tübingen with a group of young Catholic scholars for a lengthy conversation. To Barth's astonishment the party included a real Bultmannite, but there was also a scholar who knew Calvin and was sympathetic to him. For Barth the conversation ended promisingly with the question, 'Should we now really sit round our table as "separated" brothers or sisters or not, and if so, to what degree?'[113] He continued to study the literature on the Council during his summer holidays in the Valais mountains – first with the family of his son Christoph, then with that of his son Markus. He was glad to go to mass on Sundays, and in general took delight in other aspects of his life, which was blossoming out yet again. 'Because of the cold water from the mountains, my morning shower is particularly refreshing, and for such an old gentleman I run through the country very well. The wine here is also quite drinkable.'[114]

Barth's preoccupation with post-conciliar Catholicism reached its crowning climax in the autumn of 1966. Since Barth had had to refuse the invitation in 1963 to be an observer at the last sessions of the Second Vatican Council, Cardinal Bea now asked him to pay the visit which had not been possible then and to gather some first-hand information about the significance and meaning of the Council. Barth in fact received a most courteous invitation. So at the end of September he ventured on a six-day *peregrinatio ad limina apostolorum*. He was accompanied on the journey by his wife and his doctor,

Alfred Briellmann. 'From the other side we were accompanied, guided, introduced, taught, and occasionally entertained and cheered in more secular fashion in turn by Bishop Willebrands . . . by the cultivated P. Magnus Löhrer from Einsiedeln, and occasionally also by Mgr Salzmann.'[115] Barth's visit to Rome consisted 'for the most part in a series of conversations with small groups of Jesuits, Dominicans, etc., based on two sets of questions' – one a series of criticisms and the other seeking information 'on nine of the various texts of Vatican II'. I discussed all these with various groups. I only came up against somewhat grim faces with Ottaviani and Parente (in the Holy Office!).[116] Unfortunately, 'I must also be somewhat critical in recalling my evening conversation with Cardinal Bea. I was in fact surprised that I did not hear his good case supported by even better theology, and therefore, as my companion said to me afterwards, reacted with somewhat nervous gestures.'[117] 'As far as I recall, the most cheerful of these meetings was the one with the Jesuits on the roof of their Gregorian Institute, where from my seat in the autumn sun I constantly had the cupola of St Peter's immediately before my eyes and so could never forget where I was even in the stream of conversation.'[118]

He never did forget this – as is indicated by the questions which he put. They all turned especially on the point: 'Where is the *distinction* between Christ as the Lord, the King and the Judge, and his *church*?' He caused considerable confusion by his acute question: 'If Mary is termed the "model of the lay apostolate" *and* the "queen of the apostles", does this not mean that the lay apostolate *is superior* to all other forms of the apostolate in the church?!' On this visit to Rome Barth also spent some hours in the faculty of 'our Waldensian brothers in the faith'. On the last day he also took part in an international congress of Catholic theologians. 'I was greeted with applause by those present . . . was personally introduced to the Cardinals who were there (as though I were their equal, except that I did not have the right hat) . . . and was seated in a chair on the same level.' Immediately after that 'there was a confidential conversation with my colleagues Rahner, Ratzinger and Semmelroth, in which I asked them to whisper in my ear their somewhat different views of Mariology'.[119]

'The dramatic climax of our days in Rome, if not the occasion with the most significant theological content, was of course our reception in the innermost sanctuary of the Roman Catholic Church' – by

Pope Paul VI, in the Vatican, who 'literally received us with open arms'.[120] He 'impressed me as a noteworthy and indeed lovable man, but I felt rather sorry for him. After a little speech praising me, he began with an almost touching comment about how difficult it was to bear and to handle the keys of Peter which had been entrusted to him by the Lord.'[121] 'I then ventured . . . also to put to him one or other of the questions I had brought with me, e.g. about my theological status as one of the *fratres sejuncti*, which is what we are constantly called in the Council documents. Would he agree that in this formula the word *fratres* should be underlined? He seemed to agree with that. We also touched on the difficult point of Mariology: the Pope had heard that I would prefer Joseph, the foster-father of Jesus, as the primal image of the nature and the function of the church, rather than the *ancilla Domini* who was later elevated to the rank of queen of heaven. He assured me that he would pray that in my advanced age I should be given a deeper insight in this matter.' At the conclusion of the hour-long audience Barth gave the Pope four of his books – 'produced from an old briefcase which accompanied me to the Barmen Synod of 1934'.[122] The Pope in turn gave him a facsimile of the Codex Vaticanus. Immediately after the audience Barth visited the tombs of John XXIII and Pius XII. The general impression which he brought back from this visit was that 'the church and theology over there are more on the move than I had imagined'[123] – and at any rate, 'The Pope is not the Antichrist!'[124]

Barth went even further in the hand-written dedications in the books he gave to Pope Paul. He in fact anticipated his earnest hope for a Christianity reunited on the basis of a renewed, Protestant-Catholic church when in one of them he confessed, '*In communi servitio unius Domini Paulo Sexto episcopo, servo servorum Dei, dedicavit hunc librum frater sejunctus Karl Barth*' ('In common service of the one Lord, this book is dedicated to the Bishop Paul VI, the humblest servant of God, by his separated brother Karl Barth').

The visit to Rome 'stimulated me to return for a while to academic activity, at least in the form of a small seminar'.[125] Because of his illnesses, in 1964, Barth had had to drop his various discussion groups, but for the winter semester of 1966–67 he again announced a seminar (or, as he now preferred to say, a colloquium), which took place on Saturdays in the new theological seminar building on the Nadelberg. He no longer conducted seminars as he had done in earlier years, with an introduction followed by a student's paper and a discussion of it. He now went back to the method which he had introduced to his seminars in 1959: 'a round-table conference with four alternate participants in each session'.[126] The theme of the seminar this winter was the constitution *Dei Verbum (De divina revelatione)* of the previous Council, which Barth thought to be particularly important and which he felt to be generally good. He invited the Catholic scholar Joseph Ratzinger from Tübingen for the last session, and the questions which were still unanswered were put to him. At the request of the Dominican Yves Congar from Strasbourg, whom Barth had also met in Rome, Barth summed up the result of the seminar in an 'eirenic-critical' article (*'Conciliorum Tridentini et Vaticani I inhaerens vestigii?!'*) in which he showed that, contrary to its own assertions, Vatican II in parts went far beyond the Council of Trent and the First Vatican Council.

The unfinished Dogmatics

During this winter Barth resolved to have published at least a 'worked-out fragment' from the incomplete fourth (ethical) part of his *Doctrine of Reconciliation*, which had been left almost untouched since he had stopped lecturing on dogmatics. The reason for the publication of this particular extract was that he wanted to give some support to the few people who were pressing for a revision of baptismal practice – especially in 'the "Protestant" Churches of Germany and Switzerland which, with solemn and authoritative appeal to a sacrosanct order, will not even consider alternative practical solutions to what has obviously become an increasing problem'.[127] In the summer of 1968, since Barth had the impression that this blind insistence on the primacy of infant baptism was especially strong in the Rhineland, he appealed to President Beckmann in a direct communication to open up discussion of the various doctrines of baptism and to carry before him 'the cross which is without doubt laid upon you as bearer of the leading office in the church to shoulder visibly in the service of our Lord, instead of as a sign of your power'.[128] The other reason for producing the fragment was Barth's concern to speak 'once again', by means of his explanation of baptism as responsible baptism, 'of the responsibility laid on the church and on the Christian'. For 'today there is much ready talk (too much and too ready) about the world which is supposed to have come of age in relation to God. However that may be, I am much more interested in the man who ought to come of age in relation to God and the world, i.e. the mature Christian and mature Christianity, their thought, speech and action, in responsibility to God, in living hope in him, in service to the world, in free confession and in unceasing prayer.'[129]

After the insertion of some new excursuses, this fragment still made a volume of 247 pages (ET 226). Barth dedicated it 'with great gratitude' to his wife Nelly, 'with whom I am now able to celebrate a really harmonious "evening of my life" – Philemon and Baucis, as they are in the book'.[130] Over the last months they had come together again, and after all that had happened they were granted some time in which they could deepen their relationship in more tranquil circumstances. Nelly Barth did more than take great trouble over nursing her husband. She also found more leisure to read his works and went with him often to his various meetings.

Barth was well aware of the risk in producing his controversial doctrine of baptism. 'I can foresee that with this book, which by human reckoning will be my last considerable publication, I shall once again find myself in a position of some loneliness in the theological and ecclesiastical scene, which I first entered almost fifty years ago. I am conscious of making a bad exit with it. So be it. The day will come when people will do me justice on this question, too.'[131]

The book was in fact Barth's 'last considerable publication'. It was also the last part of his *Church Dogmatics* that he could produce. And so the *Dogmatics* now remained, 'in spite of its not inconsiderable bulk' (9185 pages), an *opus imperfectum*, nine times as long as Calvin's *Institutes* and almost twice as long as the *Summa* of Thomas Aquinas! 'How often in the last years I have been asked about the non-appearance of the remaining parts of the *Church Dogmatics* which had been announced.' Some of the questioners 'put before me the example of the eighty-five-year-old Adenauer'; Barth replied to them, 'Is that how you want it?'[132] 'I have put others to confusion by raising the counter-question whether they have read and studied the material already available, and if so how much and how thoroughly. . . . Others I have reminded of the unfinished nature of most of the mediaeval *Summae* as well as many cathedrals. To others again I have pointed out that Mozart's premature death interrupted work on the *Requiem* in the middle of the *Lacrimosa*. . . Finally, I have called the attention of others to the fact that not only in holy scripture, but also in *Church Dogmatics* II, 1, perfection is the epitome of the divine attributes, so that it is better not to seek or to imitate it in a human

work. Naturally these were and are excuses, and rather presumptuous ones as far as the comparisons are concerned. They conceal the
simple fact that I have gradually begun to lose the physical energy
and mental drive necessary to continue and to complete the work
which I had started . . . For the "late Barth", which I now am, it is
indeed too late to do this in worthy fashion.'[133]

So the second part of the ethics of reconciliation (IV, 4) remained
uncompleted, and the planned volumes on the doctrine of redemption (eschatology) were never begun. On the one hand Barth
thought that a good deal could be inferred 'indirectly and even
directly from the earlier volumes about the much asked-after sphere
of eschatology'.[134] On the other, he thought that perhaps this theme
would have had to be developed as a whole and thought through in
detail. Without doubt, Barth would gladly have devoted himself to
this work. He would have come to it at a time in which interest in the
subject had been newly aroused elsewhere in theology. But he
thought that had he been able to present his arguments on eschatology he would still, 'at least to begin with', have been 'as alone in this
field as I was with the other main arguments of the *Church Dogmatics*'.[135] He also supposed this in view of the writings appearing as
a result of the new interest in eschatology. He found Teilhard de
Chardin least acceptable. 'Again and again apologetics at the root of
all gnosticism! For it seems to me unmistakable that Teilhard de
Chardin is an almost classic case of Gnosticism, in the context of
which the gospel cannot possibly thrive. The reality which is supposed to be manifest and to be believed in is . . . the deity of "evolution".'[136] He also had his suspicions of Moltmann's *Theology of Hope*:
namely over the 'single line' on which he makes 'the whole of
theology end up in eschatology'. 'Salvation comes . . . from the
knowledge of "the *eternally* rich God".* Compared with this, Moltmann's God seems to me to be a bit poor.'[137] He also had questions
for Pannenberg: Was he not building his house on the 'quicksand of
yesterday and on the "historical" reckonings of probability which
are so common today'? Was not his Christ merely the 'symbol of the
presupposition of a general anthropology, cosmology and
ontology'?[138]

---

*Barth was particularly fond of the phrase 'der ewig reiche Gott' (the eternally rich God). It
comes from the second verse of the well-known hymn 'Now thank we all our God', which is
quoted several times in this book, where the English translation 'this bounteous God' is rather
weaker and does not allow the emphasis Barth gives to the 'eternally' here.

How did Barth himself mean to understand eschatology? 'I can only give an indication: the "old" and "new" worlds are indirectly identical, the new already present in the old in that its reconciliation in Jesus Christ has already taken place. What is still to come is its manifestation (i.e. "apocalyptic" eschatology!)' – its general, final, universal revelation![139] In other words: ' "Eternal" life is not another, second life beyond our present one, but the reverse side of *this* life, as God sees it, which is hidden from us here and now. It is this life in relationship to what God has done in Jesus Christ for the whole world and thus also for us. So we wait and hope – in respect of our death – to be made *manifest* with him (Jesus Christ who is raised from the dead), in the glory of judgment, and also of the grace of God. That will be the *new* thing: that the veil which now lies over the whole world and thus over our life (tears, death, sorrow, crying, grief) will be taken away, and God's counsel (already accomplished in Jesus Christ) will stand before our eyes, the object of our deepest shame, but also of our joyful thanks and praise. I would like to describe it by quoting a verse of one of old Gellert's fine hymns:

> Then in the light there shall appear
> What in the dark I saw,
> All will be wonderful and clear
> That puzzled me before.
> My soul shall see with thanks and praise
> The meaning in the course of days.'[140]

Barth himself said that he had not had the last word in his *Church Dogmatics*. Certainly not! 'I see . . . the *Church Dogmatics*, not as a conclusion but as the opening of a new conversation' – about the question of the right course for theology.[141] This was the contribution which Barth thought he had made with his *Dogmatics*. And so he could gratefully note that they had been taken up, but also see with resignation during his last days that they were not being heeded. 'Who reads them? I need not complain. As far as I can see they are read by a considerable number of pastors, a good collection of non-theologians – and Roman Catholics. But Protestant academic theology? Especially in Germany? And most especially systematic theology? I don't weep even the smallest tear over it.'[142] Sure of his cause and what he had accomplished, even in view of the marked lack of interest in his discoveries, he felt that he could say quietly that his *Church Dogmatics* 'have to wait their time'.[143] But it was a joy and a satisfaction to him that a large number of pastors were using them and reading them. These pastors, their work and their calling were continually before his eyes as he wrote. And it was one of his great delights to have some pastors as faithful friends, like Hellmut Traub;

the Swabians Helmut Goes and Gotthilf Weber; Karl Handrich from the Pfalz; the Schwenzels, husband and wife, from Hessen; Karl Steinbauer from Bavaria; Werner Koch and Martin Rohkrämer from the Rhineland; Hannelotte Reiffen at work in East Germany, and many more.

In the *Dogmatics* Barth had been concerned with interpreting and explaining the gospel. And if there was any good in them he felt that it could only be his constant new references to the gospel, the gospel which 'has made itself felt without my efforts and despite them, while I have smoked my pipe and read the Bible and other good books, thought about things and then put my relevant expectorations on paper'.[144] 'Indeed, sometimes I am almost afraid when I see to what degree free unmerited grace has prevailed over my life, work and activity and in it: this grace is almost like an alien event, setting itself up in remarkable opposition to the quite unheroic process which I have pursued day by day and year by year, just thinking a little way ahead and always rather out of breath . . . about whatever seemed to me to come next, and always under the impression that I was dragging a long way behind what really should be done. And again and again I have been preoccupied with the thought of the many people whose life is spent, unlike mine, in the same toil, or even greater, and who remain in darkness or semi-darkness . . . It is nice to become "famous". But in the end, and in the last resort, who wants to become and to be "famous"?'[145] Because Barth understood the origin of his *Dogmatics* in this way, he could see their contents as being themselves relative and wanted them understood in this way. 'In heaven we shall know all that is necessary, and we shall not have to write on paper or read any more.'[146] 'Indeed, I shall be able to dump even the *Church Dogmatics* , over the growth of which the angels have long been amazed, on some heavenly floor as a pile of waste paper.'[147] He thought of the future fate of his eleven honorary doctorates in the same way: in heaven he would 'certainly have to hand them all in at the cloakroom'.[148]

The editing of this last section of the *Church Dogmatics* marked the end of Barth's larger works. He realized this with some regret. But he also saw 'that I have certainly written more books than any other living theologian'.[149] And he saw that there were 'a terrifying number of books about me on either side of the ocean'. 'Few theologians can ever have become the object of so much research and description during their lifetime.' 'Occasionally I feel like someone who has a particularly interesting ailment, surrounded on the operating table by numerous older and younger dignitaries in white coats, and having to listen now to this one and now to that saying what he has discovered, according to the degree of his professional understanding, about the make-up and condition of my various organs and their origins in my earlier history.'[150] When Barth virtually withdrew from productive work, he did so with the hope and the wish that later generations of theologians would do good work in fulfilling the task laid upon them. 'Let each one in his own field see to the same task that I attempted, to the glory of God and his neighbour. I hope he will do it a little bit better, indeed very much better, than I.'[151] Barth felt that it was important for his readers and those who researched into him to understand that in his writings he wanted to accomplish as careful a piece of thinking as possible, and was never playing merely with thought. 'It is good to think that the *Dogmatics* have emerged not only from my studies but also from a long and often difficult struggle with myself and with the problems of the world and of life. So if they are to be understood properly, they should be read not only with theoretical interest, but in an attempt to join me in the response to practical issues which has been my concern over all the past years.'[152]

'In a narrow space'

Barth was to produce no more substantial works. 'Now in every respect my feet can only move in a narrow space . . . Gone are the journeys, the running, the walking or even the riding that I used to do; gone is all the talking to larger groups; gone is my participation in conferences and all that sort of thing. Everything has its time, and for me everything of that kind seems to have had its time.'[153] Only smaller steps were possible. Occasionally Barth wrote another article, as for instance the newspaper article for Easter 1967 on 'The Mystery of Easter Day' (which consists in the 'existence of a new man, the free man'!!). On the whole, however, he was 'hardly a producer any more, but a keen consumer of spiritual goods of every quality'.[154] He read 'more widely than I had been able to before'. He was not so fond of writing letters and did not write them often; when he did, they were 'in the form of extended postcards'.[155] Nor could he cope with so many visitors; he preferred to have a few regular ones.

One person who now came to see him frequently and with whom he was delighted to talk was the systematic theologian Eberhard Jüngel, who had been teaching in Zürich since the winter of 1966-67. Jüngel was one of the young men whose progress Barth followed hopefully, because of his attempt to re-express the doctrine of God presented in the *Church Dogmatics*, against a background of study with Rudolf Bultmann and Ernst Fuchs. Jüngel helped to establish a new understanding between Barth and Fuchs, though they still had their problems with each other, and this understanding developed further when on 11 December 1965 Fuchs paid a visit to the Bruderholz. In the summer semester of 1967 Barth felt strong enough to announce another seminar; on Calvin. He chose Calvin because he wanted to present him as *the* ecumenical theologian among the Reformers, and his doctrine of the Holy Spirit and faith in particular, because he thought that this was the best of Calvin's theology.

He went to stay in the Valais again in June, and 'in old age embarked on a very remarkable new friendship, with the poet Carl Zuckmayer. I visited him in . . . Saas-Fee and then had a lively correspondence with him.' In the spring of the next year Zuckmayer paid Barth a return visit in Basle – 'and it was extremely good to see him between my solid walls of books. He is quite a man! And he can be very serious and very cheerful.' Barth was suddenly taken seriously ill in the Valais mountains in the summer of 1967 – he felt himself close to death – and unexpectedly had to make a 'night journey by ambulance from a considerable height somewhere in the Valais straight down into the Bürgerspital in Basle'.[156] But he recovered remarkably quickly.

Soon he was again deeply immersed in questions relating to Roman Catholicism. He wrote a newspaper article about the prohibition against Jesuits in the Swiss Federal Constitution and an open letter to a young, progressive Catholic theologian who in his view was being far too forceful: 'The truth stops being the truth where it is not put forward and expressed in love.' In the summer he had spoken in the 'Mariastein'* group, and now he engaged in some 'conversations with a lively group of Catholic assistant priests from Basle and round about'[157] (he himself reported on one of them in the Catholic journal *Orientierung*). On another occasion he met the Freiburg

*Mariastein is a Benedictine monastery near Basle. It became the focal point for a group of Roman Catholic intellectuals in Basle who were concerned to further reform in the church.

Catholic theologian Adolf Kolping and his students for a conversation. He was involved in a correspondence with Karl Rahner and even with 'His Holiness' Pope Paul VI, which was partly answered by the Pope himself and partly by Cardinal Cicognani. Barth had suggested to the Pope that Romans should be produced in a Vatican edition* and then learnt that this had just been done. So he wrote again at the end of September 1968, saying that he was glad that 'in this special case, too, thoughts in Rome and in Basle (if for a moment I may mention these two places in the same breath) may, whether fortuitously or not, have in fact moved in the same direction'. Barth also wrote at length about the question of natural revelation in connection with the so-called 'pill encyclical', and he told the Pope that according to his understanding of the Bible neither the natural law nor the conscience could be considered as 'sources of revelation'. Understandably, the theme of the colloquium during the winter of 1967–68, 'which took place in the third semester of my modest academic revival',[158] was again a Catholic one, the constitution *Lumen gentium* (on the church) from the Second Vatican Council.

Also before the beginning of the semester, on 22–23 October, he took part in a conference of the authors of the Festschrift for his eightieth birthday. In a word of greeting to them he remarked, *'Res severa verum gaudium.* True joy is a serious matter,' and could only be found if one 'stuck to one's guns' and like the knight in Dürer's famous picture, 'between death and the devil', rode straight through the hostile fronts of the present day. It was no use looking for some tedious compromise; a breakthrough was the only answer.

On 13 December he put himself at the disposal of the Mennonites at Bienenberg (Basle Land), to speak in answer to a series of questions. Here he welcomed the old Baptist movement with its protest against the 'national church', indeed – 'a bit of Pentecostalism is the salt of the earth and cannot do us any harm'. Nevertheless, he gave a warning against over-anxious bigotry: 'It is important that there should be people who rejoice in God.' What delighted him most in Christianity today, he said, was the move towards the Bible, unity and the knowledge that Christianity was not a private or a religious concern but a concern for the *world*. After the Six Day War of 1967 the question of Israel split even his friends into two camps: he

---

*The reference is to an edition of the text of the Epistle to the Romans produced specially for the Pope to give as a present; it was illustrated and in a special binding.

remarked that it was necessary to make a distinction between one's own political assessment of the situation and the biblical view of the people of Israel. Of course the foundation of the state of Israel was not to be seen as an analogy to the conquest under Joshua and thus as a sign that God cannot let his people be defeated. 'Yet we can read in the newspapers: "God keeps his promise".'

During this winter, however, there was a further crisis in Barth's health. First of all, 'in December 1967 my dear wife Nelly suddenly found herself at the end of the resources which she had drawn on faithfully and zealously all her life long'.[159] She was almost seventy-five, and had to go into hospital for two months, while her husband went to stay with their daughter's family. From there, he too had to go into hospital – because of severe pneumonia. Nevertheless, on 28 February, four days after he came out of hospital, he appeared at Leuenburg, 'in the midst of the hilly world of the canton of Basle Land' to give a lecture on 'The Church in Renewal', along with Hans Urs von Balthasar. In it he developed the thought that, 'If the church were not in renewal, not being reformed – if it were not essential for the church to live in renewal . . . then it would not be a church at all.' The audience was remarkable: 'Five Roman Catholic bishops and one Old Catholic and the corresponding "hierarchs" of the Evangelical Church Federation and the representatives of two semi-official commissions for "conversations" . . . Everyone was happy. And God's sun shone down in astonishment, but in a friendly way, over it all. Is the millennium really round the corner? The fact that Mozart was played twice could also be a pointer in this direction. I recommended that the Lord Bishops should do something about his beatification, if not canonization.'[160]

Barth also ventured to start a colloquium in the summer semester of 1968. For one last time he wanted to question and consider the 'church fathers of the nineteenth (and also the twentieth?!) century by means of Schleiermacher's *Speeches*'.[161] At the same time he wanted this to be his contribution to the celebration of the bicentenary of the birth of Schleiermacher – he was worried because the 'Basle faculty has arranged no other commemoration'.[162] During the summer, in a 'postscript' to an anthology of Schleiermacher texts, Barth then gave a survey of the chequered history of his relationship with this great theologian, whom he had first welcomed so enthusiastically and then criticized so vehemently, without being able to get away from him and without solving the questions he

posed. It seemed 'that for all my opposition I could never think
about Schleiermacher without feeling the way that Doctor Bartolo
puts so well in *The Marriage of Figaro*: "An inner voice always spoke to
his advantage".'[163] Indeed, he even thought that 'I can imagine a
very happy reunion with Schleiermacher in heaven.'[164]

At the end of the 'postscript' Barth also told of his dream – which
he had also occasionally mentioned in conversations – that someone,
and perhaps a whole age, might be allowed to develop a 'theology of
the Holy Spirit', a 'theology which now I can only envisage from
afar, as Moses once looked on the promised land'.[165] He was thinking of a theology which, unlike his own, was not written from the
dominant perspective of christology, but from that of pneumatology,
and in which the concerns of the theology of the eighteenth and
nineteenth centuries were not so much repeated and continued as
understood and developed further.

After the end of the semester and the 'postscript', and then a
conversation with Wuppertal students under the direction of their
Professor Fangmeier, Barth felt very wretched. He suffered from
severe depressions. Sometimes in the midst of them he would say
somewhat ironically that he was now 'really curious to see what "the
bounteous God" might still have in mind for the rest of my days'.[166]
On 21 August, the day when the Russians marched into Prague,
Barth's life was suddenly seriously threatened by a constriction of
the bowel, and was saved again by an emergency operation: 'quite a
grim affair', which was complicated by pneumonia. He returned
home relatively soon, in September, 'weary and still always sickly'.
He could no longer think of continuing with the colloquium which he
had planned for the winter – on his own doctrine of election (*Church
Dogmatics* II,2). Nor could he go to Darmstadt, as planned, 'where I
(not Ebeling, Fuchs, or any of these specialists in hermeneutics and
cybernetics, with their talk of "speech events") was to receive a
"Sigmund Freud Prize" (yes, that too) in praise of the "eloquence of
my academic prose"'.[167] This honour also delighted him, as did his
elevation to be a 'Membre Associé de l'Académie des Sciences
Morales et Politiques de l'Institut de France', which had happened
shortly beforehand.

102. *The last picture of Barth, eighty-two, taken in his study on 6 December 1968.*

'The last word – a name'

Despite everything, Barth could still read books of all kinds – for example he came across one by Wilhelm Dantine and Kurt Lüthi ('NB, published by Christian Kaiser Verlag') 'in which the profound question "Is Barth obsolete?" was discussed from a variety of standpoints'.[168] It was also possible for him to produce a few short pieces. For a French newspaper he answered the question 'What does Jesus mean to you?' with the remarkable confession: 'For me Jesus Christ is precisely (no more and no less and none other than) what he was, is and will be for the church which he calls and commissions . . . everywhere and always – and by virtue of the message entrusted to it for all men, for the whole world.'[169] Then he made tape recordings for two broadcasts planned for the beginning of 1969 on Swiss radio: on one he gave impressions and observations as a listener to 'Catholic and Protestant Sermons on the Radio', and on the other he gave an account of his understanding of the term 'liberal', and especially liberal theology: he understood it in a way that enabled him to say boldly, 'I myself am also a liberal – and perhaps even more liberal than those who call themselves liberals.'[170] He also accepted an invitation to take part in a series 'Music for a Guest' which was also broadcast by Swiss radio, in the middle of November. He asked for nothing but Mozart, and in between the music talked about his career. He ended with the words: 'The last word which I have to say as a theologian and also as a politician is not a term like "grace", but a name, "Jesus Christ". *He* is grace, and he *is* the last, beyond the world and the church and even theology . . . What I have been concerned to do in my long life has been increasingly to emphasize this name and to say: There is no salvation in any other name than this. For grace, too, is there. There, too, is the impulse to work, to struggle, and also the impulse towards fellowship, towards human solidarity. Everything that I have tested in my life, in weakness and in foolishness, is there. But it *is* there.'[171] Then he asked for the end of the *Missa Brevis* in D Major to be played: *Agnus Dei, qui tollis peccata mundi, miserere nobis, dona nobis pacem.*

There was much talk of Mozart, and also of Thomas Mann and Friedrich Schiller, when the writer Albrecht Goes came to visit Barth at the end of November: he was the brother of Helmut Goes, a Swabian pastor who had been well known to Barth for years. On 3

December Barth had a visit from the Catholic professor Johannes Feiner, who brought with him a request to give a lecture in the middle of January 1969 for the ecumenical week of prayer in the Paulus Academy in Zürich, before a forum of Catholic and Reformed Christians. The request attracted Barth. He chose the theme 'Setting Out — Being Converted — Confessing' himself, and immediately began work on the lecture. In it he wanted to say something about understanding — not so much between the churches as between the progressives and the conservatives in the different churches. He understood the three terms in the title as characteristic of the 'one movement in which the church finds itself'.[172] In his view, this one movement always involved turning towards something new and therefore turning away from something old (though the search for the new did not happen arbitrarily, and any 'no' to what had gone before could only be a 'friendly and cheerful no'). At the same time this movement always involved a return to the old (though this was not identical with any past epoch, but only with Jesus Christ, who of course is also 'the new' and who at the same time encourages men to be grateful for past ages). His work was punctuated by reading books by Gertrud Lendorff, which are set in Old Basle.

On 7 December he spent the evening with his assistant and Frau Busch. As he had done on so many evenings recently, he read one or two sermons from the earliest period at Safenwil, listened to some Mozart, smoked a pipe and drank some wine; at the end of it they all sang Advent chorales together, and by himself he sang some of the children's songs by Abel Burckhardt which he had learnt in his early childhood: they included one in which the 'Lord Jesus' is praised because he 'dearly loves his lambs' and another which contains the words

> Now I gladly go to sleep,
> I've enjoyed the day,
> God has truly cared for me . . .

On 8 December — it was the second Sunday in Advent — he enjoyed hearing a Catholic sermon on the radio on the subject of Mary's conception. He spent the rest of the day with his wife at the Zellwegers, and from there Max Zellweger drove him over to visit Charlotte von Kirschbaum in her nursing home, as he did every Sunday. On the way he spoke of his death remarkably often and even wanted to talk about the details of his funeral. On Monday 9 December he

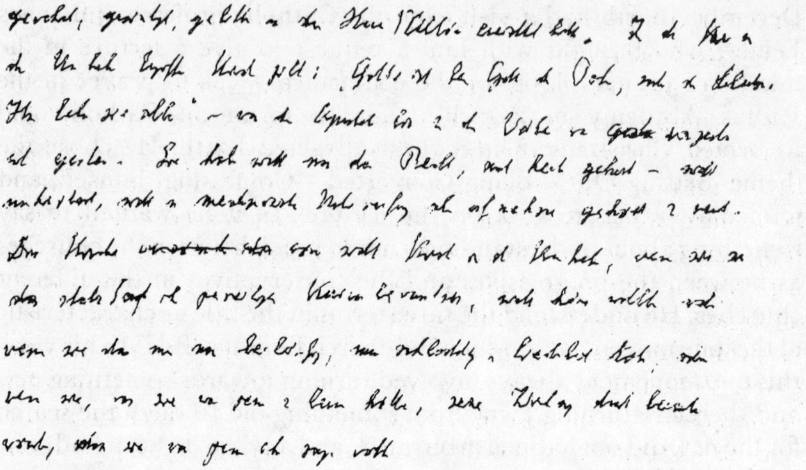

103. The last passage of Barth's last lecture, written on the evening of 9 December 1968. The draft breaks off in mid-sentence.

spent the day working on his lecture again. He was still at work in the evening when he was interrupted by two telephone calls, about nine o'clock. One was from his godson Ulrich Barth, to whom he quoted a verse from a hymn which spoke comfortingly about the Christian hope. The other person who wanted to speak to him so late at night was his friend Eduard Thurneysen, who had remained faithful to him over sixty years. They talked about the gloomy world situation. Then Barth said, 'But keep your chin up! Never mind! "He will reign!" '* When the telephone rang he had been writing a few sentences of the draft for his lecture in which he was saying that in the church it is always important to listen to the Fathers who have gone before in the faith. For ' "God is not a God of the dead but of the living." In him they all live' – from the Apostles down to the Fathers of the day before yesterday and of yesterday.[173] Barth did not go back to his draft which he had left in the middle of a sentence, but put it aside until the next day. However, he did not live that long. He died peacefully some time in the middle of the night. He lay there as though asleep, with his hands gently folded from his evening prayers. So his wife found him the next morning, while in the

*A saying of Christoph Blumhardt.

background a record was playing the Mozart with which she had wanted to waken him.

A little earlier he had written in a letter: 'Looking back, I have no serious complaints about anyone or anything: except my own failures today, yesterday, the day before yesterday and the day before that – I mean my failures in real gratitude. Perhaps I still have bitter days ahead, and certainly my death will come sooner or later. One thing remains, for me to remember and impress upon myself, in respect of yesterday and all the days which have now gone before, and again in respect of all those which may follow, and of that last day which is certainly coming: "Do not forget the good that he has done!" '[174] Barth had also put in his notes some sentences which did not find their way into the letter: 'How do I know whether I shall die easily or with difficulty? I only know that my dying, too, is part of my life . . . And then – this is the destination, the limit and the goal for all of us – I shall no longer "be", but I shall be made manifest before the judgment seat of Christ, in and with my whole "being", with all the real good and the real evil that I have thought, said and done, with all the bitterness that I have suffered and all the beauty that I have enjoyed. There I shall only be able to stand as the failure that I doubtless was in all things, but . . . by virtue of his promise, as a *peccator justus*. And as that I shall be able to stand. Then . . . in the light of grace, all that is now dark will become very clear.'

On 13 December Karl Barth was buried in the Hörnli cemetery in Basle. Only his family and closest friends attended the funeral, at which his last parish minister from the Bruderholz and his last assistant gave addresses; his sons Markus and Christoph spoke some words from the Bible at the graveside. On 14 December there was a memorial service in Basle Cathedral, which was packed to overflowing. It was broadcast live on the radio. The speakers were Max Geiger, the Dean of the Theological Faculty, and Lukas Burckhardt, President of the Basle Cantonal Council; also Helmut Gollwitzer, representing the German churches and universities; Josef Hromádka, representing the churches of Eastern Europe; Hans Küng, as a Catholic theologian; Eberhard Jüngel, representing the youngest generation of scholars; and Willem A. Visser't Hooft, representing the World Council of Churches. A performance of the first movement of Mozart's flute concerto in G major was given between the memorial speeches. At the very beginning the words of Psalm 103 were read by Werner Pfendsack, pastor of the cathedral:

'Praise the Lord, O my soul, and all that is in me praise his holy name! Praise the Lord, O my soul, and forget not all his benefits!' And the service ended with the hymn 'Now Thank We All Our God', the second verse of which with its reference to 'this bounteous God', had always been a favourite of Barth's. And so the final words:

> All praise and thanks to God
> The Father now be given,
> The Son, and him who reigns
> With them in highest heaven,
> The one eternal God,
> Whom earth and heaven adore;
> For thus it was, is now,
> And shall be evermore.

Family Tree, Maps and
Chronological list
of Barth's Major Works

The family tree and maps are intended simply to help the reader to follow the details of the narrative and are therefore incomplete in some respects.

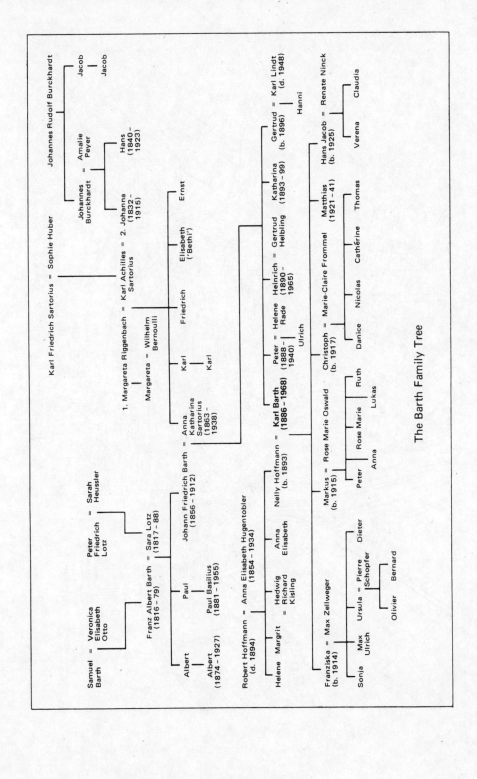

The Barth Family Tree

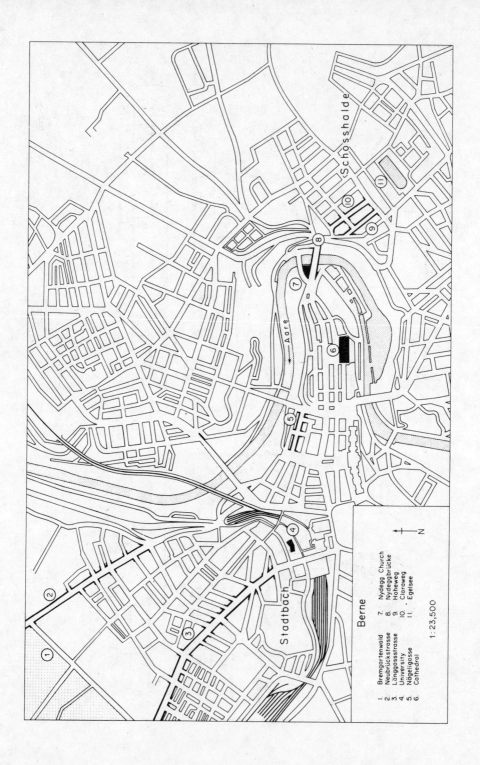

Berne

1. Bremgartenwald
2. Neubrückstrasse
3. Länggasstrasse
4. University
5. Nägeligasse
6. Cathedral
7. Nydegg Church
8. Nydeggbrücke
9. Hoheweg
10. Claraweg
11. Egelsee

1:23,500

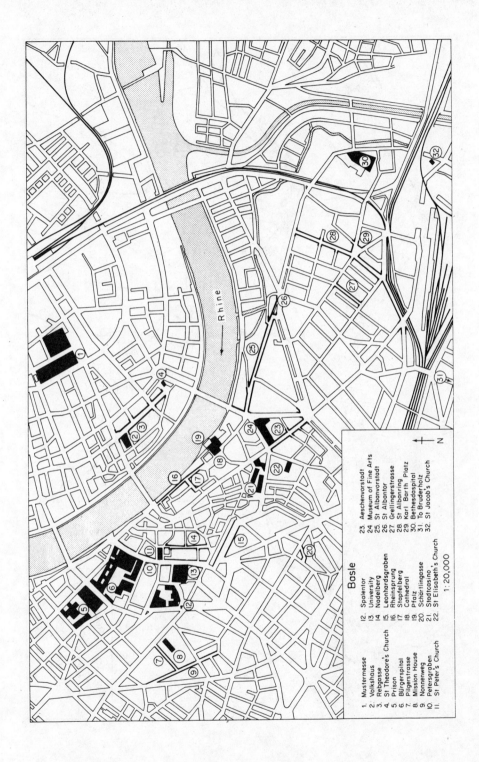

Basle

1. Mustermesse
2. Volkshaus
3. Rebgasse
4. St Theodore's Church
5. Prison
6. Bürgerspital
7. Pilgerstrasse
8. Mission House
9. Nonnenweg
10. Petersgraben
11. St Elisabeth's Church
12. Spalentor
13. University
14. Nadelberg
15. Leonhardsgraben
16. Rheinsprung
17. Stapfelberg
18. Cathedral
19. Pfalz
20. Schürlingsgasse
21. Stadtcasino
22. St Peter's Church
23. Aeschenvorstadt
24. Museum of Fine Arts
25. St Albanvorstadt
26. St Albantor
27. Grellingerstrasse
28. St Albanring
29. Karl Barth Platz
30. Bethesdaspital
31. To Bruderholz
32. St Jacob's Church

1:20,000

Rhine

N

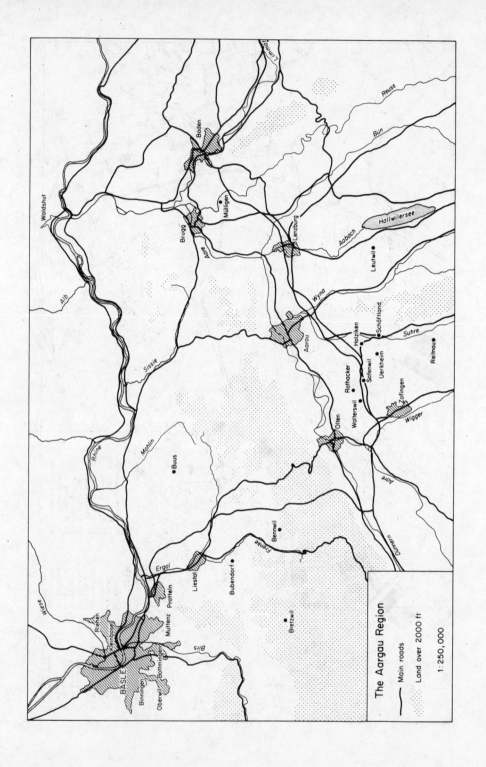

The Aargau Region

— Main roads

Land over 2000 ft

1 : 250,000

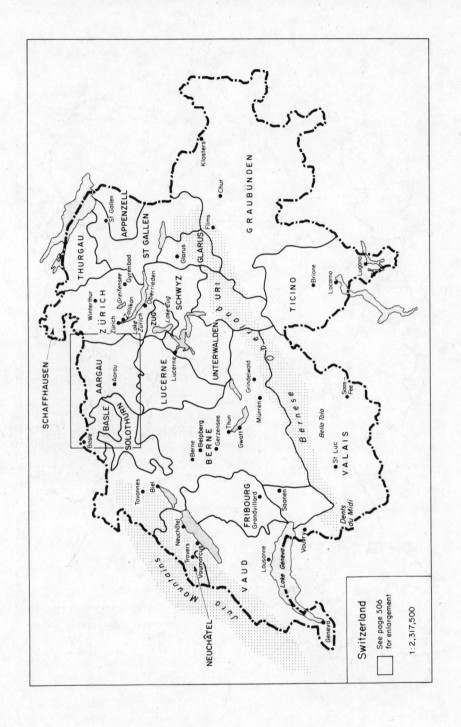

Switzerland

See page 506
for enlargement

1:2,317,500

Norderney Baltrum

Rügen

Putbus

Greifswald

Lübeck

Hamburg

NETHERLANDS

Bremen

EAST GERMANY

Osnabruck

Hanover

Berlin

POLAND

Münster

Bielefeld
(Bethel)

W E S T

Essen
Bochum Dortmund

Wuppertal Ruhr

Dusseldorf Barmen
Elberfeld

Göttingen

Halle

Leipzig

Cologne

Bonn

Rhine

Marburg Treysa

Giessen

Eisenach

Jena

Dresden

BELGIUM

Tambach

LUXEMBOURG

Moselle

Wiesbaden Frankfurt am Main

CZECHOSLOVAKIA

Mainz

Main

Darmstadt

Bamberg

Bayreuth

FRANCE

Heidelberg

Erlangen

Nuremberg

G E R M A N Y

Strasbourg

Stuttgart

Bad Boll

Tübingen

Augsburg

Freiburg

Munich

Basle

SWITZERLAND

A U S T R I A

I T A L Y

Germany

1:6,106,000

Chronological list of Barth's Major Works

This list gives, as far as possible in chronological order, original publication details and English translations of Barth's major works.

'Was sollen wir tun?', *Christliche Welt* 23, 1909, 236f.

'Moderne Theologie und Reichgottesarbeit', *Zeitschrift für Theologie und Kirche* 19, 1909, 317–21

'Der christliche Glaube und die Geschichte', *Schweizerische Theologische Zeitschrift* 1 and 2, 1912

'Der Glaube an den persönlichen Gott', *Zeitschrift für Theologie und Kirche* 24, 1914, 21–32, 65–95

Suchet Gott, so werdet ihr Leben!, G. A. Bäschlin 1917 (with Eduard Thurneysen)

Der Römerbrief (first edition), G. A. Bäschlin 1919

Briefwechsel Karl Barth – Eduard Thurneysen, 1913–1921, Evangelischer Verlag 1973 (this and a second volume covering the period from 1921–1930 supersede the earlier *Briefwechsel Karl Barth – Eduard Thurneysen, 1914–1925*, Siebenstern Taschenbuch 71, 1966; ET *Revolutionary Theology in the Making*, edited by James D. Smart, John Knox Press, Richmond, Va and Epworth Press 1964, which contains extracts only)

Der Römerbrief (second edition), Christian Kaiser Verlag 1922; ET *The Epistle to the Romans*, Oxford University Press 1935

Das Wort Gottes und die Theologie, Christian Kaiser Verlag 1924; ET *The Word of God and the Word of Man*, Hodder 1928, reissued Harper Torchbooks, New York 1957 (lectures 1916–1924)

Komm, Schöpfer Geist!, Christian Kaiser Verlag 1924; ET *Come, Holy Spirit*, T. & T. Clark and Round Table Press, New York 1935 . (with Eduard Thurneysen)

Die Auferstehung der Toten, Christian Kaiser Verlag 1924; ET *The Resurrection of the Dead*, Hodder and F. H. Revell Company, New York 1933

Erklärung des Philipperbriefes, Christian Kaiser Verlag 1927; ET *The Epistle to the Philippians*, SCM Press and John Knox Press, Richmond, Va 1962

Prolegomena zur Christlichen Dogmatik. Die Lehre vom Worte Gottes, Christian Kaiser Verlag 1928

Die Theologie und die Kirche, Christian Kaiser Verlag 1928; ET *Theology and Church*, SCM Press 1962

Fides quaerens intellectum, Christian Kaiser Verlag 1931; ET *Anselm: Fides quaerens intellectum*, SCM Press and John Knox Press, Richmond, Va 1960

Briefwechsel Karl Barth-Eduard Thurneysen, 1921–1930, Evangelischer Verlag 1974

Die Kirchliche Dogmatik I, 1, *Die Lehre vom Wort Gottes*, Christian Kaiser Verlag 1932; ET *Church Dogmatics* I, 1, *The Doctrine of the Word of God*, T. & T. Clark and Scribner, New York 1936, revd edn 1975

Theologische Existenz heute, Christian Kaiser Verlag 1933; ET *Theological Existence Today*, Hodder 1933

Offenbarung, Kirche, Theologie, Theologische Existenz heute 9, 1934; ET *God in Action*, T. & T. Clark and Round Table Press, New York 1936

Nein! Antwort am Emil Brunner, Theologische Existenz heute 14, 1934; ET in *Natural Theology*, Bles 1946, which also contains Brunner's article

Credo, Christian Kaiser Verlag 1935; ET *Credo*, Hodder and Scribner, New York 1936

Die grosse Barmherzigkeit, Christian Kaiser Verlag 1935; ET *God's Search for Man*, T. & T. Clark and Round Table Press, New York 1935 (with Eduard Thurneysen)

Karl Barth zum Kirchenkampf, Beteiligung-Mahnung-Zuspruch, Theologische Existenz heute (new series) 49, 1956; ET of pp. 1–60, *The German Church Conflict*, John Knox Press, Richmond, Va and Lutterworth Press 1965 (a collection of Barth's statements on the German church struggle)

Theologische Fragen und Antworten, Evangelischer Verlag 1957 (collected articles)

Gotteserkenntnis und Gottesdienst, Evangelischer Verlag 1938: ET *The*

Knowledge of God and the Service of God, Hodder 1938

Die Kirchliche Dogmatik I, 2, *Die Lehre vom Wort Gottes*, Evangelischer Verlag 1939; ET *Church Dogmatics* I, 2, *The Doctrine of the Word of God*, T. & T. Clark and Scribner, New York 1956 (publishers remain the same for further volumes of the *Dogmatics* and are not therefore cited)

Die Kirchliche Dogmatik II, 1, *Die Lehre von Gott*, 1940; ET *Church Dogmatics* II, 1, *The Doctrine of God*, 1957

La Confession de la Foi de l'Église, Delachaux et Niestlé 1940; ET *The Faith of the Church*, Meridian Books, New York 1958 and Collins Fontana 1960

Kurze Erklärung des Römerbriefes (1941), Christian Kaiser Verlag 1956; ET *A Shorter Commentary on Romans*, SCM Press and John Knox Press, Richmond, Va 1956

Die Kirchliche Dogmatik II, 2, *Die Lehre von Gott*, 1942; ET *Church Dogmatics* II, 2, *The Doctrine of God*, 1957

Die Kirchliche Lehre von der Taufe, Theologische Studien 14, 1943; ET *The Teaching of the Church regarding Baptism*, SCM Press 1948

Eine Schweizer Stimme, Evangelischer Verlag 1945 (political talks and writings, 1938–1945)

Die Kirchliche Dogmatik III, 1, *Die Lehre von der Schöpfung*, 1945; ET *Church Dogmatics* III, 1, *The Doctrine of Creation*, 1958

Die Protestantische Theologie im 19. Jahrhundert. Ihre Geschichte und Vorges-chichte, Evangelischer Verlag 1947; ET *Protestant Theology in the Nineteenth Century*, SCM Press and Judson Press, Valley Forge 1972

Dogmatik im Grundriss, Christian Kaiser Verlag and Evangelischer Verlag 1947; ET *Dogmatics in Outline*, SCM Press 1949

Die Kirchliche Dogmatik III, 2, *Die Lehre von der Schöpfung*, 1945; ET *Church Dogmatics* III, 2, *The Doctrine of Creation*, 1961

Fürchte dich nicht!, Christian Kaiser Verlag 1949 (sermons 1934–1948)

Die Kirchliche Dogmatik III, 3, *Die Lehre von der Schöpfung*, 1950; ET *Church Dogmatics* III, 3, *The Doctrine of Creation*, 1961

Die Kirchliche Dogmatik III, 4, *Die Lehre von der Schöpfung*, 1951; ET *Church Dogmatics* III, 4, *The Doctrine of Creation*, 1961

Against the Stream, Shorter Post-War Writings 1946–1952, SCM Press and The Philosophical Library, New York 1954 (this includes a number of works published in the series Theologische Studien)

Rudolf Bultmann: Ein Versuch, ihm zu Verstehen, Evangelischer Verlag

1952; ET 'Rudolf Bultmann – An Attempt to Understand Him', in *Kerygma and Myth* II, SPCK 1962, 83–162

Christus und Adam, Evangelischer Verlag 1952; ET *Christ and Adam*, Harper & Row, New York 1957

Die Kirchliche Dogmatik IV, 1, *Die Lehre von der Versöhnung*, 1953; ET *Church Dogmatics* IV, 1, *The Doctrine of Reconciliation*, 1956

Die Kirchliche Dogmatik IV, 2, *Die Lehre von der Versöhnung*, 1955; ET *Church Dogmatics* IV, 2, *The Doctrine of Reconciliation*, 1958

Die Menschlichkeit Gottes, Theologische Studien 48, 1956; ET *The Humanity of God*, Collins and John Knox Press, Richmond, Va 1961 (which also contains translations of *Evangelische Theologie im 19. Jahrhundert*, Theologische Studien 49, and *Das Geschenk der Freiheit*, Theologische Studien 39)

W. A. Mozart 1756–1956, Evangelischer Verlag, 1956; ET in *Religion and Culture: Essays in Honour of Paul Tillich*, Harper & Row, New York and SCM Press 1959, 61–78

Brief an einen Pfarrer in der DDR, Evangelischer Verlag 1958

Den Gefangenen Befreiung, Evangelischer Verlag 1959; ET *Deliverance to the Captives*, SCM Press and Harper & Row, New York 1961

Die Kirchliche Dogmatik IV, 3, 1, *Die Lehre von der Versöhnung*, 1959; ET *Church Dogmatics* IV, 3, 1, *The Doctrine of Reconciliation*, 1963

Die Kirchliche Dogmatik IV, 3, 2, was published in 1960; ET 1965

Der Götze wackelt, Evangelischer Verlag 1961 (collected articles)

Einführung in die evangelische Theologie, Evangelischer Verlag 1962; ET *Evangelical Theology*, Weidenfeld & Nicholson 1963

Rufe mich an!, Evangelischer Verlag 1965; ET *Call for God*, SCM Press and Harper & Row, New York 1967

Ad limina apostolorum, Evangelischer Verlag 1967

Die Kirchliche Dogmatik IV, 4 (fragment), 1968; ET *Church Dogmatics* IV, 4, 1969

Letzte Zeugnisse, Evangelischer Verlag 1969

Note: Evangelischer Verlag is also described as EVZ Verlag, and in more recent imprints has become Theologischer Verlag (TVZ Verlag)

Notes and Indexes

Introduction
to Notes

In all cases, references have been kept as brief as possible; books, journals and names have been abbreviated in the manner indicated below. Where no author is given, quotations come from Karl Barth himself. As this section is primarily for the purpose of substantiation and further research, all the references to German originals have been kept and the corresponding pages of English translations, where they have been made, are also given. Quotations from still unpublished letters and other unpublished work of Barth are based on the copies or originals to be found in the Barth archives in Basle. For full details of published material, see the chronological list of Barth's works.

General Abbreviations

Antwort	Festschrift for Barth's seventieth birthday, 1956
Beginnings	*Anfänge der Dialektische Theologie*, Christian Kaiser Verlag 1963; ET *The Beginnings of Dialectical Theology*, edited by James M. Robinson, John Knox Press, Richmond, Va 1968
CB	Christoph Barth
CvK	Charlotte von Kirschbaum
CW	*Christliche Welt*
ET	English translation
EvTh	*Evangelische Theologie*
KRS	*Kirchenblatt für die reformierte Schweiz*
MB	Markus Barth
MZ	Max Zellweger
Obit.	Published obituaries

*RGG*³	*Die Religion in Geschichte und Gegenwart* (third edition)
SdG	*Stimme der Gemeinde*
T	Eduard Thurneysen
ThExh	Theologische Existenz heute
ThSt	Theologische Studien
ZTK	*Zeitschrift für Theologie und die Kirche*
ZZ	*Zwischen den Zeiten*

Abbreviations of Barth's Works

ABT	Autobiographical texts
I	(Autobiographical sketch) *Fakultätsalbum der Evangelisch-theologischen Fakultät Münster*, 1927
II	'Lebenslauf', *Schweizer Köpfe*, 1945
III	(Autobiographical sketch) *Fakultätsalbum der Evangelisch-theologischen Fakultät Bonn*, 1946
IV	*Selbstdarstellung* (Self-portrait), 1964
V	(The beginning of the memoirs which Barth started in 1966)
VI	Karl Barth, *How I Changed my Mind*, edited by John D. Godsey, John Knox Press, Richmond, Va 1966 and St Andrew Press 1969 (first published in English)
VII	'Rückblick', in *Das Wort sie sollen lassen stahn, Festschrift für Albert Schädelin*, 1950, 1ff.
BB	*Briefwechsel Karl Barth–Rudolf Bultmann, 1922–1966*, TVZ 1971
BT	*Briefwechsel Karl Barth–Eduard Thurneysen, 1914–1925*, 1966; ET *Revolutionary Theology in the Making*, 1964 (= *RevT*)
BT I	*Briefwechsel Karl Barth–Eduard Thurneysen, 1913–1921*, 1973
BT II	*Briefwechsel Karl Barth–Eduard Thurneysen, 1921–1930*, 1974
ChD	*Prolegomena zur Christlichen Dogmatik. Die Lehre vom Worte Gottes*, 1927

Conv.	Conversations (shorthand notes or tape recordings of 'conversations' between Karl Barth and various groups)
I	In Stuttgart, March 1954
II	With pastors and lay people from the Pfalz, September 1953
III	With Christian booksellers in Flims, 24 June 1962
IV	With the Württemberg brotherhood, 15 July 1963
V	With Göttingen students, 12 October 1963
VI	With youth chaplains from the Rhineland, 4 November 1963
VII	With Tübingen students, 2 March 1964
VIII	With Wuppertal students, 1 July 1968
IX	With Swiss Methodist preachers, 16 May 1961
	With representatives of the pietists, 6 October 1959
GA	Gesamt-Ausgabe, published since 1971 by TVZ Verlag, Zürich
KD	*Kirchliche Dogmatik*; ET *Church Dogmatics*
Kirchenkampf	*Karl Barth zum Kirchenkampf, Beteiligung-Mahnung-Zuspruch*, 1956; ET of pp.1–60, *The German Church Conflict*, 1965
Lect.	Collections of lectures
I	*Das Wort Gottes und die Theologie*, 1924; ET *The Word of God and The Word of Man*, 1957
II	*Die Theologie und die Kirche*, 1928; ET *Theology and Church*, 1962
III	*Theologische Fragen und Antworten*, 1957
IV	*Eine Schweizer Stimme 1938–1945*, 1945,
V	*Der Götze wackelt*, 1961
LZ	*Letzte Zeugnisse*, 1969
Minutes	Minutes of the Safenwil church committee (made by Karl Barth)
'Nachwort'	'Nachwort', in *Schleiermacher-Auswahl*, Siebenstern Taschenbuch 113–14, 1968
ProtT	*Die Protestantische Theologie im 19. Jahrhundert. Ihre Geschichte und Vorgeschichte*, 1947; ET *Protestant Theology in the Nineteenth Century*, 1972

RevT	see *BT*
Rom. I	*Der Römerbrief* (first edition), 1919
Rom. II	*Der Römerbrief* (second edition), 1922; ET *The Epistle to the Romans*, 1935
Serm.	Collections of sermons
I	*Suchet Gott, so werdet ihr Leben!*, 1917
II	*Komm, Schöpfer Geist!*, 1924; ET, *Come, Holy Spirit*, 1935
III	*Die grosse Barmherzigkeit*, 1935; ET in *God's Search for Man*, 1935
IV	*Fürchte dich nicht!*, 1949
V	*Den Gefangenen Befreiung*, 1959; ET *Deliverance to the Captives*, 1961
VI	*Rufe mich an!*, 1965; ET *Call for God*, 1967

Notes

1 Childhood, 1886–1904

1. ABT I
2. ABT II
3. Ibid.
4. ABT V
5. Obit. F. A. Barth
6. ABT V
7. ABT II
8. ABT V
9. Obit. Sara Barth
10. ABT V
11. F. Barth, *Christus unsere Hoffnung*, 1913, 325
12. Ibid., vi
13. ABT II
14. To E. Sartorius, 2 January 1949
15. Ibid.
16. ABT V
17. To G. Merz, 5 October 1948
18. 'Nachwort', 292
19. ABT V
20. To E. Sartorius, 4 June 1949
21. ABT II
22. ABT V
23. Lecture 'Der 3. August 1833', 1 May 1901
24. ABT V
25. Ibid.
26. To T, 22 September 1931
27. To T, 26 May 1928
28. Obit. Anna Barth
29. ABT II
30. *ProtT*, 124; ET 143
31. Ibid; ET 143f.
32. *W. A. Mozart 1756/1956*, 1956, 48f.
33. To W. Kaegi, 2 January 1944
34. To H. Barth, 3 March 1955
35. Serm. IV, 300
36. To Renate Barth, 18 March 1956
37. ABT V
38. To E. Sartorius, 5 August 1955
39. ABT V and to E. Sartorius, 1 January 1948
40. To E. Rickli, 21 March 1950
41. *KD* IV, 2, 125; ET 112f.
42. 'Nachwort', 295
43. Conv. IX
44. ABT I
45. Conv. VIII
46. ABT II
47. ABT I
48. To Dora Scheuner, 20 June 1940
49. Obit. Anna Barth
50. To Daniel Barth, 6 April 1960
51. Interview with H. Fischer-Barnicol, 1964
52. F. Barth, *Christus unsere Hoffnung*, 4
53. To G. Lindt, 17 July 1940
54. To G. Lindt, 30 December 1939
55. To G. Lindt, 17 August 1944
56. Serm. V, 64; ET 64
57. To G. Lindt, 17 August 1944
58. 'Dankesworte', *EvTh* 1966, 169
59. To CB, 14 April 1949
60. 'Philosophie und Theologie', in *Festschrift H. Barth*, 1960, 106
61. To his family, 13 August 1947
62. Serm. V
63. 'Gesprek over Rome-Reformatie', in *Libertas ex veritate*, 1965
64. *Beginnings*, 40; ET 37
65. ABT I
66. ABT II
67. A. von Tavel, *70 Jahre Freies Gymnasium*, 1934, 129
68. Ibid., 70
69. ABT I
70. To G. Pfister, 29 November 1941
71. To E. Huber, 14 January 1951, and to

the Zellweger family, 29 June 1947
72. To Marie-Claire Barth, 22 March 1959
73. To Marie-Claire Barth, 14 February 1960
74. ABT I
75. ABT II
76. *W. A. Mozart*, 7, and *LZ*, 17
77. ABT I
78. ABT II
79. ABT I
80. ABT V
81. 'An meine Freunde in Japan', Spring 1956
82. To CB, 28 April 1956
83. ABT VII, 1
84. To W. Spoendlin, 4 January 1928
85. ABT I
86. See n.23
87. To E. Sartorius, 7 August 1941
88. To A. v. Erlach, 21 February 1942
89. ABT I
90. ABT V
91. Ibid.
92. Obit. Johanna Sartorius
93. Obit. Elisabeth Sartorius
94. ABT V
95. To his parents (1899?)
96. To E. Rickli, 21 March 1950
97. *ChD*, IX
98. See n.23
99. ABT V
100. To his grandmother, 24 December 1903 (?)
101. To E. Sartorius, 2 January 1944
102. To M. Feldmann, 16 September 1950
103. To E. Huber, 14 January 1951
104. ABT I
105. *LZ*, 16
106. See n.103

107. ABT I
108. ABT II
109. To H. Scholz, 24 May 1953
110. Conv. VIII
111. Ibid.
112. To Anna Barth (1899?)
113. ABT I
114. ABT II
115. ABT I
116. Obit. Anna Barth
117. To Anna Barth (1899?)
118. E. Bethge, *Dietrich Bonhoeffer*, 1967, 217; ET, Collins 1970, 132
119. To A. Hirzel, 22 July 1957
120. To MB, 27–29 November 1963
121. See n.119
122. To G. Bohnenblust, July 1953
123. ABT VII, 1f.
124. ABT II
125. See n.122
126. ABT IV
127. To J. Jaggi, 1 August 1951
128. ABT VII, 3
129. F. Barth, in the Foreword to the second edition of R. Aeschbacher, *Seid Täter des Wortes*, 1910, Vff.
130. ABT I
131. See n.127
132. 'Systematische Theologie', in *Lehre und Forschung an der Universität Basel*, 1960, 35f.
133. ABT I
134. See n.132
135. See n.127
136. ABT III
137. To his parents, 11 July 1904
138. To H. Petersen, 21 July 1960
139. ABT I
140. Ibid.

2   At university and as an assistant pastor, 1904–1911

1. ABT I
2. Ibid.
3. Interview with H. Fischer-Barnicol, 1964; ABT IV; 'Nachwort', 290
4. ABT IV
5. 'Nachwort', 290f.
6. Interview with H. Fischer-Barnicol, 1964
7. See n.5
8. ABT IV
9. See n.6
10. 'Nachwort', 291

11. See n.6
12. ABT IV
13. ABT I
14. 'Nachwort', 290
15. ABT I
16. Sermon, 13 October 1912
17. ABT I
18. To W. Spoendlin, 16 November 1904
19. Present list sent to K. Barth's grandmother
20. To W. Spoendlin, 28 November 1904
21. Ibid.

22. To A. Koechlin, 5 January 1945
23. To L. Christ, 27 October 1951
24. 'Brief an Oskar Farner zum 70. Geburtstag', in: O. Farner, *Erinnerungen*, 1954, 111
25. *KD* IV, 3, ix; ET xiii
26. 'E. Thurneysen zum 60. Geburtstag', in *Basler Nachrichten*, 11 July 1968
27. P. Gruner, *Menschenwege und Gotteswege*, 1942, 170
28. To CB, 11 July 1942
29. ABT I
30. *BT* II, 288; *RevT* 195
31. Ibid.
32. ABT I
33. 'Nachwort', 290f.
34. To Agnes von Zahn, 23 December 1935
35. *KD* I, 2, 734; ET 655
36. See n.34
37. To E. Scholz, 6 January 1957
38. 'Nachwort', 291
39. See n.34
40. ABT I
41. See n.6
42. See n.34
43. ABT IV
44. 'Nachwort', 290
45. 'Nachwort', 291
46. Lect. II, 240; ET 238
47. *Feuille Centrale de la société suisse de Zofingue*, 48th year, 279f.
48. To W. Spoendlin, 11 June 1907
49. To R. Pestalozzi, 30 December 1949
50. To G. Dalsgaard, 28 July 1956
51. *LZ*, 17f.
52. To G. Dehn, 13 September 1962
53. To W. Spoendlin, 29 May 1906
54. To G. Dalsgaard, 14 February 1960
55. To K. Huber, 13 December 1948
56. To G. Dalsgaard, 19 May 1943
57. Conv. VII
58. ABT I
59. ABT V
60. ABT I
61. Conv. VII
62. ABT I
63. Conv. VII
64. ABT I
65. Conv. VII
66. To W. Spoendlin, 6 January 1908
67. ABT I
68. To W. Spoendlin, 4 November 1907
69. Conv. VII
70. ABT I

71. To A. Graf, 18 March 1955
72. To W. Spoendlin, 21 June 1908
73. ABT I
74. Lect. II, 265; ET 256
75. Ibid., 240; ET 238
76. ABT I
77. Conv. VIII
78. ABT I
79. Lect. II, 265; ET 257
80. Ibid., 267; ET 258
81. Interview with H. Fischer-Barnicol, 1964
82. Ibid.
83. Lect. II, 279; ET 267
84. See *BT* II, 386; *RevT* 247
85. To W. Spoendlin, 21 June 1908
86. ABT I
87. To W. Spoendlin, 11 August 1908
88. ABT I
89. ABT II
90. To J. Rathje, 27 April 1947
91. To Dora Rade, 7 April 1940
92. To M. and Dora Rade, 7 October 1939
93. ABT I
94. 'Aus einem Teller', in *Gemeinde-Blatt Genf*, 1909, no. 32
95. ABT I
96. See n.26
97. To W. Jannasch, 28 November 1949
98. ABT I
99. KD IV, 1, 427; ET 387
100. ABT I
101. *ZThK* 1909, 319f.
102. Lect. II, 279; ET 267
103. ABT IV
104. See n.90
105. ABT II
106. Lect. II, 241; ET 238
107. To W. Spoendlin, 19 November 1909
108. ABT I
109. 'Christ ist Geboren!', *Gemeinde-Blatt Genf*, 1909, no. 33
110. Sermon, 3 July 1910
111. ABT I
112. Sermon, 9 July 1911
113. 'Etwas über die Kirche', *Gemeinde-Blatt Genf*, 1910, no. 39
114. To F. J. Leenhardt, 14 February 1959
115. To A. Keller, 20 May 1956
116. Sermons, 14 April 1911; 7 August 1910; 1 January 1910; 3 June 1908; 3 July 1910; 22 May 1910; 1 January 1910; 22 May 1910; 30 October 1910; 1 January 1910
117. See n.113

118. 'Pour la dignité de Genève', *Basler Nachrichten*, 1911, no. 119
119. 'Konfirmation-Abende', *Gemeinde-Blatt Genf*, 1910, no.37
120. To W. Spoendlin, 26 January 1910
121. 'Gott im Vaterland', *Gemeinde-Blatt Genf*, 1910, no.38
122. 'John Mott und die christliche Studentenbewegung', *Zofinger Zentralblatt*, 1910–1911, no.6
123. 'Nachwort', 292. See his diary, 29 August 1909: 'Plundering expedition in grandfather's library'
124. 'Nachwort', 292
125. To H. Thielicke, 7 November 1967

126. ABT I
127. *KD* IV, 1, 316; ET 287
128. 'Die christliche Glaube und die Geschichte', *Schweizer Theologische Zeitschrift*, 1912, 70, 72
129. ABT I
130. 'Vorträge von John Mott', *Basler Nachrichten*, 1911, no.47; see n.122
131. See n.118 and 'Wir wollen nicht, dass dieser über uns herrsche!', *KRS*, 1911, no.21
132. 'Über die Grenze!', sermon, April 1917, 11
133. 'Wir wollen nicht . . . '
134. To W. Spoendlin, 19 June 1911

3   The years in the parish of Safenwil, 1911–1921

1. ABT I
2. To a pastor, 1 April 1940
3. *BT* I, 375
4. E. Thurneysen, *BT*, 18f.; *RevT*, 12
5. ABT II
6. ABT I
7. ABT II
8. *LZ*, 19
9. E. Thurneysen, *BT*, 19, 29; *RevT*, 12, 22
10. *BT* I, 188; *RevT*, 41
11. *BT* I, 223
12. See n.9
13. Minutes, 4 September 1912
14. Ibid., 27 July 1911 (addition)
15. Sermon, 22 September 1912
16. Interview with H. Fischer-Barnicol, 1964
17. 'Nachwort', 293
18. Sermon, 3 December 1911
19. See n.15
20. *Homiletik*, 1966, 98
21. Sermons, 5 April 1912; 29 September 1912; 29 January 1911; 20 August 1911
22. *BT* I, 176
23. To a pastor, 17 September 1953
24. *BT* I, 61
25. Ibid., 269f.
26. Ibid., 393; see 238
27. Minutes, 28 August 1918
28. Lect.V, 113
29. ThExh 37, 29f.
30. *BT* II, 341; *RevT*, 230
31. To W. Spoendlin, 25 November 1910
32. J. Fangmeier, *Erziehung in Zeugenschaft*, 1964, 25

33. *BT* I, 271
34. Minutes, 29 December 1911; 31 March 1914
35. Minute book of the Aargau Church Council, 24 March 1920
36. *BT* I, 258
37. Ibid., 220
38. Ibid., 361
39. *BT* II, 144; I, 357; *RevT*, 133
40. Ibid., I, 30; *RevT*, 88
41. *BT* II, 232; *RevT*, 172
42. Conv. IV
43. To E. Wilhelm, 27 April 1960
44. See minutes, 9 June 1916; *BT* I, 142
45. *Generalbericht der evangelisch-reformierten Kirche des Kantons Aargau*, 1921, 14
46. *BT* I, 80
47. 'Gesprek over Rome-Reformatie', in *Libertas ex veritate*, 1965; *BT* I, 217, and letter to Pastor Grolimund, 8 January 1934
48. ABT I
49. *Prof. D. F. Barth*, Berne 1912, 9
50. M. Lauterburg, Preface to F. Barth, *Christus unsere Hoffnung*, XVII
51. *BT* I, 26
52. 'Nachwort', 292
53. ABT I and 'Nachwort', 292
54. *Kirchen- und Dorfgeschichte von Safenwil*, 1966, 48
55. F. Barth, *Christus unsere Hoffnung*, 19f.
56. To Peter Barth, 29 August 1912
57. Lecture, 'Evangelium und Sozialismus', 1 February 1914
58. *BT* I, 21; *RevT*, 27
59. Conv. IV
60. *BT* I, 3

61. To W. Spoendlin, 20 June 1913
62. *BT* I, 84
63. 'Eduard Thurneysen zum 60. Geburtstag', *Basler Nachrichten*, 11 July 1948
64. ABT I
65. E. Thurneysen, *BT*, 18; *RevT*, 11
66. E. Thurneysen, *BT* I, 524
67. *BT* II, 406
68. *BT* I, 85
69. *BT* II, 614
70. See n.63
71. See n.65
72. 'Lebendige Vergangenheit', in *Festschrift für E. Thurneysen zum 70. Geburtstag*, 1958, 12f.; *RevT*, 71
73. Ibid., *RevT*, 72
74. Introduction to E. Thurneysen, *Das Wort Gottes ünd die Kirche*, 1971, 227ff.
75. *BT* I, 212
76. Ibid., 158
77. G. Merz, *Wege und Wandlungen*, 1961, 254f.
78. To K. L. Schmidt, 14 April 1939
79. *BT* I, 86
80. ABT II
81. *BT* I, 144, 192
82. Ibid., 159
83. Ibid., 232
84. 'Nachwort', 293
85. See n.16
86. *KD* I, 1, 75; ET 74
87. *KD* II, 1, 714; ET 633
88. 'Reformierte Theologie in der Schweiz', in *Festschrift für G. C. Berkouwer*, 1965, 36
89. To. H. Schädelin, 20 December 1961
90. ABT VII, 3f.
91. 'Nachwort', 293
92. *KD* I, 1, 75; ET 74
93. *Bericht von der XV. Aarauer Studenten-Konferenz*, 1911, 3
94. ABT VII, 2
95. Obit. M. Gerwig, 1965, 8
96. *KD* IV, 3, IX; ET xiii
97. *BT* I, 70; *RevT*, 30
98. To W. Spoendlin, 22 December 1913
99. '*Die Hilfe, 1913*', in *CW*, 1914, 777
100. Sermons, 1914. GA Reihe I, 1974, 365f., 168, 23, 241, 42, 47, 193
101. *Homiletik*, 1966, 98
102. ABT II
103. 'Nachwort', 293
104. To W. Spoendlin, 4 January 1915
105. ABT I
106. ABT VII, 4
107. See n.103
108. *BT* I, 19
109. See n.103
110. ABT I
111. See n.106
112. *KD* III, 4, 515; ET 450 (the congress took place on 24 November 1912)
113. Conv.IV
114. ABT II
115. See n.106
116. *BT* I, 30; *RevT*, 18
117. To W. Spoendlin, 4 January 1915
118. *LZ*, 41f., and 'Ein Wort an das aargauische Bürgertum', in *Neuer Freier Aargauer*, 191, no.157
119. To P. Barth, 18 May 1914
120. See n.117
121. ABT I
122. See n.63
123. To Dora Rade, 17 April 1940
124. *Beginnings*, 42; ET 39
125. Ibid., 48f.; ET 45
126. Ibid, 45; ET 41
127. 'Auf das Reich Gottes warten', in *Der freie Schweizer Arbeiter*, 1916, no.47
128. *BT* I, 39; *RevT*, 28f.
129. To his sons, 17 September 1955
130. *BT* I, 62
131. Ibid., 33
132. Ibid., 79; *RevT*, 31
133. Ibid., 238
134. Lect. I, 27; ET 42
135. 'Kirchenkritik vom "Flohmart"', in *Basler Nachrichten*, 11–12 December 1965
136. *BT* I, 143; *RevT*, 37
137. Ibid., 88; *RevT*, 34
138. See n.135
139. *BT* I, 103
140. Ibid., 106f.
141. Ibid., 122; *RevT*, 36
142. To W. Spoendlin, 18 January 1916
143. To W. Spoendlin, 7 January 1916
144. Lect. I, 15; ET 24
145. See n. 45, 21
146. *BT* I, 10; *RevT*, 26
147. Ibid., 46; *RevT*, 29
148. Ibid., 83; *RevT*, 33
149. Ibid., 157
150. Ibid., 252, 247
151. Lect. I, 101f.; ET 100ff.
152. To P. Barth, 29 April 1932
153. To W. Scherffig, 20 August 1949
154. See n.127

155. M. Mattmüller, *Ragaz* II, 1968, 220ff., 228f.
156. Ibid., 229
157. ABT I
158. *BT* I, 110f.
159. ABT I
160. *BT* I, 144f.
161. 'Nachwort', 294
162. *BT* I, 525; *RevT*, 75
163. See n.161
164. *BT* I, 145; *RevT*, 37
165. See n.63
166. See n.161
167. 'Nachwort', 294f.
168. ABT II
169. ABT I
170. *LZ*, 19
171. 'Nachwort', 295
172. *LZ*, 19
173. ABT II
174. M. Mattmüller, *Ragaz* II, 245
175. *BT* I, 236; *RevT*, 43
176. Conv. VIII
177. 'Nachwort', 295
178. *BT* I, 148
179. ABT I
180. 'Nachwort', 295
181. *Systematische Theologie*, 1960, 136
182. *Rom.* I, 299
183. Ibid., 39, 25
184. Ibid., 35f.
185. Ibid., 97, 118, 25, 264
186. *Rom.* II, 223; ET 241
187. Lect. II, 241; ET 239
188. *Rom.* I, 24f.
189. *BT* I, 148
190. Ibid., 159
191. Lect. I, 29; ET 43, 45
192. *BT* I, 223
193. Ibid., 189; *RevT*, 41
194. Ibid., 247f.
195. Serm. I, 98, 102ff.
196. 'Das, was uns nicht geschehen soll', in *Neuer Freier Aargauer*, 1919, no.188 (the reading follows Barth's autograph correction)
197. ABT II
198. 'Dankesworte', *EvTh*, 1966, 618
199. Conv. VIII
200. *LZ*, 44f.
201. *BT* I, 229; *RevT*, 42
202. Conv. VIII
203. Minutes, 18 December 1917
204. Conv. VIII
205. *BT* I, 224

206. W. Vischer zum 60. Geburtstag', *KRS*, 1955, 134
207. 'Prof. Fritz Lieb', *Basler Nachrichten*, 22 October 1958
208. 'Ein Brief an den Jubilar (F. Lieb)', *EvTh*, 1962, 282f.
209. *BT* I, 264; *RevT*, 70
210. Ibid., 281
211. Preface to German reprint of *Rom.* I, 1963
212. *BT* I, 300; *RevT*, 45
212. Ibid.
214. Ibid., 321
215. Minutes, 10 August 1919
216. See n.208
217. To E. Sartorius, 14 December 1944
218. *BT* I, 313, 350; *RevT*, 48
219. Ibid., 325
220. *BT* II, 105; *RevT*, 110
221. *BT* I, 343; *RevT*, 47
222. G. Dehn, *Die alte Zeit, die vorigen Jahre*, 1964, 217
223. G. Merz, *Wege*, 240f.
224. *BT* I, 344; *RevT*, 47
225. Lect. I, 51, 36; ET 299, 277
226. M. Mattmüller, *Ragaz* II, 255
227. G. Merz, *Wege*, 240f.
228. ABT I
229. To G. Dehn, 16 July 1957
230. ABT I
231. To H. Scholz, 2 August 1954
232. *BT* I, 367; *RevT*, 48
233. Ibid.
234. Ibid., 368; *RevT*, 48
235. See n.211
236. See n.211
237. *BT* I, 441
238. 'Grusswort', in *Medicus Viator, Festschrift für R. Siebeck*, 1959, 1
239. Serm. II, 253, 210, 226, 259, 243f.; ET 275, 227, 244, 280, 264
240. ABT I
241. To H. Hag, 16 February 1945
242. To Agnes von Zahn, 23 December 1935
243. *BT* I, 379f.; *RevT*, 50
244. To a colleague, 23 December 1940
245. 'Nachwort', 295
246. ABT I
247. 'Dank und Reverenz', *EvTh*, 1963, 339f.
248. See n.244
249. *BT* I, 398; *RevT*, 51
250. 'Nachwort', 295
251. Lect. I, 79; ET 64

252. See n.247
253. 'Nachwort', 295
254. ABT I
255. 'Nachwort', 295
256. ABT I
257. *BT* I, 435; *RevT*, 173
258. Quoted by G. Merz, *Wege*, 244
259. *BT* I, 435; *RevT*, 173
260. See n.211
261. 'Nachwort', 295
262. *Rom.* II, XIX; ET 15
263. *BT* I, 463; *RevT*, 56
264. Ibid., 481; *RevT*, 58
265. Ibid., 471
266. Ibid., 492
267. Ibid., 508; *RevT*, 59
268. *Rom.* II, XIX; ET 15
269. *BT* I, 493
270. Ibid.
271. See n.208
272. ABT IV
273. *BT* I, 448; *RevT*, 55
274. Ibid., 438; *RevT*, 54
275. See n.247
276. *Die Menschlichkeit Gottes*, 1956, 5ff.; ET
     The Humanity of God, 1961 (page
     references are to the Collins Fontana
     edition of 1967), 35ff.
277. *BT* I, 485
278. *Rom.* II, 18, 6, 73; ET 42, 30, 98
279. Ibid., 12, 244, 84, 118; ET 36, 260,
     109, 141

280. Lect. V, 112
281. *KD* II, 1, 715f.; ET 634f.
282. See n.211
283. ABT II
284. *ChD*, IX
285. 'Dankesworte', *EvTh*, 1966, 616f.
286. To CB, 29 September 1949
287. *BT* I, 407
288. Ibid., 315
289. Ibid., 408
290. Ibid., 312
291. Ibid., 270
292. *Rom.* II, XIX; ET 15
293. *BT* II, 489; I, 429
294. See n.211
295. ABT I
296. *BT* I, 468
297. 'Reformierte Theologie in der
     Schweiz', 36
298. *BT* I, 488
299. *BT* I, 458
300. *Generalbericht der evangelisch-reformierten
     Kirchen des Kantons Aargau*, 1921, 12, 44
301. *BT* I, 497
302. Ibid., 526
303. Ibid., 477
304. Ibid., 526
305. ThExh 37, 23
306. *BT* I, 525
307. *BT* II, 235
308. ABT II

4   *Professor of theology in Göttingen and Münster, 1921–1930*

1. ABT II and ABT I
2. To W. Spoendlin, 21 December 1921
3. *BT* II, 8; *RevT*, 76
4. ABT VII, 5f.
5. Serm. II, 31; ET 31
6. *BT* II, 8; *RevT*, 76
7. 'Nachwort', 291
8. ABT II
9. ABT I
10. 'Nachwort', 296
11. Circular letter, May 1961
12. Interview with H. Fischer-Barnicol,
    1964
13. *BT* II, 91; *RevT*, 105
14. Ibid., 81; *RevT*, 101
15. Ibid., 91; *RevT*, 105
16. Ibid., 40
17. Ibid., 134

18. Ibid., 97
19. Ibid., 105; *RevT*, 110
20. Ibid., 81
21. To H. Stoevesant, 29 August 1959
22. ABT I and *BT* II, 34, 75
23. ABT II
24. ABT I
25. *BT* II, 35; *RevT*, 61
26. Ibid., 6, 37, 9; *RevT*, 77
27. *BB*, 215
28. ABT I
29. Preface to reprint of *Rom.* I, 1963
30. *BT* II, 127
31. Ibid., 22; *RevT*, 80
32. Conv. VII
33. *Die Auferstehung des Toten*, 1924, ⁴1953,
    III (not in ET)
34. See n.2

35. *BT* II, 164, 252, 329
36. Ibid., 72
37. Ibid., 20; *RevT*, 79
38. W. Trillhaas, 'Karl Barth in Göttingen', in *Festschrift für M. Doerne*, 1970, 364
39. ABT II
40. *BT* II, 9
41. See n.12
42. *BT* II, 86; *RevT*, 104
43. Ibid., 9; *RevT*, 77
44. Ibid., 329; *RevT*, 222
45. 'Zwischenzeit', in *Magnum*, April 1961
46. See n.2
47. ABT I
48. See n.2 and *BT* II, 33
49. See n.2 and *BT* II, 125
50. See n.2
51. Lect. II, 264f.; ET 256
52. See n.12 and *BT* II, 21; *RevT*, 80
53. *BT* I, 504 and II, 22
54. See n.2
55. *BT* II, 59f.; *RevT*, 92f.
56. See n.12
57. *BT* II, 77
58. To F. Bolgiani, 12 August 1963; *BT* II, 6; to O. Cullmann, 12 August 1963
59. *BT* II, 211
60. *KD* IV, 3, 20; ET 20
61. See n.2 and *BT* II, 23
62. *BT* II, 41ff.; *RevT*, 82ff.
63. Ibid., 73; *RevT*, 99f.
64. Ibid., 35
65. Ibid., 46; *RevT*, 88
66. Conv. VII
67. *BT* II, 46f.
68. Conv. VII
69. Ibid.
70. *BT* II, 48f.; *RevT*, 89f.
71. 'Nachwort', 301
72. *BT* II, 50
73. Introduction to E. Thurneysen, *Das Wort Gottes und die Kirche*, 1971, 227
74. 'Lebendige Vergangenheit', in *Festschrift für E. Thurneysen zum 70. Geburtstag*, 1958, 13f.; *RevT*, 72
75. *BT* II, 500
76. Ibid., 64; *RevT*, 95
77. Ibid., 80; *RevT*, 101
78. Ibid., 643, 98
79. ABT I
80. *BT* II, 116; *RevT*, 115
81. To M. Neeser, 27 December 1949
82. Lect. I, 99, 102, 113, 123; ET 97, 101, 117, 134

83. Ibid., 133, 147, 140; ET 149, 169, 158
84. *BT* II, 102, 105
85. See n.81
86. *BT* II, 103; *RevT*, 108
87. Lect. I, 158, 178, 165; ET 186, 217, 197
88. *BT* II, 105; see *RevT*, 108
89. Ibid., 111f.; *RevT*, 112
90. Ibid., 116; *RevT*, 115
91. To K. Stoevesandt, 8 August 1952
92. Conv. VIII and *BT* II, 121
93. To K. H. Miskotte, 12 July 1956
94. *ProtT* 570, 572; ET 625
95. *BT* II, 307
96. *KD* IV, 1, 585; ET 525
97. *BT* II, 379, 213
98. Ibid., 151; *RevT*, 138
99. Ibid., 132, 124; *RevT*, 125, 120
100. Conv. VIII and *BT II*, 132f.; *RevT*, 126
101. ABT IV
102. *BT* II, 30; *RevT*, 82
103. ABT IV
104. ABT VII, 5
105. 'Abschied', *ZZ*, 1933, 536
106. To Kroner Verlag, 7 March 1954
107. See n.81 and *BT* II, 329
108. *Die Menschlichkeit Gottes*, 6f.; ET 37f.
109. E. Thurneysen, *BT* II, 204; *RevT*, 156
110. Conv. VII
111. To T, 9 August 1931, and ABT I
112. *BT* II, 110
113. See n.105
114. *Rom.* II, XXIV; ET 20
115. 'Abschied', 537
116. *BT* II, 129, and to G. Merz, 5 May 1950
117. W. Trillhaas (see n.38), 365
118. E. Wolf, 'Der Christian Kaiser Verlag', in *125 Jahre Christian Kaiser Verlag*, 1970, 140
119. See n.115
120. Lect. III, 14, 17
121. Agnes von Zahn, *Adolf von Harnack*, 1936, 534f.
122. *LZ*, 22
123. See n.45
124. *BT* II, 198; *RevT*, 198
125. Ibid., 130; *RevT*, 124f.
126. Ibid., 131; *RevT*, 125
127. *LZ*, 42f.
128. Conv. VIII
129. ABT II
130. ABT I
131. *BT* II, 130

132. ABT I
133. *Die Auferstehen der Toten*, 59; ET *The Resurrection of the Dead*, Hodder 1933, 110
134. See n.81
135. Lect. I, 180, 188, 200f.; ET 221, 233, 251, 253
136. *BT* II, 286, 209; *RevT*, 193
137. Ibid., 232; *RevT*, 172
138. Ibid., 232ff.; *RevT*, 172
139. 'Nachwort', 297
140. *BT* II, 223, 235; *RevT*, 168, 175
141. 'Nachwort', 296f.
142. *Beginnings*, 175, 184; ET 142, 150
143. *BT* II, 231; *RevT*, 171
144. Introduction to H. Heppe, *Dogmatik*, 1935; ET *Dogmatics*, Allen & Unwin 1950, 5f.
145. *BT* II, 224; *RevT*, 168
146. Ibid., 251; *RevT*, 182
147. Ibid., 254; *RevT*, 185
148. Ibid., 253; *RevT*, 185
149. Ibid., 328f.; *RevT*, 221
150. Ibid., 302; *RevT*, 203
151. 'Nachwort', 297
152. *BT* II, 213; *RevT*, 162
153. Ibid., 221; *RevT*, 166
154. Ibid., 251; *RevT*, 182
155. Ibid., 303, 252
156. Ibid., 287ff.; *RevT*, 194ff.
157. Ibid.; *RevT*, 197
158. 'Menschenwort und Gotteswort in der christlichen Predigt', *ZZ*, 1925, 127
159. *BT* II, 289; *RevT*, 196
160. Circular letter, 25 May 1960 (Barth wrongly dates the meeting in 1922)
161. *BT* II, 291, 285; *RevT*, 196, 193
162. Ibid., 306f.; *RevT*, 206; 'Nachwort', 299; Conv. VII (Barth wrongly dates the meeting in 1922)
163. *BT* II, 306f.; *RevT*, 206
164. Ibid., 330; *RevT*, 222f.
165. Lect. II, 283; ET 270
166. *BT* II, 331; *RevT*, 225
167. Ibid., 236; *RevT*, 175
168. Ibid., 313ff.
169. Kutter to Barth 16 June 1925
170. See n.74
171. ABT I and *BT* II, 359; *RevT*, 235
172. *BB*, 50
173. *BT* II, 336
174. Ibid., 255, 166, 238
175. Ibid., 383
176. Ibid., 615
177. Serm. V, 7; ET 18

178. To E. Sartorius, 2 January 1944
179. To L. Christ, 18 May 1952
180. *BT* II, 370f.; *RevT*, 241
181. *BB*, 56; *BT* II, 377f.
182. *BT* II, 397f.
183. Ibid., 393
184. Ibid., 400
185. Ibid., 291
186. Ibid., 397
187. Ibid., 377
188. To Agnes von Zahn, 23 December 1935
189. *KD* I, 2, 403f.; ET 367f.
190. *BB*, 50, 53
191. *BT* II, 390
192. Ibid., 396
193. Ibid., 396f.
194. Ibid., 650
195. Ibid., 398
196. To A. Lüpkes, 21 May 1944
197. *BT* II, 398, 365
198. To K. Heim, 12 June 1928
199. To Wuppertal teachers, 26 October 1957
200. *BT* II, 639
201. 'Gesprek over Rome-Reformatie', in *Libertas ex veritate*, 1965
202. ABT II
203. *KD* III, 3, 462; ET 399
204. *BT* II, 680
205. Ibid., 409
206. To Rheinfelder, 14 July 1962
207. *BT* II, 409
208. Ibid., 423
209. Lect. II, 226, 228; ET 227, 228
210. *BT* II, 411
211. Ibid., 413ff.
212. Lect. II, 372, 384; ET 343, 349
213. *BT* II, 429
214. Ibid., 557
215. *Erklärung des Philipperbriefes*, 1927, ⁵1947, Foreword and 98f.; ET *The Epistle to the Philippians*, 1962, Preface and 101f.
216. *BT* II, 407
217. Ibid., 442
218. Ibid.
219. Ibid., 435
220. Ibid., 436, 448
221. Ibid., 441
222. Ibid., 390
223. *ChD*, VII
224. Ibid., VI
225. Interview with H. Fischer-Barnicol, 1964

226. ABT IV
227. *ChD*, 25, 112, 16
228. Ibid., VIIIf.
229. *KD* I, 1, VI; ET xi
230. *ChD*, VII
231. Ibid., V, VIII
232. *BT* II, 516f.
233. To W. Spoendlin, 4 January 1928
234. 'Rechtfertigung und Heiligung', *ZZ*, 1927, 285, 290
235. Lect. III, 35, 37
236. *BT* II, 499
237. Ibid., 490f.
238. Ibid., 500f.
239. Ibid., 507
240. Ibid., 639
241. Lect. II, 286f.; ET 273
242. *BT* II, 535ff.
243. Lect. II, 349; ET 322
244. Lect. II, 344; ET 319; to K. Heim, 12 June 1928
245. Lect. II, 361; ET 331
246. *BT* II, 523
247. To P. Althaus, 12 February 1958
248. *BT* II, 506
249. Ibid., 598, 558f.
250. Ibid., 578
251. *BB*, 90
252. To T, 22 February 1931
253. *Antwort*, 871
254. To MB, 26 February 1963
255. *BT* II, 615
256. *Ethik*, 1928, GA II, 10
257. Ibid., 18, 29, 81, 82, 79, 92ff.
258. *BT* II, 638
259. Ibid., 628
260. Ibid., 652
261. E. Przywara, in *Gespräch zwischen den Kirchen*, 1956, 7f.
262. *BT* II, 652f.
263. Lect. III, 61
264. *BT* II, 659f.
265. 'Die Lehre von der Sakramenten', *ZZ*, 1929, 429
266. *KD* IV, 4, VIII; ET viii
267. Testimonial, June 1940
268. 'Italienische Eilreise' (manuscript account of his trip by Karl Barth)
269. ABT VI, 39f.
270. To T, 30 May 1929
271. Ibid.

272. *BT* II, 668
273. Ibid., 678
274. *Zur Lehre vom Heiligen Geist*, 1930, 39f., 95; ET *The Holy Ghost and the Christian Life*, Frederick Muller 1938, 34f., 76
275. *BT* II, 555
276. To T, 2 April 1931
277. *BT* II, 590, 578
278. Conv. VIII
279. 'Zwischenzeit', in *Magnum*, April 1961
280. 'Universitätslehrer – eine Gefahr?', *Göttingen Universitäts-Zeitung*, July 1947
281. See n.279
282. To J. Scheiwiler, 11 December 1943
283. See n.279
284. See n.279
285. Lect. V, 31, 28
286. Opinion on dissertation by G. Schmidt, 2 April 1952
287. 'Bemerkungen zu H. M. Müllers Lutherbuch', *ZZ*, 1929, 563
288. *BT* II, 210, 113; *RevT*, 161, 114
289. Preface to reprint of *Rom.* I, 1963
290. See n.279
291. Conv. VII
292. *BB*, 70
293. 'Abschied', *ZZ*, 1933, 536f.
294. Ibid.
295. *BT* II, 688
296. Conv. VII
297. *BT* II, 716
298. Conv. VII
299. To H. W. Bartsch, 20 March 1959
300. Conv. VII
301. *BB*, 70
302. *Ethik*, 1928, GA II, 74
303. *BT* II, 700
304. *BB*, 101
305. 'Abschied', 538
306. *Nein!*, ThExh 14, 7f.; ET *Natural Theology*, Bles 1946, 71
307. See n.305
308. *KD* III, 4, VIII; ET xii
309. *Nein!*, 7f.; ET 70
310. See n.305
311. *BT* II, 482
312. Ibid., 693
313. To E. Scholz, 6 January 1957
314. *BB*, 102
315. See n.279

5   *The years at Bonn, 1930–1935*

1. *RGG*³ I, 1359f.

2. *BT* II, 117

3. To Professor Becker, 14 August 1947
4. To H. Weber, 24 June 1950
5. *BT* II, 677
6. To K. L. Schmidt, 4 February 1941
7. *BT* II, 677
8. To E. Wolf, 28 July 1961
9. To E. Wolf, 31 July 1952
10. To CB, 7 June 1954
11. To T, 22 February 1931
12. To T, 20 March 1930
13. Ibid.
14. To T, 24 November 1931
15. To T, 29 May 1931
16. To K. Takizawa, 4 August 1958
17. *Antwort*, 911
18. Ibid., 874
19. *BT* II, 225
20. Dietrich Bonhoeffer, *Gesammelte Schriften* I, 1958, 19; ET *No Rusty Swords,* Collins and Harper and Row, New York 1965, 120
21. ABT VI, 38
22. To T, 8 March 1931
23. To T, 24 November 1931
24. Speech in Lambeth Palace, 4 July 1956
25. *BB,* 160f.
26. CvK to T, 14 June 1930
27. *BB,* 160f.
28. Opinion on dissertation by James Leitch, March 1952
29. To Erik Wolf, 27 November 1968
30. 'Brief an K. Heim', *ZZ*, 1931, 451
31. *Fides quaerens intellectum,* 1931, ²1958, 7; ET *Anselm: Fides quaerens intellectum,* 1960, 7
32. ABT VI, 43
33. *Anselm*, 21, 26, 59, 30; ET 22, 40, 60, 35
34. Ibid., 10; ET 11
35. H. Scholz, in *Antwort,* 866f.
36. To H. Kraemer, 29 November 1952
37. To T, 10 December 1930
38. Conv. V
39. Conv. VII
40. *BB,* 118
41. *BB,* 105–29
42. 'Die Not der evangelischen Kirche', *ZZ,* 1931, 91, 100, 115, 116
43. To T, 22 February 1931
44. 'Die Not der evangelischen Kirche', 122, 120
45. To O. Dibelius, 17 May 1956
46. To T, 22 February 1931
47. Ibid.
48. To T, 8 March 1931

49. *KD* I, 1, VI; ET xi
50. *Anselm,* 10; ET 11
51. ABT VI, 43
52. Ibid., 43
53. ABT IV
54. *KD* I, 1, VII; ET, xiii
55. 'Abschied', *ZZ,* 1933, 537
56. The quotations here come from a German draft of a Preface to the English edition of *Dogmatik im Grundriss;* the Preface was not, however, included in *Dogmatics in Outline* when it was published.
57. 'Systematische Theologie', in *Lehre und Forschung an der Universität Basel,* 1960, 38
58. *KD* I, 1, VII; ET xii
59. Ibid.
60. *KD* I, 1, 41, 43, 313, 318, 323, 404; ET 42, 43, 295, 301, 315, 333
61. To T, 9 January 1931
62. *KD* I, 1, 168f.; ET 162
63. To T, 29 May 1931
64. Ibid.
65. 'H. Gollwitzer', *SdG,* 1966, 284
66. Quoted in E. Bethge, *Dietrich Bonhoeffer,* 216f.; ET 132
67. To T, 2 July 1931
68. To H. U. von Balthasar, 25 January 1930
69. *KD* I, 2, 924; ET 827
70. *KD* I, 1, VIIIf.; ET xiii
71. Ibid., 257f., 234; ET 243f., 223
72. 'Replik an Prof. D. Dr. G. Wobbermin', *Theologische Blätter,* 1932, 221f.
73. 'Protestantismus der Gegenwart', *Jugend und Krisis der Kultur,* 1932
74. To T, 24 November 1931
75. In K. Kupisch, *Karl Barth,* 1971, 75
76. To E. Wolf, 15 November 1965
77. 'Abschied', 543
78. To O. Dibelius, 17 May 1956
79. To E. Wolf, 15 November 1965
80. See n.77
81. 'Warum führt man den Kampf nicht auf der ganzen Linie?', *Frankfurter Zeitung,* 15 February 1932
82. Lect. III, 94, 96
83. 'Die Theologie und die Mission in der Gegenwart', *ZZ,* 1932, 191, 202, 197
84. Preface to the English edition of *Rom.* II, vf.
85. To T, 23 December 1932
86. *Die Kirche Jesu Christi,* ThExh 5, 3f.

87. To L. Kreyssig, 18 September 1950
88. ABT VI, 44
89. Circular letter, May 1968
90. To T, 23 December 1932
91. To T, 21 December 1928
92. To T, 23 December 1932
93. To S. Barth, 23 December 1959
94. *ProtT*, V; ET 11
95. To T, 23 December 1932
96. *ProtT*, 65f., 379, 424; ET 99f., 425, 473
97. Ibid., VI; ET 12
98. To A. Keller, 18 September 1947
99. ABT VI, 45
100. Interview with H. Fischer-Barnicol, 1964
101. 'Ein Brief an den Jubilar', *EvTh*, 1962, 283
102. *LZ*, 34f.
103. Lect. IV, 258
104. *Kirchenkampf*, 62
105. Ibid.
106. ABT VI, 45
107. To K. Ihlenfeld, 4 June 1955
108. ABT II
109. Lect. III, 138, 143
110. Lect. IV, 91
111. See n.75
112. Conv. VIII
113. To T, 27 June 1933
114. CvK to T, 2 June 1933
115. *Kirchenkampf*, 31; ET 45
116. *Theologische Existenz heute*, 1933, 15; ET *Theological Existence Today*, Hodder 1933, 34
117. To T, 27 June 1933
118. Conv VII
119. *Theologische Existenz heute*, 3, 24, 30; ET 9, 51, 62
120. ABT VI, 46
121. *EvTh*, 1963, 390
122. To T, 3 July 1933
123. To T, 27 June 1933
124. *Für die Freiheit des Evangeliums*, ThExh 2, 10, 13
125. ABT VI, 45
126. See n.115
127. *Lutherfeier 1933*, ThExh 4, 4
128. *Kirchenkampf*, 31; ET 42
129. *Reformation als Entscheidung*, ThExh 3, 3
130. To T, 16 October 1933
131. To T, 25 August 1933
132. 'Abschied', 539
133. Ibid., 544
134. See n.129
135. *Lutherfeier 1933*, 3

136. Ibid., 22ff.
137. *Der deutsche Kirchenkampf*, 1937, 12
138. W. Niemöller, *Wort und Tat im Kirchenkampf*, 1969, 72
139. Ibid., 70, 71, 73
140. *Lutherfeier 1933*, 3, 17
141. *BB*, 152f.
142. *BB*, 138
143. D. Schmidt, *M. Niemöller*, [2]1960, 104
144. *Die Kirche Jesu Christi*, 6
145. *BB*, 140
146. To T, 16 November 1933
147. *Lutherfeier 1933*, 3
148. Ibid., 5
149. To T, 29 November 1933
150. *Lutherfeier 1933*, 3
151. To T, 16 November 1933
152. Dietrich Bonhoeffer, *Gesammelte Schriften* II, 1959, 135f.; ET *No Rusty Swords*, 238f.
153. D. Schmidt, *M. Niemöller*, 121
154. *BB*, 140
155. 'Niemöller', in *Basler Kirchenbote*, November 1945
156. To M. Niemöller, 7 January 1962
157. *KD* I, 2, 64; ET 58
158. *Die Kirche Jesu Christi*, 16, 3
159. To E. Steffens, 10 January 1934
160. *Gebete*, 1963, 5
161. Lect. IV, 259f.
162. *Kirchenkampf*, 32f.; ET 43f.
163. To W. Niesel, 31 December 1954
164. *Gottes Wille und unsere Wünsche*, ThExh 7, 3ff., 9, 6ff.
165. Ibid.
166. To T, 8 January 1934
167. *Gottes Wille und unsere Wünsche*, 25
168. See n.166
169. To J. Baillie, 3 December 1937
170. Interview with H. Fischer-Barnicol, 1964
171. ABT II
172. *Gottes Wille und unsere Wünsche*, 4
173. CvK to T, 26 January 1934
174. *Gottes Wille und unsere Wünsche*, 4
175. *Kirchenkampf*, 19; ET 29
176. 'Ein Brief an den Jubilar', 284
177. Manuscript travel report by KB and CvK
178. 'Erica Küppers', *SdG*, 1966, 301
179. *Offenbarung, Kirche, Theologie*, 13, 34; ET *God in Action*, 1936, 39f.
180. *Der gute Hirte*, ThExh 10, 14, 19; ET in *God's Search for Man*, T. & T. Clark and Round Table Press, New York 1935,

1–12, 13–25
181. Conv. VII
182. To W. Niemöller, 17 October 1953
183. Conv. VII
184. Ibid.
185. 'Barmen – damals und heute', *Kirche und Mann*, May 1954
186. See n.182
187. Conv. VII
188. See n.185
189. *KD* II, 1, 194, 196f.; ET 172ff.
190. 'Brief an Eberhard Bethge', *EvTh*, 1968, 555
191. *Nein!*, ThExh 14, 11, 4; ET 67
192. Ibid., 7, 4f., 56; ET 70, 67f., 121
193. Ibid., 32; ET 99, and Conv. VIII
194. To R. Barth, 8 June 1964
195. ABT VI, 44
196. Ibid., 41
197. Conv. VII
198. To K. Kupisch, 10 February 1956
199. To H. Vogel, 5 September 1956
200. D. Bonhoeffer, *Gesammelte Schriften* II, 136f.; *No Rusty Swords*, 238f.
201. To A. Finet, 25 January 1956
202. To T, 24 March 1932
203. Preface to P. Maury, *La prédestination*, 1957, 6f.
204. To MB, 8 March 1953
205. To G. Dehn, 16 April 1957
206. To T. List, 16 February 1954
207. To CB, 29 December 1959
208. To Anna Barth, 5 August 1935
209. 'Erica Küppers', *SdG*, 1966, 301f.
210. Ibid.
211. *Der Christ als Zeuge*, ThExh 12, 4, 25; ET *God in Action*, 1936, 102, 109, 116; Lect. III, 189, 192, 195
212. To T, 22 October 1934
213. *KD* II, 1, 197; ET 175
214. To T, 23 November 1934
215. Lecture, 1 December 1934
216. To Erik Wolf, 16 March 1946
217. To M. Niemöller, 29 June 1946

218. To J. Beckmann, 20 July 1949
219. See n.216
220. *Die evangelische Kirche in Deutschland nach dem Zusammenbruch des Dritten Reiches*, 1945, 33
221. *Some Remarks on the Allied Policy*, 21 July 1946
222. *Drei Predigten*, ThExh 17, 5
223. To H. von Soden, 5 December 1934, and *BB*, 266f.
224. ABT II and *BB*, 262
225. *Kirchenkampf*, 75
226. In *Antwort*, 877
227. To T, 24 December 1934, and Serm. VI, 89; ET 88
228. Plato, *Apology*, 29D, 30A, 30D
229. To T, 24 December 1934
230. *BB*, 157
231. K. Kupisch, *Karl Barth*, 91
232. Ibid.
233. W. Niemöller, *Kampf und Zeugnis der Bekennenden Kirche*, 1948, 230
234. To E. Imobersteg, 15 March 1946
235. To P. Humburg, 9 February 1935, and W. Niesel, 24 January 1948
236. *Das Evangelium in der Gegenwart*, ThExh 25, 16f.
237. *Credo*, 1935, 150f., 5f., 46, 16, 46, 37, 113; ET *Credo*, 1936, 174f., 2, 4f., 48, 18, 49, 38, 218
238. W. Niemöller, *Kampf und Zeugnis*, 246
239. To H. Hesse, 30 June 1935
240. Quoted by W. Niemöller, *Kampf und Zeugnis*, 238
241. See n.239
242. Ibid.
243. *Das Evangelium in der Gegenwart*, 33, 31, 34
244. 'Dankesworte', *EvTh*, 1966, 618
245. To T. Creighton, 28 December 1946
246. W. Niemöller, *Kampf und Zeugnis*, 231
247. ABT II
248. See n.244
249. To K. Huber, 13 December 1948

6   The years from 1935 to 1946 in St Albanring, Basle

1. ABT II
2. Quoted in W. Niemöller, *Wort und Tat im Kirchenkampf*, 171
3. To E. Sartorius, 3 August 1935
4. To E. Wolf, 30 July 1935
5. Ibid.
6. ABT II

7. 'E. Thurneysen zum 60. Geburtstag', *Basler Nachrichten*, 11 July 1948
8. See n.4 and letter to Nelly Barth, 1 August 1935
9. Lect. III, 217, 225
10. To J. Hromádka, 6 June 1964
11. Lect. III, 233, 237

12. Ibid., 260f.
13. To H. Traub, 29 September 1935
14. 'Reformierte Theologie in der Schweiz', *Festschrift für G. C. Berkouwer*, 1965, 33f.
15. To A. Koechlin, 28 June 1944
16. See n.13 and letter to W. Niesel, 21 August 1936
17. See n.15
18. *Evangelium und Gesetz*, ThExh 32, 5, 11
19. CvK to Albert Lempp, 10 October 1935
20. To E. Fuchs, 15 November 1935
21. To K. Preiswerk, 18 January 1936
22. To K. Hesse, 16 November 1935
23. To his sons, 20 December 1953
24. *Kirchenkampf*, 74
25. See n.21
26. To his sons, 20 December 1953
27. To Frau Prof. N. N., 7 August 1937
28. To A. Keller, 27 June 1936
29. To A. Koechlin, 26 June 1939
30. 'Zum Andenken an E. Vischer', *KRS*, 21 February 1946, 54f.
31. To CB, 18 September 1960
32. *KD* IV, 3, IX; ET xii, and to E. Wolf, 30 July 1935
33. See notes 22 and 7
34. 'Prof F. Lieb', *Basler Nachrichten*, 22 October 1958, and 'Ein Brief an den Jubilar', *EvTh*, 1962, 284
35. To the Basle Kuratel, 19 February 1944
36. 'W.Vischer zum 60. Geburtstag', *KRS*, 28 April 1955, and letter to K. Immer, 27 February 1937
37. To M. Schoch, 17 October 1967, and to G. Lindt, 12 December 1936 and 12 July 1940
38. To Dr Gessler, 28 July 1936
39. 'Reformierte Theologie in der Schweiz', 36
40. To W. Lüthi, 17 October 1939
41. *Die Kirche Jesu Christi*, ThExh 5, 3. See Preface, Serm. III
42. *Nein!*, ThExh 14, 62; ET 127
43. To J. Beckmann, 31 March 1947
44. *Gebete*, 1963, 6
45. To W. Vischer, 29 February 1948
46. To W. Vischer, 18 March 1955
47. *KD* III, 4, 400; ET 352
48. ABT VI, 47, and letter to H. Hesse, 26 July 1937
49. M. Buber to Karl Barth, 21 September 1936

50. To W. Niesel, 19 January 1936
51. To H. Asmussen, 11 August 1935
52. To R. Grosche, 1 August 1935
53. *Kirchenkampf*, 34; ET 45
54. ABT VI, 46
55. See n. 53
56. To H. Dohle, 19 August 1960
57. To M. Niemöller, 29 June 1946
58. *Kirchenkampf*, 91
59. Lect. IV, 260
60. To K. Immer, 27 February 1937
61. Intro. to A. Frey, *Der Kampf der evangelischen Kirche in Deutschland*, 1937, 8
62. *Kirchenkampf*, 66
63. See n.60
64. To W. Niesel, 21 August 1936
65. To A. Koechlin, 28 June 1944
66. To Pastor Hellbardt, 10 January 1937
67. *KD* I, 2, 260; ET 239
68. To G. Spörri, 26 March 1936
69. *EvTh*, 1936, 205ff.
70. *ProtT*, 124; ET 145
71. To K. Hesse, 16 May 1936
72. ABT II
73. To W. Niesel, 21 August 1936
74. ABT II
75. ABT VI, 38f.
76. From CvK to R. Karwehl, 27 May 1936
77. *Calvinfeier 1936*, ThExh 43, 7
78. *KD* II, 2, 168; ET 154
79. Preface to P. Maury, *Prädestination* (German edition), 1959, 5
80. *Gottes Gnadenwahl*, ThExh 47, 3, 6, 10, 13
81. 'Bericht über unsere Herbstreise in den Osten', by CvK
82. CvK to Pierre Maury, 18 October 1936
83. Lect. III, 284f.
84. Ibid., 67f.
85. *Gotteserkenntnis und Gottesdienst*, 1938, 7, 44, 5f., 68f.; ET *The Knowledge of God and the Service of God*, 1938, 6f., 10, 35ff., 71ff.
86. To E. Wolf, 30 March 1937
87. To H. Hesse, 29 March 1937
88. See n.86
89. To G. Henderson, 8 October 1937
90. ABT VI, 40
91. To W. A. Visser't Hooft, 22 July 1937
92. To K. L. Schmidt, 7 August 1937
93. To H. Hesse, 26 July 1937
94. *KD* I, 2, 327; ET 299f.
95. Ibid., 743, 890, 967; ET 660, 795, 876

96. *KD* I, 1, IXf.; ET xiv
97. Conv. X
98. ABT VI, 51
99. *KD* II, 1, 200; ET 179
100. Conv. VII
101. *KD* II, 1, 150, 157; ET 141, 147
102. See n.93
103. Obit. Dr A. Frey, *Schweizerische Evangelische Pressedienst*, 7 November 1955
104. *KD* III, 4, X; ET xiv
105. See n.103
106. To A. Koechlin (?), 1 September 1938
107. To Pastor Spiro, 12 March 1952, and to P. Maury, 12 October 1938
108. *Gotteserkenntnis und Gottesdienst*, 215; ET 229
109. To Principal Fyfe, 3 April 1938, and to Herr Voigt, 18 April 1938
110. To G. Bell, 31 May 1946
111. To W. G. Meyer, 13 April 1938
112. *Rechtfertigung und Recht*, ThSt 1, 3
113. Ibid., 7, 20, 41, 43, 45
114. Lect. IV, 11
115. *Kirchenkampf*, 60; ET 76
116. Ibid., 57; ET 71
117. Ibid., 58, 79; ET 73
118. To P. Maury, 12 October 1938
119. To H. Vogel, 19 September 1938
120. To A. Keller, 17 October 1938, and Lect. V, 152
121. To B. Vasady, 9 November 1938, and Lect. V, 150
122. See n.118 and Lect. V, 150f.
123. 'Noch einmal: Frieden oder Gerechtigkeit?' *KRS*, 24 November 1938
124. ABT VI, 48
125. To H. Thomas, 19 June 1947
126. Lect. IV, 90
127. *Die evangelische Kirche in Deutschland nach dem Zusammenbruch des Dritten Reiches*, 1945, 59
128. ABT VI, 53
129. To a pastor in Berne, 22 January 1939
130. 'Ein Brief', in *Wege des Friedens, Festschrift für Gertrud Kurz*, 1960, 15
131. Ibid., and letter to M. Niemöller, 9 July 1946
132. To P. Vogt, 2 June 1943
133. To M. Niemöller, 9 July 1946
134. To P. Vogt, 21 May 1950
135. To F. Lieb, 20 February 1964
136. To MB, 8 March 1939
137. ABT VI, 52
138. *Die Souveränität des Wortes Gottes*, ThSt 5, 16f., 21
139. To a colleague in Holland, 27 February 1939
140. To students in Leiden, 27 February 1939
141. To K. L. Schmidt, 7 April 1939
142. *KD* II, 1, 288; ET 257
143. Ibid., 362f.; ET 322ff.
144. To Dorothy Sayers, 7 September 1939
145. To W. A. Visser't Hooft, 13 April 1939
146. H. Gollwitzer, *Forderungen der Freiheit*, ²1964, 338
147. To CB, 3 August 1939
148. Lect. IV, 164
149. To F. Zellweger, 7 September 1939
150. To G. Lindt, 18 September 1939
151. See n.149
152. ABT VI, 52
153. To G. Lindt, 2 January 1943
154. To A. Bronkhorst, 27 April 1940
155. 'Das christliche Geheimnis und das menschliche Leben', *Junge Kirche*, 1956, 204
156. *The Faith of the Church*, Collins Fontana 1960, 26, 27, 27f., 129, 57, 38
157. To Pastor Maller, 22 February 1942
158. To O. Weber, 20 June 1949
159. *KD* II, 2, VII; ET ixf.
160. Ibid., 13, 108, 115, 133, 177, 182, 291, 466; ET 13, 103, 115, 163, 167, 197, 207, 415
161. To CB, 31 May 1941
162. *KD* II, 2, 564, 598, 640; ET 509, 543, 576
163. See n.161
164. To H. Oprecht, 17 January 1942
165. To Dr Tökés, 25 September 1940
166. Lect. IV, 8
167. To H. Oprecht, 7 March 1941
168. Lect. IV, 136
169. Ibid., 111f.
170. Ibid., 102
171. Ibid., 12
172. Ibid., 164, 166
173. ABT VI, 53
174. See n.164
175. Lect. IV, 109
176. Ibid., 8f.
177. To W. A. Visser't Hooft, 24 January 1940; to C. Westphal, 20 March 1940; to P. Barth, 20 March 1940
178. Lect. IV, 113
179. To A. Bronkhorst, 27 April 1940
180. ABT II and ABT VI, 53

181. To E. Sartorius, 10 September 1940
182. ABT VI, 53
183. Conv. II
184. ABT VI, 53
185. See n.181
186. Peter Barth's 'Lebenslauf' by Karl Barth, 1940
187. See n.181
188. See n.183
189. To Dora Scheuner, 10 June 1940; see notes 186, 181
190. Lect. IV, 157, 215
191. To Pastor Maller, 22 February 1942, and to G. Ott, 10 May 1941
192. To E. Sartorius, 10 September 1940
193. Lect. IV, 171
194. Conv. IV
195. Lect. IV, 167
196. To the Press Division of the Army Staff, 3 May 1941
197. Lect. IV, 155
198. ABT VI, 53
199. ABT V
200. Lect. IV, 99
201. See n.164; to F. Frei, 31 January 1942
202. See n.164
203. 'Politiker fragen die Kirche', in *In Extremis*, 1940, 181
204. E. Bonjour, *Geschichte der schweizerischen Neutralität* V, 1970, 185
205. To 'Pumchen', 22 December 1940
206. *Kurze Erklärung des Römerbriefes*, 1956, 5f., 22f. ET *A Shorter Commentary on Romans*, 1956, 7f., 20
207. Lect. IV, 167, 178
208. To Pastor Studer, 10 May 1941
209. To E. von Steiger, 11 June 1941
210. Lect. IV, 209f., 218ff.
211. To Dr Bally-Gerber, 6 August 1941
212. To Pastor Roduner, 17 May 1941
213. To Oberst Bäschlin, 22 September 1941
214. To Pastor Roduner, 14 June 1942
215. To R. Freymond, 25 January 1946
216. To W. Spoendlin, 29 June 1941; to A. Frey, 2 July 1941; to K. Takizawa, 28 May 1949
217. To E. Sartorius, 11 May 1944
218. ABT VI, 51
219. To W. Loew, 16 February 1946
220. To A. Cochrane, 16 March 1953
221. To the teachers of H. J. Barth, 6 May 1942
222. See n.215
223. To MZ, 10 October 1943
224. To 'Pumchen', 28 October 1943
225. Lect. IV, 367
226. To Helene Barth, 22 January 1944, and 'Welchen Buch halten Sie für wesentlich?', *Basler Nationalzeitung*, 1934f22u. To T, 9 August 1931
228. *KD* III, 2, 96; ET 83
229. To Nelly Barth, 17 August 1941
230. To Dr Rothmund, 26 November 1941
231. Lect. IV, 240f.
232. Ibid., 243
233. Ibid., 242
234. To J. Glenthoj, 7 September 1956
235. *KD* II, 2, VI; ET ix
236. *KD* III, 1, Preface and 1; ET ix, 3
237. Ibid., Preface; ET ix
238. Ibid., 1, 46, 44, 103, 258, 207, 377; ET 3, 44, 42, 94, 228, 183ff., 330
239. Lect. V, 112
240. Lect. IV, 245f.
241. Ibid., 269
242. Ibid., 285, 279f.
243. Ibid., 299f.
244. To Pastor Maller, 22 February 1942; sermon on Daniel 9.18 (1942) and 'Unser Malaise muss fruchtbar werden', *Weltwoche*, 21 December 1943
245. Barth manuscript, 'Thesen zur Flüchtlingshilfe', autumn 1942
246. Letter of 6 March 1947
247. To K. L. Schmidt, 6 August 1942
248. To A. von Erlach, 17 July 1957
249. To CB, 5 August 1942
250. To F. Frei, 31 January 1942
251. To A. Frey, 27 October 1942
252. Lect. IV, 306
253. To C. Maurer, 5 October 1943
254. To K. L. Schmidt, 3 July 1942
255. *Die Kirchliche Lehre von der Taufe*, 40, 39; ET *The Teaching of the Church regarding Baptism*, 1948, 54, 52
256. To W. A. Visser't Hooft, 9 May 1943
257. To U. Barth, 30 September 1943, and to J. de la Harpe, 21 September 1943
258. To K. L. Schmidt, 15 January 1944
259. To O. Farner, 11 December 1943
260. To W. Gut, 21 February 1944, and to A. Keiler, 7 May 1944
261. To G. Lindt, 31 December 1943
262. To G. Lindt, 12 December 1936
263. To L. Ragaz, 22 April 1944, and from Ragaz to KB, 27 April 1944
264. To P. Vogt, 28 June 1944
265. To the Swiss-Soviet Union Society, 22 March 1945

266. To R. Freymond, 25 January 1946
267. To A. Keller, 21 July 1944
268. Lect. IV, 330f.
269. To G. Schmidt, 20 July 1944
270. Lect. IV, 330f.
271. Ibid., 334ff.
272. To M. von Heyer, 27 September 1945
273. Lect. IV, 397, 392
274. ABT VI, 54
275. To Dr Sonntag, 21 June 1945
276. To K. Müller, 9 June 1945
277. ABT VI, 54
278. To F. Siegmund-Schultze, 11 May 1945
279. To P. Vogt, 28 March 1945
280. See n.278
281. *Auslegung von Matt. 28, 16–20*, 1945, 3, 12
282. Lect. IV, 371ff.
283. ABT VI, 53f.
284. To G. Weber, 16 May 1945
285. To J. L. Leuba, 6 July 1944
286. *Kirchenkampf*, 89
287. *Kirchenkampf*, 92
288. To G. Weber, 28 June 1945

289. To G. Ott, 7 March 1960
290. ABT VI, 54f.
291. 'Und vergib uns unsere Schuld', *Weltwoche*, 14 September 1945
292. *Die evangelische Kirche in Deutschland nach dem Zusammenbruch des Dritten Reiches*, 22
293. To A. Keller, 28 September 1945
294. See n.291
295. 'Que pensez-vous du diable et des anges?' in *Jeunesse*, December 1960
296. ABT VI, 55
297. To E. Bizer, 10 October 1946
298. To O. Fricke, 30 October 1945
299. See n. 292, 37
300. To H. Asmussen, 8 June 1946
301. To M. Hottinger, 18 January 1946
302. To C. Schmid, 18 May 1956
303. To W. Loew, 16 February 1946
304. 'Ein Rückblick auf das Jahr 1945', *Schweizer Radio-Zeitung*, 1946, no. 2
305. To Erik Wolf, 16 March 1946
306. To Broxil Koch, 12 March 1946
307. Lect. IV, 414f.

7   The years from 1946 to 1955 in Pilgerstrasse 25, Basle

1. To R. Siebeck, 19 January 1946
2. ABT VI,56
3. To C. Milville, 12 November 1945
4. To A. von Erlach, 3 March 1945
5. 'Prof. K. Barths Gruss an die deutschen Studenten', *Bonner Universitäts-Zeitung*, 18 October 1946
6. CvK to Gertrud Staewen, 5 June 1946, and Barth to his family, 17 May 1946
7. To A. Frey, 24 May 1946, and to his family, 17 May 1946
8. To G. Lindt, August 1954
9. *Some Remarks on Allied Policy*, 1946, and Lect.V, 98f.
10. To his family, 9 May 1947
11. To his family, 7 July 1946
12. To Frau Goeters, 16 May 1953
13. To his family, 17 May 1946
14. *Dogmatik im Grundriss*, 1947, 5f.; ET *Dogmatics in Outline*, 1949, 7
15. Ibid.
16. To A. Frey, 24 May 1946
17. *Dogmatik im Grundriss*, 109, 84ff., 77, 110; ET 93, 72ff., 66f., 93
18. See n.16
19. 'Abschiedsgruss an die Bonner Studenten', in *In Extremis*, 1946, 71f.

20. CvK to E.Wolf, 17 June 1946
21. To his family, 2 June 1946
22. To his family, 26 May 1947
23. To the Basle Department of Education, 5 September 1946
24. *Die christliche Verkündigung im heutigen Europa*, 1946, 11, 17
25. *Christengemeinde und Bürgergemeinde*, 1946, 55, 14, 13, 29; ET 'The Christian Community and the Civil Community', in *Against the Stream*, 1954, 21, 27, 42, 49
26. Conv. VIII
27. To his family, 26 July 1946
28. See n.23
29. Conv. IV and letter to Erik Wolf, 27 November 1968
30. To K. Seifert, 23 December 1946
31. To M. Niemöller, 29 June 1946 and 7 June 1946
32. 'Die deutsche Frage heute', *Journal de Genève*, 1946, no. 303
33. To G. Dehn, 26 October 1947
34. To M. Eras, 6 April 1947
35. 'Ein Rückblick auf das Jahr 1945', in *Schweizer Radio-Zeitung* 1946, no. 2
36. See n.33

37. See n.30
38. CvK to E.Wolf, 7 November 1947
39. Lect. V, 115
40. To CB, 25 February 1948
41. To CB, 24 November 1947
42. To CB, 1 April 1947
43. *Gespräche nach Amsterdam,* 1949, 30
44. To E. Sartorius, 1 April 1947
45. *Die Schrift und die Kirche,* ThSt 22, 7, 19
46. To N. Ehrenström, 1 April 1947, and
    E. Sartorius, 1 April 1947; the text is in
    The Universal Church in God's Design
    (Study volume for Amsterdam 1948),
    SCM Press 1948
47. See n.10
48. To C. Milville, 22 September 1947; to
    Rose Marie Barth, 16 May 1947; to his
    family, 1 August 1947
49. *Die christliche Lehre nach dem Heidelberger
    Katechismus,* 1948, 7f.; ET *The
    Heidelberg Catechism for Today,* John
    Knox Press, Richmond, Va 1969; see
    n.10
50. *Die christliche Lehre,* 12f., 60, 16; ET
    18f., 21f.
51. To his family, 1 August 1947, and to
    C. Milville, 22 September 1947
52. From CvK to O. Knobloch, 23
    January 1960
53. To G. Dehn, 20 September 1947
54. To his family, 13 August 1947
55. *Die Kirche zwischen Ost and West,* 1949,
    30f.; ET in *Against the Stream,* 145
56. See n.54 and letters to H.Obendiek, 15
    August 1947, and L. Dennenberg, 27
    March 1959
57. *BB,* 287ff.
58. *KD* III, 2, 524, VIII, 47, 36; ET 437,
    xf., 41, 32
59. Ibid., VII; ET ix
60. Letter of 13 March 1954
61. To H. Diem, 27 November 1949
62. To W. Baumgartner, 12 July 1950
63. To W. Vischer, 29 February 1948
64. To CB, 11 August 1949
65. To CB, 25 March 1951
66. To MB, 11 February 1964
67. To G. Lindt, 31 December 1944
68. To E. Sartorius, 1 January 1948
69. To CB, 13 December 1947
70. To CB, 16–17 January 1948 and 14
    February 1948
71. To W. Niesel, 8 August 1950
72. To W. Scherffig, 20 August 1949
73. To R. Karwehl, 28 May 1949

74. To CB, 16–17 January 1948
75. To K. Jaspers, 21 February 1953
76. To K. Seifert, 7 January 1948
77. To CB, 1 May 1948
78. Seminar report, 9 January 1950
79. Seminar report, 1951
80. To H. Ott, 21 July 1950
81. *Die christliche Gemeinde im Wechsel der
    Staatsordnungen,* 1948, 55ff.; ET in
    Against the Stream, 101f.
82. Ibid., 10, 57, 23, 35, 45; ET 104, 57,
    70, 92
83. To H. Mochalski, 25 April 1948
84. To G. Traub, 5 December 1948
85. See n.81, 57f., 75; ET 104, 123
86. To A. Koechlin, 20 September 1948
88. See n.81, 66; ET 113
89. To W. Lüthi, 13 June 1948
90. See n.81, 66; ET 114
91. See n.81, 69; ET 116
92. To the parish of Wattwil, 25
    December 1948
93. To CB, 6 November 1948
94. To CB, 15 February 1949
95. *Die Kirche zwischen Ost und West,* 3, 10f.;
    ET in *Against the Stream,* 132
96. CvK to K. Seifert, 31 January 1948
97. ABT VI, 57f.
98. *LZ,* 25f.
99. To CB, 10 August 1948, and *The First
    Assembly of the World Council of Churches.
    The Official Report,* SCM Press 1949
100. To CB, 30 September 1948, and G.
    Lanzenstiel, 28 November 1949
101. To G. Merz, 5 October 1948
102. To K. Handrich, 3 April 1953
103. To CB, 30 September 1948
104. Ibid.
105. ABT VI, 58
106. See n.101
107. *Die Wirklichkeit des neuen Menschen,*
    ThSt 27, 3
108. See n.103
109. *Gespräche nach Amsterdam,* 24
110. See n.101
111. See n.93
112. Ibid.
113. See n.94
114. Hans Urs von Balthasar, *Karl Barth:
    Darstellung und Deutung seiner Theologie,*
    1962; ET *The Theology of Karl Barth,*
    Holt, Rinehart and Winston: New
    York 1971
115. To F. Gehrig, 5 December 1948
116. To CB, 30 December 1948

117. See n.94
118. Ibid.
119. To CB, 23 June 1949
120. To H. Weber, 23 May 1949
121. To H. Stratenwerth, 5 April 1960
122. To CB, 11 August 1949
123. To Dr Studer, 19 September 1950
124. To CB, 7 January 1950
125. To CB, 30 December 1948
126. See n.116
127. *KD* III, 3, VIf.; ET xiii
128. Ibid., V; ET xi
129. Ibid., VI, 47; ET xii, 41
130. See n.94
131. To F. Herzog, 21 May 1949
132. CvK to CB, 11 June 1949
133. *KD* III, 3, VI; ET xii
134. To O. Weber, 20 June 1949
135. To R. Pestalozzi, 30 December 1949
136. Letter of 17 December 1949
137. To H. Gollwitzer, 8 January 1950
138. *Humanismus,* ThSt 28, 13ff., 21f.
139. To CB, 29 September 1949
140. Ibid.
141. To CB, 24 November 1949
142. To G. Gloege, 26 November 1949
143. To CB, 26 February 1950
144. To CB, 7 June 1954, and to MB, 11 August 1950
145. To H. U. von Balthasar, 25 January 1950
146. See n.143
147. To CB, 7 January 1950
148. To CB, 26 February and 28 March 1950
149. To CB, 22 December 1950
150. To A. Gilg, 23 November 1956
151. To CB, 7 May 1950
152. To CB, 21 September 1950
153. See n.137
154. To D. Schellong, 12 October 1950 and to H. Weber, 15 October and to H. Weber, 15 October 1950
155. *KD* IV, 1, 858; ET 768
156. To his sons, 14 September 1953
157. To CB, 25 March 1951, and Conv. VII
158. To H. Weber, 15 October 1950, and to V. Vinay, 15 October 1950
159. To CB, 25 March 1951
160. See n.155
161. See n.159
162. Seminar report, 1950–51
163. See n.159
164. To Gerty Pestalozzi, 3 January 1951

165. To H. J. Iwand, 29 April 1951
166. Ibid.
167. To CB, 2 June 1951
168. To CB, 13 July 1951
169. To CB, 25 August 1951
170. To G. Harbsmeier, 29 November 1952
171. To T. L. Haitjema, 14 May 1949
172. To the convention of Reformed Preachers, 26 April 1949
173. To CB, 23 June 1949
174. To R. Will, 28 December 1946
175. To H. Scholz, 2 August 1954
176. To K. L. Schmidt, 2 June 1948
177. To P. Vogt, 10 January 1953, and to Dr Krueger, 16 November 1953
178. CvK to H. Gollwitzer, 19 October 1952
179. To CB, 24 November 1949
180. To CB, 7 May 1950
181. Introduction to O. Weber, *Karl Barths Kirchliche Dogmatik,* 1950, 6; ET *Karl Barth's Church Dogmatics,* Lutterworth Press 1953, 10
182. *KD* III, 4, IX; ET xii
183. Ibid.
184. Conv. VI
185. See n.181, 5; ET 9
186. To CB, 2 June 1951
187. *KD* III, 4, VII; ET xi
188. Jacket copy of *KD* III, 4
189. Ibid., and *KD* III, 4, 31, 745, 58, 63; ET 29f., 648, 53, 59
190. See n.186
191. See n.165
192. *KD* IV, 1, 83; ET 79
193. To CB, 13 July 1951
194. *KD* IV, 1, 171ff., 336f., 379f., 738f., 769; ET 157ff., 305, 344, 725f., 757f.
195. *KD* IV, 1, Preface; ET ix
196. To B. Gherardini, 24 May 1952
197. *BB,* 200, and to A. Bronkhorst, 28 December 1952
198. To C. H. Ratschow, 2 January 1958
199. To G. W. Bromiley, 1 June 1961
200. *KD* IV, 1, 858f.; ET 769
201. To H. Müller, 7 April 1961
202. D. Bonhoeffer, *Letters and Papers from Prison, The Enlarged Edition,* SCM Press and Macmillan, New York 1971, 286
203. To J. Glenthøj, 7 September 1956, and Conv. II
204. To M. P. van Dijk, 29 December 1952
205. To G. C. Berkouwer, 30 December 1954
206. To CB, 18 November 1950

207. To CB, 21 September 1950
208. To CB, 18 November 1950, and Lect. V, 150ff.
209. To CB, 22 December 1950
210. 'Barmen', in Bekennende Kirche, Festschrift für M. Niemöller, 1952, 9
*211. ABT VI, 62f.
212. To T. Schnyder, 8 June 1958
213. To G. Jacob, 18 February 1955
214. To M. Feldmann, 16 September 1950
215. To M. Feldmann, 10 February 1951
216. To CB, 25 August 1951
217. To H. Weber, 15 October 1950, and to CB, 25 August 1951
218. To Berne friends, 21 December 1951
219. See n.216
220. KD III, 4, 782; ET 684
221. To A. Bereczsky, 6 January 1952
222. To A. Bereczsky, 16 September 1951
223. To CB, 18 January 1952
224. To the British Ambassador, 14 January 1952
225. To CB, 9 March 1952
226. To H. Obendiek, 25 March 1952
227. See n.225
228. 'Du sollst dir kein Bildnis noch irgendein Gleichnis machen', Basler Nachrichten, no. 32, 22 January 1952
229. KRS, 3 July 1952
230. To G. Casalis, 13 October 1952
231. 'Nachwort', 298 and ABT IV
232. 'Nachwort', 298
233. ABT IV
234. Conv. II
235. To CB, 25 November 1951
236. KD IV, 1, Foreword; ET ix
237. To W. Herrenbrück, 15 February 1952
238. To G. Gloege, 26 November 1949
239. See n.235
240. Seminar report, 17 January 1953
241. To CB, 9 March 1952
242. To S.Neill, 18 March 1953
243. CvK to W. Simpfendörfer, 16 May 1952
244. Rudolf Bultmann: Ein Versuch, ihn zu Verstehen, 1952; ET 'Rudolf Bultmann – An Attempt to Understand Him', in Kerygma and Myth II, 1962, 83–162
245. BB, 197
246. See n.241
247. Preface to new edition of Rudolf Bultmann and Christus und Adam, 1964, 5
248. To G. Ebeling, 7 December 1952
249. See n.241

250. See n.240
251. Circular letter, 20 May 1952
252. 'Moglichkeiten liberaler Theologie heute', Schweizer Theologische Umschau, 1960, 97
253. To G. Merz, 16 March 1953
254. Published in Freies Christentum, 1953
255. To his sons, 22 May 1953
256. To MB, 8 March 1953
257. Ibid.
258. To E. Wolf, 31 July 1951
259. To MB, 4 April 1953
260. To his sons, 22 May 1953
261. ABT VI, 62
262. See n.258
263. KD II, 2, Preface to English edition
264. To E. Wolf, 18 March 1955
265. See n. 259
266. KD IV, 2, VI; ET ix
267. Ibid.
268. Ibid., 30, VII, 578ff., 462, 770, 918ff.; ET 29, x, 511ff., 411, 690, 824ff.
269. Ibid., VII; ET x
270. KD IV, 3, 1, IX; ET xiii
271. Conv. IX
272. To his sons, 12 July 1953
273. To G. and Liselotte Schwenzel, 28 July 1953
274. To E. Kühler, 5 April 1960
275. To H. Scholz, 24 May 1953
276. See n.260
277. To CB, 25 August 1951
278. CvK to Nelly Barth, 26 July 1951
279. See n.277
280. To S. Neill, 11 March 1953
281. 'The Christian Hope', Episcopal Church News, Richmond, Va, 6 April 1952
282. 'Kirchen schliessen Bekanntschaft', Die Woche, 1952, 44
283. To his sons, 14 September 1953
284. To K. Seifert, 7 October 1953, and to W. Simpfendörfer, 12 May 1954
285. To E. Wolf, 3 October 1953
286. Ibid.
287. Das Geschenk der Freiheit, ThSt 39, 21f.; ET in The Humanity of God, 87
288. See n.285
289. To W. A. Visser't Hooft, 18 October 1953
290. To G. Lindt, 24 February 1955
291. To U. Barth, 19 March 1954
292. To H. Scholz, 2 August 1954
293. To his sons, 9 March 1954
294. See n.291
295. To F. Herzog, 13 February 1954

296. To his sons, 20 December 1953
297. To A. von Erlach, 22 November 1949
298. Seminar Report 1953–54
299. To MB, 19 August 1954
300. To MB, 9 May 1954
301. See n.296
302. See n.293
303. To MB, 11 February 1964
304. To CB, 13 July 1954
305. To his sons, 22 December 1954
306. To MB, 12 July 1954
307. See n.304
308. To his sons, 19 September 1954
309. To G. Lindt, August 1954
310. To G. Gherardini, 18 September 1954
311. *W. A. Mozart 1756/1956*, 1956, 49
312. To J. Souček, 4 August 1954
313. Postscript to J. Hromádka, *Evangelium für Atheisten*, 1969, 62
314. To his sons, 17 March 1955

315. See n.305
316. To G. Heinemann, 19 November 1954
317. 'Gerstenmaier auf den Stehkragen', *Gesamtdeutsche Rundschau*, 18 March 1955
318. To M. Niemöller, 28 January 1955
319. To H. Schmidt, 20 November 1954
320. CvK to H. E. Tödt, 19 June 1955
321. Lect. V, 205
322. To H. H. Brunner, 30 August 1955
323. To H. Kuwada, 22 January 1963
324. To Dora Scheuner, 7 September 1956
325. To G. Merz, 28 August 1956, and to H. Vogel, 9 March 1960
326. To CB, 21 September 1950
327. To Daniel Barth, 8 July 1954
328. To Gertrud Staewen, 15 July 1954
329. *KD* IV, 2, X; ET xii
330. To H. Hesse, 27 October 1954

8   The years from 1955 to 1962 in Bruderholzallee 26, Basle

1. To P. van Buren, 18 November 1955
2. To his sons, 20 October 1955
3. Circular letter, May 1968
4. To MB, 24 August 1959
5. ABT VI, 75
6. To R. Ley, 31 August 1955
7. To B. Vischer, 19 July 1955
8. To MB, 21 April 1956
9. *W. A. Mozart 1756/1956*, 1956, 8
10. To E. Wolf, 26 December 1955
11. *W. A. Mozart*, 37, 39, 38, 44
12. ABT VI, 71f.
13. To R. Morgenthaler, 15 October 1963
14. To K. Lüthi, 22 June 1963
15. To MB, 21 April 1956; to D. Mendt, 22 April 1956; to G. Heipp, 23 March 1956
16. Conv. V
17. To MB, 21 April 1956, and to CB, 28 April 1956
18. To G. Lindt, 16 February 1955; to G. Merz, 28 April 1956; to his sons, 21 December 1955
19. To J. Scheiwiler, 22 January 1944
20. To. H. van Oyen, December 1968
21. To H. Barth, 3 March 1955
22. To Renate Barth, 18 March 1956
23. To H. Obendiek, 25 March 1952
24. ABT VI, 61
25. To his sons, 14 September 1953; ABT VI, 61
26. To H. Scholz, 2 August 1954

27. To W. Niesel, 31 December 1954
28. Serm. V, VII; ET 11
29. Ibid., 189
30. To A. von Erlach, 17 May 1955, and to H. Scholz, 2 August 1954
31. Serm. VI, 8f., 69; ET 10ff., 87ff., 24, 68; to K. Scherf, 5 April 1960
32. Serm. V, VII; ET 11
33. To MB, 15–16 July 1957 and to M. Schwarz, 1 August 1955
34. *KD* IV, 3, 1, VIII; ET xiii
35. To his sons, 21 December 1955
36. To B. Nagy, 18 November 1955
37. *KD* IV, 3, 1, VIII; ET xii
38. To P. B. Barth, 28 October 1951
39. To CB, 7 June 1954
40. To E. Imperatori, 14 July 1955
41. To CB, 28 April 1956. The Buddhist was Japanese, not Indian
42. To MB, 21 April 1956, and to K. H. Miskotte, 12 July 1956
43. 'An meine Freunde in Japan', 1956, and to F. W. Camfield, 7 October 1947
44. 'An meine Freunde in Japan', 1956
45. Ibid.
46. Speech in Lambeth Palace, July 1956
47. To T. A. Gill, 10 August 1957
48. To H. Vogel, 5 September 1956
49. CvK to K. G. Steck, 5 July 1956
50. To his sons, 14 September 1953
51. To his sons, 17 September 1955, and to CB, 16 September 1956

52. ABT VI, 69f.

53. H. Küng, *Rechtfertigung*, 1957, 12; ET *Justification*, Burns & Oates 1964, xviii

54. To K. H. Miskotte, 12 July 1956

55. To CB, 16 September 1956, and to T. H. L. Parker, 10 July 1956

56. *KD* IV, 3, 1, IX, ET xiii

57. To E. Barth, 13 August 1956, and to CB, 16 September 1956

58. Interview with H. Fischer-Barnicol, 1964

59. *Die Menschlichkeit Gottes*, ThSt 48, 7, 3, 10, 15; ET 34, 38, 33, 46f., 49

60. *Evangelische Theologie im 19. Jahrhundert*, ThSt 49, 3; ET in *The Humanity of God*, 9

61. To W. Herrenbruck, 13 July 1963

62. *KD* IV, 3, 8f.; ET 8

63. Ibid., VIIf.; ET xif.

64. Ibid., 47; ET 44

65. Ibid., 872; ET 762

66. Ibid., 550; ET 477f.

67. To his sons, 26 December 1956

68. 'Uns fehlt das Bewusstsein der eigenen Relativität', *Die Woche*, 1963, no.4

69. To R. von Bergen, 10 November 1956; see n.67

70. To F. Flückiger, 1 December 1956

71. To J. Bäschlin, 22 July 1957

72. To A. von Erlach, 17 July 1957

73. *Brief an einen Pfarrer in der DDR*, 1958, 6

74. To H. Ott, 17 July 1957

75. To MB, 15–16 July 1957

76. CvK to friends, 17 June 1957

77. Seminar report 1957–58

78. Seminar report 1955–56

79. Testimonial for E. Jüngel, 1958

80. See n.77

81. 'Zum Kernwaffenproblem', *SdG*, 1957, 262

82. 'Antwort an Radio Warschau', *KRS*, 1957, 191

83. To his children, 28 July 1958

84. To H. Simon, 25 September 1958

85. To his children, 12 October 1958

86. To Sun Bum Yun, 16 June 1958

87. To K. Stoevesandt, 25 July 1958

88. See n.85

89. Ibid.

90. To J. Hamel, 23 March 1959, and *Laudatio* for G. Wieser, 1957

91. Postscript to J. Hromádka, *Evangelium für Atheisten*, 1958, 63

92. To MB, 11 February 1964

93. To J. Hromádka, 18 December 1962 and 10 July 1963

94. *Brief an einen Pfarrer in der DDR*, 11, 15, 28

95. To A. von Erlach, 26 May 1959

96. To Marie-Claire Barth, 22 March 1959

97. CvK to MB, 1 May 1959

98. Circular letter, May 1959

99. 'Philosophie und Theologie', in *Philosophie und christlicher Existenz, Festschrift für Heinrich Barth*, 1960, 93ff.

100. To W. Weischedel, 9 May 1960

101. To his children, 28 July 1958

102. To MB, 15 July 1957

103. To R. Siebeck, 8 October 1957; to his children, 12 October 1958; to R. Karwehl, 13 March 1952

104. To CB, 25 May 1958

105. To A. von Erlach, 18 December 1958

106. To MB, 24 August 1959; to CB, 8 January 1961; to MB, 24 December 1957; to his children, 28 July 1958

107. See n.85

108. To C. W. Kegley, 9 July 1960

109. To MB, 20 December 1958

110. To MB, 15–16 July 1957

111. See n.77

112. To F. J. Leenhardt, 14 February 1959, and to CB, 8 June 1959

113. To CB, 11 November 1957

114. ABT VI, 62

115. To Rose Marie Barth, 31 December 1959

116. To CB, 29 December 1959, and from CvK to G. Barczay, 6 December 1959

117. Conv. VII and IX

118. To G. Wolff, 2 September 1959

119. To Erik Wolf, 7 March 1960, and to K. Handrich, 7 March 1960

120. *KD* IV, 3, VII; ET xi

121. To CB, 29 December 1959, and to MB, 27 September 1959

122. To CB, 6 April 1960

123. Circular letter, 15 May 1960

124. To MB, 24 August 1959, and to H. Vogel, 9 March 1960

125. 'Die theologische Fakultät', *Basler Nachrichten*, 26 June 1960

126. 'Die Theologie in der heutigen Welt', *Basler National-Zeitung*, 26 June 1960

127. *KD* IV, 4, IX; ET viiif.

128. To CB, 18 September 1960

129. To G. Casalis, 31 August 1960

130. Conv. IX

131. *BB*, 199
132. 'Protokoll des Gesprächs zwischen KB und Vertretern der Brüdergemeine,' *Civitas praesens*, 1961, no.13
133. To E. Käsemann, 3 January 1960
134. To Rose Marie Barth, 7 April 1961
135. ABT VI, 68
136. To G. Ebeling, 29 July 1959
137. To R. Karwehl, 26 December 1960
138. To A. Hege, 3 April 1962
139. To U. Smid, 11 December 1962
140. To F. Middendorf, 5 April 1962
141. Television interview for the BBC; German text in *Junge Kirche*, 1961, 276
142. In *Zürcher Woche*, 28 July 1961
143. Conv. VI
144. Conv. III
145. To CB, 6 April 1960

146. To MB, 24 December 1960
147. To G. Casalis, 31 August 1960
148. To CB, 25 May 1958
149. To CB, 8 January 1961
150. To A. Bereczky, 18 July 1961
151. To E. Wolf, 28 July 1961
152. *Einführung in die evangelische Theologie*, 1962, 7
153. To H. Goes, 17 July 1962
154. To K. H. Miskotte, 16 July 1962
155. To H. Gollwitzer, 31 July 1962
156. To MB, 11 February 1962
157. See n.154
158. *Einführung in die evangelischen Theologie*, 7f.; ET *Evangelical Theology: An Introduction*, Fontana Books 1965, 5
159. Ibid., 7, 11, 14, 65, 155, 182, 224; ET 5, 9, 14, 65f., 134, 154, 192

9 The years of retirement, 1962–1968

1. Circular letter, 25 May 1964
2. *KD* III, 4, 707f.; ET 615f.
3. *KD* IV, 4, VIII; ET viii
4. ABT VI, 71
5. To W. A. Visser't Hooft, 18 October 1953
6. To MB, 11 February 1962
7. To MZ, 19 May 1962
8. 'Remembrances of America', *The Christian Century*, 1963, 1,7ff.
9. 'Uns fehlt das Bewusstsein der eigenen Relativität', *Die Woche*, 1963, no.4
10. See n.8
11. To H. Goes, 17 July 1962
12. To E. Hubacher, 6 June 1962
13. See n.11
14. To H. Gollwitzer, 31 July 1962
15. To G. Dehn, 13 September 1962
16. To A. Hirzel, 28 November 1962
17. To H. Dietzfelbinger, 27 October 1962
18. To E. Wolf, 8 November 1962
19. See n.14
20. 'Systematische Theologie', in *Lehre und Forschung an der Universität Basel*, 1960, 37
21. To CB, 27 February 1963, and to A. Hirzel, 28 November 1962
22. See n.18
23. Conv. VI
24. To CB, 27 February 1963
25. To MB, 26 February 1963
26. To MB, 27–29 November 1963

27. To E. Wolf, 14 August 1963
28. To N.N., 31 October 1963
29. To O. Cullmann, 30 October 1963
30. Conv. VII
31. Conv. IV
32. Ibid.
33. To CB, 27 February 1963
34. To G. Casalis, 28 October 1963
35. See n.26
36. *LZ*, 65f.
37. To H. H. Brunner, 21 November 1963, and to CB, 18 June 1963
38. Conv. VII
39. Foreword to new edition of *Rudolf Bultmann* and *Christus und Adam*, 1964
40. Ibid.
41. To CB, 13 March 1964
42. Circular letter, May 1964
43. Conv. VI
44. Conv. VII
45. To CB, 18 June 1963
46. Conv. VII
47. To B. A. Willems, 6 March 1963
48. See n.45. Barth's 'Überlegungen zum Zweiten Vatikanischen Konzil' appeared *inter alia* in *Zwischenstation, Festschrift für K. Kupisch*, 1963, 9ff.
49. 'Dank und Reverenz', *EvTh*, 1963, 337
50. To MB, 26 February 1963
51. 'Dank und Reverenz', 341f.
52. See n.45
53. See n.26
54. 'Das Christentum und die Religion',

KRS, 1963, 181f.

55. 'Reformierte Theologie in der Schweiz', in *Festschrift for G. C. Berkouwer*, 1965, 28
56. See n.26
57. 'Das Gebot des gnädigen Gottes', in *Festschrift for K. H. Miskotte*, 1961, 280, and to K. H. Miskotte, 12 July 1956
58. To MB, 11 February, 1964
59. To D. Schellong, 5 March 1963
60. *KD* IV, 4, VIII; ET viii
61. Circular letter, 25 May 1964
62. To A. de Quervain, 28 April 1965
63. To R. Karwehl, 8 November 1964
64. See n.60
65. To E. Jüngel, 3 November 1965
66. To E. Wolf, 15 November 1965
67. To G. Schwenzel, 8 November 1965
68. To R. Karwehl, 5 November 1965
69. See n.67
70. To E. Wolf, 15 November 1965
71. Circular letter, May 1967
72. To Frau Brunner, 7 March 1966
73. To M. Gabriel, 14 January 1966, and to A. de Quervain, 28 April 1965
74. To N. N., 20 December 1961
75. To M. Löhrer, 18 August 1966
76. Circular letter, May 1968
77. See n.68
78. *KD* IV, 4, VIII; ET viii
79. See n.76
80. To M. Fischer, 26 October 1962
81. Circular letter May 1968 and to R. Karwehl, 1 February 1967
82. See n.76
83. *Gebete*, 1963, 7f.
84. To *Das Werk*, 23 April 1959
85. To Honemeyer, 13 July 1968
86. *LZ*, 54f.
87. To J. Lombard, 24 August 1954
88. To E. Wolf, 15 November 1965
89. Circular letter, May 1968
90. To MB, 26 February 1963
91. Circular letter, June 1966
92. See n.88
93. To P. Vogelsanger, 4 April 1966
94. To E. Jüngel, 3 November 1965
95. To W. Querl, 30 September 1968
96. *EvTh*, 1966, 619
97. To E. Wolf, 21 May 1966
98. *Ad limina apostolorum*, 1967, 9
99. Ibid.
100. To A. Grau, 16 March 1966
101. *KD* IV, 4, VIII; ET viii
102. See n.98, 9f.

103. Ibid., 10
104. 'Autorität der Freiheit', in *Nachrichten aus dem Kösel Verlag*, F.26, 1967, 23
105. 'In diesem Zeichen wirst du nicht siegen', *Orientierung*, 1967, 267
106. See n.89
107. See n.98, 18
108. 'Überlegungen zum 2. Vatikanischen Konzil', 15f.
109. See n.89
110. Ibid., and *Ad limina*, 17
111. See n.105
112. See n.98, 18
113. To H. Küng, 27 June 1966
114. To E. Busch, 10 July 1966
115. See n.98, 11
116. To E. Wolf, 3 October 1966
117. To J. G. M. Willebrands, 11 October 1966
118. See n.98, 13
119. Ibid., 27, 35, 15
120. Ibid.
121. To E. Schlink, 21 October 1966
122. See n.98, 18
123. See n.116
124. See n.122
125. *KD* IV, 4, IX; ET viii
126. Seminar report, 4 January 1961
127. *KD* IV, 4, XI; ET ixf.
128. To J. Beckmann, 29 June 1968
129. *KD* IV, 4, X; ET ixf.
130. Circular letter, May 1968
131. *KD* IV, 4, X; ET xii
132. *KD* IV, 4, VII; ET vii, and to MB, 26 February 1963
133. *KD* IV, 4 VII, IX; ET viif.
134. Ibid.
135. To W. A. Visser't Hooft, 8 March 1953
136. To G. Casalis, 18 August 1963
137. To J. Moltmann, 17 November 1964
138. To W. Pannenberg, 7 December 1964
139. See n.135
140. To W. Rüegg, 6 July 1961
141. See n.8
142. To C. H. Ratschow, 2 January 1958
143. To W. Herrenbrück, 13 July 1963
144. To M. Fischer, 26 April 1956
145. Circular letter, May 1961
146. To J. Lombard, 24 March 1955
147. To H. J. Iwand, 27 July 1953
148. To K. H. Miskotte, 16 July 1962
149. To J. M. Lochman, 30 October 1961
150. To M. Storch, 26 April 1964; to M. Neeser, 27 December 1952, and

Preface to reprint of *Rom.* I, 1963
151. See n.145
152. To N.N., 31 October 1963
153. Circular letter, May 1967
154. Circular letter, May 1964
155. See n.153
156. Circular letter, May 1968
157. Ibid.
158. To H. Gollwitzer, 7 November 1967
159. See n.156
160. To K. P. Gertz, 29 February 1968
161. 'Nachwort', 290
162. To G. Müller, 27 November 1968
163. 'Nachwort', 297f.
164. Ibid., 310
165. To CB, 14 May 1968
166. To R. Karwehl, 1 February 1967
167. To R. Karwehl, 30 October 1968
168. Ibid.
169. *LZ*, 7
170. *LZ*, 33f., 27
171. *LZ*, 30f.
172. *LZ*, 61
173. *LZ*, 71
174. Circular letter, May 1968

Index of Names

Index of Places

Index of Subjects

An asterisk denotes a reference to an explanatory footnote

Acknowledgments for Illustrations

Karl Barth Archives, Basle: 2, 3, 4, 5, 6, 7, 8, 9, 10, 11, 12, 16, 17, 18, 19, 20, 21, 23, 25, 27, 28, 29, 33, 35, 38, 39, 40, 41, 42, 48, 49, 50, 52, 53, 54, 59, 60, 62, 63, 64, 66, 67, 68, 69, 71, 73, 74, 75, 76, 77, 78, 80, 84, 86, 87, 89, 91, 92, 93, 94, 95, 96, 97, 98, 99, 100, 101, 103; Bildarchiv Foto, Marburg: 13, 14, 15; Bilderdienst Süddeutscher Verlag: 47; Eberhard Busch, Uerkheim: 34; Ex Libris Verlag, Zürich: 24, 61; Helmut Gollwitzer, Berlin: 90; Peter Heman, Basle: 82; Photo Höflinger, Basle: 1; Franz Hubmann- Magnum: 81; Christian Kaiser Verlag, Munich: 22, 30, 32, 37, 45, 55, 70, 88; Gertrud Lindt, Gümlingen: 36; Bernhard Moosbrugger, Zürich: 102; Maria Netter, Basle: 65, 72, 83, 85; Phaidon Press, London: *Frontispiece;* Städtisches Museum, Göttingen: 31; Gertrud Staewen, Berlin: 44, 56, 57, 58; Karl Gerhard Steck, Münster: 29, 43, 51; Ullstein Bilderdienst: 26; Peter Walter, Gelterkinden: 46.